# Juniper(r) Networks Secure Access SSL VPN Configuration Guide

**Neil R. Wyler** Technical Editor
**Trent Fausett**
**Kevin Fletcher**
**Patrick Foxhoven**
**Mark J. Lucas**
**Kevin Miller**
**Kevin Peterson**
**Brad Woodberg**

| KEY | SERIAL NUMBER |
| --- | --- |
| 001 | HJIRTCV764 |
| 002 | PO9873D5FG |
| 003 | 829KM8NJH2 |
| 004 | BPOQ48722D |
| 005 | CVPLQ6WQ23 |
| 006 | VBP965T5T5 |
| 007 | HJJJ863WD3E |
| 008 | 2987GVTWMK |
| 009 | 629MP5SDJT |
| 010 | IMWQ295T6T |

PUBLISHED BY
Syngress Publishing, Inc.
Elsevier, Inc.
30 Corporate Drive
Burlington, MA 01803

Juniper(r) Networks Secure Access SSL VPN Configuration Guide

Printed in the United States of America
1 2 3 4 5 6 7 8 9 0

ISBN 13: 978-1-59749-200-3

Publisher: Amorette Pedersen
Acquisitions Editor: Andrew Williams
Technical Editor: Neil Wyler
Project Manager: Gary Byrne

Page Layout and Art: SPI
Copy Editors: Michelle Lewis and Audrey Doyle
Indexer: Nara Wood
Cover Designer: Michael Kavish

For information on rights, translations, and bulk sales, contact Matt Pedersen, Commercial Sales Director and Rights, at Syngress Publishing; email m.pedersen@elsevier.com.

# Technical Editor and Contributing Author

**Neil R. Wyler** (JNCIA-SSL, JNCIS-FWV, JNCIS-M) is an information security engineer and researcher located on the Wasatch Front in Utah. He is currently doing contract work for Juniper Networks, working with the company's Security Products Group. Neil is a staff member of the Black Hat Security Briefings and Def Con hacker conference. He has spoken at numerous security conferences and been the subject of various online, print, film, and television interviews regarding different areas of information security. He was the lead author and technical editor of *Aggressive Network Self-Defense* (Syngress, ISBN: 1-931836-20-5) and coauthor of *Configuring Juniper Networks NetScreen & SSG Firewalls* (Syngress, ISBN: 1-59749-118-7).

# Contributors

**Trent Fausett** (JNCIA-FWV, JNCIA-SSL) is a network engineer with Valcom (the longest standing Juniper reseller) in Salt Lake City, UT. He was previously doing contract work for Juniper Networks for the SSL VPN primary Technical Assistance Center. He did extensive work with improving the Juniper SSL VPN knowledge base and helped publish the SSL VPN resolution guides available on the Juniper support site today. He is currently finishing up a bachelor's degree in Computer Science.

**Kevin Fletcher** (CISSP) works for Juniper Networks in technical marketing and was formerly a product manager at Neoteris, the inventor of the first SSL VPN appliance. He has spent the last several years building and evangelizing SSL VPNs and works closely with organizations all over the world as they design and deploy their next-generation remote access control solutions. Kevin's primary areas of expertise include HTTP, SSL/TLS, PKI, AAA, network management, Web security, and overall solution design. He has over 10 years' network management and security experience and holds a bachelor's degree from Purdue University in Telecommunications Networking.

**Patrick Foxhoven** (JNCIS-FWV, JNCIA-IDP, JNCIA-SSL, ECDP, MCP+I, CCNA) is the chief information officer of CentraComm Communications, a leading managed security service provider (MSSP) and Juniper Networks Elite J-Partner based in Findlay, OH. Patrick has over 12 years of diverse professional experience in telecommunications, managed security, and mission-critical networking fields encompassing a unique mix of multisite networking, security, hosting, wireless, and consulting strategies for solutions aimed at medium-sized through Fortune 500 accounts. Prior to joining CentraComm, Patrick served as vice president of a regional Internet service provider with five physical network points of presence in Ohio serving over 2,500 customers. He has hands-on proficiency and multiple industry certifications.

**Mark J. Lucas** (MCSE and GIAC Certified Windows Security Administrator) is a senior system administrator at the California Institute of Technology. Mark is responsible for the design, implementation, and security of high-availability systems such as Microsoft Exchange servers, VMWare ESX hosted servers, and various licensing servers. He is also responsible for the firewalls protecting these systems. Mark has been in the IT industry for 10 years. Mark lives in Tujunga, CA, with his wife, Beth, and the furry, four-legged children, Aldo, Cali, Chuey, and Emma.

**Kevin Miller** (JNCIA-SSL, CCSP, CCNP, CCDP, MCSE) is a network architect with Herman Miller Inc., an international office furniture manufacturer. From his home office in Huntsville, AL, he provides network design, configuration, and support services throughout Herman Miller's network. His specialties include Juniper's SSL concentrators and Cisco routers, switches, firewalls, wireless and Web content services. Kevin's background includes significant experience with both security and quality-of-service technology.

**Kevin Peterson** (CISSP, JNCIA-SSL) is an SSL VPN specialist for the eastern region (U.S.) with Juniper Networks and has been working with the Juniper SSL VPN for over four years. Kevin's background includes positions as a security product manager and a senior security architect at McKesson Information Solutions, a support engineer at Microsoft, and an avionic systems technician with the United States Air Force Special Operations Command in England. He has also authored multiple security white papers and presented at notable security conferences, including the RSA Security Conference, HIPAA Summit, The Institute for Applied Network Security, and the Healthcare Information Management Systems Society (HIMSS). Prior system and security certifications include MSCE, MCP+I, MCT, CNA, CCNA and GSEC.

Kevin resides in Alpharetta, GA, with his family, Patricia, Siobhan, and Conor.

**Brad Woodberg** (JNCIS-FWV, JNCIS-M, JNCIA-IDP, JNCIA-SSL, JNCIA-UAC, Packeteer Expert, CCNP) is a security consultant at Networks Group Inc. in Brighton, MI. At Networks Group his primary focus is designing and implementing security solutions for clients ranging from small businesses to Fortune 500 companies. His main areas of expertise include network perimeter security, intrusion prevention, security analysis, and network infrastructure. Outside of work he has a great interest in proof-of-concept vulnerability analysis, open source integration/development, and computer architecture.

Brad currently holds a Computer Engineering bachelor's degree from Michigan State University and participates with local security organizations; he also mentors and gives lectures to students interested in the computer network field. He was a contributing author to *Configuring Juniper Networks NetScreen & SSG Firewalls* (ISBN: 1-597491187), published by Syngress Publishing.

# Contents

# Introduction

## Why This Book Was Written

When I first discovered that in the near future I would be working closely with the Juniper Networks SSL VPN, I did what, I assume, most people do when confronted with a new piece of technology. I started researching. It was a frustrating process to say the least.

For days I pored over Web site after Web site, grasping at every scrap of information I could find to help familiarize myself with the appliance that would soon become a large focus of my professional time. There were plenty of sales documents on the Juniper Web site, but I wanted technical information, and that information was hard to find.

Eventually, I went through several training classes on the appliance and had all the resources of the Juniper Technical Assistance Center (JTAC) at my disposal. I was saturated with technical information, but there was still the nagging feeling that I wasn't as prepared as I would have liked.

So fast forward to today. The book that you're currently reading is for all people wanting to know more before they touch the Juniper Networks SSL VPN—for example, the administrator or engineer configuring it for the first time or the guy whose support contract just expired and needs an answer now. Of course, the book is also a desk reference for the seasoned SSL VPN administrator.

I hope this book provides you with everything now that I wish I had when I first started working with this technology.

# Juniper Networks and the SSL VPN

In 2000 a company called Neoteris Inc opened its doors and soon became the market leader for SSL VPN products using what it called its Instant Virtual Extranet (IVE) platform.

Neoteris was purchased in late 2003 by NetScreen Technologies, a company already known for its firewall, IPSec VPN, and intrusion detection products, for approximately $265 million.

NetScreen found itself in a similar situation only a few months later when it was purchased by Juniper Networks for approximately $3.4 billion.

All of these acquisitions meant the SSL VPN product, and its customers, changed hands several times. It is not uncommon when speaking to other users of the Juniper Networks SSL VPN to hear them refer to it as "the Neoteris box" or "NetScreen Device." Several other names commonly heard, and used, are "the SA" or "Secure Access device" and lastly, "the IVE."

You will see us use several of these names interchangeably throughout this book; none are what we would consider incorrect, though the references to Neoteris and NetScreen are dated.

> **NOTE**
>
> For a short time Neoteris was known as DanaStreet after the Dana Street Roasting Company, where the company founders would often meet to discuss their ideas about an SSL VPN solution. A nod to this can still be seen today in the URL rewrite on the device. For example, the URL for the Admin page of the SSL VPN is rewritten as https://secure.yourcompany.com/dana-na/auth/url_admin/welcome.cgi.

## Resources Beyond This Book

While we hope this book is all you'll need to get your Secure Access device up and running, there are other resources you may want to take a look at.

- **Secure Access Admin Guide** This nearly 1000 page document covers a significant amount of information on the Juniper Networks SSL VPN. While not always the plain English you might be looking for, and lacking in visuals, it is a great resource and is updated with each new version of the IVE OS. You can find the Admin Guide for IVE OS 6.0 at www.juniper.net/techpubs/software/ive/6.x/6.0/. Previous, and future, releases will use the same URL scheme.

- **JuniperForum.com** This is a fantastic forum, run by Jay Austad (Username: signal15) of FishNet Security, that has thousands of members worldwide using a wide range of Juniper Networks products. If you have questions about anything Juniper Networks related and/or want to hear the experiences of other Juniper Networks customers, this is the place to do it. The posts are regular and the information is high quality. Several of the authors of this book are regulars on this forum as well.

# Introduction to VPNs

In the past when a business wanted to connect their network to machines in a remote location they were forced to use expensive leased lines in order to receive what, by today's standards, was less than satisfactory performance.

With the wide spread deployment of the Internet, and ever increasing broadband rates, the ability to connect remote network resources using the Internet became more appealing than the high cost leased solution.

While the use of public resources made the cost of remote connectivity substantially lower, it also presented a new problem, security. The use of a public network to transmit private data opened the door to issues of privacy and data integrity, and one way of dealing with these problems is a virtual private network (VPN).

Probably the simplest definition for a VPN is a private network that at some point utilizes public resources, most commonly the Internet. It is a system that allows for the authentication and encryption of data between two endpoints. This allows businesses to maintain the security and privacy of a leased network, while enjoying the cost and speed benefits made available by the Internet.

As shown in Figure 1, once the VPN tunnel is created, different types of users and resources can be accessed through the tunnel. Mobile devices, such as PDA's, are able to access company e-mail servers so they can keep in touch with clients and business associates; server to server sharing can take place, and sales records can be uploaded to a company database on the fly.

**Figure 1** A VPN Tunnel Passing through the Internet Cloud

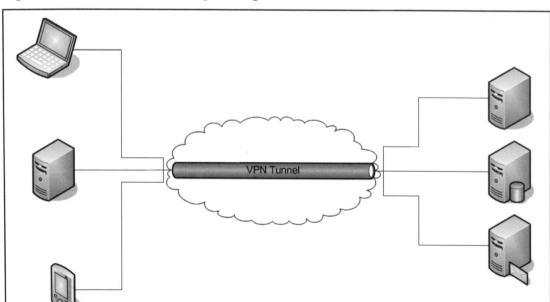

This access, and the security that is required, is provided by the use of strong encryption. While there are numerous protocols for creating VPNs two common methods are IPSec and SSL, which we will discuss here.

# IPSec

IPSec is, and has been, considered by many to be the standard protocol for use with VPNs. Created in 1995, and having undergone several revisions, IPSec is a protocol suite that answered many of the questions concerning data confidentiality and integrity that had plagued network administrators. By using encryption the information could be sent securely across the wire without fear of interference or interception. IPSec also provided the user with the ability to authenticate the party they were communicating with, adding an extra layer of security, and peace of mind.

IPSec consists of two Layer 3 protocols: Authentication Header (AH) and Encapsulating Security Payload (ESP).

The Authentication Header ensures authentication and integrity of the IP datagram. To do this it creates what is known as a Hash Message Authentication Code (HMAC) based on the secret key, payload, and parts of the IP header information and then adds itself to the packet. Figure 2 is a diagram of an authentication header packet.

**Figure 2** AH Packet

| 0 - 7 bit | 8 - 15 bit | 16 - 23 bit | 24 - 31 bit |
|---|---|---|---|
| Next Header | Payload Length | Reserved | |
| Security Parameters Index (SPI) | | | |
| Sequence Number | | | |
| Hash Message Authentication Code(HMAC) | | | |

The first 8 bits make up the Next Header field, this field specifies the protocol of the data being transferred. The next 8 bits specify the length of the payload, and is followed by 16 bits of reserved space. The next 32 bits is the Security Parameters Index (SPI) which provides the information on what parameters were used for this packet. The next 32 bits are the Sequence Number, which helps defend against possible replay attacks. And finally, the last 96 bits are the HMAC, which provides the integrity information for the packet.

The Encapsulating Security Payload protocol can ensure not only the authentication and integrity of the IP datagram but also the confidentiality. After the packet is encrypted and the HMAC is calculated, the ESP header is created and added to the packet. Figure 3 shows an example of an ESP packet.

**Figure 3** ESP Packet

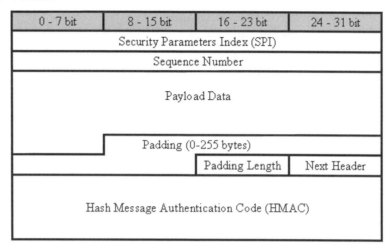

| 0 - 7 bit | 8 - 15 bit | 16 - 23 bit | 24 - 31 bit |
|---|---|---|---|
| Security Parameters Index (SPI) | | | |
| Sequence Number | | | |
| Payload Data | | | |
| Padding (0-255 bytes) | | | |
| | | Padding Length | Next Header |
| Hash Message Authentication Code (HMAC) | | | |

The SPI and sequence number fields follow the same format, and purpose as above. Payload Data is the actual data being transferred. Since IPSec uses block ciphers the payload may require some padding in order to make the payload a multiple of the block length. The pad length is then added, followed by the Next Header field, and finally the HMAC is added.

IPSec supports two operational modes: *transport mode* and *tunnel mode*.

In Transport Mode only the data that is being transmitted is encrypted, the IP header is not modified, and the routing is left intact. This mode is used in host to host communication.

In Tunnel Mode both the data and IP information are encrypted and are then encapsulated within a new IP packet in order to be routed. This mode is primarily used for host-to-network or network-to-network communications. Figure 4 shows the different IPSec modes.

**Figure 4** Differences in Packets in Different IPSec Modes

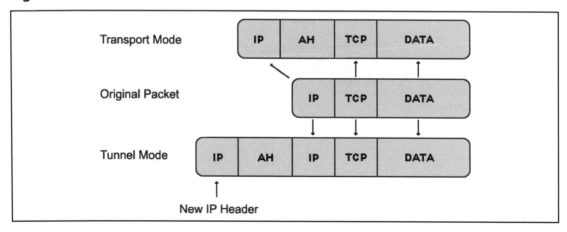

IPSec is a fantastic protocol, but does have some drawbacks when used with a VPN. With an IPSec VPN you need to configure or install client software in order to connect to the VPN. Once the client is installed and configured IPSec is secure, however, you're now tied to the workstation with the client software in order to access and resources provided by the tunnel.

# SSL

We aren't going to have a book about an SSL VPN without a little discussion about the protocol that makes it possible, Secure Sockets Layer, or SSL. SSL is the most widely deployed security protocol in the world. It's what allows most people to feel safe making purchases online or using online banking, and you'd have a hard time finding someone that uses the Internet regularly that's unfamiliar with the little lock in the corner of their browser.

SSL was originally created by Netscape in 1994 in order to protect Web traffic for use with e-commerce, and it has since undergone a number of revisions. It provides confidentiality, integrity, and authentication between two hosts with the use of encryption.

As shown in Figure 5 SSL runs above TCP/IP but below other higher level protocols like HTTP and LDAP. It uses TCP/IP on behalf of the higher level protocols, and allows a server and client to authenticate to one another in order to establish an encrypted connection.

**Figure 5** Location of SSL

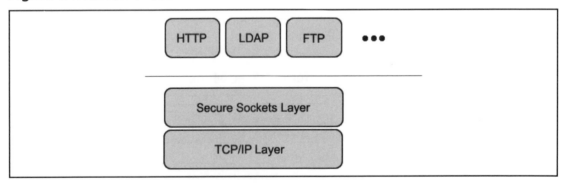

SSL is a layered protocol and we'll focus a bit more on two of the main layers, the SSL Record protocol and SSL Handshake protocol. The SSL Record protocol is responsible for the encapsulation of the higher level protocol data, while the SSL Handshake protocol is responsible for the authentication and negotiation of the encryption algorithm and keys between the client and server in order to establish a secure communication, this is accomplished using the SSL Record protocol.

- **SSL Record Protocol** All encryption for SSL is handled by this protocol. The SSL Record protocol defines a standard format to be used for the transmission of data. These Records contain the message type, version, length, and encapsulated data. They are 8 bytes in length, and do to this fixed length a pad is sometimes necessary.

- **SSL Handshake Protocol** This protocol is used to establish a secure connection between the communicating hosts. The handshake allows the server to authenticate itself to the client using public key techniques, as well as client to server in some cases, and then allows for creation of symmetric keys for use with encryption, decryption, and integrity checking.

Here is a brief summary of the steps involved in the SSL Handshake (see Figure 6):

1. The client sends a message to the server in order to initiate a session. The message includes the SSL version, random data generated by the client, session identifier, cipher settings, and compression method.

2. The server responds to the client request by returning the same parameters used by the client. It will also send the server certificate, or server key exchange if no certificate is available, and a request for the client certificate if a server resource requiring authentication is requested.

3. The client initiates a client key exchange by creating a *premaster secret* and encrypting it with the server's public key and sending it to the server. The client now returns the client certificate if one has been requested. It may also verify its certificate by sending data encrypted using its private key so that the server can verify that the client is indeed the owner of the certificate.

4. The server and client both generate a *master secret* based off of the shared premaster secret and use the master secret to generate the *session keys*. These are symmetric keys used to encrypt and decrypt the data throughout the session.

5. The client and server send a message to each other stating that all future communications will be encrypted using the session keys, and the handshake is complete.

**Figure 6** SSL Handshake Step-by-Step

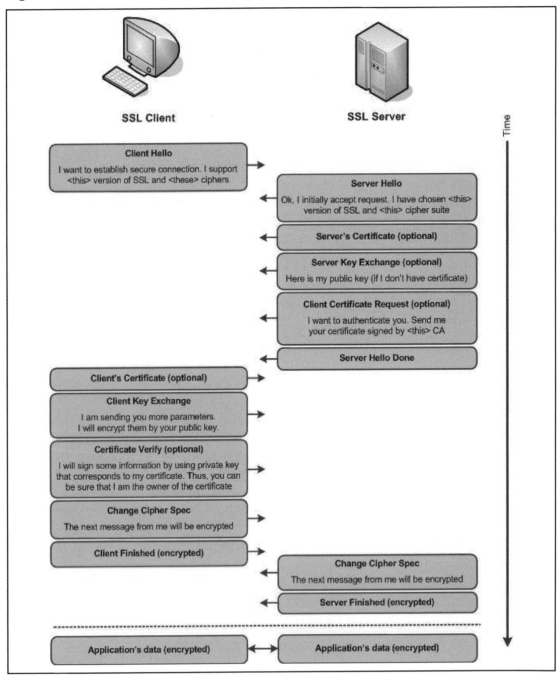

With an SSL VPN there is no need for client software and configuration. Since you can use any browser to connect to the VPN, you can access private resources from anywhere with a browser that supports SSL. Whether at home, an internet café, or an airport kiosk, the widespread use of SSL makes connecting to company resources secure and easy.

## IPSec VPN vs. SSL VPN

An IPSec VPN is fantastic, and is a great choice when you're looking for an always on, dedicated connection, from Network-to-Network across the Internet cloud. It takes more maintenance and time to deploy but is a solid solution.

However, in this battle the SSL VPN seems to be taking on, and surpassing, IPSec as the choice for more and more VPN solutions. There are several reasons this may be the case; the cost associated with deploying an SSL VPN, the relatively low maintenance involved in administrating the device, and the increased control of resources.

Because an SSL VPN uses a Web browser for access there is no maintenance performed on the client side as long as a supported browser is being used, this saves countless man hours and in turn money. It is also a cross platform solution; if the operating system has a supported browser installed then the resources can be accessed. Detailed access control can be used; different users can be given different levels of access rather than being allowed access to more resources than are absolutely necessary.

## What Is the IVE?

All Juniper Networks Secure Access appliances are built upon the Instant Virtual Extranet (IVE) platform. An extranet is an extension of a corporate network to mobile users, telecommuters, or partners that is provided over a secure connection. The Juniper Networks SSL VPN provides this connection through a standard SSL enabled browser.

Once a user has been authenticated they can make requests for resources to the IVE. The IVE, acting as a middle man between the external user and internal company resources, makes requests on behalf of the authenticated user. Any resources the user is permitted access to are passed to the IVE, which then passes the resource on to the remote user. This provides an excellent layer of security since the IVE is the only device ever communicating with the internal resources on the corporate network.

Users are able to access internal websites, file servers, e-mail, Terminal Services sessions, and telnet and/or SSH sessions all through their browser.

Here is a brief summary of how the IVE works:

1.  The end user connects to the IVE using an SSL enabled browser, is authenticated, and makes a request for a specific resource.

2.  The IVE logs the request, terminates the connection to the user, and requests the resource from the internal server using the appropriate protocols.

3.  The internal server receives the request from the IVE and returns the requested resource back to the IVE using the appropriate protocols, where it is logged and the connection to the server is terminated.

4.  The IVE prepares the resource for external transmission, initiates a connection to the requesting user and transmits the requested resource encapsulated in SSL.

5.  The end user receives the connection from the IVE and the requested resource is delivered.

# Where Is the IVE Deployed?

In most situations the IVE will be deployed on the internal side of the corporate firewall, but as networks have endless possibilities the IVE may be deployed in a number of ways. Let's discuss several of them.

## One-Arm, No DMZ

One of the simplest solutions for deploying the IVE is to attach only the internal interface of the IVE to the internal network. The firewall can then be configured in one of two ways.

First, it can allow only SSL traffic destined for the IVE to reach it, dropping all other types of traffic to the IVE. The IVE then acts as a proxy for any connections to internal resources. Or second, the firewall can forward all SSL traffic regardless of destination to the IVE; this allows the IVE to resources based upon User ID and the requested service. Figure 7 is an example of one-arm no DMZ deployment.

**Figure 7** One-Arm, No DMZ Deployment

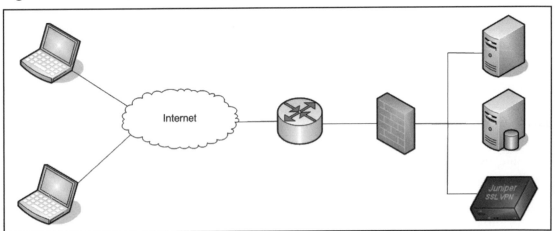

## Two-Arm, DMZ

If you are using a network which has an established DMZ, the IVE can be deployed in a 'Two-Arm, DMZ' format (see Figure 8). With this type of setup you will be using both the internal and external interfaces of the IVE. The external interface is connected to the DMZ, while the internal interface is connected to the internal network.

This setup is similar to the above in that you configure the firewall to forward SSL traffic to the IVE where it acts as a proxy for any connections to internal resources.

**Figure 8** Two-Arm, DMZ Deployment

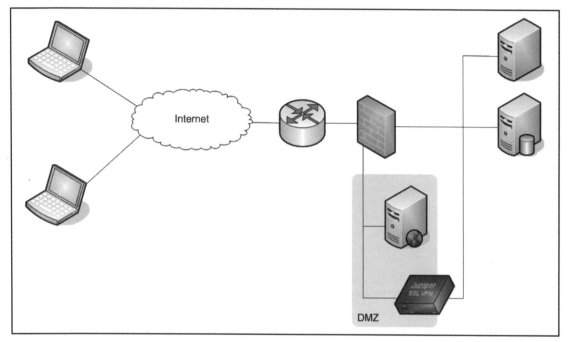

> **NOTE**
>
> If you'd like to administer the IVE from the external interface you'll have to enable administrator access in order to do so. You can do this by logging into the AdminUI and navigating to **Administrators | Admin Realms | <Realm Name> | Authentication Policy | Source IP** and check the box where it reads "**Enable administrators to sign in on the External Port**".

## *Two-Arm, Two DMZ*

Another possible deployment is to create a second DMZ for the internal IVE connection. Again you are going to be using both the internal and external interfaces. The external interface is connected to the public DMZ, and the internal interface is connected to the internal DMZ (see Figure 9).

With this setup you are adding an additional layer of security by placing the firewall between the internal interface and the internal network allowing the firewall to help prevent any unintentional access to resources due to an IVE misconfiguration.

**Figure 9** Two-Arm, Two DMZ Deployment

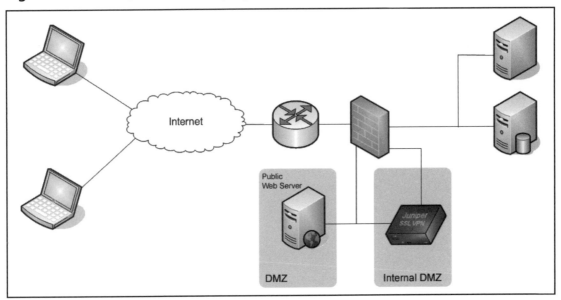

The IVE supports an enormous range of features that you can use in your deployment. Unlike some other vendors that make completely separate builds for their software (so that you have to download a different version of software for a certain combination of features), the IVE has just one package that you install, with each feature activated by a license key.

Each license key is a string of words that is applied to the IVE. Rather than having to enter a complex list of random characters generated by an algorithm, Juniper has chosen to go with a different model which uses a collection of seven words to form the license key. The main advantage here is for administrators because this is easier to enter (particularly if you need to exchange the license key over the phone!).

# IVE Platforms

Since not all business needs are the same the Juniper Networks SSL VPN comes in several different platforms. The product range is sufficient to cover small business to service provider access and features. No matter which device is purchased, all Juniper Networks Secure Access devices are hardened appliances running a proprietary web server from an AES-encrypted hard drive.

For the sake of space, and not turning this section into a marketing rant, we will note the features of the different platforms briefly, however more detailed information on these platforms can be found at www.juniper.net/products_and_services/ssl_vpn_secure_access/index.html

## Secure Access 700

- Designed for small to mid-sized businesses
- Up to 25 Concurrent Users, based on licensing
- Includes 'Network Connect'
- Core Clientless Access is gained through the purchase of the Advanced License

## Secure Access 2000

- Designed for Medium enterprises
- Secure Remote Intranet and Extranet access
- Includes Core Clientless Access
- Up to 100 Concurrent Users, based on licensing
- Secure Meeting with license purchase
- Can be paired with another SA2000 in a cluster, with license
- Secure Application Manager and Network Connect, with license
- Central Manager is gained through purchase of the Advanced License

## Secure Access 4000

- Designed for Medium to Large enterprises
- Secure Remote Intranet and Extranet access
- Includes Core Clientless Access
- Up to 1000 Concurrent Users, based on licensing

- Secure Meeting with license purchase
- Can be paired with another SA4000 in a cluster, with license
- Secure Application Manager and Network Connect, with license
- Hardware based SSL Acceleration, with license
- Instant Virtual Systems, with license
- Central Manager is gained through purchase of the Advanced License
- SA4000 FIPS Hardware also available

## Secure Access 6000

- Designed for Large enterprises
- Secure Remote Intranet and Extranet access
- Includes Core Clientless Access
- Includes Hardware based SSL Acceleration
- Includes Hot-swappable drives
- Up to 2500 Concurrent Users, based on licensing
- Secure Meeting with license purchase
- Can be paired with multiple SA6000's in a cluster, with license
- Secure Application Manager and Network Connect, with license
- Central Manager is gained through purchase of the Advanced License
- SA6000 FIPS Hardware also available

As you can see from the information above there are a multitude of options for any business. With the use of different types of licenses, these platforms can be tailored to suit the needs of any enterprise. A lot of these features do depend on what licenses are purchased, and installed, on the IVE so let's discuss them now.

# License Types

As we mentioned previously, the different features for the IVE are activated by license keys. The following licenses are available for the different IVE devices:

- **Baseline** The Baseline license essentially defines how many concurrent users can be connected to the IVE at a time. This allows you to access the baseline features such as Web and file access. It also provides limited support for external authentication such as Active Directory, Lightweight Directory Access Protocol (LDAP), and RADIUS. The number of users that you can get for a particular license will depend on the platform of the unit itself.

- **Advanced** This opens up many more features on the box, including all authentication types, complex/custom expressions, Secure Virtual Workspace, Central Manager, log filtering, and much more. Just like the Baseline license, this license defines how many concurrent users can access the device.

- **Secure Account  Manager (SAM) and Network Connect** The SAM/Network Connect license activates the SAM and Network Connect feature sets, which allow you access to two of the IVE's most powerful features. In addition, the Terminal Services features are activated in this license (they used to be part of the SAM license, but Juniper combined the SAM and Network Connect licenses into one license). See Chapters 5 and 7 for a thorough discussion of these features.

- **Secure Meeting** One very popular feature is the Secure Meeting feature set, which allows you to host online meetings. This product is similar to Web-Ex, but it is much more lightweight and allows you to do everything from present (share your desktop or applications) to providing remote control. This is a popular feature for everything from performing presentations to providing technical support.

- **Advanced Endpoint Defense: Malware Protection (for Additional Users)** This license allows for coverage for additional users if you are beyond the number of licenses that your appliance supports for performing Advanced Endpoint Defense (provided by WholeSecurity). This feature allows you to actually check a connecting user's machine to ensure that it isn't infected with keyloggers, Trojans, and more. See Chapter 8 for a complete discussion of Advanced Endpoint Defense.

- **Clustering** The Clustering license is required if you are going to cluster multiple IVE devices for additional redundancy. This license covers active/passive and active/active deployments (additional hardware is needed). You will obviously need multiple IVEs to perform clustering. For more discussion about performing clustering, see Chapter 14.

- **SSL Acceleration** If you have an SA 4000 or SA 6000 box, you can purchase this license to offload some SSL encryption/decryption to a hardware card which will handle these features specifically. This allows you to increase your IVEs' throughput. This license will allow you to activate this feature.

- **ICE (In Case of Emergency)** This license is sure to be popular with organizations concerned with disaster recovery. In the event of a disaster that might prevent employees from coming to work, you might still want them to connect to the IVE from another location. The problem is that you probably did not account for such a large number of users connecting to the IVE at a single time, which might overwhelm your license ability. In response, Juniper has produced the ICE license, which will allow you to accommodate a larger number of users to connect to the IVE for a predefined period to help with business continuity.

- **SSL Instant Virtual Systems (IVS)** If your organization is a service provider or is quite large to the point where administration to your IVE is widespread, you might be interested to know of a feature called IVS, which allows you to create virtual IVEs so that you can run multiple IVEs on a single box.

# Summary

The IVE is a fantastic and feature rich device and in order to understand how it all works together you need to start at the beginning. In this chapter we discussed the origins of the juniper Networks SSL VPN or IVE and how it became part of the Juniper Networks product line. We also discussed IPSec and SSL, how they work, and what the benefits to using SSL over IPSec for your VPN solution are.

Once we understood why we might need an SSL VPN we needed to know where the device should be deployed in our network and we discussed what some of those methods are. Finally we discussed the different types of Juniper Networks Secure Access devices and what features and licenses are available.

Now that we've discussed where the IVE comes from, and where and how we might want to deploy it, we need to get the device initially configured for use in our network; we will discuss this topic in Chapter 2.

—Neil R. Wyler

# Chapter 1

## Defining a Firewall

### Solutions in this chapter:

- Why Have Different Types of Firewalls?
- Back to Basics: Transmission Control Protocol/Internet Protocol
- Firewall Types

☑ Summary

☑ Solutions Fast Track

☑ Frequently Asked Questions

# Introduction

When most people think about Internet security, the first thing that comes to mind is a firewall, which is a necessity for connecting online. In it's simplest form, a firewall is a chokepoint from one network (usually an internal network) to another (usually the Internet). However, firewalls are also being used to create chokepoints between other networks in an enterprise environment. There are several different types of firewalls.

# Why Have Different Types of Firewalls?

Before we delve into what types of firewalls there are, we must understand the present threats. While there are many types of threats, we only discuss a few of them in this chapter, paying the most attention to those that can be mitigated by firewalls.

Ensuring a physically secure network environment is the first step in controlling access to your network's data and system files; however, it is only part of a good security plan. This is truer today than in the past, because there are more ways into a network than there used to be. A medium- or large-sized network can have multiple Internet Service Providers (ISP's), virtual private network (VPN) servers, and various remote access avenues for mobile employees including Remote Desktop, browser-based file sharing and e-mail access, mobile phones, and Personal Digital Assistants (Pads).

# Physical Security

One of the most important and overlooked aspects of a comprehensive network security plan is physical access control. This matter is usually left up to facilities managers and plant security departments, or outsourced to security guard companies. Some network administrators concern themselves with sophisticated software and hardware solutions to prevent intruders from accessing internal computers remotely, while at the same time not protecting the servers, routers, cable, and other physical components from direct access. To many "security-conscious" organization's computers are locked all day, only to be left open at night for the janitorial staff. It is not uncommon for computer espionage experts to pose as members of cleaning crews to gain physical access to machines that hold sensitive data. This is a favorite ploy for several reasons:

- Cleaning services are often contracted out and their workers are often transient, so your company's employees might not know who is a legitimate member of the cleaning company staff.

- Cleaning is usually done late at night when all or most company employees are gone, making it easier to surreptitiously steal data.

- The cleaning crew members are paid little attention by company employees, who take their presence for granted and think nothing of them being in areas where the presence of others would normally be questioned.

Physically breaking into a server room and stealing a hard disk where sensitive data resides is a crude method of breaching security; nonetheless, it happens. In some organizations, it may be the easiest way to gain unauthorized access, especially for an intruder who has help "on the inside."

It is beyond the scope of this book to go into detail about how to physically secure your network, but it is important for you to make physical access control the outer perimeter of your security plan, which means:

- Controlling physical access to the servers

- Controlling physical access to networked workstations

- Controlling physical access to network devices

- Controlling physical access to the cable

- Being aware of security considerations with wireless media

- Being aware of security considerations related to portable computers

- Recognizing the security risk of allowing data to be printed

- Recognizing the security risks involving floppy disks, CDs, tapes, and other removable media

There are also different types of external intruders who will physically break into your facility to gain access to your network. Although not a true "insider," because he or she is not authorized to be there and do not have a valid account on the network, this person still has many of the advantages (refer to the "Internal Security Breaches" section.) Your security policy should take into account the threats posed by these "hybrid" intruders. Remember, someone with physical access to your servers has complete control over your data. Someone with physical access to your authentication servers owns everything.

# Network Security

Virtual intruders can access your network from across the street or from halfway around the world. They can do as much damage as a thief that breaks into your company headquarters to steal or destroy data, and are much harder to catch. The following sections examine specific network security risks and ways to prevent them.

For a number of years, firewalls were used to divide an organization's internal network from the Internet. There was usually a demilitarized zone (DMZ), which contained less valuable resources that had to be exposed to the Internet (e.g., Web servers, VPN gateways, and so forth), and a private network that contained all of the organization's resources (e.g., user computers, servers, printers, and so forth). Perimeter defense is still vitally important, given the ever-increasing threat level from outside the network. However, it is no longer adequate by itself.

With the growth of the Internet, many organizations focused their security efforts on defending against outside attackers (i.e., those originating from an external network) who are not authorized to access the systems. Firewalls were the primary focus of these efforts. Money was spent building a strong perimeter defense, resulting in what Bill Cheswick from Bell Labs famously described years ago as, "A crunchy shell around a soft, chewy center." Any attacker who succeeded in getting through (or around) the perimeter defenses, would have a relatively easy time compromising internal systems. This situation is analogous to the enemy parachuting into the castle keep instead of breaking through the walls. Perimeter defense is still vitally important, given the increased threat level from outside the network; however, it is simply no longer adequate by itself.

Various information security studies and surveys have found that the majority of attacks come from inside an organization. Given how lucrative the sale of information can be, people inside organizations can be a greater threat than people outside the organization. These internal threats can include authorized users attempting to exceed their permissions, or unauthorized users trying to go where they should not be. Therefore, an insider is more dangerous than an outsider, because he or she has a level of access to facilities and systems that the outsider does not. Many organizations lack the internal preventive controls and other countermeasures to adequately defend against this threat. Wide open networks and servers sitting in unsecured areas provide easy access to the internal hacker.

The greatest threat, however, arises when an insider colludes with a structured outside attacker. With few resources exposed to the outside world, it is easier for the bad guys to enlist internal people to do their dirty work. The outsider's skills combined with the insider's access could result in substantial damage or loss to the organization.

# Attacks

Attacks can be divided into three main categories:

- **Reconnaissance Attacks** Hackers attempt to discover systems and gather information. In most cases, these attacks are used to gather information to set up an access or a Denial of Service (DOS) attack. A typical reconnaissance attack might consist of a hacker pinging Internet Protocol (IP) addresses to discover what is alive on a network. The hacker might then perform a port scan on the system to see which applications are running, and to try to determine the operating system (OS) and version on a target machine.

- **Access Attacks** An access attack is one in which an intruder attempts to gain unauthorized access to a system to retrieve information. Sometimes the attacker has to gain access to a system by cracking passwords or using an exploit. At other times, the attacker already has access to the system, but needs to escalate his or her privileges.

- **DOS Attacks** Hackers use DOS attacks to disable or corrupt access to networks, systems, or services. The intent is to deny authorized or valid users access to these resources. DOS attacks typically involve running a script or a tool, and the attacker does not require access to the target system, only the means to reach it. In a Distributed DOS (DDOS) attack, the source consists of many computers that are usually spread across a large geographic boundary.

# Recognizing Network Security Threats

In order to effectively protect your network, you must consider the following question: From who or what are you protecting it? In this section, we approach the answer to that question from three perspectives:

- Who are the people that break into networks?

- Why do they do what they do?

- What are the types of network attacks and how do they work?

First we look at intruder motivations and classify the various types of people who have the skill and desire to hack into others' computers and networks.

## Understanding Intruder Motivations

There are probably as many different specific motives as there are hackers, but the most common intruder motivations can be broken down into a few broad categories:

- **Recreation** Those who hack into networks "just for fun" or to prove their technical prowess; often young people or "antiestablishment" types.

- **Remuneration** People who invade the network for personal gain, such as those who attempt to transfer funds to their own bank accounts or erase records of their debts, and "hackers for hire" who are paid by others to break into the network. Corporate espionage is also included in this category.

- **Revenge** Dissatisfied customers, disgruntled former employees, angry competitors, or people who have a personal grudge against someone in the organization.

The scope of damage and the extent of the intrusion is often tied to the intruder's motivation.

# Recreational Hackers

Teen hackers who hack primarily for the thrill of accomplishment, often do little or no permanent damage, perhaps only leaving "I was here" messages to "stake their claims" and prove to their peers that they were able to penetrate your network's security.

There are also more malevolent versions of the fun-seeking hacker. These cyber-vandals get their kicks out of destroying as much of your data as possible or causing your systems to crash.

**NOTE**

The following is one example of a recreational hacker:

October 17, 2005 (Computerworld)—Using a self-propagating worm that exploits a scripting vulnerability common to most dynamic Web sites, a Los Angeles teenager made himself the most popular member of community Web site *MySpace.com* earlier this month. While the attack caused little damage, the technique could be used to destroy Web site data or steal private information, even from enterprise users behind protected networks.

The unknown 19-year-old, who used the name 'Samy,' put a small bit of code in his user profile on MySpace, a 32-million-member site, most of whom are under age 30. Whenever Samy's profile was viewed, the code was executed in the background, adding Samy to the viewer's list of friends and writing at the bottom of their profile, "Samy is my hero."

## Profit-Motivated Hackers

Hackers who break into your network for remuneration of some kind—either directly or indirectly—are more dangerous. Because money is at stake, they are more motivated than other hackers to accomplish their objective. Unfortunately, the number of these hackers are increasing dramatically, especially with the profitability of identity theft. Furthermore, because many of them are "professionals", their hacking techniques could be more sophisticated than those of the average teenage recreational hacker.

Monetary motivations include:

- Personal financial gain
- Corporate espionage
- Third-party payment for the information obtained

Those motivated by the last goal are almost always the most sophisticated, and the most dangerous. money is often involved in the theft of identity information. Identity thieves can be employees who have been approached by any number of malicious organizations and offered money or merchandise or even threatened with blackmail or physical harm.

In some instances, hackers go "undercover" and seek a job with a company in order to steal data that they can give to their own organizations. To add insult to injury, these "stealth spies" are then paid by your company at the same time they're working against you.

There are also "professional" freelance corporate spies that can be contracted to obtain company secrets, or they might do it on their own and auction the data off to competitors.

These corporate espionage agents are often highly skilled. They are technically savvy and intelligent enough to avoid being caught or detected. Fields that are especially vulnerable to the threat of corporate espionage include:

- Oil and energy
- Engineering
- Computer technology
- Research medicine
- Law

Any company on the verge of a breakthrough that could result in large monetary rewards or worldwide recognition, should be aware of the possibility of espionage and take steps to guard against it.

*Phishing,* the new information gathering technique, is spreading and becoming more sophisticated. Phishing e-mails either ask the victim to fill out a form, or directs them to a Web page designed to look like a legitimate banking site. The victim is asked for personal information such as credit card numbers, social security number, or other data that can then be used for identity theft. There has been at least one insidious phishing scheme that uses a Secure Sockets Layer (SSL) certificate so that the data you give to the hacker is safely encrypted on the network.

---

**NOTE**

"Cybercrime on the rise, survey finds. Criminal attacks online are on the upswing and they are getting stealthier," according to Symantec.

By Amanda Cantrell, *CNNMoney.com* staff writer

March 7, 2006: 11:51 AM EST

NEW YORK (*CNNMoney.com*) - Cybercrime is on the rise, and today's attacks are often silent, hard to detect and highly targeted, according to a new survey.

Danger in the ether

Symantec (down $0.57 to $15.96, Research), which makes anti-virus software for businesses and consumers, found a notable increase in "cybercrime" threats to computer users, according to the latest installment of its semiannual Internet Security Threat Report. Cybercrime consists of criminal acts performed using a computer or the Internet. Symantec also found a rise in the use of "crimeware," or software used to conduct cybercrime.

Cybercriminals are also getting more sophisticated. Attacks designed to destroy data have now given way to attacks designed to steal data outright, often for financial gain, according to the survey, which covers the six-month period from July 1, 2005 to December 31, 2005. Eighty percent of all threats are designed to steal personal information from consumers, intellectual property from corporations, or to control the end user's machine, according to Symantec.

Moreover, today's attackers are abandoning large-scale attacks on corporate firewalls in favor of targets such as individual desktop computers, using Web applications that can capture personal, financial, and confidential information that can then be used for financial gain. That continues a trend Symantec found in its survey covering the first half of 2005."

# Vengeful Hackers

Hackers motivated by the desire for revenge are also dangerous. Vengeance seeking is usually based on strong emotions, which means that these hackers could go all-out in their efforts to sabotage your network.

Examples of hackers or security saboteurs acting out of revenge include:

- Former employees who are bitter about being fired or laid off, or who quit their jobs under unpleasant circumstances.

- Current employees who feel mistreated by the company, especially those who are planning to leave soon.

- Current employees who aim to sabotage the work of other employees due to internal political battles, rivalry over promotions, and the like.

- Outsiders who have grudges against the company, such as dissatisfied customers or employees of competing companies who want to harm or embarrass the company.

- Outsiders who have personal grudges against someone who works for the company, such as employees' former girlfriends or boyfriends, spouses going through a divorce, and other relationship-related problems.

Luckily, the intruders in this category are generally less technically talented than those in the other two groups, and their emotional involvement could cause them to be careless and take outrageous chances, which makes them easier to catch.

**N**OTE

New Directions in Malware

Kaspersky Labs reports on extortion scams using malware:

"We've reported more than once on cases where remote malicious users have moved away from the stealth use of infected computers (stealing data from them, using them as part of zombie networks, and so forth) to direct blackmail, demanding payment from victims. At the moment, this method is used in two main ways: encrypting user data and corrupting system information.

Users quickly understand that something has happened to their data. They are then told that they should send a specific sum to an e-payment account maintained by the remote malicious user, whether it be EGold, Webmoney or some other e-payment account. The ransom demanded varies significantly depending on the amount of money available to the victim. We know of cases where the malicious users have demanded $50, and of cases where they have demanded more than $2,000. The first such blackmail case was in 1989, and now this method is again gaining in popularity.

In 2005, the most striking examples of this type of cybercrime were carried out using the Trojans GpCode and Krotten. The first of these encrypts user data; the second restricts itself to making a number of modifications to the victim machine's system registry, causing it to cease functioning.

Among other worms, the article discusses the *GpCode.ac* worm, which encrypts data using 56-bit Rivest, Shamir, & Adleman (RSA). The whole article is interesting reading.

Posted on April 26, 2006 at 01:07 PM on *www.schneier.com*."

## Hybrid Hackers

The three categories of hacker can overlap in some cases. A recreational hacker who perceives himself as having been mistreated by an employer or in a personal relationship, could use his otherwise benign hacking skills to impose "justice," or a vengeful ex-employee or ex-spouse might pay someone else to do the hacking.

It is beneficial to understand the common motivations of network intruders because, although we might not be able to predict which type of hacker will decide to attack our networks, we can recognize how each operates and take steps to protect our networks from all of them.

Even more important than the type of hacker in planning our security strategy, is the type of attack. In the next section, we examine specific types of network attacks and ways in which you can protect against them.

---

**NOTE**

Social engineering, also known as people hacking, is a means for obtaining security information from people by tricking them. The classic example is calling up a user and pretending to be a system administrator. The hacker asks the user for his or her password to perform some important maintenance task. To avoid being hacked via social engineering, educate your user community that they should always confirm the identity of any person calling them, and that passwords should never be given to anyone over e-mail, instant messaging, or the telephone.

It is beyond the scope of this book to address social engineering and ways to educate employees against it. However, SysAdmin, Audit, Network, Security (SANS) Institute (*http://www.sans.org*) has both full courses and step-by-step guides to help with this process.

---

# Back to Basics: Transmission Control Protocol/Internet Protocol

Transmission Control Protocol/Internet Protocol (TCP/IP) is the network protocol that pushes data around the Internet. (Other protocols you may have heard of are Windows NETBeui, Mac Appletalk, and Novell IPX/XPS, however none of these concern us). You don't need to understand the intricacies of TCP/IP; however, a basic understanding will make your firewall deployment much easier.

TCP/IP is based on the idea that data is sent in packets, similar to putting a letter in an envelope. Each packet contains a header that contains routing information concerning where the packet came from and where it is going (similar to the address and return address on an envelope), and the data itself (the letter contained in the envelope). Figure 1.1 illustrates a typical TCP/IP packet.

**Figure 1.1** Layout of a Typical TCP/IP Packet

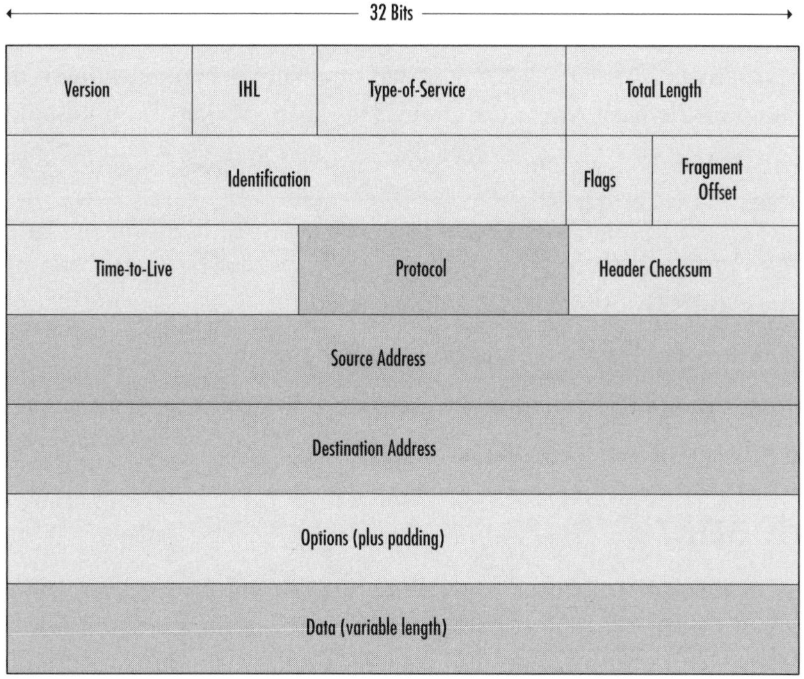

| 32 Bits | | | |
|---|---|---|---|
| Version | IHL | Type-of-Service | Total Length |
| Identification | | | Flags / Fragment Offset |
| Time-to-Live | | Protocol | Header Checksum |
| Source Address | | | |
| Destination Address | | | |
| Options (plus padding) | | | |
| Data (variable length) | | | |

- **Version**  Indicates the version of IP currently used.

- **IP Header Length (IHL)**  Indicates the datagram header length in 32-bit words.

- **Type of Service**  Specifies how an upper-layer protocol wants a current datagram to be handled, and assigns various levels of importance to datagrams.

- **Total Length**  Specifies the length, in bytes, of the entire IP packet, including the data and header.

- **Identification**  Contains an integer that identifies the current datagram. This field is used to help piece together datagram fragments.

- **Flags**  Consists of a 3-bit field of which the two low-order (least significant) bits control fragmentation. The low-order bit specifies whether the packet can be fragmented. The middle-order bit specifies whether the packet is the last fragment in a series of fragmented packets. The third or high-order bit is not used.

- **Fragment Offset**  Indicates the position of the fragment's data relative to the beginning of the data in the original datagram, which allows the destination IP process to properly reconstruct the original datagram.

- **Time-to-live**  Maintains a counter that gradually decrements down to zero, at which point the datagram is discarded. This keeps packets from looping endlessly.

- **Protocol**  Indicates which upper-layer protocol receives incoming packets after IP processing is complete.

- **Header Checksum**  Helps ensure IP header integrity.

- **Source Address**  Specifies the sending node.

- **Destination Address**  Specifies the receiving node.

- **Options**  Allows IP to support various options, such as security.

- **Data**  Upper-layer information.

# TCP/IP Header

The "envelope" or header of a packet contains a great deal of information, only some of which is of interest to firewall administrators, who are primarily interested in source and destination addresses and port numbers. Only application proxies deal with the data section.

## IP Addresses

Source and destination addresses reference the exact machine a packet came from and the corresponding machine receiving the packet. These addresses are in the standard form of four sets of three-digit numbers separated by periods (i.e., the IP version 4 standard). Table 1.1 shows the various classes of IP addresses.

**Table 1.1** IP Address Classes

| Class | Start Address | Comment |
| --- | --- | --- |
| A | 0.0.0.0 | Standard internet addresses available to all users, except private 10.0.0.0 subnet |
| B | 128.0.0.0 | Standard internet addresses available to all users, except private 172.16.0.0 – 172.31.255.255 range |
| C | 192.0.0.0 | Standard internet addresses available to all users, except private 192.168.0.0 subnet |
| D | 224.0.0.0 | Multicast address class |
| E | 240.0.0.0 | Research and limited broadcast class |

As noted in the table, there are three sets of addresses known as *private addresses* and there are three subnets designated as private: 10.0.0.0 to 10.255.255.255, 172.16.0.0 to 172.31.255.255, and 192.168.0.0 to 192.168.255.255. By definition, these subnets, cannot be routed on the Internet.

There is also a group of IP addresses known as *self-assigned addresses*, which range from 169.254.0.0 to 169.254.255.255. These addresses are used by the OS when no other address is available, making it possible to connect to a computer on a network that doesn't automatically assign addresses (Dynamic Host Configuration Protocol [DHCP]), and there are no valid *static IP addresses* that can be typed into the network configuration. All routers, switches, firewalls, and other appliances are designed to stop these addresses.

One address is reserved as the *loopback address*. Address 127.0.0.1 refers to the machine itself, and is generally used to confirm that the TCP/IP protocol is correctly installed and functioning on the machine.

Networks 224.0.0.0 to 254.255.255.255 are reserved for special testing and applications. While Internet-routable, the standard organization or individual does not generally use them. The Class D network provides *multicast* capabilities. A multicast is when a group of IP addresses is defined in such a way as to permit individual packets to have a destination address of all the machines, rather than a single machine. Class E is for research by particular organizations and has *limited broadcast* capabilities. A *broadcast* is when a single device sends out a packet that has no particular recipient. Instead, it goes to every machine on the subnet. On standard (non-Class E) networks, this is defined by address 255.255.255.255. The Class E network is different and is not accessible to devices on the other classes of networks.

While there are legitimate uses for broadcasts (e.g., obtaining a DHCP address), we want to keep them to a minimum. To this end, all routers and firewalls block broadcasts by default. Too many broadcasts will slow network performance to a crawl.

Every device on the Internet must have a unique IP address. If a device has a valid IP address (i.e., not a private, non-routable address or self-assigned address) and is not behind a firewall, it is available for connection to any other device on the Internet. A computer in Berlin can print to a printer in London. A mail server in Chicago can deliver e-mail directly to a machine in Singapore.

This ubiquitous communication and ability to transfer data directly from one machine to another is what makes the Internet so powerful. It is also what makes it so dangerous. It is impossible to stress strongly enough that no machine on the public Internet is hidden. No machine is safe from detection. Firewalls are the only method of safely hiding a device on a private network, while still providing access to the Internet as a whole.

Firewalls are able to hide a device by doing *address translation*. Address translation is when firewalls convert a valid Internet address to a private address on a private subnet. Almost all firewalls do this type of address translation, which has several advantages:

- **An Additional Layer of Security** Without the firewall in place to do the translations, Internet addresses can't communicate with the private network and vice versa.

- **Expansion of Available IP Addresses** Not every device in your organization needs to be accessible from the Internet. User workstations require access to the Internet, but do not need to have incoming traffic originating on the Internet. They only require responses to inquiries sent out. Most firewalls handle this by converting every internal address to a single, Internet-routable address. This address is usually the address of the firewall itself, but does not necessarily have to be.

- **Ability to Completely Hide a Device from the Internet** Is it necessary to have your printers available to the Internet? Does that Web server that is only available to employees at their desks, need to have an Internet address? The answer to both questions is probably "no." With a firewall capable of address translation, both of these examples can be assigned a private address with no translation to the outside. The device is hidden from anyone on the public Internet and is completely inaccessible.

## IP Half-Scan Attack

*Half scans* (also called *half-open scans* or *FIN scans*) attempt to avoid detection by sending only initial or final packets rather than establishing a connection. Every IP connection starts with a Synchronous (SYN) packet from the connecting computer. The responding computers respond with a SYN/Acknowledgement (ACK) packet, which acknowledges the original packet and establishes the communication parameters. SYN/ACK continues until the end of the communication when a *FIN packet* is sent and the connection is broken. A half scan starts the SYN/ACK process with a targeted computer but does not complete it. Software that conducts half scans, such as Jakal, is called a *stealth scanner*. Many port-scanning detectors are unable to detect half scans.

## IP Spoofing

*IP spoofing* involves changing the packet headers of a message to indicate that it came from an IP address other than the true source. The spoofed address is normally a trusted port that allows a hacker to get a message through a firewall or router that would otherwise be filtered out. Modern firewalls protect against IP spoofing.

Hackers use spoofing whenever it is beneficial for one machine to impersonate another. It is often used in combination with another type of attack (e.g., a spoofed address is used in the SYN flood attack to create a "half-open" connection. The client never responds to the SYN/ACK message, because the spoofed address is that of a computer that is down or doesn't exist. Spoofing is also used to hide the true IP address of the attacker in ping of death, teardrop, and other attacks. IP spoofing can be prevented using source address verification on your firewall.

## Denial-of-Service Attacks

In February 2000, massive DOS attacks brought down several of the biggest Web sites, including *Yahoo.com* and *Buy.com*. DOS attacks are a popular choices for Internet hackers who want to disrupt a network's operations. The objective of DOS attackers is to bring down the network, thereby denying service to its legitimate users. DOS attacks are easy to initiate, because software is readily available from hacker Web sites and warez newsgroups that allow anyone to launch a DOS attack with little or no technical expertise.

> **NOTE**
>
> *Warez* is a term used by hackers and crackers to describe bootlegged software that has been "cracked" to remove copy protections and made available by software pirates on the Internet, or in its broader definition, to describe any illegally distributed software.

The purpose of a DOS attack is to render a network inaccessible by generating a type or amount of network traffic that will crash the servers, overwhelm the routers, or otherwise prevent the network's devices from functioning properly. DOS can be accomplished by tying up the server's resources (e.g., by overwhelming the central processing unit (CPU) and memory resources. In other cases, a particular user or machine can be the target of DOS attacks that hang up the client machine and require it to be rebooted.

> **NOTE**
>
> DOS attacks are sometimes referred to in the security community as *nuke attacks*.
>
> Distributed DOS (DDOS) attacks use intermediary computers (called *agents*) on which programs (called *zombies*) have previously been surreptitiously installed, usually by a virus or Trojan (see below). The hacker activates these zombie programs remotely, causing the intermediary computers (which can number in the hundreds or even thousands) to simultaneously launch the actual attack. Because the attack comes from the computers running the zombie programs— which could potentially be on networks anywhere in the world—the hacker is able to conceal the true origin of the attack.

It is important to note that DDOS attacks pose a two-layer threat. Not only could your network be the target of a DOS attack that crashes your servers and prevents incoming and outgoing traffic, but your computers could be used as the "innocent middlemen" to launch a DOS attack against another network or site.

The Domain Name Server (DNS) DOS attack exploits the difference in size between a DNS query and a DNS response, in which all of the network's bandwidth is tied up by bogus DNS queries. The attacker uses the DNS servers as "amplifiers" to multiply the DNS traffic.

The attacker begins by sending small DNS queries to each DNS server, which contain the spoofed IP address of the intended victim (see "IP Spoofing" in this chapter). The responses returned to the small queries are much larger in size, so if there are a large number of responses returned at the same time, the link will become congested and DOS will take place.

One solution to this problem is for administrators to configure DNS servers to answer with a "refused" response (which is much smaller than a name resolution response) when they receive DNS queries from suspicious or unexpected sources.

**NOTE**

Detailed information on configuring DNS servers to prevent this problem are contained in the U.S. Department of Energy's Computer Incident Advisory Capability information bulletin J-063, available at *www.ciac.org/ciac/bulletins/j-063.shtml.*

## Notes from the Underground…

### IP Version 6

You may have heard of IPv6, the new standard for Internet communications. This standard was devised to address several problems with IPv4, primarily the limited number of possible addresses available. IPv4 supports $4.3 \times 10^9$ (4.3 billion) addresses, while IPv6 supports $3.4 \times 10^{38}$ addresses. The roll out of IPv6 is occurring slowly, as more computers and network appliances become IPv6-compatible. For the foreseeable future, IPv4 will be the de facto standard. What you learn in this book will still largely apply to IPv6. Firewall concepts, filtering theories, and deployment strategies will change little, if at all.

IPv6 does not use the same classes of addresses as IPv4. Instead, there are three classes: unicast, multicast, and anycast. Broadcasts are not supported; however, multicast accomplishes nearly the same end.

Also, IPv6 has only two reserved addresses, one for internal protocol implementation and a loopback address. All other addresses are free for use on the public Internet.

The question which should come to mind is, "If my firewall supports IVv6, and I really don't use it, do I need to worry about configuring it?" The short answer is "yes."

There are already exploits that take advantage of IPv6. If firewalls supporting IPv6 are configured incorrectly, they will pass unimpeded through your firewall. Remember, IPv6 is designed to travel over the same network as IPv4. All it needs are routers, switches, and firewalls that support IPv6. Most new network appliances support IPv6.

## Source-Routing Attack

TCP/IP supports *source routing,* which is a means to permit the sender of network data to route the packets through a specific point on the network. There are two types of source routing:

- **Strict Source Routing** The sender of the data can specify the exact route (rarely used).

- **Loose Source Record Route (LSRR)** The sender can specify certain routers (hops) through which the packet must pass.

The source route is an option in the IP header that allows the sender to override routing decisions normally made by the routers between the source and destination machines. Network administrators use source routing to map the network or to troubleshoot routing and communications problems. It can also be used to force traffic through a route that will provide the best performance. Unfortunately, hackers can also exploit source routing.

If the system allows source routing, an intruder can use it to reach private internal addresses on the Local Area Network (LAN) (normally not reachable from the Internet), by routing the traffic through another machine that is reachable from both the Internet and the internal machine. Source routing should be, and is disabled on most routers to prevent this type of attack. If it is not disabled on your router, disable it now.

# TCP/UDP Ports

A port number is a virtual "mail slot" on each of these machines. Applications running on computers listen to the Internet for incoming information on these ports. Certain applications listen on certain ports. The Internet Assigned Numbers Authority (IANA [*www.iana.org*]) defines these ports (e.g., Web servers listen on ports 80 and 443 and File Transfer Protocol (FTP) servers listen on port 21. Hyper-text Transfer Protocol (HTTP), Hyper-Text Transfer Protocol Secure sockets (HTTPS), and FTP are examples of IPs. You will never find a legitimate FTP server listening on port 80. Ports 1 to 1023 are considered well-known ports, and have clearly defined IP's. Ports 1024 through 49151 are *registered ports*. Specific software vendors have registered these ports for use by their specific applications. Ports 49152 to 65535 are *dynamic ports*. These have no specific registration and can be used by any application at any time. Using either or both application and gateway firewalls mitigates the misuse of ports.

Ports can use either the TCP protocol or the User Datagram Packet (UDP) protocol. TCP requires a connection started with a SYN packet that receives an ACK packet in response. SYN-ACK continues until the end of the data transmission. Each ACK packet confirms the correct receipt of the SYN packet containing data. On the other hand, UDP protocols send data with no requirement for a response. UDP protocols are generally faster than TCP protocols, but there is no assurance that the data has arrived at its destination intact.

RFC 1700 documents, the official well-known port assignments, are available on the Web at *www.freesoft.org/CIE/RFC/1700/index.htm.* The IANA makes the port assignments. In general, a service uses the same port number with UDP as with TCP, although there are some exceptions. The assigned ports were originally numbered from 0 to 255, but were later expanded to 0 to 1023.

Some of the most well-known ports used are:

- TCP/UDP port 20: FTP (data)
- TCP/UDP port 21: FTP (control)
- TCP/UDP port 22: SSH
- TCP/UDP port 23: Telnet
- TCP/UDP port 25: SMTP
- TCP/UDP port 53: DNS
- TCP/UDP port 67: BOOTP server
- TCP/UDP port 68: BOOTP client
- TCP/UDP port 69: TFTP
- TCP/UDP port 80: HTTP
- TCP/UDP port 88: Kerberos
- TCP/UDP port 110: POP3
- TCP/UDP port 119: NNTP
- TCP/UDP port 137: NetBIOS name service
- TCP/UDP port 138: NetBIOS datagram service
- TCP/UDP port 139: NetBIOS session service
- TCP/UDP port 220: IMAPv3
- TCP/UDP port 389: LDAP
- TCP/UDP port 443: HTTPS
- TCP/UDP port 1433: Microsoft SQL
- TCP/UDP ports 6660–6669 and 7000: IRC (Internet Relay Chat [IRC])

## Port Scanning

A total of 65,535 TCP ports and 65,535 UDP ports are used for various services and applications. If a port is open, it responds when another computer attempts to contact it over the network. Port-scanning programs such as *Nmap* are used to determine which ports are open on a particular machine. The program sends packets for a wide variety of protocols and, by examining which messages receive responses and which don't, creates a map of the computer's listening ports.

It is not possible to turn off all listening ports. If you did, you would render the computer invisible on the network and other devices would be unable to communicate with the computer. This may be exactly what you want with a workstation, but with servers, this is impossible.

Port scanning generally does no harm to your network or system, but it does provide hackers with information they can use to penetrate a network. Potential attackers use port scans in much the same way that a car thief checks the doors of parked vehicles to determine which ones are unlocked. Although this activity in itself does not constitute a serious offense and is generally not considered illegal. However, what the person conducting the scan does with the information can present a big problem. Intensive port scanning can cause a DOS and in some cases crash the machine being scanned. Should these situations occur, the activity is illegal.

**N**OTE

The intrusion and attack reporting center at *www.doshelp.com/PC/trojanports. htm* is an excellent resource for information on ports that should be closed, filtered, or monitored, because they are commonly used for Trojan and intrusion programs.

Firewall logs are an excellent resource to analyze and to see if you are being port-scanned. Port scans generally appear as pings to various ports on one IP address after another. Port scanners are now automated so the hacker can set it to run and come back later to a report of IP addresses with listening ports.

The logs also provide evidence should legal action be taken against the scanner. Thus, logs need to be maintained and backed up in a secure manner.

## Other Protocol Exploits

The attacks discussed so far involve exploiting some feature or weakness of the TCP/IP protocols. Hackers can also exploit vulnerabilities of other common protocols, such as HTTP, DNS, Common Gateway Interface (CGI), and other common protocols.

Active-X controls, JavaScript, and VBScript can be used to add animations or applets to Web sites, or to Hyper Text Markup Language (HTML) e-mail messages, but hackers can exploit these to write controls or scripts that allow them to remotely plant viruses, access data, or change or delete files on the hard disks of unaware users. Both Web browsers and e-mail client programs that support HTML mail are vulnerable.

# Data Packet

The data portion of the packet itself can be analyzed. Gateway firewalls generally do not perform this type of analysis, or they do it in a "rudimentary" or "simplistic" manner. Application proxies are much more thorough and examine each packet that is passed through the application proxy.

Since data packets vary greatly from application to application, it is impossible within the scope of this book to describe how packets are structured and the process for examining each type. Let's take a brief look at some ways to manipulate the data packet for nefarious purposes.

## *System and Software Exploits*

*System and software exploits* allow hackers to take advantage of weaknesses of particular OSs and applications (often called *bugs*). Like protocol exploits, they are used by intruders to gain unauthorized access to computers or networks, or to crash or clog up the systems to deny service to others.

Common bugs can be categorized as follows:

- **Buffer Overflows** Many common security holes are based on buffer overflow problems. Buffer overflows occur when the number of bytes or characters input exceeds the maximum number allowed by the programmer writing the program.

- **Unexpected Input** Programmers may not take steps to define what happens if invalid input (input that doesn't match program specifications) is entered. Such input could cause the program to crash or open up a way into the system.

- **System Configuration Bugs** These are not really bugs per se, but rather they are ways of configuring the OS or software that leaves it vulnerable to penetration.

Popular software such as Microsoft's Internet Information Server (IIS), Microsoft's Internet Explorer (MSIE), Linux Apache Web Server, UNIX Sendmail, and Mac Quicktime, are popular targets of hackers looking for software security holes that can be exploited.

Major OS and software vendors regularly release security patches to fix exploitable bugs. It is very important for network administrators to stay up-to-date in applying these fixes and/or service packs to ensure that their systems are as secure as possible.

## *Trojans, Viruses, and Worms, Oh My!*

Intruders who access your systems without authorization or inside attackers with malicious motives, could plant various types of programs to cause damage to your network. There are three broad categories of *malicious code*: Trojans, viruses, and worms.

- **Trojans** The name, short for *Trojan horse*, refers to a software program that appears to perform a useful function, but in fact performs actions that the program user is not aware of or did not intend. Hackers often write Trojans to circumvent the security of a system. Once the Trojan is installed, the hacker can exploit the security holes it creates to gain unauthorized access, or the Trojan program can perform some action such as deleting or modifying files, transmitting files across the network to the intruder, or installing other programs or viruses.

  Basically, the Trojan can perform any action that the user has privileges and permissions to perform on the system. This means that a Trojan is especially dangerous if the unsuspecting user who installs it is an administrator and has access to the system files.

  Trojans can be cleverly disguised as innocuous programs, utilities, screensavers, or the like. A Trojan can also be installed by an executable script (JavaScript, a Java applet, Active-X control, and so forth) on a Web site. Accessing the site can initiate the installation of the program, if the Web browser is configured to allow scripts to run automatically.

- **Viruses** Includes any programs that are usually installed without the user's awareness and performs undesired actions. Viruses can also replicate themselves, infecting other systems by writing themselves to any disk used in the computer or sending themselves across the network. Viruses often distribute as attachments to e-mail or as macros in word processing documents. Some viruses activate immediately on installation; others lie dormant until a specific date or time, or when a particular system event triggers them.

  Viruses come in thousands of varieties. They can do anything from popping up a message that says "Hi!" to erasing a computer's entire hard disk. The proliferation of computer viruses has also led to the phenomenon of the virus hoax, which is a warning (generally circulated via e-mail or Web sites) about a virus that does not exist or does not do what the warning claims it will do. Real viruses, however, present a real threat to your network. Companies such as Symantec and McAfee make anti-virus software that is aimed at detecting and removing virus programs. Because new viruses are created daily, it is important to download new virus definition files, which contain the information required to detect each virus type on a regular basis, to ensure that your virus protection stays up-to-date. The most dangerous virus is a new, fast replicating virus for which no definition has been created. Fortunately, anti-virus companies now respond within hours of a new outbreak. Since nearly all anti-virus software has auto-update features, the new definitions are usually quickly put in place and effectively shut down the proliferation. This does not mean you are immune from infection if you have anti-virus software, it just means you are generally safe from older viruses.

Both viruses and Trojans may carry a logic bomb (i.e., a bit of malicious code designed to "explode" under certain circumstances such as performing, or failing to perform an action). The bomb can do anything from delete files to wipe a computer. The "fun" part of a logic bomb for a hacker is letting the victim believe nothing is wrong and then at a much later time damage the computer, making it more difficult to determine where and when the infection occurred.

■ A **worm** is a program that can travel across the network from one computer to another. Sometimes different parts of a worm run on different computers. Worms make multiple copies of themselves and spread throughout a network. The distinction between viruses and worms has become blurred. Originally the term *worm* was used to describe code that attacked multi-user systems (networks) and *virus* was used to describe programs that replicated on individual computers.

The primary purpose of a worm is to replicate. Worm programs were initially used for legitimate purposes in performing network management duties, but their ability to multiply quickly has been exploited by hackers, who create malicious worms that replicate wildly and might also exploit OS weaknesses and perform other harmful actions.

Unfortunately, nearly all these now contain a *root-kit*. This is a series of tools that take control of your machine and create a zombie that will do the bidding of the malicious writer. Once a root-kit is installed on your machine, your only choice is to flatten the machine and rebuild from scratch. Root-kits notoriously have subprograms that hide their presence from the OS. While there are tools such as Root-kit Revealer by SysInternals (*www.sysinternals.com*), there is no sure way to confirm that all pieces of the root-kit have been removed. Any remaining bits have the potential to reinstall the entire root-kit and begin transmitting information to the owner.

## Buffer Overflow

In general, most data packets can be manipulated in an attempt to create a *buffer overflow*, which is a specific condition in an application where more data is written to an area of memory than has been allocated. The extra data then flows into the next area of memory, where it should not be. If the application design doesn't consider this possibility, it may be possible to leverage this situation to execute the code in the second memory area. This situation can yield many unwanted results including: application hang or crash, server hang or crash, or even worst, compromise of the machine where control is given to the sender of the packet.

*White hat hackers*, people who attempt to find vulnerabilities in software and then report them to the manufacturer for correction, are constantly working to find buffer overflow errors in software and OSs. Because humans write all software and humans are prone to error, it is highly unlikely that there will ever be "perfect software" with no vulnerability. Therefore, it is in the best interest of network administrators to protect the most valuable assets with firewalls as best we can.

## Notes from the Underground...

### Do Firewalls Have Buffer Overflows?

Short answer, "Yes." However, there are far fewer than most other software, because firewalls are stripped down to the bare essentials. Firewall software is also scrutinized more closely due to the task the firewall is attempting to perform. Most firewall vulnerabilities result in DOS's rather than access violations or compromise. Firewalls are designed to *fail closed* so that the firewall cuts off network access rather than permitting unauthorized access.

Also realize that some firewalls are designed to be installed on existing OSs. If the underlying OS has vulnerabilities, your firewall will only be as good as the OS its running on.

In addition, a poorly configured firewall can leave gaping holes that a malicious person could walk through with ease. This book is a good start to configure your firewall securely; however, don't stop here. Read the manufacturer's documentation, white papers provided by the manufacture, and blogs, newsgroups, and discussion groups related to your model of firewall. Learn from other's mistakes and don't make them yourself. Most of these resources are freely available on the Web; a few searches should turn up starting points that will lead you to more resources.

To a determined hacker, discovering a firewall is tantamount to throwing down a gauntlet and posing the challenge of how to exploit the permitted access. The good news here is that such determined hackers are fewer than the *script kiddies* (less experienced hackers who rely on pre-written scripts and tools to compromise machines) who look for easy targets with well-known vulnerabilities. Therefore, be certain that the script kiddies will walk away after knocking on the door and getting no answer. Then delve into the literature mentioned above and make your network unwelcoming to even determined hackers.

# Firewall Types

There are two basic types of firewalls: Application Proxy and Gateway. Gateways are divided into packet filters and stateful inspection firewalls. These differ in function and design and have different uses in network architecture. Never try to have one type of firewall do the duty of another type. It is better to have a well-run and securely configured firewall doing its intended job, than to have something doing a job for which it wasn't designed. This is an invitation for disaster. Let's look at these firewalls and how they should be used.

# Application Proxy

An application proxy firewall takes apart each packet that comes in, examines it to see if it meets the criteria set, rewrites it, and sends it on its way. The proxy terminates the connection from the outside source and starts a new connection from the proxy to the destination. This offers great protection to the servers, because there is no direct interaction between the source and the destination. In addition, the proxy is greatly hardened against attacks and has a very small attack surface. It is very difficult for a hacker to take control of an application proxy firewall.

These firewalls are very specific and a proxy must be written for each supported application. The advantage to this is that you will have the exact needs of your particular application addressed; however, you are at the mercy of the vendor should there be an update to your application that the firewall doesn't support. Delays may occur in upgrading your application until the firewall vendor catches up.

Application proxies are usually "invisible" on the network. Often, they have no IP address themselves, or, if they do, they sometimes masquerade as the destination server. Thus, application proxies may not do address translation.

Application proxies work at the application level of the Open Systems Interconnection (OSI) model (see Figure 1.2).

**Figure 1.2** The OSI Model

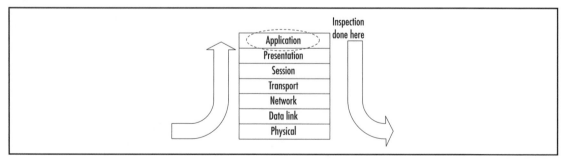

As the name implies, application proxy firewalls act as intermediaries in network sessions. The user's connection terminates at the proxy, and a corresponding separate connection is initiated from the proxy to the destination host. Connections are analyzed all the way up to the application layer to determine if they are allowed. It is this characteristic that gives proxies a higher level of security than packet filters, stateful, or otherwise. However, as you might imagine, this additional processing extracts a toll on performance. Figure 1.3 shows how packet processing is handled at the application layer before it is passed on or blocked.

**Figure 1.3** Application Proxy Data Flow

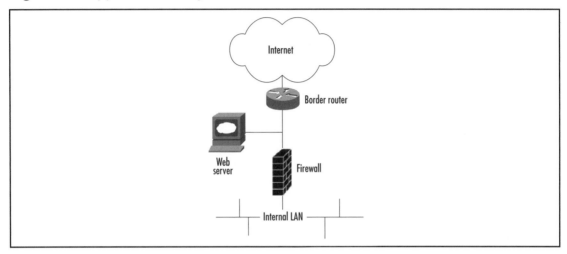

Depending on how the application proxy is written, it is possible to permit only those packets that are specific for the target application, and reject all others. Typically, these firewalls check against such factors as buffer overflows, hidden malicious code, correct source and destination IP addresses, and correct port usage using algorithms and international Internet standards. Any packet that doesn't pass the tests is rejected. This makes for very clean packets arriving at the server; however, it also requires a great deal of processing power.

# Pros

For a high level of security, an application proxy is the appliance of choice. The detail of control permitted is unmatched by any other device.

## High Security

An application proxy is generally far more secure than a gateway. By breaking down each packet to its basic parts and rewriting it, the firewall discovers and drops hidden malicious code. These firewalls can, and have, prevented zero-day attacks.

# Refined Control

Application proxies also provide the opportunity to fine tune exactly what you will let into your protected network, and, depending on the design of the firewall, what you will allow out. A *reverse proxy* handles controlling the outgoing of information. Reverse proxies can play a very important role in high security environments by examining the contents of outgoing packets for sensitive information.

# Cons

While providing high security, application proxies cannot and should not be used in every situation. There are severe drawbacks to using these devices.

## Slower Network Performance

Due to the work an application proxy must perform to dissect each packet and then rewrite it properly to pass on, they tend to be slower than a gateway. Depending on the volume of traffic across the firewall and the complexity of the data, you may see a significant performance hit with an application proxy.

## Update Schedule Governed by Vendors

Since vendors specifically write the OS of these appliances, it may take time for them to catch up to the latest release of a particular application. Until your proxy is up-to-date with the application it is protecting, you cannot update the application itself.

## Limited Control, Depending on Vendor

While some application proxies can be tweaked, others cannot. In most cases, if you are using standard protocols and the application proxy at your border to the Internet, it will not matter if you can finely control what does and doesn't enter your protected network. However, using an application proxy to protect an entire server room from the rest of the organization can prove to be disastrous if not tested. Note that neither of these scenarios are typical uses for an application proxy. Most often, an application proxy will be placed in front of a specific type of server, not at a border or subnet. (see Figure 1.4.)

**Figure 1.4** Example Positioning of an Application Proxy Firewall

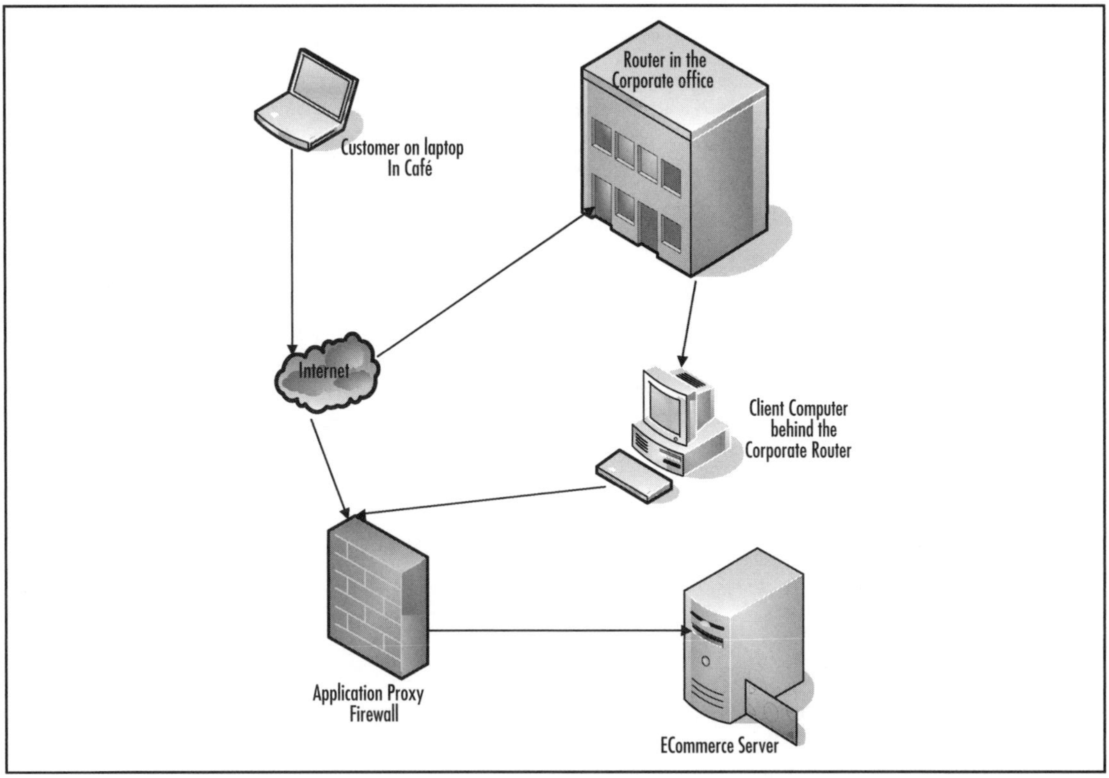

In this example, the corporate offices have a direct connection to the Internet, and there are mobile users directly on the Internet. Due to the sensitivity of the e-mail communications, all e-mail passes through Microsoft Internet Security and Acceleration (ISA [*www.microsoft.com/isaserver/default.mspx*]) server. ISA server is Microsoft's application proxy. Built for various applications including Exchange, Structured Query Language (SQL), and Terminal Server, it analyzes the data for appropriateness to the backend application, terminates the connection from the client, and establishes a new connection from ISA server to the backend Exchange. The reverse is done as the Exchange server answers the client's query.

## Tools & Traps...

### Evaluate, Test, Evaluate, and Test Again

I was offered the opportunity to evaluate a new application proxy firewall. The marketers promised this would be the "golden bullet" that would solve all our problems and prevent zero-day attacks. They also promised that their algorithms were perfectly safe and compatible with the servers we had deployed. We already had a well-configured gateway firewall in front of our servers, protecting them from the Internet and the rest of the organization. If we didn't have the option of putting this application proxy device at the border, we would place it in-line with the gateway in front of the servers.

To start, we weren't certain that there were significant risks to our servers from zero-day attacks. We patched early and often and the number of ports open to the local network was small, even with a smaller subset open to the Internet. All of these ports were well-known and well-established protocols.

I used my own workstation as a guinea pig. I could afford to be offline; our production servers could not. Within 5 minutes, Outlook stopped talking to the Exchange server; my e-mail was offline. In my mind, I could hear the mail users screaming and the phones ringing off the hook if we had listened to the marketers and placed this inline with the gateway, as they suggested. The application proxy had "decided" that the packets between Outlook and Exchange didn't match what it considered a legitimate protocol.

I examined both the Web interface to the application proxy device and the logs, to determine if I could figure out why it thought this was unacceptable traffic and if I could fix or reconfigure the logic to mark these packets as acceptable. Alas, neither was possible.

Beware of placing such black boxes in your environment. Not knowing how they work or why they mark traffic as unacceptable can be almost as destructive as an attack. Having to explain why the device you put on the network performed a DOS against the network it was meant to protect, is no fun. Faced with a choice between two devices, one that logged everything it did and why, and one that did its thing with little or no feedback to you, I'd always go with the first.

# Gateway

By far, the most commonly deployed firewall is the gateway. This firewall examines the source and destination addresses and ports, and determines if the packet meets the designated rules to pass through the firewall to the servers. There are various levels of gateways. Some are extremely simplistic and only filter packets by port, others can filter by IP address and port, and still others perform various checks on the legitimacy of some or all IPs. Gateways come in two flavors: packet filters and stateful inspection gateways. Let's examine each in turn.

# Packet Filters

These are basic firewalls with very little flexibility or functionality. Often, these are built into OSs, such as Mac OS X, to provide rudimentary protection for the individual workstation. Windows and Linux have more advanced firewalls built in. Windows firewall has some features of stateful inspection, while Linux has IPChains, which can be used as a full-function firewall. Packet filters also have their place in the network architecture. Network routers will function as packet filters.

## Technical Description

In its most basic form, a *packet filter* makes decisions about whether to forward a packet based only on information found at the IP or TCP/UDP layers (transport and network layers, respectively, in the OSI model. See Figure 1.1). In effect, a packet filter is a router with some intelligence. However, a packet filter only handles individual packets; it does not keep track of TCP sessions. Thus, it is poorly equipped to detect spoofed packets that come in through an outside interface. These specifically crafted packets will pretend to be part of an existing session by setting the ACK flag in the TCP header. Packet filters are configured to allow or block traffic according to source and destination IP addresses, source and destination ports, and type of protocol (TCP, UDP, Internet Control Message Protocol [ICMP], and so on).

While rudimentary, packet filters can provide an effective barrier that reduces your *attack surface*. An attack surface, in network speak, refers to the number of ports you have available for someone to try to exploit. A Web server, which is only serving unencrypted pages, only requires port 80 open to the Internet. Using a packet filter, you can block all incoming traffic except that destined for port 80. You have just reduced your attack surface from 65535 ports to 1. While any hacker worth their salt will find your single open port, you have greatly reduced their toolset for breaking into your machine. In addition, if there is vulnerability, even a zero-day vulnerability, on one of the other ports, it will be impossible to reach *from the outside*.

Another example of packet filter use involves limiting the IP addresses permitted to contact a server. Let's assume you have a business that has a specific subnet, 192.168.50.x. Your financial application server should only provide services to this subnet. Simply block all other traffic. Now, the only way someone can get to your application server is to be on your specific subnet. Packet filters usually have their own address and address translation.

The ultimate example of a simplistic port-only packet filter is the old Microsoft Windows TCP/IP filter available in advanced network properties. This is so simplistic, it is only worthwhile to use in a few cases.

Figure 1.5 shows an example using a router as a packet filter. This situation is often found in academia where open communication is considered more important than security. In this case, the router selectively blocks certain protocols that are determined to be dangerous, and all other traffic is permitted. In this case, the blocked protocols are insecure because they transmit usernames and passwords in clear text, or, they can be used by hackers to gain control over machines. Simple Network Management Protocol (SNMP) can transfer various commands to devices. These commands range from information gathering to actual control of the devices. IRC is a common protocol used by hackers to communicate with zombies. Blocking this at the border, both incoming and outgoing, removes a control channel for hackers should a machine inside become compromised. Telnet and FTP are protocols that transmit both data and authentication credentials in clear text. Telnet is a remote command-line protocol and FTP is used to transfer files to and from servers. Better choices are Secure Shell (SSH) and Secure File Transfer Protocol (SFTP) both of which encrypt data and authentication. Simple Message Block (SMB) file sharing, while not insecure in and of itself, has been found to have numerous vulnerabilities in the implementation in Windows and older Linux system. These vulnerabilities can be used to compromise machines, and therefore should be blocked at the border router. Also note the Peer-to-Peer (P2P) file sharing, which is not uncommon in academic settings and should be taken into consideration when designing network security.

**Figure 1.5** Using a Router as a Packet Filter

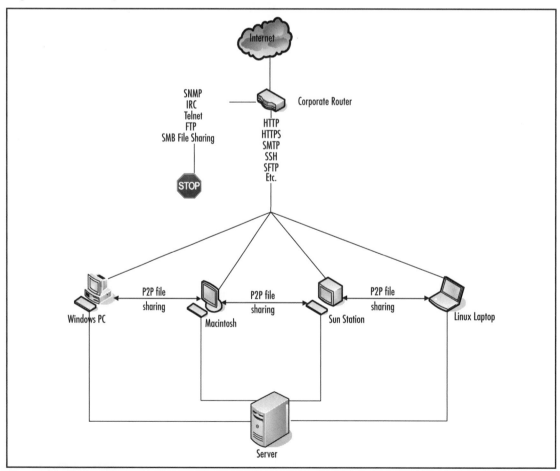

# Pros

Packet filters are extremely useful in certain situations. Primarily they should be deployed at the perimeter of your organization where coarse filtering is the best option.

## Speed

Packet filters are extremely fast. Since they only examine the destination port and/or the source/destination IP address, they have very little work to do. Simple packet filters are an excellent choice if you have an extremely high traffic resource that must process packets in and out very quickly. A high-traffic Web site is an ideal application for a packet filter. You can also throw a packet filter at your corporate border. Perhaps you only need ports such as SSH (22) or Remote Desktop Protocol (RDP) (3365) open for remote administration and VPN for remote access by users. Perfect. None of the cons below applies to these protocols and you don't need anything fancy to get the job done.

## Rapid Implementation

Quick deployment is also a major plus to packet filters. As long as you know the necessary ports and/or subnets, you can have a packet filter set up in literally minutes. There are no complicated rule sets and no extra protocols to deal with. What ports do you need open and where can the traffic come from? Answer those two questions and you are on your way.

# Cons

While packet filters have the advantages of speed and simplicity, they suffer from problems of security and other limitations that more complicated firewalls do not.

## Less Secure

Because packet filters are basic and do simple packet inspection, they are less secure than an application proxy. They pass through anything arriving from a permitted subnet to a permitted port, no questions asked.

## Port Limitations

Packet filters do not track where an incoming packet came from, or insure that the return packet goes to the same location (see "Stateful Inspection"). This also means that the conversation cannot be moved from lower static ports to higher dynamic ports. Remember the high dynamic ports we discussed earlier? Many applications use these after making the initial handshake and the two machines agree how to communicate. The application will request a move to higher ports to free up the lower static ports for other initial handshakes. With a packet filter, this requires opening most, if not all, of the dynamic ports, which, of course, makes the firewall useless.

The Windows mail application, Outlook, and its corresponding server, Exchange, demonstrate this very well. Initial communications are started on TCP port 135. Once the connection is established and authenticated, Exchange requests that the communication be moved up to ports around 5000. By default, this could include any number of possible ports that would require too many holes in the packet filter.

FTP, a "standard" protocol, can behave strangely with a packet filter. Since communication happens on port 21 but data transfer is switched to port 20, many packet filters fail to correctly pass FTP packets; therefore, the file transfer is interrupted.

# Stateful Inspection

The Stateful Inspection gateway is the standard type of firewall deployed to protect servers and other network resources. There are many companies that provide this type of firewall with varying degrees of features. For now, let's look at how these firewalls work in general.

## Technical Description

Stateful inspection is important to security because it provides a deeper level of filtering than Access Control Lists (ACL's) found in routers, which may only filter based on header information. Firewalls that perform stateful inspection analyze individual data packets as they traverse the firewall. In addition to the packet header, stateful inspection also assesses the packet's payload and looks at the application protocol. It can filter based on the source, destination, and service requested by the packet. The term "stateful inspection" refers to the firewall's ability to remember the status of a connection and thereby build a context for each data stream in its memory. With this information available, the firewall is able to make more informed policy decisions.

Stateful inspection is several steps below an application proxy and much better than a packet filter. In this case, the firewall keeps track of the TCP SYN/ACK packets that initiate and continue the conversation between two machines in a *connection table*. UDP protocols are monitored in a similar fashion, but the table is far less complete, because there is no detailed information. Stateful inspection firewalls also handle IPs such as Generic Route Encapsulation (GRE) and Protocol 47 used in VPN communications, and ICMP.

All of these types of firewalls have the concept of "inside" versus "outside." While there may be several insides that have various levels of security (private, users, DMZ, and so forth), there is only one outside and it is completely untrusted. By default, nothing is permitted to cross the firewall from the outside. Conversely, devices on a higher security interface, such as users, are permitted access to a lower security interface such as DMZ or outside. All of these parameters are configurable; however, before we begin discussing the configuration, let's get a better understanding of how a firewall decides what can and cannot pass through.

## The Inspection Process

The inspection of TCP/IP packets is a multi-step procedure. What follows is a summary of the steps, not necessarily in order (see Figure 1.6):

1. A packet arrives at the outside interface. It is checked for *permitted* or *denied* ports and IP addresses. Note that stateful inspection firewalls require both a port and an IP address. IP addresses can be in the form of a single machine, group of IP addresses, or "any," meaning any valid IP address on the specified network.

2. The firewall checks the source IP address for validity. This feature prevents spoofed packets from being transmitted, by allowing only packets whose source addresses match the subnet of the firewall's incoming interface or routing table. Therefore, if the packet has inconsistent information concerning its origins, it is unlikely that it is legitimate and is dropped.

3. The firewall compares the ports and addresses to the ACL, and either clears the packet for further processing or drops the packet.

4. The packet's *from* and *to* addresses, as well as other tracking information, is recorded in a table for reference when a return packet is sent. Stateful inspection firewalls keep track of who is talking to whom. This is extremely important for the correct use and protection of the dynamic ports. Should the packet be part of an ongoing connection, there is an entry in the connection table and the packet information is compared to the table for consistency.

5. If the packet is a well-known protocol such as SMTP (Internet mail), HTTP (Web), or FTP (file transfer), the packet may be checked against the IANA standards or a vendors private standards for compliance. This insures that packets containing malformed data are dropped and do not reach the servers where they may cause harm. This is not, however, equivalent to the application proxy's inspection of packet data. Application proxies inspect data contained in the packet to conform to a specific application's requirements and rewrite the packet. Stateful inspection firewalls simply look for standards compliance and only address translation. They do not wholesale rewrite the packet. They are not application-specific nor do all stateful inspection firewalls perform this type of check.

6. Finally, the firewall rewrites the destination IP address from the valid Internet address to the private address, and sends it on its way.

**Figure 1.6** Stateful Packet Inspection Example

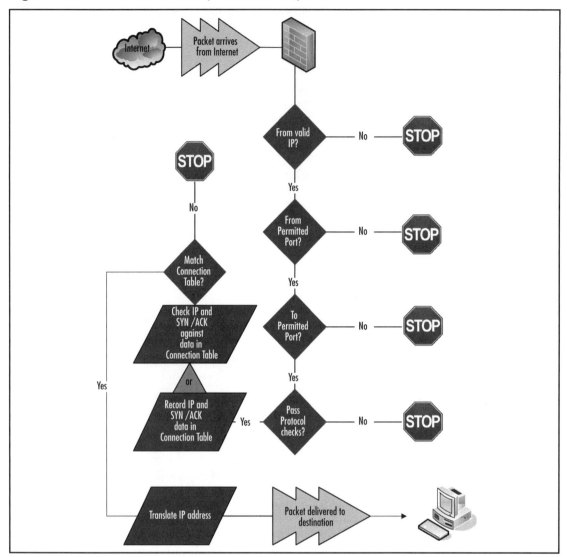

Packets sent from the inside to the outside follow a similar process:

1.  The firewall checks for a valid IP address and permitted IP address destinations. By default, most firewalls assume that a higher security interface is permitted to access any location outside the firewall. However, this can be overridden and best practices suggest doing this.

2.  A comparison is done between the outgoing packet parameters and the entries in the connection table. The firewall confirms that the entries match and that the packet is headed to the appropriate destination.

3. The firewall may confirm the outgoing protocols, although in most cases, firewalls assume that trusted networks use valid protocols.

4. Addresses are translated and the packet is sent on its way to the destination.

## Stateful Inspection Gateway Features

Let's take a look at some of the features that make the Stateful Inspection Firewall so popular. While not every model of firewall will contain all, or even most of these features, some will be in nearly every one:

- **Purpose-built OS** Eliminates the weaknesses found in most general OSs. Because the firewall's OS has a single purpose—filter TCP/IP traffic from one interface to another—it does not have extras that could be leveraged as a point of entry for compromise. It also means that the OS that does the filtering can be separated completely from a Graphical User Interface (GUI) interface for configuration and maintenance.

- **Connection Table** The method the firewall uses to provide stateful packet filtering, which analyzes each packet to ensure that only legitimate traffic traverses the interface. This is the module that maintains the connection table and validates destination and source addresses.

- **Universal Resource Locator (URL) Filtering** Can limit URLs accessed by the user's base on a policy defined by the network administrator or a security policy. This feature can be considered a reverse proxy. Users inside the firewall can be prevented from accessing certain Web sites based on the address of the Web site.

- **Content Filtering** Can block ActiveX or Java applets. This is a simplistic application filter that is beginning to blur the line between application proxies and gateways. The firewall can block either specific ActiveX and/or Java applets, or all such applets.

- **Network Address Translation (NAT) and Port Address Translation (PAT)** Hides internal addressing from the Internet and makes more efficient use of private address space. As stated above, this is the standard for gateways. As both a security measure and a way to extend a limited Internet address space, NAT turns valid Internet addresses into private addresses. PAT can be used to redirect a standard port (e.g., HTTP Port 80) to a non-standard port (Port 8080). This is often used for security or to mask the service from other internal machines.

- **Cut-through Proxy** Authenticates users accessing resources through the firewall. With a single authentication event, the firewall permits users to access file and print services that would otherwise be inaccessible outside the firewall.

- **VPN** Capable of handling mobile user access and site-to-site VPN's utilizing Data Encryption Standard (DES), 3DES, and Advanced Encryption Standard (AES) methods. Thus, a mobile user creates an encrypted "tunnel" from his computer to the firewall, permitting secure access to the resources behind the firewall, as if the computer was physically behind the firewall.

- **Intrusion Detection**  Enables the firewall to protect against various forms of malicious attacks, as well as the ability to identify attacks via attack "signatures." Yet another feature that makes the stateful inspection firewall appear a bit like an application proxy. Remember, these are general validations of the protocols and are not specific for a given application. Application proxy firewalls are written for specific applications and do much more precise checks on each data packet.

- **DHCP**  Can act as a DHCP client and/or server. While not so much a security feature, it provides the opportunity to automatically assign IP addresses to machines inside the firewall, which eliminates the need for a second device. There are some arguments against using this feature, because if an intruder gains access to your private network and is able to automatically obtain a valid IP address, it makes it much easier to begin the malicious work. (If an intruder has access to your private network, you have much larger concerns.)

- **Routing Functionality**  Can support static routes, Routing Information Protocol (RIP), and Open Shortest Path First (OSPF). Not strictly a security feature, but an elimination of other network appliances that must be maintained.

- **Support for Remote Authentication Dial-in User Server/Service (RADIUS)** or **Terminal Access Controller Access Control System Plus (TACACS+)** Authenticating, authorizing, and accounting for users passing through the firewall, or to enable authentication for those connecting to the management interfaces. RADIUS and TACACS+ are basic, cross-platform authentication services that eliminate the need to maintain multiple sets of usernames and passwords that increase security.

- **Failover**  Provides a resilient, high-availability solution in case of failure. A network is only useful if it is available. Providing failover not only protects against hardware failure, but also against failure due to a DOS attack or other non-destructive interruption of service.

# Pros

Stateful inspection firewalls are the best balance between the performance of a packet filter and the security of an application proxy. There's a wide selection of these firewalls available and they have few, if any drawbacks.

## Networking Standard

A stateful inspection firewall is the de facto standard for network protection at this time. Installing less is not a wise move without good reason (e.g., a requirement for the fastest possible data transfer while maintaining some protection for the internal network).

## Performance and Protection

The balance of performance versus protection between a packet filter and an application proxy is excellent. Since stateful inspection is the current standard, most vendors support this type of firewall and offer it in many levels of data transfer rates and cost.

# Cons

There are very few reasons not to use a stateful inspection firewall; however, there are a few possible considerations.

## Lower Data Transfer Rates Than a Packet Filter

As stated above, there is performance degradation over a packet filter. Tables are maintained and logic is used to parse the access lists, costing memory and processor power.

## Lack of Fine Control

Fine control of application proxies is lost in favor of better performance. Stateful inspection firewall software is written to be generic (i.e., usable in nearly any environment), whereas application proxies are specific and therefore provide fine control for the specific applications.

# Summary

The number and variety of threats on the Internet increase every day. With increased connection speeds and the wide availability of fast connections, hackers have more access to more potential targets than ever before. Weaknesses in the TCP/IP protocol combined with weaknesses in the OSs provide "hooks" for malicious persons to gain control of valuable resources for fun and profit.

Data is pushed around the Internet using the TCP/IP protocol. The protocol uses headers as envelopes for the data, and firewalls use the information in these headers to control what data is permitted through to the protected servers and what data is dropped.

Two types of transmission protocols create the headers. TCP protocol uses SYN and ACK packets to confirm the successful receipt of data. UDP protocol sends the data off with no regard whether the information reaches its intended target or not. Packet filter firewalls disregard much of the packet information and permit/block based solely on the port number and/or destination/source IP address. Both application proxies and stateful inspection firewalls create tables of source and destination addresses and ports, and monitor communications based on these tables.

Application proxy firewalls are written to the specifications of particular applications, and the selection of a particular application proxy is mostly determined by the type of application server being protected. Fine control of information is favored over performance.

Packet filters favor speed over control. They are basic and only monitor if a particular source or destination address or port is permitted through. A particular port can be used for any type of information, not just the information for which the port was defined. Packet filters are favored when performance outweighs all other considerations.

Stateful inspection gateways are the best balance of application proxy fine control and packet filter performance. They are the standard for most network infrastructures. While they are generic and can be used in any environment, they often provide good basic inspection of various IPs to maintain network integrity.

# Solutions Fast Track

## Why Have Different Types of Firewalls?

- ☑ Physical access

- ☑ Network access

- ☑ Reconnaissance, Access, DOS attacks

- ☑ Hacking for fun and profit/Identity theft

- ☑ Trojans, viruses, and worms

# Back to Basics: Transmission Control Protocol/Internet Protocol

- ☑ Packet structure
- ☑ IP addresses
- ☑ TCP/UDP ports, their uses, and vulnerabilities
- ☑ Data packet vulnerabilities

# Firewall Types

- ☑ Fine control of data
- ☑ Written for specific applications
- ☑ Performance sacrificed for data integrity
- ☑ At mercy of vendor for updates supporting application updates
- ☑ High performance, high data transfer rates
- ☑ Block/permit based solely on Internet address and/or port number
- ☑ Least secure of the technologies
- ☑ Extremely quick to implement
- ☑ Excellent balance between Application Proxy and Packet Inspection
- ☑ Provides good generic data integrity
- ☑ Widely supported
- ☑ Monitors data destinations and ports
- ☑ Provides support for transmissions changing from low-static ports to high-dynamic ports without loss of connection

# Frequently Asked Questions

**Q:** Can I deploy a firewall in my environment?

**A:** Almost undoubtedly. No matter what your environment, deploying a firewall to protect your infrastructure from the hostile Internet is a wise move. With proper planning, a firewall will improve your security and reduce your attack surface without degrading your data transfer performance or causing unwanted communication problems.

You may begin by using your existing router to block unneeded or vulnerable services. Check, check, and recheck to ensure whatever ports you block will not turn off vital business services. There is nothing worse than making a change in the name of security and then having the CEO who is on an important business trip, call angry and in a panic because he or she cannot obtain the data needed.

**Q:** What type of firewall should I deploy?

**A:** Ultimately, only you can answer this question. Consider what you are trying to protect, where in your network infrastructure you are planning to place the firewall, and how much control you want to exert over the data transmission.

**Q:** Can I deploy more than one type of firewall?

**A:** Absolutely. Defense in depth is standard practice, like putting a lock on your motorcycle so that the wheels cannot roll, putting a second lock on the steering column so it cannot be turned, chaining the motorcycle to an immovable object, and activating an alarm that will sound if moved. The more hoops a malicious person must jump through to obtain access to your valuable resources, the less likely that person will bother. Figure 1.7 shows a highly protected network where the most valuable resources are completely isolated, not only from the Internet, but also from the users.

In the figure, untrusted servers may be servers run by a consultant or other third party. The public access Web application servers could be e-commerce servers housing customer private information such as credit card numbers. User access servers could be mail servers or file servers for use inside the organization. Protected private application servers could house organizational financial information or employee records. Note that in this particular setup, it would likely be necessary to have VPN access between the users and the Web application servers so that authorized users could access the credit card data.

By dividing the network in this way, it is unlikely that the compromise of one portion of the network will result in the compromise of the entire network. With this type of strict division of networks, most users would not be able to access sensitive information. It also limits the damage that an internal user can do, even with sophisticated hacking tools.

**Figure 1.7** Defense In-Depth Example

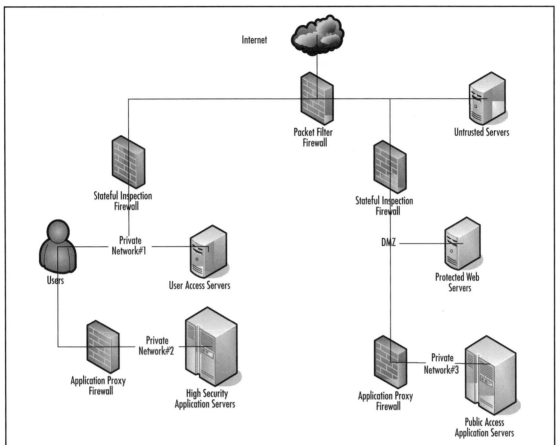

**Q:** Where should I put the various firewalls?

**A:** Packet filters are best deployed at the border of your organization, between your final router and your Internet Service Provider (ISP). This is where all of the traffic in and out of your organization occurs. Performance is essential here, and fine control is nearly impossible due to the variety of protocols and information types passing through. The packet filters will most likely be set to accept most connections and only deny some potentially dangerous ones such as Telnet. Outbound, you may wish to block the IRC ports. Hackers often use IRC to communicate with the malicious software (*bots*) that they install on compromised machines.

Stateful inspection gateways can be used internally to further protect subnets and filter the information coming in from the Internet. Stateful inspection gateways are often used to protect a more secure area (e.g., financials) from the rest of the organization.

Finally, application proxies are used to protect your most valuable applications from attack. An e-mail application proxy is a good example of this type of deployment. The proxy can be configured to not only accept e-mail from certain locations, but also to filter for unwanted data and protect internal data from either accidental or purposeful transmission outside the organization. There are even e-mail proxies which scan every e-mail for keywords or attachment types that could contain valuable private data. The proxies stop this data cold.

**Q:** If I deploy all three types of firewalls exactly to the best practices, will I be 100 percent safe?

**A:** Nothing short of using wire cutters to cut the cables connecting you to the Internet, will keep any network 100 percent safe from outside threats. Even if you took this step, you still have people inside that could compromise your data. You cannot ignore patching your internal computers nor can you ignore patching your firewall. You must maintain vigilance and check your firewall logs for problems. DOS attacks can still render your communications to the Internet impossible. However, you will be better protected with a firewall than without.

**Q:** What if a hacker manages to take control of a machine inside my firewall?

**A:** This is every network and system administrator's greatest nightmare. Several steps can be taken to mitigate the damage such a situation would cause.

1. Use host-based firewalls such as IPChains or Windows Firewall to limit the access one machine has to other machines. This limits the available ports available for a hacker to exploit from the compromised machine.

2. Monitor your network with intrusion detection systems (IDS) such as Snort (*www.snort.org*), which will alert you to malicious behavior before it spreads.

3. Monitor your important systems for unauthorized changes with system auditing and third-party products such as Tripwire (*www.tripwire.com*).

**NOTE**

To fully explore an IDS is far beyond the scope of this book and has filled several volumes by itself. Two places to start learning more about intrusion detection are SANS (*www.sans.org/resources/idfaq/*) and WindowSecurity (*www.windowsecurity.com/whitepaper/info/misc/network-intrusion-detection.html*).

4. Divide your network following the example above to minimize the possibility of a single compromise permitting access to every system.

5. Employ *bastion hosts* to access the most valuable systems. Bastion hosts are machines who's sole function is to provide an access portal to other, more vulnerable systems. These machines must be individually secured and hardened, because they are always in a position of being attacked or probed. This means that before placement, a bastion host must be stripped of unnecessary services, fully updated with the latest service packs, hot fixes, and updates, and isolated from other trusted machines and networks to eliminate the possibility that its compromise would allow for connection to (and potential compromise of) the protected networks and resources. This also means that a machine being used for this purpose should have no user accounts relative to the protected network or directory services structure, which could lead to enumeration of your internal network. See Figure 1.8 for placement and use.

**Figure 1.8** Bastion Host Placement and Use

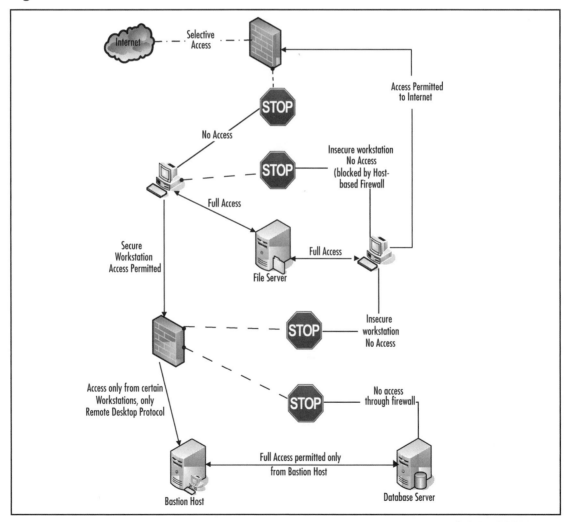

**Q:** It would be easier for me to administer my firewall via HTTP or Telnet. Why are clear text protocols so dangerous?

**A:** There are numerous versions of a type of tool called a *packet sniffer* available. A packet sniffer captures the TCP/IP packets passing between devices and records the data. These devices can be used to "steal" data as it travels across the network. The sniffer captures individual data packets and allows hackers to view and analyze the message contents and packet headers. Should you use a plain text protocol, not only will all the commands be passed for a potential intruder to see, but so will your username and password. It would then be trivial for an intruder to access your firewall and change the configuration to suit his needs.

> **NOTE**
>
> Packet sniffers are also called *protocol analyzers* or *network analyzers*. Sniffer and Sniffer Pro are two packet-sniffer products marketed by Network Associates.

Here is a plain text capture of a packet from a Web site captured on TCP Port 80:

```
HTTP/1.1 200 OK
Accept-Ranges: bytes
Date: Sun, 11 Jun 2006 02:49:58 GMT
Content-Length: 450
Content-Type: text/plain
Server: Apache/1.3.33 (Darwin)
Last-Modified: Thu, 04 May 2006 16:02:47 GMT
ETag: "eb1be3-1c2-445a25a7"
Via: 1.1 netcache03 (NetCache NetApp/5.5R6)
{
configURL = "http://configuration.apple.com/configurations/internetservices/
dotmackit/1/clientConfiguration.plist";
  accountInfoURL = "https://www.mac.com/WebObjects/Info.woa/wa/XMLRPC/accountInfo";
  signUpURL = {
    en = "http://www.mac.com";
    ja = "http://www.mac.com/WebObjects/Welcome.woa/wa/default?lang=ja&cty=JP";
  };
  referralLookupURL = "http://homepage.mac.com/dotmackitsupport/Referrals";
  otherParameters = {};
}
```

As you can see, this is completely legible. If there was a username and password in this conversation, it would be available. (*www.mac.com*).

Here is an encrypted session captured on TCP Port 443. This was captured by accessing *https://www.mac.com*, my personal page:

As you can see, this is completely illegible. This was transmitted with 128-bit encryption, which is nearly unbreakable. This is typical of any encrypted protocol, HTTPS, SSH, SFTP, and so forth. While it is not necessarily easy to sniff network traffic, it can be done. Particularly vulnerable are unencrypted wireless connections, Internet Café's, and networks connected via hubs rather than switches. Therefore, never, under any circumstances, enable clear text protocols on a network connection to important data or the devices protecting that data.

# Chapter 2

# Setup

**Solutions in this chapter:**

- **Initial CLI Setup**
- **Initial Web Setup**
- **Certificates**
- **Security and System Settings**

☑ **Summary**

☑ **Solutions Fast Track**

☑ **Frequently Asked Questions**

# Introduction

As you can see by the size of this book, you can design and configure quite a bit when it comes to the Juniper Secure Sockets Layer (SSL) virtual private network (VPN). Fortunately, you must complete relatively few tasks to get the box up and running on your network. In this chapter, we will focus on those initial steps that involve everything you need to know to get the IVE up and running. We will then go into some detail about IVE licensing (features and support), as well as certificates and other system wide settings to be configured on the IVE.

The tools we discuss in this chapter will enable you to get your box up and running on the network. Unlike some other appliances, you do very little through the command-line interface (CLI) on the Juniper IVE. Juniper has left most of the configuration to its AdminUI, which you can access in virtually any Web browser. The CLI is basically enabled to allow for the initial setup, as well as for some last-resort troubleshooting techniques which you may have to employ if you lose your connection to the IVE or are locked out for one reason or another. In any event, you will find that the IVE provides you with the tools you need to set up your IVE, as well as maintain the system that your organization will no doubt rely heavily upon.

# Initial CLI Setup

We start our IVE endeavor with a task in which many of you no doubt have much experience: the command line. Although this may seem like an odd place to start the configuration, Juniper has good reason for beginning the initial configuration at this spot. Essentially, you accomplish all IVE configuration within the AdminUI, which is a Web-based interface that allows you to configure all of the IVE's great aspects. But before we can configure the device through a Web browser, we must make some initial configurations on the IVE to give it basic network information, as well as set up a login account (we actually will need to complete a few more steps, but not many). Like many other appliances, the IVE does not waste system resources (software or hardware) on providing a keyboard, video, and mouse (KVM) interface with a graphical user interface (GUI) such as a desktop. Rather, Juniper has designed the underlying operating system to be as lightweight as possible, so it can maximize the IVE's performance for its intended purpose (which is to deliver applications and remote access securely to remote users). To help incorporate this feature, Juniper uses a simple console-based setup to configure the IVE.

## IVE Console Setup

On the front of every IVE model is a console serial port which is an RS-232 DB9 male connector. Your IVE should come with a console cable to connect to a serial port on a workstation, laptop, or server. Many newer-model computers do not have an RS-232 serial port built in, so you may have to use a USB-to-Serial converter or an Ethernet-to-RS-232 DB9 converter, which you should be able to find in a good local computer store or at an online retailer (such as Newegg, www.newegg.com). The IVE follows the same connection properties as many other manufacturers, and it uses the following settings for the serial connection:

- Bits per second: 9600

- Data bits: 8

- Parity bits: None

- Stop bits: 1

- Flow control: None

You can use your favorite terminal emulator program to manage the serial connection on your workstation. HyperTerminal is popular because it comes with many distributions of Windows, but TeraTerm and Minicom are also popular for other platforms. At this point, you can go ahead and power up your box with your console cable connected to your machine. In the following sections, we will discuss how to set up the console connection as well as how to perform the initial configuration steps.

## Configuring HyperTerminal for Connecting to the IVE Console Port

We will start our configuration with an example using HyperTerminal in Microsoft Windows. If you are using a different application, consult the documentation for that application to perform the same steps. If you are already familiar with setting up your machine to perform console connections, there are no surprises here and you can skip this example.

1. Go to **Start | Run** and enter **hypertrm.exe**.

2. You will be prompted with a **Connection Description** window. Enter a **Name** to give to this session and click **OK**.

3. You will be asked to define some properties of the connection. There is really only one value that we are concerned with here, and that is the **Connect Using** value. Expand the drop-down menu and look for the COM port that you are plugged into on your machine. If there are multiple COM ports, you might have to try each one to determine the right port. When you have a single physical RS-232 port on your machine, this is often COM1, but it can be different, especially if you have to use a USB-to-RS-232 converter to make the connection.

4. After you have selected the appropriate COM port, click **OK**.

5.  The last thing you will have to do before you connect is to configure the properties of the session, as we described earlier. This means you will set the following properties:

    Bits per second: 9600
    Data bits: 8
    Parity bits: None
    Stop bits: 1
    Flow control: None

6.  Click **OK**, and assuming that you entered the right information you should be connected. If your IVE has already had a chance to power on, press **Enter**, which should bring up the Initial Configuration message:

```
Welcome to the initial configuration of your server!
NOTE: Press 'y' if this is a stand-alone server or the first
machine in a clustered configuration.
If this is going to be a member of an already running cluster
press n to reboot. When you see the 'Hit TAB for clustering options'
message press TAB and follow the directions.
Would you like to proceed (y/n)?
```

## Initial Configuration

In this example, we will configure the IVE for the first time. When you access an IVE that has not been configured, you will be given a message asking you whether you would like to proceed with the configuration. Assuming you say yes, you will have a few tasks to perform:

- Agree to the license.
- Apply an Internet Protocol (IP) address, subnet mask, and default gateway for the internal interface.
- Define Primary and optionally secondary domain name system (DNS) servers.
- Define a domain name.
- Provide an address for a Windows Internet Name Service (WINS) Server (optional).
- Create a default admin name and password.
- Provide the common name for the IVE.
- Generate a self-signed certificate.

1. After you have connected to the console and the IVE has booted up, you will be asked whether you wish to perform the initial configuration steps. Type **y** and press **Enter**.

2. You will be prompted with the license agreement. You can type **y**, **n**, or **r**. These stand for Yes, No, and Read, respectively. After you have read the license agreement by typing **r**, type **y** and press **Enter** to agree to the license agreement and to continue.

3. You will be prompted for the **IP Address** of your IVE's internal interface. Enter the IP address that you wish to define for the IVE and press **Enter**.

4. Define the **Subnet Mask** that will be applied to the internal interface and press **Enter**.

5. Define the **Default Gateway** for the internal interface. The IVE does not act exactly like a router, but it must have routing knowledge to your internal network. If you do use an external interface, the IVE will maintain a separate default route for the external interface, but we will configure that in the AdminUI.

6. The IVE will prompt you to define **Primary** and **Secondary DNS Servers**. These DNS servers are typically internal DNS servers, but if you do not have internal DNS servers you can use the DNS servers your Internet service provider (ISP) gives you. Enter the **Primary DNS Server** and press **Enter**. If you have a **Secondary DNS Server** for redundancy, enter its IP address; otherwise, just press **Enter**.

7. If your organization uses WINS for name resolution, you can provide the IP address of the **WINS Server**; otherwise, just press **Enter**.

8. The IVE will force you to create a default **username** and **password** for the Admin account which you will initially use to configure the AdminUI. Later, you can choose to use another mechanism to provide Admin authentication (such as a RADIUS [Remote Authentication Dial-in User Service] server or Active Directory), but initially, you must configure an Admin account that is located locally on the IVE. To do so, you must first provide an **Admin Name** as well as an **Admin Password** at the respective prompts. Your password must be at least six characters long.

9. You will be prompted for the **Common Name** for the IVE, which will be used to connect to the IVE. This is typically configured as the fully qualified domain name (FQDN, such as vpn.mycompany.com); this could also be an IP address, but it is usually the former because users usually connect to the IVE by the DNS name rather than the IP address. In the end, this step isn't too important because you will most likely provide your own valid certificate rather than use the self-signed certificate,

but either way, define the **Common Name** that you would like to apply to the IVE for the self-signed SSL certificate.

10.  Define the **Organization Name** that will be used in the certificate.

11.  You will be asked to enter some **Random Data** that will be used to generate the self-signed certificate. Just enter a bunch of random characters (30 or so) and press **Enter**. You must create a certificate in the initial configuration because the IVE requires secure access to the IVE via HTTPS, which must use a certificate.

12.  When you see the following message, you will have completed the initial configuration on the IVE, and you can proceed to configure the IVE in the AdminUI:

```
Congratulations! You have successfully completed the initial set up of
your server.
To administer the system, please browse to an appropriate URL:
https://<IVE-IP-Address>/admin (note the 's' in https://)
Example: https://10.10.22.34/admin
If a DNS name already exists for this IVE, you can also use:
https://<IVE-Host-Name>/admin
Example: https://IVE.mycompany.com/admin
```

# Initial Web Setup

As you can see, you simply configure the basics on the IVE console to get the box up and running. In this section, we will cover the basic steps you should configure on the box now that you have access to the AdminUI. Note that most of the aspects of IVE configuration will be broken out into individual sections in this book, so this chapter is not going to go into much detail, but rather will cover the issues you will most likely need to know to get the basics set up before expanding into the other parts of the configuration.

## Accessing the IVE through the WebUI

Now that you have the device up and running (and we assume you have it on your network), you should be able to access the IVE from your machine. Simply open a Web browser and enter the following in the URL field: **https://<ipaddress>/admin**, where <ipaddress> is the IP address you assigned to the internal port of the IVE in the console setup. Your browser will prompt you to continue because it will not "trust" the certificate (different browsers go about this differently), but for now, just accept the certificate and continue. You will be brought to the IVE default Admin page, which will look like Figure 2.1.

**Figure 2.1** Accessing the Admin Sign-in Page

Enter the Admin username and password that you configured on the console during the initial setup and click the **Sign In** button. You will then be brought to the AdminUI. The first time you connect to the AdminUI, you will see a sidebar tip sheet that lists some tasks you will need to perform (see Figure 2.2). We will cover those in the next few examples.

**Figure 2.2** Initial AdminUI When You First Connect to the IVE

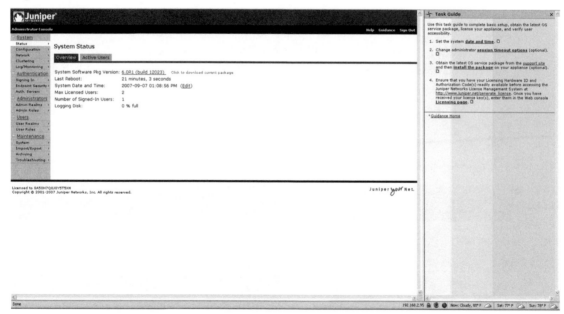

# Configuring Date and Time

In this example, we will configure the date and time for your IVE. Configuring the date and time is a very important task, and it is more than just good practice. The IVE relies on time settings being accurate for a number of functions (particularly with SSL and certificate validation). Of course, the IVE also uses the date and time to record a timestamp in each log entry, so if there is a problem you will want to know that the correct time is on your IVE.

1.  In the **AdminUI**, go to the **Status** page, which is the default page you will be brought to each time you log into the IVE. You will see a **System Date and Time** label, with the **Edit** field beside it. Under those fields, you will see the date and time to which the IVE is currently set. If this value is not accurate, you should definitely reset it. You may also wish to incorporate a feature such as **NTP** to automatically manage the time of your device for you. Click the **Edit** button to continue.

2.  You will be brought to the Date and Time screen. The first thing you should do is set the **Time Zone** if it is different from your time zone. Click **Save Changes**. Go back into the Date and Time screen. If you configure multiple steps at once, you will most likely end up misconfiguring your time.

3.  You have two options for defining the time. You can **Use NTP Server**, in which case you must define the **NTP Server** (either hostname or IP address) as well as define an **Update Interval** (in minutes) to update the server. Click **Save Changes**.

4.  Your other option is to just **Set Time Manually**, which allows you to define the time without having an external update source. You can either define the **Date** and **Time** in the mm/dd/yyyy hh:mm:ss (with selecting A.M./P.M.) format; or you can just click **Get from Browser** which will automatically populate this field (see Figure 2.3). Click **Save Changes**.

**Figure 2.3** Configuring Date and Time on the IVE

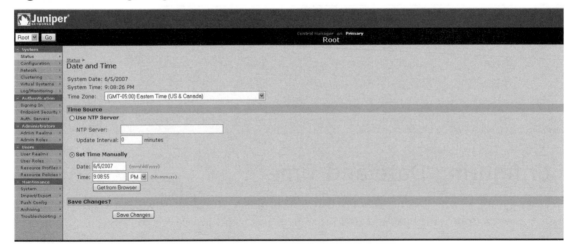

# Configuring Licensing on the IVE

The IVE has multiple options as far as licensing for the device, but before you can enter a license key, you must generate a license. Most likely, your Juniper reseller will provide you with an authorization code generated by Juniper to create the license. You use this authorization code in combination with the serial number or hardware ID of the box to generate the license.

## Generating a License on the Juniper Web Site

After you have purchased an IVE or an additional license from a Juniper reseller, you should be provided an e-mail with an attached PDF which will contain an authorization code. This code is a 16-character code which would look like the following: *RAdu-CNet-nJep-NAmV*. Once you generate the license, you will receive another e-mail which will provide you with the actual license key to apply to your IVE. In this example, we will show you how to generate a license key for your IVE assuming that you have an authorization code:

1. Go to www.juniper.net/customers/support/ and click on **Contracts & Product Management** on the left-hand side of the Web page. You will be forced to log into the Juniper support page. If you do not already have a login, contact the Juniper Technical Assistance Center (JTAC) at 1-888-314-JTAC to have an account set up (they can also generate the license for you if you would like). Sign into the Juniper support site.

2. Click on **License Key Generator** when you are brought to the **Contract and Product Management** page.

3. Select the **Secure Access SSL VPN** from the product's drop-down menu. Juniper has provided license generation for most of its products through this same mechanism, so you must be sure to apply your license to the appropriate platform. Click **Go**. Note that should you ever need to generate a license for an RMA device, you will follow this same procedure, but go to **Generate License Keys for RMA Device** rather than selecting the SSL VPN from the drop-down menu.

4. Provide the hardware ID for your IVE. This code is available at the console (just console in and press **Enter**, which will bring up a menu that will list the hardware ID), or you can view the hardware ID for your IVE on the licensing page of your IVE at **System | Configuration | Licensing**. The hardware ID (which is different from the serial number for your IVE) looks something like SA50ARM0J0DAL3ML. Provide the hardware ID in the **Licensing Hardware ID** field and the authorization code in the **Authorization Code** field, and click **Generate**. See Figure 2.4, which shows how this is configured within the IVE.

5. Assuming that your auth code and hardware ID check out, you will be brought to a page where you can either download the license key and/or have it e-mailed to you.

**Figure 2.4** Generating License Keys on the Juniper Support Page

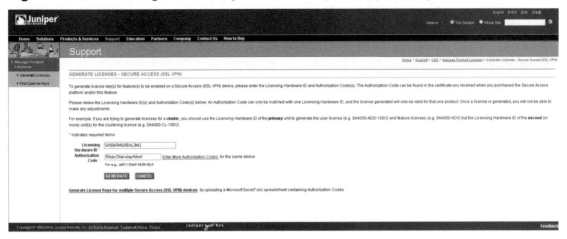

6. Once you have the license key, you will want to apply it to your IVE. To do so, go to the AdminUI of the IVE. You apply the license at **System | Configuration | Licensing**.

7. Enter one license key per line in the **License Key** text box. Once you add the licenses to the IVE, click **Add**. Assuming that you applied the correct licenses to the IVE, you should see them appear in the **Installed Licenses Detail**. Because licenses are tied to a hardware ID, make sure you are applying the correct license to the correct box. If you are still having a problem applying the license, you should contact JTAC at 1-888-314-JTAC. Figure 2.5 shows how the license is applied to the IVE.

8. Once you add the license key(s) you will see new features open in the configuration.

**Figure 2.5** Adding Licenses to the IVE

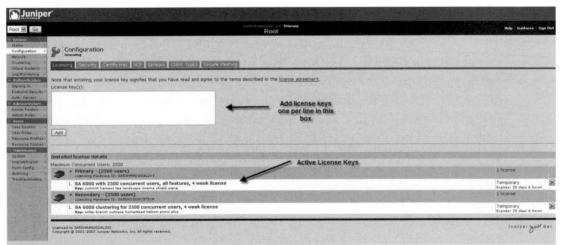

**NOTE**

If you have a cluster of IVE devices, you must make sure you apply the correct license to the correct box. When you get your authorization codes, one will be for the primary device, and the other will be for the cluster device. Just keep track of which hardware ID is applied to which auth code so that when you apply the licenses to the correct box you won't have any issues.

# Network Settings in the AdminUI

The console setup for the IVE allows you to configure some basic tasks to get the IVE up and running to the point of management, but you will most likely have to perform many other tasks to get your IVE where it needs to be before you start configuring the user-related settings. In this section, we will focus on those tasks, which include configuring the external and management ports, routing, DNS/name resolution, virtual ports, certificates, interface settings, and more! We will go through the purpose of each configuration task as well as provide an example of how to configure those tasks.

## Configuring IVE Interfaces in the WebUI

All IVEs have at least two interfaces, which are known as the internal and external interfaces. Some IVE platforms come with a separate management port so that you can dedicate a specific interface for management (this is often seen as a security feature because you can completely separate management from the normal network interfaces). Note that you don't necessarily have to use the internal, external, and management (where applicable) interfaces. You have different deployment options for configuring the IVE, so you might require only one interface which will be the internal interface to handle the external and internal connections. Some organizations might prefer to have the IVE segment the external and internal traffic on the network by dedicating separate interfaces. Regardless of the setup, you will most likely need to make some tweaks to your IVE network configuration, so we will discuss those changes here.

### Configuring the IVE Physical Ports

By default, the external port on the IVE is disabled. To be able to use the external port, you must first install the licensing that was purchased with the IVE. You can enable the external port as well as configure other properties of the interface by performing the following steps (see Figure 2.6, which accompanies this example):

1. Navigate to **System | Network | <Port> | Settings**. In this example, we will select the **External Port**.

2. **Enable** the port. No matter what you configure elsewhere, you will not be able to activate the settings until you enable the port.

3. Define the **IP Address** for this interface. One important thing to note is that if you are using an active/passive cluster, you can only configure this at node level; you must configure everything else at the cluster level (we will discuss this at length in Chapter 14).

4. Define the **Subnet Mask** (in dotted decimal format) on the node, which will define the network boundary for this host.

5. The IVE requires a **Default Gateway** for each interface on the box. This is because depending on the traffic direction (which the IVE handles automatically), it must maintain separate default routes for the different networks in which the IVE has an interface. Note that you can define static routes if necessary (which we will discuss shortly).

6. Each interface has some advanced settings. First, define the **Link Speed**, which allows you to define the Port Speed and Duplex settings. You can either define the respective port speed/duplex setting, or just leave the setting at **Auto** to have the interface automatically determine the settings based on the settings of the other device.

7. Next is the **ARP Ping Timeout**. This is essentially how long the IVE should take to wait for a response to an ARP request. The default value is 5 seconds; you should not modify this value unless JTAC specifically directs you to, or you have a reason to, as modifying it may result in instability.

8. The last value that you configure on the interface is the maximum transmission unit (**MTU**) setting. This determines how large the IVE packets can be. The default value is 1,500 bytes, which is the standard for Ethernet. You should not change this value unless you have a specific need to, as doing so will result in instability.

9. Click **Save Changes** to apply the settings.

**Figure 2.6** Configuring a Port on the IVE

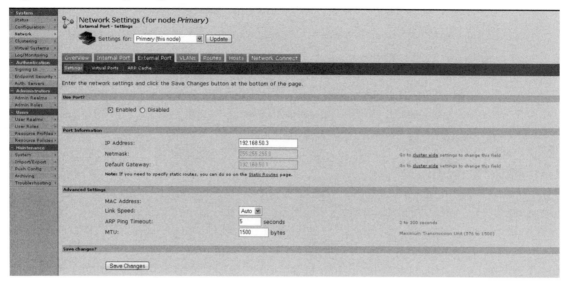

## Configuring Virtual Ports

The IVE allows you to configure virtual ports so that the IVE can listen on more than one IP address. This is commonly used with Passthrough Proxy (a Web option that we will discuss in Chapter 9), or if you want to assign different certificates to different DNS names on the IVE. In this example, we will configure a virtual port on the external interface. One thing to note is that if you are configuring this on an active/passive cluster, you must configure the interface on the cluster level rather than the node level.

1. Go to **System | Networking | <Interface> | Virtual Ports**. In this example, we will configure this on the external port. If you are configuring the virtual port in an active/passive cluster, you must configure this on the cluster level.

2. Click **New Port** to configure a new interface.

3. You need to configure only two values on a virtual port, which are the **Name** for the port and the **IP Address** that the port will be assigned. The rest of the settings will be inherited by the interface that the virtual port is a member of (e.g., the netmask, default gateway, etc.).

4. Click **Save Changes**.

## Configuring Static ARP Entries

In some cases, you may have a reason to configure a static ARP entry on the IVE rather than allowing for dynamic ARP to take place for a particular host. One example is if you want to protect your IVE from ARP spoofing, by configuring a static ARP entry for a server or gateway. You configure static ARP entries on an interface-by-interface basis. Typically, it is not recommended that you do this, but if you have a specific reason to do so, you may want to proceed with these steps:

1. Go to **System | Network | <Interface> | ARP Cache**.

2. Define the **IP Address** for the ARP entry that you would like to configure.

3. Define the **MAC Address** to which the IP address will map. This Media Access Control (MAC) address is the MAC address of the device which is assigned the IP address. Note that if the device is ever replaced, or even if the interface card is changed, you must manually reset this mapping.

4. Click **Add** to add the mapping to the table.

## Configuring Static Routes

Sometimes a single default route per interface will not be adequate for your network. For instance, let's say you have two internal routers which route to different internal networks. Because of this, if you need to support routing to different networks through those different gateways, you will have to configure separate routes for the destination networks to point them to the respective router that should be handling the routing. Otherwise, if you define a single default route, you will either lose the ability to reach certain networks, or implement suboptimal routing, as you will route to one router, which will have to pass the traffic to the correct router rather than just going directly to that router in the first place! One important concept to remember with configuring static routes is that you *must* configure routes on the appropriate interfaces, so it is important to keep track of which interface you are configuring. Figure 2.7 also accompanies this example to show you how the configuration should look.

1. Navigate to **System | Network | Routes**.

2. Select which interface you would like to configure the routes for by selecting that interface from the drop-down menu labeled **View Route Table For:**. Click **Update** if you had to change the interface so that you can see the routes for the appropriate interface. See Figure 2.7.

**Figure 2.7** Viewing a Routing Table on a Particular Interface

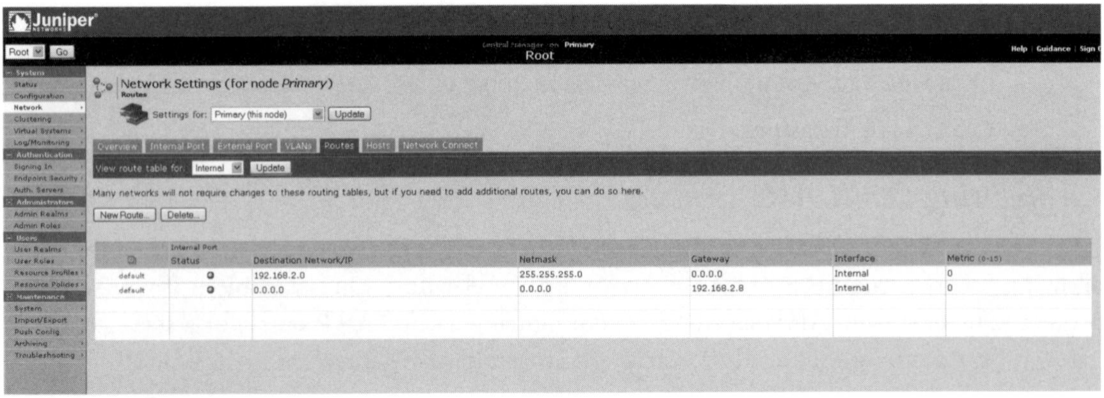

3. Click the **New Route** button to configure a new route on the interface.

4. Define the network that you want to configure the route for by configuring the **Destination Network/IP**.

5. Define the accompanying **netmask** for that interface.

6. The **Gateway** is the next hop to which the IVE should forward the traffic to. You must set this value so that the IVE knows what the next hop should be for this route.

7. Define the **Interface** to which you would like to apply the route.

8. Define the **Metric** for this route. A route is active if the IVE can reach the next hop. So, if you have multiple routes to the same network, you must use the **Metric** to define which route should be preferred. This value can be between 0 and 15.

9. Click **Add to <Interface> route table** to save the changes. See Figure 2.8 for an example of configuring a static route.

**Figure 2.8** Configuring a Static Route

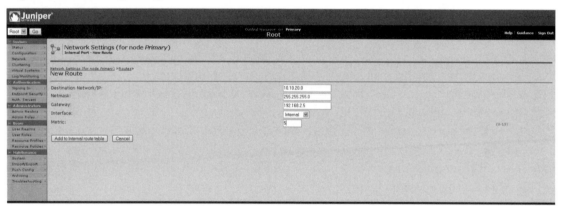

## Configuring Static Host (Name) Entries

Occasionally, you may need to configure a hostname entry manually into the IVE. You can do this to override other name server responses, or if you don't have a name server, you would have to configure the server to handle these requests here. In this example, we will configure a static hostname in the IVE:

1. Navigate to **System | Network | Hosts** to go to the Host Mapping table.

2. Define the **IP Address** which will map to the names you configure.

3. Configure what **Names** will map to the IP address that you configured. You can configure multiple names in a single entry by separating the hostname entries with commas.

For instance, you could say *email, email.company.local, email.company.com*, all within a single entry.

4. If you want, you can define a **Comment** for the entry, which is recommended to help define administration of the box.

5. Click **Add** to save the entry.

# Certificates

Certificates are part of the SSL security suite, so it is obvious that we must apply certificates to the IVE. Certificates and public key infrastructure (PKI) seem to strike fear into the hearts of many administrators, but they are not as bad as many may initially feel. For a complete discussion of certificates, visit http://en.wikipedia.org/wiki/X.509.

As you may remember, the IVE had you create a self-signed certificate when you initially set up the IVE. This was necessary because the IVE must use SSL, and therefore must have you generate the certificate when you set up the device. Of course, a self-signed certificate isn't exactly ideal for long-term IVE management. The biggest problem with self-signed certificates is that they are not going to be "trusted" by any client's Web browser, which will trigger a warning (this varies from browser to browser). The other problem is that because they are not trusted, users will be used to clicking Accept for a trusted certificate, so it would be easy to sneak a false certificate across a user and perform a man-in-the-middle attack. Therefore, it is recommended that you get a certificate that is signed by a trusted certificate authority (CA), such as VeriSign, Thawte, Entrust, and so on. The advantage is that most Web browsers already trust several CAs, so by having them sign your certificate, you can ensure that your IVE is who it claims to be.

The IVE supports certificates for much more than just SSL encryption. For instance, you can configure the IVE to authenticate clients with certificates (client certificates) as well as restrict access to resources based on client certificates and much more. In this section, we will focus primarily on configuring the IVE to use the certificates for SSL, but not to authenticate users (we will cover authentication servers in Chapter 4.)

## Generating a CSR

One of the first steps that you will have to perform when getting a certificate signed by a trusted CA is to generate a Certificate Signing Request (CSR). The CSR essentially creates the private key which is stored securely on the IVE, as well as generating a public key which will be presented to the CA to sign. The certificate will have several properties which you must configure when you generate a CSR. Figure 2.9 accompanies this example.

1. Navigate to **System | Configuration | Certificates | Device Certificates**.

2. Click **New CSR** to begin the CSR process.

3. You must define several fields in this example, including the following:

**Common Name**  This is the name the user will use to refer to the IVE. This is typically a DNS name such as vpn.mycompany.com or secure.mycompany.com. It can alternatively be an IP address, but this is not common. Most likely, you will use a DNS name. Note that the common name must match the DNS name that you configure (what the users reference the IVE by); otherwise, users will get a warning with the certificate.

**Organization Name**  This is the name of your organization. Many people configure this using their company name if their organization is a business.

**Org Unit Name**  This is the name of the department to which this is allocated. Often this will be something such as IT, Accounting, or Sales. But it doesn't really have too much significance, as long as it matches what you will set with your CA when you're getting the CSR signed.

**Locality**  This is the city or other local notation for where this device is going to be located.

**State**  This is the full written name (not two-letter acronym) for your state or province.

**Country**  This is the two-letter country code for your country.

**Email Address**  This is typically an administrator/administrative e-mail address which can be used to help identify a contact point relating to the certificate.

4. Enter some random data into the **Random Data** field that will be used to help ensure that the certificate is based on random data. See Figure 2.9, which accompanies this example.

5. Click **Create CSR**.

**Figure 2.9** Creating a CSR in the IVE

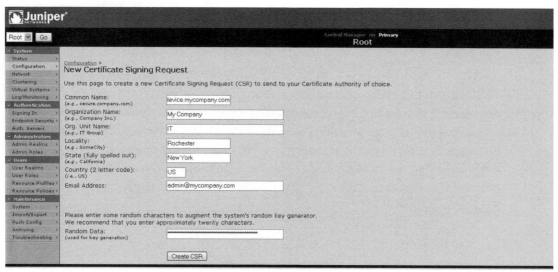

Once you click **Create CSR**, the IVE will generate the CSR. You will be brought to the next screen, which will show you the generated CSR. You will need to copy that section of the certificate and enter it in the CSR field when you are generating the signed certificate with the CA. This is going to vary between different CAs, so you will need to follow your CA's instructions. If you have problems with that step, you should contact your CA.

**TIP**

You do not necessarily need to use the CSR generated on the IVE to get a signed certificate on the IVE, but this method is recommended. You could generate a CSR on another device and have it signed through the same mechanism, but the problem with that method is that the private key must be handled outside the IVE, and you must come up with a method to generate the public/private key pair (such as OpenSSL).

6.  Once you have your public key of your certificate signed by your CA, it is most often delivered to you in a .txt file or .crt file in .pem format. Download the certificates to your local machine, and then go back into the IVE to upload the certificate.

7.  If you have already closed out of the IVE, go to **System | Configuration | Certificates | Device Certificate** and click on the CSR to import the certificate.

8.  As shown in Figure 2.10, you can click on the **Browse** button next to the **Signed Certificate**. This will bring up the browser window so that you can select the signed certificate on your local machine.

9.  Click **Import** to apply the certificate to the device. If you try to apply a certificate that doesn't match the CSR private key, you will receive an error, but if everything applies successfully you should be all set. You can always check to make sure that your IVE is presenting the correct certificate by browsing to the IVE and double-clicking the padlock icon (typically located in the URL bar) and view the certificate properties to make sure that it is the new certificate [the date is most often the best indicator]).

**Figure 2.10** Generated License

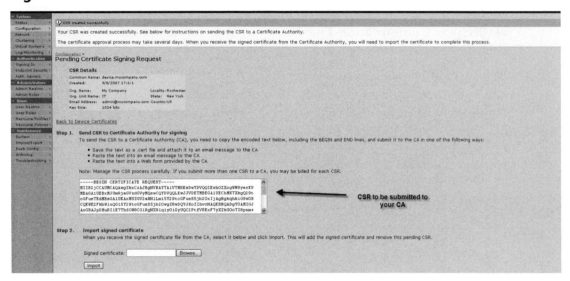

## Importing a Signed Certificate (without CSR)

In some cases, you may wish to generate the CSR off the IVE, have the CSR signed, and then import both the private key and the public (signed) key to the IVE. Juniper accommodates this type of setup. You perform this step slightly differently than you would generating the CSR. We will assume that you will already have your certificate and private key ready to be installed. See Figure 2.11, which accompanies this example.

1. Go to **System | Configuration | Certificates | Device Certificates** and click **Import Certificate & Key**.

2. You can upload the certificates in a few different formats. These essentially depend on how the certificate was created:

    **Certificate & Private Key in one file**  If the certificate includes the private key option allows you to upload a cert file that includes both keys. Click **Browse** to select the certificate on your local machine. Assuming that you encrypted the private key with a password (recommended), you must enter the password in the **Password Key** field.

    **Certificate & Private Keys in separate files**  Quite often, you will have two different files for your public and private keys. That way, your private key is never sent to the signing authority. In this case, you will have to select your **Certificate File** to upload it to the IVE, and then select the **Private Key** file to upload that (**Browse** for both files to select them and upload the files to the IVE). Assuming that you have a password assigned to the private key, you will need to enter that password so that the private key can be accessed.

**System Configuration** You can also import a license key from an IVE system configuration binary. To do this, you will need to click **Browse** under **Import via System Configuration File** and, if you assigned a password to the system configuration, enter the password in the **Password** field.

3. Next to each option is an **Import** button, so simply click **Import** next to each option you want to upload. If there is a problem with the upload, you will know immediately when the IVE reports back the status. The IVE will instruct you what the issue is with the upload. Most often it is an incorrect password, or you are trying to upload the certificate in the wrong format.

**Figure 2.11** Importing a Certificate into the IVE without the Use of a CSR

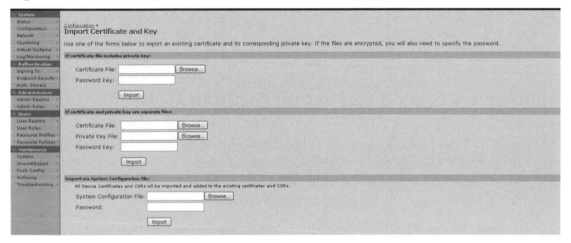

## *Assigning a Certificate to a Port*

Once you have a certificate loaded onto the IVE, you will need to assign it to a port before the IVE will present it to a user attempting to connect to the IVE. The reason you must assign a certificate to a port and the IVE doesn't automatically perform that step (assuming you have multiple ports) is because you may have different FQDNs which resolve to those different ports, so you must make sure you apply the correct certificate to the correct port; otherwise, the user will receive a warning that the certificate does not match the browsed name. In this example, we will apply the certificate to a port (note that you do this in the same way you apply the certificate to a virtual port, physical interface, or cluster VIP if you are using active/passive clustering):

1. Navigate to **System | Configuration | Certificates | Device Certificates** and click on the certificate you would like to apply to a port.

2. Click the **Ports** to which you want to apply the certificate. These are organized into internal ports and external ports. You can apply a certificate to multiple ports, so simply select the ports to which you want to apply the certificate, and click the **Add** button next to the respective Internal/External section. The port should appear in the **Selected Virtual Ports** for the respective Internal/External section; see Figure 2.12.

3. Click **Save Changes**.

**Figure 2.12** Applying Certificates to Ports

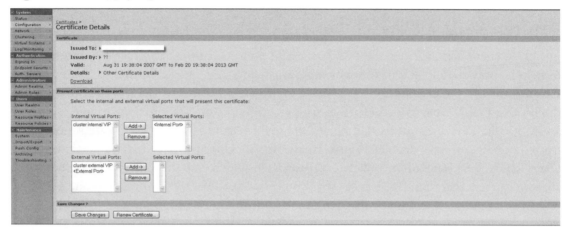

> ## Warning
>
> Certificates do have a lifespan which is determined when you create them. This is often one or two years. Once a certificate expires, your clients will receive a warning. To prevent unnecessary calls to your help desk, you should keep track of when the certificate will expire, to make sure you can renew the certificate before this happens. To renew a certificate go to **System | Configuration | Certificates | Device Certificates** and click on the appropriate **Certificate**. At the bottom of the certificate screen is a **Renew Certificate** button. If you have your CA renew the certificate that you originally loaded, your CA will provide you with a new certificate file (which is just a re-signed copy of the public key for your certificate so that it has a new expiration date). You simply need to load this certificate to the IVE by clicking **Browse** to locate the certificate, and if there is encryption on the file itself, you will need to enter the password in the **Password Key** field and click **Import**, which will renew your certificate. You can ensure that the correct certificate is loaded by browsing to your IVE and double-clicking the padlock in the URL bar (for most browsers) to examine the certificate and make sure it follows the correct expiration date.

# Other Certificates

The IVE has a few other uses for certificates than just SSL encryption to client browsers. The IVE can also use certificates to authenticate clients, as well as signing Java applets and determining the authenticity of sites that clients are browsing for beyond the IVE. We will cover certificate-based authentication in Chapter 4 and Java applet signing in the Chapter 9. In the following section, we will briefly discuss how trusted server CAs are implemented and why they are configured on the IVE.

## Trusted Server CAs

Just like a client Web browser, the IVE has several preinstalled trusted server CA certificates to help identify signing authorities which are trusted to sign certificates. Go to **System | Configuration | Certificates | Device Certificates | Trusted Server CAs** to view the list that the IVE has loaded. If a user tries to browse to an SSL site that is signed with a CA that the IVE does not trust, the user will get a warning that the certificate is not trusted (unless you have disabled **Allow Browsing to Untrusted SSL sites** under **Users | User Roles | <UserRole> | Web | Options**, in which case the user would *not* be allowed to view that site). But let's say that you do want to trust a particular signing CA (e.g., if you have an internal CA that you want to trust any certificates signed by that CA). You will want to import the CA cert to the IVE as a trusted server CA so that the IVE will trust it. To do so, perform the following steps:

1.  Navigate to **System | Configuration | Certificates | Device Certificates | Trusted Server CAs**. Click **Import Trusted Server CA**.

2.  Load the certificate from your local machine by clicking **Browse** to locate the certificate on your machine.

3.  Click **Import** to import the CA certificate.

> **NOTE**
>
> Trusted server CA certificates can expire just like regular certificates. This usually isn't a problem with public CAs because their certificates last for a very long time, and Juniper will handle loading their new CA certs when they are released (with new firmware versions). The issue you are more likely to run into is that if you upload a trusted server CA (such as through an internal CA) and that cert expires, you must be sure to renew the certificate just like you would a device certificate, or else users will not be able to trust any certificates that that CA had signed.

# Security and System Settings

The IVE has some system-wide settings that are helpful to know about, particularly when you are first setting up the IVE. Although these steps are not mandatory, they are helpful to be aware of, because they can alter the behavior of the IVE itself. In this section, we will cover those options that are configured in the IVE and applied system-wide.

## Security Settings

Most IVE configuration is broken down into granular configuration locations that you can customize across different realms, roles, and resource; but some settings are applied system-wide and apply to user experience when it comes to security and the IVE. It is recommended that you look at these settings when you are setting up an IVE to help ensure that these default settings are what you intend. You can locate the following settings under **System | Configuration | Security**:

- **Allowed SSL and TLS Versions** As SSL technology has evolved, there have been several different versions which provide more security and fix previous vulnerabilities and weaknesses. The problem is that older Web browsers may not support these newer standards, so you may want to strike a balance between usability and security. The different options are as follows:

  - **Accept only TLS v1** This setting maximizes security, as Transport Layer Security (TLS) v1 is considered stronger than SSL v1 and v2.

  - **Accept SSL v3 and TLS v1** This provides better security than SSL v2, but it allows for either SSL v3 or TLS v1, which makes it more likely that browsers will be able to support the protocol. This is the default setting.

  - **Accept SSL v2, SSL v3, and TLS v1** You should use this setting only when you must be able to support SSL v2 browsers. Because SSL v2 has known vulnerabilities, it is recommended that you do not select this option.

- **Allowed Encryption Strength** Although the individual algorithms that are supported are one factor when it comes to security, we also have to worry about the encryption strength (or the length of the encryption key). Typically, the longer the encryption key, the more secure the communication; however, it also requires more resources on the computer to be able to process the keys. Also, some longer key lengths are not supported in some browsers, so just like the SSL/TLS algorithm that you choose, you must also select what key length you want to support so that the IVE can talk to clients. Here are your choices:

  - **Accept only 168-bit and greater** This is the strongest encryption key length, but it might exclude some browsers from being able to connect if they are not capable of supporting that key length.

- **Accept only 128-bit and greater** This option is likely to provide adequate security and the most compatibility with client Web browsers. This is the default.

- **Accept 40-bit and greater** This option allows you to provide the most compatibility with user Web browsers, but at a decrease in security.

- **Custom SSL Cipher Selection** Key length is not exactly indicative of security all by itself. You also have to factor in what algorithm is being used (e.g., AES/3DES, AES, DES, RC4, or RC2). Therefore, the IVE allows you to select what algorithms/key lengths are accepted on a case-by-case basis. The green highlighted encryption ciphers/strengths are recommended for FIPS deployments.

- **Do Not Allow Connections from Browsers That Only Accept Weaker Ciphers** This option allows you to completely prevent users from being able to connect to the IVE when they do not meet the encryption strength. If you do not have this option selected, the IVE will allow the user to connect only to give the user a message indicating there is an issue. This option is left off by default because it allows users to remediate their browsers, but if you have it enabled, users will simply not be able to connect.

- **SSL Handshake Timeout Option** By default, the IVE will consider an SSL handshake to be timed out if the handshake doesn't complete in 60 seconds. Sometimes users over slow links or with very slow computers may take longer to complete the SSL handshake, so you may have to alter this value.

- **Delete All Cookies at Session Termination** This option allows you to determine what happens to IVE cookies on the user's machine when the user signs out. Two cookies are stored on the user's machine, so you may want to have the browser delete the cookies:

  - **Delete This********Delete all cookies at session termination**

  - **Preserve cookies at session termination** This option will save the cookies on the user's machine rather than delete them, which will save the last realm the user selected (useful if you have multiple realms on a sign-in policy so that they automatically get the same realm), as well as the last sign-in URL cookie. This is the default.

  - **Include IVE Session Cookie in URL** This setting typically affects a user's ability to launch applications (such as JVM) through the IVE. By including the session cookie in the URL, the user should not have an issue launching these applications, particularly when using Mozilla as a browser.

- **Include session Cookie in URL. Default.**

■ **Do not include session cookie in URL** This option is viewed by many as a security enhancement because it will not include the IVE session cookie in the URL. You should note that it may cause some disruption to some IVE functions when it comes to launching applications through your Web browser.

■ **Lockout Options** You can control whether an IP address should be locked out of the IVE if the user fails too many authentication attempts. Of course, this can also be affected by your authentication server as well. For instance, if you have the IVE set to use LDAP as an authentication server, and it is set to lock out users if they fail two authentication attempts in 30 minutes, that may preclude the IVE settings.

■ **Rate** This is the number of attempts per minute that will trigger an IP address to be locked out. You can set this between 1 and 4,294,967,295 attempts per minute. The default is 3.

■ **Attempts** Alternatively, you can determine how many attempts will result in an IP address being locked out. By default, this is 180, but it can be between 2 and 4,294,967,295.

■ **Lockout Period** This is the period for how long the IP address should be locked out. By default, it is set to 2 minutes, but you can set it between 1 and 10,080 minutes.

■ **Last Login Options** This determines what the user might see on his portal page regarding his last session when he logs into the IVE. You can choose to show these options or not; they are disabled by default:

■ **Show last login time on user's bookmark page**

■ **Show last login IP address on user's bookmark page**

## System Options

The IVE has some other system options that don't directly relate to IVE security but do impact how the IVE functions. These options may vary between different hardware platforms and software versions. The options are located under **Maintenance | System | Options**:

■ **Automatic Version Monitoring** This option allows the IVE to notify you in the AdminUI of critical security patches for the IVE that should be installed to fix a vulnerability or bug. To perform this check, the IVE must report to Juniper to report some information. If you do not want the IVE communicating with Juniper, you should disable this option.

- **Enable GZIP Compression**  This setting allows compression policies to be enforced by using GZIP compression for HTTP traffic (assuming that the client browser supports it). This can help reduce the amount of data that is sent between the IVE and the client, which is particularly helpful if you have low-bandwidth links. See Chapter 9 for more information on enabling compression.

- **Enable SSL Acceleration**  This option is available to systems that have an SSL acceleration card and an SSL acceleration license. If you have these features, you should enable this option to help improve system performance. Note that this setting will reboot the IVE when this option is saved.

- **Enable Java Instrumentation Caching**  This feature allows the IVE to cache Java instrumentation, which can help improve performance because redundant data may not have to be downloaded.

- **Show Auto-Allow**  This feature will display the Auto-Allow setting in the bookmark configuration for roles (e.g., Web, File, SAM, etc.). This is nice because it will create the resource policies for you to allow access to these resources, but you may find it better to just configure these settings in Resource Profiles that can perform the equivalent operations. Either way, this option is good to enable.

- **External User Records Management**  If you are finding that your system is becoming stressed with disk space issues, you may want to limit how many user records should be maintained in the system. You can set the number of records that will be saved in the system with the following options:

  - **Persistent user records limit**  This is the number of user sessions that will be stored on the IVE.

  - **Number of user records to delete when the limit is exceeded**  This option allows you to define how many user records will be deleted when the limit is exceeded. Note that you can click the **Delete Records Now** button to manually delete the additional records.

  - **Enable automatic deletion**  This option allows the IVE to automatically delete the user records when the limit is exceeded. Without this option enabled, you will have to manually click the **Delete Records Now** button to reduce the number of records.

- **End-User Localization**  This option allows you to specify what language to use for the IVE for client sessions. You can either select an appropriate language, or set the IVE to Automatic, which will present whichever language is being used on the user browser (this is the default).

# Summary

The IVE has many different features that you can customize and configure at many different points. But before we go through all of the fine details of all the bells and whistles, we need to get the IVE up and running, which is what we covered in this chapter. We began by exploring how you must initially configure the IVE on the serial console along with what values are configured. Once the IVE is up and running, there are still some primary tasks which you must undertake in the AdminUI. These tasks include configuring other ports, certificates, security settings, and other system options. All of these options set the stage for the rest of the configuration that you will be performing later in your IVE administration.

# Solutions Fast Track

## Initial CLI Setup

☑ The IVE must initially be configured on the serial console before you can manage the device via the Web interface.

☑ You should have several different pieces of information when you are setting up your IVE, including IP address, subnet mask, gateway, and other name server settings.

☑ You configure a single admin account on the CLI which will be used to log into the IVE Web interface.

## Initial Web Setup

☑ The IVE admin interface is located at https://<ipaddress>/admin.

☑ You can configure additional network settings, or edit those settings that you configured on the CLI.

☑ It is very important to set the date and time on the IVE.

## Certificates

☑ Device certificates are used to validate IVE identity as well as encrypt traffic using PKI.

☑ The IVE can assign different certificates to different ports.

☑ You can manually upload certificates to validate client authenticity as well as authenticate server identity.

# Security and System Settings

☑   The IVE allows you to configure system-wide security settings such as SSL protocol version, encryption strength, and algorithm used.

☑   You can define whether the IVE will keep or remove cookies that are generated on a user's machine.

☑   You can implement several options to enhance IVE performance and management, such as SSL acceleration, GZIP compression, and Auto-Allow features.

# Frequently Asked Questions

**Q:** I configured my device on the serial console, but I still cannot connect the AdminUI after I completed the setup. What should I do?

**A:** You should try to perform some of the IVE console troubleshooting steps, such as checking whether you can ping the default gateway or other devices on the network. Checking the ARP table also helps. You can configure other options such as link speeds/duplex values, IP address, subnet mask, and gateway configuration.

**Q:** I purchased a SAM and Network Connect license, but I can't find those features on the IVE. What do I do?

**A:** You must apply the SAM/Network Connect license that will open these features.

**Q:** Getting publicly signed certificates is expensive. I see that I don't need to have a public certificate. Why do I want one?

**A:** Without a valid certificate, users will not be able to verify the IVE's authenticity. Therefore, the clients would be susceptible to an SSL man-in-the-middle attack. Visit www.sans.org/reading_room/whitepapers/threats/480.php for more information.

**Q:** We have an internal SSL site that users access through the IVE, and it brings up warning messages that the SSL certificate is not trusted. What can I do?

**A:** If you control access to the CA cert, upload it to the IVE as a trusted server CA to help prevent user confusion or SSL man-in-the-middle attacks (because users will be used to clicking past the warning message if you don't have a trusted certificate).

**Q:** I am trying to recover a certificate from a system configuration file so that I have access to both the private and the public key without having to generate a new CSR and have a new certificate signed. What can I do?

**A:** Your best option is to perform a certificate import from a system configuration file. See the "Certificates" section of this chapter to perform those steps.

**Q:** I want to prevent users with browsers that don't support SSL v3 or TLS from connecting to the IVE. What do I need to do?

**A:** This option is enabled by default. The IVE will only allow sessions to be created on SSL v3 and TLS, but will not support SSL v1 or SSL v2.

**Q:** Can I configure authentication servers from the IVE console?

**A:** No, you can only configure authentication servers through the WebUI, although you can create local administrator accounts on the IVE console.

**Q:** I lost my administrator credentials and need access to the IVE. What can I do?

**A:** You can create a temporary login account to log into the IVE by going to the IVE console and choosing **Create Super Admin Session**. This will provide you with a URL to browse to along with a login token that is good for three minutes (you need to log in before the token expires, but once you are logged in, the session will be good for as long as it normally would be for an admin session).

# Chapter 3

# Realms, Roles, and Resources

**Solutions in this chapter:**

- **Introducing Realms, Roles, and Resources**
- **Configuring Realms**
- **Configuring Roles**
- **Configuring Resources**

☑ **Summary**

☑ **Solutions Fast Track**

☑ **Frequently Asked Questions**

# Introducing Realms, Roles, and Resources

Realms, roles, and resources are known to the vast majority of IVE administrators as simply the "3 Rs." The reason for this is simple: One builds on the other in a way that can't be separated, with the realm being perhaps the easiest to define and ultimately getting much more granular as you work your way down through roles and resources. That is the order we need to go in if we are to fully understand and appreciate the overall benefit of this architecture.

So, what are the 3 Rs? They are quite simple (see Figure 3.1):

- **Realms** simply define the authentication, authorization, and auditing services for a specific group of users, along with the ability to map those users to each of their roles. Realms can even apply a wide array of authentication policies to ensure that users are only allowed to log in under the specific conditions that have been allowed by the administrator. To the user, the primary contact with realms is the sign-in page, and each user can authenticate to only one realm at a time.

- **Roles** are what users ultimately belong to. If you are an employee in the accounting department with a management title, your roles are probably something like Everyone, Accounting, and Management. Since you have mapped to all three roles, once you are logged in you will simply see the sum of all the allowed resources. Just like realms, individual roles may be restricted from view, depending on the various policies implemented by the administrator.

- **Resources** are anything on your network that remote users need to access. As an administrator, you will decide what should or should not be allowed for each of the users, using realms and roles as the gatekeepers to the individual resources. To be a bit more specific and to provide a nice overview of what the IVE is capable of delivering, the various resources that might be found within any role can include:

**Web** These are Web pages delivered via the IVE's rewrite engine, which would simply show up as hyperlinks on the user's IVE homepage.

**Hosted Java Applet** The IVE can actually accept a wide variety of Java applets that can be uploaded straight to the IVE instead of an internal Web server, then delivered straight to the client from a single Web bookmark. Because the applets are designed to be cross-platform (Windows, Mac, and Linux), the very fact that the IVE can deliver them on demand and rewritten to enable all external communication to flow over SSL only is a very key feature that is often overlooked. Common applets include RDP

(Windows Terminal Services), JICA (Citrix Java Client), 3270/5250 (mainframe), and FTP (file transfer).

**Files** Windows and Unix/NFS file shares are natively supported so that file shares can be made accessible to clients through their Web browsers. Novell file shares can also be accessed as long as the Novell server is set up to emulate either Windows or NFS file share, which is easily accomplished.

**Secure Application Manager (SAM).** Client/server applications such as Microsoft Outlook communicating with Exchange require more than Web portal access—they require the ability to communicate directly from the client to the server, hence the client/server designation. SAM is the IVE's answer to this basic demand. SAM is actually divided into two types: JSAM and WSAM. We won't cover all the pros and cons of each right now, since that is tackled later on. Just remember that there are two types and that only one can be enabled during any single user logon.

**Terminal Services** If you have either Windows Terminal Servers or Citrix Metaframe Servers, you will want to learn all you can about the IVE's support for terminal services. Configuring these on the IVE will give clients the ability to have hyperlinks to specific terminal servers or published applications, thereby making it very easy to deploy complex applications to remote users.

**Meetings** Secure Meeting provides a nice, simple way for groups of users to interact through a secure meeting environment, including the ability for anyone in the meeting to share individual applications or even their entire desktop. Want more? Users can allow someone else to control their PCs, chat with others, or interact using a virtual whiteboard.

**Network Connect** This is your replacement for your legacy IPSec client. It provides a full Layer 3 connection (the client gets an IP address from the corporate LAN). Network Connect automatically downloads and installs itself on demand and runs on Windows, Mac, and Linux workstations. It is great for Voice over Internet Protocol (VoIP) applications and other applications that can benefit from the added performance of a Layer 3 connection. Furthermore, as with most of the aforementioned resources, the capabilities are so varied that we have to cover them in a separate chapter.

Of course there is actually much more to it, but at least you now have the general idea before we start to dive too much deeper. The rest of this chapter introduces you to the key features and focuses in on the often overlooked administrative goodies, along with providing the more basic how-to procedures that you will need just to get you started.

**Figure 3.1** Combined Relationship Between Realms, Roles, and Resources

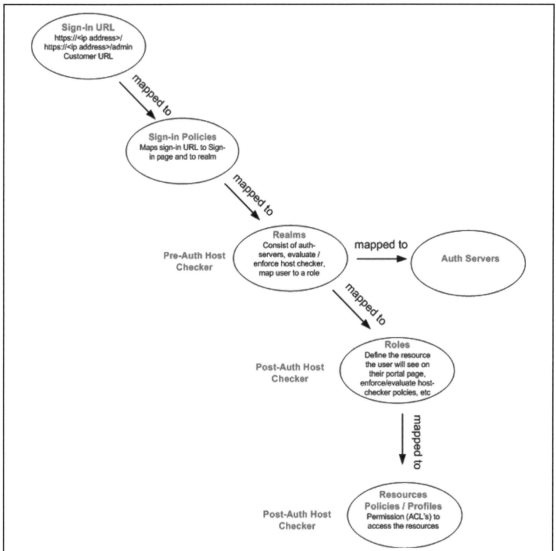

# Configuring Realms

Realm configuration is perhaps the first part of the IVE where you get to turn your creativity loose in terms of both overall security and user experience. The realm configuration stage is the time to really start thinking about how you would like to fashion the user experience. There is no particular right way for a realm to be designed; each organization may follow its own convention. You could simply start off with Users, which would certainly encompass everyone and make for a very simple starting place, or you might want to map it to the larger divisions of your company, such as EMEA, APAC, and Americas for the large multinational crowd. Although you can certainly change the realms at a later date, a little up-front planning can certainly save you some work in the future.

# Selecting and Configuring General Settings

In the spirit of keeping things simple, we will use Employees and Contractors as our two starting realms. As you can see in Figure 3.2, we simply selected **Users, User Realms**, **New Authentication Realm** and are in the midst of defining our new Employees realm. But now let's look at this from the best-practices point of view to learn what would provide us the greatest benefit to administrators and users alike. We will jump right past the all-too-easy Name and Description fields and go straight to the Servers section, explaining each continuing option in more detail as we go along.

**Figure 3.2** New User Authentication Realm

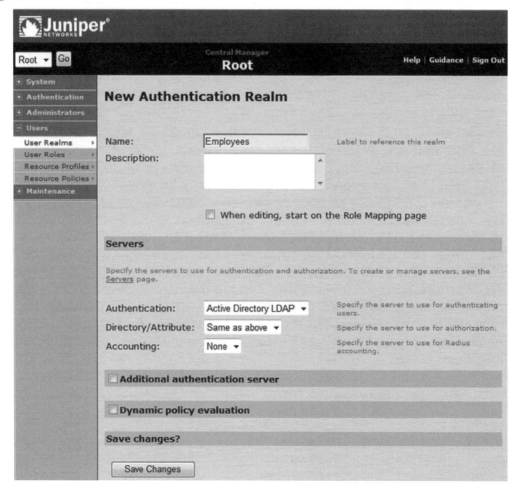

First, you won't have anything in the drop-down list if you haven't already defined at least one authentication server (see Chapter 4). Because we are really looking to turn this into a best-practices opportunity for this new realm, here is the "typical" order of preference that pretty much any IVE administrator or consultant would advise you to use:

1. **Token Authentication or Certificates.** If your corporate policy is that no employee shall have remote access unless he or she is authenticated with a token or certificate, this is the choice you will select from your drop-down list. Pretty much every token authentication system uses RADIUS anyway, whereas RSA SecureID would use either its proprietary protocol or the built-in Steel-Belted RADIUS component from Juniper.

2. **Active Directory LDAP.** If you are running Active Directory, you should have configured it as an LDAP server. If you created it using the Active Directory/ Windows NT option, go back and recreate it as LDAP, selecting **Active Directory** as the custom LDAP server type. You will need this for the authorization piece anyway (the next box down), so you might as well go ahead and use it for authentication, especially since it also offers a much more robust password management feature.

**NOTE**

The Advanced License is required for password management. If you are running an SA4000 or SA6000, this license is almost certain to be a requirement. The Advanced Licenses option is not available on the SA700.

Prior to configuring an LDAP server instance where Password Management is required, you will need an Admin Distinguished Name (DN) and password, as covered in the Authentication Servers chapter. If your responsibilities do not include being the LDAP administrator, you will need to work with the LDAP admin to get this account set up. The DN will look something like "CN=SSLV PN,CN=Users,DC=company,DC=com". *Again, the full admin account is required only when password management will be used; otherwise, a user account with standard permissions will be sufficient (assuming that the account has permissions to search your LDAP structure when performing group/attribute matching).*

If the Active Directory administrator does not want to create an account with Admin permissions (many frown on this), the following explicit permissions can be used (configured inside Active Directory):

1. **User Account.** Create a normal user account and place that account in a group as **Primary Group** (just to eliminate the possibility that it is not using the Domain Users' group). Give this user permissions for

**controlling computers**. Grant the user **Create Computer Objects** and **Delete Computer Objects** Access Control Entries (ACEs).

2. **Computer Account.** From the **Active Directory Users and Computers** snap-in, click **Advanced Features** on the **View** menu so that the **Security** tab is exposed when you click **Properties**. Right-click the **Computers** container, then click **Properties**. On the **Security** tab, click **Advanced**. On the **Permissions** tab, click **Add**, and **add the created user** to the list of permission entries. Make sure the **This object and all child objects** option is displayed in the **Apply onto** box. From the **Permissions** box, click to select the **Allow** check box next to the **Create Computer Objects** and **Delete Computer Objects** ACEs, and then click **OK**.

3. Restart the IVE services to ensure that the account has been updated, and then run a policy trace to see whether the "Join to Domain" was successful.

___

3. **Active Directory/Windows NT.** If Windows NT is all you have, this is the option you will use. If you are using Active Directory, again we will say that the second option is your best all-around choice. The only exception to this rule is if you have Active Directory and you also need to support cross-domain authentication. In that case, you can use this as the authentication server while still assigning LDAP for the Directory/ Attribute option. But even then you will not be able to retrieve anything but groups, and password management will be limited: no early warning and no feedback if the entered password does not match the assigned password policy.

4. **RADIUS.** Actually, this one could probably tie for the second spot in our list here, but because not everyone runs RADIUS, we will just leave it here at the bottom of the two. But if you do have RADIUS and would like to use it for primary authentication, this is certainly the way to go.

5. **Local.** No matter how many authentication options the IVE has (there are currently 10 types), this choice will always be in the bottom two for any authentication realm. After all, who wants to go into a Web UI to create and maintain potentially thousands of user accounts that aren't usable by any external system? Still, the Local option can actually come in handy for your contractor realm(s) because you can easily define a few vendor accounts and then enable or disable them as needed, especially since you have the option to automatically disable the account once the vendor has signed in. Use this option sparingly.

6. **Anonymous.** You can use the anonymous server to provide unauthenticated access. Yes, you read that correctly: *unauthenticated*. Absolutely no username/password

access is required—just type in the correct URL and you are through. Still, in some use cases this makes sense and the IVE does add a nice layer of application security in this mode that would take a great deal of time and money to replicate with custom extranets. But if you go this route, you need to make sure that your idle timeouts and other realm, role, and resource restrictions have been thoroughly evaluated and policies put in place that would limit the damage that a remote attacker could achieve. If you are new to information security, you might want to seek some highly qualified advice before opening this option to the public.

## Directory/Attribute

You need to have defined an LDAP or RADIUS server instance before anything will show up in the drop-down. If your authentication server is of the LDAP variety, this option will automatically be set as "Same as above," which of course would be LDAP. If your authentication server is set as RADIUS, you will have the option to use either your LDAP server or the attributes from RADIUS. The most common setting here is to use your LDAP server for authorization, as you will come to appreciate much more as we move on to the topic of role mapping.

## Accounting

This is just for RADIUS accounting. The nice thing here is that you don't have to use RADIUS for either of the previous two options while still being able to leverage your RADIUS logging.

So to recap, unless you are new to security, and we welcome you if you are, you probably already noticed that we just covered the basic authentication, authorization, and accounting (AAA) configuration options for the entire realm; notwithstanding all the more specific user, admin, and system logs that are handled by the built-in Syslog and SNMP mechanisms. Of course you will now want to go right back and do the same for the "Contractors" realm or any other realms that you can dream up.

And now that the basics are out of the way, you can stop right now and go on to the "Roles" section and still be just like the vast majority of the IVE configurations currently in production, or you can look a bit further down the configuration screen to see what other clever tricks lie in store and continue to get the most out of the IVE.

## Additional Authentication Server

As you will see when you select this option (see Figure 3.3), this is really focused on realms that require single sign-on to back-end applications, even though the user initially signs on with something other than the same authentication server that is being used by those internal applications.

**Figure 3.3** Specifying an Additional Authentication Server for SSO

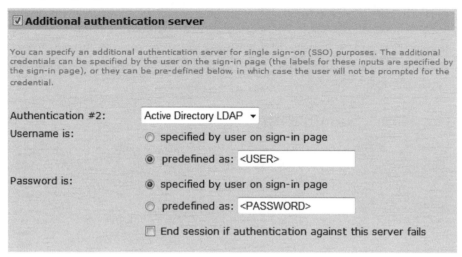

One of the more common examples of this is where the realm is configured to use tokens for authentication (as in SecureID or Certificates). Since token passwords are good for one use only and certainly don't match the user's Active Directory password, they are of absolutely no use to anything once the user has successfully signed in. So, what we do here is to simply enable the second authentication server—this time using Active Directory—to automatically match the exact same username that the user used when he or she signed against the token server, which the IVE has conveniently stored in memory for each unique user as the <USER> variable, thereby prompting the user on the logon page to also enter his or her Active Directory password. The bottom line here is that the user will have only three fields to enter: username, token password, and Active Directory password.

There are two other notable benefits to this option as well:

- Users would be advised that their Active Directory passwords were about to change and then could change the passwords themselves.

- A server such as RSA SecurID could be put in to "PINless" mode so that users would not have to remember their own token PINs, given that their Active Directory passwords would now fulfill the "what you know" component of the two-factor scenario.

Also, by deselecting the **End session if authentication against the server fails** check box at the bottom of this section, we are still allowing the user to sign in even if he or she uses the wrong Active Directory password, though they certainly won't have single sign-on to any back-end system, since the stored <PASSWORD2> variable would not be correct. To clarify further, <PASSWORD2> is what we would use for single sign-on because it is the password that we collected from the second authentication server. <PASSWORD> is the variable that we could have brought down from the primary authentication server, which in our scenario here would have been the token password, which of course would have been useless to us.

## Dynamic Policy Evaluation

This is perhaps one of the least used features of the IVE, but it should not be bypassed or forgotten. Simply use this option whenever you have made configuration changes and you want them to be applied across the realm on a regular basis, without the user having to log out and then back in (see Figure 3.4).

**Figure 3.4** Dynamic Policy Evaluation

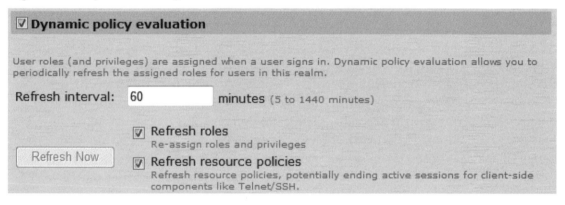

**Tip**

If your IVE environment is already approaching its maximum limits, you might want to use dynamic policy evaluation sparingly (if at all), because the increased processing could impact overall system performance. This option would not apply to Web and File resource policies, because they are checked with each request from a user thus it would not make any sense to apply this option for changes to those resource policies.

The trend for most administrators is to leave the dynamic policy evaluation set to the default state, which is off.

# Selecting and Configuring Authentication Policies

Everywhere you go you'll find policies and procedures. But what is a policy? Isn't it a statement about what will and will not be tolerated under certain conditions? In the case of the IVE, the *procedure* would be what you tell the users to do to get access: Go to this URL and enter your credentials. A *policy*, on the other hand, will lay down the law that you can't get access unless you are in strict compliance with the rules. The IVE has policies, and the authentication policy allows you to uniquely define a large list of things that are either coming from the users or their PCs that must be compliant with your stated policy before they will be allowed to use this realm. If a user is not compliant, this realm will be off limits to that user … simple as that.

Well, maybe not *that* simple. There is one thing that needs to be understood about authentication policies, and it is a pretty important detail: You have to learn and appreciate how an authentication policy will impact the login process, especially when multiple realms are tied to a single login page. The reason this is so important is that if you have two or more realms tied to a single login URL and then apply authentication policies to one or more of them, the user could get security popups for realms that she does not care to log in to. The user could ultimately be allowed to sign in to her realm, but do you really want that user complaining about all the unnecessary security warnings that have nothing to do with her? As you read the rest of this book, remember to pay particularly close attention to your sign-in policies and endpoint security rules, since forgetting to do so could end up causing you more time re-architecting your IVE implementation.

In Figure 3.5 you will see seven submenus, each defining the criteria that our users need if they are to gain access to this realm.

**TIP**

A common trick used with realm authentication policies is to apply them in a way that will ensure that a user only has access to one realm per URL, despite the fact that the administrator may have assigned two or more realms to the single login page, thus leaving the user with the nice drop-down menu to select from during each logon. By applying these tests to one or more of the realms, the realm that fails to match the requirement will simply not be accessible to the user, at which point the realm selection drop-down disappears and the user is left with just the one approved realm.

**Figure 3.5** Realm Authentication Policies

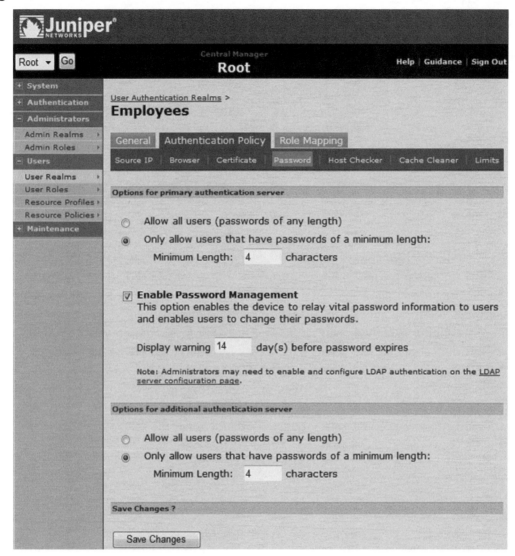

Just so you don't think you have déjà vu once we get to our discussion of roles, you will see a very similar list that will apply to the individual roles, minus the Password and Limits tabs.

## Password Management: Realm Restriction

If you want to enable password management for your Active Directory server, there are a few things you need to know. An obvious first is that you must ensure that the **Enable Password Management** check box is selected. The second, and much less obvious, thing is that the Active Directory server must be configured for LDAPS mode if it is going to actually allow the users to change their passwords. The reason for this is that the standard LDAP port 389 is not encrypted, so it is hardly what we would want all the users changing their passwords over. Instead we want the IVE to seamlessly switch over to the LDAPS (TCP port 636) during password change events, which requires only that LDAPS be properly set up on the IVE. Don't sweat the details here; nice clean documents available from both Microsoft and Juniper Networks will walk you through the exact steps for this configuration.

## Host Checker: Realm Restriction

Of course, Host Checker is covered in much more detail in the Endpoint Security chapter, but there is still something worth noting here: Selecting **Evaluate Policies** will only write a log entry that the user passed or failed at the realm, whereas selecting **Require and Enforce** will write the log entries and restrict the user session if the user is not compliant. If you really like to build reports from your syslog servers, you can actually use Host Checker for some basic software inventory.

## Limits: Realm Restriction

This is an absolutely must-have setting if you're going to use the anonymous authentication server. Without this setting to limit the maximum number of users for this particular realm, you could end up having so many anonymous connections used that there are none left for the other realms. For example, if you had an anonymous realm configured to only allow access to a remote access enrollment server and someone kept establishing new connections without dropping his old session, you could end up having every concurrent user license used, even though only a small fraction of your actual user population might be connected. It also doesn't hurt to use the limits to ensure that there are always enough seats left for the Admin realm, or else you might find yourself having to go to the serial console to get access because all the user licenses are in use. Both of these cases are obviously not good, and both have certainly happened to even experienced IVE administrators. Instead of becoming a related statistic of administrators who configured their systems to lock out users and themselves, simply put a reasonable limit on this realm while also using the idle and session timers within the associated roles.

# Selecting and Configuring Role Mapping

At its most basic level, *role mapping* is nothing more than assigning all the roles you created to just the users that need access to each of them. Sounds simple, right? It can be, if you use your LDAP or RADIUS authorization servers to their fullest, as you will see.

Of course, in the examples that follow, you will no doubt notice that we already have some roles defined, even though we haven't covered role creation yet. Okay, so we cheated just a bit to keep things flowing, thus avoiding the whole "chicken and egg" conundrum as we navigate you systematically through the IVE admin UI. If you are using this book to configure your very first IVE, now would be a good time to do the same.

As you can see by looking at Figure 3.6, we are basically starting off on our role mapping with a clean slate. From here, we will build some custom role mappings so that the list of roles can be properly mapped using the authorization servers from this realm.

**Figure 3.6** Role Mapping Overview Page

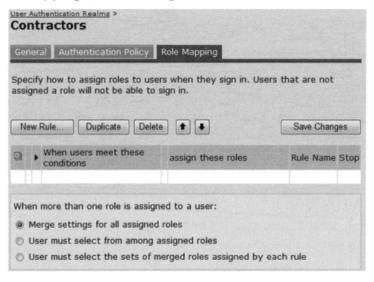

Before we begin, we need to explain a bit about the radio button selection option at the bottom of Figure 3.6, which is known as Permissive Merge. In this case, the default option is the standard setting for the overwhelming majority of all IVE administrators: **Merge settings for all assigned roles**. Now if a user maps to multiple roles, they will get the sum total of all those roles. It's clean. It's easy. It's simply the best default option for nearly every configuration. Play with the other settings if you like, but you will probably come to the same conclusion and will likely use the last two options exclusively for administrators and help desk realms, if at all.

The second common thing to pay particular attention to is the Stop column, also shown in Figure 3.6 but selected when the rule is actually created: **Stop processing rules when this rule matches** (see Figure 3.7). This setting is basically saying that if the user does map to this rule, we need to stop any further role-mapping exercises in what could be a very long list of rules to follow. This is great for user roles that you absolutely know should only map to the one role; just put the role at the top and select the **Stop** option. To follow that same line of thought, in most cases this would imply that the rules with the Stop option should be closer to the top of the list because this would reduce the overhead of IVE (i.e., give faster performance) due to the fact that it would not be processing role-mapping rules that the user would not have access to anyway. However, the simple fact is that there is no perfect guideline to dictate the order under which all of this should be designed, and you are encouraged to study your own roles and apply them in the most efficient order. Whatever you do, make sure that you come back and study this option to ensure that both security and performance are part of your decision process.

**Figure 3.7** Rule Baseline Criteria

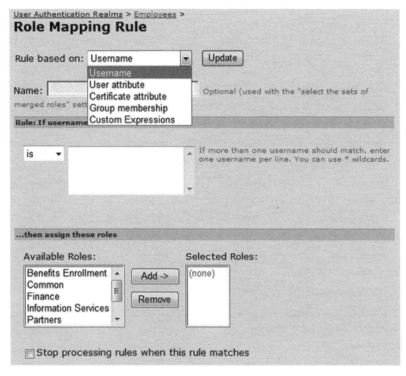

**T**IP

If the permissive merge is not working to your liking—for instance, if resources are showing up that you believe should not—there are basically two places to go to validate your logic: the current IVE admin guide, which is publicly available has a fairly long list of the permissive merge guidelines/ criteria, and the IVE's Policy Trace tool, which will show the exact details of how the user was mapped to each role.

Now select the **New Rule** button and be prepared to unleash the power of the IVE's authorization engine! To build each rule, you need to first know on what you want to base that rule: username, user attribute, certificate attribute, group membership, or custom expression. You should note that the role-mapping options will be based on the type of authentication server being used for that particular realm, so you will get different options if you are using LDAP as the authentication source rather than SecureID.

Here's how each would be used:

- **Username.** Although this is seen in many production configurations, many would say that it shouldn't be seen at all. All you are doing here is assigning a particular username to a role. This might be good for a quick demo, but it doesn't really scale to anything but a few users. However, if there isn't a group or other attribute that can be easily used to map a few users to a role, this is all we really have left. Use sparingly.

- **User attribute.** Here's where the IVE's role mapping really begins to shine, so this is the starting point for any best-practice implementation. We select **User attribute** from the drop-down list and select the **Update** button to the right. Once the screen changes, use the **Attribute** drop-down to select any attribute that exists in the IVE's Server Catalog (populating the IVE's Server Catalog is explained below). If you want to assign everyone whose title starts with anything close to manager, vice president, or director, as shown in the user's Active Directory properties, simply use the **Title** attribute, followed by the **Is** drop-down, followed by entering the various titles in the text field, as shown in Figure 3.8. Just don't forget that you can also use * wildcards in the text field.

**Figure 3.8** Mapping Users by LDAP Attribute

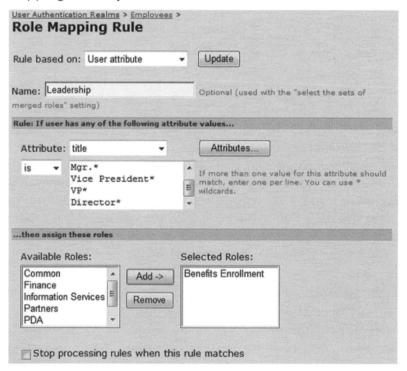

# Optimizing User Attributes

Readers with a high degree of familiarity with Active Directory or LDAP will certainly understand the level of integration that we just went over and are probably already thinking of other clever ways to make full use of this feature. For those who aren't, here is a more in-depth view of LDAP to help get you started down the same path.

The thing about Active Directory Users and Computers (ADUC), the standard admin tool for managing Active Directory user accounts, is that it really doesn't show all the user attributes. For that we need a real LDAP browser, which Microsoft has in the form of its very own ldp.exe utility. Many others are available for download over the Internet, several of which are completely free. For this exercise, however, we will stick with the Microsoft utility (ldp.exe, which is part of the Windows XP SP2 support tools available for download from Microsoft's Web site).

In Figure 3.9 we can see the LDAP view of a single user account, including any custom schema extensions that might have been applied and that are now revealing more than ADUC would show. In this particular example, we don't have any schema extensions to pick from, but we do have one attribute that isn't already in the IVE's Server Catalog: msNPAllowDialin. So what is this attribute? If we go back to ADUC and select the **Dial-in** tab for any user account, we will see a radio button to allow or deny access; that is the msNMPallowDialin attribute. Since we aren't at all interested in using the Microsoft dial-in service, we can now select the **Allow access** option and test for it during the IVE logon to see if it is set to True or False, with True being the allowed setting.

**Figure 3.9** Mapping Users by LDAP Attributes

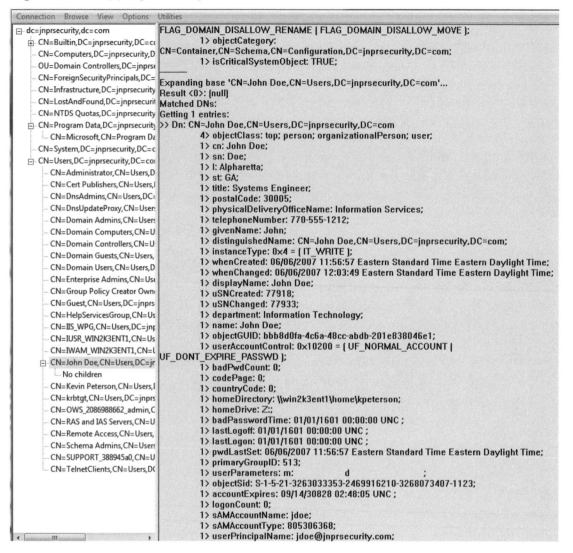

So now back to the IVE, where we will add the newly discovered msNPAllowDialin attribute to the IVE Server Catalog. To do this, we simply select the **Attributes** button from the **Role Mapping Rule** screen (Figure 3.8), enter the attribute name (in this case **msNPAllowDialin**), and select **Add Attribute** (see Figure 3.10). Now each time the user logs in, the IVE will not only check for all the default attributes but also the newly assigned msNPAllowDialin attribute.

**Figure 3.10** Adding LDAP Attributes to the IVE

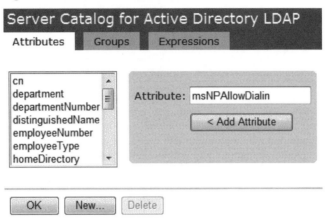

To see how the IVE sees this information coming from the Active Directory server, we can run the IVE's built-in policy trace tool, which is located under the **Troubleshooting**, **User Sessions**, **Policy Tracing** menu, to record the user's logon session (covered in more detail in the Troubleshooting chapter). In Figure 3.11 we can see the Policy Trace output of a single user logon. If we match up the attributes from Figure 3.9, it becomes clear—after a little bit of studying and comparing of the two—that the IVE is able to extract from Active Directory precisely the attribute values that we ask it to. For now, we are simply using this to map certain users to a role; later we will look at how to use the attributes to dynamically build use bookmarks, custom messages, and even static IP address assignments for Network Connect!

## Figure 3.11 Using the IVE Policy Trace for LDAP

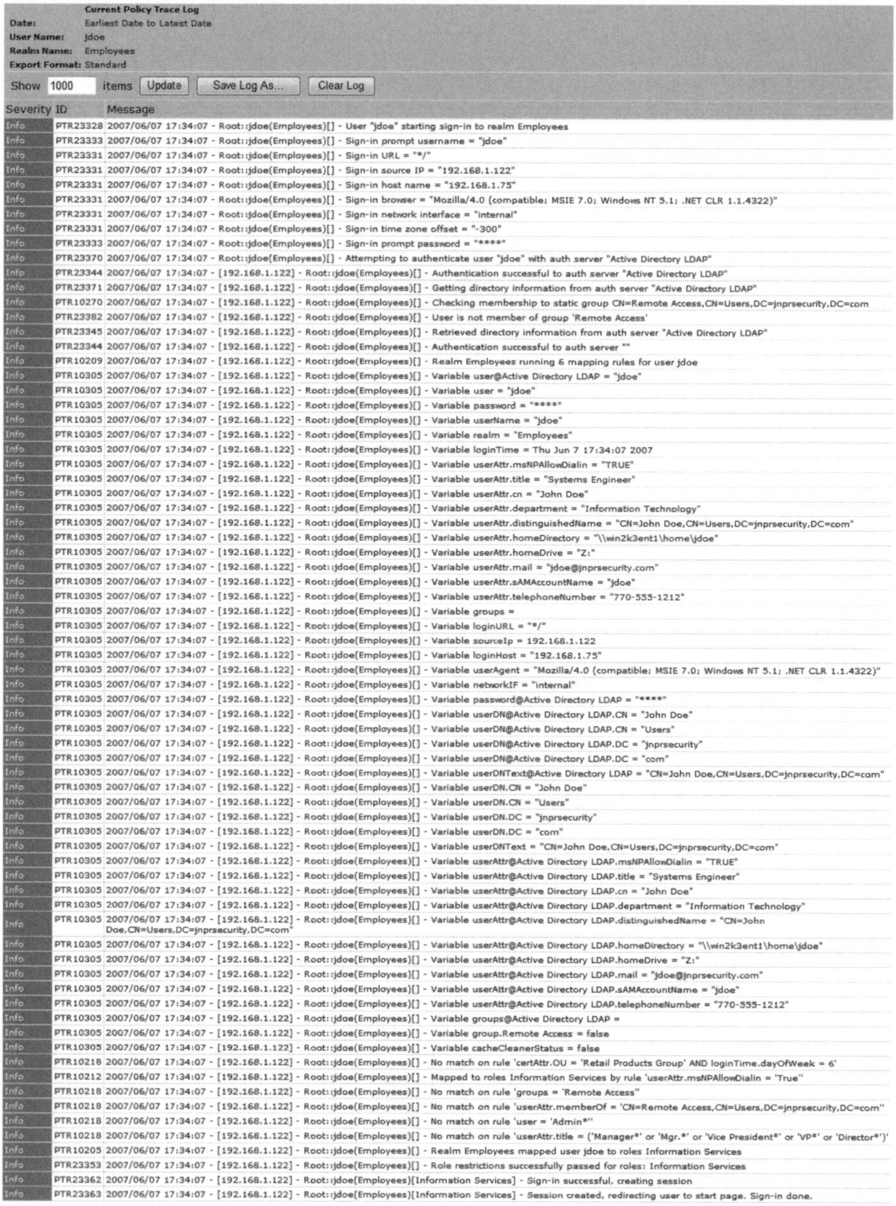

```
Current Policy Trace Log
Date:           Earliest Date to Latest Date
User Name:      jdoe
Realm Name:     Employees
Export Format:  Standard

Show [1000] items  [Update]  [Save Log As...]  [Clear Log]

Severity ID    Message
Info  PTR23328 2007/06/07 17:34:07 - Root::jdoe(Employees)[] - User "jdoe" starting sign-in to realm Employees
Info  PTR23333 2007/06/07 17:34:07 - Root::jdoe(Employees)[] - Sign-in prompt username = "jdoe"
Info  PTR23331 2007/06/07 17:34:07 - Root::jdoe(Employees)[] - Sign-in URL = "*/"
Info  PTR23331 2007/06/07 17:34:07 - Root::jdoe(Employees)[] - Sign-in source IP = "192.168.1.122"
Info  PTR23331 2007/06/07 17:34:07 - Root::jdoe(Employees)[] - Sign-in host name = "192.168.1.75"
Info  PTR23331 2007/06/07 17:34:07 - Root::jdoe(Employees)[] - Sign-in browser = "Mozilla/4.0 (compatible; MSIE 7.0; Windows NT 5.1; .NET CLR 1.1.4322)"
Info  PTR23331 2007/06/07 17:34:07 - Root::jdoe(Employees)[] - Sign-in network interface = "internal"
Info  PTR23331 2007/06/07 17:34:07 - Root::jdoe(Employees)[] - Sign-in time zone offset = "-300"
Info  PTR23333 2007/06/07 17:34:07 - Root::jdoe(Employees)[] - Sign-in prompt password = "****"
Info  PTR23370 2007/06/07 17:34:07 - Root::jdoe(Employees)[] - Attempting to authenticate user "jdoe" with auth server "Active Directory LDAP"
Info  PTR23344 2007/06/07 17:34:07 - [192.168.1.122] - Root::jdoe(Employees)[] - Authentication successful to auth server "Active Directory LDAP"
Info  PTR23371 2007/06/07 17:34:07 - [192.168.1.122] - Root::jdoe(Employees)[] - Getting directory information from auth server "Active Directory LDAP"
Info  PTR10270 2007/06/07 17:34:07 - [192.168.1.122] - Root::jdoe(Employees)[] - Checking membership to static group CN=Remote Access,CN=Users,DC=jnprsecurity,DC=com
Info  PTR23382 2007/06/07 17:34:07 - [192.168.1.122] - Root::jdoe(Employees)[] - User is not member of group 'Remote Access'
Info  PTR23345 2007/06/07 17:34:07 - [192.168.1.122] - Root::jdoe(Employees)[] - Retrieved directory information from auth server "Active Directory LDAP"
Info  PTR23344 2007/06/07 17:34:07 - [192.168.1.122] - Root::jdoe(Employees)[] - Authentication successful to auth server ""
Info  PTR10209 2007/06/07 17:34:07 - [192.168.1.122] - Root::jdoe(Employees)[] - Realm Employees running 6 mapping rules for user jdoe
Info  PTR10305 2007/06/07 17:34:07 - [192.168.1.122] - Root::jdoe(Employees)[] - Variable user@Active Directory LDAP = "jdoe"
Info  PTR10305 2007/06/07 17:34:07 - [192.168.1.122] - Root::jdoe(Employees)[] - Variable user = "jdoe"
Info  PTR10305 2007/06/07 17:34:07 - [192.168.1.122] - Root::jdoe(Employees)[] - Variable password = "****"
Info  PTR10305 2007/06/07 17:34:07 - [192.168.1.122] - Root::jdoe(Employees)[] - Variable userName = "jdoe"
Info  PTR10305 2007/06/07 17:34:07 - [192.168.1.122] - Root::jdoe(Employees)[] - Variable realm = "Employees"
Info  PTR10305 2007/06/07 17:34:07 - [192.168.1.122] - Root::jdoe(Employees)[] - Variable loginTime = Thu Jun 7 17:34:07 2007
Info  PTR10305 2007/06/07 17:34:07 - [192.168.1.122] - Root::jdoe(Employees)[] - Variable userAttr.msNPAllowDialin = "TRUE"
Info  PTR10305 2007/06/07 17:34:07 - [192.168.1.122] - Root::jdoe(Employees)[] - Variable userAttr.title = "Systems Engineer"
Info  PTR10305 2007/06/07 17:34:07 - [192.168.1.122] - Root::jdoe(Employees)[] - Variable userAttr.cn = "John Doe"
Info  PTR10305 2007/06/07 17:34:07 - [192.168.1.122] - Root::jdoe(Employees)[] - Variable userAttr.department = "Information Technology"
Info  PTR10305 2007/06/07 17:34:07 - [192.168.1.122] - Root::jdoe(Employees)[] - Variable userAttr.distinguishedName = "CN=John Doe,CN=Users,DC=jnprsecurity,DC=com"
Info  PTR10305 2007/06/07 17:34:07 - [192.168.1.122] - Root::jdoe(Employees)[] - Variable userAttr.homeDirectory = "\\win2k3ent1\home\jdoe"
Info  PTR10305 2007/06/07 17:34:07 - [192.168.1.122] - Root::jdoe(Employees)[] - Variable userAttr.homeDrive = "Z:"
Info  PTR10305 2007/06/07 17:34:07 - [192.168.1.122] - Root::jdoe(Employees)[] - Variable userAttr.mail = "jdoe@jnprsecurity.com"
Info  PTR10305 2007/06/07 17:34:07 - [192.168.1.122] - Root::jdoe(Employees)[] - Variable userAttr.sAMAccountName = "jdoe"
Info  PTR10305 2007/06/07 17:34:07 - [192.168.1.122] - Root::jdoe(Employees)[] - Variable userAttr.telephoneNumber = "770-555-1212"
Info  PTR10305 2007/06/07 17:34:07 - [192.168.1.122] - Root::jdoe(Employees)[] - Variable groups =
Info  PTR10305 2007/06/07 17:34:07 - [192.168.1.122] - Root::jdoe(Employees)[] - Variable loginURL = "*/"
Info  PTR10305 2007/06/07 17:34:07 - [192.168.1.122] - Root::jdoe(Employees)[] - Variable sourceIp = 192.168.1.122
Info  PTR10305 2007/06/07 17:34:07 - [192.168.1.122] - Root::jdoe(Employees)[] - Variable loginHost = "192.168.1.75"
Info  PTR10305 2007/06/07 17:34:07 - [192.168.1.122] - Root::jdoe(Employees)[] - Variable userAgent = "Mozilla/4.0 (compatible; MSIE 7.0; Windows NT 5.1; .NET CLR 1.1.4322)"
Info  PTR10305 2007/06/07 17:34:07 - [192.168.1.122] - Root::jdoe(Employees)[] - Variable networkIF = "internal"
Info  PTR10305 2007/06/07 17:34:07 - [192.168.1.122] - Root::jdoe(Employees)[] - Variable password@Active Directory LDAP = "****"
Info  PTR10305 2007/06/07 17:34:07 - [192.168.1.122] - Root::jdoe(Employees)[] - Variable userDN@Active Directory LDAP.CN = "John Doe"
Info  PTR10305 2007/06/07 17:34:07 - [192.168.1.122] - Root::jdoe(Employees)[] - Variable userDN@Active Directory LDAP.CN = "Users"
Info  PTR10305 2007/06/07 17:34:07 - [192.168.1.122] - Root::jdoe(Employees)[] - Variable userDN@Active Directory LDAP.DC = "jnprsecurity"
Info  PTR10305 2007/06/07 17:34:07 - [192.168.1.122] - Root::jdoe(Employees)[] - Variable userDN@Active Directory LDAP.DC = "com"
Info  PTR10305 2007/06/07 17:34:07 - [192.168.1.122] - Root::jdoe(Employees)[] - Variable userDNText@Active Directory LDAP = "CN=John Doe,CN=Users,DC=jnprsecurity,DC=com"
Info  PTR10305 2007/06/07 17:34:07 - [192.168.1.122] - Root::jdoe(Employees)[] - Variable userDN.CN = "John Doe"
Info  PTR10305 2007/06/07 17:34:07 - [192.168.1.122] - Root::jdoe(Employees)[] - Variable userDN.CN = "Users"
Info  PTR10305 2007/06/07 17:34:07 - [192.168.1.122] - Root::jdoe(Employees)[] - Variable userDN.DC = "jnprsecurity"
Info  PTR10305 2007/06/07 17:34:07 - [192.168.1.122] - Root::jdoe(Employees)[] - Variable userDN.DC = "com"
Info  PTR10305 2007/06/07 17:34:07 - [192.168.1.122] - Root::jdoe(Employees)[] - Variable userDNText = "CN=John Doe,CN=Users,DC=jnprsecurity,DC=com"
Info  PTR10305 2007/06/07 17:34:07 - [192.168.1.122] - Root::jdoe(Employees)[] - Variable userAttr@Active Directory LDAP.msNPAllowDialin = "TRUE"
Info  PTR10305 2007/06/07 17:34:07 - [192.168.1.122] - Root::jdoe(Employees)[] - Variable userAttr@Active Directory LDAP.title = "Systems Engineer"
Info  PTR10305 2007/06/07 17:34:07 - [192.168.1.122] - Root::jdoe(Employees)[] - Variable userAttr@Active Directory LDAP.cn = "John Doe"
Info  PTR10305 2007/06/07 17:34:07 - [192.168.1.122] - Root::jdoe(Employees)[] - Variable userAttr@Active Directory LDAP.department = "Information Technology"
Info  PTR10305 2007/06/07 17:34:07 - [192.168.1.122] - Root::jdoe(Employees)[] - Variable userAttr@Active Directory LDAP.distinguishedName = "CN=John Doe,CN=Users,DC=jnprsecurity,DC=com"
Info  PTR10305 2007/06/07 17:34:07 - [192.168.1.122] - Root::jdoe(Employees)[] - Variable userAttr@Active Directory LDAP.homeDirectory = "\\win2k3ent1\home\jdoe"
Info  PTR10305 2007/06/07 17:34:07 - [192.168.1.122] - Root::jdoe(Employees)[] - Variable userAttr@Active Directory LDAP.homeDrive = "Z:"
Info  PTR10305 2007/06/07 17:34:07 - [192.168.1.122] - Root::jdoe(Employees)[] - Variable userAttr@Active Directory LDAP.mail = "jdoe@jnprsecurity.com"
Info  PTR10305 2007/06/07 17:34:07 - [192.168.1.122] - Root::jdoe(Employees)[] - Variable userAttr@Active Directory LDAP.sAMAccountName = "jdoe"
Info  PTR10305 2007/06/07 17:34:07 - [192.168.1.122] - Root::jdoe(Employees)[] - Variable userAttr@Active Directory LDAP.telephoneNumber = "770-555-1212"
Info  PTR10305 2007/06/07 17:34:07 - [192.168.1.122] - Root::jdoe(Employees)[] - Variable groups@Active Directory LDAP =
Info  PTR10305 2007/06/07 17:34:07 - [192.168.1.122] - Root::jdoe(Employees)[] - Variable group.Remote Access = false
Info  PTR10305 2007/06/07 17:34:07 - [192.168.1.122] - Root::jdoe(Employees)[] - Variable cacheCleanerStatus = false
Info  PTR10218 2007/06/07 17:34:07 - [192.168.1.122] - Root::jdoe(Employees)[] - No match on rule 'certAttr.OU = 'Retail Products Group' AND loginTime.dayOfWeek = 6'
Info  PTR10212 2007/06/07 17:34:07 - [192.168.1.122] - Root::jdoe(Employees)[] - Mapped to roles Information Services by rule 'userAttr.msNPAllowDialin = 'True'
Info  PTR10218 2007/06/07 17:34:07 - [192.168.1.122] - Root::jdoe(Employees)[] - No match on rule 'groups = 'Remote Access'
Info  PTR10218 2007/06/07 17:34:07 - [192.168.1.122] - Root::jdoe(Employees)[] - No match on rule 'userAttr.memberOf = 'CN=Remote Access,CN=Users,DC=jnprsecurity,DC=com''
Info  PTR10218 2007/06/07 17:34:07 - [192.168.1.122] - Root::jdoe(Employees)[] - No match on rule 'user = 'Admin*''
Info  PTR10218 2007/06/07 17:34:07 - [192.168.1.122] - Root::jdoe(Employees)[] - No match on rule 'userAttr.title = ('Manager*' or 'Mgr.*' or 'Vice President*' or 'VP*' or 'Director*')'
Info  PTR10205 2007/06/07 17:34:07 - [192.168.1.122] - Root::jdoe(Employees)[] - Realm Employees mapped user jdoe to roles Information Services
Info  PTR23353 2007/06/07 17:34:07 - [192.168.1.122] - Root::jdoe(Employees)[] - Role restrictions successfully passed for roles: Information Services
Info  PTR23362 2007/06/07 17:34:07 - [192.168.1.122] - Root::jdoe(Employees)[Information Services] - Sign-in successful, creating session
Info  PTR23363 2007/06/07 17:34:07 - [192.168.1.122] - Root::jdoe(Employees)[Information Services] - Session created, redirecting user to start page. Sign-in done.
```

Of course all this is just a starting point. It is just as easy to build a rule that says if the user's phone number starts with a certain area code, that user should be mapped to the roles that users in that particular city would find most useful (for example, LDAP attribute *telephoneNumber is 770** maps the users to the Atlanta office role). Isn't this better than creating and maintaining endless Windows security groups for each and every remote access need?

So, in Figure 3.12 we have gone ahead and built a fairly broad set of role-mapping rules for the Employees realm, using custom expressions, attributes, groups, and even single usernames. You should also notice that in the first rule that we set the **Stop** flag, thus preventing anyone who matches the first rule from attempting to map to any subsequent rules. Not only is this a great security feature, but for very large implementations (thousands of concurrent users, each mapped to many roles), it can actually provide increased logon performance because each user logon processes fewer role mapping rules.

### TIP

For those of you who love to tweak the performance of everything you get your hands on, consider the order of each rule and the number of users who will map to each rule, followed by the application of the Stop flag to immediately stop processing at the point that those users will gain no more benefit from continuing down the list.

**Figure 3.12** Multiple Attribute, Group, and Username Role Assignment

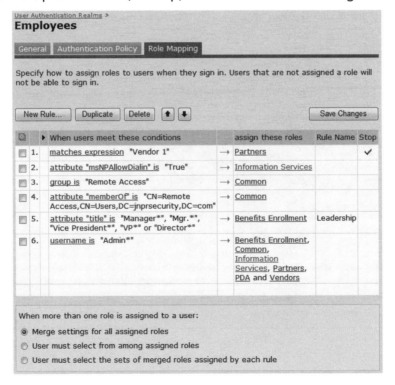

**TIP**

For those who have very large Active Directory infrastructures, consider the following best practices:

If your Active Directory spans multiple forests, make sure that your LDAP configuration is pointing to the Global Catalog server(s) because this will be required for the IVE to locate all user objects.

To optimize the user authentication process, especially when hundreds or thousands of users are logging on in a very compressed period of time, consider using the *memberOf* attribute for role mapping (rule 4 of Figure 3.12). With this rule you are simply comparing what was already extracted during the user's logon (find the *memberOf* attribute in Figure 3.9 and you will see the *cn=* for that user). Of course, we also have to make sure that the *memberOf* attribute was added to the IVE's Server Catalog, as shown in Figure 3.10.

# Admin Realms

Admin realms are configured basically the same way as user realms, with a few less options. The default, however, is to use the IVE's local authentication server instead of pointing to internal authentication servers. But this is easily changed: Simply point the admin realm to a different authentication server.

## Damage & Defense...

### Admin Port Access

The default setting on the IVE is to allow administrative access via the internal port. In configurations where the external port is enabled, administrators can enable administration over that port as well. To prevent an attacker from accessing the IVE over the Internet, it is wise to use the various admin realm Authentication Policy settings to further restrict admin access, such as limiting the administrators to a select range of IP addresses or only after a thorough Host Checker scan.

# Configuring Roles

The User Roles are where we define what type of access users who map to the role will have. Just because we enable one of the access features at the role, doesn't give them access to resources. Resource Policies is where we allow access, which will be discussed later in this chapter. Roles are designed to be simple to understand. After all, everyone in the workplace has a job to do, and each job can be classified into at least one role. For example, the very fact that someone is an employee of a company will likely entitle them to be in the Everyone role, but the fact that the employee is also in the accounting department will further define the person as belonging to the Accounting and perhaps even the Benefits Administration roles. Now all we have to do is roll up our sleeves and start defining these roles within the IVE, right? Actually, there are many things to consider when we implement roles in a best-practice configuration, and here is where we will provide some guidance that will hopefully save you hours of confusion and reworking.

## User Roles

First, we aren't going to create or even cover a single Web, client/server, file, or terminal services bookmark in this chapter. Readers who are already familiar with the IVE, perhaps going back several years, will likely be confused by this approach. But trust us, there is a better way, and that method will be covered in the following chapters as part of Resource Profiles. For now, we will focus on the best structure for a single role, including building on the LDAP integration that we covered in the chapter on realms. So, if you somehow managed to skip right past our discussion on realms, now would be a good time to review it, particularly if you aren't already using LDAP for authorization.

## General Settings

The obvious—if not highly intuitive—first step to creating a new user role is to simply go to the **User Roles, New User Role** screen and provide a nice, friendly name and description for the new role you want to define, followed by checking any of the features that this group will ultimately have access to. Once this is done, as shown in Figure 3.13, you will be able to further refine settings for this role. From this point through the rest of the roles discussion, we will simply go through each tabbed page and subpage to reveal what is most important, along with what often gets missed.

**Figure 3.13** Multiple Attribute, Group, and Username Role Assignment

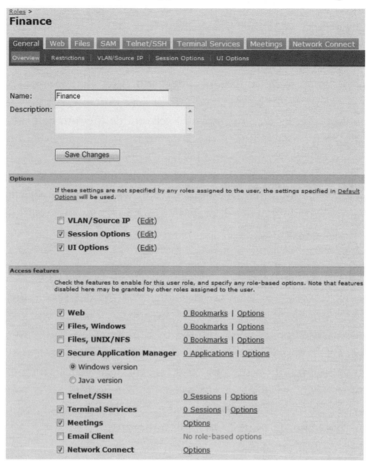

Just remember, we can always go back and change anything we like in any of the roles. If we wanted to change our role name at a later date to, say, Finance and Accounting, we could certainly do so, and any links associated with this role would be updated accordingly, such as the role mappings under the realm settings.

# Role Restrictions

The important thing to remember about any role restriction is that it only affects the role to which we are assigning it. That is, role restrictions aren't inherited back up to the realm in any way, as shown in Figure 3.1. So if the goal is to keep users from even signing in unless they are compliant, we must to go back to the realm restrictions and apply our restrictions there. Where the role restrictions gain their power is through the ability to limit users' access to this one particular role, while possibly still allowing them access to all the resources that are defined through their other roles. For example, John Doe might be mapped to the Accounting role and yet fail the Host Checker policy for antivirus, which is a requirement to get access to this role, but he could still be allowed to gain access to the remediation role, which contains antivirus software downloads and other support files and would obviously not have the same Host Checker restriction applied to it.

## VLAN/Source IP

If any virtual ports or VLANs have been configured (under Network Settings), each realm can be assigned to any available virtual port or VLAN. A common implementation approach for this feature is to assign a unique source IP so that logging will better reveal which role the user was assigned to. Furthermore, for implementations that require a firewall to be placed behind the IVE to provide additional security, the ability to have a unique source IP address for each role means that the security team can provision the rules faster and much more granularly overall.

**TIP**

For large implementations that have a modern firewall behind a heavily loaded IVE, leveraging the per-role source IP should be investigated as a potential benefit of reducing the overall load on the IVE to provide higher end-user throughput, since the reduction of Access Control List processing on a heavily utilized IVE can be significant.

## Session Options

Everything on the Session Options menu is used to tune how that particular role will behave when it comes to a wide variety of settings, including session lifetimes, roaming, persistent sessions (working across browser instances), password caching, idle timeouts, and several others. Each of the options is quite simple to understand and is conveniently described within the admin UI, just above each setting.

However, there are a few settings that we should probably focus on a bit more; these are the session lifetime values. These values, which are all part of the Session Lifetime section, include Idle Timeout, Max. Session Length, and Reminder Time. If we set these too high, we create a security issue. Set them too low and our users will start complaining. If we don't already have one that we can apply on a role-by-role basis, we probably need to get one approved through our chain of command so that everyone understands the balance between security and convenience.

A key thing to remember about session options is that whenever the role is being used in conjunction with an anonymous authentication server realm, the session lifetime variables should be set as low as they can possibly go without disrupting the typical user scenario. This is because anonymous users are not authenticated to the IVE but still consume a user access license for each and every session.

# UI Options

Let's take a look at some of the UI options.

## Headers

This section is worth spending some time on. The first thing that we can change is the header graphics, which are what the user will see at the top of his or her IVE homepage. In our scenario, we would certainly want users to see the standard company logo whenever they log in (using the default logon page settings) but perhaps see a different graphic once they have logged in. So, by placing a graphic that simply says Accounting, we could allow users to see that they are indeed in the Accounting role and feel quite special that someone cared enough to recognize it. Of course, this then has to be the first role that those users map to, because the header the user sees is only applied based on the user's first role. If we can't find the perfect background color to match the graphic so that the color is uniform all the way across the top, we can use one of several freeware utilities (www.tomaweb.com/color-codes.asp) that can quickly help us find the true HTML Hex color code. While we're at it, we might as well go ahead and change the browsing toolbar logo to match the company instead of leaving it at the default Juniper icon.

## Start Page

The Custom page option is best used when there is only one role that the user maps to and that user needs to be very focused on one particular Web page, such as a physician who only ever needs to go to a hospital's physician portal, or a large group of users who only need access to Citrix Web Interface. Once this option is enabled, the user will not see the standard IVE homepage (bookmarks page) and might or might not be able to get to the IVE homepage, depending on the way the administrator has configured the browsing toolbar.

## Bookmarks Panel Arrangement

This should be one of the first things that every administrator changes. For some reason the default setting is set to align everything on the left, which really has them all aligned right down the middle, since there is nothing to the right. Not only is this a waste of screen real estate, it causes users to have to scroll more than they need to, and it's fixing these little things that make the users much happier with their IT leadership. Of course, users can also change these to their own liking if they have access to the Preferences option on the User Toolbar.

## Personalized Greeting

The default option is pretty good. It basically provides the user with the message: "Welcome to the Secure Access SSL VPN, *<USER>*", where *<USER>* is replaced with whatever name the user signed in with. So if John Doe signed in as *jdoe*, the message will read "Welcome to the Secure Access SSL VPN, jdoe." Again, that's not bad, but we can do better by simply disabling the standard greeting and instead using the **Show notification message** option. Here we simply enter whatever message we like, followed by the user attribute variable that we captured during that user's logon—for example, "You are currently logged on as *<userAttr.cn>*," where the LDAP *cn* could be John Doe. Of course, LDAP implementations vary, so it could be *<userAttr.name>* or something else along those lines; your LDAP browser will reveal the truth on that one.

We could even go on to include other variables to create additional messages just for that user, such as "Please confirm that all of the following information is correct by notifying the help desk of any incorrect information. The information we currently have for you is:

> Work Phone: *<userAttr.telephoneNumber>*
>
> E-Mail Address: *<userAttr.mail>*
>
> Department: *<userAttr.department>*
>
> Title: *<userAttr.title>*

As we covered in the Realms chapter, the user of these attributes requires that they are first added to the IVE's Server Catalog. Also, adding different fonts or external links will require the use of HTML tags.

Figure 3.14 provides an example of what you might enter in the admin UI and what it might then look like for the logged-in user.

**Figure 3.14** Per-User Welcome Message Using LDAP Attributes

```
You are currently logged on as, <userAttr.cn>
<BR>
Please review your personal information below and notify the <a
href="http://updateinfo.company.com/update.asp">helpdesk</a> of any changes.
<BR><BR>
Title: <font size="1", color="blue"><userAttr.title></font><BR>
Phone Number: <font size="1", color="blue"><userAttr.telephoneNumber></font><BR>
eMail Address: <font size="1", color="blue"><userAttr.mail></font><BR>
Department: <font size="1", color="blue"><userAttr.department></font>
<BR><BR>
```

**Welcome to the Secure Access SSL VPN**

You are currently logged on as, John Doe
Please review your personal information below and notify the helpdesk of any changes.

Title: Systems Engineer
Phone Number: 770-555-1212
eMail Address: jdoe@jnprsecurity.com
Department: Information Technology

# Standard Options

The **User can add bookmarks, User can add sessions, User can add applications** option exists in one form or another for Web, terminal services, SAM, Telnet/SSH, and files. The standard practice for larger installations is to leave this option disabled. Not only does it require more open access to the network and increase training for users, but additional overhead is created by having to synchronize perhaps tens of thousands of per-user bookmarks across all clustered IVEs that can cause performance issues, especially in WAN environments. System administrators often want to use this option for themselves, although it is typically not any more relevant to open it for their roles than for those of their users. Just add a role for system administrators and define each and every bookmark under **Resource Profiles** so that the entire team of system administrators continues to have all the bookmarks that the entire team needs. There is even a nice procedure, available from Juniper for the asking (too large to cover here), on how to create just one bookmark that will then prompt the administrator to connect to any terminal server on the network! The Web option of "User can type URLs in the IVE browse bar" can be used to access Web pages, file shares, or terminal services.

To access resources from the IVE browse bar, where bookmarks have not already been defined for the user and the browse bar has been enabled for the user's role:

- Microsoft Terminal Services: rdp://*<hostname or IP address>*
- Citrix Presentation Server: ica://*<hostname or IP address>*
- Web Page: http://*<URL or IP address>*
- Windows File Shares: \\*<hostname or IP address>*

# Meeting Options

Secure Meeting is one of the key features that most IVE administrators will quickly say they can't imagine being without. Let's take a look at the tool's advantages:

- Allows individual applications or the entire desktop to be securely shared in a web meeting, including the ability to pass control to any meeting attendee. And yes, the user who relinquished control to someone else can always seize control back.

- Since all connections exist only between the client and the IVE over SSL, administrators don't have to worry about what information might leak out through third-party meeting service providers.

- Personal Meeting can be configured so that each users automatically have their own personal meeting URLs enabled whenever they log on. For example, each time John Doe logs in, he will have https://secure.company.com/meeting/jdoe or even https://secure.company.com/meeting/John.Doe enabled and ready for use. This is very convenient for John because he can now put this URL at the bottom of every e-mail signature, and whenever he is logged in and started his meeting, everyone can join in.

- Support Meetings quickly establish a two-person meeting with desktop sharing and remote control enabled and secure chat and annotations disabled.

- Cost. Many administrators claim that the cost of the Secure Meeting license is recovered in a matter of months because costly service provider fees are reduced and use by the help desk and other departments has a positive impact on support calls.

- Integrates with the authentication servers to allow users to easily select their attendees. However, most seem to prefer just creating the meeting, let the IVE automatically send the invite directly to them, and then forward the invite along using their preferred messaging/calendar client.

The disadvantages are:

- It is not a replacement for large-scale meetings such as large-scale corporate earnings meetings or sales presentations.

- Meetings cannot be recorded for future playback. However, recordings done by any clients using their local workstations could be used.

- Integrated video and audio are not supported.

# Admin Roles

Like user roles, there are also roles for administrators only. These roles dictate what administrators can alter within the IVE admin UI. By default, there are two predefined admin roles: .Administrators and .Read-Only Administrators. Together, these mark the beginning of the delegated admin feature, which you would probably miss if you never went any further by selecting the **Administrators, Admin Roles, New Admin Role** option and tried to build your own delegated admin group. After all, .Administrators is a wide-open security setting, whereas .Read-Only is at the other end of the spectrum. There simply has to be something in between.

Now that we have covered realms and roles quite a bit, you can probably build your own delegated admin role without any assistance. But just in case, here is a recap of the steps needed:

- Make sure that there is a unique user available to assign to the new restricted realm. If you try to do this with your default admin account, you could very well find out that you locked yourself down and would be required to establish a new admin account via the serial console.

- Create a new Admin role, being as specific as you can for each permission you want to grant or deny. Anything set at Deny will not be seen by the delegated administrators once they log in, so they could have a very clean admin interface. Also, resources created by delegated administrators will not work if those administrators do not also have permission to modify the resource policy ACL for that resource. In other words, if the full administrator has a locked-down ACL for a resource, the delegated admin can create all the bookmarks she wants and still not get the application to work, which is just as it should be … from a security point of view. This is no different than a trusted user on your network trying to access a resource that you have restricted by your firewall. You control the gateway in, and no matter how may shortcuts or bookmarks they create, they just aren't getting any further until you open up the ACL for them.

- Create a Role Mapping rule (under the Admin realm) that assigns your delegated admin user(s) to the new delegated admin role.

- Test to make sure that the target users are sufficiently locked down.

# Configuring Resources

If you go back to Figure 3.1, you will notice that Resources are at the bottom. Yeah, we are almost done with this Realms, Roles, and Resources discussion and can soon move on to the really cool stuff! But before we get there, we need to introduce the overall concept of resources, which will help set the stage for Resource Profiles and Resource Policies actually being extended to the extranet. Figure 3.15 is an example of a resource profile using an Outlook Web access template.

**Figure 3.15** A Resource Profile Using an Outlook Web Access Template

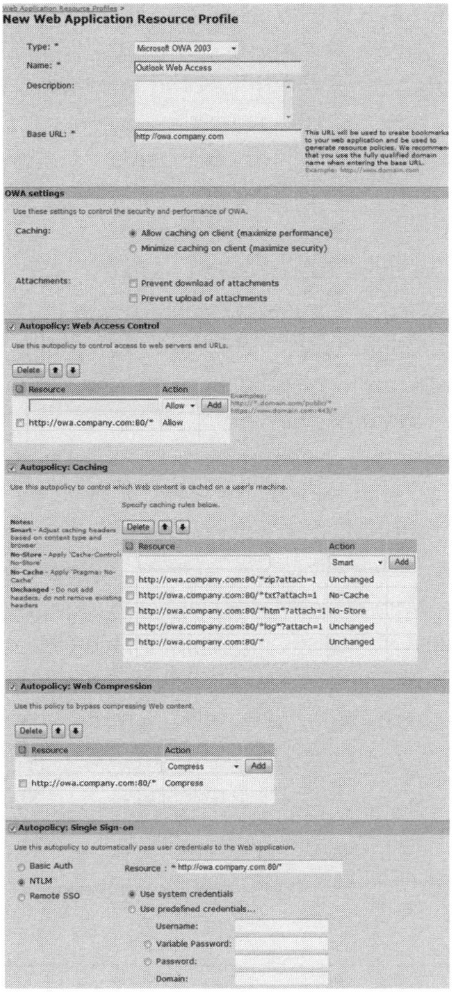

So, what is a resource to the IVE? It's exactly what it is to everything else in the information technology arena: a place you go—Web servers, terminal servers, file servers, and so on—to get information. It's the end of the line...everything we have been building up to. Now it's time to start building our rules so that not only can we provision these resources to the users, but we can do so securely and without causing the IVE administrator to work too hard as the requests for access to all the various resources start rolling in. That's the goal: security and simplicity!

# Introducing Resource Profiles

As we have been navigating our way through the various User Roles settings, we have been asking that you disregard the fact that you can create bookmarks within each and every role.

Now *resource profiles* are your new best friend. Just imagine if you had to create a link to a web page (like Outlook Web Access, for example) inside of one of the roles. Simple enough; so what's the problem? Now imagine that you had to create the same link for another group in another role … and another … and another … and another … ! Now you see the problem. Wouldn't it be easier to create the bookmark once and then assign it to the roles? Of course it would be. That's what Resource Profiles do: Create it once and assign it to all the roles!

But wait, there's more! There's actually another problem with creating the bookmarks within the role itself: There are these things called *resource policies* (more on these in a minute) that not only have to be addressed to some degree with each resource that you make available, but they are almost nowhere to be found within the roles themselves. Again, resource profiles save the day by bringing all the resource policies to us, and all on the same page! Finally, the settings for some of the more advance and common applications are already built into the resource profiles as templates.

Figure 3.15 provides a nice example of this concept. At the top all we had to do is say that this was going to be an Outlook Web Access 2003 server, with a URL of http://owa. company.com. The resource profile took care of auto-filling the hostname through the various other resource settings for us: Web Access Control, Rewriting, Java Access Control, Caching, Compression, and Single Sign-On, and so on (some of which are not shown in Figure 3.15, since they are not required as part of the Outlook Web Access template). Once we save this page and answer the simple question of what roles we would like to assign this resource to, the policies, known as *Autopolicies* to the IVE, will manage to put all these policies and bookmarks where they belong, as you can see in Figures 3.16–3.18.

**T**IP

Notice in the first resource profile in Figure 3.16 that we once again use the IVE's LDAP attribute for *<userAtttr.cn>* to bring forward the user's full name. Now the user won't get just some generic "My Portal" link but actually something like "John Doe's Employee Portal."

**Figure 3.16** Resource Profile Overview Page

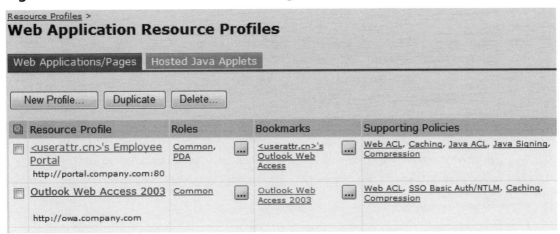

Selecting the **Common** role hyperlink (see Figure 3.16) will take us to the Common role **Web Bookmarks** (see Figure 3.17).

**TIP**

It is possible to have each user's workstation names and/or IP addresses stored in Active Directory so that a single Terminal Services Resource Profile bookmark can be implemented that will extract only that user's workstation identity and provide a direct terminal services bookmark (or bookmarks, should they have more than one). The attribute would look something like *<userAttr. workstation1>*. This allows users to connect directly to their office workstations, and only their workstations, whenever they use the IVE. You can import these workstation names into LDAP using tools such as Microsoft's SMS Server and other custom scripts (unfortunately, discussion of these is well outside the scope of this book).

**Figure 3.17** Resource (Web Application) Profiles Linked to Common Role

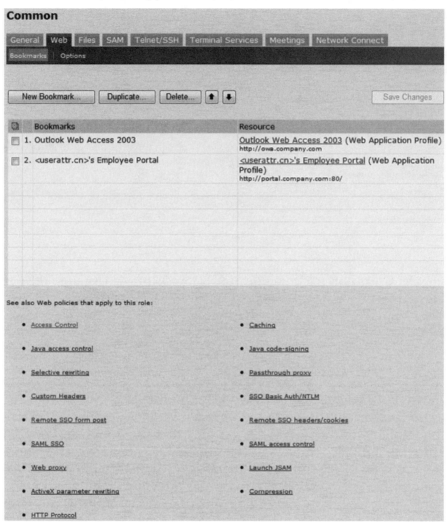

By selecting the **Access Control** link (see Figure 3.17), we are taken to the associated Web ACL under the resource policies (see Figure 3.18).

**Figure 3.18** Resource Autopolicies (Web ACL)

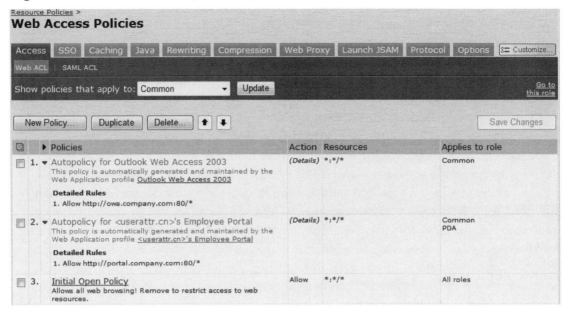

## NOTE

You will click the blue arrow to the left of each Autopolicy to see the exact rules that are being carried forward. Notice that the Action column displays *(Details)*, letting you know that the detailed rules define the resources that are allowed through.

## Damage & Defense...

### Initial Open Policy

The Initial Open Policy shown in Figure 3.18 being set for all roles basically means that the first two ACLs are not really needed, since the wide-open third one is letting everything through anyway. Therefore, it is a common security practice to set this to Deny so that only preceding rules that specifically allow traffic will pass.

# Introducing Resource Policies

Conveniently located just below the Resource Profiles on the admin UI, you will find the resource policies. Thankfully, as you have just seen with resource profiles and Autopolicies, you should not have to go digging deep into this section very often. Still, there will be times you will, and we at least owe you a brief overview of the structure so that your time in this section will be at a minimum.

The first thing to notice is that no matter which resource policy you select that has an expansion arrow next to it (Web, Files, SAM, Telnet/SSH, Terminal Services, Network Connect, and Meetings), they all have more or less a common structure: Access Control at the top, Options at the bottom, with Web and Files having more than enough extra unique policies to keep you busy for the next month if you let yourself go that deep, which, thankfully, you don't really have to—at least not right now. Access Control should be more or less well understood at this point, whereas the common thread for Options is the IP-based matching for Hostname-based policy resources, which is simply saying that the IVE will compare the IP address that a user enters (if you even allow that option for your users) against the actual hostname (as it is cached by the IVE) to determine if there is a match. If there is a match and there is no other ACL blocking it, the IVE will consider this a policy match against the allowed hostname and will allow the session to continue.

As we move into the various chapters that cover the resource types in more detail, you will gain much more exposure to the individual resource policies. As you review these upcoming chapters, take note of the Autopolicies for the resource profiles and where they place themselves within their associated resource policies.

# Summary

Realms, roles, and resources are the 3 Rs. They go hand in hand and together establish the core of the IVE's administrative experience. Those who truly understand the IVE and can bring out its full potential have done so only because they took the time to understand and appreciate the unique interdependencies between these concepts, including the relationship with Endpoint Security, Sign-In Policies, and Authorization Servers. No matter how many times you review it, this chapter will not answer every question you may eventually have on the 3 Rs, but neither will the Admin Guide or even the remainder of this book. What this chapter should have provided is a thorough overview and at least a high-level understanding of how realms, roles, and resources operate together to deliver a secure, dynamic, and convenient remote access environment to any trusted employee or partner.

# Solutions Fast Track

## Introducing Realms, Roles, and Resources

- ☑ Remember that realms, roles and resources (the 3 Rs) are interdependent, with whatever changes you make to realms impacting roles, which in turn impact resources.

- ☑ Hosted Java Applet support allows administrators to upload common Java applets that are then stored on the IVE and delivered to the client as a secure means of accessing client/server applications through a standard Web browser.

- ☑ Administrative realms and resources can be configured to provide highly granular delegated administration.

## Configuring Realms

- ☑ Pay close attention to Sign-in Policies and Endpoint Security checks when you're configuring realms, preferably in a test group to start off.

- ☑ When LDAP (including Active Directory) is already in place, this will likely be the best option for realm authorization, even if the authentication server was set up as Active Directory/Windows NT (AD/NT). AD/NT can only provide group information, whereas LDAP, including Active Directory LDAP, can provide access to per-user attributes.

- ☑ The Realm Authentication Policy can provide access restrictions to the entire realm, which basically means that the user can't even attempt to sign on unless the workstation he or she is on is in full compliance.

☑ Role mapping is best when LDAP or RADIUS is used for authorization, because each can provide per-user information back to the IVE that goes well beyond the simple group information of a Windows NT server.

☑ "Merge setting for all assigned roles," or permissive merge, is the standard used by almost all administrators for the vast majority of users.

# Configuring Roles

☑ A single user can belong to one or 100 roles, it really doesn't matter.

☑ Use "Stop processing rules when this rule matches" as a way to increase the login performance of the IVE (for large environments) or to simply ensure that a particular user or group (role) will not accidentally map to any of the following roles in the role-mapping sequence (under realms).

☑ Meetings are a good way to bring groups of people together in a secure online workspace.

☑ Consider changing the UI options to best provide meaningful information to users as well as cleaning up some of the default options to match your environment. A common best practice is to change the Bookmark Panel Arrangement from having everything in the left column to a more balanced left and right column display.

# Configuring Resources

☑ When possible, *do not* configure bookmarks and other resources within the roles. Instead, configure all resource using resource profiles and allow the autopolicies to handle the resource policies for you.

☑ If users have their office-based workstations listed in LDAP/Active Directory, a single bookmark that replaces the regular hostname or IP address with something like <userAttr.userworkstation1> will build a unique bookmark for just that user when he or she logs in. Likewise, a file share bookmark pointing the user straight to his or her home directory, which would also be listed in Active Directory, can be created by creating a single bookmark with the variable <userAttr.homedirectory>. In all cases, the user will only be given a bookmark if the values existed in Active Directory.

☑ Citrix is a great way to get to touch client/server applications, and the IVE provides a wide range of support for Citrix Web Interface and Metaframe Presentation Server, including single sign-on, client software deployment, and Java ICA fallback for cross-platform support.

☑ Every resource has an ACL that can be applied to it and should be reviewed closely during the design stage. Delete the "Initial Open Policy" as soon as possible.

☑ Be careful what you enable compression for. In many cases, enabling compression can actually slow down an application, especially if the Web application is delivering content that can't be highly compressed. Try to understand your applications and what they are delivering.

☑ Enable Java Code Signing to prevent users from seeing a security warning each time the access any Java Applets.

# Frequently Asked Questions

**Q:** Why do I see a drop-down box on the user sign-in page?

**A:** You have two or more realms configured and assigned to the same sign-in URL under Signing In, Sign-in Policies.

**Q:** I want to use a token for authentication but also want to provide single sign-on to back-end applications. How can I do this?

**A:** Configure an additional authentication server, likely LDAP, and then switch the password variable from *<PASSWORD>* to *<PASSWORD2>* so that the user's LDAP password is presented to the back-end server, not the token (one-time use) password.

**Q:** I enabled Password Management but the user is unable to change his or her password and it is nearing expiration. What is wrong?

**A:** For password management to function, LDAPS must be enabled on the LDAP server. Both Microsoft and Juniper provide detailed instructions on how to support this and are available from either company's support site.

**Q:** I enabled Host Checker to test my workstation's antivirus software, but it doesn't show that I have failed, even when the antivirus software is disabled. What's wrong?

**A:** Check to see if you selected Evaluate Policies or Require and Enforce. Only Require and Enforce will give you the results you are looking for. Also check the logs to see what information is being returned to the IVE as this should help you to narrow down the cause.

**Q:** I need to provide remote access to a particular vendor but want to ensure that all vendor access is controlled by the internal firewall. I know the IVE has an ACL for all the resource types but the firewall admin and our corporate policy is very clear that all vendor access must be controlled by the firewall. How can this be supported?

**A:** Create either a new VLAN or Virtual Port (under Network) and then assign that VLAN or new Source IP to the vendor realm. The firewall admin can now ensure that all traffic that originates from that role is fully controlled by the firewall.

**Q:** The built-in Telnet/SSH client does not have an adequate screen buffer or other features I am accustomed to using with my workstation. What else is there?

**A:** Check out the commercial and open-source Java applets that best match your needs and upload them to the IVE. Note that they will now show up as Web bookmarks and not Telnet/SSH in the client UI.

**Q:** Users coming in through the IVE and hitting our intranet are unable to browse back out to external Web sites. We do have a proxy server, but I don't see how changing the proxy settings on the remote client will help. Is there any way around this?

**A:** Buried deep within the Resource Policies you will see two proxy server options: Web Proxy Policies and Web Proxy Servers. First configure your proxy server with the same settings as you would apply for a user who is accessing it from the LAN. Now configure a policy that allows the various groups of users to access that proxy server.

**Q:** I don't want every Web request from a remote session to a server that is already on the Internet to have to go through the IVE. Can the IVE just access servers on the Internet directly?

**A:** In this case it is the client browser that needs direct access to the Internet resources, but the Initial Rewrite Policy is probably still set to rewrite \*:\*/\*, which is basically saying that any URL that the IVE can see will be rewritten to point the user straight back to the IVE to retrieve the page. This is not what you want. Instead, you want to modify the default rewrite policy to only rewrite the internal resources, such as 10.0.0.0/8:\*, so that all other resources will now be directly accessible. Alternatively, you could specify specific target servers and use the "Don't rewrite content: Redirect to target web server" option.

**Q:** The performance of my Web site is painfully slow when going through the IVE. Why is that?

**A:** Check your Web caching and compression options, in that order. Caching can have a huge impact on application performance. Finally, check to see if your direct access to the server is using HTTP (SSL) instead of straight HTTP (non-SSL). SSL handshaking alone can have a huge impact on application performance, and in these cases (comparing apples to apples) the IVE will often be shown to enhance the overall performance of the SSL session, since the SA4000 and SA6000 both have dedicated SSL acceleration hardware (the SA4000 requires the SSL Acceleration license to enable the hardware acceleration feature).

# Chapter 4

# Authentication Servers

## Solutions in this chapter:

- **Local Authentication**
- **LDAP**
- **NIS**
- **ACE**
- **RADIUS**
- **AD/NT**
- **Anonymous**
- **SiteMinder**
- **Certificate**
- **SAML**

☑ **Summary**

☑ **Solutions Fast Track**

☑ **Frequently Asked Questions**

# Introduction

Many network admins are familiar with the concept of AAA: Authentication, Authorization, and Accounting. These components of a logical system control access to resources. Authentication identifies the user, authorization grants or denies that user access to a resource, and accounting records the access (or attempted access).

The IVE integrates seamlessly into many existing AAA schemes, and includes some of its own as well. These include local authentication, LDAP, NIS, ACE, RADIUS, Active Directory/ NT, anonymous, SiteMinder, certificate, and SAML authentication. (Note: SiteMinder, SAML, and certificate authentication require the Advanced License, and are subsequently not supported on the SA 700 platform.) The IVE also allows for dual-factor authentication. Dual-factor authentication is the method of using two different ways of authenticating a user. Users are authenticated through three primary methods:

- Something the user *knows*, such as a password or PIN.

- Something the user *has*, such as a hardware token.

- Something the user *is*, such as a fingerprint or other biometric.

Dual-factor authentication must include two of these three methods. The IVE supports ACE and RADIUS server authentication, which can fall under the "something the user has" category. (ACE authentication relies on a hardware token, and many token-based authentication vendors use a RADIUS server on the backend.) The IVE does not support native biometric authentication.

In this chapter, we will discuss Authentication and Authorization/Directory server configuration. Because describing the configuration of the authentication servers themselves could each generate a book of their own, we will limit our discussion to configuring the IVE to integrate with the various authentication servers. We will configure the IVE to integrate with LDAP, NIS, ACE, RADIUS, Active Directory/NT, SiteMinder, and SAML authentication servers. We will also configure local, certificate, and anonymous authentication. The latter three require no external authentication server. The authentication server configuration section in the admin console of the IVE is located at Authentication | Auth. Servers, which is the starting point of all the configuration we will do in this chapter.

# Local Authentication

Local authentication uses a local database of usernames and passwords stored on the IVE. Configuration is fairly straightforward. Select **Local Authentication** from the dropdown menu, and then click the **New Server...** button. This will bring up the local authentication server configuration options, as shown in Figure 4.1.

**Figure 4.1** New Local Authentication Configuration

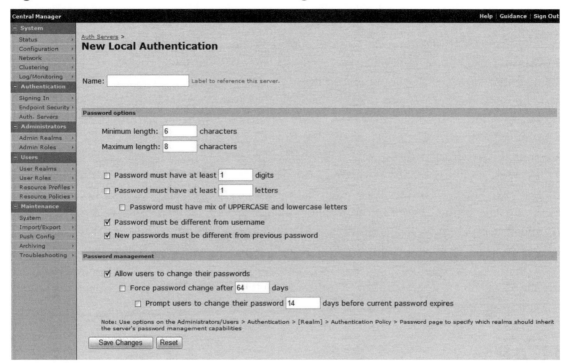

The **Name:** field is used to uniquely identify the server instance to the IVE. The name can contain only alphanumeric characters, spaces, underscores (_), hyphens (-), and periods (.).

The next section is labeled **Password options** and gives you options to restrict the types of passwords users can use. You can enforce a minimum and maximum length, as well as password complexity requirements, such as requiring that the user's password contain a minimum number of digits and/or letters, have a mix of uppercase and lowercase letters, be different from their username, be different from their previous password, or any combination of these options. By default, when creating a new local authentication server instance, the two options Password Must Be Different From Username and New Passwords Must Be Different From Previous Password are selected, and the minimum and maximum length are set to six and eight characters, respectively.

The final section in the Local Authentication configuration screen is labeled **Password management**. This section gives you the option to allow or deny users to change their password. If you choose to allow users to change their password, you can then force users to change their password after a number of days (64 is the default). If you select this option, you can choose to prompt users to change their password a number of days (14, by default) before it expires, rather than simply disabling their account with no warning when their maximum password age has been reached. In this section, only the **Allow Users To Change Their Passwords** option is enabled by default.

As with any other section of the IVE, the **Save Changes** button commits the changes on this page, and the **Reset** button resets the options to the current settings. Also, take note of the message at the bottom of the screen, which reads, "Note: Use options on the Administrators/Users > Authentication > [Realm] > Authentication Policy > Password page to specify which realms should inherit the server's password management capabilities." Even though you can configure password management options in the server instance, password management must be enabled for the realm before they can take effect. See Chapter 3 for more information.

# LDAP

LDAP stands for Lightweight Directory Access Protocol. Many authentication servers use LDAP as their protocol for authentication, including (but not limited to) Microsoft Active Directory, Sun ONE (iPlanet), Novell eDirectory, and generic LDAP servers such as OpenLDAP. Those just listed are the LDAP servers that the IVE supports natively, but LDAP is a standard protocol, so if configured properly, any LDAP server can be used with the IVE.

One thing that needs to be discussed is the way that LDAP works. We will use Active Directory as an example because it is the most widely used. If we were to look at a user in Active Directory (via Users and Computers) there would be many different settings we can set.

Some of these settings are the username, password, e-mail address, and so on. The way LDAP works is that it assigns an Attribute name to each of these settings. For example (remember we are using Active Directory as an example), we look at a user named Joe Schmoe in the domain mycompany.com. His username is jschmoe, and his e-mail address is jschmoe@mycompany.com. If we were to use an LDAP browser (there are quite a few free LDAP browsers out there, including ldp.exe, which is included in the Microsoft XP service tools) to look at the user, we would find that the LDAP attribute name for the username is sAMAccountName, and the LDAP attribute name for the e-mail address is mail. We could then use these attribute names to reference those values when configuring all kinds of things on the IVE. The ones we will cover in this chapter are the attributes for setting up the LDAP authentication server.

To configure an LDAP server, select **LDAP Server** from the dropdown menu and click the **New Server…** button. This brings up the LDAP configuration screen (see Figure 4.2).

**Figure 4.2** New LDAP Server Configuration

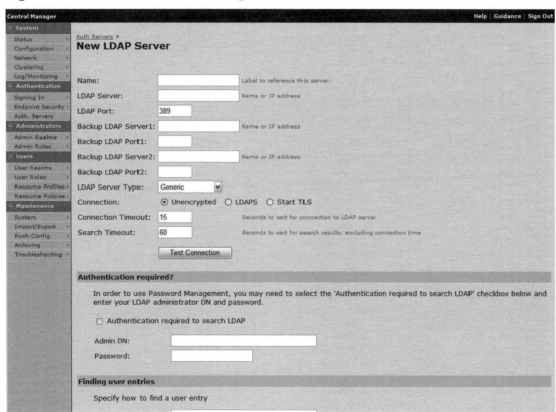

The following are included in the window:

- **Name:** This field, as mentioned previously, is the unique identifier of this server instance. Be sure to give your servers meaningful names when creating them since it can be tedious to have to go back to your list of authentication servers to determine which server type you are selecting when configuring a realm. For example, for LDAP servers, you could include LDAP in the name. Users won't see the server name, so make the name meaningful to you, the admin.

- **LDAP Server:** This field is where you enter the DNS name or IP address of the LDAP server. We recommend using the IP address, in case any DNS issues occur in your network.

- **LDAP Port:** The port used by LDAP, by default, is 389. If your LDAP implementation uses a different port, you will need to enter that number here.

- The **Backup LDAP Server** and **Backup LDAP Port** sections provide you with the ability to designate backup LDAP servers. In the event the primary LDAP server does not respond, the IVE will try to connect first to Backup LDAP Server1 and then to Backup LDAP Server2. Again, we recommend using an IP address rather than a DNS name in these fields.

- **LDAP Server Type:** This dropdown menu lets you select Generic, Active Directory, iPlanet, or Novell eDirectory. If your LDAP implementation is not listed, select Generic. Note that when using a Generic-type LDAP server, not all password management functions are supported. Table 4.1 lists management functions that are supported based on the LDAP server type:

**Table 4.1** LDAP Server Password Management Functions Supported

| Function | Active Directory | iPlanet | Novell eDirectory | Generic |
|---|---|---|---|---|
| Authenticates user | unicodePwd | userPassword | userPassword | userPassword |
| Allows user to change password if licensed and if enabled | Server tells us in bind response (uses ntSecurityDescriptor) | If passwordChange == ON | If passwordAllow Change == TRUE | Yes |
| Logs out user after password change | Yes | Yes | Yes | Yes |
| Forces password change at next login | If pwdLastSet == 0 | If passwordMustChange == ON | If pwdMust Change == TRUE | |
| Password expired notification | userAccount Control== 0x80000 | If Bind Response includes OID 2.16.840.1.113730.3.4.4 == 0 | Check date/time value in password ExpirationTime | |
| Password expiration notification (in X days/hours) | If pwdLastSet−now() < maxPwdAge−14 days (maxPwdAge is read from domainattributes) displays warning if less than 14 days | If Bind Response includes control OID 2.16.840.1.113730.3.4.5 (contains date/time) (IVE displays warning if less (IVE than 14 days) | If now()−password ExpirationTime < 14 days (IVE displays warning if less than 14 days) | |
| Disallows authentication if account is disabled/locked | userAccountControl== 0x2 (Disabled) accountExpires userAccount Control == 0x10 (Locked) lockoutTime | Bind ErrorCode: 53 "Account Inactivated" Bind Error Code: 19 "Exceed Password Retry Limit" | Bind ErrorCode: 53 "Account Expired" Bind ErrorCode: 53 "Login Lockout" | |

*Continued*

**Table 4.1 Continued.** LDAP Server Password Management Functions Supported

| Function | Active Directory | iPlanet | Novell eDirectory | Generic |
|---|---|---|---|---|
| Honors "password history" | Server tells us in bind response | Server tells us in bind response | Server tells us in bind response | |
| Enforces "minimum password length" | If set, IVE displays message telling user minPwdLength | If set, IVE displays message telling user password MinLength | If set, IVE displays message telling user passwordMinimum Length | |
| Disallows user from changing password too soon | If pwdLastSet – now() < minPwdAge, then we disallow | If passwordMinAge > 0, then if now() is earlier than passwordAllowChange Time, and is disallowed | Server tells us in bind response | |
| Honors "password complexity" | If pwdProperties == 0x1, then enabled. Complexity means the new password does not contain a username, first or last name, and must contain characters from 3 of the following 4 categories: English uppercase, English lowercase, Digits, and Non-alphabetic characters (e.g., !, $, %) | Server tells us in bind response | Server tells us in bind response | |

The **Connection:** section gives you radio button options to select: **Unencrypted**, **LDAPS**, or **Start TLS**. These settings pertain to the communication between the IVE and the LDAP server. **Unencrypted** is the default option. Note that when using **LDAPS** or **Start TLS**, the LDAP server must have a certificate installed on it, and you must modify the **LDAP Port** (and backup server ports if applicable) to reflect the port used by LDAPS or Start TLS (**636** by default).

In the **Connection Timeout:** field, you can configure the number of seconds to wait for the LDAP server to respond before failing over to your backup servers. This is set to 15 by default.

The **Search Timeout:** option is the number of seconds (60 by default) that the IVE will wait for a response from the LDAP server after issuing a search request. This timeout does not include the time it takes the IVE to connect initially to the LDAP server.

The Test Connection button checks to see if the LDAP server you specified is responding on the port you specified. It does not test the other settings on the page.

The next section is labeled **Authentication required?**. You must select this option (if it is not selected by default) if you wish to use password management functionalities such as allowing users to change their password through the IVE or notifying them when their password is about to expire. If you select this option, you must provide the admin DN and password. DN stands for Distinguished Name. It is how LDAP locates the user within the directory. Think of it as the logical "location" within the directory structure. The admin DN is the Distinguished Name of a user account that has administrative privileges in the domain (in Microsoft Active Directory, this is a Domain Admin account). If your LDAP server is Microsoft Active Directory, you can specify the admin DN in the *DOMAIN\ USERNAME* format. Otherwise, you must specify the full DN of the admin account. For example, the DN of the default Administrator account in Active Directory is CN=Administrator,CN=Users,<Base DN> where <Base DN> is the base DN of your domain. For example, if your domain is company.com, your base DN would be DC=company,DC=com. You can use an LDAP browser to find the DN for any user account that exists in the directory. Refer to the documentation of the particular LDAP browser you are using to figure out how to get the DN (many of the LDAP browsers allow you to right-click and select Properties, or they have an option that lets you find the DN).

The next section is labeled **Finding user entries**. In this section, you specify the **Base DN:** and **Filter:** to use when searching the LDAP server for a user account. The base DN is the base DN of your domain, although you can be more specific about the location where you want the IVE to begin looking when checking user credentials. For example, suppose you only want users within a specific organizational unit (OU) of your Active Directory implementation to be able to sign in to your realm. Instead of specifying the DN of your domain (DC=company,DC=com), you can specify the DN of the OU you want to allow (CN=IT,DC=company,DC=com). The filter is used to specify the LDAP attribute for the user's username. For example, in Active Directory, the username is designated by the LDAP attribute sAMAccountName. The IVE variable <USERNAME> is assigned the value of whatever a user enters when signing in to the IVE. So, for Active Directory, the **Filter:** entry should be entered as samAccountname=<USERNAME>. For iPlanet, the LDAP attribute for the username is uid, so the **Filter:** section in that case would be uid=<USERNAME>.

The final section is labeled **Determining group membership**. When configuring role-mapping rules, you can assign roles based on the groups that a user belongs to. This section is where you configure how the IVE determines a user's group membership.

It includes the following:

- **Base DN:** This field is similar to the field by the same name in the **Finding user entries** section. The **Base DN:** is where you specify where the IVE should begin looking when it is determining group membership. For example, if you have a Groups OU where you keep all of your groups, you could specify here CN=Groups,DC=company,DC=com. The field is also like the **Filter:** field in the previous section. Typically, this field will be filled in as cn=<GROUPNAME>. This will use the LDAP attribute cn as the name of the group. If we were to look at the group via an LDAP browser, we would see that the Domain Users group would look like this: cn=Domain Users, dc=mycompany,dc=com.

- **Member Attribute:** The member attribute is the LDAP attribute that specifies the members of a group. Note that this is not an attribute of a user account, but rather an attribute of a group object. In Active Directory, the attribute used to identify members of a group is simply "member." In iPlanet, it is uniquemember, and in eDirectory it is "uniquemember". Note that if you have specified Active Directory as the LDAP server type, you will have the option to select **Reverse Group Search**. If selected, this option allows you to query a user object for its group attribute, rather than searching the group object for its member attribute. When using Active Directory as the LDAP server, the attribute that identifies the groups a user belongs to is memberOf, which is the attribute used for the reverse group search.

- **Nested Group Level:** This is the maximum depth that the IVE will search for a group. This allows you to search for groups that are nested in other groups. If you have a member of a nested group, this option must allow you to search through as many nested groups as needed.

- **Nested Group Search:** This section gives you two options: **Nested Groups In Server Catalog** and **Search All Nested Groups**. If you select **Nested Groups In Server Catalog**, you must specify all the groups within a nest in the server catalog to be able to role-map. If you have a vast domain with many users and nested groups, you may want to utilize this option if you have performance issues with users authenticating. If you select **Search All Nested Groups**, the IVE will do exactly that. While this is much more flexible, as you do not have to specify all the groups within a nest, it can cause performance issues with authentication in particularly large domains.

The server catalog is accessible once you have successfully created an LDAP server instance. The phrase *Server Catalog* in the **Determining group membership** section becomes a hyperlink that will take you to the Server Catalog. Clicking the server catalog link will allow you to test the configuration of the LDAP server instance. If you are able to search for group within the server catalog, you have properly configured the LDAP server.

# NIS

NIS authentication is used to authenticate users against a Unix NIS server. Configuration is very straightforward. You simply designate the name of the server instance (for reference in the IVE), the name or IP address of the NIS server, and the NIS Domain (see Figure 4.3).

**Figure 4.3** New NIS Server Configuration

One note regarding NIS authentication: You can only use NIS if the passwords are stored on the NIS server using Crypt or MD5 formats.

# ACE

ACE authentication is used to integrate with an RSA ACE server. An ACE server allows users to authenticate using a hardware or software token, which uses a one-time password. ACE integration with the IVE is very simple to configure. The majority of the configuration is done on the ACE server itself. The IVE simply needs the sdconf.rec config file from the ACE server's Agent Host record for the IVE. You can only have one ACE server instance configured at one time.

If you have a cluster of IVEs, you will need to create an agent host for each of the IVEs in the cluster. Because the configuration is synced between the IVEs in the cluster, you will only need to generate one sdconf.rec file from the agent host file of the primary node in the cluster. Once you have imported the config file, you will need to log in using ACE from each of the nodes in the cluster. The easiest way to do this is to manually log in to each node one at a time using the newly configured ACE server.

To configure an ACE server, select **ACE Server** from the dropdown menu and click the **New Server...** button. This brings up the ACE configuration screen (see Figure 4.4).

**Figure 4.4** New ACE Server Configuration

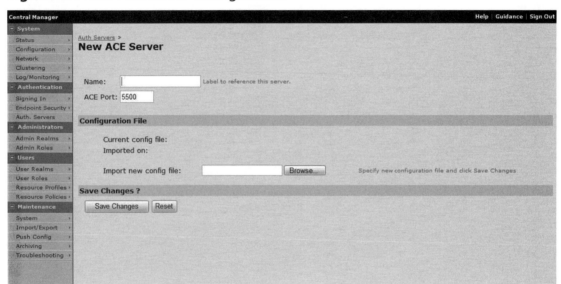

Specify the name of the server instance in the **Name:** field.

The **ACE Port:** field lets you designate the default port used to communicate with the ACE server. This is set to 5500 by default, and should only be changed if the ACE server is configured to listen on a different port. Note that this field is only used if the port is not specified within the sdconf.rec file.

The **Configuration File** section is used to upload the configuration file from the ACE server (named sdconf.rec) by default. After you have successfully imported the configuration file, the **Current config file:** and **Imported on:** sections will be populated. To upload the configuration file, manually enter the location of the file or click the **Browse** button to locate it.

# Radius

RADIUS (Remote Authentication Dial-In User Service) is a protocol used for AAA (Authentication, Authorization, and Accounting). The IVE can use a RADIUS server to authenticate users, as well as perform role-mapping based on RADIUS attributes. The IVE must be configured as a client on the RADIUS server.

To configure a RADIUS server instance, select **RADIUS Server** from the dropdown menu, and click the **New Server...** button. This brings up the RADIUS configuration screen (see Figure 4.5).

**Figure 4.5** New RADIUS Server Configuration

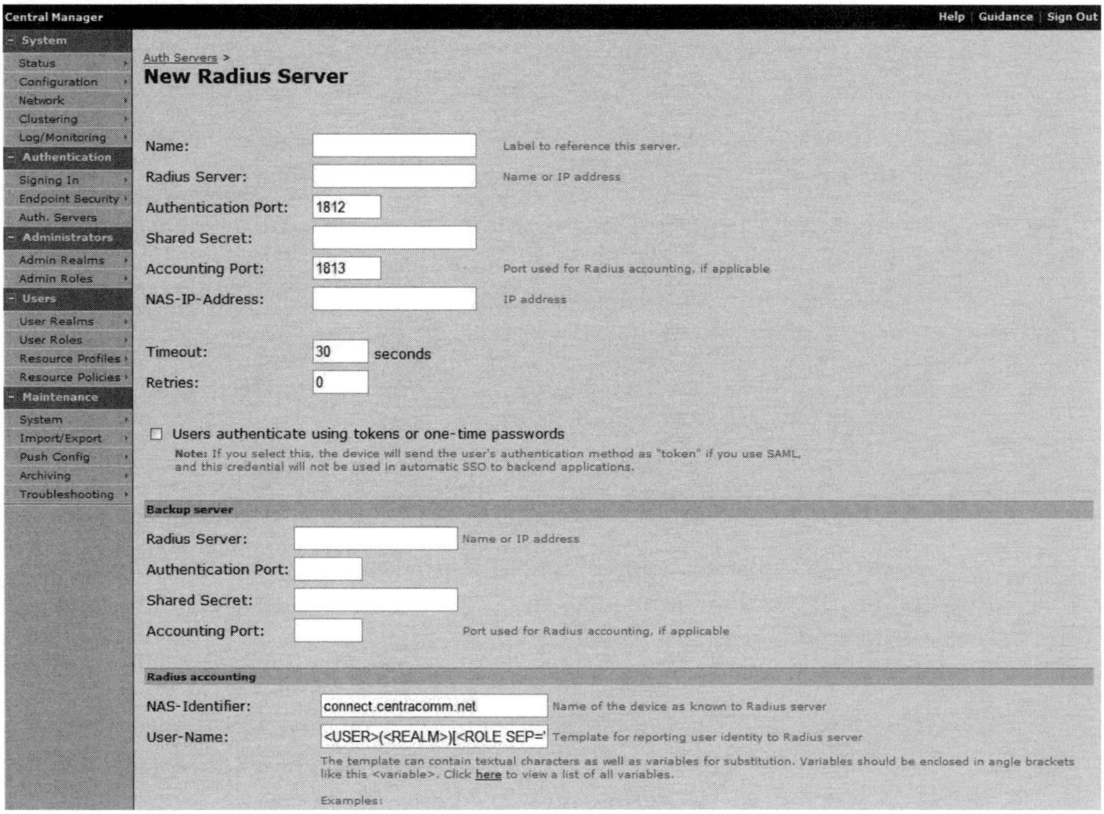

The following are included in the window:

- **Name:** The name of this server instance.
- **Radius Server:** The DNS name or IP address of the RADIUS server. Once again, we recommend using the IP address in case of DNS issues on the network.

- **Authentication Port:** This is the port with which the IVE communicates to the RADIUS server for authentication purposes. The default is 1812, and should only be changed if your RADIUS server is operating on a different port.

- **Shared Secret:** The shared secret is set on the RADIUS server. The IVE needs the shared secret in order to communicate with the RADIUS server.

- **Accounting Port:** Set this to 1813. It should only be changed if your RADIUS server's accounting service listens on a different port.

- **NAS-IP-Address:** This field lets you control the NAS-IP-Address value that is sent to the RADIUS server. This is useful in cluster situations, where you want the same IP address to be sent, regardless of which IVE originates the request. If this field is left empty, the NAS-IP-Address will be the IP address of the IVE's internal port.

- **Timeout:** This is the length (in seconds) that the IVE will wait for a response from the RADIUS server before timing out. The default is 30 seconds.

- **Retries:** This is the number of times the IVE will try to connect to the RADIUS server if the first attempt fails. The default value for this field is 0.

- **Users authenticate using tokens or one-time passwords:** This checkbox should be used if you do not want the password entered by a user to be used for any SSO (Single Sign On)-enabled applications. Typically, you will want to select this option if you are using one-time passwords (such as a hardware or software token).

- The **Backup server** section lets you specify a secondary RADIUS server to be used if the primary server is unreachable.

- The **Radius accounting** section gives you the ability to specify how the IVE reports user session information back to the RADIUS server for accounting purposes.

- **NAS-Identifier:** The NAS-Identifier is the name that identifies the IVE to the RADIUS server. The default value for this field is the hostname of the IVE (specified under System | Network | Overview). If there is no value set for the IVE's hostname, the IVE will use Juniper IVE as the NAS-Identifier.

- **User-Name:** This is the format in which the IVE will report the user's username to the RADIUS accounting service. The default value for this field is <USER>(<REALM>)[<ROLE SEP=",">]. Using this format, a user with the username jdoe in the realm IT Staff with the roles IT Admin and Domain Users would be recorded by the RADIUS server as jdoe(IT Staff)[IT Admin, Domain Users].

- **Interim Update Interval:** This value is the interval (in minutes) at which the IVE will send an interim update to the RADIUS server. The data in the interim update is cumulative, meaning it contains the total since the beginning of the session, rather than since the last interim message.

- The **Custom challenge expressions** section gives you the option to enter custom challenge expressions to allow the IVE to integrate with different RADIUS implementations. The IVE searches the Access-Challenge packet from the RADIUS server and issues the appropriate challenge to the user. It is not likely that you will need to utilize this field. However, if you are using CASQUE authentication with a CASQUE player, you will need to enter **:([0–9a–zA–Z/+=]+):** in the Generic Login field and check the checkbox next to it.

# AD/NT

Active Directory/Windows NT native authentication is supported on the IVE using NTLM (v1 or v2) or Kerberos-based authentication. Active Directory group membership can be used for role mapping on the IVE as with LDAP.

To configure an AD/NT server instance, select **Active Directory / Windows NT** from the dropdown menu, and click the **New Server...** button. This brings up the AD/NT configuration screen (see Figure 4.6).

**Figure 4.6** New Active Directory/Windows NT Server Configuration

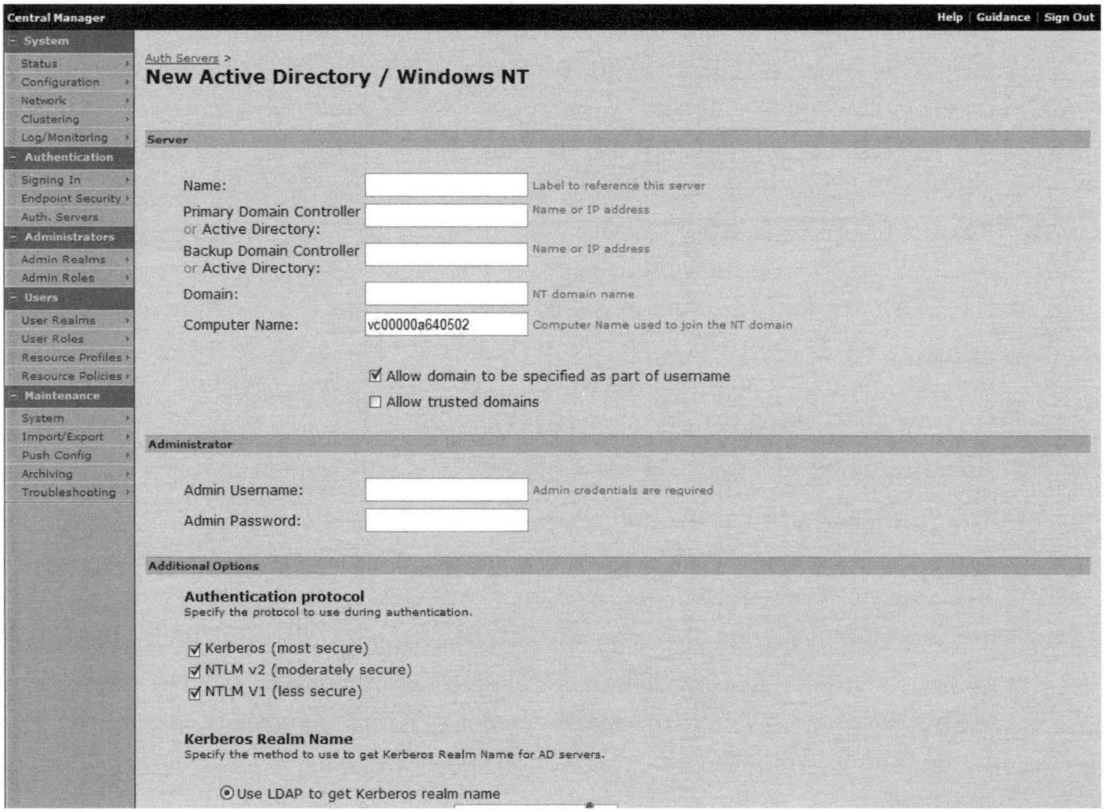

The following are included in the window:

- **Name:** As with the rest of the authentication servers, a unique name must be entered for the AD/NT server.

- **Primary Domain Controller:** Enter the DNS name or the IP address of the primary domain controller in the domain. As stated before, we recommend using the IP address should any DNS issues arise on the network.

- **Backup Domain Controller:** If there is a backup domain controller in the domain, you can enter the information in this field.

- **Domain:** Enter the NT domain name of the domain. This name is a little confusing since it is not the full domain name but the NT domain name. If my internal domain name were mycompany.com, my NT domain name would be MYCOMPANY. If this name is entered incorrectly, authentication will fail.

- **Computer Name:** Enter the name of the computer object for the IVE that will be added to the computers container in AD. Because the IVE uses a Linux-based OS, a winbind process occurs between the AD domain and the IVE. The IVE is added as a computer object in the AD domain.

- Two more options can also be enabled: **Allow Domain To Be Specified As Part Of Username** and **Allow Trusted Domains**. The first option lets a user enter their username in the following format (once again using mycompany.com as the example domain): mycompany\jschmoe. This is helpful if users are already used to logging in using that format. The second option allows users from trusted domains to also be able to authenticate.

- **Admin Username:** Here, enter the username of the administrator account with the access to look up users in the domain. The easiest way to configure an account is to make it a domain admin in the domain since that account has the correct privileges the account will need. The privileges needed by the administrator in this field are the following: the ability to create/delete objects in the computers container, reset passwords, and modify permissions.

- **Admin Password:** Enter the password for the admin account in this field.

- The **Authentication Protocol** section is used to select the protocol(s) that the domain can use to authenticate users. Select the protocols that will be needed for authentication.

- The last section is used to specify the Kerberos realm name. You can either specify the realm name manually, or select the radio button to have LDAP find the realm name for you. If the realm name is specified incorrectly, user authentication will fail.

# Anonymous

The anonymous server allows users to access the IVE and its resources without ever needing to provide a username and password. The user enters a specific sign-in URL (that then references the Anonymous Server), and the IVE bypasses the standard sign-in page, presenting the user with the welcome page.

To configure an Anonymous server instance, select **Anonymous Server** from the dropdown menu, and click the **New Server...** button. This brings up the Anonymous Server configuration screen (see Figure 4.7).

**Figure 4.7** New Anonymous Server Configuration

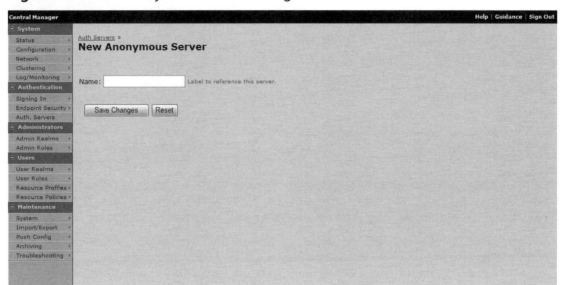

The only configuration needed for an anonymous server is to give it a unique server name.

# SiteMinder

The IVE can integrate with a SiteMinder policy server. The complete configuration instructions for SiteMinder are outside the scope of this book. For more detailed configuration instructions, please refer to the documentation of the SiteMinder policy server itself.

To configure a SiteMinder server instance, select **SiteMinder Server** from the dropdown menu, and click the **New Server...** button. This brings up the SiteMinder configuration screen (see Figure 4.8).

**Figure 4.8** New SiteMinder Server Configuration

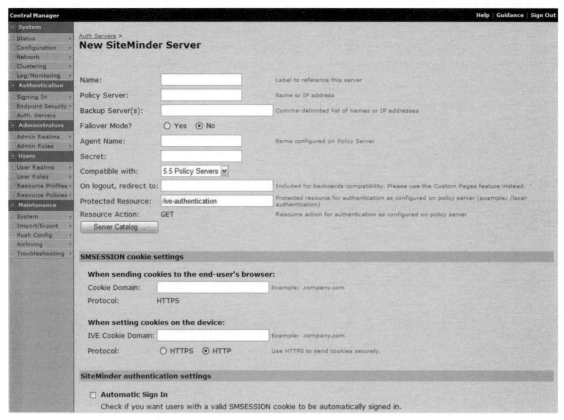

The following are included in the window:

- **Name:** As with the rest of the authentication servers, a unique name must be entered for the SiteMinder server.

- **Policy Server:** This is the hostname or IP address of the SiteMinder Policy Server used to authenticate users.

- **Backup Server:** A comma-delimited list of the servers that should be used in case the first Policy Server is unreachable. The Failover Mode is used to specify whether the IVE should always use the main policy server or if it should round-robin load share across all the servers defined.

- **Agent Name and Secret:** The name and shared secret configured in the SiteMinder agent.

- The **Compatible With** option specifies what version of SiteMinder you are integrating with (5.5 or 6.0). The On Logout, Redirect To option is a URL that can be specified to direct users to when they sign out of the IVE. If this is left blank, the default IVE users page is used.

- The **Protected Resource** references what was specified on the SiteMinder server for the realm. Refer to the IVE Documentation bundle or the SiteMinder documentation for specifics on configuring a realm in SiteMinder for the IVE.

- The only other two required options to specify are the **Cooke Domain** and **Cookie Provider Domain** (**IKE Cookie Domain**). Note that the domain names are case-sensitive, and make sure to specify domains by using a leading period (for instance, .connect.company.com).

# Certificate

The Certificate Server allows the IVE to authenticate users based on client-side certificates. This is most commonly used in conjunction with another server to authenticate users in conjunction with usernames and passwords (using the certificate to role map or provision appropriate access) or to securely and automatically authenticate users without needing to enter a username and password.

To configure a Certificate server instance, select **Certificate Server** from the dropdown menu, and click the **New Server...** button. This brings up the Certificate configuration screen (see Figure 4.9).

**Figure 4.9** New Certificate Server Configuration

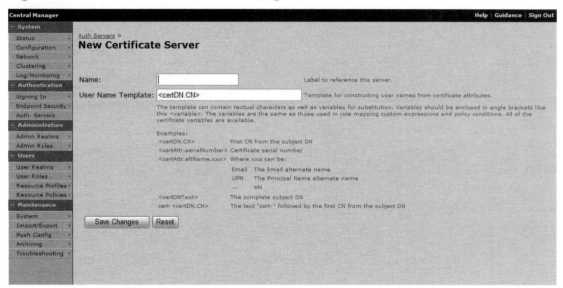

The following are part of the window that appears:

- **Name:** You must provide a unique name for the Certificate Server.
- **User Name Template:** This specifies how the IVE should generate a username. A combination of certificate variables are defined here and any combination is possible.

# SAML

Secure Access Markup Language (SAML) authentication allows the IVE to pass user and session state information to an SAML server/environment and keeps users from having to enter their credentials multiple times. The IVE can support SAML as a SAML Authority or a Receiver.

To configure a SAML server instance, select **SAML Server** from the dropdown menu and click the **New Server...** button. This brings up the SAML configuration screen (see Figure 4.10).

**Figure 4.10** New SAML Server Configuration

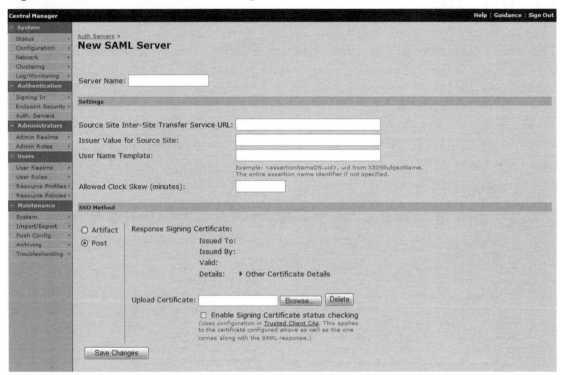

The following are included in the screen that appears:

- **Name:** Provide a unique name for the SAML Server in this field.

- The **Source Site Inter-Site Transfer Service URL** is specified based on how SAML is implemented that the IVE will participate in as well as the Issuer Value for the source site. The User Name Template is how the IVE will map the SAML assertion to the IVE User Realm (generate a username). The Allowed Clock Skew is specified in minutes and determines how much the IVE clock can differ from the source site clock.

The rest of the configuration varies according to whether an Artifact profile or a Post profile is used. Depending on which profile is used, the specified settings are self-explanatory.

# Summary

In summary, the IVE supports several different types of authentication servers with which to integrate, including local authentication, LDAP, NIS, ACE, RADIUS, Active Directory/NT, anonymous, SiteMinder, certificate, and SAML authentication. Some authentication methods (SiteMinder, SAML, and certificate authentication) require an Advanced License and are subsequently not supported on the SA700. The IVE also allows for dual-factor authentication, where authentication can take place using a username and password as well as a second factor, such as a hardware or software token.

# Solutions Fast Track

## Local Authentication

☑ A local database of usernames and passwords is stored on the IVE, so there's no need to integrate with an external authentication server.

☑ Local authentication supports password management and minimum complexity requirements.

## LDAP

☑ The IVE can integrate with most common LDAP servers, including Active Directory, Sun ONE (iPlanet), Novell eDirectory, and generic LDAP servers such as OpenLDAP.

☑ Different types of LDAP servers support different types of password management features.

## NIS

☑ The IVE can authenticate natively to a Unix NIS server.

☑ You can only use NIS if the passwords are stored on the NIS server using Crypt or MD5 formats.

## ACE

☑ The IVE can authenticate natively to an RSA/ACE server, allowing users with hardware or software one-time password tokens.

☑ The sdconf.rec file from the ACE Server's Agent Host record is required to configure ACE authentication.

☑ If an IVE cluster is used, you must manually log in to each node.

# Radius

- ☑ The IVE can use a RADIUS server to authenticate users and perform role-mapping rules based on RADIUS attributes.

- ☑ The IVE also supports RADIUS accounting as well as a variety of RADIUS attributes.

# AD/NT

- ☑ The IVE can integrate natively to an Active Directory or Windows NT Server using NTLM (v1 or v2) or Kerberos-based authentication.

- ☑ Active Directory group membership is supported for role-based mapping on the IVE.

# Anonymous

- ☑ Allows users to access the IVE without ever needing to enter a username and password.

- ☑ An Anonymous Server is referenced by a sign-in URL that then bypasses the standard sign-in page. The IVE welcome page immediately appears before the user.

- ☑ User-specific rules / role mapping / reporting isn't possible because a username is never collected.

# SiteMinder

- ☑ The IVE supports integration to a SiteMinder policy server. For more specifics on SiteMinder policy server integration, please refer to the SiteMinder documentation.

# Certificate

- ☑ Allows the IVE to authenticate users based on client-side certificates.

- ☑ Certificates can authenticate clients completely (no need to enter a username and password) or be used in conjunction with another authentication server to provision access.

# SAML

- ☑ SAML (Secure Access Markup Language) authentication allows the IVE to pass user and session state information to an external system that supports SAML and prevents the need to enter usernames and passwords multiple times.

- ☑ The IVE can support SAML as a SAML Authority or Receiver.

# Frequently Asked Questions

**Q:** How can I give access to a vendor or contractor on my network without having to create an Active Directory (or similar) account on my external authentication server?

**A:** The best way to achieve this would be to set up authentication using a local authentication server and store the usernames and passwords locally on the IVE. By utilizing either selective authentication realms or multiple sign-in URLs, this can be easily implemented by supporting both the local and external authentication of users and provisioning access appropriately.

**Q:** What RADIUS attributes are supported on the IVE?

**A:** The IVE supports a wealth of RADIUS attributes. For a specific list/description, see the FreeRADIUS Web site located at www.freeradius.org/rfc/attributes.html.

**Q:** Does the IVE support Trust Relationships in Active Directory for authentication? What about Active Directory's different types of groups?

**A:** Yes, it does support it if the Allow Trusted Domains option is checked on the AD/NT server configuration screen. The IVE also supports Domain Local Groups, Domain Global Groups, and Universal Groups in an Active Directory forest. The IVE allows only AD Security Groups, not Distribution Groups. For Windows NT, it supports Domain Local and Domain Global groups.

**Q:** I am using an anonymous server and I can't see or delete sessions of users who are logged in. Is my concurrent user license limit being exceeded?

**A:** On the Users tab of the IVE, it is not possible to view or delete sessions of a user because the IVE never collects a username. Be very cautious and/or implement user session restrictions when Anonymous Servers are being used.

**Q:** How can I make certificate-based authentication more secure?

**A:** It's strongly recommended if using certificate-based authentication to train users to close their Web browsers after signing out of the IVE. Otherwise, new browser sessions can be launched without requiring reauthentication on the IVE.

# Chapter 5

# Secure Application Manager

## Solutions in this chapter:

- **Secure Application Manager**
- **Secure Application Manager Implementation**
- **Secure Application Manager User Experience**
- **Troubleshooting**

☑ **Summary**

☑ **Solutions Fast Track**

☑ **Frequently Asked Questions**

# Introduction

Not all applications work through the Juniper Core Clientless Access Services—commonly called Web Services. Client/server applications like Lotus Notes and Microsoft Exchange, and Thin Client solutions like Microsoft Terminal Services and Citrix are good examples. These systems need an access method that is not an application-aware web proxy, which is how the Juniper content intermediation engine (CIE) works. Yet, security professionals want to maintain the vital separation provided by a hardened intermediate device. Both the Secure Application Manager (SAM) and Juniper's Terminal Services proxy can perform this task without provisioning a full VPN tunnel.

Client/server applications and Thin Client Computing (TCC) are similar in many ways. They both attempt to use server resources to minimize the client resources required and to make the best use of bandwidth that exists between client and server. However, they are very different in their approach. Client/server applications require a "fat" client that in many cases can act independently of the server. Thin-client technology on the other hand requires very little client processing because all the work of the application takes place on the server. The client portion of the technology is limited to sending input (such as mouse movements and keystrokes) to the server, and receiving output (such as screen writes) from the server.

Because of the similarities, SAM and Terminal Services will be covered back-to-back in this chapter and the next. You will notice some overlap—for example, SAM can be used to transport Citrix. But the in-depth discussion of this will be saved for the next chapter. For now, let's focus on classic client/server computing.

# Why Use SAM?

SAM is a lightweight client that provides dynamic port forwarding over SSL. But, that basic description misses some of the most important aspects of SAM. There are many features of SAM that make it an extremely useful tool for network engineers, including:

- SAM supports both Microsoft Windows and non-Windows systems. The Java version of SAM works on Windows, Mac, and Linux. A single method to provide access across multiple computer types reduces complexity and makes support easier.

- SAM can be either pre-installed on a corporate computer or dynamically delivered to connecting users. This means an enterprise or service provider need not worry about initial installs and upgrades, lowering the system's total cost of ownership (TCO).

- A slew of security features make SAM a great choice for secure remote access. Socket access can be carefully controlled to allow only the minimum traffic necessary to support the application. Everything from application validation using MD5 checksums to endpoint posturing with Juniper's Host Checker makes security a compelling reason to deploy SAM.

- SAM benefits from the IVE's rich set of logging and troubleshooting features. This gives engineers and support technicians the tools they need to identify and solve problems quickly.

- SAM does not require any additional client IP addresses because it performs Network Address Translation (NAT) on all connections through the IVE, rather than assigning the client an IP address on the internal network.

## Feature Availability

SAM is a feature that comes with the "Secure Application Manager and Network Connect" license, which can be purchased from a Juniper reseller. As with other feature licenses, the license key must be installed under **System | Configuration | Licensing**. SAM and Network Connect used to be separate licenses on the older SA products (1000, 3000, 5000). The current platforms (2000, 4000, 6000) combine these features into a single license.

SAM is not available on the Juniper Networks Secure Access 700. That platform is limited to Network Connect and Core Clientless access methods only.

## Chapter Overview

This chapter will cover Secure Application Manager. We will begin with how to select from the many different ways to deploy the software, and a few other key pre-configuration questions will be considered. Then, we will move into the implementation details of SAM, evaluating throughout how best to balance security with access.

Along the way, practical examples will show how the features can be deployed in an enterprise environment. The chapter will cover the most common problems with SAM, along with how to troubleshoot and solve these issues.

## Secure Application Manager

Network Connect sends all traffic through the VPN tunnel, limited only by access control and split tunnel lists. While intermediation is not required with Network Connect, the Core Clientless Access Service (or Web Services) is an application-aware web proxy which intermediates nearly all traffic that flows through the tunnel. SAM is the middle ground between the two. SAM can be very selective about what traffic is tunneled—based on the originating application or destination. SAM users are not assigned internal IP addresses because the IVE performs Network Address Translation (NAT) on the incoming traffic. Unlike Network Connect which builds a full SSL or IPSEC tunnel, SAM can only build SSL tunnels.

# SAM Versions

SAM comes in two versions: a Windows version (WSAM) and a Java version (JSAM). While the security and access goals of these versions are the same, the implementation is vastly different. These differences must be fully understood because the choices made before the configuration begins are critical to a successful deployment. How WSAM and JSAM select traffic to be tunneled is the most fundamental and important distinction between the two.

## WSAM

WSAM uses a Windows API in the operating system's IP stack to target traffic that should be tunneled. The IVE can be configured to tunnel traffic by originating application, by destination IP, or by a combination of destination IP and port. For example, you could configure WSAM to tunnel all Microsoft Outlook traffic (all traffic originated by the outlook.exe application); or all traffic destined to a specific host IP or network could be tunneled; or you could tunnel all tcp/1352 traffic to a specific host IP or network.

## JSAM

JSAM uses loopback addresses (127.0.0.0/8 as defined in RFC 3330) and Java Library Service Proxies (LSP) to select traffic to be tunneled. Using a source application is not an option with JSAM. For example, to tunnel traffic to ten internal Lotus Notes servers, ten loopback addresses would be assigned (either manually or automatically) and administratively mapped to the internal servers. The JSAM client would "listen" for traffic destined to one of these loopback addresses and the traffic would get tunneled. As will be described later, this method makes name resolution challenging because the client application must be able to resolve the server name to the loopback IP.

## Version Comparison

The differences between the SAM versions are summarized in Table 5.1.

**Table 5.1** Primary Functional Differences between WSAM and JSAM

|  | WSAM | JSAM |
|---|---|---|
| **Supported Clients** | Windows only, including some handheld/PDA devices | Windows, Linux, and Mac |
| **Supported Protocols** | UDP and dynamic TCP ports | Only static TCP ports |
| **Install method** | ActiveX control, Java, or preinstalled launcher | Java (must be already installed on OS) |

**Continued**

**Table 5.1 Continued.** Primary Functional Differences between WSAM and JSAM

| | WSAM | JSAM |
|---|---|---|
| **Permissions required to install client** | Local administrator rights are required to install. The Juniper installer can be pre-installed by an administrator to get around this. | User needs the right to execute Java code and the ability to edit the local HOSTS file in some configurations. |
| **Launch Options** | Must be manually launched by the user or automatically launched by the role. | Same options as WSAM. JSAM can also be launched when an application bookmark is selected. |
| **Performance** | ActiveX is considered slightly faster. | Java is considered slower and more resource intensive. |
| **Scripting** | Session start and session end scripts | None |
| **User Control** | None | Option to allow users to define their own applications, but this may be considered a security risk. |
| **SAM visibility to user** | Icon in taskbar | **DO NOT CLOSE** window must remain open throughout session. |

The choice of which version of SAM to use depends entirely on the deployment scenario. For example, if Linux and Mac clients need to connect—JSAM is the only option because WSAM does not support these operating systems. This may seem limiting at first, but really isn't. If WSAM is preferred over JSAM for Windows users, two separate roles can be configured, one for WSAM and one for JSAM. Juniper's Host Checker can be used to map Windows users to the WSAM role and all others to the JSAM role.

There are several rules to keep in mind when configuring SAM:

■  Only one type of SAM can be enabled per role. If two were possible, the user could potentially have both WSAM and JSAM active at the same time. The IVE does not stop you from mapping a user to two roles that run different SAM versions. However, when the user logs in, the first role that has SAM enabled that the user is mapped to will take priority and only that version of SAM will run.

■ JSAM does not support multiple client applications that need to communicate using the same port to different servers. For example, App1 using tcp/25 to Server1 and App2 using tcp/25 to Server2 doesn't work. To get around this, a different port can be manually or automatically selected.

The ability to support a variety of clients with JSAM is a compelling reason to seriously consider using it for all users. However, many network engineers struggle with known incompatibilities between Java versions. Unsupported or untested Java runtime environments can cause problems for users. In an environment where there is little control over the configuration of connecting computers, these incompatibilities can make support of a critical Java application very frustrating. In addition, name resolution to support the Java SAM client can be difficult to maintain which makes scaling JSAM difficult in a large enterprise.

# How to Deploy the SAM Applet to Connecting Computers?

SAM can be deployed in three ways and each has benefits and drawbacks. The client can be installed and upgraded automatically by pushing the software from the IVE to the computer upon initial connect, by using an autonomous installer, or through the Juniper Installer Service.

## Web Install/Upgrade

Both JSAM and WSAM can be automatically installed or upgraded the first time a user selects a link that loads SAM. In addition, users can be mapped to a role that automatically launches SAM (and installs if necessary). If connecting computers are "unmanaged," a web install is the only viable option. Not only is it very easy to configure, keeping the software current becomes trivial because as the Juniper IVE is upgraded, the SAM client is upgraded. The first time a user connects after an IVE upgrade, the new code is downloaded and installed automatically.

There are drawbacks to this method, however. The installer must be downloaded and run. Even though no user interaction is typically required for the install, it takes both bandwidth and additional time on initial connection. No reboot is needed, but this process can be confusing and frustrating to users who may not be expecting it. In addition, as shown in Table 5.1, the privileges of local user on the connecting computer must be considered. Figures 5.1 and 5.2 show the WSAM download and install screens that display on the connecting computer.

**Figure 5.1** WSAM Download

**Figure 5.2** WSAM Install

# Autonomous Installers

Juniper provides several downloadable WSAM installers. These can be used to install WSAM manually any time, including before a new computer is given to the user. The installers are often used by organizations who want to deploy and manage desktops using applications like BMC's Configuration Management (formerly Marimba). The IVE 6.0 installers include:

- Windows SAM for Windows 2000/XP/Vista platforms
- Scriptable Windows Secure Application Manager
- Windows SAM for PocketPC 2003SE/Windows Mobile 5.0

The primary benefit to using a pre-installed client is that there is no remote download and install needed at first connection. However, since the SAM clients are relatively small (WSAM is about 800k), this may not prove to be a compelling reason to use an installer. There is no autonomous JSAM installer.

## Juniper Installer Service

This application provides relief from the administrative privileges requirement to install SAM. This is not an installer itself, but a framework that allows the web installer to succeed when the user has restricted privileges. This service is especially useful on managed computers intended for public use (like hardened kiosks) because the environment demands greatly limited user privileges.

The big drawback of the Juniper Installer Service is that it must be pre-installed. There is no way to automatically push and launch this service—so its use is normally limited to organizations that pre-configure computers before sending them to users.

The Installer Service is designed for and works only with Juniper's software. To verify a program's authenticity, the installer checks the Authenticode digital signature of the file to make sure it was published by Juniper Networks.

# Secure Application Manager Implementation

One of the biggest advantages of the Juniper IVE is the extreme level of control over the user environment. Like Border Gateway Protocol (BGP), which is a simple protocol with lots of opportunity to customize, the many options in the IVE can be intimidating. Configuring SAM is like this too. However, if you stick to the basic procedures that Juniper recommends, you will likely have few problems. On the other hand, if you choose to leave the marked trail and hike cross-country—make sure you have a good compass and be prepared to get lost!

## Enabling SAM and Configuring Role Options

The first task is to enable SAM on the role and configure some basic role settings. The creation of user roles was covered in Chapter 3 (Realms, Roles, and Resources), so it is assumed that the role already exists.

1. To enable SAM, navigate to **Users | User Roles**. Select the name of the role to modify.

2. Check the box next to **Secure Application Manager**, and choose either **Windows version** for WSAM or **Java version** for JSAM.

3. Select the **Save Changes** button.

# Configuring SAM Role Options

These options affect both WSAM and JSAM.

1. Select the **Options** link on the **Secure Application Manager** row, or select the **SAM** tab, then the **Options** menu item.

2. Select the check boxes next to the SAM features you want to enable for the role.

The SAM options are listed here in the categories as they appear on the IVE.

**Auto-launch Secure Application Manager**    This is useful to automatically launch SAM when a user is mapped to the role. If this is not selected, users must manually select the **SAM Start** button under **Client Application Sessions** on the IVE homepage. Using this feature makes SAM more automatic and may reduce the training necessary for non-technical users.

**Auto-allow application servers**    This creates a SAM access policy (described later) that ensures any server resource lists mapped to this role are automatically permitted. While this is a somewhat useful feature, the profile creation process makes it easy to ensure an access policy is created to permit the proper resources.

# Configuring Windows SAM Role Options

The following options affect only WSAM:

- **Auto-uninstall Secure Application Manager**  This feature will uninstall WSAM when a user disconnects. While this may be desired in some cases (for example, when the client will never connect again), it is normally preferred to maintain the client on the connecting computer. Enabling this option will cause each launch of WSAM to require a download and install of the client.

- **Prompt for user name and password for intranet sites**  This option changes the Prompt for user name and password setting under Security Settings | User Authentication | Login on the Local Intranet Zone in Microsoft Internet Explorer. Use of this option assumes that IE is configured to treat intranet sites differently, which is not the default in IE.

- **Auto-upgrade Secure Application Manager**  This feature is very useful for maintaining an up-to-date WSAM client on each connecting computer. With this setting, when the IVE software is upgraded, the new WSAM client is automatically downloaded and installed on first connection. This eliminates the need for a separate software management process. You can maintain an older version of the WSAM client after an IVE upgrade by deselecting this option. This may be useful if you need to do an IVE upgrade (such as for a new feature or in response to a security vulnerability), but don't want to immediately update all the clients.

- **Session start script** After the WSAM session starts, this script is executed on the client. The script must be in a location (either local or on the network) that is accessible by the user. Session start scripts are very useful with SAM for launching fat client applications, setting environment variables, mapping drives, and more.

- **Session end script** After the SAM session ends, this script is executed. The script must be in a location (either local or on the network) that is accessible by the user. Session end scripts are useful for killing processes and performing system maintenance (such as launching backups) and cleanup.

Note that the IVE only supports the following types of scripts: BAT, CMD, and EXE. If you would like to use a Visual Basic script, you can call the VBS script from a BAT file.

## Configuring Java SAM Role Options

The following options affect only JSAM:

- **User can add applications** This feature allows users to create their own JSAM port-forwarding applications on the IVE homepage. The SAM access policy configured on the IVE is still enforced. One important note about this is that if a user creates an application, even if this setting is later disabled, the application remains in effect. So, this feature is often considered a security concern.

- **Automatic host-mapping** This option automatically creates loopback IP addresses and associates them with JSAM destinations (as defined in a resource profile). This feature edits the local HOSTS file, which often requires the user to have administrative privileges on the connecting computer. If hosts are not mapped automatically using the HOSTS file, external DNS can be used to manually associate administratively selected loopback IPs with JSAM destinations.

- **Skip web-proxy registry check** Every time JSAM launches, it checks for a web proxy in the registry. This function sometimes requires privileges, so non-privileged users may receive an error message. This option is helpful in eliminating that error message.

- **Auto-close JSAM window on sign-out** This option will automatically close JSAM when the user signs out. If this is not selected, the user must manually close JSAM.

## Configuring Role Session Options that Affect SAM

As described in Chapter 3 (Realms, Roles, and Resources), each role has a number of session options that are either inherited from the Default Options (**Users | User Roles | User**

**Roles**, then select the **Default Options…** button), or are set on the role itself. These settings affect all access features selected on the role, not just SAM.

The role options are configured under **Users | User Roles | Role | General | Session Options**. The **Max Session Length** setting is very important to SAM users. By default, a non-administrative session can remain active for the number of minutes set in this option. When a session reaches this length, the session is terminated by the IVE. The **Idle Timeout** and **Reminder Time** values don't work for SAM—these values are only for web sessions through the Core Clientless Access Service.

When the **Max Session Length** value expires, JSAM shows "Session Expired" next to a yellow diamond shape in the DO NOT CLOSE window to indicate that the session has been terminated by the IVE—without any pop-up indication. As you can see in Figure 5.3, the WSAM disconnect message is visual, but a bit cryptic. The lesson here is that the **Max Session Length** value needs to be carefully considered to avoid support calls.

**Figure 5.3** WSAM Session Timeout Pop-up

# Configuring SAM on a Role

Resource Profiles eliminate the need to separately configure each element necessary for SAM. They ensure that a critical element of the configuration (like establishing a SAM access policy that permits the traffic) is not forgotten. However, it is sometimes necessary to configure policies directly. There are several reasons for this, including:

- **Global Policies**  Rather than each resource profile creating individual autopolicies to allow access to server resource lists, it often makes sense to create a single policy supporting many profiles. This saves time and makes the IVE configuration simpler and easier to troubleshoot. For example, it may make sense to create a single SAM access policy to permit tcp/110 access to a subnet of Pop3 email servers, rather than having a bunch of SAM Resource Profiles creating separate autopolicies to allow access to individual servers.

- **Granular Security** Autopolicies from Resource Profiles are limited in that they only allow the most basic configuration: **Allow** or **Deny** on all defined resources. Custom policies can use complex logic to create exactly the access policy that is desired.

- **Additional Functionality** It is not possible to define a WSAM Bypass Application in a Resource Profile.

There is a price to pay, however. One of the main benefits of a resource profile is that it can be associated with multiple roles—in effect, sharing the application definition and making the configuration less complex. A custom defined application or destination is associated with a single role and can't be copied or assigned to other roles.

# Adding a WSAM Supported Application to a Role

This procedure creates a WSAM application and associates it to a single role. A WSAM application created on a role can not be applied to another role.

1. Navigate to **Users | User Roles | Role | SAM | Applications**. Select the **Add Application** button above the WSAM Supported Applications list.

2. The configuration here is similar to a new Application Resource Profile. From the **Type** drop-down menu, select **Custom**, **Standard,** or **Pick a Resource Profile**. Both selections require a **Name** and allow for an optional **Description**.

   - Custom enables you to create a non-standard application and requires a Filename, with an option to supply a Path to the application and an MD5 hash. See the sidebar "Using an MD5 Hash to strengthen SAM security."

   - Standard requires you to select from a list of applications, including Citrix NFuse, Lotus Notes, Microsoft Outlook/Exchange, and NetBIOS file browsing.

   - Pick a Resource Profile brings up a pop-up window that allows you to select a pre-defined profile. This serves the same function as editing a WSAM Resource Profile and adding the role to the list of Selected Roles.

**NOTE**

While this creates a WSAM application, it does not automatically create a SAM access policy. Traffic from the originating application on the WSAM client will be sent to the IVE, but will be dropped unless there is a matching access policy that specifically permits the traffic.

## Damage & Defense...

### Using an MD5 Hash to strengthen SAM security

The ability to create custom applications for Windows SAM is a great way to provide remote access to nearly any client/server application. However, this access comes at the expense of security, unless you're careful. For example, assume you create a WSAM custom application for a home-grown application called "Myapp.exe" and create an access policy that allows tcp/80 access to all internal hosts. It is very easy for a nefarious SAM user to rename any application to "Myapp.exe" and use this to attack devices inside your network. This problem can be eliminated by using an MD5 Hash.

MD5 (Message Digest version 5) is a cryptographic hash function that takes in a variable length string of characters and outputs a 128-bit number, which is often displayed as a 32-character hexadecimal number. The MD5 hash process is commonly used to verify the integrity of files. For example, a file download can be protected by a web server administrator publishing a pre-computed checksum (which is what the output of the hash is called) of a file. When a user downloads the file, they can compute the checksum of the received file. If the checksums match, the files are identical. The details of the algorithm are freely available on the Internet and aren't relevant here.

The configuration of a WSAM custom application can use the MD5 hash checksum of a file to verify that the file is correct. The WSAM client compares the checksum against the originating application. If the checksums match, traffic is permitted from that application to go through the tunnel. If they don't match, traffic is denied.

The MD5 checksum guarantees that the originating application is exactly the one the Juniper administrator intended as the source of the WSAM traffic. No one can then rename an application and slip by your security policy. However, this check also requires that all users run exactly the same version of the application—because different versions of the same application will always have different MD5 checksums.

The Juniper administrator can get a utility to calculate the MD5 hash of an application on the IVE by navigating to **User | User Roles | User Roles**.

## Adding a WSAM Allowed Server to a Role

This procedure creates a WSAM allowed servers list and associates it to a single role. An allowed servers list created on a role can not be applied to another role.

1. Navigate to **Users | User Role | Role | SAM | Applications**. The wording on the IVE is not the best, because adding an "allowed server" is equivalent to adding a WSAM destination in a Resource Profile. Select the **Add Server...** button above the WSAM Allowed Servers list.

2. The configuration here is similar to a new WSAM Destination Resource Profile. From the **Type** drop-down menu, select **Standard** or **Pick a Resource Profile**.

■ Standard requires a Name and allows for an optional Description. In the Server field, specify the destinations that the client should reach through the VPN tunnel. The destinations can be entered either as host names or in IP/netmask notation. Wildcards are permitted. In the Ports field, specify the ports that will be used to access these destinations.

The major difference from the Resource Profile definition is how the destinations are added. On the role, servers and ports are configured separately, which means that it may take several "Allowed Servers" on a role to match a Resource Profile list. For example, on a Resource Profile the following is a valid destination list:

```
10.231.76.0/24:80
10.231.77.1:443
```

To do the same list using **Allowed Servers** on a role, two separate servers would be needed: one for 10.231.76.0/24:80, and one for 10.231.77.1:443. You can see that this configuration method can be very time consuming if there are lots of destinations.

■ Pick a Resource Profile brings up a pop-up window that allows you to select a pre-defined profile. This serves the same function as editing a WSAM Resource Profile and adding the role to the list of Selected Roles.

**NOTE**

While this creates a WSAM destination, it does not automatically create a SAM access policy unless the **Auto-allow application servers** option is selected in the SAM role options. Traffic from the WSAM client will be sent to the IVE, but will be dropped unless there is a matching access policy that specifically permits the traffic.

# Adding a WSAM Bypass Application to a Role

Traffic that originates from a "Bypass Application" is never sent through the VPN tunnel. There are several reasons for configuring Bypass Applications. Here are two examples:

■ **Security** There may be a process running on a client that should never send traffic through the VPN tunnel regardless of the destination. A client-side server process (like one of the default Bypass Applications: apache.exe) is the most likely example.

- **Application split tunnel** When you are using WSAM destinations, it may be useful to have an originating application that can communicate with the destination servers without going through the VPN. For example, you could configure a destination of 1.1.1.1:23 and create a Bypass Application of telnet.exe, while allowing other telnet applications like HyperTerminal to flow through the tunnel.

The IVE comes with a list of default bypass applications but administrators can add their own on a role.

1. Navigate to **Users | User Role | Role | SAM | Applications**.
2. Select the **Add Bypass Application** button above the **WSAM Bypass Applications** list.
3. The only required field to configure is the **Filename**, but a **Name**, **Description**, and **Path** can be optionally specified. Select **Save Changes** to complete the configuration.

# Adding a JSAM-Supported Application to a Role

This procedure creates a JSAM application and associates it to a single role. A JSAM application created on a role can not be applied to another role.

1. Navigate to **Users | User Role | Role | SAM | Applications**. Select the **Add Application** button above the **JSAM Supported Applications** list.
2. The configuration here is similar to a new Application Resource Profile. From the **Type** drop-down menu, select **Custom**, **Standard**, or **Pick a Resource Profile**.

   - Custom enables you to create a non-standard application and requires a Server Name and Server Port. You can also configure the client loopback IP address and port, or allow the IVE to select one automatically. The IVE will use the server port as the client port by default. However, recall that two loopback addresses cannot listen on the same port. In order to get around this, you can manually define a different client port or set the Allow Secure Application Manager to dynamically select an available port if the specified client port is taken checkbox and let the IVE choose one for you.

   - The Standard option requires you to select from a list of applications, including Citrix NFuse, Lotus Notes, Microsoft Outlook/Exchange, and NetBIOS file browsing.

   - The Pick a Resource Profile option (which appears only when a JSAM Application Resource Profile already exists) brings up a pop-up window that allows you to select a pre-defined profile. This serves the same function as editing a JSAM Resource Profile and adding the role to the list of Selected Roles.

**NOTE**

While this creates a JSAM application, it does not automatically create a SAM access policy. Traffic from the JSAM client will be sent to the IVE, but will be dropped unless there is a matching access policy that specifically permits the traffic.

3. Enter a **Name**, which is required, and an optional **Description**.

4. Select **Save Application** to continue.

For Citrix NFuse, a little more is necessary.

1. In the **Max Session** field, enter the number of possible simultaneous Citrix client sessions for each user. This value is needed because the IVE automatically assigns this many loopback addresses to be associated with the different Citrix destinations.

2. The **Allowed Ports** field is set to 1494, 2598 by default, the standard ports for ICA (1494) and Common Gateway Protocol (2598), which supports the **Session Reliability** and **Auto-client reconnect** features.

3. Under **Connect Local Devices**, select the boxes to allow users to connect **Printers**, **Drives**, and **COM ports** during their Citrix session.

4. Select **Save Changes** to return to the JSAM Supported Applications list.

**TIP**

Only one SAM Citrix application can be applied to a role—regardless of how it is configured. In other words, if the role is using JSAM, only one JSAM Citrix application is allowed; if the role is using WSAM, only one WSAM Citrix application is allowed. Make sure your access policy for the one supported application allows access to all the servers the user will need.

For Microsoft Outlook/Exchange and NetBIOS file browsing, enter a list of servers in the **Host mapping field** if you are planning to use automatic host mapping. If using external DNS for name resolution to loopback IP, leave this field blank. Select **Save changes** to continue.

# Configuring SAM Resource Policies

In this section we'll show discuss configuring SAM resource policies and policy options.

# Configuring a SAM Resource Policy for Access Control

A flexible security policy can often make the configuration of a network device easier. Being able to create independent SAM Access Control policies allows you to take advantage of these opportunities by creating an access policy that can be shared by multiple Resource Profiles. Recall that each profile ultimately controls what each role can access by defining the originating application or by specifying the destination, so creating a common access policy doesn't necessarily give the user any additional access.

For example, assume you have ten roles defined for ten groups of users. Each role permits tcp/8080 access to a different set of servers through a WSAM Destination Resource Profile. If the corporate security policy states that incoming tcp/8080 traffic to all servers can be permitted through SAM, a single SAM Access Control policy can be configured to allow one policy to replace ten individual autopolicies built from the individual Resource Profiles. This isn't much of a savings when you have only ten roles, but becomes more significant as the number of roles increases.

1. To create a custom SAM access policy, navigate to **Users | Resource Policies | SAM | Access Control**. Select the **New Policy** button.

2. Enter a policy **Name**, which is required, and an optional **Description**.

3. Enter a list of **Resources** in the box that includes host names and IP addresses covered by the policy.

4. The **Action** button makes the policy an **Allow** or **Deny** rule.

5. Select **Save Changes** to complete the rule.

The **Used Detailed Rules** option merits special attention because it offers a very interesting way of creating a granular definition of access within a single policy. Even with detailed rules, the **Resources** list is still required. However, rather than a single **Allow** or **Deny** that affects the entire resource list, rules are built that allow or deny subsets of the Resources list based on many other factors, including group membership (based on the Role's Directory/Attribute Server), user name, login URL, Host Checker status, and so forth. Note: A detailed rule is a feature of the Advanced License. To use this feature, a license key must be installed under **System | Configuration | Licensing.**

1. To create a detailed rule, select the **Use Detailed Rules** radio button and select **Save Changes**. This creates a new tab called **Detailed Rules**. Select the **New Rule** button.

2. Select a radio button to configure the rule to either **Allow** or **Deny** socket access.

3. In the **Resources** field, create a list of destinations using either host names or IP/netmask notation, including port information. Wildcards are supported here.

4. In the **Conditions** field, create a Boolean expression that, if matched, will apply the action to traffic destined for the resources.

Interestingly, the IVE will allow the **Resources** list under **Detailed Rule** to include resources that are not part of the Access Policy Resource list. Even though this is possible, it is not a good idea because it makes the configuration difficult to understand.

Figure 5.4 is an example of a detailed rule that allows socket access to hosts in the 10.0.177.0/24 subnet when the user is a member of the Domain Administrators group and is using Microsoft IE 7.0.

**Figure 5.4** Detailed Rules Configuration

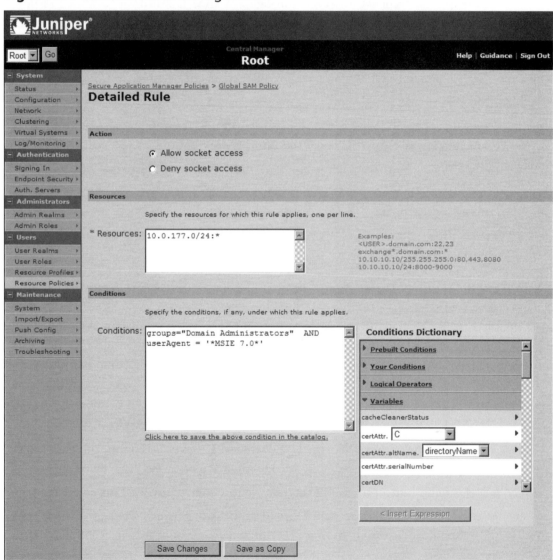

# Configuring SAM Resource Policy Options

The Resource Policy options are configured under **Users | Resource Policies | SAM | Options**. There is only one option to configure:

**IP based matching for Host name based policy resources**   When this option is enabled, the IVE looks up the IP addresses for all the host names defined in the SAM resource policy fields. It maintains a cache of this information. If a SAM user subsequently attempts to refer to a destination by IP address rather than host name, the IVE consults this cache to determine if there is a match. If so, the IVE considers the IP address to be a policy match and it can treat the request properly. If this option is not selected and a policy is created using only the server's fully qualified domain name, user access attempts directly to the server's IP address will not work.

> **NOTE**
>
> This setting does not apply to resource policy fields where wildcards are used. For example, during the creation of a WSAM application resource profile for Microsoft Outlook, it is necessary to define a list of application servers for the supporting SAM access policy. If the administrator used a wildcard (such as server?.mycorp.com) in the Resource field, the IVE does not look up IP addresses that correspond to the matching servers. So, if a WSAM user refers to server1.mycorp.com as an IP address, the request will fail.

# Configuring JSAM Autolaunch Policies

JSAM has the ability (unlike WSAM) to automatically launch in response to a user selecting a bookmark. Configuring this can be done as part of a Web Application Resource Profile. However, it is also possible to create a custom policy to do this. As with the configuration of Access Control policies, SAM Autolaunch policy configuration allows the use of detailed rules for precise control over when JSAM is launched.

1. Navigate to **Users | Resource Policies | Web | Launch JSAM**.

2. Select the **New Policy** button above the **Policies** table. A policy **Name** is required, but the **Description** field is optional.

3. The **Resources** field lists the URLs covered by the policy. The resources listed here are Web Resources since this policy is applied to a Web bookmark. So, the syntax of the resources will be like those used in Chapter 9 (Web/File Access/ Telnet/SSH). Note: Be sure to use fully qualified domain names in this field.

4.  The **Roles** control allows you to select the roles that should use the policy.

5.  The **Action** options do the following:

   ■ Launch JSAM for this URL  JSAM is launched when the user selects a bookmark that matches the URL.

   ■ Don't Launch JSAM for this URL  JSAM is not launched when a selected bookmark matches. This is useful for creating an exception to an already-configured policy. For example, you could have several bookmarks covered by a Web Resource Policy with an overall Launch JSAM policy. If all but one bookmark requires JSAM, use this option to create an exception to the overall policy to not launch JSAM for that single bookmark.

   ■ Use Detailed Rules  This provides the power (and accompanying configuration complexity) to make very detailed decisions about when to automatically launch JSAM based on many things (including group membership, username, browser type, and more).

# Configuring SAM Resource Profiles

Juniper recommends using resource profiles to configure SAM. This is the same recommendation made for Core Clientless Access Services. Resource profiles are easy and produce consistent results, making sure critical elements of the configuration aren't forgotten. In addition, one profile can be associated with several roles, making it an efficient way of sharing configurations between roles and making the IVE configuration less complex and easier to maintain. In this section, we'll cover the following methods for configuring SAM:

   ■ Client Applications Resource Profile—WSAM

   ■ WSAM Destination Resource Profiles

   ■ Client Applications Resource Profile—JSAM

   ■ Web Application Resource Profiles with rewriting options to use SAM

## Configuring WSAM Client Applications Resource Profiles

This procedure creates a WSAM application using a resource profile. Applications created as resource profiles can be applied to many roles.

1.  Navigate to **Users | Resource Profiles | SAM | Client Applications**. Select the **New Profile** button and select **WSAM** from the drop-down menu.

2.  In the **Application** drop-down menu, select one of five options:

   ■ **Custom** An application is manually defined

   ■ **Lotus Notes** Lotus Notes client

- **Microsoft Outlook**  Microsoft Outlook client

- **NetBIOS file browsing**  Microsoft file system calls over NetBIOS tcp/137

- **Citrix**  Citrix applications

    All of the pre-defined applications are configured the same way. Selecting **Custom** requires a bit more information.

3. A **Name** must be configured and there is an optional field for a **Description**. These fields are displayed only in the details section of the WSAM client and are not normally visible to the user.

    SAM Resource Profiles do not display bookmarks the way Web Resource Profiles do. To use the application, WSAM must be launched either manually by the user off the IVE homepage or auto-launched by the role at login. Once WSAM is running, the user simply runs the fat client application and the traffic is intercepted by WSAM and sent through the tunnel.

4. The **Autopolicy: SAM Access Control** is equivalent to an access list, which either allows or denies traffic flowing through the tunnel. In the **Resource** field, the traffic destinations can be entered either as host names or in IP/netmask notation. Wildcards are allowed. For example, if all Citrix servers were located on a common subnet, a good Access Control policy for Citrix may be:

```
10.23.32.0/24:1494,2598
```

Like most access lists, the order of entries is important. The IVE evaluates the entries from the top down and stops when the first match is found. Arrange the entries carefully to ensure that the access policy matches what is intended. The list can be reordered by selecting the box next to the rule to move and using the **Up** and **Down** arrows to rearrange the list.

Flexible access control is one of the most powerful elements of the Juniper IVE. The ability to use wildcards to define resources makes tight access control possible without sacrificing ease of use. Using host names with wildcards underscores the benefits of following strict naming standards—especially when it comes to shared resources (such as servers and printers). See the sidebar "Using Wildcards for Resource Definitions" later in this chapter.

---

**N**OTE

Only one SAM Citrix application can be applied to a role, regardless of how it is configured. In other words, if the role is using JSAM, only one JSAM Citrix application is allowed; if the role is using WSAM, only one WSAM Citrix application is allowed. Make sure your access policy for the one supported application allows access to all the servers the user will need.

---

5.  Select **Save and Continue**.

6.  Each resource profile is assigned to one or more roles. Assigning a profile to multiple roles is an efficient way of sharing the configuration between roles, making the configuration less complex. On the **Roles** tab, select the roles that should be assigned to this profile and select **Add**. When done, select **Save Changes**.

---

## Tools & Traps…

### Using Wildcards for Resource Definitions

When configuring the IVE, you often find yourself configuring lists of "resources." When configuring SAM, resources are *destinations*: servers or groups of servers. Because the IVE is a security device, making sure these resource lists reflect your security policy is a big deal. Making a mistake can grant unintentional access. What can be worse—the mistake can go unnoticed.

To make resource lists easier to build, the use of wildcards are often (but not always) supported in the IVE. If wildcards can be used, an inline note is displayed to the right of the field. Knowing how to build resource lists using wildcards is a useful skill for any IVE administrator. Wildcards make representing a large number of internal hosts very easy. Both host names and IP addresses can be used in resource definitions, and both have their own type of wildcard.

1.  **Host Name Wildcards**    Names entered into resource definitions can be either relative or fully-qualified domain names (FQDN). For example, "fred" and "fred.mycorp.com" are both accepted. Note: Using the fully-qualified name is always a good idea since it eliminates ambiguity. Two basic wildcards can be used for text names:

    **?** Represents a single character

    * Represents a string of characters delimited by a period "." character

    Examples are usually the best way to get an understanding of wildcards:

    **fred?.mycorp.com**    Matches fred1.mycorp.com, fred2.mycorp.com, freda.mycorp.com, and so on. Does not match fred11.mycorp.com, fred123.mycorp.com, and equivalent.

    **fred*.mycorp.com**    Matches fred1.mycorp.com, fred2.mycorp.com, freda.mycorp.com, and so on. Also matches fred11.mycorp.com, fred123.mycorp.com, and equivalent.

    **fred.\*.com**    Matches fred.domain1.com, fred.domain2.com, and so forth.

2. **IP Address Wildcards**   IP addresses entered into resource definitions can use either a subnet mask (called a netmask) or prefix-length notation. A netmask and prefix accomplish the same thing—separating the part of the IP address that is considered "the network" and the part that is considered "the host." Technically speaking, a prefix is the number of left-most contiguous bits that make up the netmask. For example, the netmask 255.255.255.0 is /24 as a prefix since there are 8 bits in each octet of the IP address and 255 equals 11111111 in binary notation

The topic of how IP addressing works is beyond the scope of this book. Several examples should suffice:

```
10.20.30.0/255.255.255.0 or 10.20.30.0/24
```

matches hosts in the range: 10.20.30.1 to 10.20.30.255.

```
10.0.0.0/255.0.0.0 or 10.0.0.0/8
```

matches hosts in the range: 10.0.0.1 to 10.255.255.255.
While not technically a wildcard, the effect of the netmask is the same.
There is good reason to be careful when using wildcards. The most important problem you can have is granting incorrect access by including hosts in the resource definition unintentionally. Experienced administrators double and triple check their resource lists to make sure that all the necessary access is granted, but no more.

# Configuring WSAM Destination Resource Profiles

With WSAM Destination Profiles, any application can send traffic through the tunnel to the destination IP addresses on the configured ports. Destination Profiles are configured like Client Application Profiles, except that no application is selected (since the profile is based on destination not application).

1. Navigate to **Users | Resource Profiles | SAM | WSAM Destinations**. Select the **New Profile** button.

2. A **Name** must be configured and there is an optional field for a **Description**. These fields are displayed only in the details section of the WSAM client and are not normally visible to the user.

3. The **WSAM Destinations** lists the IP addresses and ports that the client can send to through the tunnel. In the **Destination** field, the destinations can be entered either as host names or in IP/netmask notation.

Unlike an access list, the order of entries is not important so there are no **Up** or **Down** arrows to rearrange the list. The list of destinations is more like a VPN split tunnel list, which provides a client with a list of destinations on the other end of the VPN. With SAM, if the destination is not in the list, the traffic is sent to the local default gateway without traversing the SAM tunnel.

4. Select the **Create an access control policy by allowing SAM access to these servers** checkbox to have the IVE create an access control policy that permits the traffic in the destination list. By default, no traffic is allowed, so this is a necessary step. If it is not done, the traffic from the SAM client will be dropped when it reaches the IVE.

5. Select **Save and Continue**.

6. Each resource profile is assigned to one or more roles. Assigning a profile to multiple roles is an efficient way of sharing the configuration between roles, making the configuration less complex. On the **Roles** tab, select the roles that should be assigned to this profile and select **Add**. When done, select **Save Changes**.

# Configuring JSAM Client Applications Resource Profiles

This procedure creates a JSAM application using a resource profile. Applications created as resource profiles can be applied to many roles.

1. Navigate to **Users | Resource Profiles | SAM | Client Applications**. Select the **New Profile** button and select **JSAM** from the drop-down menu.

2. In the **Application** drop-down menu, select one of four options:

   ■ **Custom** An application is manually defined

   ■ **Lotus Notes** Lotus Notes client

   ■ **Microsoft Outlook** Microsoft Outlook client

   ■ **NetBIOS file browsing** Microsoft file system calls over NetBIOS tcp/137
   All of the predefined applications are configured the same way. Selecting **Custom** requires a bit more information.

3. A **Name** must be configured and there is an optional field for a **Description**. These fields are for administrators only—they are not displayed to the user.

4. The **Servers** field lists all the servers that the JSAM client can access. If the **Automatic host-mapping** role option is set, the JSAM client modifies the local host file of the connecting computer so that servers defined in this list are mapped to loopback IP addresses. The JSAM client listens on those addresses and sends traffic it receives through the VPN.

**TIP**

If you use external DNS for server name to loopback address resolution, make sure to statically define the loopbacks in the **Servers** field.

The inability to use wildcards in this field is one of the biggest limitations of Java SAM. A large company with hundreds of internal email servers would find creating and managing this list difficult or impossible. Using external DNS to provide a mapping between server names in this field and loopback addresses is an option and scales better than the local HOSTS file. However, that doesn't solve the problem that the list must initially be built and forever maintained. The Lotus Notes standard JSAM application will allow you to use wildcards for server definitions, but this requires the use of an external DNS system for resolution—the host file is not modified by the IVE automatically in this case.

5. Select **Save and Continue**.

6. Each resource profile is assigned to one or more roles. Assigning a profile to multiple roles is an efficient way of sharing the configuration between roles, making the configuration less complex. On the **Roles** tab, select the roles that should be assigned to this profile and select **Add**. When done, select **Save Changes**.

JSAM Client Application Resource Profiles do not display bookmarks the way Web Resource Profiles do. To use the application, JSAM must be launched manually by the user off the IVE homepage or auto-launched by the role at login. Once JSAM is running, the user simply runs the fat client application and the traffic is intercepted by JSAM and sent through the tunnel.

# Configuring SAM Rewriting Bypass with Web Application Resource Profiles

SAM can be enabled during a Web Application Resource Profile definition as a supporting policy to bypass the rewriting of the application by the IVE. This method is discussed in Chapter 9 (Web/File Access/Telnet/SSH), so only the basics will be covered here.

Using SAM in this way is a common step in troubleshooting application performance problems through the CIE. It is easy to configure SAM to bypass the intermediation engine to check if performance improves. If it does, you may want to keep SAM or work with JTAC engineers or a Juniper support partner to identify the area of the intermediation engine causing the problem.

The rewriting option is not visible by default. Select the **Show ALL autopolicy types** button in the application definition screen, and then select the box next to **Autopolicy: Rewriting Options**. Choosing either the **No rewriting (use WSAM)** or the **No rewriting (use JSAM)** option causes the server to be automatically added. For JSAM, not adding an entry in the **Client Loopback IP** field causes the IVE to automatically select an available loopback IP to be used.

One useful feature of configuring JSAM in this way is the **Launch JSAM** checkbox. This will cause JSAM to automatically launch when the web resource is selected by the user. This essentially links JSAM with the application bookmark, which eliminates the need to either launch it when the role is mapped, or manually from the IVE homepage. If the application is not used during every session, the user won't be delayed by the time taken to launch JSAM. Unfortunately, it is not possible to link WSAM to a bookmark in this way.

# Secure Application Manager User Experience

What the user sees when SAM runs depends on how the IVE is configured. When SAM is launched is one obvious example (for example, whether it runs when the role is mapped, when a bookmark is selected on the IVE homepage, or when manually launched off the IVE homepage).

The biggest difference, however, is what the SAM client looks like on the connecting computer.

- WSAM installs as an ActiveX control and creates a taskbar icon that looks like this: 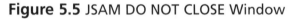. The small circles above the icon are green when traffic is being sent and received.

- JSAM runs as a Java applet and creates a **Do Not Close** window, shown in Figure 5.5.

**Figure 5.5** JSAM DO NOT CLOSE Window

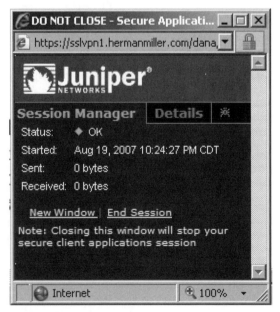

This look-and-feel difference is very important—especially when the client desktop must be carefully designed to minimize support calls. If the IVE homepage is closed, WSAM continues to run without issue and stops only when closed using the taskbar right-click menu or when the computer is shut down. Hibernating or any other event that blocks connectivity between the connecting computer and the IVE may cause WSAM to interact with the user, but these will normally cause an active client/server application to throw an error too.

On the other hand, if users attempt to close the Java window, they receive the message shown in Figure 5.6. Navigating away from the **Do Not Close** page essentially closes JSAM.

**Figure 5.6** JSAM Closure Window

# Troubleshooting

Although the troubleshooting capabilities of SAM are not as substantial as Core Clientless Access Services, both the IVE and client log a lot of information that can be used to diagnose problems.

## Secure Application Manager Troubleshooting

In this section we'll discuss several common problems that affect SAM users and some typical reasons behind these problems. We'll show you how each of the following issues is identified using tools on the IVE and client:

- **Application Doesn't Work During Initial SAM Setup** If an application has never worked before, the most obvious reason for this problem is an IVE configuration issue. Here are the typical problems:

  - **WSAM Application Profile** Incorrect file name, path, or MD5 hash specified

  - **WSAM Destination Profile** Incorrect resource list (for example, IP addresses don't match or wrong port)

  - **JSAM** No resolution between name and loopback address

  - **JSAM/WSAM** No access policy configured

- **Application Doesn't Work Following Initial SAM Setup** If an application has been working through SAM and suddenly quits, the most likely reason is a change in the environment. Here are the typical problems:
  - **WSAM Application Profile** An application upgrade caused the file name, path, or MD5 hash to change
  - **WSAM Destination Profile** A server has been readdressed or ports changed so they no longer match the resources list
  - **JSAM** A server has been readdressed and the resolution of name to loopback address is no longer correct
  - **JSAM/WSAM** A server has been readdressed but the SAM access policy was not updated with the new information so traffic is being dropped
- **Poor Application Performance** It is rare for a client/server application using SAM to run slowly through the IVE. Normally, performance problems are caused by bandwidth issues (or other network-related problems) or underpowered hardware.

# IVE-Side Troubleshooting

User Access Logs are one of the best and worst things about the IVE. The amount of log information is great and the ability to create custom queries to focus log output is very useful. However, logs can get extremely large and be very slow on a production concentrator. Even though log output is critical to troubleshooting problems, it can be a challenge. Learning how to use custom queries is essential to success. Policy tracing can be a good alternative to log access.

## Concentrator Logs

To troubleshoot SAM successfully, the critical first step is to enable SAM logging. Navigate to **System | Log/Monitoring | User Access | Settings**. Under **Select Events to Log**, ensure the **SAM / Java** box is checked. The log itself can be found from here by selecting the **Log** link on the menu, or by navigating to **System | Log/Monitoring | User Access | Log**.

## Example One

You get a call from a Lotus Notes user complaining that access to certain servers isn't working through a newly configured WSAM setup. You enable SAM logging on the IVE and see the following:

- ```
  Info JAV20022 2007-06-05 15:15:54 - ive - [2.9.19.22] Root::sam(SAM)[WSAM
  Example] - Request to connect to 10.1.3.41 port 1352 permission denied
  ```
- ```
  Info JAV20022 2007-06-05 15:15:54 - ive - [2.9.19.22] Root::sam(SAM)[WSAM
  Example] - Request to connect to 10.1.3.42 port 1352 permission denied
  ```

- ```
Info JAV20023 2007-06-05 15:05:13 - ive - [2.9.19.22] Root::sam(SAM)[WSAM
Example] - Closed connection to SERVER1 port 1352 after 0 seconds, with
320 bytes read (in 3 chunks) and 130 bytes written (in 3 chunks)
```

- ```
Info JAV20021 2007-06-05 15:05:13 - ive - [2.9.19.22] Root::sam(SAM)[WSAM
Example] - Connected to SERVER1 port 1352
```

Why are users able to access servers referred to by a server name, but are unable to access servers referred to by an IP address? A "permission denied" message is going to come from the SAM Access Control policy since that is how traffic is allowed or denied through the IVE. By default, no access is permitted through the IVE. So you suspect an access policy problem.

Navigating to the SAM Access Control policies via **Users | Resource Policies | SAM | Access Control**, you see in the Policies list that the access control is accomplished through an Autopolicy that is maintained by the WSAM Application Profile. You follow the link in the table directly to the profile definition to review the resource list.

During the Profile creation, you decided to use wildcards to allow access to all servers on port tcp/1352 and configured the resource list in this form: \*.\*:1352. Now you think the wildcards are not working as you expected. After some testing, you find that \*.\* matches host names (like SERVER1) but not IP addresses. So, you change the resource list to: \*:1352 and retry. Your permission denied messages go away and your user is now able to access e-mail.

## Policy Trace of SAM Policies

Policy tracing gives an IVE administrator the ability to focus investigation on the policies applied to a single user—as the user connects and accesses resources. This can be a very powerful tool during setup (for instance, to verify resource usage of an application) and for troubleshooting.

To use the tool, navigate to **Maintenance | Troubleshooting | User Sessions | Policy Tracing**. Enter the user name and realm to which the user will connect. Under **Events to Log**, select **SAM Policies**. You may also want to enable **Launch JSAM** under **Web Policies**. The drawback to the policy trace utility is the quantity of information it returns. Finding a policy failure can be difficult with a huge number of trace entries. It is a good idea to enable logging for only those policies you need to review. However, be prepared to expand your tracing if you fail to find the problem.

Once you have the user ready to test, select the **Start Recording** button. The user then duplicates the issue. Then select **Stop Recording** and the **View Log** button.

## Example Two

You have an existing web policy configured for your corporate Intranet. Now you find that you need to automatically launch JSAM, but the configuration change you made to the web profile isn't working. You suspect a SAM policy is involved so you enlist a volunteer to connect while you watch the IVE policy trace log.

You configure the Policy Trace utility with the user name and realm and start recording. Once the user has duplicated the issue, you stop the recording and view the log. You see the following lines:

- ```
  Info PTR23232 2007/06/05 22:01:06 - [24.96.149.252] -
  Root::sam(SAM)[JSAM Example] - Start Policy [WEBURL/LAUNCH_JSAM]
  evaluation for resource http://intranet.mycorp.com:80/
  ```

- ```
  Info PTR23233 2007/06/05 22:01:06 - [24.96.149.252] -
  Root::sam(SAM)[JSAM Example] - Applying Policy [Test]
  ```

- ```
  Info PTR23239 2007/06/05 22:01:06 - [24.96.149.252] -
  Root::sam(SAM)[JSAM Example] - Action [Don't Launch JSAM] is
  returned
  ```

- ```
  Info PTR23234 2007/06/05 22:01:06 - [24.96.149.252] -
  Root::sam(SAM)[JSAM Example] - Policy [Test] applies to resource
  ```

A policy called Test is causing JSAM not to launch, and you don't recall configuring this policy. A check of the Launch JSAM Web Policies shows a policy named Test that has been moved to the top of the list—meaning it is evaluated before the Autopolicy created by the Web Profile. Calls to other IVE administrators yield someone who admits to creating the Test policy. The policy is removed and JSAM now launches properly.

## Simulation of SAM Policies

The simulation tool isn't normally used for troubleshooting, but is very useful in creating SAM policies and shouldn't be overlooked. The tool becomes more useful as the number of policies increases because it can become difficult to determine which policies will be applied when there are tens or hundreds of policies that could potentially be applied to a user. The simulation clearly shows the policies that are applied, eliminating the guesswork.

The simulation yields similar output to the policy trace, but a user is not involved in the process. The IVE simulates the access attempt on behalf of the user and outputs the result. More information can be found on this tool in Chapter 10.

# Client-Side Troubleshooting

Client logs can be an invaluable tool in troubleshooting access issues. Users can upload logs, as described in Chapter 13 (Logging), which can then be downloaded and reviewed by administrators.

## Client Logs

Client logging is enabled and disabled on the IVE in **System | Log/Monitoring | Client Logs | Settings**. Each SAM client has different sets of logs that are accessed in different ways.

## WSAM Client Logs

The WSAM logs reside in the following directory:

```
C:\Documents and Settings\<username>\Application Data\JuniperNetworks\Secure
Application Manager
```

There are several logs in this directory, including:

- **dsSamEvent.log** This file is the most useful event log for basic troubleshooting.
- **dsSamDebug.log** This file contains very detailed debugging information used mainly by JTAC engineers.

The dsSamEvent.log file can be viewed directly from the client. To do this, launch the WSAM client by double-clicking the taskbar icon or by right-clicking on this icon and selecting **Status** from the menu, as shown in Figure 5.7.

**Figure 5.7** Launching the WSAM Client

Then, select the **Advanced** button to display the **Log** and **Tool** tabs. Select the **Event Log** tab to display the log.

## Example Three

You have a custom Telnet utility that you use through WSAM to provide remote management to UNIX servers. Suddenly, users are calling to complain that the application no longer works. A check of the IVE log shows nothing unusual (so it is unlikely to be an access policy issue) and the same users can access other applications through SAM properly (so you know they are logged in fine and SAM is working).

You ask a user to access the client log and they relay the following:

```
16:39:38 checksum mis-match detected for application
C:\WINDOWS\system32\telnet.exe, will not secure
```

You remember that your WSAM application profile includes an MD5 hash of this application. The developer of the Telnet utility is called and admits to a mid-week upgrade of the application to fix a problem.

You have two options:

1. Eliminate the MD5 hash on the application profile. This could potentially compromise security if you need tight control over which application can originate this traffic through SAM.

2. Recalculate the checksum using the new version and update the application profile.

Note: Using an MD5 hash can be difficult because it assumes that everyone is running the same version of an application. A phased migration from one version to another may require creating a second application profile or temporarily eliminating the checksum until all users are upgraded.

## JSAM Client Logs

The JSAM logs reside in the following directory:

```
C:\Documents and Settings\<username>\Application Data\Juniper Networks\Java
Secure Application Manager
```

There are several logs in this directory, including:

- **dsJSAMSummary_win1.log** This file contains only summary information. It may be useful for very basic troubleshooting, but more info is often needed.

- **dsJSAM_win1.log** This file contains very detailed debugging information.

The JSAM client is not as fully featured as the WSAM client. Access to the log entries is not available in the JSAM client. To access the log, use Windows Explorer or another tool to view the directory.

## Example Four

You have an existing web policy configured for your corporate Intranet that automatically launches and uses JSAM to bypass rewriting. Everything was working fine until today. SAM continues to launch, but the website doesn't display.

You ask a user to send you their dsJSAM_win1.log file. You sift through hundreds of log entries and finally find several that may be related:

- ```
  TunnelServer.jav:112 (06/05 21:52:55.937)[Thread-14] java.io.IOException:
  Unable to open connectionCannot open conn to remote host:port= intranet.
  mycorp.com:80
  ```

- ```
  CSUI.java:027 (06/05 21:52:55.937)[Thread-14] Application: (1) WebApp:80
  127.0.10.1 Message: Cannot open connection to intranet.mycorp.com:80
  Status: 2
  ```

You suspect that the IVE is unable to access the website, so you decide to test locally to make sure your computer can access the website. A ping shows the problem:

```
C:\>ping intranet.mycorp.com
```
Ping request could not find host intranet.mycorp.com. Please check the name and try
again.

Someone has changed the host name of the web server without telling the IVE administrator. A call to the website administrator results in an admission of the change and the new name. After updating the Web Profile, access begins to work again.

# Client Tools

Troubleshooting WSAM and JSAM on the client is different mainly because the WSAM client includes a number of built-in troubleshooting tools while the JSAM client does not. You can troubleshoot both successfully, however, by knowing where to look for problems.

## WSAM Tools

Launch the WSAM client by double-clicking the taskbar icon or by right-clicking on the icon and selecting **Status** from the menu. Then, select the **Advanced** button to display the tool tabs.

One interesting test is on the **Diagnostics** tab. Enter a URL and select the **Start Test** button. The output is the result of a number of individual tests that provide an overall health check of the client. While these results don't help diagnose problems with the IVE configuration, they can verify basic network connectivity on the connecting computer. A summary of the output is shown in Figure 5.8.

**Figure 5.8** Summary Output of WSAM Diagnostics Test

| Test Component | Result | Description |
|---|---|---|
| *IP Configuration:* | OK | Test to see if the machine's IP address is properly configured |
| *TCP/IP Connection Link status:* | OK | Tests to verify the TCP communication link |
| *Loopback Communication link:* | OK | Tests to verify the Loopback communication link |
| *Domain Name Service (DNS) availability:* | OK | This is to verify the behavior of Name space provider |
| *UDP Communication link status:* | OK | Tests to verify the UDP communication link |

## Example Five

Your WSAM users are complaining that a certain Lotus Notes server is running slowly. You know that several WSAM client tools can help in diagnosing problems with the client and network. One of the most useful is on the **Performance** tab. In the drop-down menu, select **Host:Port**. Because WSAM is used mostly for client/server applications, this option is needed most frequently. You ask the user to enter the following: Server1:1352 and enter 10 in the **Iteration** box. Select the **Run** button to start the test.

Note: It is a good idea to try this test multiple times to ensure the results are consistent.

The user tells you the tool shows an average round trip time (abbreviated Ave. RTT (ms) in the WSAM client) of 938 ms. Trying the test a few more times shows this value is relatively consistent. You know the server the user is trying to access is at a remote site. You ask the user to select a server at your main site and rerun the test. The user enters: Server2:1352. After a few attempts, the user tells you the round trip time to this destination is only 65 ms.

With these results, you suspect a problem with connectivity to the remote site. A call to the network team solves the problem—the primary circuit to the remote site is down and they are running on a backup VPN over a low-speed Internet connection.

## JSAM Tools

While there are not many client tools available on the JSAM client, don't overlook what is available from the OS and other applications. The HOSTS file, DNS, and the JVM provide information that may prove valuable during troubleshooting.

Recall that the HOSTS file is one method of mapping between server name and loopback IP. If you are relying on this to work, make sure you check the HOSTS file to determine if it is being properly updated with the JSAM hosts. On a connected client, simply view the contents of the file. It should show the mapping you have configured in the JSAM Application Profile:

```
C:\WINDOWS\system32\drivers\etc>type hosts
#[JSAM_BEGIN] IVE hosts##
127.0.10.1    intranet.mycorp.com
#[JSAM_END] IVE hosts##
```

If external DNS (rather than the HOSTS file) provides the loopback IP, you must ensure resolution is working. The *nslookup* command is an easy tool for this task:

```
C:\>nslookup intranet.mycorp.com
Server: externaldns.mycorp.com
Address: 188.23.43.222
Name: intranet.mycorp.com
Address: 127.0.10.1
```

Troubleshooting the Java VM is beyond the scope of this book. However, don't ignore the tools that come with the JVM installed on the client when working on JSAM problems. The Java console can provide helpful information.

# Summary

Secure Access Manager is an optional feature of the Juniper SSL concentrator that performs intermediation of traffic from client/server applications. Several popular client/server applications benefit from built-in support on the IVE, including Lotus Notes and Microsoft Exchange. The IVE is capable of automatically provisioning one of several SAM clients, so no initial software on the client is necessary. Both Java and ActiveX versions of SAM are available to run on the most commonly deployed operating systems: Windows, Mac, and Linux.

# Solutions Fast Track

## Secure Application Manager

☑ Use WSAM Application Profiles to configure client/server application access for one of the standard built-in applications (Lotus Notes, Microsoft Outlook, NetBIOS file browsing, or Citrix) or define your own custom application.

☑ Create WSAM Destination Profiles to allow any application to tunnel traffic through the IVE by defining flexible destination lists using a combination of host names, IP addresses, and destination ports.

☑ JSAM Application Profiles allow similar client/server intermediation access in a cross-platform environment, allowing Windows, Mac, and Linux computers to connect. JSAM features secure client/server traffic using access control policies that allow or deny access from clients based either on basic resource lists or extremely flexible and powerful detailed rules.

## Secure Application Manager Implementation

☑ The Auto-launch Secure Application Manager feature is useful to automatically launch SAM when a user is mapped to the role.

☑ The Auto-uninstall Secure Application Manager feature will uninstall WSAM when a user disconnects.

☑ The Auto-upgrade Secure Application Manager feature is very useful for maintaining an up-to-date WSAM client on each connecting computer.

## Secure Application Manager User Experience

☑ What the user sees when SAM runs depends on how the IVE is configured.

☑ If the IVE homepage is closed, WSAM continues to run without issue and stops only when closed using the taskbar right-click menu or when the computer is shut down.

☑ Navigating away from the **Do Not Close** page essentially closes JSAM.

# Troubleshooting

☑  Both the IVE and client log a lot of information that can be used to diagnose problems.

☑  Even though log output is critical to troubleshooting problems, it can be a challenge. Learning how to use custom queries is essential to success.

☑  To troubleshoot SAM successfully, the critical first step is to enable SAM logging.

# Frequently Asked Questions

**Q:** Can the IVE be configured to automatically disconnect a SAM user after a certain period of inactivity?

**A:** No—The role **Idle Timeout** setting doesn't work with either WSAM or JSAM. This setting only affects connections through the Core Clientless Access Services (Web Proxy). The **Max Session Length** timer to control session lifetime is the only option for these users, and it does not consider inactivity.

**Q:** Can I have both JSAM and WSAM applications configured on the same IVE?

**A:** Yes—both JSAM and WSAM applications can be configured. However, both JSAM and WSAM can't be enabled on the same role.

**Q:** I have a user who is mapped to multiple roles, but only one role's SAM is working. Why?

**A:** If a user maps to multiple roles with one role using WSAM and one role using JSAM, you'll have problems. The reason is that WSAM and JSAM can't run at the same time. In this case, the SAM configured on the first role the user maps to will work.

**Q:** I am using JSAM because I need non-Windows clients to connect, but I don't want the IVE to modify the local HOSTS file to resolve names to loopback addresses. What can I do?

**A:** You can use an external DNS server to resolve names to loopback addresses. Make sure to configure the IVE to use static loopback addresses for all servers so the DNS server doesn't need to change every time the application definition does.

**Q:** I have JSAM users who map to multiple roles and my applications aren't working. What's going on?

**A:** A common problem with this scenario is IP loopback address conflicts. You can work through the issues by ensuring there is no conflict by using different server names and loopbacks on different roles, but this may be confusing if they refer to the same server. A better solution may be to consolidate roles so users map to only a single role with JSAM applications applied.

# Chapter 6

# Terminal Services and Citrix

## Solutions in this chapter:

- **Terminal Services**
- **Citrix**
- **Terminal Services and Citrix Troubleshooting**

☑ **Summary**

☑ **Solutions Fast Track**

☑ **Frequently Asked Questions**

# Introduction

Windows Terminal Services (WTS) and Citrix allow users to access resources and applications on remote computers. They use a technology that provides a connection to an entire desktop or an individual application. They are examples of a type of client/server application commonly called *thin client software* or *server-based computing*.

Classic client/server applications require an independent "fat" client, whereas a thin client needs only a very small client applet to send input (e.g., mouse movements and keystrokes) to the server and receive output (e.g., screen writes) from the server. The original thin clients were graphical terminals (as compared to older text terminals called *green screens*) which began to appear in the mid-1980s with the development of the X protocol at MIT. The personal computer explosion caused graphics terminals to wane in popularity, but they were not abandoned completely. In fact, thin clients are now more popular than ever.

Although there are many benefits to thin client computing, the most commonly cited include:

- **Cost**  The cost of both hardware and administrative support can be much lower in a thin client environment. Because the application resides only on the server, upgrades and support are centralized and potentially easier as a result. In addition, much greater efficiency is possible because computing resources are shared so that systems overall (including both servers and clients together) can cost less.

- **Security**  Providing adequate security for computers in a distributed environment is a huge challenge. With thin clients, all application processing and storage can be done on the server. This centralization makes the problem of enforcing security easier.

- **Bandwidth**  The number of mobile workers is growing fast in many organizations. If these users require bandwidth-intensive applications, a thin client solution may be the only option. It is often impossible to determine exactly how much bandwidth is needed for fat client/server communications. Bandwidth in a thin client environment is deterministic because it is based on which protocol is used, as well as on display settings (e.g., screen resolution and color depth).

- **Platform independence**  Enterprises today support many different kinds of endpoints, from traditional Windows-based computers to nontraditional devices such as mobile phones. A thin client computing model gives IT organizations the ability to allow a variety of devices access to applications that run only on Windows servers.

Most thin clients run as a software application. However, many hardware thin clients (typically with no hard drive and very little memory and other computing resources) are available. Each thin client architecture differs in the way the clients and servers communicate, and this difference is important to understand how the IVE provides connectivity to support them. The most common thin client architectures available include the following:

- Microsoft Terminal Services uses Remote Display Protocol (RDP) over tcp/3389. Originally released with Windows NT 4.0, the software has changed over time to add support for local printers, more colors, sound, and local resource mappings. Windows Vista introduced some important new features, including the ability to access a single application rather than the full desktop. There are clients for almost all versions of Windows and several other operating systems, such as Solaris, Linux, FreeBSD, and Mac OS X.

- Citrix Systems' WinFrame and Presentation Server (aka MetaFrame) uses Independent Computing Architecture (ICA) over tcp/1494 and tcp/2598. At the time of this writing, the Citrix Web site listed 24 client installers for 13 groups of operating systems, ranging from MS-DOS to Vista, and including several flavors of UNIX, Mac, Java, and even mobile phone operating systems. This does not include the array of partner and open source installers available.

- X Window System (called either X11 or simply X) is the old man of thin client computing, as it was first developed by MIT in 1984. It is used most often as the graphics system in UNIX/Linux and OpenVMS server environments and it supports many different types of clients, including software clients (e.g., Reflection X and Exceed) and diskless workstations (which are somewhat confusingly called "thin clients").

- Virtual Network Computing (VNC) uses the Remote FrameBuffer (RFB) protocol to remotely control another computer. VNC is most often deployed as an application for remote technical support of both clients and servers.

# Why Use the Juniper Citrix Terminal Services Proxy?

Several thin client vendors (e.g., Citrix) offer their own solution for providing secure remote access to clients. Why, then, would someone want to use Juniper's solution? The following represents some of the several specific benefits of the IVE:

- For many people, the most important use of the Juniper Citrix Terminal Services (CTS) proxy is to provide secure and consistent remote access to both Citrix and Microsoft Terminal Services clients without regard for the endpoint or the underlying protocol. A common interface for users makes for a more supportable system for network managers.

- The Terminal Services proxy eliminates the need for additional hardware or software to allow remote access to Citrix Presentation Server or Microsoft Terminal Server. Software such as Citrix Secure Gateway or IPSec VPN clients becomes unnecessary.

- Terminal Services, such as Security Account Manager (SAM), integrates with Juniper's Host Checker endpoint posturing. This provides information on the client environment which can be used to customize the user's Citrix/Terminal Services session.

- The IVE provides a host of methods to enable thin client access, including support for a variety of client configurations: Web/no-Web, client/no-client, and so on. This breadth of options increases the chance that network managers can mimic the predeployment environment and reduce user retraining.

- Security is of primary importance to Juniper Terminal Services. The IVE includes excellent AAA (authentication, authorization, and accounting) of thin client sessions, in addition to the same logging and troubleshooting features as SAM.

# Feature Availability

The Terminal Services proxy is a feature that comes with the "Secure Application Manager and Network Connect" (SAMNC) license, which you can purchase from a Juniper reseller. As with other feature licenses you must install the license key under **System | Configuration | Licensing**. SAM and Network Connect used to be separate licenses on the older SA products (1000, 3000, and 5000). With these older products, the Terminal Services proxy was bundled with the SAM license. The current platforms (2000, 4000, and 6000) combine these features into a single license.

The Terminal Services proxy is not available on the Juniper Networks Secure Access 700. That platform is limited to Network Connect and Core Clientless access methods only. To provide thin client access on the 700, you must use Network Connect.

# Chapter Overview

The IVE supports thin client connectivity through Juniper's CTS proxy, JSAM, WSAM, Network Connect, and Hosted Java Applets. The number of choices shouldn't be surprising because it is a reflection of how many client and server configurations are possible. RDP and ICA are the most commonly deployed protocols supporting thin client users in an enterprise environment. As a result, the IVE includes native policies to support these environments and this chapter will focus on them. We will cover both Terminal Services and Citrix access methods.

We will begin with Terminal Services (TS) because the Juniper proxy can be used for both TS and Citrix clients. We will discuss the significant number of TS options, as well as configuring TS directly on a role in addition to Resource Profiles (Juniper's recommended method). We will also cover use of Hosted Java Applets to support both Citrix and TS clients.

We will then cover Citrix with explanations of the various configuration methods and tips on how to choose between them. Using Citrix Web Templates will be the focus here. As with SAM, practical examples will show how the features can be deployed, focusing on an enterprise environment.

Finally, the chapter will cover some of the most common problems with Terminal Services and Citrix, along with how to troubleshoot and solve these issues.

# Terminal Services

In 1998, Windows NT 4.0 Terminal Server Edition (codenamed Hydra) first introduced RDP for thin client computing. Since then, the technology has become much more widely available. On the server, Terminal Services is now included in Windows 2000 Server and Windows Server 2003. In addition, the Remote Assistance and Remote Desktop features of Windows XP use RDP, making it a very common protocol in enterprise networks.

The Juniper Citrix Terminal Services (CTS) proxy, often called Embedded Terminal Services Access, intermediates only RDP and ICA traffic. The proxy is similar to SAM in that it builds a Secure Sockets Layer (SSL) tunnel (not IPSec). The TS/Citrix client is not assigned an internal Internet Protocol (IP) address. The IVE performs many functions, including authentication, access control, and Network Address Translation (NAT), which creates the separation between trusted and untrusted networks that is essential for a secure system.

Version 6.0 of the IVE software has added some important new features related to Citrix and Terminal Services access. These include:

- **Intelligent client delivery and single sign-on (SSO) through CTS** Citrix users can now access published applications without SAM, with the benefit of SSO using domain credentials.

- **CTS support for Citrix Session Reliability and Auto-Client Reconnect** Citrix clients can benefit from the session keepalive and reconnect functionality added to MetaFrame Presentation Server (MPS) 3.0.

- **Granular control of Citrix local resource availability at the role level** Using Host Checker, IVE administrators can now control which resources are available to Citrix users based on the trust level of local endpoints.

- **Terminal Services RDP/JICA fallback** When you are connecting through CTS, the IVE can now attempt to launch several different clients to maximize the chance that a user can access the session, regardless of the configuration of the connecting computer.

- **Support for Windows Terminal Services Session Directory** The Juniper TS client is now aware of the Session Directory. If a session fails, a client reconnection will bypass normal load balancing and reconnect the user to the original server.

- **New end-user experience features** The IVE now supports a universal printer driver through the CTS proxy that eliminates the need to install third-party printer drivers on Terminal Servers. In addition, the IVE supports RDP version 6.0 enhancements including font smoothing, desktop composition, animated windows and menus, and more.

# Terminal Services Implementation

The configuration of the Terminal Services proxy is not difficult. This section will detail the basic procedures of each method. Juniper recommends using Terminal Services Resource Profiles because they ensure that essential elements of the configuration aren't missed. However, it is sometimes necessary to work directly with the policies, so we will cover these too.

## Enabling Terminal Services Proxy and Configuring Role Options

The first task is to enable Terminal Services on the role and configure some basic role settings. We covered user role creation in Chapter 3, so it is assumed that the role already exists.

1.  To enable Terminal Services, navigate to **Users | User Roles**. Select the name of the role to modify.

2.  Check the box next to **Terminal Services**.

3.  Select the **Save Changes** button.

### *Configuring Terminal Services Role Options*

It is important to know which access method will be used to intermediate the thin client traffic (Web, SAM, TS, or Network Connect) to know which options to configure. Refer to the appropriate chapters for coverage of options used with the other access methods. The Terminal Services role options listed here include settings that affect both Terminal Services and Citrix clients only when they connect through the Juniper Citrix Terminal Services proxy.

1.  Navigate to **Users | User Roles |** *Role* **| Terminal Services | Options**.

2.  Select the checkboxes next to the Terminal Services options you want to enable for the role.

The Terminal Services options are listed here in the categories as they appear on the IVE:

- **Citrix client delivery method** Users of the CTS proxy can use the Citrix Web client. This option controls from where the client is retrieved by the user. The options are:

    - **Download from Citrix web site** This option downloads the Web client directly from Citrix, which ensures that users always receive the most recent version. With this option, however, you lose the ability to fully test the new client before it is deployed.

    - **Download from the IVE** This option downloads a client from the IVE. It is important to note that the installer defined here is used for all roles. A new file configured here will automatically deploy to all users who use or need a Web client.

- **Download from a URL** This option allows the installer to be offered from any Web server.

The version number set on two of these options allows the IVE to know when updating the client is necessary. If the version number defined here is greater than the version on the connecting computer, the client is updated.

---

### Tools & Traps...

### Additional Policies Needed for Users to Successfully Download the Citrix Web Client

Downloading the Web client either from Citrix's Web site or from a URL is a little tricky because the IVE tunnels traffic from the client to the download site through the IVE. To make it work, you need two additional policies:

- An access policy must exist that allows users in the role to access the Web site to get the installer.

- A caching policy is needed on the role with the Action set to **Don't Cache (send "Cache Control: No Store")**.

In both cases, the **Resource** is the URL of the installer. The most recent client is available from Citrix at http://download2.citrix.com/FILES/en/products/CPSICAClients Multi/icaweb.cab.

---

### NOTE

Downloading the client from the IVE takes a little less configuration because no other policies are needed. But this means the administrator must upload the installer to the IVE, so keeping a current version is a manual process. However, many Citrix administrators want to control when a new client is made available to users (after rigorous testing, of course).

---

- **User can add sessions** This option enables three features on the IVE:
  - Users can access Terminal Servers through the IVE browse bar, by using the following syntax:

- *ica://<hostname>* for Citrix resources

- *rdp://<hostname>* for Microsoft Terminal Services or Remote Desktop connections

Users can create personal session bookmarks on the IVE home page. Like Web bookmarks, the personal session bookmarks will be available from any computer where the user signs in.

Links to Terminal Services and Citrix sessions through the IVE can be created on external Web sites, with the URL specifying the connection parameters or using session bookmarks. This is an enormously useful feature for developers of external portal sites.

---

**NOTE**

Allowing a user to add sessions does not bypass Terminal Services access control. There must be an access policy that permits the user to access the resource for the connection to succeed.

---

- **Auto-allow role Terminal Services sessions** Rather than creating a unique access policy each time a session bookmark is created to a new host, this option creates a single access policy and automatically allows new session hosts for the role. This involves only role session bookmarks defined on the IVE by an administrator, not user-created session bookmarks.

- **Allow users to enable local resources** These settings control whether user-defined session bookmarks or IVE bookmarks applied to the role can connect a computer's local resources during a terminal session. Local resources include:

  - **Drives** The client's local disk drives display under the **Other** label in My Computer on the server during the session.

  - **Printers** Printer redirection is used to route print jobs from the server to a local client printer. This can be done manually or automatically, depending on the driver that is needed to process the job. The process is automatic when the server has an appropriate driver for the local printer. Consult Microsoft's RDP documentation for details.

  - **COM ports** This performs serial port redirection so that the server can make use of modems and other devices connected to the client's Component Object Model (COM) ports. Use the Windows *change port* command to view the mappings:

    ```
    C:\WINDOWS\system32\dllcache>change port
    AUX =\DosDevices\COM1
    ```

```
COM1 = \Device\RdpDrPort\;COM1:1\tsclient\COM1
COM3 = \Device\RdpDrPort\;COM3:1\tsclient\COM3
LPT1 = \Device\RdpDrPort\;LPT1:1\tsclient\LPT1
PRN = \DosDevices\LPT1
```

- **Clipboard sharing** This feature synchronizes the client clipboard with the server clipboard, allowing a cut operation on the client and a paste on the server (and vice versa). You can use the Windows Clipbook Viewer tool (clipbrd. exe) to view the clipboard contents. Not only are text and graphics supported, but also copy and paste of files and folders.

**NOTE**

You must also configure corresponding session bookmark options to actually make the resources appear during the session.

- **Allow users to modify Display settings** These options determine whether a connecting user can change various display settings during a Terminal Services session. These settings do not apply to Citrix sessions. They include:

  - **Desktop background** The user is allowed to change the desktop background during a session.

  - **Show contents of window while dragging** If this is not selected, windows appear as an outline during a drag. This option can increase the amount of data sent from the server to the client.

  - **Menu and window animation** This enables animation that can increase bandwidth used during the session.

  - **Themes** This allows the user to configure Windows themes.

  - **Bitmap caching** This enables caching of bitmap images to improve performance by reducing the amount of data sent over the network.

  - **Font smoothing** (RDP 6.0 and later) This implements a new feature called ClearType. This technology displays fonts so that they appear clearer and smoother, especially when using an LCD monitor.

  - **Desktop composition** (RDP 6.0 and later) This implements a new feature called Windows Aero that includes features such as translucent windows, taskbar buttons with thumbnail-size window previews, and open windows viewed in a 3D stack on the desktop.

**NOTE**

You must also configure corresponding session bookmark options to actually enable these features during a session.

## Configuring Role Session Options That Affect Terminal Services

As described in Chapter 3, each role has a number of session options that are either inherited from the default options (**Users | User Roles | User Roles**, then select the **Default Options** button), or are set on the role itself. These settings affect all resources associated to the role, not just Terminal Services.

You configure the role options under **Users | User Roles |** *Role* **| General | Session** Options. The **Max Session Length** setting is very important to Terminal Services users. By default, a nonadministrative session can remain active for the number of minutes set in this option. When a session reaches this length, the IVE terminates the session. The **Idle Timeout** and **Reminder Time** values don't work for Terminal Services; these values are only for Web sessions through the Core Clientless Access Service.

When the **Max Session Length** value expires, any open Terminal Services windows show the flashing RDP network connect error warning shown in Figure 6.1, followed by the Terminal Server proxy timeout message shown in Figure 6.2.

**Figure 6.1** RDP Network Connect Error Warning

**Figure 6.2** Terminal Server Proxy Timeout Message

## Configuring a Windows Terminal Services or Citrix Session on a Role

Juniper recommends using Resource Profiles to configure both Terminal Services and Citrix sessions through the Terminal Services proxy. The Resource Profile can be associated with multiple roles—in effect, sharing the definition and making the configuration less complex. A Citrix Resource Profile includes the ability to specify a Java client as either a primary or a backup. This supports Mac and Linux users whereas the role configuration does not.

However, it is sometimes necessary to configure a session directly on a role without using a Resource Profile. In this section, we will cover the configuration of a session on a role. A session created on a role cannot be applied to another role.

1. Navigate to **Users | User Roles |** *Role* **| Terminal Services**. The list includes all the sessions assigned to a role, whether they were created on the role or as part of a Resource Profile. These sessions show up under the **Terminal Services** section of the user's IVE home page in the order in which they appear here. You can modify the order by selecting the checkbox to the left of the session name and choosing either the **Up** or **Down** arrow. Once the list is rearranged, a refresh of the user's IVE home page will reflect the new order. New sessions are always appended to the end of the list, so you may need to reorder the list as sessions are added.

2. Select the **Add Session** button. Leave the **Type** drop-down menu set to **Standard**.

3. Change the **Session Type** drop-down menu to **Windows Terminal Services**, **Citrix using Default ICA**, or **Citrix using Custom ICA**.

4. Adding a **Session Name** and **Description** are both optional.

**TIP**

The only required field on the entire page is the **Host** setting. If no **Session Name** is specified, the hostname or IP address in the **Host** field is used instead, both in the IVE configuration and on the IVE home page. A session name is essentially a bookmark. You can create multiple sessions to the same host with different parameters, using the session name to distinguish between them. For example, you can create two bookmarks—"Host1–Full Screen" and "Host1–800×600"—with the only difference being the Screen Size setting. This allows the user flexibility in choosing the configuration he prefers.

## Configuring Windows Terminal Services or Citrix Using the Default ICA

The remaining steps are nearly identical if you are configuring a Windows Terminal Services client or a Citrix client using the default ICA. In the following section, we will cover using a custom ICA with a Citrix client, beginning from this point.

1. Enter the IP address or hostname of the Microsoft Terminal Server or Citrix MPS in the **Host** field. Only a single host can be specified.

2. The **Client Port** field is optional. The client port almost never needs to be manually configured because the IVE automatically selects an available port. Be careful if you change this because if the IVE or client can't use the port configured as the client port, the session will not work.

3. The **Server Port** is also optional. Microsoft Terminal Server and Remote Desktop listen for connections on tcp/3389 and Citrix listens on tcp/1494. These are the default server ports, but it is possible to change the port on the server. If this is done, the new server port can be configured here.

4. Select the desired **Screen Size** and **Color Depth** using the drop-down menus. RDP version 6.0, which was introduced with Windows Vista and Windows Server "Longhorn," added support for 32-bit color. If you select **32-bit True-Color** in the IVE and the server does not support it, a lower color depth will automatically be used for the session. For Citrix sessions, both this setting and the client's local display settings affect the colors available. The lowest value of the two color settings is used. The default color depth on the IVE is 8-bit.

5. Under **Authentication**, enter an optional **Username** and either a **Variable Password** or a static **Password**. You can use the IVE substitution variables *<user>* and *<password>* in these fields. You can also use the *<password2>* variable if secondary authentication is enabled on the realm and you want to reference the user's password from the secondary authentication server.

6. For Citrix sessions, the **Use Domain Credentials** option enables pass-through authentication, where the user's cached credentials from his connecting computer are sent to the MPS.

## Tools & Traps...

### Using Domain Credentials for Citrix Sessions

Enabling **Use Domain Credentials** requires a bit more configuration to make sure the Program Neighborhood is able to send credentials to the server. The client's settings file (appsrv.ini) must be configured to enable SSO. This file is located in the C:\Documents and Settings\username\Application Data\ICAClient directory. Two settings must be set:

- **EnableSSOnThruICAFile=On**

- **UseLocalUserAndPassword=On**

If these settings are missing or incorrect, the user will be prompted for credentials.

7. The Start Application feature is very useful to automatically launch an application when a session begins. The **Path to application** field should be the absolute path to the application (e.g., C:\WINDOWS\system32\notepad.exe). The **Working directory** field specifies the active directory. Substitution variables are supported in these fields. For example, you can set the working directory to C:\<user>\docs.

8. For Citrix sessions, select **Session Reliability** and **Auto-client reconnect** if the Citrix MPS is configured to support this feature, which is enabled by default on MPS 3.0. When Session Reliability is used, the ICA client sends normal ICA traffic inside the Common Gateway Protocol using tcp/2598. A service on the MPS, called the Citrix XTE, relays the underlying ICA traffic to the Citrix ICA listener using tcp/1494.

9. The **Auto-launch** setting is similar to automatically launching SAM. All sessions with this option selected will automatically connect when a user is mapped to the role. The IVE home page is still displayed to the user.

10. Under **Connect Devices**, select the local resources that should be available to users during the session. The resources that can be accessed include printers, local drives, COM ports, and the Windows clipboard.

11. For Terminal Services sessions, under **Display Settings** choose which settings should be used for this session. Recall that some of these settings control what the

user can change during the session (e.g., Themes, Background, etc.) and others control how the session displays (e.g., Font Smoothing, Menu and Window animation). Refer to the **Allow users to enable local resources** role option for a description of each setting.

12. Select the **Save Changes** button to save the configuration and return to the session list.

## Configuring Citrix Using a Custom ICA

By using a custom ICA, many of the configuration elements will be defined in the file, so the IVE configuration is very simple. The remaining steps are a continuation of the role configuration from the previous section.

1. Select a **Custom ICA File** by using the **Browse** button and locating the file on your computer. This file is copied to the IVE and is downloaded to connecting computers. You can download the default ICA file by selecting the link.

---

**NOTE**

If you choose to edit the default ICA file and create your own custom ICA file, you must keep the Transmission Control Protocol/Internet Protocol (TCP/IP) as the transport driver because the IVE does not support UDP port forwarding. In addition, three parameters must be specified:

- <CITRIX_CLIENT_NAME> can be any value up to 20 characters.

- <APPDATA> specifies the location of the persistent disk cache and should be set to a valid path. The default is C:\Documents and Settings\\*username*\Application Data\ICAClient\Cache.

- <TARGET_SERVER> is the address of the Citrix MPS server. This can be a domain name system (DNS) name or an IP address.

---

Once the custom ICA is specified, refer to the steps in the earlier configuration of Citrix using the default ICA to complete the following:

2. Configure the **Session Name** and **Description** fields.

3. Configure the **Authentication** section by following the directions in steps 5 and 6.

4. Configure the **Auto-launch** setting as in step 9.

5. Select the **Save Changes** button to save the configuration and return to the session list.

# Terminal Services Session Bookmarks

Session bookmarks are very important to the Citrix and Terminal Services configuration. A session bookmark is similar to a Web bookmark in that it launches a Terminal Services session like the Web bookmark launches a URL. However, session bookmarks define not only the target server, but also many other connection parameters. The options available for a session bookmark vary with the type of connection. For example, an RDP session bookmark includes window settings (size and color depth), applications to run, SSO information (the username and password the IVE passes to the server), local resource mapping, and more.

# Configuring Terminal Services Resource Policies

In this section, we'll show you how to configure terminal services resource policies for access control and how to configure terminal services policy options.

## Configuring a Terminal Services Resource Policy for Access Control

All traffic through the Juniper Terminal Services proxy must be permitted by an access policy. These policies can be created automatically during the creation of a Resource Profile or session bookmark. Alternatively, you can create an access policy manually. There are two primary reasons to configure a policy manually:

- The corporate security policy permits a single access policy to support multiple sessions. For example, if all Terminal Servers are located in one subnet, a single access policy allowing tcp/3389 to that subnet may be preferred over individual auto-policies, each supporting a single server.

- Manually configured access policies benefit from the ability to define Detailed Rules, which give the IVE administrator much greater control over what traffic is allowed or denied. Note that Detailed Rules is a feature of the Advanced license. To use this feature, you must install a license key under **System | Configuration | Licensing**.

To create a Terminal Services Resource Policy for access control, follow these steps:

1. Navigate to **Users | Resource Policies | Terminal Services | Access Control**. This list includes all the active access control policies. Recall that access policies are evaluated from the top down, with the first match of a resource determining the action performed. You can reorder the list by selecting the box next to the rule to move and using the **Up** and **Down** arrows to rearrange the list. Select the **New Policy** button to create a new policy.

2. Enter a policy **Name** which is required, and an optional **Description**.

3. Enter a list of **Resources** in the field that includes hostnames and IP addresses covered by the policy.

4. The **Action** button makes the policy an Allow or Deny, or allows the use of Detailed Rules.

5. Select **Save Changes** to complete the rule.

## Configuring Terminal Services Policy Options

You configure the Resource Policy options under **Users | Resource Policies | Terminal Services | Options**. There is only one option to configure: **IP based matching for Hostname based policy resources**. Just like the SAM policy option of the same name, when this option is enabled the IVE looks up the IP addresses for all the hostnames defined in the Terminal Services Resource Policy fields. It maintains a cache of this information. If a Terminal Services user subsequently attempts to refer to a destination by IP address rather than hostname, the IVE consults this cache to determine whether there is a match. If so, the IVE considers the IP address to be a policy match and it can treat the request properly. If this option is not selected and a policy is created using only the server's fully qualified domain name (FQDN), user access attempts directly to the server's IP address will not work.

**IMPORTANT**

This setting does not apply to Resource Policy fields where wildcards are used. However, because wildcards are used much less frequently with Terminal Services policies, this setting is not as critical as it is when using SAM.

# Configuring Terminal Services Resource Profiles

Juniper recommends using Resource Profiles to configure Terminal Services. This is the same recommendation made for both SAM and Core Clientless Access Services. Resource Profiles are easy and produce consistent results, making sure critical elements of the configuration aren't forgotten. In addition, one profile can be associated with several roles, making it an efficient way to share configurations among roles and making the IVE configuration less complex and easier to maintain.

1. Navigate to **Users | Resource Profiles | Terminal Services**. Select the **New Profile** button.

2. In the **Type** drop-down menu, select the type of profile to create: **Windows Terminal Services**, **Citrix using Default ICA**, or **Citrix using Custom ICA**. Complete the steps for the selected profile type and then continue with the steps listed shortly for all profiles.

For Terminal Services and Citrix using the default ICA:

1.  Enter a profile **Name**, which is required, and an optional **Description**.

2.  Enter the IP address or hostname of the Microsoft Terminal Server or Citrix MPS in the **Host** field. Only a single host can be specified.

3.  The **Server Port** is optional. Microsoft Terminal Server and Remote Desktop listen for users on tcp/3389 and Citrix uses tcp/1494. These are the default server ports, but it is possible to change the port on the server. If this is done, the new server port can be configured here.

4.  Check the **Create an access control policy** box to have the IVE automatically create a Terminal Services access policy that allows traffic to the host.

For Citrix using a custom ICA:

1.  Select a **Custom ICA File** by using the **Browse** button and locating the file on your computer. This file is copied to the IVE and is downloaded to connecting computers. You can download the default ICA file by selecting the link. Refer to the **Configuring Citrix using Custom ICA** procedure under the earlier "Configuring a Windows Terminal Services or Citrix Session on a Role" section for more information about modifying the default ICA file.

**NOTE**

The **Host** and **Server Port** fields are not available when using a custom ICA file. You must specify this information in the [Default] section of the ICA file. For example, the field could be:
*Address=MyMPS.mycorp.com:1494*

2.  Check the **Autopolicy: Terminal Services access control** box to create a policy allowing Citrix traffic to your MPS servers. The **Resources** can be entered either as hostnames or in IP/netmask notation. For example, to permit traffic to the example MPS server discussed earlier, the resource list would include MyMPS.mycorp. com:1494. Select the **Add** button to add the resource to the list.

For all profiles:

1.  To use a Java applet as either the primary or backup client for this profile, check the **Enable Java Support** box. Having Java available is helpful if ActiveX is blocked, not functional, or not supported.

2.   In the **Applet to use** drop-down menu, select a Java client or select **Edit List** to upload a new one. See the "Uploading a Hosted Java Applet" sidebar for more information.

3.   Selecting the client automatically fills in the **HTML** field. You need to modify the contents of this field to successfully use the Java client:

   a.   Replace instances of __PLEASE_SPECIFY__ with the filename that contains the applet's compiled applet subclass. Because many Java clients use custom parameters, consult the applet documentation for information on which values to use. For the Citrix client, the value is *com.citrix.JICA*.
   For properJavaRDP, the value is *net.propero.rdp.RdpApplet.class*.

   b.   To reference the server configured in the **Host** field, use the following:

   ```
   <param name="Address" value="<<HOST>>">
   ```

4.   Select whether to use this Java applet as the primary or backup client by selecting one of the two radio buttons. If **Use this Java applet as a fallback mechanism** is selected, the client will be used only if the Windows client fails to launch. If **Always use this Java applet** is selected, the Java client is used exclusively (i.e., the Windows client does not become the backup).

5.   Select **Save and Continue**.

6.   Each Resource Profile is assigned to one or more roles. Assigning a profile to multiple roles is an efficient way to share the configuration between roles, making the configuration less complex. On the **Roles** tab, select the roles that should be assigned this profile and select **Add**. When done, select **Save Changes**.

7.   A bookmark named the same as the profile is automatically created. On the **Bookmark** tab, you can add additional bookmarks if necessary.

## Tools & Traps...

## Uploading a Hosted Java Applet

You can upload a Java client in several areas of the IVE (e.g., while creating a Terminal Services profile, when configuring a Hosted Java Applet, and on the Web Resource Profiles page). Many Java clients are available for download. Two examples of frequently used clients are:

- properJavaRDP, an open source Java RDP client. The software is based on rdesktop, a SourceForge project. properJavaRDP works on Windows, Linux, and Mac computers. See http://properjavardp.sourceforge.net/ for more information. You can download the latest version at http://sourceforge. net/project/showfiles.php?group_id=90078.

- The Citrix Java client is a widely deployed Java ICA client. The client is small, about 517KB, which makes downloading fast. The client requires a Java-compliant Web browser with Java 2 Standard Edition (J2SE), version 1.4.x or 1.5.x. The Microsoft JVM is no longer supported. You can download the latest version from www.citrix.com/English/SS/downloads/details. asp?dID=2755&downloadID=20731&pID=186.

Here is the process to upload the new applet:

1. Download the client installer you want to upload to the IVE.

2. From the **Java Applets** window, select the **New Applet** button.

3. Enter a name in the **Name** field.

4. Use the **Browse** button to select the client from your workstation.

5. Use the **Uncompress jar/cab file** option if your file is compressed.

6. Select **OK** to finish.

# Configuring Terminal Services and Citrix Using a Hosted Java Applet

Hosted Java Applets are custom clients developed by software companies and open source developers. Although Juniper does not support the applets themselves, this feature offers an interesting alternative client. The major benefit of a Java client to Terminal Services and Citrix users is the ability to execute and run the software on non-Windows computers. Any computer that runs a JVM is theoretically able to run a Java TS or Citrix client.

However, as every experienced network engineer knows, there are serious problems with Java version incompatibility. Any organization that plans to use Java needs to consider this issue carefully. The incompatibility problems may not be a concern if the clients will be corporate computers, where the software installations are centrally managed and the configurations are standardized. Any upgrade of either the JVM or the Java client should be rigorously tested prior to deployment.

You need to preinstall Java on the computer for the Java client to run. A JVM is not standard software that comes with Windows, so you cannot assume that the proper environment exists on all connecting computers. You can use the Juniper Host Checker application in these cases to determine whether Java is installed and make sure it is the proper version. If not, Host Checker can help with client remediation by providing links and instructions for users to self-install the software, if they can. Normally, administrative rights are needed to install Java.

In addition, the user must have rights to run Java code, which is not guaranteed, especially on public PCs, kiosks, and other hardened computers. Routers, firewalls, and other network devices (e.g., network intrusion prevention systems) that provide Internet access to client computers must not run filtering software that blocks Java code.

Assuming that all the requirements for Java to work can be met, setup of the Java applet for RDP and ICA is relatively straightforward. Once complete, the Hosted Java Applet bookmark appears under the Web bookmarks on the IVE home page.

1. Navigate to **Users | Resource Policies | Web**. Select the **New Profile** button. In the **Type** drop-down menu, select **Hosted Java Applet**.

2. Enter a policy **Name**, which is required, and an optional **Description**.

3. In the **Applet to use** drop-down menu, select a Java client or select **Edit List** to upload a new one. See the "Uploading a Hosted Java Applet" sidebar for more information.

4. Select the **Autopolicy: Java Access Control** option to create a Java access policy to allow access to the Citrix MPS and Windows Terminal Server. The servers can be entered either as hostnames or in IP/netmask notation, followed by an optional port. Wildcards and substitution variables are supported. For example, the field could include:

```
10.10.24.0/24:3389
<user>.mycorp.com:3389
```

   or:

```
10.10.24.0/24:1494,2598
<user>.mycorp.com: 1494,2598
```

5. Select **Save and Continue** to continue.

6. On the **Roles** tab, select one or more **Available Roles** and choose **Add**. Select **Save Changes** to continue.

7. On the **Bookmark** tab, select **New Bookmark**.

8. Enter a bookmark **Name**, which is required, and an optional **Description**.

9. Select the **Generate HTML** button which populates the **HTML code** field. This field must be modified for the bookmark to work. There are several things to do at a minimum:

   ■ Replace instances of __PLEASE_SPECIFY__ with the filename that contains the applet's compiled Applet subclass. Because many Java clients use custom parameters, consult the applet documentation for information on which values to use. For the Citrix client, the value is *com.citrix.JICA*. For properJavaRDP, the value is *net.propero.rdp.RdpApplet.class*.

■    Within the body of the applet, specify the hostname of the Microsoft Terminal Server or Citrix MPS. For example: *<param name="Address" value="server. mycorp.com">*.

10.    Under **Display Options**, check the **Bookmark opens new window** box if you want the bookmark to launch a new window when invoked. If selected, choose whether to display the toolbar and address bar. You may want to suppress the display of these features on kiosks and other public computers where control of the desktop is required.

11.    Select which roles the bookmark should be associated with. When selecting a subset of roles, the interface is similar to the **Roles** tab.

12.    Select the **Save Changes** button to complete the profile definition.

# Terminal Services User Experience

From the IVE home page, the user selects a bookmark to launch a Terminal Services session. Bookmarks set to auto-launch require no user input—they start automatically when the user is mapped to the role. If the user is familiar with Terminal Services, retraining should be unnecessary because the Juniper proxy is basically transparent. The only significant difference is that a Remote Desktop Connection client doesn't run and the user can't configure per-session options because these are configured on the bookmark.

Table 6.1 shows the key combinations supported through the Juniper Terminal Services proxy.

**Table 6.1** Supported Terminal Server Key Combinations through the IVE

| Key Combination | Description |
| --- | --- |
| **CTRL + ALT + END** | Opens the Windows Security dialog box, which allows users to change their password, log off, and so on. Equivalent to local **CTRL + ALT + DEL**. |
| **ALT + INSERT** | Cycles through active programs. Equivalent to local **ALT + ESC**. |
| **ALT + PAGE UP/DOWN** | Changes focus of the active program. Equivalent to local **ALT + TAB** and **ALT + SHIFT + TAB**. |
| **ALT + HOME** | Shows the Start menu. Equivalent to local **CTRL + ESC**. |
| **ALT + DELETE** | Displays the active window's menu |
| **CTRL + ALT + BREAK** | Switches between windowed and full-screen mode |

If the user is provided with a browse bar on the IVE home page and a Terminal Services access policy permits RDP traffic to the server, he can create a session by entering a URL in the form **rdp://<hostname>**. This simple syntax doesn't allow the user to specify screen size, color depth, or any of the other session options.

If the **User can add sessions** option is selected in the **Role** options, users can create their own Terminal Services bookmarks on the IVE home page.

# Citrix

There is no shortage of ways for an administrator to configure the IVE to support Citrix clients. Citrix is supported through the IVE using the Core Clientless Access Service, JSAM, WSAM, Terminal Services proxy, and Network Connect. The availability of the various access methods makes it likely that organizations can find one that fits well in their environment. However, navigating through the choices can be intimidating.

How do you choose which access method is best for your environment? What are the criteria to use in deciding? Not surprisingly, there is not a simple answer to this. However, there are some good rules of thumb that experienced administrators and consultants use. The selection of which method to use is less about configuration convenience and more about the current environment, and what type of clients and features must be supported.

Here are some typical questions consultants ask as they gather information to make recommendations on the proper deployment model for Citrix connectivity through the IVE. Remember that the recommendations here don't consider many other aspects of the environment that are important to making an informed decision.

Typical questions asked about the current environment:

- Does an existing Citrix installation already use a Web interface (NFuse/WebInterface)?

- Is NFuse used for only a few connections (the Citrix desktop and several published applications), or is NFuse used heavily for many applications?

Discussion:

If the Citrix Web interface is lightly used, the desktop and published applications can become session bookmarks on the IVE home page, eliminating the need for NFuse entirely. In this case, configure the IVE with Terminal Services Resource Profiles. If, however, there are many applications on NFuse or users really like this interface, you can maintain it by configuring the IVE with Citrix Web Templates to access the NFuse server, selecting among the template options based on the features you want.

Here are some typical questions asked about client and feature support:

- Are clients Windows only, or must Mac and Linux clients be supported too?

- What rights do users have on connecting computers?

- Are connecting computers managed by the organization, or are they public computers?

- What client software already exists on the computer?

- What client does the organization wish to use: Web, Java, or Program Neighborhood?

Discussion:

Any configuration method supports Windows clients. Non-Windows computers require a Java interface. The best choice is to use Terminal Services Resource Profiles with a Java client defined.

Most ICA client installations require administrative rights on the connecting computer. Web (ActiveX) and Java client installs depend on the browser security settings and not the rights of the user. Once installed, however, none of the connectivity methods require administrative rights. For public PCs where there is no guarantee that the user has administrator rights, use a Terminal Services Resource Profile (ActiveX) or a Hosted Java Applet. Because of the way the Juniper Terminal Services client is downloaded, ActiveX settings in the browser don't affect the ability to install the Web client, which makes it a good choice for public PCs.

For managed computers, some services (e.g., WSAM and Network Connect) can be preinstalled and the Juniper Installer Service can be used to allow upgrades of preinstalled software without requiring administrative rights. Any method should work fine under these controlled circumstances.

## Tools & Traps…

### A Summary of Citrix Configuration Methods

It is helpful to have in one place a list of all the ways you can configure Citrix, along with the path through the IVE menu system to configure each.
    To configure Citrix as a Terminal Services session on a role:
        **Users | User Roles | Role | Terminal Sessions | Sessions | Add Session**
            Citrix using default ICA
            Citrix using custom ICA
    To configure Citrix NFuse as a JSAM application on a role:
        **Users | User Roles | SAM (Java) | Applications | Add Application**
            Citrix NFuse
    To configure Citrix with a WSAM Resource Profile:
        **Resource Profiles | SAM | Client Applications**
            **WSAM | Citrix**

Continued

```
          To configure Citrix with a Terminal Services Resource Profile:
              Resource Profiles | Terminal Services | New Profile
                  Citrix using default ICA
                  Citrix using custom ICA
          To configure Citrix as a Hosted Java Applet:
              Resource Profiles | Web | New Profile
                  Hosted Java Applet
          To configure Citrix with a Web Template:
              Resource Profiles | Web | New Profile
                  Citrix Web Interface/JICA
                  Java ICA Client with NFuse
                  Java ICA Client without NFuse
                  Non-Java ICA Client with NFuse
                      ICA client connects over CTS client
                      ICA client connects over WSAM
                      ICA client connects over JSAM
```

Table 6.2 lists the various configuration methods and includes some important information to consider when selecting the best method to use. Recall that the Content Intermediation Engine (CIE) is the proxy that the Juniper Core Clientless Access Service uses.

**Table 6.2** Intermediation and Client Support for Each Available Citrix Configuration Method

| Citrix Configuration Method | Intermediation Method | Java Client (Non-Windows Support) | Custom ICA Files |
| --- | --- | --- | --- |
| Terminal Services session configured on a role | CTS | No | Yes |
| NFuse as a JSAM application configured on a role | JSAM | Yes | No |
| WSAM Resource Profile | WSAM | No | No |
| Terminal Services Resource Profile | CTS | Yes, via Java Primary or Fallback | Yes |
| Hosted Java Applet | CIE | Yes | No |
| Web Template, Java ICA with NFuse | CIE | No | No |
| Web Template, Java ICA without NFuse | CIE | No | No |

**Continued**

**Table 6.2 Continued.** Intermediation and Client Support for Each Available Citrix Configuration Method

| Citrix Configuration Method | Intermediation Method | Java Client (Non-Windows Support) | Custom ICA Files |
|---|---|---|---|
| Web Template, non-Java ICA with NFuse using CTS | CTS | No | No |
| Web Template, non-Java ICA with NFuse using WSAM | WSAM | No | No |
| Web Template, non-Java ICA with NFuse using JSAM | JSAM | Yes | No |
| Network Connect | None | N/A | N/A |

# Citrix Client Types

Four Citrix client types work through the IVE: Java applets, the Citrix Program Neighborhood, the Citrix Program Neighborhood Agent, and ActiveX (Web) clients. Regardless of the configuration method, which client software is used follows this order:

1.  The Java client runs if it is configured as the primary client in the IVE config (via Hosted Java Applets or as an option when configuring Citrix as a Terminal Services Resource Profile).

2.  If the Program Neighborhood client exists on the client, it runs.

3.  If the Web client exists, it runs. If not, the IVE attempts to install it via ActiveX.

4.  If the Web install fails, the Java client is run if it is configured as a fallback (Terminal Services Resource Profile only).

Table 6.3 compares the features available to each available client.

**Table 6.3** Feature Availability of Citrix Clients without NFuse

| Citrix Client | SSO | Seamless Windows | App-Based Load Balancing |
|---|---|---|---|
| Java applet | IVE bookmark SSO | Yes | Yes |
| ActiveX (Web) | IVE bookmark or domain credentials SSO | No | No |
| Program Neighborhood | Domain credentials SSO | Yes | Yes |
| Program Neighborhood Agent | No | Yes | Yes |

# Citrix Load Balancing

The IVE supports Citrix load balancing when a Citrix administrator is using a custom ICA file to return the address of a master browser server (which performs the load balancing). The master browser server keeps track of all the servers in the Citrix farm that run a particular published application. In response to an ICA client connection, the master browser sends to the client the IP address of the "least busy" server, which the client then connects to directly.

Because the IVE can also provide ICA files to users, the IVE administrator can implement load balancing in a similar way. By using a custom ICA file (available only with Terminal Services Resource Profiles or configured on a role), the master browser address can be returned instead of the application server.

> **NOTE**
>
> For load balancing to work through the IVE, the response from the master browser must be an IP address, not a hostname. To ensure that this happens, disable the **Enable XML service DNS address resolution** option during setup of the Citrix master browser server.

Although the IVE does not support using NFuse-based load balancing, other appliance-based load balancing solutions that frontend the MetaFrame Presentation Server may work.

# Citrix Single Sign-on

Single sign-on (SSO) is the ability of the IVE to pass credentials to the Citrix server, which eliminates the need for the user to manually enter his username and password. The user is prompted for credentials only if those supplied by the IVE to the Citrix server fail.

There are two places where the credentials sent to the Citrix server can originate: from the client or from the IVE. When the client supplies the credentials, they are always the locally cached Windows domain credentials. When the IVE supplies the credentials, they can be those entered by the user on the Sign-in page, static credentials defined on the session bookmark, or static credentials configured as parameters inside the hosted applet HTML.

Both the Program Neighborhood client and the Juniper CTS Web client support SSO using domain credentials. Using domain credentials for SSO will work only if the connecting computer is a member of the domain and the appsrv.ini file has both **EnableSSOnThruICAFile** and **UseLocalUserAndPassword** set to "on". Refer to the "Using Domain Credentials for Citrix Sessions" sidebar earlier in this chapter.

The Juniper CTS client supports IVE supplied credentials configured on the bookmark. Figure 6.3 is an example of using the credentials entered by the user on the Sign-in page.

**Figure 6.3** Configuring IVE-Supplied Credentials for SSO

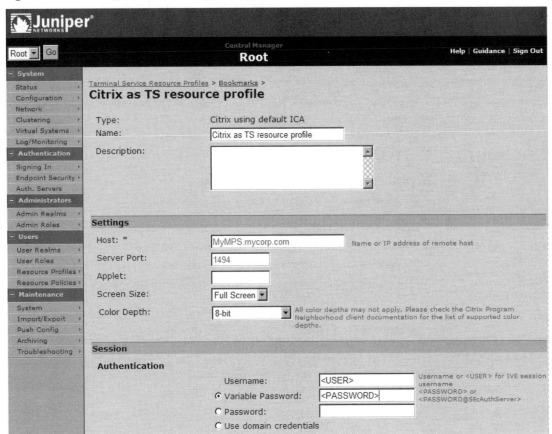

If SSO is used with published applications using a Terminal Services session bookmark, the windows are not "seamless," meaning that the application appears to be running inside a Windows desktop. In contrast, seamless windows make a remote application look like it is running on the local desktop. Even though the application works properly without seamless windows, the appearance of the surrounding desktop can be confusing to users and can make switching between applications running on the local desktop and on the server more difficult.

# Citrix Implementation

Citrix Web Templates provide administrators with an easy way to configure Citrix access through the Juniper Terminal Services proxy and SAM (both JSAM and WSAM). The templates are intended for organizations that have the Citrix Web interface (MPS NFuse) in their environment, or when a Web server is hosting the ICA files. When the IVE sees an ICA file being sent to the user (e.g., in response to a user selecting an ICA bookmark on an NFuse server), the IVE automatically launches the appropriate transport mechanism to enable the access.

Juniper recommends using templates to configure Citrix, rather than configuring the application on a role with supporting Resource Policies. One significant benefit to templates is the ability to use SSO to pass credentials and other information to the Citrix server. The template automatically passes the correct values based on the version of MPS. In addition, because this method can support a Java ICA client, it allows access from Mac and Linux computers without the security concerns surrounding JSAM with custom ICA files.

# Configuring Citrix
# with a Web Template (Resource Profile)

It is important to note that you can assign only one Citrix Web Template to a role at a time. This means that two NFuse servers can't be available simultaneously to a single user. For situations that require two internal NFuse servers (e.g., during a migration), user groups on an authentication server can be used in role mappings to separate connecting users to the correct role. Moving users between groups will then move them from one NFuse environment to another.

1. Navigate to **Users | Resource Profiles | Web** and select the **New Profile** button. Select **Citrix Web Interface/JICA** from the **Type** drop-down menu.

2. A **Name** must be configured and there is an optional field for a **Description**. The **Name** is automatically used as the name of the session bookmark, but it can be changed.

3. In the **Web Interface (NFuse) URL** field enter the complete URL for the MPS NFuse server. This field could also be a Web server that the IVE can use to download Citrix Java applets and .cab files. Because this URL is used to create bookmarks and profiles, the field should contain the fully qualified URL including the prefix (e.g., http://nfuse.mycorp.com).

4. Select the radio button corresponding to type of Citrix installation you have:

   - **Java ICA Client with Web Interface (NFuse)**

   - **Java ICA Client without Web Interface (NFuse)**

   - **Non-Java ICA Client with Web Interface (NFuse)** This option requires that you specify which type of ICA client access to use because the non-Java traffic cannot use the CIE. This setting is completed later.

   - **Non-Java ICA Client without Web Interface (NFuse)** You cannot select this option because it is only supported using SAM Resource Profiles. Follow the link in the IVE to configure a profile. We covered this configuration in Chapter 5 in the "Configuring WSAM Client Applications Resource Profiles" section.

5. In the **Web Interface (NFUSE) version** drop-down menu, select the version of Citrix you are using. This setting is used to automatically configure values sent to the MPS through SSO. Don't forget to update this setting and the corresponding SSO policy when you upgrade your MPS.

6. The **MetaFrame servers** field must include all the servers that the ICA clients will use. You can enter the servers either as hostnames or in IP/netmask notation, and wildcards are supported. After entering the server, select the **Add** button to add the server to the list. Repeat this step to add additional servers. The IVE uses this list to automatically create an access policy for the profile, depending on the type of client used.

7. For Java ICA clients, you have the option to "re-sign" the Java ICA client applet using the IVE's code-signing certificate by selecting the **Sign applets with uploaded code-signing certificate(s)** box. This is sometimes necessary if the applet is signed with a certificate root that your clients do not normally trust. Re-signing the applet will avoid security warnings on the client when the applet is downloaded.

8. For non-Java ICA clients, because only Java clients can use the CIE, you must choose which method the IVE will use to send traffic to the MPS server. This choice is used to create an appropriate access policy to permit the traffic. The options are:

   - **ICA client connects over CTS client** This creates a Terminal Services access control policy.

   - **ICA client connects over WSAM** This creates a WSAM access control policy.

   - **ICA client connects over JSAM** This creates a JSAM access control policy. JSAM also requires that you specify the number of MetaFrame servers and the ports used. This is needed for the IVE to assign the correct number of loopback addresses and ports in the access policy.

---

**NOTE**

Recall that only one SAM Citrix application can be applied to a role, regardless of how it is configured. In other words, if the role is using JSAM, only one JSAM Citrix application is allowed, and if the role is using WSAM, only one WSAM Citrix application is allowed. Make sure your access policy allows access to all the servers the user will need.

---

9.  For non-Java ICA clients, under **Connect Devices**, select which local resources should be available to users through the Citrix session. The resources that can be accessed include printers, local drives, COM ports, and the Windows clipboard.

10. The **Autopolicy: Web Access Control** checkbox is selected by default and a **Resource** has already been added for the NFuse URL defined earlier.

11. To enable SSO so that the user is not prompted for a username/password when connecting, select the **Autopolicy: Single Sign-on** checkbox. The MetaFrame version choice selected previously has configured most of the common labels used with Citrix. You must at least set the user's domain name by clicking on **[Please-fill-this-in]** in the Value column. Remove the existing text and enter the user's domain name. When done, click the **Accept Changes** check button at the end of the row.

    These settings create two SSO policies that you can find in **Users | Resource Profiles | Web | SSO Form POST** and **Users | Resource Profiles | Web | SSO Cookies/Headers**.

12. Select **Save and Continue**.

13. Each Resource Profile is assigned to one or more roles. On the **Roles** tab, select the roles that should be assigned this profile and select **Add**. When done, select **Save Changes**.

The Bookmarks tab allows you to customize the Web bookmark that is automatically created. See Chapter 9 for information on customizing the bookmark.

# Citrix User Experience

Citrix bookmarks may appear on the IVE home page in several places, or not at all, depending on the configuration. Table 6.4 provides a comparison of the configuration methods and when bookmarks are displayed.

**Table 6.4** Availability of Citrix Bookmarks on IVE Home Page by Configuration Method

| Citrix Configuration Method | Bookmark on IVE Home Page? | SAM Required |
| --- | --- | --- |
| Terminal Services session configured on a role | Yes, under Terminal Services | No |
| NFuse as a JSAM application configured on a role | No | JSAM, requires launch |

**Continued**

**Table 6.4 Continued.** Availability of Citrix Bookmarks on IVE Home Page by Configuration Method

| Citrix Configuration Method | Bookmark on IVE Home Page? | SAM Required |
| --- | --- | --- |
| WSAM Resource Profile | No | WSAM, requires launch |
| Terminal Services Resource Profile | Yes, under Terminal Services | No |
| Hosted Java Applet | Yes, under Web Bookmarks | No |
| Web Template, Java ICA with NFuse | Yes, under Web Bookmarks | No |
| Web Template, Java ICA without NFuse | Yes, under Web Bookmarks | No |
| Web Template, non-Java ICA with NFuse using CTS | Yes, under Web Bookmarks | No |
| Web Template, non-Java ICA with NFuse using WSAM | Yes, under Web Bookmarks | WSAM, launches automatically |
| Web Template, non-Java ICA with NFuse using JSAM | Yes, under Web Bookmarks | JSAM, launches automatically |
| Network Connect | No, requires NC launch | No |

# Launching Terminal Services Sessions and Java Applets from an External Site

Both Terminal Services sessions (including Citrix sessions using CTS) and Hosted Java Applets are able to launch directly from a URL placed on an external Web site. This feature is very useful to developers of external Web portals where use of the IVE home page is not desired. It allows authenticated access (users are still prompted for login credentials) via the IVE without the look and feel of the IVE.

Administrators can create URLs that include all the session parameters, or reference a predefined IVE bookmark. If you are using custom sign-in pages, there are caveats for using external links to sessions.

## Terminal Services Syntax

To provide all the session details manually, create a Terminal Services session using the following syntax:

```
https://<IVE_hostname>/dana/term/winlaunchterm.cgi?<param1>=<value1>&<param2>=<value2>
```

To link directly to a Terminal Services or Hosted Java Applet bookmark, use the following syntax:

```
https://<IVE_hostname>/dana/term/winlaunchterm.cgi?bmname=<bookmarkName>
```

Table 6.5 shows several of the most useful parameters. These parameters are not case-sensitive.

**Table 6.5** Parameters for Creating URLs to Terminal Services Sessions

| Parameter | Description |
| --- | --- |
| Host | Required. This is the hostname or IP address of the Windows Terminal Server or Citrix MPS. |
| Type | Type of connection, either Windows or Citrix |
| serverPort | Port on which the server listens. Defaults are 3389 for Windows TS and 1494 for Citrix. |
| User | Username, either literal (e.g., Dave) or variable (e.g., <user> or <username>) |
| Password | Password, either literal (e.g., MyPass) or variable (e.g., <password>) |

Here are some examples:

```
https://myive.mycorp.com/dana/term/winlaunchterm.cgi?host=10.1.2.1&type=Citrix
```

```
https://myive.mycorp.com/dana/term/winlaunchterm.cgi?host=ts1.mycorp.com&type=
Windows&user=Dave
```

```
https://myive.mycorp.com/dana/term/winlaunchterm.cgi?host=ts2.mycorp.com&type=
Windows&user=<username>&password=<password>
```

# Terminal Services and Citrix Troubleshooting

Successful troubleshooting requires a combination of tools and a logical approach to the problem. The IVE and client operating system provide several important tools, especially the IVE and client logs which we will discuss here.

> **NOTE**
>
> A single time source on the network that synchronizes the clocks on clients, servers, and network devices makes log analysis much easier. Consistent time can provide vital information about the order of a failure when reviewing multiple logs. The Network Time Protocol (NTP) and Simple Network Time Protocol (SNTP) are good choices for time synchronization.

# IVE-Side Troubleshooting

As described in the preceding chapter, User Access logs are a challenge on the IVE. The amount and quality of information is excellent, but the logs are large and access can be very slow on a busy IVE. Use custom queries to focus log output and consider policy tracing as an alternative to log access.

## IVE Logs

As always, the first step is to enable logging. Navigate to **System | Log/Monitoring | User Access | Settings**. Under **Select Events to Log**, ensure that the **Secure Terminal** box is checked. The **Web Requests** event must be logged to troubleshoot Terminal Services access through the Web proxy (CIE)—like a Hosted Java Applet. You can find the log from here by selecting the **Log** link on the menu, or by navigating to **System | Log/ Monitoring | User Access | Log**.

### *Example 1*

You are trying to get a new open source Java client to work and things aren't going well. You have configured the Web profile and the bookmark appears on the IVE home page, but selecting it only results in a new browser window with a small Java X in the upper left-hand corner.

After trying the client, you access the IVE User Access log to see whether you can see the problem:

```
Info WEB24302 2007-06-12 22:35:00 - ive - [2.9.1.2] Root::user(TS/Citrix)[TS/
Citrix Example] - Applet file '/dana-cached/webapplets/vc0/rewritten/applet_3/test.
class' is not found.
Info WEB24302 2007-06-12 22:34:59 - ive - [2.9.1.2] Root::user(TS/Citrix)[TS/
Citrix Example] - Applet file '/dana-cached/webapplets/vc0/rewritten/applet_3/test.
class' is not found.
Info WEB23656 2007-06-12 22:34:59 - ive - [2.9.1.2] Root::user(TS/Citrix)[TS/
Citrix Example] - User 'user' is accessing applet file: '/dana-cached/webapplets/
vc0/rewritten/applet_3/log4j-java1.1.jar'.
```

```
Info AUT22670 2007-06-12 22:34:15 - ive - [2.9.1.2] Root::user(TS/Citrix)[TS/
Citrix Example] - Login succeeded for user/TS/Citrix from 2.9.1.2.
```

The log shows that the user is launching the Java applet, but notice that an applet file seems to be missing. You recall being confused about how to configure the HTML in the bookmark creation of the Hosted Java Applet for Terminal Services. To get through the config, you replaced the __PLEASE_SPECIFY__ with *test* just so that you could save the bookmark. It wasn't clear from the IVE what the value was supposed to be. You now know that the value is the filename that contains the applet's compiled Applet subclass. So, you consult the Web site where you downloaded the client and find the filename you need.

Going back to the bookmark in the Web Resource Profile, you reselect **Generate HTML**, which resets the code back to the default. You replace the text with the correct filename and retest. Users can now access the TS session using the Java client.

## Policy Trace of Terminal Services Policies

Policy tracing gives an IVE administrator the ability to focus an investigation on the policies applied to a single user, as the user connects and accesses resources. This can be a very powerful tool during setup (e.g., to verify resource usage of an application) and for troubleshooting.

To use the tool, navigate to **Maintenance | Troubleshooting | User Sessions | Policy Tracing**. Enter the username and realm to which the user will connect. Under **Events to Log**, select **Terminal Services Policies**. You may also want to enable **Web Policies** and **SAM Policies**, depending on the client type you are troubleshooting. The drawback to the policy trace utility is the quantity of information it returns. Finding a policy failure can be difficult if there are a huge number of trace entries. It is a good idea to enable logging for only those policies you need to review. However, be prepared to expand your tracing if you fail to find the problem.

Once you have the user ready to test, select the **Start Recording** button. The user then duplicates the issue. Then select **Stop Recording** and the **View Log** button to see the trace.

# Client-Side Troubleshooting

Even though TS and Citrix client logs can be an invaluable tool in troubleshooting access issues, don't overlook the operating system event logs.

## Terminal Services Client Logs

The IVE administrator must enable logging first or the client logs do not exist. You enable and disable client logging on the IVE in **System | Log/Monitoring | Client Logs | Settings**. Under **Enable client-side logging for the following features:** ensure that the **Terminal Services** box is checked. On the client, the Terminal Services logs reside in the C:\Documents and Settings\ <username>\Application Data\Juniper Networks\Juniper Terminal Services client directory.

The log file in this directory is dsTermServ.log. Users can upload logs to the IVE that administrators can then download and review.

Terminal Services client logs aren't easy to use. A file from a busy client will include hundreds or thousands of entries, most completely meaningless. Every IO event is logged, showing the read and write of bytes sent to and from the server. This consumes much of a file from a working client. Source and destination ports are shown in the log, which is useful for checking for possible filtering devices on the network (e.g., routers, firewalls, etc.).

A good idea for evaluating any client log is to get a good file searching tool such as FIND or GREP, which can be very helpful in limiting the output. Use redirection commands to send output of these commands to a new file. On a Windows operating system, the > and >> symbols send output from a command to a file. The "pipe" character (|) allows redirection to other commands. For example, this command sends all lines in the Terminal Services log that contain the string *fail* to another find command which prints all lines that contain the string *10.1.1.1*:

```
Find "fail" dsTermServ.log | find "10.1.1.1"
```

## Example 2

Ever since you configured Terminal Services, one group of users has been complaining that they lose connection to the server after a short time. You know the users who complain map to the same role. Because it always happens to these users, you suspect a timeout issue but don't know for sure. You are away from your desk and can't access the IVE log, so you take a seat at an affected user's computer and access dsTermServ.log.

Toward the end of the file, you see the following log entries:

```
2007/06/12 17:01:09.343 dsTermServ: t1488 "DebugId" 'worker' [Debug] worker:
Closing conn 003AF540 due to session timeout
2007/06/12 17:03:39.703 dsTermServ: t1488 "DebugId" 'worker' [Debug] worker: Got a
redirect, probably due to session timeout
```

This confirms your suspicion and you let the user know the problem will be fixed within minutes of you returning to your desk. A change to the **Max Session Length** setting on the role solves the problem.

## Citrix Client Logs

Citrix access isn't an access method like SAM and Terminal Services. Citrix clients use Juniper's Web proxy, SAM, and Terminal Services proxy to connect. So, whatever IVE feature the client uses to connect must be enabled for logging.

You enable and disable client logging on the IVE in **System | Log/Monitoring | Client Logs | Settings**. Select one or more of the following depending on how the clients connect:

■    Windows Secure Application Manager

■    Java Secure Application Manager and Applet Rewriting

■    Terminal Services

When you enable logging for Terminal Services, the Citrix client adds log files to the following location: C:\Documents and Settings\<USERNAME>\Application Data\Juniper Networks\Juniper Citrix Services Client.

The log file in this directory is dsCitrixServ.log. Like the Terminal Services log, this file is filled with debug information, so it isn't easy to use.

# Summary

The IVE provides many ways to support secure remote thin client access, and choosing between them based on needed features can be difficult. This chapter provided the context needed to understand the issues involved, along with guidance on making the decision. The Terminal Services proxy, which comes bundled with the SAMNC license, performs intermediation of ICA and RDP traffic to Windows Terminal Servers and Citrix MPS.

Both Terminal Services and Citrix client software can be automatically downloaded to connecting users. This chapter described which client is used and the features supported with each client. Hosted Java Applets allow administrators to deploy custom client software supporting non-Windows computers. The chapter also covered the configuration of these applets and the common problems with Java.

Citrix can be configured on the IVE to work through the Web proxy, SAM, TS, and Network Connect. This chapter focused on using Citrix Web Templates, the Juniper recommended method of configuring Citrix when NFuse is used or when a Web server is hosting ICA files. The chapter also described ways to access both Citrix and Terminal Services sessions using a bookmark on an external site, which allows portal developers great flexibility.

# Solutions Fast Track

## Terminal Services

- ☑ Version 6.0 of the IVE software has added some important new features related to Citrix and Terminal Services access.

- ☑ Terminal Services access control policies limit access from thin clients to only the destination servers and ports that are necessary. Integration with the Host Checker application allows detailed rules to be created, giving very granular control of access policy.

- ☑ Terminal Services bookmarks control the thin client session look and feel, and give the administrator fine control over what users see and do during a session.

## Citrix

- ☑ Citrix Web Templates provide an easy and consistent method of configuring ICA client access to Citrix servers, supporting both ActiveX and Java connectivity.

- ☑ The IVE ability to use Hosted Java Applets enables administrators to deploy custom thin client software provided by independent software vendors and open source developers.

# Terminal Services and Citrix Troubleshooting

☑ Extensive IVE and client logs provide abundant information for troubleshooting access issues through the Juniper Citrix Terminal Services proxy.

☑ IVE administrators use policy tracing to create a verbose log of all policies applied to a user and the policy results, as the user logs in and accesses resources.

# Frequently Asked Questions

**Q:** I'm unable to get the Hosted Java Applet parameters shown in the book to work in my environment. What's wrong?

**A:** Many Java applets use their own special parameters. Consult with the developer of the applet to determine the syntax for parameters such as hostname and window size.

**Q:** I am allowing smart card redirection on my Microsoft Terminal Server, but Juniper clients aren't able to use this feature. What's wrong?

**A:** Some of the recently added redirection features of Microsoft Terminal Server aren't supported through the Juniper Terminal Services proxy. Specifically, redirection of audio, smart cards, and time zones doesn't work.

**Q:** I'm trying to troubleshoot a user's Citrix connection, but I can't find log entries on the client or IVE that shows an issue.

**A:** Keep in mind that the problem may not be related to the IVE. For example, if a user tries to create a Citrix session with an account that has not been granted the "Allow log on through Terminal Services" right the connection will fail, but not because of an issue with the IVE. Don't expect to see these failures in the logs.

**Q:** I've configured my Citrix session to **Use Domain Credentials**. But my Citrix users are still prompted for a username/password. What's wrong?

**A:** There are two things to check. First, make sure the appsrv.ini file is configured for SSO as described in the "Using Domain Credentials for Citrix Sessions" section. Second, make sure the connecting computer is a member of the domain. Both of these cause the unwanted prompt.

# Chapter 7

# Network Connect

## Solutions in this chapter:

- **Network Connect**
- **Network Connect Troubleshooting**

☑ **Summary**

☑ **Solutions Fast Track**

☑ **Frequently Asked Questions**

# Introduction

Until recently, companies that wanted to provide remote access to the corporate network used an IPSec VPN concentrator. Connecting computers ran VPN client software to establish an encrypted tunnel to the concentrator. This worked well for many years (IPSec was first standardized in 1995 in RFC 1825) and IPSec proved to be a good way to create both site-to-site and remote access virtual private networks (VPNs).

As time passed, however, the traditional IPSec VPN became more difficult to deploy and maintain. Remote workers and corporate IT managers faced a rising tide of problems with IPSec, including:

- New types of endpoints began to emerge. Since the IPSec VPN required client software, each new device required a new client. Modern remote workers need the flexibility to build VPNs from any endpoint, including pocket PCs and mobile phones.

- As Internet broadband popularity ballooned, so did the security requirements needed to keep the network safe. Firewalls (blocking ports and performing address translation) and other network access devices (such as proxy servers) posed serious challenges to building a successful VPN, frustrating both remote workers and IT support personnel.

- VPN access is no longer considered "nice to have." Years ago in many organizations, only a few traveling workers were allowed remote access and their expectations were low because VPN was compared to dial-up access. This has completely changed. In a growing number of organizations, nearly everyone has VPN access and it is now considered critically important.

- The difficulty of deploying and maintaining client software has risen with the number of remote workers. Manually updating a few dozen computers was acceptable if a new version of concentrator software was needed to fix newly-discovered security vulnerabilities. With today's mobile workforce, large organizations can't possibly rely on manual updates. Even corporate software management applications don't work well for remote workers, since most require VPN connectivity before an update can be done.

- One of the well-known limitations of IPSec is a lack of support for multicast traffic. Many new multimedia applications won't work over traditional IPSec VPNs. As these applications move from peripheral to business critical, the need for multicast support becomes essential.

As these and other problems became more and more difficult to get around, corporations began looking to SSL, or in Juniper's case a hybrid IPSec/SSL solution. Network Connect is the IVE client most commonly compared to a traditional IPSec VPN. This software builds either an IPSec or SSL encrypted tunnel to provide connectivity between client and IVE.

# Why Use Network Connect?

When a company decides to move away from an IPSec client VPN, they typically want a full encrypted IP tunnel—because that's the only option they had with their old hardware. Other chapters in this book show how the Juniper IVE can be used to provide as little to as much access as is needed using Core Clientless Access Service, Secure Application Manager, or the Citrix Terminal Services (CTS) proxy.

When full IP connectivity is required, Juniper's Network Connect is the right choice. This software solves many of the most difficult problems faced with providing remote connectivity over IPSec. To be specific:

■ Network Connect clients exist for Windows, Mac OS X, and Linux. In version 6.0 of the IVE software, a new client is available for 64-bit Windows. The software can be automatically installed the first time a user attempts to log on and automatically updated each time the IVE software is updated—essentially eliminating the need for a corporate software distribution system to maintain the client. Some companies choose to preinstall the client so the user doesn't have to download and install the client. The Juniper Installer Service is helpful when the user has limited privileges on the computer.

■ The Network Connect software first tries to build a tunnel with IPSec (which is faster) and automatically switches to SSL if IPSec doesn't succeed. This ensures the connecting user has the best chance to successfully create the tunnel. Of course, there will still be places where both IPSec and SSL are blocked, but these are rare compared to how often a traditional IPSec client was blocked.

■ Access control is clearly one of the most powerful features of the Juniper IVE. With Network Connect, users can be limited at both Layer 3 (hostname or IP address/ subnet, with wildcards) and Layer 4 (ports/protocols). In addition, tight integration with Juniper's Host Checker software allows access to be limited based on the posture of the connecting computer. Access control on many popular IPSec concentrators was notoriously difficult to configure, so it was rarely implemented. Many organizations controlled access using a firewall placed between the concentrator and the internal network. This is still possible, but no longer essential.

■ Unlike traditional IPSec VPNs, Network Connect multicast mode supports streams up to 2 Mbps over a tunnel. The IVE functions as an Internet Group Management Protocol (IGMP) version 3 proxy—issuing multicast joins and leaves for the Network Connect client.

# Feature Availability

Network Connect is a feature that comes with the "Secure Application Manager and Network Connect" license (SAMNC), which can be purchased from a Juniper reseller. As with other feature licenses, the license key must be installed under **System | Configuration | Licensing**. SAM and Network Connect used to be separate licenses on the older SA products (1000, 3000, 5000). The current platforms (2000, 4000, 6000) combine these features into a single license.

Network Connect is also available on the Juniper Networks Secure Access 700. That platform is limited to Network Connect and Core Clientless access methods only.

# Chapter Overview

This chapter will cover the configuration and troubleshooting of Network Connect, along with the various options to customize and control the user's environment. We'll start with a description of the newest features of Network Connect from version 6.0 of the IVE software.

The configuration sections will begin with several global settings needed for Network Connect. The importance of these settings in various configuration scenarios will be explained. Then, how Network Connect is configured on a role is described. This section will include a list of the possible configuration options and how each is used.

We'll also cover several "special case" options—including Graphical Identification and Authentication (GINA), multicast, the command line launcher, and running Network Connect in the various IVE clustering scenarios. Finally, the troubleshooting section will describe some of the common problems you are likely to encounter with Network Connect, how to recognize the problems both on the IVE and client, and how to resolve them.

# Network Connect

The really impressive thing about Network Connect is that it is able to morph into an IPSec VPN endpoint or an SSL VPN endpoint, without requiring any interaction from the user. This is significant not because of the underlying technical details, but because of the flexibility gained to allow administrators to select the appropriate method to suit a specific deployment scenario.

IPSec operates at the network layer of the OSI Reference Model, which allows it to achieve better performance than SSL. However, it is more susceptible to being blocked by a firewall. SSL operates at the application layer using HTTPS which is available in all standard web browsers. SSL is a little slower, but is nearly ubiquitous. Both IPSec and SSL make the remote user appear to be part of the extended network by assigning an internal IP address.

Version 6.0 of the IVE software has added some important new features to Network Connect. These include:

- An enhanced split tunneling option that allows users to access local resources (including printers, servers, and more) while connected to the corporate network. Because most networks these days use "internal" addressing (based on RFC 1918), address overlap between the corporate network and the user's network can be a common problem.

- A new 64-bit Windows client is available for users who need the increased processing power of this advanced operating system. High-end applications for design, drafting, and even gaming are being released. While not common yet on corporate networks, these computers are connecting more often remotely because more users are moving to 64-bit hardware at home as the need to break the 4 GB memory barrier becomes important. The new client is not a true 64-bit client—it is a 32-bit application that has been "ported" to run on a 64-bit computer.

- The Network Connect Command Line Launcher now supports certificate authentication, which makes PKI capabilities available across all access methods. Even though this is not a common method of creating a Network Connect session, the launcher is invaluable when a VPN must be built in a script.

Many veteran IVE administrators have used the Network Connect packet logging feature for troubleshooting in previous versions of IVE software. Version 6.0 has removed this feature because of the negative impact it had on performance. However, TCP Dump can still be used to log packets. See the Troubleshooting section of Chapter 10 for more information on this utility.

# Network Connect Implementation

Network Connect is probably the easiest access method on the IVE to configure. This section will detail the basic configuration procedures and give advice about how to use the options to support various deployment scenarios.

## Network Connect Global Configuration

There are two global settings which affect all roles that have the Network Connect feature enabled. Except when configuring active/active multi-site clustering, these options should not be changed.

1. Navigate to **System | Network | Network Connect**. The **IP Address Filter** is set by default as*, the wildcard that matches all IP addresses. For a stand-alone and active/passive cluster, this value does not need to be changed. This value is important for an active/active multisite cluster. The filter is used to define which IP addresses are assigned by Network Connect from the IP address pool. If this doesn't make sense, don't worry because the filter will be described later in the **Configuring Network Connect with IVE Clustering** section.

2. The Network Connect Server IP Address is set by default to 10.200.200.200. This should not be changed unless it is requested by Juniper Technical Support. The address is used by the Network Connect process to communicate internally to the IVE—roughly analogous to a loopback address. It does not need to be routable in your environment and you will never see traffic going to or coming from this address. There are only two rules that govern how this address is selected:

- The address must be the same on all IVEs in a cluster.

- The address must not be part of any IP address pool or DHCP scope used by Network Connect users.

# Enabling Network Connect and Configuring Role Options

The first task is to enable Network Connect on the role and configure some basic role settings. The creation of user roles was already covered in Chapter 3 (Realms, Roles, and Resources), so it is assumed that the role already exists.

1. To enable Network Connect, navigate to **Users | User Roles**. Select the name of the role to modify.

2. Check the box next to **Network Connect**.

3. Select the **Save Changes** button.

## *Configuring Network Connect Role Options*

Role options are settings that affect Network Connect users who are mapped to the role after authentication. If a user is mapped to more than one role which has Network Connect enabled, only the options on the first role mapped affect the user's session.

1. Select the **Options** link next to the **Network Connect** row or select the **Network Connect** tab, then the **Options** menu item.

2. Select the radio buttons and check boxes next to the Network Connect options you want to enable for the role as discussed in this section.

The Network Connect options are listed here in the categories as they appear on the IVE.

**Split Tunneling Modes** Establishing a split tunnel gives the administrator control over what traffic the client sends through the tunnel. If split tunneling is enabled, a list of routes (defined in a Network Connect Resource Policy described later) is downloaded to the client. Only traffic destined to those networks is tunneled and all other traffic is sent unencrypted out the computer's network interface. In addition, the split tunnel configuration allows the administrator to decide whether or not to permit the client to access local resources (such as printers and local servers) while they are using Network Connect.

There are five options. The names don't make it easy to decipher how each method operates, so a description of each is provided:

- **Disable Split Tunneling**  All traffic is sent through the tunnel regardless of the destination. All traffic, whether or not it is destined for the corporate network, is encrypted and tunneled. This is often configured to increase security by eliminating the possibility that the client can be attacked from the Internet during a Network Connect session, as well as serve as a bridge to the corporate network. This mode centralizes processing of Internet traffic which can be useful for accounting, filtering, and more. The drawback to this mode is that additional processing is required on both the client and IVE (because all traffic is encrypted) and latency increases because Internet traffic is not following the most efficient path. This may become a problem for users connecting to an IVE over low speed or high latency links (for example, international circuits). As a security feature, this option also monitors the client's route table. If there are any changes to the routes on the client machine while Network Connect is running, the session is terminated.

**NOTE**

With Vista's strong host model enabled, local area network traffic won't go through the Network Connect tunnel even if split tunneling is disabled.

- **Allow access to local subnet**  This option allows users to access their local subnet (based on the IP address and netmask of the client's network interface). However, all other traffic is sent through the tunnel. Split tunneling is still disabled, but an exception is made for local traffic. If there is an IP address overlap between the client's network and the corporate network, connectivity problems will occur. The Network Connect Split Tunneling Policies are not used.

- **Enable Split Tunneling**  In this mode, the split tunnel list is downloaded to the client. Traffic to destinations in the list is tunneled, while other traffic is sent unencrypted out the client's network interface. This is done by preserving the routing to the user's internal network and adding the split tunnel list to the client's route table with a default gateway as the Network Connect interface. If there is an IP address overlap between the two networks, connectivity problems will occur.

- **Enable Split Tunneling with route change monitor** This is similar to the previous option, except that any change to the local route table during the Network Connect session causes the session to be terminated. This is typically deployed as a security precaution.

- **Enable Split Tunneling with allowed access to local subnet** New in version 6.0, this mode downloads the split tunnel list to the client, allows traffic outside the list to be sent directly by the client, and allows the client to access local resources.

**Auto-Launch Network Connect** More often than other features of the IVE, Network Connect is used by itself as a one-to-one replacement for a traditional IPSec VPN client. Used in this way, administrators want to emulate the look-and-feel of the previous client to help minimize the retraining necessary for users. This option automatically launches Network Connect when the user is mapped to the role after authentication. If this option is not selected, the user is required to manually launch Network Connect off the IVE homepage.

**Auto-Uninstall Network Connect** Like a similar SAM option, this feature will uninstall Network Connect when a user disconnects. While this may be desired in some cases (for example, when the client will never connect again), it is normally preferred to maintain the client on the connecting computer. Enabling this option will cause the client to download and install each time Network Connect is launched. Juniper recommends against enabling this option when GINA is used.

**Enable ToS Bits Copy** The IP header contains a field called *ToS* (Type of Service) which was defined as early as 1981 in RFC 791, originally including two parts: an IP Precedence often used for queuing, and ToS, which reflects the packet's need for delay, reliability, throughput, and cost. This field was later reused by IETF as the *Differentiated Services* (DiffServ) field, containing codepoints (DSCP) to affect how the packet should be queued throughout the network. This field is often set by applications like voice over IP (VoIP) softphones that require priority handling to minimize latency and jitter.

With a VPN, the entire packet (including the IP header with the ToS field) is encrypted—which essentially hides the ToS markings from network devices that are processing the encrypted packet. The **Enable TOS Bits Copy** option copies the field from the cleartext IP header into the encrypted IP header, so the packet can be handled properly even though it is encrypted.

**NOTE**

This option is not supported on 64-bit Vista clients.

Enabling this option may require that Windows users of Network Connect reboot when the client is initially installed.

Enabling this option requires that you disable the **Replay Protection** option described in the **Creating Network Connect Connection Profiles** section. Also, see the sidebar titled "How ToS Affects Replay Protection" later in this chapter for more information.

**Multicast**  Many multimedia applications like video conferencing use IP multicast traffic to make more efficient use of bandwidth. This option causes the IVE to act as a multicast proxy, which allows multicast applications to work over a Network Connect tunnel. When a user requests to join a multicast group, the IVE sends an IGMP join message to the network. The IVE keeps track of which clients are in which multicast groups, and responds to IGMP polls on behalf of the client. Note: With Network Connect multicast support enabled, if the IVE is connected to a Layer 2 (not routing) switch, the switch must support IGMP v3.

**Install GINA with Network Connect**  GINA (Graphical Identification and Authentication) is a DLL that is loaded with the *Winlogon* process and handles user interaction before Windows logon (for example, reacting to **Control + Alt + Delete**) and launches the Windows Shell. A Network Connect session can be started during Windows logon using this option. See the *Using GINA with Network Connect* section later in this chapter for more information.

If selected, the IVE administrator can also choose whether or not to require Network Connect to start when the user logs in to Windows. Select the radio button next to the desired option:

- **Require NC to start when logging into Windows**  Network Connect is automatically launched every time a Windows user logs on.

- **Allow user to decide whether to start NC when logging into Windows**  This option gives the user control over whether or not to launch Network Connect at each Windows startup.

**Session Scripts**  Network Connect supports session start and end scripts for Windows, Linux, and Mac clients. Specify the fully-qualified path to the script in the appropriate **Session start script** field. After Network Connect launches, both scripts are copied to the client from this location. Scripts can be local to the client, or accessed remotely from network storage (such as a file share).

The Network Connect client keeps a local copy of the end script after the session starts to ensure that the script can run successfully if the connection were to fail.

## Tools & Traps...

### Running Scripts on Windows Network Connect Clients

There are several important things to know when configuring scripts to work with Windows clients.

- As previously stated, the scripts can either be local or accessed remotely from a file share. Using a file share eliminates the need to keep a local version of the script up-to-date. However, for Windows scripts to copy properly, the connecting computer must be a member of the same domain as the source of the script, and the user's credentials must have the rights necessary to access the script.

- Keep in mind what auxiliary files and applications are called by scripts running on the client. If files are large, it can be a good idea to keep a local copy of the file to avoid having to download it to the client. For example, to run a KiXtart script on a Windows client, it may be wise to keep a copy of the Kix interpreter (Kix32.exe) locally on the client. This allows the script to run more quickly since the executable doesn't need to be accessed over a potentially low-speed Internet connection.

- Network Connect will only run scripts with BAT, CMD, or EXE extensions. Other types of scripts (such as a Visual Basic script with a VBS extension) must be launched from a batch file.

- Select the **Skip if GINA Enabled** option to ignore the Windows session start script if GINA is used. This is most often needed to avoid having the same script execute twice, which would happen if the normal Windows log-on script is identical to the session start script.

## Configuring Role Session Options that Affect Network Connect

As described in Chapter 3 (Realms, Roles, and Resources), each role has a number of session options that are either inherited from the Default Options (**Users | User Roles | User Roles**, then select the **Default Options…** button), or are configured on the role itself. These settings affect all resources associated to the role, not just a single feature like Network Connect.

The role options are configured under **Users | User Roles | Role | General | Session Options**. The *Max Session Length* setting is very important to Network Connect users.

By default, a non-administrative session can remain active for the number of minutes set in this option. When a session reaches this length, it is terminated by the IVE. The *Idle Timeout* and *Reminder Time* values don't work for Network Connect—these values are only for Web sessions through the Core Clientless Access Service.

When Network Connect is running, Windows users will see a taskbar icon that looks like this: ▨ The small circles above the icon are green when traffic is being sent and received.

When the *Max Session Length* timer expires, three things display to the user:

1. The Network Connect task bar icon turns light gray: ▨

2. Windows may display a warning bubble near the taskbar saying the connection has been unplugged:

> ⓘ **Local Area Connection**  ✕
> A network cable is unplugged.

3. The *session timed out* error window appears as shown in Figure 7.1.

**Figure 7.1** Network Connect Session Timed Out Notification

## Configuring Other Role Options that Affect Network Connect

Network Connect doesn't require other IVE functions because the "full tunnel" makes the proxy of application traffic unnecessary. Even so, in all cases the IVE launches some type of Start page. By default, the start page is the IVE homepage that shows *Welcome to the Secure Access SSL VPN* or whatever welcome message the IVE administrator defines. Or, a custom page can be referenced as the start page. This can be good or bad, depending on your situation.

Launching a start page after Network Connect loads is a good thing if the IVE administrator wants to provide users with an application portal. The IVE homepage can be easily populated with the most useful applications and can be customized based on who the user is (by username or group membership) or through integration with Host Checker (by installed applications).

If, on the other hand, the IVE administrator wants as little interaction as possible with the user, a start page is a nuisance. If you are trying to emulate as closely as possible what the user experiences when they are directly connected to the internal network, no start page is desired. Unfortunately, you're out of luck—the start page can't be disabled.

The custom page option can be used to make the best of the situation. Redirecting users to the corporate Intranet can serve as a visual indicator that Network Connect successfully connected. Or, a corporate welcome page can be built to provide users with the latest news, announcements, and so on.

To configure the *Start page* option, navigate to **Users | User Roles | User Roles | Role | General | UI Options**. Select **Bookmarks page** for the standard IVE homepage, or **Custom page** to redirect Network Connect users to a different URL.

---

**NOTE**

To use a custom page, the Web access feature must be enabled for the role (**Users | User Roles | User Roles | Role | General | Overview**). If this isn't done, the user will be redirected to the IVE homepage regardless of how the *Start page* option is configured. Refer to Chapter 12 (Sign-in Policies) for more information about using a custom page.

---

It is also possible to launch Network Connect manually using (on a Windows machine) **Start | Programs | Juniper Networks | Network Connect**. This method launches a mini-browser window with the log-on prompt. After authentication, the Network Connect icon will appear in the system tray and there is no start or IVE homepage displayed to the user. This method is useful if connecting to corporate resources via a "fat" client (such as MS Outlook). However, if there are applications on the IVE homepage that the user needs, this wouldn't be the best method.

---

Tools & Traps...

**Disabling the Rewriting of Web Content through Network Connect**

Even though a Network Connect tunnel is established, the custom start page and any URLs followed by selecting bookmarks off the IVE homepage are intermediated through the Core Clientless Access Services feature. This may not be desired, especially if you are using Network Connect because a Web application you need doesn't work through the Content Intermediation Engine (CIE).

To disable the rewriting of this content, a selective rewriting resource policy is needed.

1. By default, the selective rewriting tab is not visible. Navigate to **Users | Resource Policies | Web** and select the Customize button: ⠿ Customize...

2. Select the **Rewriting** checkbox and the **Selective Rewriting** checkbox as shown in Figure 7.2.

3. Select the **Rewriting** tab (now visible). Select the **New Policy** button.

4. Enter a **Name** and an optional **Description**.

5. Enter *:* in the **Resources** field. This is a wildcard that matches all hosts and all ports.

6. Under **Roles**, select the **Policy applies to SELECTED roles** radio button. Under **Available Roles**, highlight the role used for Network Connect and select the **Add** button to move the role to the **Selected Roles** column. Important: Be sure that **Policy applies to ALL roles** is *not* selected. If it is selected by mistake, roles that depend on the Core Clientless Access Services feature will stop working!

7. For the action, select the **Don't rewrite content: Redirect to target web server** radio button.

8. Select **Save Changes** to complete the policy.

With this policy in place, no content is rewritten by the CIE for users mapped to the Network Connect role.

**Figure 7.2** Customizing the Web Resource Policies View to See the Selective Rewriting Policies

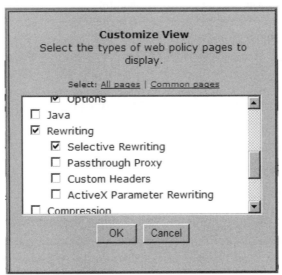

# Configuring Network Connect Resource Policies

Resource policies are where the bulk of the configuration work is done for Network Connect. These policies are applied to one or more roles.

## Configuring a Network Connect Resource Policy for Access Control

All traffic through Network Connect must be permitted by an access policy. By default, there is a Network Connect access policy applied to all roles that permits traffic to all hosts over all ports. This policy can be removed if the default is not desired. Or, new policies can be created which are attached to the top of the list, making the new policy evaluate before the default.

It is important to note here that the access policies are evaluated like this:

1. If the role does not match, evaluate the next policy in the list.

2. If the role matches and the resource does not match, evaluate the next policy in the list.

3. If the role matches and the resource matches, perform the action.

4. If no policy permits the traffic, drop the packet.

To create a Network Connect Access Policy:

1. Navigate to **Users | Resource Policies | Network Connect | Network Connect Access Control**. This list includes all the access policies, which are evaluated from the top down with the first match of role and resource combined determining the action performed. The list can be reordered by selecting the box next to the rule to move and using the **Up** and **Down** arrows to rearrange the list. Select the **New Policy...** button to create a new policy.

2. Enter a policy **Name,** which is required, and an optional **Description**.

3. Enter a list of **Resources** in the field, which are hostnames and IP addresses covered by the policy. See the sidebar *Network Connect ACL Syntax Change* for more information.

4. The **Action** button makes the policy an **Allow** or **Deny** rule, or allows you to **Use Detailed Rules**.

5. Select **Save Changes** to complete the rule.

The *Use Detailed Rules* option merits special attention because it offers a very interesting way of creating a granular definition of access within a single policy. Even with detailed rules, the *Resources* list is still required. However, rather than a single *Allow* or *Deny* that affects the entire resource list, rules are built that allow or deny subsets of the *Resources* list based on many other factors, including group membership (based on the Role's Directory/Attribute Server), user name, log-on URL, Host Checker status, and more. Note: *Detailed rules* is a feature of the Advanced License. To use this feature, a license key must be installed under **System | Configuration | Licensing**.

1. To create a detailed rule, select the **Use Detailed Rules** radio button and select **Save Changes**. This creates a new tab called **Detailed Rules**. Select the **New Rule** button.

2. Select a radio button to configure the rule to either **Allow** or **Deny** socket access.

3. In the **Resources** field, create a list of destinations using either hostnames or IP/netmask notation, including port information. Wildcards are supported here. Note: All resources in this list must also be defined in the **Resources** field in the regular resource policy.

4. In the **Conditions** field, create a Boolean expression that, if matched, will apply the action to traffic destined for the resources.

## Tools & Traps...

### Network Connect ACL Syntax Change

A big change to the way ACLs are defined took effect with IVE version 5.3. Prior versions of IVE code allowed resource lists like this:

```
*:80,123
```

In IVE version 5.3 and beyond, a resource list that specifies a port number without a protocol is not accepted and an "Invalid Resource!" warning message is displayed. The correct way to create this resource list would be:

```
TCP://*:80, 123
UDP://*:80, 123
```

Only 15 ports are permitted per line. If more than 15 ports are required, create a second line with the same syntax. For example:

```
TCP://*:1,2,3,4,5,6,7,8,9,10,11,12,13,14,15
TCP://*:16,17,18, etc
```

If the IVE is upgraded from 5.2 to 6.0, the ACLs are automatically converted to the new format.

# Configuring a Network Connect Connection Profile

A Network Connect Connection Profile contains nearly all of the connection-specific parameters needed by clients when they connect. This includes IP address assignment, transport settings, DNS, and proxy information.

To create a Network Connect Connection Profile:

1. Navigate to **Users | Resource Policies | Network Connect | NC Connection Profiles**. This list includes all the policies, which are evaluated from the top down with the first match of role determining the settings applied to the connecting user. The list can be reordered by selecting the box next to the policy to move and using the **Up** and **Down** arrows to rearrange the list. Select the **New Profile...** button to create a new profile.

2. Enter a profile **Name,** which is required, and an optional **Description**.

3. In the *IP address assignment* section, select the radio button for **DHCP Server** or **IP Address Pool**. IP pool addresses can be specified using range syntax (for example, 10.20.1.1-255 or 10.20.4.1-7.255), or in network/netmask format (for example, 10.20.1.0/24 or 10.20.4.0/22).

    Juniper recommends that the IP addresses used for Network Connect reside on the same IP subnet as the internal interface of the IVE. If this isn't possible (if, for instance, the IVE internal interface and the IP pools must reside in different subnets), static routes to the NC client subnets must be added to routers.

    Juniper also recommends using internal (RFC 1918) addresses. Addressing is usually not a problem as long as a large enough address space is allocated in advance. The IP address space assigned to users needs to be large enough to supply an address to each connecting client. If addresses aren't available, new users are denied access.

    Active/active multi-site clustering poses some challenges because a common IP address pool is not supported. See the *Using Network Connect in an Active/Active Multisite Cluster* section later in this chapter for details on configuring address pools to support this scenario, including an addressing example.

4. The *Connection Settings* section specifies the protocols used for transport, encryption, and compression. For transport, select either **ESP** or **oNCP/NCP**.

    It is important for the IVE administrator to understand the differences between the two transport modes: Encapsulating Security Payload (ESP) and Juniper's Optimized Network Communications Protocol (oNCP).

    Note: NCP is an older protocol used only with Windows clients. oNCP supports Windows too, but also Mac and Linux clients. Unless the auto-select feature has been disabled (**System | Configuration | NCP**), oNCP is used first and will only fail over to NCP in cases where an oNCP connection is not possible (such as when a Web proxy is required). Disabling NCP auto-select is no longer supported by Juniper Technical Support.

ESP (defined in RFC 2406) is one of the key protocols of IPSec, and utilizes traditional encryption and authentication methods (AES/SHA1/MD5) to provide confidentiality, origin authentication, integrity, and anti-replay protection. In contrast, oNCP uses SSL encryption methods (RC4-128). Table 7.1 shows the default protocols and ports used by the two transport protocols.

**Table 7.1** Network Connect Transport Mode Port Requirements

| Transport Mode | Encryption | Protocol/Port |
|---|---|---|
| ESP | IPSEC with AES/SHA1/MD5 | udp/4500 |
| oNCP | SSL with RC4-128 | tcp/443 |

The default transport mode is ESP, which is faster than oNCP. However, the ports needed to establish an ESP session are often blocked. This is normally not a problem because if ESP fails for any reason to establish a connection, NCP is automatically used as a backup method. However, if oNCP/NCP is selected as the transport method, ESP is not tried if an oNCP connection fails.

5. If ESP is maintained as the transport method, the IVE administrator can customize the following values:

   1. **UDP port** By default, the port used by ESP is udp/4500 (per RFC 3948). This port can be changed by modifying this field. However, keep in mind that all devices between the client and IVE must permit traffic on this new port. It may be tempting to change this to a commonly open port (such as udp/53, which is normally used for DNS) in an attempt to increase a client's ability to connect from more locations. However, this is an intentional attempt to bypass security policy and is not recommended. In addition, many Intrusion Protection Systems (IPS) are application-aware and can recognize and block an attempt to use a different port in this way.

   2. **ESP to NCP fallback timeout** This value is the number of seconds the IVE waits before establishing an oNCP connection if ESP is unable to make a connection. The default is 15 seconds.

   3. **Key lifetime (time based) and (bytes transferred)** Encryption keys must be changed periodically to maintain confidentiality. The key lifetime can be

based on time (minutes) or an amount of data (bytes) transferred. Both sides of the VPN negotiate this value, with the lowest value configured being used for the session. Setting this value low (which frequently changes the encryption keys) can increase the CPU overhead on the IVE. The default is 20 minutes, with no byte limit.

## WARNING

Be careful changing these values. In particular, make sure the ESP *Key Lifetime* is greater than the *NCP Idle Connection Timeout* (**System | Configuration | NCP**). If it isn't, Network Connect sessions may randomly disconnect.

4. **Replay Protection** Anti-replay protection is enabled by default with this checkbox. This setting protects against replay attacks, where a hacker intercepts and retransmits data. With this option selected, the IVE drops packets that have already been received and packets that are out of order. This option must be disabled if *Enable TOS Bits Copy* is being used.

## Tools & Traps...

### How ToS Affects Replay Protection

Packets with ToS information in the header may be processed differently by network devices (including routers, switches, and firewalls) than those that don't. For example, a router may provide a priority queue for VoIP traffic that allows these packets to exit the router before other packets in an attempt to minimize latency. While this priority handling is necessary to maintain voice quality, packets may be reordered in the process.

However, when ESP *Replay Protection* is selected, out of order packets are automatically dropped when they reach the IVE. This is why it is critical that ESP *Replay Protection* is disabled in the **NC Connection Profile** when the **Enable TOS Bits Copy** option is selected in the **Network Connect** role options.

5. For Encryption, select either **AES/SHA1** or **AES/MD5**. Both are cryptographic hash functions that take in a variable length string of characters and output a fixed length number. MD5 (Message Digest version 5) generates a 128-bit number, which is often displayed as a 32-character hexadecimal number. SHA-1 (Secure

Hash Algorithm-1) outputs a 160-bit number. There is much debate about the benefits and drawbacks of each, but both are widely used.

6. Select either **Compress** or **No Compression** to control whether the tunneled data between IVE and Network Connect client is compressed. The type of compression used depends on the transport selected. ESP uses LZO compression (named for its creators Lempel-Ziv-Oberhumer, LZO compression is very fast at decompressing data) and oNCP uses a deflate compression algorithm (similar to what is used in the/popular PKZIP product, deflate attempts to balance compression and decompression performance).

7. In the **Roles** section, select one of the following radio buttons:

   ■ **Policy applies to ALL roles** All users, regardless of role, will match this profile.

   ■ **Policy applies to SELECTED roles** Only users mapped to roles in the *Selected roles* list will match this profile. The *Available roles* list must include the roles for this to be effective.

   ■ **Policy applies to all roles OTHER THAN those selected below** All users except for those who map to the *Selected roles* will match the profile. The *Available roles* list must include the roles for this to be effective.

8. Select **Save Changes** to complete the policy and return to the list of connection profiles.

## Configuring NC Connection Profile DNS Information

A connection profile may need to be modified beyond the initial configuration to customize how name resolution is accomplished on the Network Connect client. The administrator can choose to override the default DNS/WINS information sent to the client, and even the order in which name resolution is done on the client.

1. From the *Network Connect Connection Profile* screen (**Users | Resource Policies | Network Connect | NC Connection Profiles)**, select the profile to modify.

2. Select the **DNS** tab.

3. Unless the values are changed here, the IVE sends to Network Connect clients the name resolution settings defined on the **System | Network | Overview** screen. If desired, enter IP addresses for primary and secondary DNS servers, a DNS domain list (multiple domains may be separated by a comma), and a name or IP address for a WINS server. Note: When a Network Connect client connects to the IVE, the client saves its original DNS server information before accepting the DNS servers sent from the IVE. Once the session terminates, the original values are restored.

4. Select the **Auto-allow IPs in DNS/WINS settings (only for split-tunnel enabled mode)** checkbox to have the Network Connect client automatically tunnel traffic to the DNS/WINS servers, even if they are outside the split tunneled network. For example, if your split tunnel network list is 10.0.0.0/8 and your DNS server is 172.16.20.1, the traffic to your DNS server will not be encrypted and sent over the tunnel. This option will automatically include name servers in the split tunnel list.

5. When split tunneling is enabled, the IVE administrator can decide in which order the DNS servers should be searched. Either the client's or the IVE's DNS servers can be searched first, followed by the other; or visa versa. Select the appropriate radio button for either **Search client DNS first, then the device** or **Search the device's DNS servers first, then client.** If split tunneling is disabled, all traffic (including DNS requests) flows through the IVE so the IVE DNS server is used, and search order doesn't matter.

## Configuring NC Connection Profile Proxy Information

Some IVE administrators may require that Network Connect clients use a proxy server to access either the Internet or internal Web applications once they connect to the IVE. However, Network Connect does not support the browser's ability to automatically detect proxy servers (such as DHCPINFORM or WPAD). Instead, an NC Connection Profile can be used to define an explicit proxy server, or a Proxy Automatic Configuration (PAC) file can be used—but these can not be used together.

1. From the *Network Connect Connection Profile* screen (**Users | Resource Policies | Network Connect | NC Connection Profiles)**, select the profile to modify.

2. Select the **Proxy** tab.

3. The default is for **No proxy server** to be used. To have clients download a PAC file from a server, select the **Automatic** radio button and specify the URL to the PAC location in the **Server address** field. Clients poll servers periodically to update PAC files and the default update interval is 5 minutes. This can be changed by modifying the *Update Frequency* field. The frequency can be set as low as 1 minute. If the value is changed to 0, the client will never poll for an updated PAC file.

4. To manually configure a proxy server, select the **Manual Configuration** radio button and enter the hostname or IP address of the server in the **Server** field. The port must be changed to match what is used on the proxy server software. Microsoft Proxy Server uses port 8080 by default.

Some locations (for instance, hotels and other public hotspots) require that Network Connect clients use a proxy server to connect to the IVE. In this case, all HTTP traffic including NCP to the IVE can be sent through the proxy.

# Configuring Network Connect Split-Tunneling Networks

It is necessary for any VPN client to know what traffic to encrypt and send through the tunnel and what traffic, if any, can be sent out the local network interface. Split-tunnel networks provide the Network Connect client with this information through a list of IP addresses and networks defined on the IVE.

The split tunnel list by itself does not allow clients to connect. A corresponding access policy to allow the traffic must exist or traffic to the destinations defined in the list will be denied and dropped.

To create a split tunnel list:

1. Navigate to **Users | Resource Policies | Network Connect | Split-tunneling Networks**. This list includes all the policies, which are evaluated from the top down with the first match of role determining the settings applied to the connecting user. The list can be reordered by selecting the box next to the policy to move and using the **Up** and **Down** arrows to rearrange the list. Select the **New Policy...** button to create a new split tunnel list.

2. Enter a policy **Name,** which is required, and an optional **Description**.

3. Create the split tunnel list by entering destinations in the **Resources** field using IP/netmask notation. This is simply a list of IP hosts and networks, so protocol and port information can't be included here. Multiple networks can be added to the list, one entry per line.

4. In the **Roles** section, select one of the following radio buttons:

   - **Policy applies to ALL roles**  All users, regardless of role, will match this policy

   - **Policy applies to SELECTED roles**  Only users mapped to roles in the *Selected roles* list will match this policy. The *Available roles* list must include the roles for this to be effective.

   - **Policy applies to all roles OTHER THAN those selected below**  All users except for those who map to the *Selected roles* will match the policy. The *Available roles* list must include the roles for this to be effective.

5. The **Action** radio buttons makes the policy either a simple *Allow access* list, or detailed rules can be configured that base the split tunnel list on many other factors, including group membership (based on the Role's Directory/Attribute Server), user name, log-on URL, Host Checker status, and more. Figure 7.3 is an example of basing the split tunnel list on the user's browser type.

**Figure 7.3** Split Tunnel List Based on User's Browser Type

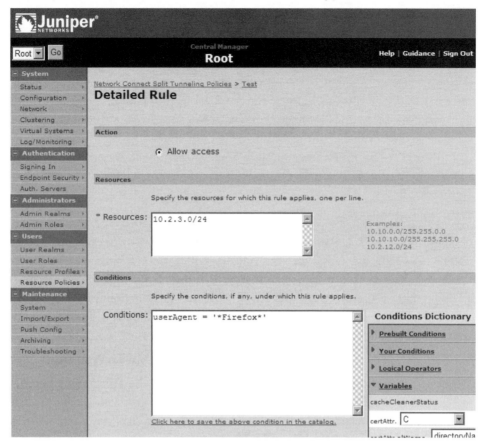

6.  Select **Save Changes** to complete the rule.

The Network Connect client modifies the local client route table so networks defined in the split tunnel list are sent to the Juniper Network Connect Virtual Adapter and all other traffic is sent to the local physical interface. Consider the following example where the client's LAN address is 10.123.100.12 and the client's local gateway is 10.123.100.1. The output has been modified to make it more readable. This command shows the client's routing table before a Network Connect session has been established, demonstrated in Table 7.2.

```
C:\>route print
```

**Table 7.2** Client Routing Table Before Establishing a Network Connect Session

| Network Destination | Netmask | Gateway | Interface | Metric |
| --- | --- | --- | --- | --- |
| 0.0.0.0 | 0.0.0.0 | 10.123.100.1 | 10.123.100.12 | 20 |
| 10.123.100.0 | 255.255.255.0 | 10.123.100.12 | 10.123.100.12 | 20 |

Once the Network Connect client creates a connection to the IVE, the client is assigned the address 10.211.101.48. This command shows the client's routing table, which illustrates the split tunnel mode selected (**Enable Split Tunneling**) and the effect of the split tunnel list (10.0.0.0/8). Notice that traffic to the local subnet (10.123.100.0/24) is sent to the IVE because of the lower metric. Internet traffic is sent to the client's default gateway because split tunneling is enabled (see Table 7.3).

```
C:\>route print
```

**Table 7.3** Client Routing Table with Split Tunnel Mode Selected

| Network Destination | Netmask | Gateway | Interface | Metric |
|---|---|---|---|---|
| 0.0.0.0 | 0.0.0.0 | 10.123.100.1 | 10.123.100.12 | 20 |
| 10.0.0.0 | 255.0.0.0 | 10.211.101.48 | 10.211.101.48 | 1 |
| 10.123.100.0 | 255.255.255.0 | 10.123.100.12 | 10.123.100.12 | 20 |
| 10.123.100.0 | 255.255.255.0 | 10.211.101.48 | 10.211.101.48 | 1 |

# Network Connect Implementation Options

Several additional implementation options deserve special attention because they can be extremely useful in certain deployment scenarios.

## Using GINA with Network Connect

The Graphical Identification and Authentication (GINA) dynamic-link library is responsible for implementing the Windows interctive authentication policy. After it is loaded by the *Winlogon* process, GINA interacts with users to gather credentials information. It also does many other things including displaying the legal notification dialog box, displaying the last log-on name, and processing **Control + Alt + Delete**. The standard version of GINA supplied by Microsoft, Msgina.dll, can be replaced or "chained" to other GINAs by third parties (such as Novell's NetWare client, NWGINA).

This is an important topic for IVE administrators because it is sometimes necessary for a client to create a Network Connect session during the Windows log-on procedure. To support this, Network Connect works with GINA to initiate a Network Connect tunnel to the IVE during logon.

For example, assume you have a help desk that supports remote corporate computers. Periodically, these computers need to be replaced and the new computer administratively added to the domain. This process requires the computer to be "on the network" during the first logon in order for the credentials to be verified by a domain controller. Network Connect with GINA makes this possible and eliminates the need to have the computer on-site to perform the task.

GINA is enabled in the Network Connect role options (**Users | User Roles | *Role* | Network Connect**). When this option is selected, the IVE administrator must decide whether to require Network Connect to launch at Windows logon, or whether the user can decide to launch Network Connect at each logon.

The following points are important:

- Juniper recommends that the **Auto–Uninstall Network Connect** role option should not be enabled on roles where GINA is used.

- GINA does not support certificate authentication.

- Windows Vista has completely replaced GINA with Credential Providers, which is a more flexible way of performing the same functions. This was done to make it easier for third parties to supplement the Windows log-on architecture with additional functionality like Smart Card integration. As a result, GINA does not work with Vista.

- In older versions of IVE software, Single Sign On (SSO) was possible, linking Network Connect with the Windows credentials. In IVE version 5.4 and later, Single Sign On is no longer supported with Network Connect GINA.

## Tools & Traps...

### GINA Chaining and Uninstalling Network Connect GINA

GINA DLLs can call other GINA DLLs. This process is called GINA chaining. When Network Connect GINA is installed, it evaluates the other GINA DLLs to see if they are compatible. If they are, NC GINA is installed at the end of the chain. The user receives a warning message if the other GINAs are not supported.

When Network Connect GINA is uninstalled, things get a little tricky. If Network Connect GINA was the last one installed, it can easily uninstall independent of any others. However, if Network Connect GINA is in the middle of the chain, all the GINAs following the Network Connect GINA must be uninstalled first.

# Using the Network Connect Command Line Launcher

The ability to launch Network Connect from a command line was added as a feature to IVE version 5.4. This client command line utility allows a session to be created in batch files, scripts, and custom-built applications. In fact, the NC launcher can be bundled with an application that requires Network Connect access, making VPN-ready applications easier to develop and deploy.

Version 6.0 of the IVE software added support for certificate authentication. However, the NC Launcher is not a fully-functional client. The utility does not currently support Host Checker and Cache Cleaner applications—so if these are required on a role, the user will not map properly. In addition, because the command line utility is not interactive, users can't be prompted to select between roles. As a result, the **Users must select from assigned Roles** must not be enabled if more than one role is available.

The launcher syntax is:

```
nclauncher [-url Url] [-u username] [-p password] [-r realm] [-help] [-stop]
[-signout]
[-version] [-d DSID] [-cert client certificate]
```

Two parameters deserve more information.

- The *client certificate* parameter must be the string in the *Issued To* field of the certificate. When a certificate is specified, both the *-url* and *-r* parameters are required. Certificate authentication must be configured (for example, a trusted client CA is configured on the IVE) and the sign-in page specified in the *-url* must map to a realm that uses certificate authentication.

- DSID is used to pass a cookie to the NC Launcher from a different authentication mechanism. This is typically used when an enterprise Single Sign On (SSO) system is deployed.

# Using Network Connect in an Active/Active Multisite Cluster

IP address allocation must be configured properly when Network Connect is deployed in an active/active multisite cluster. The IP address assigned to the Network Connect user must be valid for the site. However, the Network Connect Resource Profiles (which specify the IP address pool space) are replicated between nodes in the cluster. So, the resource profile address pool must be configured to contain *all* of the address space for *all* the cluster members. The problem is this: how does the IVE know which IP address to assign?

IP Address Filters (**System | Network | Network Connect**) serve to identify those addresses in the pool that should be locally assigned—all other addresses in the pools are ignored. These filters are *not* replicated between cluster members, so the configuration here is unique to each node in the cluster.

For example, a company has four IVEs in an active/active cluster and needs address pools for about 1,000 users each. Recall that each local IVE needs adequate space to be able to assign addresses to all users in the event of a failure. Each IVE is assigned a network with a /16 mask, which provides plenty of addresses to support all the clients in the cluster if necessary.

The networks are assigned as shown in Table 7.4. Notice that all the networks assigned to the cluster members are configured in the address pool (**Users | Resource Profiles | Network Connect | NC Connection Profiles**). Also note that the IP address filter of each IVE includes only the range to be assigned at that location.

**Table 7.4** Sample Network Connect Address Allocation

| IVE | Addresses Pool Configured on ALL Cluster Members | IP Address Filter |
| --- | --- | --- |
| New York | 10.20.0.0/16 | 10.20.0.0/16 |
| San Francisco | 10.21.0.0/16 | 10.21.0.0/16 |
| Seattle | 10.22.0.0/16 | 10.22.0.0/16 |
| Chicago | 10.23.0.0/16 | 10.23.0.0/16 |

The final item to configure for the cluster is to ensure that routing works. Recall that the addresses assigned to Network Connect clients should be on the same network as the IVE internal interface, or a static route needs to be defined to ensure the rest of the network knows the IVE interface is the proper route toward the address pool.

# Network Connect Client Distribution

Network Connect is not "clientless." Client software must be installed on the connecting computer either automatically or manually.

## Web Install/Upgrade

The NC client can be automatically installed or upgraded the first time Network Connect is launched. This can happen when a user selects the Network Connect link off the IVE homepage or when a user is mapped to a role that has the **Auto-launch Network Connect** option selected.

If connecting computers are "unmanaged," a Web install is the only viable option. Not only is it very easy to configure, keeping the software current becomes trivial because as the Juniper IVE is upgraded, the NC client is upgraded. The first time a user connects after an IVE upgrade, the new code is downloaded and installed automatically.

There are drawbacks to this method, however. The installer must be downloaded and run. Even though no user interaction is typically required for the install, it takes both bandwidth and additional time on initial connection. No reboot is usually required (unless GINA or ToS options are configured), but this process can be confusing and frustrating to users who may not be expecting it. In addition, administrative privileges of the NC user on the connecting computer are required.

## Autonomous Installers

Juniper provides several downloadable Network Connect Installers. These can be used to install Network Connect manually any time—including before a new computer is given to the user. The installers are often used by organizations who want to deploy and manage desktops using applications like BMC's Configuration Management (formerly Marimba). The IVE 6.0 installers include:

- Network Connect for Windows
- Network Connect for 64-bit Windows
- Network Connect for Mac OS X
- Network Connect for Linux

These installers are available by navigating to **Maintenance | System | Installers**. The primary benefit to using a pre-installed client is that there is no remote download and install needed at first connection. However, since the NC clients are relatively small (Windows NC is 729k), this may not prove to be a compelling reason to use an installer.

## Juniper Installer Service

This application provides relief from the administrative privileges requirement to install Network Connect. This is not an installer itself, but a framework that allows the Web installer to succeed when the user has restricted privileges. This service is especially useful on managed computers intended for public use (such as hardened kiosks) because the environment demands greatly limited user privileges.

The Installer Service is designed for and works only with Juniper's software. To verify a program's authenticity, the installer checks the Authenticode digital signature of the file to make sure it was published by Juniper Networks.

In 6.0, Juniper has added an MSI package for the Juniper Installer Service. This package can be used to push the installer service to users via SMS or other deployment software.

There is no "Juniper recommended" way of pushing out the package, but the MSI package makes this possible.

# Network Connect Troubleshooting

Successful troubleshooting requires both tools and a logical approach to the problem. The IVE and client OS provide several important tools, especially the IVE and client logs, which will be described here.

> **NOTE**
>
> A single time source on the network that synchronizes the clocks on clients, servers, and network devices makes log analysis much easier. Consistent time can provide vital information about the order of a failure when reviewing multiple logs. NTP or SNTP are good choices for time synchronization.

## IVE-Side Troubleshooting

As described in previous chapters, User Access logs are a challenge on the IVE. The amount and quality of information is excellent, but the logs are large and access can be very slow on a busy IVE. Use custom queries to focus log output and consider policy tracing as an alternative to log access.

### IVE Logs

As always, the first step is to enable logging. Navigate to **System | Log/Monitoring | User Access | Settings**. Under **Select Events to Log**, ensure the **Network Connect** box is checked. The log itself can be found from here by selecting the **Log** link on the menu, or by navigating to **System | Log/Monitoring | User Access | Log**.

### Example One

You receive a call from the help desk that no Network Connect users are able to establish a new connection. Existing users continue to work fine. New users are receiving the message shown in Figure 7.4.

**Figure 7.4** Network Connect Error

You look up the message in the *WSAM and Network Connect Error Messages* document available on the Juniper Customer Support Center Web page (www.juniper.net/techpubs/ software/ive/6.x/errormsgs/6.0-NC_WSAM_ErrMsgs.pdf). The result is shown below in Figure 7.5.

**Figure 7.5** Error Message Explanation from Juniper

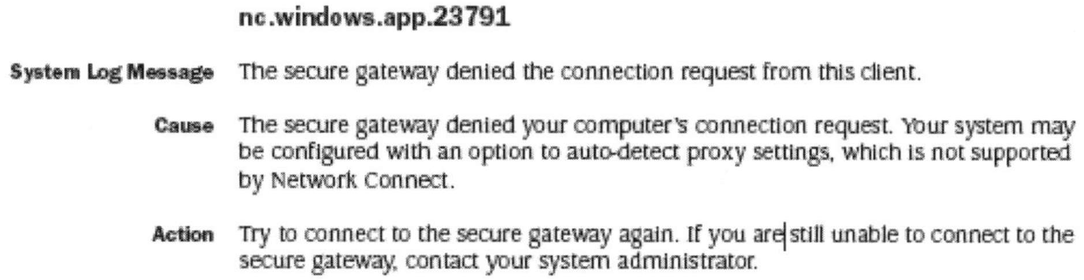

**nc.windows.app.23791**

| | |
|---|---|
| **System Log Message** | The secure gateway denied the connection request from this client. |
| **Cause** | The secure gateway denied your computer's connection request. Your system may be configured with an option to auto-detect proxy settings, which is not supported by Network Connect. |
| **Action** | Try to connect to the secure gateway again. If you are still unable to connect to the secure gateway, contact your system administrator. |

You quickly realize that this document won't be any help to you! Actually, the document is an excellent source during troubleshooting and normally provides insight into the problem. However, because *nc.windows.app.23791* is a very common "catch-all" error, the document doesn't include much detail.

You access the IVE User Access log to see if you can determine the problem. The problem is easily found:

```
Minor NWC23466 2007-09-09 21:02:21 - ive - [10.123.2.3]
Root::Myname(Users)[Users] - Network Connect: IP address cannot be allocated
to user Myname. Solution: Check IP Address Pools / DHCP server state.
```

A check of the DHCP server (defined in **Users | Resource Profiles | Network Connect | NC Connection Profiles**) shows that the scope has no more addresses to assign. Creating a larger scope on the server solves the problem.

## Policy Trace of Network Connect Policies

Policy tracing gives an IVE administrator the ability to focus investigation on the policies applied to a single user—as the user connects and accesses resources. This can be a very powerful tool during setup (for example, to verify resource usage of an application) and for troubleshooting.

To use the tool, navigate to **Maintenance | Troubleshooting | User Sessions | Policy Tracing**. Enter the username and realm to which the user will connect. Under **Events to Log**, select **Network Connect Policies**. You may also want to enable **Pre-Authentication**, **Authentication**, and **Role Mapping** if you are troubleshooting a log-on problem; or enable **Web Policies** to troubleshoot problems with the Start page.

The drawback to the policy trace utility is the quantity of information it returns. Finding a policy failure can be difficult if there are a huge number of trace entries. It is a good idea to enable logging for only those policies you need to review. However, be prepared to expand your tracing if you fail to find the problem.

Once you have the user ready to test, select the **Start Recording** button. The user then duplicates the issue. Then select **Stop Recording** and the **View Log** button to see the trace.

# Client-Side Troubleshooting

Even though Network Connect client utilities and logs can be invaluable tools in troubleshooting access issues, don't overlook the operating system event logs.

## *Network Connect Client Logs*

The IVE administrator must enable logging first or the client logs do not exist. Client logging is enabled and disabled on the IVE in **System | Log/Monitoring | Client Logs | Settings**. Under **Enable client-side logging for the following features,** ensure the **Network Connect** box is checked. The Network Connect logs reside in the following directories:

- **Windows client** C:\Documents and Settings\<user>\Application Data\Juniper Networks\Network Connect x.x.x\

- **Vista client** \Users\<user>\AppData\roaming\Juniper Networks\Network Connect x.x.x\

- **Linux client** ~/.juniper_networks/network_connect/

- **Macintosh client** ~/Library/Logs/Juniper Networks/Network Connect/

The log files in this directory are NetworkConnect.log, NCService.log, and NCAdmin.log. Users can upload logs to the IVE which can then be downloaded and reviewed by administrators. Client logs can be accessed easily on Windows computers using the NC Troubleshooting software by accessing **Start | Programs | Juniper Networks | Network Connect x.x.x | NC Troubleshooting**, as shown in Figure 7.6. From the **Logs** tab, select the **Explore Log Files** button. This brings up the proper log directory in Windows Explorer.

**Figure 7.6** Network Connect Troubleshooting Tool

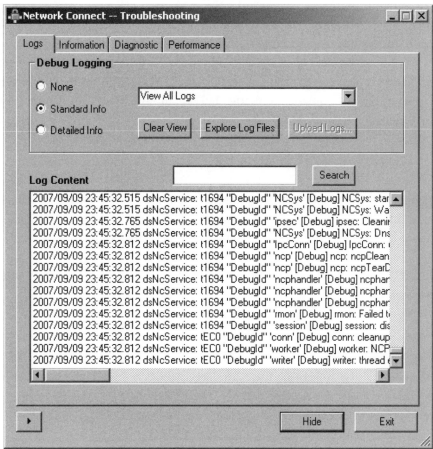

The same interface is available by right-clicking on the Network Connect icon in the taskbar, then selecting **Advanced View** as shown in Figure 7.7. Select the **Logs** tab, then the **Explore Log Files** button.

**Figure 7.7** Network Connect Right-Click Menu

Network Connect client logs aren't easy to use. A file from a busy client will include hundreds or thousands of entries. A good idea for evaluating any client log is to get a good file searching tool like FIND or GREP which can be very helpful in limiting the output. Use redirection commands to send output of these commands to a new file. In Windows, the > and >> symbols send output from a command to a file. The "pipe" character (|) allows redirection to other commands. For example, this command sends all lines in the Network Connect log that contain the string "fail" to another find command which prints all lines that contain the string "10.1.1.1":

```
Find "fail" NetworkConnect.log | find "10.1.1.1"
```

## Example Two

You're configuring Network Connect for the first time but access isn't working. The Network Connect client launches properly, but applications can't access hosts beyond the IVE. You suspect an access list problem. After checking the IVE, the access policy looks fine.

After enabling Network Connect client logging on the IVE, you connect with a test computer and review NetworkConnect.log. You don't see any failures, but the following log entry doesn't look right:

```
2007/09/10 07:59:32.609 dsNetworkConnect: t834 "DebugId"
'DSSetupInitializeParam()' [Debug] DSSetupInitializeParam():
Parameter[1]:split-tunneling-routes=10.0.0.0|255.255.255.0,
```

You recognize that the split tunnel list should be 10.0.0.0/255.0.0.0 instead of the /24 subnet mask that is actually configured on the IVE. This explains your lack of access to internal hosts. Changing the split tunnel list fixes the problem.

# Summary

For organizations looking to replace their existing IPSec VPN concentrator and maintain the same base functionality, Network Connect is the right choice and this chapter described many of its benefits. Network Connect builds an encrypted IP tunnel like its predecessor, but the ability to use SSL solves many of the problems that afflict IPSec-only concentrators.

IVE administrators don't have to worry about how to deploy and maintain client software. In addition, Network Connect support for Mac OS X, Linux, and 64-bit Windows means that a single access method is available to nearly everyone throughout the organization. Administrators no longer need to build and maintain (and secure) a separate access method for Mac users in the Marketing Department and application developers running Linux.

Network Connect users benefit from many features unavailable in traditional concentrators, including proxy server support, which makes connecting from many public areas possible for the first time. Using SSL means that VPN access works from inside most networks without firewall modification, so traveling workers don't need to contact every local firewall administrator to request support for IPSec.

The IVE administrator will find that Network Connect is not difficult to configure. For most deployment scenarios, there are fewer things to configure on the IVE to support Network Connect than for SAM or Terminal Services. This chapter covered how to configure Network Connect in a variety of situations, including using features like GINA. The chapter also discussed how to troubleshoot NC using both IVE and client logs.

# Solutions Fast Track

## Network Connect

- ☑ The role *Max Session Length* value must be carefully chosen to ensure Network Connect users aren't disconnected too quickly.

- ☑ A *Selective Rewriting* policy must be configured if the IVE administrator doesn't want the CIE to intermediate traffic for Network Connect users for bookmarks accessed off the IVE homepage.

- ☑ GINA can be used to create a Network Connect tunnel during Windows logon. However, Vista doesn't support GINA.

- ☑ Active/active multisite clustering requires IP address pools that include all the addresses to be assigned by every IVE in the cluster. IP Address Filters are used to make sure only locally routable addresses are assigned by each IVE.

# Network Connect Troubleshooting

☑ Extensive IVE and client logs provide abundant information for troubleshooting access issues with the Network Connect client. However, OS logs shouldn't be ignored.

☑ IVE administrators can use policy tracing to create a verbose log of all policies applied to a user and the policy results—as the user logs in and accesses resources.

# Frequently Asked Questions

**Q:** I've enabled the role option to support Multicast traffic over Network Connect, but my application is not working. What could be wrong?

**A:** There are several things to consider. Network Connect multicast will only work automatically if L2 switches connected to the IVE internal interface support IGMP v3. If the switches only support IGMP v2, you need to enable static IGMP snooping group membership to make sure multicast is forwarded to the IVE internal interface. Also, only the following multicast groups are supported over Network Connect: 224.0.0.0/8, 232.0.0.0/8, 233.0.0.0/8, and 239.0.0.0/8. Make sure your multicast address is contained in one of these ranges. Refer to RFC 3171 for guidelines on assigning multicast addresses.

**Q:** I've selected the **Enable TOS Bits Copy** option on the role to support Network Connect users with softphones. However, my users experience packet loss—poor voice quality, slow application response, and so on. What's wrong?

**A:** The problem is caused by ESP *Replay Protection*. This security feature drops encrypted packets that arrive at the IVE out of order. The *Enable TOS Bits Copy* option is copying the ToS information set by the softphone to the encrypted packet header. During the transmission of these packets to the IVE, the network is queuing the packets in response to the ToS information, which results in them arriving out of order—and dropped. Disable ESP *Replay Protection* when the *Enable TOS Bits Copy* option is configured.

**Q:** Why can't I launch a Visual Basic script as a Network Connect session start script?

**A:** Network Connect will only run scripts with BAT, CMD, or EXE extensions. If you want to run any other type of command, you must call it from a batch file or application.

**Q:** Why won't GINA work with Vista?

**A:** Windows Vista has completely replaced GINA with a similar log-on architecture called Credential Providers. It allows third party developers to more easily integrate with the *Winlogon* process. Network Connect doesn't currently support Credential Providers.

# Chapter 8

# Endpoint Security

## Solutions in this chapter:

- **Host Checker**
- **Cache Cleaner**
- **Secure Virtual Workspace**
- **IVE/IDP Integration**

☑ **Summary**

☑ **Solutions Fast Track**

☑ **Frequently Asked Questions**

# Introduction

Network security has always been somewhat of a moving target for security administrators. In the early days of networking, network security had more to do with securing your resources locally and preventing outside threats to your internal resources. Today, as various forms of remote access have become popular, your job of securing your network extends far beyond your Internet router. As corporate computing assets spend more time outside the office, they are much more exposed to potential threats. Furthermore, many organizations must provide access to internal resources to users and devices that are outside their realm of control. All of these factors make it much more difficult to ensure that remote users (whether corporate assets or not) are not bringing more into your network than you expect. As direct access to resources (both server and workstation) has become less common to attackers due to firewalls and network address translation (NAT), attackers have shifted their tactics to use subtler methods of compromise, such as worms, Trojans, spyware, and other browser and operating system exploits to gain control of internal systems through trusted assets.

Although all this talk of new exploits and clever attackers may sound frightening, there is some good news. While attackers have been improving their tactics, so have network security companies such as Juniper Networks. In this chapter, we will focus on several tools that you have at your disposal within the IVE. As you will soon discover, the IVE offers many ways to extend the security of your network and your corporate access policies far beyond your Internet connection, and thus ensure that your network is secured from internal and external threats.

In this chapter, we will focus on four main tools that the IVE provides to help secure your network. These tools are Host Checker, Cache Cleaner, Secure Virtual Workspace, and IVE/IDP integration. The latter of which actually is a bit more of a network security device, but it does allow you to help protect your network and hosts connecting into your network.

# Host Checker

We will begin our discussion of how the IVE can extend your network's security to hosts connecting to your network through the IVE by introducing a very powerful tool called Host Checker. Host Checker is essentially an application that is automatically provisioned to clients that connect to your network through the IVE. Host Checker does exactly what its name implies. It ensures that the host that is connecting to your network meets a certain set of criteria before it can gain access to resources. You can deploy Host Checker to end systems in many ways, and as it has with all of its products, Juniper has emphasized granular control and implementation of this feature to empower you to have a wide variety of scalable options for deployment. In this section, we will begin by discussing how Host Checker works and is deployed, and various options and tools that you have at your disposal. We will also spend some time discussing custom Host Checker policies and rules, as well as support for the Trusted Computing Group's (TCG's) Trusted Network Connect (TNC). These features allow you to expand you ability to ensure end-system compliance in just about any way you can imagine with the use of customized checks.

# Host Checker Functionality

Host Checker can run on Windows, Macintosh, and Linux machines and is delivered to clients in a similar fashion as other clients that the IVE provides, such as Network Connect. Windows clients running Internet Explorer can get Host Checker through either ActiveX or Java (ActiveX will be tried first), whereas Windows clients running a browser other than Internet Explorer, or running Internet Explorer with ActiveX disabled, will get Host Checker delivered via Java. Both Mac and Linux clients will get Host Checker delivered via Java.

Host Checker's capabilities vary among the different platforms (Windows, Mac, and Linux). This is due in part to the fact that one operating system may have features which are unique to the other two operating systems (e.g., Windows has a Registry, whereas Mac and Linux don't). At this point, Windows has the most support by far for different host checks, but it is likely that Juniper will expand its features to other platforms in the future.

Host Checker is available on all IVE platforms, regardless of license; however, some features, such as the use of detailed rules, can be used only with the Advanced license.

# Host Checker Components

You will mainly be concerned with two Host Checker components: policies and rules. A Host Checker policy is composed of rules that essentially evaluate to true or false. Based on the logic that you incorporate into a policy, it in turn will be evaluated to either true or false. You use policies to control what the user can access through the IVE. These policies can be referenced at the realm, role mapping, role, and resource levels; so throughout the IVE, you reference policies (which are composed of rules), but not the rules themselves.

In addition to policies and rules, you will be concerned with a few other Host Checker components. These are the system-wide Host Checker properties, endpoint security updates/definitions, and Advanced Endpoint Defense, all of which we will cover throughout this section.

## Host Checker Policies and Rule Types

As we mentioned earlier, a Host Checker policy is referenced throughout the configuration, and is composed of Host Checker rules (including rule logic and remediation actions). We will focus primarily on rules in this section because a policy is essentially a collection of one or more rules, logic, and remediation actions. Figure 8.1 outlines how you apply Host Checker to various parts of the configuration. We will cover how to apply Host Checker to each level later in this chapter, but it is helpful to understand how these checks are applied at each level before we get into an in-depth discussion:

- **Realm level** At the realm level, you select one or more Host Checker policies to evaluate a client's compliance at this level. By default, if you select multiple policies, the IVE will evaluate these as a Logical AND (meaning you must pass all policies), but you can select **Allow Access to Realm if Any ONE of the Selected Require and Enforce Policies Is Passed**, which will be treated like a Logical OR between the different policies (so you have to pass only one to get access to the realm). Each policy references Host Checker rules which define the individual checks. Each policy will also implement its own logic (either **All of the Above Rules** [evaluates rules with Logical AND logic], **Any of the Above Rules** [evaluates with Logical OR logic], or **Custom Expression**, which you define). Each Host Checker policy can additionally define its own remediation action.

- **Role mapping level** If you have the Advanced license, you can define a custom expression that is matched at the role mapping level. When the client signs into the realm, the client is evaluated against role mapping rules in that realm to determine whether it matches a particular rule to get access to the defined roles for that rule. To match at the role mapping level is to use a custom expression. Within that expression, you define your own logic to determine which Host Checker policies are evaluated, and with what logic. Additionally, you can evaluate other logic as well within this same expression. Each policy will also implement its own logic (either **All of the Above Rules** [evaluates rules with Logical AND logic], **Any of the Above Rules** [evaluates with Logical OR logic], or **Custom Expression**, which you define). Each Host Checker policy can additionally define its own remediation action.

- **Role level** You can evaluate Host Checker compliance at the role level to allow users access to different roles based on whether they comply with Host Checker rules. You reference which Host Checker policies will be evaluated in each role. If you select **Allow users whose workstations meet the requirements specified by these Host Checker policies** and select multiple Host Checker policies, Host Checker will evaluate the policies as a Logical AND; however, if you select **Allow access to the role if any ONE of the selected policies is passed**, the policies will be evaluated as a Logical OR. Each policy references Host Checker rules which define the individual checks. Each policy will also implement its own logic (either **All of the Above Rules** [evaluates rules with Logical AND logic], **Any of the Above Rules** [evaluates with Logical OR logic], or **Custom Expression**, which you define). Each Host Checker policy can additionally define its own remediation action.

- **Resource policy level** If you have an Advanced license, you can apply Host Checker checks at the resource level so that users can access resources only if they comply with Host Checker policies for that resource. Applying Host Checker at the resource policy level is very similar to defining a check at the role mapping level. You use a custom expression to define what Host Checker policies should be evaluated to be able to access this resource. You can define your own logic to be applied if you want to evaluate multiple Host Checker policies. Each policy references Host Checker rules which define the individual checks. Each policy will also implement its own logic (either **All of the Above Rules** [evaluates rules with Logical AND logic], **Any of the Above Rules** [evaluates with Logical OR logic], or **Custom Expression**, which you define). Each Host Checker policy can additionally define its own remediation action.

**Figure 8.1** Applying Host Checker Policies at Different Levels

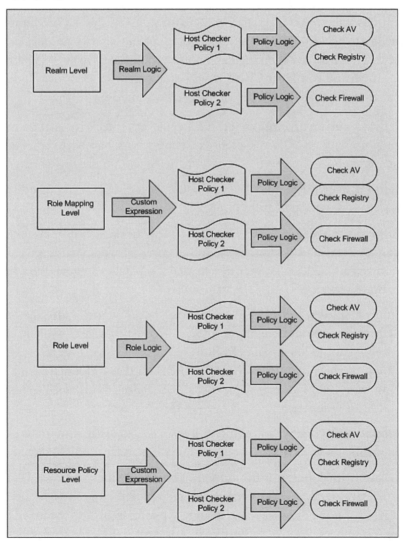

As we mentioned at the beginning of this chapter, Windows, Mac, and Linux have different Host Checker rule checks because each operating system is different, so we will break these down into the different host checks for each operating system.

## Windows Host Checks

Host Checker has the most support for performing checks on the Windows operating system (Windows 98 through Vista). Juniper has provided support for both predefined and custom host checks. Predefined host checks are used to verify compliance with checks such as antivirus, antispyware, and operating system version. These are precompiled checks that use a combination of file, process, and Registry key checks to ensure compliance. Host Checker will use different types of checks to verify different types of applications. This is because different applications will create different files, Registry checks, and so on. Juniper has to create the predefined checks on a case-by-case basis. Custom checks are checks that you can manually create to check for a wide range of system properties, which we will discuss shortly. You can install and run Host Checker with any privilege level on Windows. Host Checker is capable of the following types of checks on Windows:

- **Predefined antivirus checks** Host Checker can check to confirm whether a system is running an antivirus client (just about every antivirus software you can imagine is supported) as well as whether the signatures are up-to-date.

- **Predefined firewall checks** Host Checker can check to see whether the end system is running a client firewall.

- **Predefined malware checks** This predefined check is used to ensure that you are running an antimalware program. Although most antivirus/antispyware applications function as antimalware, Juniper has created a separate category for a few select antimalware vendors.

- **Predefined spyware checks** This section checks to make sure that you are running various antispyware applications which help protect your machine from spyware infection. This doesn't check to see whether you have spyware. If you want something to check your PC manually to ensure that it doesn't have a spyware infection, you should look at deploying the Advanced Endpoint Defense application through Host Checker (discussed later in this chapter).

- **Predefined OS checks** You can check to make sure that computers connecting to your network are of a particular operating system and, in some instances, service pack.

- **Predefined third-party NHC check** You can define your own host check by using the Host Checker API, which will reference the check to be performed. This can also be a host check that you may purchase or acquire from a third-party vendor. This check will be a dynamic link library (DLL) file that must be deployed on the client machine, and you will define the path that the DLL exists in for Host Checker to launch.

■ **Custom ports** This check can verify whether a port (or list/range of ports) is in use on the client machine. This check can be useful in conjunction with the firewall check, because the firewall check only verifies whether the machine is running a firewall, not what ports it may be listening on.

■ **Custom process** This check is used to determine whether a process is running on a client end system. You may want to use this check to ensure that an application is running (such as a corporate compliance checking application, or an application that isn't predefined in Host Checker). You can also check to make sure that an application isn't running on an end machine. For example, say a new worm is spreading throughout the Internet and runs a process on an end system called Replicate.exe. You can use this host check to make sure this process is not running on the end system, or else trigger another event to happen or prevent the user from connecting.

> **WARNING**
>
> The process check will check to see whether a process is running on the end system, but there are a few caveats that you should note. First, you can change the name of an application such as Notepad.exe to whatever you want, so a user could potentially disable the application you are checking for, and rename Notepad.exe to that application name and run it, which would still result in the user passing that host check. To help prevent this, Juniper can calculate the MD5 hash of an application's .exe file to make sure that it is in fact the same application you want to check for (you will have to calculate the MD5 hash of the application and enter that hash value into Host Checker's MD5 field). The only issue with this approach is that applications may change quite often, which will change the MD5 hash (e.g., getting an updated or new version of an application). You can enter multiple MD5 hashes to check for this, but this may not be that easy to manage. The same is true for file checks.

■ **Custom file** You can provide a check to ensure that a file is present or not present on an end system. Additionally, you can check to see when the file was modified, or what version it is if that meta-information is present (Windows only). The file can also be calculated against an MD5 hash.

■ **Custom Registry setting** Host Checker allows you to check whether a Registry key is present within the Windows Registry. This can be useful for checking end system configurations, and is a popular method for making sure a connecting machine is a corporate asset by checking for a Registry key that you bury deep in the Registry (often pushed out through Group Policy).

- **Custom NetBIOS** This check allows you to verify the NetBIOS name on a system. You can list multiple NetBIOS names.

- **Custom MAC address** You can check to verify that a connecting machine has a particular Media Access Control (MAC) address. For instance, you might want to make sure that any connecting machine is an HP machine that is using the HP (Compaq) OUI, which is 00:0B:CD:xx:xx:xx.

- **Custom machine certificate** This allows you to verify that a Windows machine connecting to your network matches a valid certificate. Note that you must specify who issued the certificate to verify the validity of the connecting machine. This is a new feature as of IVE 6.0.

- **Custom remote IMV** If you plan to use the TNC architecture in your IVE, you will need to implement IMV rules to help evaluate these checks. Note that this option is visible only after you have created an IMV server and IMV policy.

## Damage & Defense...

### Verifying Asset Identity

Administrators are often tasked with providing a mechanism to grant different levels of access based on whether the machine that is connecting to the network is truly a corporate asset. You can use Host Checker to help verify the identity of a machine connecting to the IVE in several different ways. The most popular mechanisms to verify machine identity are machine certificates, Registry keys, NetBIOS names, and MAC addresses. So, with these different options, which is the best one to select? If you are most concerned with security, you will want to use machine certificates (or at least machine certificates with the other methods discussed). Machine certificates are the most preferred method because NetBIOS names can be changed or spoofed, Registry keys can be modified, and MAC addresses can be spoofed, but machine certificates are not considered "spoofable." It is possible that someone with appropriate rights on a machine could copy the certificate and apply it to another machine, but you can always revoke a certificate, which is something you cannot do with the other methods of verifying a device. Of course, using certificates means you must have a public key infrastructure (PKI) in place, so you will need to make sure you have a mechanism to generate, verify, and revoke certificates.

## *Mac Host Checks*

Because this isn't a Windows-only world, the IVE has provided basic support for checking compliance of machines connecting on Macintosh end systems. Although this list is brief at the moment, it is likely that Juniper will be expanding the different types of host checks in the future, as the Macintosh becomes more and more popular.

- **Custom ports** This check can verify whether a port (or list/range of ports) is in use on the client machine. This check ensures that multiple ports are either open or closed on the end system.

- **Custom process** This check is used to determine whether a process is running on a client end system. You may want to use this check to ensure that an application is running (such as a corporate compliance checking application, or an application that isn't predefined in Host Checker). You can also check to make sure that an application isn't running on an end machine. For example, say a new worm is spreading throughout the Internet and runs a process on an end system called Replicate.exe. You can use this host check to make sure this process is not running on the end system, or else trigger another event to happen or prevent the user from connecting.

- **Custom file** You can provide a check to ensure that a file is present or not present on an end system. Additionally, you can check to see when the file was modified. The file can also be calculated against an MD5 hash.

## *Linux Host Checks*

Linux currently has the same support for host checks as the Macintosh. It is likely that these checks will be expanded in the future as the popularity of Linux continues to grow.

---

**T**ɪᴘ

Each Host Checker policy can have a separate component for Windows, Macintosh, and Linux so that you can apply only one policy to be evaluated in the IVE, and the IVE will evaluate the appropriate rules for the client machine's operating system.

---

# Host Checker Policy Logic and Remediation

Juniper has drastically enhanced the power of Host Checker policies by enabling the creation of logic to create complex matching criteria (see Figure 8.2). Host Checker allows you to enforce AND, OR, NOT logic to rules to determine whether the policy evaluates to true or false (remember that you reference policies, not individual rules, within the IVE configuration). You have essentially three different options when configuring logic within a policy:

- **Require all of the above rules** This means all rules in a specific policy must evaluate to true or else the policy will evaluate to false. For example, the logic for this option would look like (Rule1 AND Rule2 AND Rule3).

- **Require any of the above rules** This means as long as at least one rule in the policy evaluates to true, your policy will evaluate to true. For example, the logic for this option would look like (Rule1 OR Rule2 OR Rule3).

- **Require custom expression** This option means you must define the custom expression for matching the rules using the AND, OR, NOT logic. This gives you great flexibility for defining your own custom logic into an expression. For example, you could make a complex rule with the following logic: ((Rule1 OR Rule2) AND (NOT Rule3)).

**Figure 8.2** Host Checker Policy Logic and Remediation

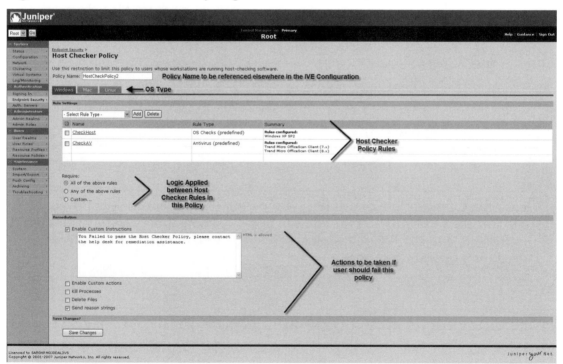

## Remediation Actions

Juniper offers several actions that you can perform in any combination to help customize the response to a failed user authentication. Please keep in mind that these are executed only when the user fails authentication, not when the user passes authentication. Here is a list of the various options that you can configure on a policy-by-policy basis:

- **Enable Custom Instructions** Custom instructions are in the form of a pop-up message that will appear in the user's browser when the user fails authentication. You can include HTML in the failed message to help customize the experience, and even offer links to other Web pages for remediation or additional information.

- **Enable Custom Actions** Custom actions essentially means you should evaluate other policies if the user fails this policy. This allows you to create chains of policies. This is different from the logic that you employ within a policy, because this essentially instructs the IVE to evaluate other policies should the user fail to pass this policy. When you evaluate other policies, the outcome of the user's compliance will be transferred to the new policy that you choose to evaluate. For instance, say you fail to pass one policy (PolicyA) and its custom action is to evaluate PolicyB. If you pass PolicyB, you will have passed the host check, even though you just failed PolicyA. We will discuss this in more detail later in this chapter.

- **Kill Processes** This option will kill a running process on the user's machine should the user fail to authenticate on this policy. You obviously have to be careful with this option, as it could create some major problems on the user's computer. One example of where this might be an attractive option is to check to see whether a machine is infected with a new worm that has been spreading throughout the Internet, and to kill that process if you detect it running on the user's machine. You can also specify the MD5 hash of the process that you want to kill (it checks the .exe file to compute the hash).

- **Delete Files** If a host check policy fails, you can trigger the IVE to delete a file on the end machine's operating system. You must define the path to the file that you want to delete. You can optionally define an MD5 hash on the file to ensure that it matches the exact file you want to delete.

- **Send Reason String** This option will display what checks failed to the user should the user fail to pass the host checks for this policy. This message will be displayed in the Web browser in the screen that accompanies a failed policy check. For example, say you have a rule in a policy called CheckAV which checks to make sure the antivirus client is running and signatures are up-to-date. If you have the Send Reason String option enabled, and the user fails authentication, the user would receive a message stating "CheckAV evaluated to False." You may or may not want to give these messages to users. Sometimes it is better to enable custom instructions, because you can always see what evaluated to true or false in the user access logs, or within a policy trace.

# Host Checker Options

Host Checker has a number of system-wide options that you can enforce to help provide enhanced security to your network. This section outlines these behaviors in Host Checker. You can find all of these options on the **Authentication | Endpoint Security | Host Checker** page within the AdminUI:

- **Perform Check Every** This option allows you to dynamically reevaluate client compliance at a certain time interval. By default, this is set to reevaluate the client every 10 minutes. This is a powerful feature because the client is always evaluated when it first connects, but you typically want to ensure that the client complies with your security policy throughout the duration of the session (and doesn't do something like turn on antivirus protection so that it can connect to the IVE and then turn it off after it connects). By enabling this option, you can perform a check as often as every minute to ensure that the client complies with the checks. If the client no longer complies with the configured security policies, the appropriate actions based on the policies will be taken. Note that you must enable dynamic policy evaluation for Host Checker for this to take effect.

- **Client-Side Process Inactivity Timeout** You can determine how long the IVE should wait before it forces a timeout when the user is trying to process Host Checker tasks. For instance, if the user logs into the IVE which starts the Host Checker process but then decides to go to a new Web site, or if the user is downloading Host Checker over a very slow link, how long should the IVE wait until it considers the process to be timed out? By default, this is 20 minutes, which is quite a long time. If you notice that you are consuming too many resources while users are logging in with Host Checker, you may wish to decrease this interval.

- **Auto-Upgrade Host Checker** This instructs the IVE to upgrade Host Checker whenever a new version is available. This typically happens when you upgrade your IVE firmware. You must be running the same version of the IVE firmware for Host Checker to work properly, so you would want to enable this only if you did not want users to upgrade their code for some specific reason.

- **Perform Dynamic Policy Re-evaluation** This option will trigger Host Checker to force a realm-level dynamic policy refresh to make sure the user has the appropriate policy actions based on the outcome of the host check if the user's status changes.

- **Create Host Checker Connection Control Policy** This option applies only to Windows hosts, and has Host Checker act as a pseudo-firewall. It will essentially disable all inbound Transmission Control Protocol (TCP) connections to the host that is connecting to the IVE, but will allow all outbound TCP connections. Some administrators may wish to disable inbound connections to prevent the host from being able to have one foot in the internal network and one foot outside the network when connected to the IVE. Note that you must have administrative rights on your end host for this to work.

■ **Enable Advanced Endpoint Defense: Malware Protection**  Although it is nice to be able to check to see whether antivirus, antispyware, or antimalware software is running, doing so doesn't actually tell you whether the machine is infected with malicious software, just whether the application is running. Juniper has partnered with WholeSecurity to provide you with the ability to scan a Windows end system to make sure common threats such as keyloggers, Trojans, and other malware are not present on the end system. By selecting this option, you will enable Advanced Endpoint Detection on the system. This will not actually apply any changes to Host Checker, but rather will create the policies automatically which you can apply to Host Checker. We will discuss this in more detail later in this chapter.

You can configure two additional behavioral options for Advanced Endpoint Defense software:

■ **Enable Silent Enforcement of Signature Scan**  This option means the user will not be notified when the software detects a piece of malware running on the system. Administrators will be notified within the logs.

■ **Enable User Control over Disabling Behavior Blocker**  By default, the user will not have control over stopping the Endpoint Defense process from blocking applications it deems to be malware. You may or may not want to disable this so that the user has control over this. By default, users do not have control.

# Host Checker Definition Updates

Because Host Checker is responsible for being able to check for software and accompanying definitions that are dynamically changing, it must also have a mechanism that supports updating its definitions to be able to accommodate the new definitions. As of Version 5.4, Juniper included two new features which allow you to do exactly that. They are Virus Signature Version Monitoring and Endpoint Security Assessment Plug-ins. We will cover both of these in this section.

## Virus Signature Version Monitoring

Juniper used to support file checking only for the last modified date to check whether the files were up-to-date. The version monitoring feature allows you to ask Host Checker to make sure the signature definitions are considered up-to-date according to the antivirus software vendor. To do this you must perform two tasks. You must create a rule to check for predefined antivirus clients (make sure to enable the **Virus signatures must be up to date** option; we will demonstrate this in an example later in this chapter). Next, you must set up the virus signature updates system-wide. To do so, follow these steps:

1. Go to **Authentication | Endpoint Security | Host Checker**.

2. Expand the **Virus signature version monitoring** menu.

3. Select the **Auto-Update virus signature list**.

4. By default, the **Download path** is set to https://download.juniper.net/software/ av/uac/avupdate.dat. Leave this as is unless you have a specific reason to change it (e.g., if the Juniper Technical Assistance Center [JTAC] instructed you to do so).

5. The IVE is configured to check for updates for virus signatures every 30 minutes by default. If you want to change the frequency, define the custom **Default Interval**.

6. You must provide your Juniper support credentials in the IVE configuration. If you do not have a Juniper Support account already, you should contact either JTAC (1-888-314-JTAC) or your Juniper reseller to set up an account. You must provide your **Username** and **Password**. This connection will be performed with HTTPS, so you need to make sure the IVE will be able to connect to the Juniper download server.

7. Click **Save Changes**.

---

**NOTE**

Alternatively, you can configure the IVE to manually install the pattern update. To do so you must download the file to your local machine. Under the **Virus Signature Version Monitoring** menu, simply click the **Browse** button and locate the file on your local machine. Then click **Save Changes**. Note that you do not have to have the auto-update virus signature list, download path, download interval, or username/password to be able to update manually.

---

## Endpoint Security Assessment Plug-in Update

Signature updates are not the only updates you can apply to the IVE. Because the IVE supports version-specific checks for different antivirus, firewall, antispyware, antimalware, and operating system checks, the IVE must be able to support host checks of new versions of these applications when they come out. Before IVE 5.4, you could update the list of predefined host checks only by upgrading the entire IVE firmware. This caused a problem, because many organizations had to perform extensive testing before they could simply upgrade to support new host checks. To help solve this, Juniper integrated this feature as a manual update patch that you can apply, called the Endpoint Security Assessment Plug-in (or ESAP update for short). At the time of this writing, you must go to the Juniper download site for the IVE software and download the ESAP update to your local machine. Here are the steps to follow:

1. Go to www.juniper.net/customers/csc/software/. Note that you will have to sign into the Juniper support site with a valid account.

2. Click the **SSL VPN (IVE)** hyperlink to download the IVE code. You must have a valid support contract to be able to download the software.

3. Click the **ESAP** link on the right side of the page. You will be brought to another page that lists all of the ESAP plug-in versions, with the highest number being the most current. Download that update to your local machine by right-clicking on the appropriate update and selecting **Save As**, or **Save Link As** depending on your Web browser.

4. After you have downloaded the software update, upload and apply it to the IVE by going to **Authentication | Endpoint Security | Host Checker**.

5. Under the **Manage Endpoint Security Assessment Plug-in Version** section, click the **Browse** button, and select the ESAP update on your local machine.

6. If you want to upload and apply the ESAP update, select **Set as active after upload**. If you simply want to upload the update and not apply it, do not check this option.

7. Click the **Upload** button.

---

**NOTE**

The IVE will indicate which update is active under the Currently Active ESAP version (see Figure 8.3). You can select a different version to use by selecting it and clicking **Active**. If you want to remove a version, select it and click the **Delete** button. Note that if you are using a predefined definition that is referenced in the version you are trying to delete, or if you try to downgrade to an older version of an ESAP that does not support a particular predefined check, the IVE will throw an error message. You will need to remove the reference to this object in your Host Checker rules. For example, if you are using a predefined definition for Trend Micro Officescan 8 and you want to roll back to an older ESAP update that doesn't have the definition for Trend Micro OfficeScan 8, you will have to remove the reference to the object in the Host Checker rule to which it is referenced to roll back the ESAP.

---

**Figure 8.3** The Juniper Support Page for Downloading ESAP Updates

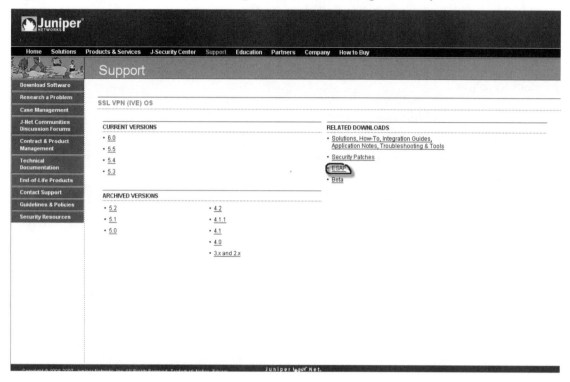

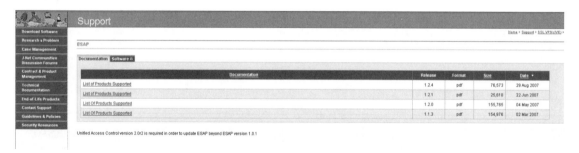

# Configuring Host Checker Rules

So far, we have discussed the properties and options that apply to Host Checker, but we have not discussed how to make Host Checker rules. In this section, we will discuss how to configure a few different types of Host Checker rules.

# Configuring a Host Checker Policy

Before you can create individual Host Checker rules, you must create a Host Checker policy. Creating a policy is quite simple. In this example, we will create a Host Checker policy into which we can use put Host Checker rules.

1. Navigate to the **Authentication | Endpoint Security | Host Checker** page.

2. Under the **Policies** section, click **New**.

3. This will bring you to a new screen which should have the Host Checker tab selected by default. You must define a **Name** for the Host Checker policy, which will be referenced elsewhere in the IVE configuration.

4. Click the **Continue** button, which will create the policy and bring you into the **Rule configuration** screen.

# Host Checker Policies or Rules?

One question you may be asking yourself is whether you should create multiple Host Checker policies with individual rules (one rule per policy), or whether you should create one or a few policies with multiple Host Checker rules within them. This is an interesting question that doesn't necessarily have a one-size-fits-all answer. Remember that only Host Checker policies can be referenced within the IVE, not individual rules. Also, rules cannot be referenced by anything other than the policy in which they exist, so you cannot reference one rule by multiple policies.

So, now you're probably still wondering what the best approach is. Here are some tips that will help you formulate your implementation:

- Start by verbally defining the behavior you want Host Checker to evaluate. Creating a flow chart can also be very helpful for both design and documentation purposes.

- Typically, the best place to implement logic is within the Host Checker policy itself. You can configure the IVE to match multiple policies, but you are limited in the logic which you can implement across multiple policies (typically it is an AND/OR logic at that level). Therefore, if you need complex logic to evaluate multiple rules, it is best to have the rules within a single policy where you can define the logic to determine whether the policy passes.

- Remember that the logic defined in the Host Checker policy determines whether the client passes the policy. For instance, the client may not pass any rules within Host Checker, but may still pass the policy if you were to use a custom expression that used the appropriate logic to indicate that not passing any host checks indicates that you pass the policy.

- Try to find rules that you can apply in multiple places. For instance, if you know you want to implement two rules—CheckAV, for checking that the client is running an antivirus client, and CheckAsset, for checking whether the machine is a corporate asset—across the board, it would be helpful to put them into a single policy rather than mixing them with other rules, because you might have to define complex logic to get the correct implementation.

- Unless you have only a few host checks to perform, it is usually best not to implement a single rule per policy, but rather to use logic to collapse multiple rules within a policy. This is because you have to reference the policies, not the rules, elsewhere in the configuration, and having too many policies makes it more difficult to manage.

## Configuring a Predefined Antivirus Rule

In this example, we will configure a Host Checker rule which will evaluate a Windows machine to ensure that it is running one of a list of approved antivirus clients for MyCompany's corporate security policy. These antivirus products include F-Secure Anti-Virus version 6, McAfee VirusScan 9, and Trend Micro OfficeScan Client 8 with up-to-date antivirus signatures. We will assume that you have already enabled the automatic virus signature updates. See Figure 8.4 for the AdminUI of this check.

To configure this example, follow these steps:

1. Go to **Authentication | Endpoint Security | Host Checker** and either select an existing policy, or create a new policy as discussed earlier in this section.

    Note that you can set up different checks for different operating systems within the same policy, but in this case, we are going to be doing a **Predefined Antivirus** check under the **Windows** tab.

2. Under the **Rule Settings** section, expand the **Select Rule Type** drop-down menu, select **Predefined Antivirus**, and click **Add**.

3. Define a **Rule Name** (no spaces!) and then select the various antivirus products that you want to check for. When you select multiple antivirus products within a single rule, the IVE essentially treats the selection within the rule as a logical OR. So, for instance, in this example we are going to select **F-Secure Anti-Virus version 6**, **Sophos Anti-Virus 7**, and **Trend Micro OfficeScan Client v7** and **v8** and then click **Add**. We will also enable the **Virus signatures must be up to date** checkbox. This rule will essentially be evaluated as the following: (You must be running F-Secure Anti-Virus 6 OR McAfee VirusScan 9 OR Trend Micro Office Scan Client 8) AND your signatures must be up-to-date.

4. Click **Save Changes**.

**Figure 8.4** Configuring a Host Checker Antivirus Rule

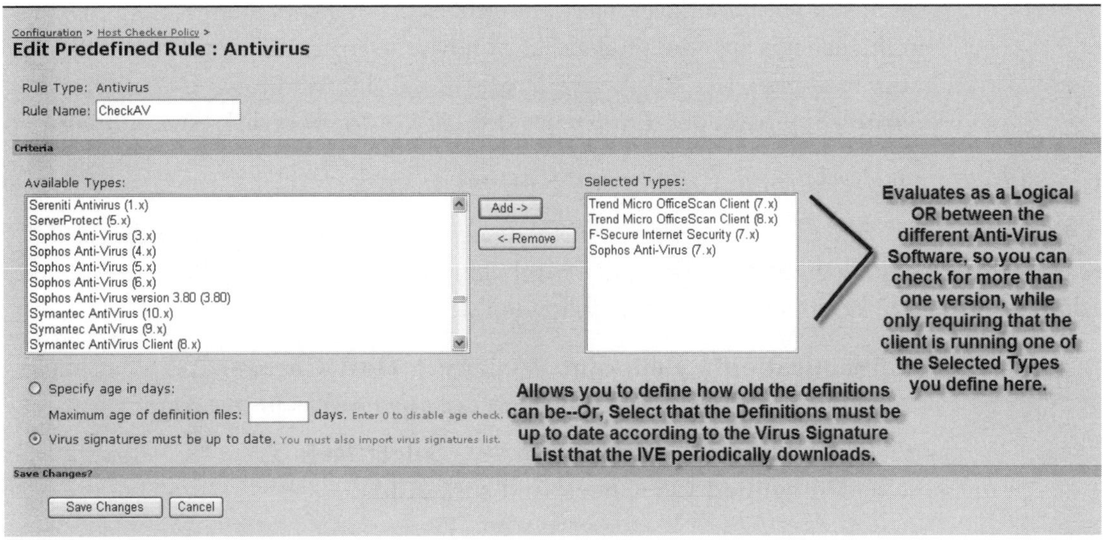

## Configuring a Predefined Firewall Rule

In this example, we will create a host check rule to see whether the client is running the Windows XP Server Pack 2 firewall on its machine:

1. Go to **Authentication | Endpoint Security | Host Checker** and either select an existing policy, or create a new policy as discussed earlier in this section.

2. Under the **Rule Settings** section, expand the **Select Rule Type** drop-down menu, select **Predefined Firewall**, and click **Add**.

3. Define a **Rule Name** (no spaces) and then select the appropriate firewall products to check for. If you select multiple objects, Host Checker evaluates them as a logical OR between the different firewall products, so you have to match only one to pass the rule. In this example, select **Microsoft Windows Firewall (xP SP2)**, click **Add**, then click **Save Changes**.

## Configuring a Predefined Antispyware Rule

In this example, we will create a host check to see whether Ad-Aware Professional 6.0, Windows Defender 1.0, or Webroot Spy Sweeper Enterprise 3.0 has been predefined:

1. Go to **Authentication | Endpoint Security | Host Checker** and either select an existing policy or create a new policy as discussed earlier in this section.

2. Under the **Rule Settings** section, expand the **Select Rule Type** drop-down menu, select **Predefined Spyware**, and click **Add**.

3.  Define a **Rule Name** (no spaces) and then select the appropriate spyware products to check for. If you select multiple objects, Host Checker evaluates them as a logical OR between the different spyware products, so you have to match only one to pass the rule. In this example, select **Ad-Aware Professional 6.0**, **Windows Defender 1.0**, and **Webroot Spy Sweeper Enterprise 3.0**, click **Add**, then click **Save Changes**.

## Configuring a Predefined Operating System Check Rule

In this example, we will check the end systems that are connecting to make sure they are either Windows XP or Windows Vista, and are not running a version of the Windows Server Edition software. To do so we perform the following steps:

1.  Go to **Authentication | Endpoint Security | Host Checker** and either select an existing policy, or create a new policy as discussed earlier in this section.

2.  Under the **Rule Settings** section, expand the **Select Rule Type** drop-down menu, select **Predefined OS Check**, and click **Add**.

3.  Define a **Rule Name** (no spaces) and then select the appropriate OS versions. If you select multiple objects, Host Checker evaluates them as a logical OR between the different operating systems. In this example, select **Windows XP**, **Windows XP 64-bit**, and **Windows Vista**. We can additionally select which service pack we want to detect, but that is not necessary, and you can just ignore the service pack level for this example. Click **Save Changes**.

## Configuring a Custom Port Rule

In this example, we will check to see whether the client machine connecting to the IVE is listening on TCP port 12345, which is the port that NetBus uses to allow remote control of a machine. We want to make sure this port is not being used, along with TCP port 22 for SSH and TCP ports 5900–5910 for VNC.

1.  Go to **Authentication | Endpoint Security | Host Checker** and either select an existing policy, or create a new policy as discussed earlier in this section.

2.  Under the **Rule Settings** section, expand the **Select Rule Type** drop-down menu, select **Custom Ports**, and click **Add**.

3.  Define a **Rule Name** for the port checks. The IVE will access either a single port number, a list of port numbers (delimited by commas, no spaces), port ranges (e.g., 1000–1100), or a combination of ports and port ranges. In this example, we are looking to match 22,12345, and 5900–5910, so our string would be "22,12345,5900–5910" in the **Ports** field. In this example, we want to make sure the user is not listening on these ports, so we select **Deny**, but if we wanted to make sure a client was listening on a particular port we would select **Required**.

4.  Click **Save Changes**.

## *Configuring a Custom Process Rule*

In this example, we will make sure hosts connecting to the IVE are running an application called CompMon.exe, which performs health checks on a user's computer and reports back to a central server when the connection is available. We want to make sure this application is running and that a user did not disable it. To do so, we implement a custom process check (see Figure 8.5).

1.  Go to **Authentication | Endpoint Security | Host Checker** and either select an existing policy, or create a new policy as discussed earlier in this section.

2.  Under the **Rule Settings** section, expand the **Select Rule Type** drop-down menu, select **Custom Process**, and click **Add**.

3.  Define a **Rule Name** for the process check. Next, we enter **CompMon.exe** in the **Process Name** field, and select **Required** because we want to make sure the user is running the application. Selecting **Deny** would mean we wanted to make sure the user wasn't running this application.

4.  We want to make sure a user doesn't simply rename an application such as Notepad.exe, and that the process we are detecting is in fact the corporate CompMon.exe. To enforce the certainty, we will use MD5 calculations to make sure it is indeed the correct file. There are two different versions of this application: one that runs on Windows XP and one that runs on Windows 2000. These applications are slightly different, so we need to calculate different MD5 hashes for each program. We will use the application MD5 Calculator 1.0, which is available from www.softpedia.com/get/System/File-Management/MD5-calculator.shtml, to calculate the MD5 hash of the CompMon.exe files. In this example, the Windows XP hash was "121E8AF1B95CFEA9FA6C45730A0 3138A" and the Windows 2000 hash was "5FF400758907BEF18B2653BF7970857C". We will enter those values on separate lines in the **MD5 Checksums** box.

---

**NOTE**

You can use wildcard values within the process name. The * wildcard will match any character up to a "." or the end for the name, and a "?" will match a single character. We would enter *.**exe** to check for any process with the .exe extension, and **testapp**\*.**exe** to match testapp, followed by any characters, with the .exe extension. Alternatively, we could match any process that is called syscontrol.* with any extension. An example of using "?" would be if we wanted to match any version of an application that follows the format CustomApp<Version><Platform>.exe. So, for instance, the process name might look like CustomApp7WinXP.exe. If we only wanted to match for any Windows XP version of the app, we might use the expression *CustomApp?WinXP.exe*.

---

5.  Click **Save Changes**.

**Figure 8.5** Configuring a Custom Process Check

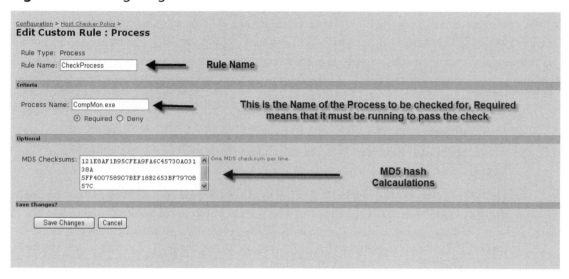

## Configuring a Custom File Check

In this example, we want to check that our antispyware software has up-to-date definitions. Currently, the IVE supports version checking for antivirus only, so to check that our antispyware software is up-to-date, we will check to see when the definition file was last modified. Figure 8.6 shows how the following example is configured in the AdminUI.

1. Go to **Authentication | Endpoint Security | Host Checker** and either select an existing policy, or create a new policy as discussed earlier in this section.

2. Under the **Rule Settings** section, expand the **Select Rule Type** drop-down menu, select **Custom File**, and click **Add**.

3. Define a **Rule Name** for the file check. We must define the filename with a path. This is important because Host Checker must know where to look for the file. In this example, we want to look in the user's program files directory. We can use an environment variable to help us define this file check because different systems may have this directory in a different place. So, in our example we will be checking for the definition files for Ad-Aware, which are located at <%ProgramFiles%> Ad-Aware SE Personaldefs.ref.

4. We will also define that this file has been modified within the past five days to ensure that definitions are up-to-date. We will not define a minimum version because we want to make sure the files are current, and version numbers may change too quickly. We also do not want to define an MD5 check because this

will change with every update, and thus it would not be good to manage in this example.

5.  Click **Save Changes**.

**Figure 8.6** Configuring Host Checker File Checks

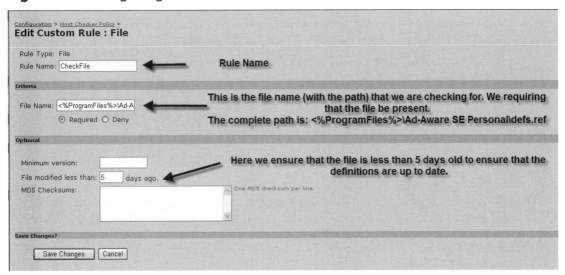

The following Windows environment variables for file checks are based on the published environment variables Juniper provides in its Admin Guide (you can use these variables within the File Name field to define dynamic paths based on variable names):

- **<%APPDATA%>** This maps to the Application Data directory of the currently logged-in user. For instance, if the user's name was gwashington and his document folder was C:\Documents and Settings\gwashington, *<%APPDATA%>* would be the same as writing *C:\Documents and Settings\gwashington\Application Data*.

- **<%windir%>** This variable links to the Windows Install directory. For instance, on a computer where Windows is installed on the C: drive, this would map to C:\Windows.

- **<%ProgramFiles%>** This maps to the Program Files definition for the user's machine. When you install Windows on the C: drive, this would map to C:\Program Files.

- **<%CommonProgramFiles%>** This maps to the Common Files directory within Program Files. On a Windows machine where the Windows Install directory is on the C: drive, this would look like C:\Program Files\Common Files.

- **<%USERPROFILE%>** This links to the user's profile, which is typically stored under the username within the Documents and Settings folder. So, for a user who is named gwashington and is on a machine on which the home drive is C: this would look like C:\Documents and Settings\gwashington.

- **<%HOMEDRIVE%>** This maps to the operating system's home drive. On a machine where the user installs Windows on the C: drive, this would be C:\.

- **<%Temp%>** This is the folder where temporary files are stored for a particular user. It is located within the user's profile, so for a user named gwashington, it would be C:\Documents and Settings\gwashington\Local Settings\Temp.

You can reference the following Macintosh and Linux environment variables in file checks:

- **<%java.home%>** On the Macintosh, this would typically default to the following location: /System/Library/Frameworks/JavaVM.framework/Versions/1.6.0/Home. On Linux, this would typically default to the following location: /local/local/java/j2sdk1.6.0_01/jre.

- **<%java.io.tmpdir%>** On the Macintosh, this would typically be found in the following location: /tmp. On Linux, this would typically be found in the following location: /tmp.

- **<%user.dir%>** On the Macintosh, this would typically be found in the following location: /Users/<username>. On Linux, this would typically be found in the following location: /home-shared/<username>.

- **<%user.home%>** On the Macintosh, this would typically be found in the following location: /Users/<username>. On Linux, this would typically be found in the following location: /home /<username>.

## Creating a Custom Registry Key Check

Registry keys are typically used to define system and application properties on a Windows machine. They are usually configured by applications and not manually by administrators, but creating a custom Registry key can be a good mechanism for identifying an asset. This is attractive because it is much easier than deploying a PKI. In addition, the Registry can be restricted, so users cannot modify it without appropriate rights.

In the following example, we will configure a Registry check based on the following Registry key being present: HKEY_LOCAL_MACHINE\SYSTEM\CurrentControlSet\

Services\Company\CompanyAsset, with a value of 1. See Figure 8.7, which follows this example, for configuring the Registry key check in the AdminUI.

1. Go to **Authentication | Endpoint Security | Host Checker** and either select an existing policy, or create a new policy as discussed earlier in this section.

2. Under the **Rule Settings** section, expand the **Select Rule Type** drop-down menu, select **Custom Registry Setting**, and click **Add**.

3. Define a **Rule Name** for the policy (no spaces) and then select the appropriate **Registry Root Key**. Your choices are:

   HKEY

   HKEY_LOCAL_MACHINE

   HKEY_USERS

   HKEY_CURRENT_USER

   HKEY_CURRENT_CONFIG

   HKEY_CLASSES_ROOT

4. Next, define a **Registry Subkey**, which is where the registry entry is located. In this example, this would be under \SYSTEM\CurrentControlSet\Services\Company.

5. Define the actual **Name** of the Registry object itself, which in this example would be CompanyAsset.

6. Registry keys can come in different types: either as a string, binary, or DWORD key. You must define which **Type** of key you are looking for. This is the same type of key you specified when you created the key. In this example, we will call it a string.

7. Define the actual **Value**, which in this example will be 1.

8. If you are checking for a minimum version of an application, in which case you would be checking for a number (e.g., a version is greater than 3), you would define your **Value** as the minimum version, and select the **Minimum Version**. In this example, we will not select this.

9. Click **Save Changes**.

**Figure 8.7** Configuring a Registry Key Check

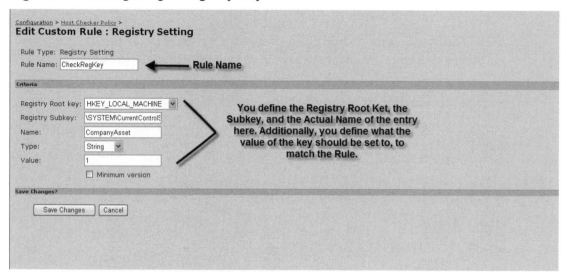

## Configuring a NetBIOS Check

If you want to check whether a machine connecting to the IVE has a particular IVE, you can use a NetBIOS check. In the following example, we will check to see whether a machine's NetBIOS name is President:

1. Go to **Authentication | Endpoint Security | Host Checker** and either select an existing policy, or create a new policy as discussed earlier in this section.

2. Under the **Rule Settings** section, expand the **Select Rule Type** drop-down menu, select **Custom NetBIOS**, and click **Add**.

3. Define a **Rule Name** for the device you want to check for (no spaces), and specify the value of the NetBIOS name that you want to detect. You can enter multiple names on separate lines, but you cannot use wildcard characters. For this example, we will enter **President** in the **NetBIOS Names** box.

4. Select whether you want to **Require** the value listed in the rule to pass the check, or whether you want to **Deny** any session where the host check matches the values listed.

5. Click **Save Changes**.

## Configuring a Custom MAC Address Check

Under certain circumstances, you may wish to configure a host check rule to check for a particular group of MAC addresses on the machines connecting to your network. You can actually glean some interesting information when you know a MAC address. This is because MAC addresses have a special format which indicates who manufactured the card. You can get more information on this process at http://standards.ieee.org/regauth/oui/index.shtml. In this example, we will search for any MAC address that was manufactured by Intel with an OUI of 00:18:DE, or the MAC address 00:19:FC:11:A8:CA:

1. Go to **Authentication | Endpoint Security | Host Checker** and either select an existing policy, or create a new policy as discussed earlier in this section.

2. Under the **Rule Settings** section, expand the **Select Rule Type** drop-down menu, select **Custom MAC Address**, and click **Add**.

3. Define a **Rule Name** for this MAC address check.

4. Define the actual MAC addresses that you want to check for. You can enter one MAC address statement per line, and you can use wildcard characters in the **MAC Addresses** field. In this example, we will enter **00:18:DE:\*:\*:\*** and **00:19:FC:11:A8:CA**.

5. For this example we will select **Require** because we want to make sure the user will pass the check if he matches. If we selected **Deny** the user would not pass if he matched the check.

6. Click **Save As**.

## Configuring a Custom Machine Certificate Check

One way to enhance your network's security is to ensure that you trust the machines that connect to your network, or give different levels of access based on whether you have control of the asset that is connecting to the IVE. Although Registry keys, MAC addresses, and NetBIOS names could be valid ways to check a machine, they can all be spoofed quite easily. Machine certificates are another way to check a machine to ensure that it is a company asset. Of course, you can already use user certificates in the realm, role, or resource policy restrictions, which don't use Host Checker at all. In this example, we will use machine certificates to confirm that a machine is indeed a member of Active Directory. We will assume that you have already added your certificate authority (CA) signing certificate into the **Trusted Client CA** section of the IVE (we discussed this earlier in the book).

1. Go to **Authentication | Endpoint Security | Host Checker** and either select an existing policy, or create a new policy as discussed earlier in this section.

2. Under the **Rule Settings** section, expand the **Select Rule Type** drop-down menu, select **Custom Machine Certificate**, and click **Add**.

3. Define a **Rule Name** for this machine certificate check.

4. Specify the **Select Issuer Certificate**, which will be a **Trusted Client CA** certificate that you have previously loaded to the IVE.

5. You can optionally specify whether the IVE should evaluate other properties of the certificate to narrow down the range of what you want to accept (e.g., not just authenticate whether the certificate is valid). Note that the IVE will validate the certificate no matter what, but you can specify certain properties of a certificate that you would like to match. These variables are properties of the certificates themselves. For instance, you can match a CN, DN, DC, OU, or e-mail address. You enter the variable you want to check for in the **Certificate Field**, specify the actual value you expect to be present to match the check in the **Expected Value** field, and then click **Add** to add this check. You can configure multiple checks. One good way to help you determine what checks are matching or failing is to do a policy trace, which will show you all of the properties of the cert that are matching or failing to match, along with the values that are delivered to the IVE. This is a good tool to use to help you tune your policy.

6. Click **Save Changes** to apply the changes and save your check.

---

**NOTE**

If you have multiple machine certificates on the machine that is logging into the IVE, Host Checker will send the first machine certificate it finds in the certificate store to the IVE to validate the certificate against the issuer certificate you configured for the Host Checker rule.

---

## Configuring a Third-Party NHC Check

The third-party NHC check is somewhat deprecated these days with the introduction of the TNC architecture to the IVE (which provides a standard API to configure truly custom Host Checker checks on an end system). However, you may still wish to use the Host Checker API to configure your own checks (because this is a very powerful tool), and therefore, you may still want to implement this type of rule. Configuring the actual Host Checker checks is outside the scope of this book, but luckily, Juniper has developed a document to provide you information on how to configure these checks on the end system. This document is located at www.juniper.net/support/, under the IVE Documentation section (requires login). The document that you will want to reference is the Host Checker API Guide. In this example, we will configure a third-party Host Checker rule in a Host Checker policy:

1. Go to **Authentication | Endpoint Security | Host Checker** and either select an existing policy, or create a new policy as discussed earlier in this section.

2. Under the **Rule Settings** section, expand the **Select Rule Type** drop-down menu, select **Custom: 3rd Party NHC Check**, and click **Add**.

3. Define a **Rule Name** for this third-party check.

4. Define a **Vendor Name** for the third-party check. This is typically defined as the vendor for which this host check is applied.

5. The most important step is to define the location of the DLL file that Host Checker will call to perform this check. This file must already be located on the client system for the IVE to be able to call the DLL. When the IVE calls the DLL, the DLL will perform the check (based on the code in the DLL; see the Host Checker API Guide), and then will return a value to Host Checker to indicate the success or failure of the check. Define the appropriate path to the DLL file which will perform the check in the **Path to NHC DLL** field.

6. Click **Save Changes**.

## Uploading a Third-Party Host Checker Policy to the IVE

You can create more than individual Host Checker rules on the IVE. Juniper has provided you with an interface to deploy your own (entire) third-party policy to the IVE. You should reference the IVE Endpoint Defense Guide located at www.juniper.net/support in the IVE Documentation menu. This guide will provide you with the appropriate information for configuring these third-party policies. Covering how to configure a third-party policy is outside the scope of this book, but we will cover how to upload the policy to the IVE.

1. Go to **Authentication | Endpoint Security | Host Checker** and click **New 3rd Party Policy**.

2. Define a **Name** by which to reference the policy.

3. Upload the policy files that you have zipped on your local machine, by clicking **Browse** and locating the files on your local machine.

4. Define any **Remediation** actions just as you would for other Host Checker policies (see the section "Configuring Host Checker Policies," earlier in this chapter).

5. Click **Save Changes** to upload the policy files and apply them.

# Host Checker TNC Architecture

IVE 6.0 now supports the new Trusted Network Connect (TNC) standard, which was developed by the Trusted Computing Group (TCG). The TNC standard is a design document for an architecture to be able to evaluate user machines across different authenticating platforms. The TCG developed the TNC standard to solve the issue of different vendors each having their own API to perform host checks. Just like the early days of networking when many different companies developed their own communication protocols (e.g., IP, IPX, Banyan Vines, AppleTalk, DECNet, etc.), so have many companies developed their own host-checking standards and created their own host-checking APIs. The problem with having no industry standards is that it really halts innovation, because each company has to essentially reinvent the wheel. By creating a standard API, companies can create their own host checks which can be used across different platforms. The host checks are not the only part of the IVE platform that applies to the TNC standard. The IVE also incorporates communication which occurs between the IVE and the backend server that can evaluate and enforce the host checks. To get more information about the TNC standard and the TCG, visit www.trustedcomputinggroup.org/home. In this section, we will cover how to configure the TNC implementation on the IVE.

There are essentially three main steps for configuring the TNC. You must first set up a connection to the IMV server that contains all of the checks on the back end. Next, define a policy that references the policy to be applied on the IMV server. Lastly, you must define a Host Checker rule that references an IMV policy configured on the IVE so that when this rule is called, Host Checker will know how to proceed with evaluating the end system by referencing the appropriate IVE policy.

## Configuring an IMV Server

The first task you should perform when configuring the TNC architecture is to configure an Integrity Measurement Verifier (IMV) server. This server is the backend server to which the data collected in the host check will be sent to evaluate whether the user passes the check. The IVE is not an IMV, but acts as a proxy between the client system and the IMV. In this example, we will configure an IMV server.

1. Go to **Authentication | Endpoint Security | Host Checker**. Click **New Server** under **Remote IMV** to create the new server.

2. Define a **Name** for the server that will be referenced elsewhere in the configuration. Optionally, configure a description for the IMV server to help identify it for administrative purposes.

3. Define the hostname or IP address of the IMV server in the **Host** field. Note that this must match whatever is defined in the IMV server certificate as the "hostname"; otherwise, the IVE will not trust the certificate.

4. Define the **Port** number for which the IMV server is listening for the IMV server connections.

5. Define a preshared secret key which will be used between the IMV server and the IVE.

6. Click **Save Changes**.

**T**ɪᴘ

Note that IVE/IMV communication is performed using SSL encryption, so the IVE and IMV servers must have certificates that are signed from CA server(s) that each device trusts. You could do this by using certificates signed by a well-known CA such as VeriSign or Thawte, or you could use a private CA such as an Active Directory CA, or just generate your own CA and sign the certificates with an SSL application such as OpenSSL. For more information on OpenSSL go to www.openssl.org.

## Configuring an IMV Policy

Now that you have configured an IMV server, you can configure an IMV policy. This is a policy that can be referenced elsewhere in the configuration to evaluate user compliance. Your policy will be used to reference other policies elsewhere in the configuration. In this example, we will create an IMV policy on the IVE:

1. Navigate to the **Authentication | Endpoint Security | Host Checker** page. Then click **New IMV** under the **Remote IMV** section.

2. Define a **Name** for the IMV policy. Optionally, define a **Description** for this policy.

3. The next step is very important to get correct (not that you should get any other step incorrect, but this is very easy to overlook). You must make sure that the **IMV Name** matches the same name as the name defined on the IMV server.

4. Each policy will be assigned to at least a **Primary IMV** server, and can additionally be mapped to a **Secondary IMV** server. We intentionally defined the IMV server before the policy because they must be defined in this step.

5. Click **Save Changes**.

## Configuring IMV Rules

Once you have defined an IMV server and policy, you will have a new Host Checker rule type available which will be called a **Remote IMV** rule. In this example, we will show you how to implement this rule in your IVE. Note that you must have at least one remote IMV Host Checker rule to be able to evaluate an end system with the TNC architecture.

1. Go to **Authentication | Endpoint Security | Host Checker** and either select an existing policy, or create a new policy as discussed earlier in this section.

2. Under the **Rule Settings** section, expand the **Select Rule Type** drop-down menu, select **Custom Remote IMV**, and click **Add**.

3. Define a **Rule Name** for the IMV rule, which will be referenced elsewhere in the configuration.

4. Define the **IMV Policy** for this rule. Essentially, the IMV works as follows. Host Checker sees that it has to evaluate an IMV rule, and that rule references an IMV policy. In the IMV policy, there is information about which policy on the appropriate IMV server should be evaluated (e.g., this is the **IMV Name** field which defines the name of the check that is located on the IMV server; the IMV policy also references the appropriate **IMV Server**). Select this IMV policy from the drop-down menu.

5. Click **Save Changes** to apply this rule.

**TIP**

A custom IMV rule essentially acts just like a Host Checker rule. You evaluate an IMV rule within a Host Checker policy, and you can apply the same logic to evaluate regular Host Checker policies (both predefined and custom) as you normally would in a Host Checker policy. For instance, you can define a Host Checker policy that references a predefined antivirus check, firewall check, and IMV check. You can then apply the appropriate logic to the Host Checker policy, just like you normally would (see the next section on evaluating multiple Host Checker rules), and therefore perform complex logic within a Host Checker policy combining both local and remote policy checks.

## Configuring Policy Logic to Evaluate Multiple Host Checker Rules

Now that we have discussed how to create the various Host Checker rules, we have a certain dilemma. How can we configure some logic into Host Checker so that the user will pass a policy based on the outcome of more than one rule? In this example, we will discuss the different options you have to help you evaluate your rules. See Figure 8.8 for how this example would look in the AdminUI. We will assume that we have four Host Checker rules configured within the policy as follows:

- **Rule 1** CheckAV, which checks to see whether the client is running an accepted antivirus client with up-to-date signatures

- **Rule 2** CheckRegKey, which checks to see whether the client is a corporate asset by checking to see whether it has a unique Registry key located within its Registry

- **Rule 3** CheckFirewall, which checks to see whether the client is running an accepted firewall client

- **Rule 4** CheckPorts, which checks to make sure that the client is not listening on any well-known backdoor ports

1. Navigate to the policy onto which you would like to configure the policy logic. This is under **Authentication | Endpoint Security | Host Checker**. Then click on the policy on which you would like to configure the logic.

2. You have three options for defining logic. We discussed these briefly earlier in the chapter. They are **Require: All the above rules** (Logical AND between the rules of the policy—therefore, all rules must evaluate to true; otherwise, the policy will evaluate to false); **Any of the Above Rules** (Logical OR between the rules so that only one rule will have to evaluate to true for the policy to evaluate to true); and **Custom Expression** (for which you can define your own logic).

3. In this example, we will define our own custom logic. We will say that if CheckRegKey and CheckAV are true, the user will pass the policy check, OR if CheckAV and Check Firewall and CheckPorts all evaluate to true (meaning that the asset is not a corporate asset, but it meets our antivirus, firewall, and port security criteria), the user will pass the policy. Therefore, we will select **Custom Expression** under the **Require** field.

4. Enter the following value into the **Custom Expression** text box: **(CheckRegKey AND CheckAV) OR (CheckAV AND CheckFirewall AND CheckPorts)**.

5. Define the additional options you wish to perform as remediation actions if the user should fail the check.

6. Click **Save Changes**.

**Figure 8.8** Configuring Custom Expressions for Evaluating Host Checker Policies

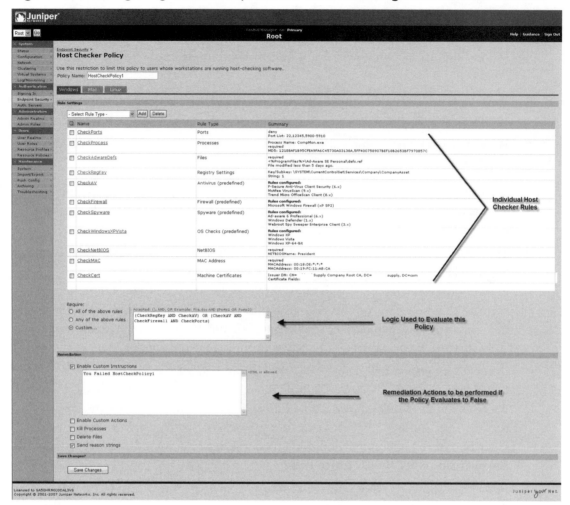

## Configuring Policy Chaining

Another way to extend logic on the IVE Host Checker is to configure Host Checker policy chaining. Although the AND, OR, NOT logic is usually quite effective for performing host checks, there is another mechanism which may be attractive for evaluating host checks. This technique is often referred to as policy chaining. This works by stating that as a remediation action, should you fail to evaluate one policy, you should evaluate another policy to see whether you pass that check. This is slightly different from using logic, because the remediation policy will not be evaluated unless the primary policy fails. In this example, we will configure a Host Checker policy called EmployeeAsset to evaluate another policy if it is not able to pass the user. One important thing to note is that the secondary policy you evaluate can only be a policy which evaluates third-party checks, or other checks, such as the Advanced Endpoint Defense, and Secure Virtual Workspace (not standard policies). Here are the policy and rule properties:

- **Policy 1** Contains a rule that checks for a Registry key which is a custom key that indicates a corporate asset. If this key is detected the policy passes. If the policy fails, Policy 2 is evaluated.

- **Policy 2** Contains a rule that checks for an Advanced Endpoint Defense rule. If the user passes the check, the user will be considered a corporate asset; otherwise, the user will fail that check.

1. Navigate to the policy on which you would like to configure policy chaining by going to **Authentication | Endpoint Security | Host Checker** and clicking the policy on which you want to create a policy chain (see Figure 8.9). This will be the "root" policy, which is initially called by Host Checker. Note that you must already have a separate policy created to chain to before you configure the IVE to evaluate the secondary policy if that policy fails.

2. Define whatever rules and logic you want to use to evaluate this policy. In this case, we will use the CheckReg rule which will check to see whether the user has a Registry key in his Registry which determines whether the machine is a company asset.

3. Select **Enable Custom Actions** under the **Remediate** section. This will expand a new portion of the AdminUI which will show two columns: one with **Available Policies** and one with **Selected Policies**. In this example, we will select **Advanced Endpoint Defense: Malware Protection** as the selected policy that we want Host Checker to evaluate if Policy1 fails. This policy will not be evaluated if Policy1 passes.

4. Save the policy by clicking **Save Changes**.

**Figure 8.9** Configuring Policy Chaining

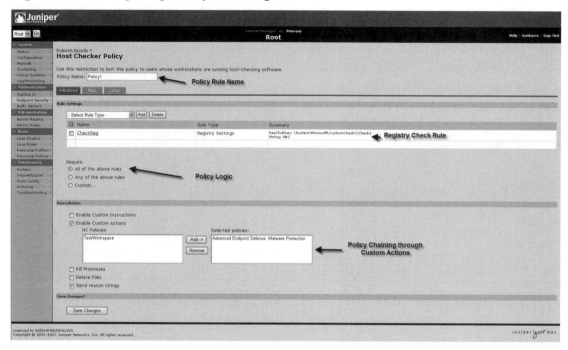

# Advanced Endpoint Defense

Although Host Checker may have some nice capabilities when it comes to checking for antivirus, antispyware, and other client-side security applications, it is often too cumbersome to check for individual worms or viruses on a client machine. And although you can check for the presence of antivirus and antispyware applications, it doesn't mean the machine is not infected. One way to perform some automated checks is to utilize the Advanced Endpoint Defense checks. These actually download a separate application from WholeSecurity (now Symantec) that performs different host checks to make sure you comply with these checks (i.e., no malicious software is found) before you are allowed to access whatever resource has been configured to initiate the check. In this section, we will discuss how to enable this check, as well as how to apply policies.

## *Enabling Advanced Endpoint Defense*

Before you can apply any policies for Advanced Endpoint Defense, you must enable this application system-wide. To do this perform the following steps:

1.    Navigate to **Authentication | Endpoint Security | Host Checker**.

2.    Check **Enable Advanced Endpoint Defense: Malware Protection**.

3. This will trigger two new options to appear: **Enable Silent Enforcement of Signature Scan** (no end user involvement) and **Enable User Control over Disabling Behavior Blocker** (no end user involvement). These are both optional. The first check will allow you to scan without the user's involvement for the scan. The second option for determining whether to allow the user to unblock applications, which the WholeSecurity module has detected as a threat. This allows manual user intervention into your policy. If you want to enable these options, simply select them where appropriate.

4. Click **Save Changes**.

## Applying Advanced Endpoint Defense Policies

When you enable the Advanced Endpoint Defense configuration in Host Checker, it automatically creates three Host Checker policies (note that these cannot be edited). These policies are:

- **Advanced Endpoint Defense Malware Protection Behavior Blocker** This check monitors the system for known keyloggers and screen-capture applications on the user's machine. This check will disable such applications. Note that you must have Local Admin rights to run this, and it is currently only supported on Windows 2000 and XP.

- **Advanced Endpoint Defense Malware Protection Category One Threats (Trojan Horses and Key Loggers)** As the name implies, this is a check for applications such as Trojans, worms, spyware, malware, and viruses. This is supported for Windows 98, ME, NT4, 2000, and XP.

- **Advanced Endpoint Defense Malware Protection Category Two Threats (Monitoring Applications and Remote Controls)** This policy checks for applications that may be doing remote monitoring such as VNC, or other applications that allow remote control of a machine. These may or may not be legitimate applications, but they are applications which could be used to control an end system.

You cannot edit these policies on the IVE; you can only determine where to apply them. Once you enable the Advanced Endpoint Defense product, it will automatically create these policies. Just like other Host Checker policies, you can enable them at the realm, role mapping, role, and resource levels. In this example, we will implement all three checks at the realm level:

1. Navigate to the realm for which you would like to apply these checks by selecting **Users | User Realms | <RealmName> | Authentication Policy | Host Checker**.

2. Enable the **Require and Enforce** checkbox next to each of the three Advanced Endpoint Defense policies on the screen, and click **Save Changes**.

## Damage & Defense...

### Utilizing Advanced Endpoint Defense

Advanced Endpoint Defense can help you provide an additional level of security for your network by protecting against clients that may be infected by certain malicious applications. One thing to understand when deploying Advanced Endpoint Defense is that it needs to download some files each time it connects. Over slower links, this may dramatically increase the time it takes to sign in to the IVE. Additionally, the user's machine must be able to access Update.wholesecurity.com to be able to download update files to the client machine to be able to function properly. We highly recommend that you test Advanced Endpoint Defense before you deploy it to make sure it meets your needs.

# Applying Host Checker Policies to the IVE

Now that we have discussed all of the different options you have for configuring Host Checker policies and rules, we can discuss how the Host Checker policies are actually applied to the IVE configuration. We can apply the Host Checker policies primarily in four places. In this section, we will discuss each of those, along with the motivation for applying the Host Checker rules at those levels. The four places you can apply Host Checker policies are as follows:

- Realm level
- Role mapping level
- Role level
- Resource level

## Applying Host Checker to the Realm Level

In this section, we will discuss applying Host Checker at the realm level. There are two ways to do this. One way is to just evaluate the client, which will not download to the user's machine if the user does not already have it. If the user does have it, it will trigger Host Checker to evaluate. The other option is to require and enforce at the realm level. When you apply Host

Checker at the realm level with require and enforce, you are essentially saying you want Host Checker to evaluate the client *before* the client enters credentials on the IVE. So essentially, when the client browses to the IVE, the client will immediately download the IVE Host Checker policy which will evaluate the client to see whether it is passing the host check. This occurs before the client is able to see the login page, which you can use to your advantage in case the client's machine is not compliant or is infected with a keylogger/malware to prevent the theft of credentials. This can be especially powerful when combined with the Advanced Endpoint Defense feature to do a quick scan of the end-user machine before the user signs in.

One thing you must keep in mind when host checking at the realm level is that if you have multiple realms in the same sign-in policy, the user may see a message related to a host check for a different realm when he connects to that sign-in policy. This is because the IVE must evaluate Host Checker before the user signs into the IVE (before a realm is selected), so if you have require and enforce enabled, the IVE will display an error message that may not apply to that user. If this is a problem for your organization, consider either moving the host checks to a different level (e.g., the role level) or using separate sign-in policies to place different realms at different URLs so that users won't get other policies applied to them. Again, this matters only at the realm level. Of course, using multiple URLs does require an Advanced license, so that is something to keep in mind.

## Configuring Host Checker Enforcement at the Realm Level

After you have defined the Host Checker policies, you must apply them to the IVE (see Figure 8.10). If you wish to apply them at the realm level, follow these steps:

1. Go to **Users | User Realms | <UserRealm> | Authentication Policy | Host Checker**.

2. In this window, you will see of the policies you have configured on the IVE. There are two categories for the actions you can configure for the Host Checker policies. One is to **Evaluate** policies, and the other is to **Require and Enforce**. Each row will have those options, along with the policy name you wish to select. You can select what enforcement you want to provide on a policy-by-policy basis. By default, the IVE will use Logical AND logic if you have multiple Host Checker policies configured for a realm with Require and Enforce. This means that if you have Policy1 and Policy2 set to Require and Enforce on the realm, you must pass both checks or you will not be able to log into the realm.

3. If you want to make it so that you have to pass only a single policy of the multiple policies configured at the realm level, you can specify the option to **Allow access to realm if any ONE of the selected "Require and Enforce" policies is passed**. This option will essentially treat all selected policies in the realm as a Logical OR.

4. Click **Save Changes**.

**Figure 8.10** Applying Host Checker at the Realm Level

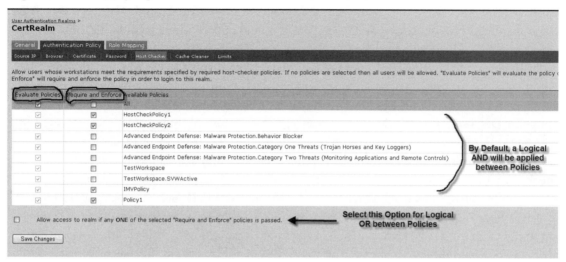

# Applying Host Checker Policies to the Role Mapping Level

Applying Host Checker policies at the realm level isn't always ideal for a variety of reasons. One reason we already discussed is that clients may see Host Checker remediation messages that don't apply to their realm. One way to evaluate user/machine compliance before users get access to roles is to perform the compliance check during the role mapping process. Note that to do this you must have an Advanced license, because it requires the use of custom expressions/detailed rules within the role mapping, which is an Advanced license feature. One thing to note is that unlike doing the policy check at the realm level, this check will not be performed before a user enters his credentials, because the role mapping function is not performed until after the user signs in.

## Configuring a Host Check Policy Evaluation at the Role Mapping Level

In this example, we will apply a Host Checker policy at the role mapping level to evaluate a user for compliance before he is mapped to a role in the realm on which the role mapping is configured. Of course, because this check is performed at the role mapping level, it must be configured on a realm-by-realm basis. Also, you must ensure that you are at least **Evaluating** at the realm level so that Host Checker gets downloaded to the client machine. If you are not Evaluating or Requiring and Enforcing at the realm level, Host Checker will not be loaded at this point, so it cannot evaluate policies configured at this level. We will assume you already have three policies configured in this example: Policy1, Policy2, and Policy3. See Figure 8.11 for how to configure host checking at the role mapping level.

1. Navigate to the **Role Mapping** screen for the realm on which you would like to apply the host check by selecting **Users | User Realms | <RealmName> | Role Mapping**.

2. Click **New Rule** to create the new rule for the role mapping.

3. Select **Custom Expressions** from the **Rule based on** drop-down menu and click **Update**.

4. This will refresh the Role Mapping screen, which will now display the **Expressions** button; click the **Expressions** button. This will bring up the new **Expressions** window. Note that you can select which expression you would like to edit by expanding the **View** drop-down menu in the **Expressions** window. If you want to create a new expression, just make sure the **View** section has **New** selected.

5. You will see an **Expression Dictionary** on the right-hand side of the screen. Under the **Variables** menu, you will see many variables, but we are specifically looking for the **hostCheckerPolicy** variable. When you expand this, you will see an example of the Host Checker custom expression.

6. A Host Checker custom expression essentially goes as follows: *hostCheckerPolicy = expression*. The expression is based on simple logic. If you wanted to just evaluate whether Policy1 evaluates to true, the expression would be *hostCheckerPolicy = "Policy1"*. If you wanted to evaluate whether Policy1 or Policy2 evaluates to true, the expression would be *hostCheckerPolicy = ("Policy1" or "Policy2")*. If you wanted to evaluate where (Policy1 and Policy2 and Policy3), the expression would be *hostCheckerPolicy = ("Policy1" and "Policy2" and "Policy3")*.

7. Click **Save Changes**.

8. You will now be back on your role mapping configuration page for the rule you were creating. You will see the name of the expression you just created in the **Available Expression** window; **Add** it to the **Selected Expression**.

9. Select the **Roles** to which you want to apply role mapping. If you want to have role mapping stop on this rule, select the **Stop processing rules when this rule matches** option.

10. Click **Save Changes**.

**Figure 8.11** Applying Host Checker at the Role Mapping Level

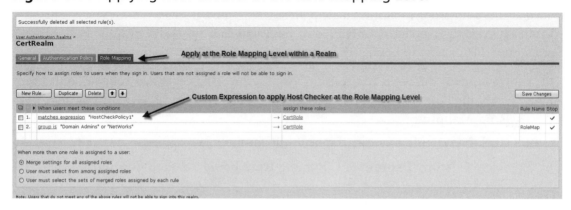

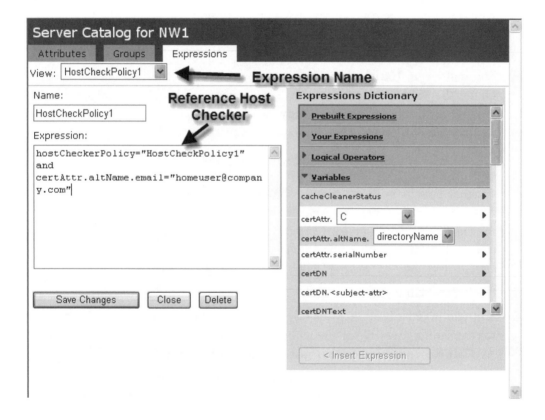

**Figure 8.11 Continued.** Applying Host Checker at the Role Mapping Level

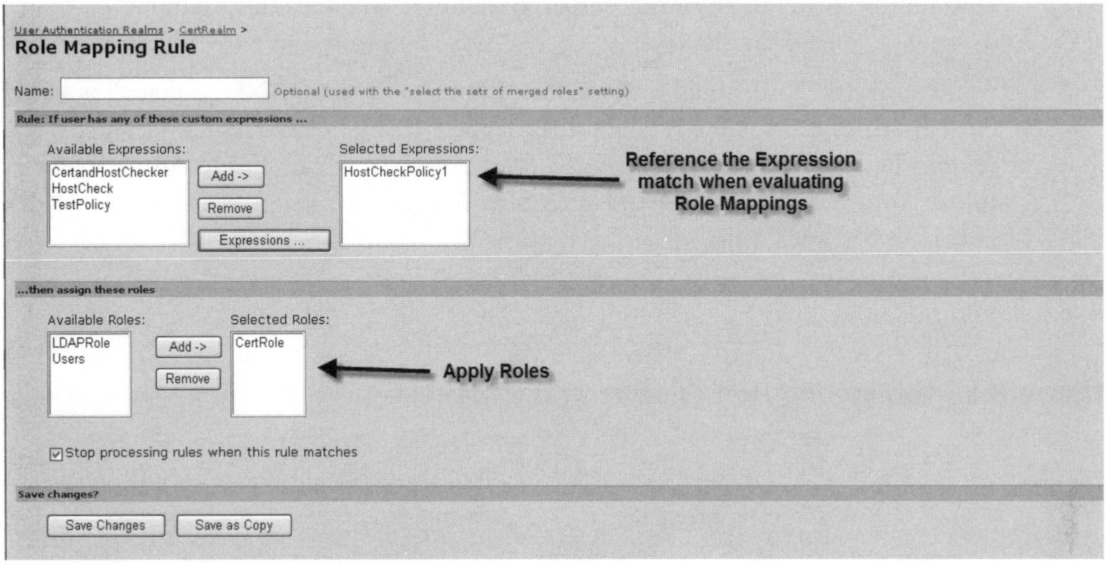

# Applying Host Checker Policies to the Role Level

We will now cover another popular way to apply Host Checker rules, which is to apply them at the role level. Essentially, you can configure a set of Host Checker policies that will be applied to the connecting user/machine before users get access to certain roles. This allows you to configure different access based on the state of a user's attempted session. For instance, you could put a Host Checker policy at the role level of a role which gives Network Connect access to a user. That way, the user might gain some access to the IVE when he doesn't pass the requirements, but won't be able to directly connect to your network with Network Connect. But when the user meets the compliance of your security policies, the user will get access to the Network Connect role. This allows you, the administrator, to dynamically assign access based on the level of compliance of the user who is connecting (on top of the regular controls you might implement, such as group and attribute matching within role mapping policies).

## Configuring Host Checker at the Role Level

In this example, we will apply two Host Checker policies, called HostCheckPolicy1 and HostCheckPolicy2, to the role:

1. Navigate to **Users | User Roles | <RoleName> | General | Restrictions | Host Checker**.

2. Change the **Role Host Checking** setting from **Allow all users (Host Checker not required)** to **Allow users whose workstations meet the requirements specified by these Host Checker policies**.

3. Select the Host Checker policies you want to evaluate in the role level, and click the **Add** button to add them to the **Selected Policies** menu. In this example, we want to evaluate Policy1 and Policy2, so we will add them to the role (see Figure 8.12).

4. At this point, the IVE would evaluate the policies as a Logical AND so that all policies must evaluate to true for the role to be mapped. If any policy failed under that setting, the role would not be mapped. Alternatively, you can enable **Allow access to the role if any ONE of the selected policies is passed**, which evaluates the policies as a Logical OR.

5. Click **Save Changes**.

**Figure 8.12** Configuring Host Checker at the Role Level

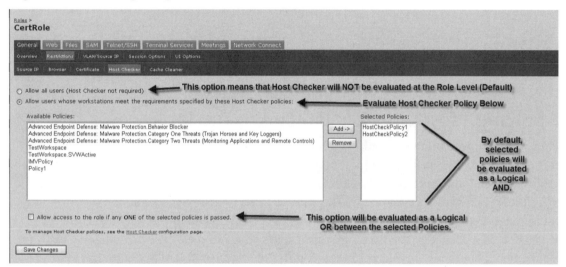

**Role Mapping Host Checker or Role-Based Host Check**

You might be a bit confused about the difference between applying Host Checker at the role mapping level and at the role level. The main difference is that if you apply Host Checker at the role level, it will be applied across any role mapping rule across every realm which references that role. But say you have a role that you map to several different realms and you want only certain realms to do a host check when the role is being mapped. Or you want to do a host check on only certain groups of users when they get mapped to the role. In these scenarios, role level host checking wouldn't give you a choice. If you configured the host check at the role mapping level, you could do this on a role mapping by role mapping basis, which offers much more flexibility. Ultimately, it depends on your needs and whether you have the Advanced license, because that is required to do a custom expression.

# Applying Host Checker Policies at the Resource Level

If you have the Advanced license, you have one more option for applying Host Checker policies, which is to apply them at the resource level. This gives you the greatest level of granularity, to define access on a resource-by-resource basis. Because you use a custom expression to map Host Checker policies to the resource level, you can add more logic than just the Host Checker policy; you can add other variables as well. This mapping can allow you to apply host checking policies across the entire configuration, because you can apply them on a resource-by-resource basis.

## Configuring a Resource Policy Level Host Check

In this example, we will apply a Host Checker policy which we will call HostCheckPolicy1 to a resource which will allow Network Connect access to an internal server to 192.168.2.50 on TCP port 22. Note that Host Checker must be running for it to be able to evaluate any policy. This means that if you do not already have Host Checker running, the client will not be able to pass a Host Checker policy. You can have launched a Host Checker policy either at the realm level (either selecting **Evaluate** or **Require and Enforce**) or at the role level.

1. Navigate to **User | Resource Policies | Network Connect | Network Connect Access Control**. In this example, we are using Network Connect as the type of access we are configuring, but you can apply this to any type of access (e.g., Web, file, SAM, etc.).

2. Click **New Policy**.

3. Define a **Name** by which to reference the resource policy in the IVE. You can optionally define a **Description** for the resource policy (this is recommended for administrative purposes).

4. Define the resource you would like to match. In our case, we will enter **tcp://192.168.2.50:22**.

5. Select the roles to which you wish to apply this resource profile. Of course, you have the option to either **Apply Policy to All Roles**, **Apply Policy to Selected Roles**, or **Apply Policy to all roles OTHER THAN those selected**.

6. Choose **Use Detailed Rules**.

7. Click **Save Changes** to bring you to the **Detailed Rules Page**.

8. In the **Detailed Rules Page** you will want to define the resource to match to. In most cases, this will be the same resource you define in the main rule, but you can break these out into more specific rules if necessary.

9. Define the conditions to match, which are based on the **Conditions Dictionary**. In this case, we will be using the **hostCheckerPolicy** variable, but you can choose additional variables if you like.

10. Enter **hostCheckerPolicy = "HostCheckPolicy1"**.

11. Click **Save Changes**.

# Troubleshooting Host Checker

Host Checker can be a blessing for network security, but it can also be painful for your helpdesk. But fear not, as there are many facilities to help you understand why Host Checker is failing a check or behaving in a particular fashion. First, we want to point out a few documents that are of interest when it comes to troubleshooting.

All of the following documents are located on Juniper Networks' IVE documentation page:

- Host Checker Configuration Guide
- Host Checker Troubleshooting Guide
- Host Checker API Guide
- Endpoint Defense Guide

Now, what are you to do when a user calls in who fails a Host Checker check? If the user has already failed, the easiest thing you can do is check the user access logs. As long as default options for the log records are set, you will be able to see some high-level information for why a user failed a Host Checker policy. If you have an Advanced license, you can define a filter or query to help narrow down user activity in the user access log. For instance, you can use one of the following queries to look for a Host Checker event for a particular user:

```
id = "AUT22923" AND user = <USERNAME>
```

or

```
user=<USERNAME>
```

The second option will search for all events for a particular user, to help give a holistic view of the user's session, not just a look at the Host Checker results.

Although the user access logs are a good facility for helping to identify easy problems in the user's session, sometimes you need a bit more detail. Luckily, the IVE can provide you with granular information on each check to help you determine why a user is failing a host check (e.g., what rule the user fails on), or why the user is getting only some roles but not others. It does this via the policy tracing feature, a feature we discuss throughout this book. Policy traces can provide you with lots of information that you can use to determine the root cause of your issue. Of course, policy traces must be turned on before you can glean information from them, so they usually require some coordination between you and the user. When you launch a policy trace to troubleshoot Host Checker, you typically need to enable only the Pre-Authentication and Role Mapping options. However, if you are applying Host Checker checks at the resource policy level, you should make sure that whatever resource policy type for which you evaluate Host Checker rules is enabled (e.g., Web or Network Connect). It's also often helpful to have the Authentication option checked, although that is not always required.

User access logs and policy traces should give you some clues as to why your user is failing authentication, but you may have to do some investigative work on your own to be able to isolate the reason why a particular rule is failing. For example, we have seen where Host Checker predefined antivirus checks fail, because they are also checking for up-to-date signatures, and the corporate antivirus license subscription ran out, so new signatures were no longer downloaded (thus, the check fails). But most of the time, you can look at what rule the user is failing, and that should point you in the right direction to remediate that condition.

When all else fails, it will probably be best to get Juniper involved. There are a few logs which are quite useful when opening a case with Juniper. In fact, you can look through these logs yourself. They are a bit cryptic, but if you pay close attention you might be able to discover the reason a check is failing. These logs include:

- **dsHostCheckerLog** This log lists information relating to the Host Checker process running itself, and can provide some information into why the host check is or is not functioning correctly. This is located in the user's profile Application Data directory. This file is typically located at C:\Documents and Settings\ <UserName>\Application Data\Juniper Networks\Host Checker.

- **EPCheck.log** This file contains all the information regarding why a user did or did not pass a host check. This log is a bit cryptic, but if you are feeling brave you might want to review it before you decide to submit it to JTAC. You can find this file in the user's Application Data directory, which is typically located under C:\Documents and Settings\<UserName>\Application Data\Juniper Networks\EPCheck\.

- **dsHostCheckerProxy.log**  This log is present only if you are using the Host Checker preauthentication feature to perform a connection to the IVE before the user actually logs into the machine. This log is located under C:\Documents and Settings\<UserName>\Application Data\Juniper Networks\Host Checker.

# Cache Cleaner

Whenever a user browses a Web page, the page is sent to the user's machine where it is usually stored on the hard drive in a Temp directory. This means that even after a user has stopped browsing a Web site, parts of the site are still locally stored on the user's machine. Therefore, even though content may have been transmitted on an encrypted channel (SSL), it is most likely stored unencrypted. If someone were to get the user's machine, he may be able to access these files. Although that should be somewhat of a concern, a bigger concern is what happens if the user accesses the IVE from a machine that is not his, such as a kiosk or other public computer. Then these sensitive files will most likely be left on the machine.

To help combat this potential security issue, Juniper has deployed an application called Cache Cleaner. Just as the name implies, its primary job is to clean the Web browser cache (or other directories as well) of any content that is being stored during the IVE session, thus clearing the user's "tracks" on the machine so that another user won't be able to access the cached content. In this section, we will discuss the various aspects of Cache Cleaner, how it is deployed, and the options that apply to Cache Cleaner that dictate how it will behave on the user's machine.

## Cache Cleaner Deployment

Just like other applications that run on the IVE, Cache Cleaner is deployed via ActiveX, Installer Service, or Java. It can be automatically deployed through the user's Web browser. If the user is running Mac or Linux, it must be installed via Java; otherwise, it can be installed via ActiveX (if the browser is Internet Explorer and ActiveX is enabled) or the Juniper Installer Service. Cache Cleaner only runs on Microsoft Windows, but you can install it and run it regardless of the user rights on the machine (as long as either ActiveX or Java is enabled). One thing to note is that unlike Host Checker, only one Cache Cleaner policy is configured on the IVE; however, it can be deployed at different locations on the IVE. You can run Cache Cleaner at the following points of a user's connection to the IVE:

- **Evaluate before user accesses the sign-in page**  This is configured at the realm level and forces Cache Cleaner to run before the user gets to log into his sign-in page. This can help with security, but if you have other realms on the same sign-in page, users who want to log into those realms will notice Cache Cleaner running.

- **Realm level**  This will launch Cache Cleaner after the user is mapped to the realm in the authentication process. This is typically known as just loading Cache Cleaner but not executing it.

- **Role level** If you just enabled loading but not executing at the realm level, you can instruct the IVE to actually require that Cache Cleaner be running at the role level.

- **Role mapping level** You cannot launch Cache Cleaner from the role mapping level, but you can make sure it is running at this level. This helps to ensure that the client is in compliance with your security policies.

- **Resource policy level** This functions similar to the role mapping level, except this is configured at the resource policy level. You can make sure the client is still in compliance before he can access individual resources.

# Cache Cleaner Options

Cache Cleaner has several options which you can configure system-wide on the IVE. In this section, we will cover how to configure these options, which are located under **Authentication | Endpoint Security | Cache Cleaner** in the AdminUI:

- **Cleaner Frequency** This is how often Cache Cleaner will run and clear the content located on the user's machine. By default, this is 60 minutes, and you can run it in intervals of from 1–60 minutes. This will clear the content you have defined to be cleared in the **Browser Cache** and **Files and Folders** cache, which we will cover later in this section.

- **Status Update Frequency** This checks how often the IVE will update its status with the IVE. This is useful when checking to see whether the user is running Cache Cleaner in the configuration (e.g., at the role, role mapping, and resource levels). The more frequent the checks, the more likely you are to catch whether the user is out of compliance, but that also requires more resources to perform the status updates. The default value is every 15 minutes, and you can set it from between 1 and 60 minutes.

- **Client-side Process, Login Activity Timeout** This value defines how long the IVE should wait before considering Cache Cleaner communication to be timed out. This occurs if the user navigates away from the IVE or closes the Web browser when connecting to the IVE before signing in. The other may happen if the user is connecting over a slow link in which he hasn't completely downloaded the client before the timeout finishes.

- **Disable AutoComplete of Web Addresses** This check will disable the Web browser from using cached values when the user types a URL in the browser bar. This may be desirable because a malicious URL might have been left behind in the browser cache. If a user starts to enter the URL, it will pop up, and without looking closely the user might be tricked into selecting this site. Note that this changes a Registry key which is changed back at the end of the session. This works only for Internet Explorer.

- **Disable AutoComplete of Usernames and Passwords** This option is used to prevent passwords from being saved in the browser bar, which could leave behind credentials on a machine. This is functional only in Internet Explorer, and it modifies a few Registry keys which it resets when you log out.

- **Flush All Existing AutoComplete Passwords** This option deletes any passwords that have been previously cached within Internet Explorer. You have two choices when implementing this option:

  - **For IVE Session Only** This will remove any previously stored credentials from the browser cache, but will store them so that when the session completes, the credentials will be placed back in the cache.

  - **Permanently** This will delete the credentials permanently.

- **Uninstall Cache Cleaner at Logout** Normally Cache Cleaner will not completely remove itself when you sign out of the session. You can select this option to remove Cache Cleaner when the user signs out.

## Cache Cleaner Content Clearing Techniques

You have two options for identifying content that you wish to clear as part of the Cache Cleaner content cleaning function. Both options are configured under **Authentication | Endpoint Security | Cache Cleaner**.

The first option is Clear Browser Cache. This technique clears browser cache objects based on where they came from. The browser uses a combination of either hostname, FQDN, or IP address to find content that should be removed. The problem with this configuration is that the IVE does not perform DNS resolution on the objects, so if an object is referenced by IP address rather than the hostname with which it is represented in the IVE config, that content will not be removed. Sometimes your organization may be required by a regulation to only remove this content, and this option will allow you to perform just that and remove objects from a particular domain. Note that you can use wildcards in this field, and you can define objects one per line. For example, the following values are proper objects that you can enter in the Browser Cache box:

- www.example.com
- 192.168.2.0
- mailserver
- mailserver.company.com
- *.company.com

The second option is Files and Folders. The IVE allows you to define files or folder that you want Cache Cleaner to clear out. These can be defined as either individual files (e.g., individual files in the cache), or entire folders (and optionally subfolders). Firefox can only remove directories defined in the Cache Cleaner file and directory, and not the clearing based on domain names/hostnames/IP addresses. If you only define the filename, Cache Cleaner will look for the files in the default Web browser cache directory; otherwise, you can define an entire path from which to remove the contents. For instance, the following are valid options which you can enter in **File or Folder Path**. For each item you configure, you can optionally define to **Clear Subfolders**. Additionally, you can use wildcards at the end of the path to define that all files below a path should be removed.

- C:\Windows\Temp

- <USERHOME>\* (this keyword will map to the user's home directory)

- <IETEMP>\* (this keyword will map to the user's Temp directory in his user profile; e.g., C:\Documents and Settings\joeuser\Local Settings\Temporary Internet Files)

One option you have at your disposal is to Clear Folders only at the end of the session. This option is attractive because if you clear content that was being used (e.g., cookies that keep session state), you could impact the user's experience. Also, you should not remove the DSPREAUTH because it will cause Cache Cleaner issues. If you do not select this option, the IVE will have Cache Cleaner clear the defined cache files to the cleaner frequency you defined earlier. Figure 8.13 shows an example of how you can configure Cache Cleaner options within the AdminUI.

**Figure 8.13** Configuring Cache Cleaner Using the Files and Folders Method

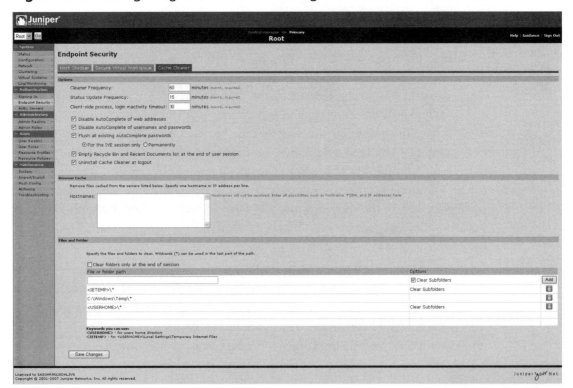

# Implementing Cache Cleaner

You can implement Cache Cleaner in a few different locations. Just like Host Checker, you essentially run Cache Cleaner from the realm level, but you do not necessarily have to start enforcing Cache Cleaner policies until different levels. Additionally, you can make sure Cache Cleaner is running in different locations in the IVE. For instance, you can make sure it is running before a user can have access to a resource so that you can ensure that the user doesn't have access to the resource when he doesn't comply with your security standards.

## *Applying Cache Cleaner at the Realm Level*

In this example, we will configure Cache Cleaner to run at the realm level. This example is important, because if you are using Cache Cleaner, you must enable it at the realm level to load; otherwise, you will not be able to run it at other levels.

1.  Go to **Users | User Realms | <UserRealm> | Authentication Policy | Cache Cleaner**.

2.  You have three options for configuring Cache Cleaner at the realm level:

    ■   **Disable Cache Cleaner** This is the default option, and will not load or run Cache Cleaner. This means you will not be implementing Cache Cleaner on this realm.

    ■   **Just Load Cache Cleaner** This option loads Cache Cleaner but does not launch the process. You would choose this option if you want to run Cache Cleaner at the role level. When you choose this option, Cache Cleaner will be downloaded to the user's machine after authentication but before role mapping. This is a good way to implement Cache Cleaner when you have multiple realms mapped to the same sign-in policy. This is preferable because you don't have to have users download Cache Cleaner who do not need to launch it. For example, if you have two realms on the same sign-in policy and one policy uses Cache Cleaner but the other does not, if you choose to load and run Cache Cleaner, both clients will download Cache Cleaner because that option takes place before the user logs into the IVE. Therefore, when any realm in a sign-in policy has that option, all other realms will, at the very least, download the client.

    ■   **Load and Enforce Cache Cleaner** This option will both download Cache Cleaner and launch it before the user logs into the IVE. This option is appropriate if you want Cache Cleaner to start running from the beginning of the session, no matter what roles the user is mapped to. As we mentioned in the preceding option, because this launches Cache Cleaner before the user logs in, if you have this enabled on a realm which is in a sign-in policy with other realms, those other realms will also be forced to download Cache Cleaner (see Figure 8.14).

3.  Click **Save Changes**.

**Figure 8.14** Configuring Cache Cleaner at the Realm Level

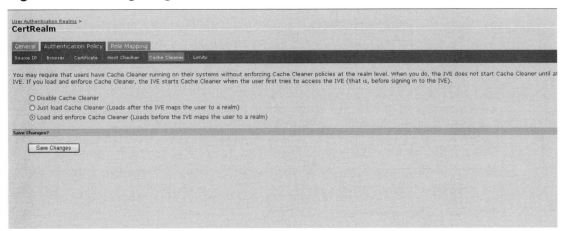

## Configuring Cache Cleaner Checks at the Role Mapping Level

You can check to make sure Cache Cleaner is running at the role mapping level so that a user does not get mapped to a role unless he is running Cache Cleaner. This option requires configuring a custom expression, which will check to see whether Cache Cleaner is running. Of course, custom expressions require an Advanced license.

1.  Navigate to the **Role Mapping** screen for the realm to which you would like to apply the host check by selecting **Users | User Realms | <RealmName> | Role Mapping**.

2.  Click **New Rule** to create the new rule for the role mapping.

3.  Select **Custom Expressions** from the **Rule based on** drop-down menu and click **Update**.

4.  This will refresh the Role Mapping screen, which will now display the **Expressions** button; click the **Expressions** button. This will bring up the new Expressions window. Note that you can select which expression you would like to edit by expanding the **View** drop-down menu in the Expressions window. If you want to create a new expression, just make sure the **View** section has **New** selected.

5. You will see an **Expression Dictionary** on the right-hand side of the screen. Under the **Variables** menu, you will see many variables, but we are specifically looking for the **cacheCleanerStatus** variable. When you expand this, you will see an example of the Cache Cleaner custom expression.

6. You essentially have two options for this custom expression. You can check to see whether Cache Cleaner is running or not running. Typically, you will be checking to see whether it is running, so your statement would look like this: *cacheCleanerStatus=1* (*cacheCleanerStatus=0* would mean it is not running). Of course, you can add additional statements to the expression as well to make a complex expression.

7. Click **Save Changes**.

8. You will now be back on your role mapping configuration page for the rule you were creating. You will see the name of the expression you just created in the **Available Expression** window. **Add** it to the **Selected Expression**.

9. Select the **Roles** to which you want to apply the role mapping. If you want to have the role mapping stop on this rule, select the **Stop processing rules when this rule matches** option.

10. Click **Save Changes**.

---

**N**OTE

If you want to make sure the user is actually running Cache Cleaner at the role mapping level, you must select **Load and Enforce** at the realm level; otherwise, Cache Cleaner will be downloaded but not executed, so a check to see whether it is running will result in a false or 0 value returned.

---

## Configuring Cache Cleaner at the Role Level

An alternative to executing Cache Cleaner at the realm level is to launch it at the role level. You would want to do this when you want to force only some users that are configured within a realm to run Cache Cleaner. For instance, you might want only users who map to a role with Web access to launch Cache Cleaner, and users who map to a Network Connect role not to access this feature. In this example, we will configure Cache Cleaner to launch at the role level.

1. Go to **Users | User Roles | <RoleName> | General | Restrictions | Cache Cleaner**.

2. Check the **Enable Cache Cleaner** option. As the page indicates, you must have set the realm to **Just Load Cache Cleaner** so that Cache Cleaner will be downloaded and initialized on the user's machine; otherwise, it will not work at the role level.

3. Click **Save Changes**.

## Configuring a Cache Cleaner Check at the Resource Policy Level

You can ensure that users trying to get access to a particular resource are running Cache Cleaner so that they do not leave behind any data on their machine when the session ends. If you have an Advanced license, you can create custom expressions which allow you to configure a check to ensure that Cache Cleaner is running at the resource policy level. In this example, we will configure a check at the resource policy level to make sure Cache Cleaner is running. We will perform the check for a Network Connect policy, but you can do this for any resource policy.

1. Navigate to **User | Resource Policies | Network Connect | Network Connect Access Control**.

2. Click **New Policy**.

3. Define a **Name** by which to reference the resource policy in the IVE. You can optionally define a **Description** for the resource policy (this is recommended for administrative purposes).

4. Define the resource which you would like to match. In our case, we will enter **tcp://192.168.2.50:22**.

5. Select the appropriate roles to which you wish to apply this resource profile. Of course, you have the options to either **Apply Policy to All Roles**, **Apply Policy to Selected Roles**, or **Apply Policy to all roles OTHER THAN those selected**.

6. Choose **Use Detailed Rules**.

7. Click **Save Changes** to bring you to the **Detailed Rules Page**.

8. In the **Detailed Rules Page** you will want to define the resource to match to. In most cases, this will be the same resource you define in the main rule, but you can break these out into more specific rules if necessary.

9. Define the conditions to match, which are based on the **Conditions Dictionary**. In this case, we will be using the **cacheCleanerStatus** variable, but you can choose additional variables if you like.

10. Enter **cacheCleanerStatus = 1**.

11. Click **Save Changes**.

> **NOTE**
>
> If you want to make sure the user is actually running Cache Cleaner at the resource policy level, you must select **Load and Enforce** at the realm level, or you must have selected **Just Load Cache Cleaner** at the realm level and enabled Cache Cleaner at the role level so that it is already running. Otherwise, Cache Cleaner will be downloaded but not executed, so a check to see whether it is running will result in a false or 0 value returned.

# Secure Virtual Workspace

One problem that a lot of administrators have difficulty solving is how to provide external access to corporate resources without exposing those resources to compromise. Whether it be by regulation, corporate security policy, or just administrative preference to not allow unprotected access to corporate resources externally, it is a problem administrators have had to deal with. For instance, the IVE allows you to configure file shares which can be accessible through the Web interface. The problem with this is that although it does provide your users with access to the files, they can download them to their local machines. This is particularly a concern if the machines which these files are downloaded to are not corporate controlled assets. So, how can you provide security for your intellectual property without completely shutting down external access? The answer is a wonderful feature of the IVE, called Secure Virtual Workspace.

Secure Virtual Workspace (SVW) essentially creates a virtual environment which looks just like the standard desktop for users to work in. SVW is much more than just another desktop, however. It not only allows you to control what the user can access on the local machine (e.g., network shares, Flash drives, printers, etc.), but it also allows for users to work on documents in a protected environment. This allows you, the administrator, to grant remote access to corporate resources with the knowledge that the documents will be secured on the local machine. This includes preventing users from saving the files to local machines, and many more options that we will discuss at length in this section. Note that SVW does require that the IVE have an Advanced license.

## Secure Virtual Workspace Options

Because the SVW offers users a desktop-like experience, it must be able to provide a wide range of behaviors. Thus, you have many different options when it comes to configuring an SVW instance. Actually, we should mention that SVW is more like Host Checker than Cache Cleaner in the sense that you can actually configure different SVW policies in the

IVE and apply them to different users. This gives you very granular control over the user experience based on the level of access you would like to provide. In this section, we will cover the various options you can configure within an SVW policy. You can see these options by going to **Authentication | Endpoint Security | Secure Virtual Workspace** and clicking **New Secure Virtual Workspace Policy**, which will bring you to the **New Policy** screen with the following options:

- **Name** You must define a name for your SVW policy which will be referenced elsewhere in the configuration (e.g., at the realm level where you map the realm to this policy).

- **Permissions** These are various configuration options that you may enable for the user's sessions:

  - **Printers** This option will allow the user access to network printers that are installed on the device. This allows you to prevent users from printing documents on network printers while in the virtual workspace.

  - **Restricted View of Files** This option will restrict users to only be able to see the Documents and Settings, Program Files, and Windows system folders (e.g., C:\Documents and Settings, C:\Program Files, and C:\Windows folders). This is not recommended if the user's computer has partitioned drives where applications are installed in other partitions, because the user will not be able to access these. (Default)

  - **Removable Drives** This option allows users to insert removable media (e.g., USB drives) into their machines and view the media within the SVW. Some organizations consider this to be a potential security threat because users could upload or download content to these removable media devices.

  - **Network Share Access** This option allows you to specify whether the user can access network share drives within the SVW session. Some people view the ability to view such drives as a potential security threat because users could download or upload content to/from them into the SVW session.

  - **Switch to Real Desktop** This option will allow users to switch between the virtual desktop and their real desktop while the SVW session is open. If you want to prevent users from being able to switch back and forth, disable this option so that they will have to exit the SVW session to resume their normal desktop. (Default)

  - **Desktop Persistence** By default, the IVE will erase all of the resources that it uses on the user's machines (i.e., SVW working directories). This will mean that if a user saves a file to his SVW desktop, when he logs into the SVW on that same machine it will be gone, and the desktop will be in the default state. If you would like the user to be able to have desktop persistence, where the files are restored when the user restores a session on the same virtual desktop, select this option. Desktop Persistence will encrypt the contents of a user's session on the local machine so that when he reconnects to the SVW on the same machine he can get the files back. Note that the user must use a password to encrypt the session; if multiple users use the same password, they could potentially access the other's data. Also note that this works only on NTFS-formatted drives. The user will be prompted for the password to restore the session if this option is selected. If he does not enter the correct password, he will not be able to restore the saved session.

■ **Applications** You can restrict the applications users can use within an SVW environment to help protect your users and network from performing unauthorized actions while connected within the SVW environment. By default, all applications are allowed. Juniper also has some special definitions for the following applications which you can enable/disable as an option:

   ■ **Control Panel** You can enable user access to the Control Panel while in the SVW session. For security reasons, many administrators prefer that users cannot access this feature, so it is off by default.

   ■ **Run Menu** This option will allow the Run menu to be displayed within the Start menu. Because the Run menu can allow users to run commands and access resources, this option is disabled by default.

   ■ **Registry Editor** You can allow users the option to be able to edit the Registry (with regedit32.exe) while they are within an SVW session. If you do not foresee your users needing to edit the Registry (or have applications edit the Registry), it is best to disable this option.

   ■ **Task Manager** The Windows Task Manager is a utility that allows you to be able to view running processes and other system resource information. By default, this option is disabled for users that are within the SVW.

   ■ **Command Windows** This option allows the user to run the cmd.exe command-line utility. Like the Run menu, this can give users the ability to run commands and other applications through the command-line interface (CLI). This is disabled by default for security purposes within the SVW.

   ■ **Custom Applications** One of the powerful features at your disposal is the ability to define what applications should and should not be allowed to run within the SVW. There are two sections for Custom Applications: Applications to Allow and Applications to Deny. You define an application by its filename (e.g., notepad.exe or Word.exe), but as an additional security measure, you can define an MD5 hash with the process name so that the user cannot spoof the process (e.g., rename Virus.exe to Word.exe). Additionally, wildcards can be used. Some examples of applications that you could allow include * (allows any application); CorporateApp*.exe (matches CorporateApp, plus any other characters until the "." is reached. This file must be an .exe file); and *__safe.exe__ (matches Esafe.exe, as well as prosafe.exe).

---

**NOTE**

---

If an application is defined under both Custom Applications (Allowed) and Applications to Deny, the deny will take precedence. This allows you to use wildcards in the Allowed section, and then explicitly deny applications within the Applications to Deny section. So, if you defined Outlook.exe in the Custom Applications (Allowed) section and defined *.exe in the Applications to Deny section, Outlook.exe along with any other .exe file would not be able to execute.

---

- **Security** This menu allows you to define security levels enforced within the SVW environment:

  - **Encryption** This is the encryption scheme used to encrypt files written to disk in the SVW environment. By default, it is set to 128 bits, although you can set it to 192 bits or 256 bits.

  - **IE/Outlook Extensions to allow** This allows you to define DLL files which Outlook can execute. By default, all extensions are allowed, although you can restrict this to specific extensions to allow. Any not explicitly defined will be denied.

- **Options** These are session-specific properties that you can apply to the SVW environment:

  - **Idle Timeout** This value defines how much inactivity would deem the SVW session idle, and thus end the session. This can be configured independent of other session timeouts on the IVE, but if the user's IVE session expires, the SVW session will also expire.

  - **Desktop Wallpaper Image** You can upload a bitmap (.bmp) file to the IVE that will serve as the user's background when he is connected to the SVW session. This can help the user identify which desktop he is working in by incorporating a logo or some other sign to identify the user's session.

- **Desktop Background Color** By default, this is a light blue color; however, you can define the color to be used as the background if you do not have a background image. Or, if your background image does not fill the entire screen, this background color will fill the rest of the background.

- **Sign-in URL to use SVW** If you want the SVW to redirect you to a different sign-in URL, you can specify a separate URL in this field; otherwise, you can just leave it as "-" to keep it on the same policy that the user logged into.

- **Remediation** Just like a Host Checker policy, you have some remediation options available to enforce should the SVW use if the user's machines do not support the requirements that are configured in the policy. For instance, if the SVW cannot launch a session because the user's machine does not meet the SVW requirements, it can trigger a remediation action. Additionally, Host Checker policies can be evoked during the SVW session, so a failure in compliance can result in those remediation actions as well. These actions include:

  - **Enable Custom Instructions** This provides a user with a Web page with a message that you can provide to inform the user that there is a problem. Because you can include HTML in the message, you can customize the page that appears and give the user hyperlinks for support and remediation.

  - **Enable Custom Actions** This option allows you to reference another policy to evaluate should the SVW policy fail to evaluate.

  - **Remediate** This allows you to perform remediate rules which are configured within the IMV configuration.

  - **Kill Processes** This option will kill a running process on the user's machine should he fail to authenticate on this policy. You obviously have to be careful with this option as it could create some major problems on the user's computer. One example of when this might be an attractive option is to check to see whether a machine is infected with a new worm that has been spreading throughout the Internet, and to kill that process if you detect it running on the user's machine. You can also specify the MD5 hash of the process that you want to kill (it checks the .exe file to compute the hash).

  - **Delete Files** If an SVW policy fails you can trigger the IVE to delete a file on the end system's operating system. You must define the path to the file that you want to delete. You can optionally define an MD5 hash on the file to ensure that it matches the exact file that you want to delete.

- **Send Reason Strings** This option will display what checks failed to the user should they fail to pass the SVW policy. This message will be displayed in the Web browser in the screen that accompanies a failed policy check. You may or may not want to give these messages to users. Sometimes it is better to enable custom instructions, because you can always see what evaluated to true or false in the user access logs, or within a policy trace.

## Configuring a Secure Virtual Workspace Policy

So, now that we have reviewed the various configuration options for SVW, let's set up an example to review the configuration. In this policy, we want SVW to create a secure desktop, with no access to network shares, printers, or remote storage. We do want users to be able to switch between the real and virtual desktops, but no session persistence, and a restricted view of files. We will give users access to Word.exe, Excel.exe, and iexplorer.exe, but no other applications will be allowed. No access will be given to the Control Panel, Registry, command line, Run menu, or Task Manager. We will leave the "Options" to their default values, but we will **Enable Custom Instructions** and **Send Reason Strings** should the user fail the policy, along with instructions for remediation.

At this point, we're ready to configure the example. Figure 8.15 accompanies this configuration example.

1. Navigate to **Authentication | Endpoint Security | Secure Virtual Workspace**. Click **New Secure Virtual Workspace Policy** to create a new policy.

2. **Name** this policy SVWPolicy1.

3. Configure the following settings for the **Permissions**:
   - Printers: Unchecked
   - Restricted View of Files: Checked
   - Removable Drives: Unchecked
   - Network Share Access: Unchecked
   - Switch to Real Desktop: Unchecked
   - Desktop Persistance: Unchecked

4. Under the **Application** section configure the following:
   - Control Panel: Unchecked
   - Run Menu: Unchecked

- Registry Editor: Unchecked
- Task Manager: Unchecked
- Command Window: Unchecked
- Custom Applications: (one per line), such as Word.exe, iExcel.exe, and Iexplorer.exe.
- Applications to Deny: (Empty)

5. Leave the **Security** settings to their default values:

- Encryption(AES) Keylength: Left to the default value 128
- IE/Outlook extensions to allow: *

6. Leave the **Options** settings to the default values:

- Idle Timeout: 30 minutes
- Desktop Wallpaper: (Empty)
- Desktop Background Color: #FF9966
- Sign-in URL to use in SVW: -

7. Remediation:

- Enable Custom Instructions: Checked
- "Your computer does not meet the compliance checks to allow you to run the Secure Virtual Workspace, please call the corporate help desk for additional assistance at 888-111-1234."
- Enable Custom Actions: Unchecked
- Remediate: Unchecked
- Kill Processes: Unchecked
- Delete Files: Unchecked
- Send Reason Strings: Checked

8. Click **Save Changes** to save the policy.

**Figure 8.15** Configuring Secure Virtual Workspace Policies

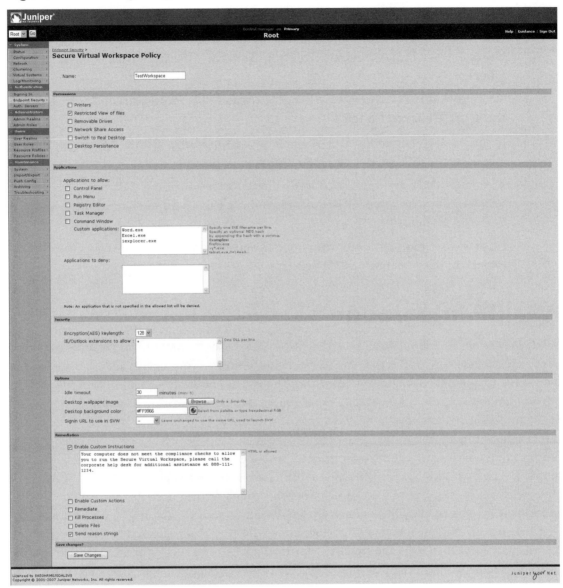

## Applying a Secure Virtual Workspace Policy

SVW policies are just like Host Checker policies (in fact, SVW used to be configured within Host Checker). You can configure them at the same locations within the IVE as other Host Checker policies, as we discussed earlier in this chapter. In this example, we will apply

SVWPolicy1 at the role level to launch the SVW for users after they are mapped to the SVWUser role. To perform this setup, follow these steps:

1. Go to the role to which you would like to apply the SWV policy by selecting **Users | User Roles | <UserRole> | General | Restrictions | Host Checker**.

2. Select **Allow users whose workstations meet the requirements specified by the Host Checker Policies**.

3. If you are assigning more than one policy, you can enable **Allow Access to the role if any ONE of the selected Policies is passed**.

4. At the very least, you must select the SVW policy you created earlier in this section, which in our case is the **SVWPolicy1**, and click the **Add** button to add it to the **Selected Policies** list.

5. Click **Save Changes**. Now when users are mapped to the role it will launch the evaluation of the defined SVW policy.

# IVE/IDP Integration

While we are on the subject of endpoint security, we felt that it would be valuable to mention a relatively new feature of the IVE which can help to provide your clients and your network with some exceptional security. One issue that security administrators grapple with when providing remote access, is how to let "clean" traffic into the network while protecting against malicious traffic. Even if you know every one of your users by name, you can't be certain that they are not bringing things that aren't business-related into your network. Quite often an unsuspecting user might become infected with spyware or some other worm which will propagate itself without the user knowing it. Although Host Checker and Advanced Endpoint Defense can help you extend your security beyond your IVE and firewall, they cannot block attacks that are generated by hosts which are legitimately connected to the IVE and transmitting on allowed ports. Say, for instance, you allow users who pass Host Checker to gain Network Connect access. If they were infected by a worm, the worm may try to propagate itself into your internal network. In the past, many administrators have implemented firewalls or an IDS/IPS to help protect their networks from such attacks. The problem with this solution is that a firewall can only allow/deny traffic based on ports, and so a worm propagating across an allowed port is not prevented from spreading. Alternatively, a good IPS system may be able to stop an attack, but that doesn't impose any action on the user. For instance, the IPS might stop the worm from making propagation attempts, but that user is still going to be connected through Network Connect and still sending those propagation attempts through. Wouldn't it be great if you could provide some integration between an IPS system that can detect attacks and the IVE which grants users access to your network?

Such a question led Juniper to integrate two of its products to work in unison to help protect your network from external threats. This integration is between the Juniper IVE and its IPS system, the IDP. Essentially, IVE/IDP integration works as follows. The IVE is deployed as you would usually design it to be implemented in your network (note that this integration does not have to happen at initial deployment, and can happen after the IVE is in production). You should be running a Juniper IDP sensor that is at least at 4.0 firmware and managed by the Juniper NSM. The IDP sensor can be deployed in two different modes: Inline and Sniffer (Tap). In any case, the IDP must be able to see the traffic as it flows into the network; otherwise, it will not work. This is because it is the IDP that performs the attack detection, not the IVE, and traffic is not duplicated through another path from the IVE to the IDP, so it must be detected within the real stream (see Figure 8.16).

**Figure 8.16** IDP/IVE Integration with Inline and Sniffer Modes

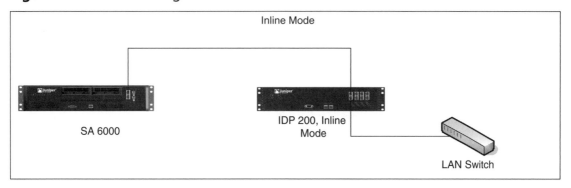

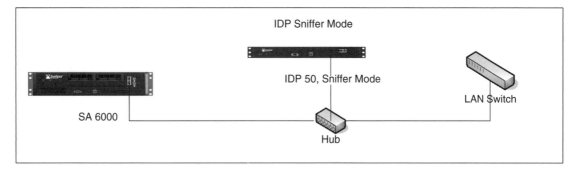

The main difference between the Inline and Sniffer (Tap) modes is how the traffic flows to/through the IDP. In Inline mode, the IDP sensor physically sits between two network segments on which it actively enforces policies. This means that all traffic actually passes through the IDP much like it would a firewall. The IDP examines the traffic to detect whether it is malicious (based on your IDP policy) and will perform whatever action is configured. The strength of this deployment is that it can actually prevent attacks from occurring by stopping them right in the IDP before they are allowed to progress further into the network. This method varies slightly from Sniffer mode deployment. Sniffer mode essentially means that the IDP will not be inline with the traffic, but will still be able to see the traffic. This is typically accomplished by using a hub or creating a SPAN session on a network switch which will duplicate the traffic it sees on a particular interface, and forward it to the IDP. The advantage here is that the IDP does not directly impact the traffic as it does not sit inline with it. That means that if the IDP were to fail, it wouldn't affect the flow of traffic (although the IDP 50, 200, 600, and 1100 have features that allow them to fail open in both hard failures, such as a power failure, and soft failures, such as a graceful restart or internal process failure). The main disadvantage with not having an IDP sensor inline is that you cannot stop the traffic per se. There is also a chance that the traffic may not make it to the IDP (e.g., if your switch drops some packets). Once a packet is sent, the IDP cannot stop it because it does not sit inline; however, it can send TCP resets to both the client and/or the server to reset the connections. We will examine how Inline and Sniffer modes affect IVE/IDP integration in the next section.

# IDP/IVE Signaling

Here is where we will detail why getting the Juniper IDP is better than using a different IPS product in your network. As we discussed earlier, the IDP must be able to see the traffic as it passes through the network to be able to either enforce an action on the traffic itself, or signal back to the IVE. The IDP does two things when it detects an attack on the network. First, it performs whatever action it is configured to perform within its policies. This may include dropping the traffic, sending TCP resets, or not performing any action at all. Obviously, if you are in Sniffer mode, your options are more limited in terms of what the IDP can do to the traffic, because it cannot stop it from traversing the network. Next, after the IDP has performed its action on the attack, it will send a signal back to the IVE to inform it of the attack that took place. Now, the IDP does not know which user the attack came from, and sends the session information back to the IVE (e.g., source port, source address, destination port, destination address, attack, etc.), and the IVE uses the port and address information to do a lookup and determine which IVE session generated this traffic. This works similar to how a firewall performs NAT and references sessions in the state table. Once the IVE determines who the attack came from, it can evaluate a policy on the IVE to determine what should happen to that user session. The options range from logging the attack on the IDP, to assigning the user to a remediation role, or even terminating the user session entirely. This integration means that you can not only protect against the attacks themselves, but also prevent future attacks through the IVE. Of course, you have a great deal of flexibility to determine what should be considered worthy of performing an action on a user session. In the next section, we will discuss how to set up IVE/IDP integration on the IVE side.

# Configuring the IVE for IDP Integration

In this section, we will discuss how to configure the IVE to talk to an IDP sensor for IVE/IDP integration. We must note a few things here. First, only the IDP stand-alone sensor models are supported for this integration; IDP is not currently supported on the ISG with IDP modules. Also, the IVE can map to multiple IDP sensors, but each IDP sensor can map to only one IVE device. We will start our discussion with the configuration for establishing communication between the IVE and IDP sensor.

## Establishing Communication

In this example, we will establish communication between the IVE and IDP sensor. Note that you must have the IDP configured before you configure the sensor on the IVE for this to work properly. See Figure 8.17 for the configuration in the AdminUI.

1.  Navigate to **System | Configuration | Sensors | Sensors**. Click **New Sensors**.

2.  You will be brought to the **New Sensor** configuration page. Define the **Name** for the sensor that will be referenced elsewhere in the configuration.

3.  Define the **IP Address** or resolvable **Hostname** for the IDP sensor in the **Hostname** field.

4.  The default **Port** which the IVE/IDP communicate on is TCP 7103. If you have any firewalls or any other device that would hinder communication on this port between the IVE and IDP, you must make sure this port is open or else the communication will not work.

5.  Now for the **One-time Password**. This is a password that you actually configure on the IDP sensor during the ACM configuration (**Under the IVE OTP** section) you actually have to go through the ACM and when you get to the summary page, copy the *hashed* value for the OTP and place it into the IVE's **One-time Password** field. So, to emphasize this, you *must* use the hashed password in the IVE field and *not* the plaintext password that you typed into the IDP for this to work. For example, if you entered **onetimepassword** into the IDP, the hashed value may be 3h7mzAhhdovJEqB4hWfpOzbm1rJvfkIKhXX2CqSt, which is what you would enter into the IVE. If you enter the plaintext password, it will not be able to establish communication with the sensor.

6.  Define what IP addresses the IDP will monitor in the attacks from the IVE. You can define these IP addresses on a line-by-line basis (using the same convention you would use for defining IP addresses and network masks elsewhere in the configuration), or you can use the *<default>* keyword, which will monitor any IP addresses that belong to the IVE (e.g., internal interface IP addresses including

VLANs, Network Connect ranges including DHCP ranges handed out through Network Connect, etc.).

7. Define the minimum **Severity Filter** to which attacks will be notified from the IDP to the IVE.

8. Click **Save Changes**.

**Figure 8.17** Configuring an IDP Sensor in the IVE for IDP/IVE Integration

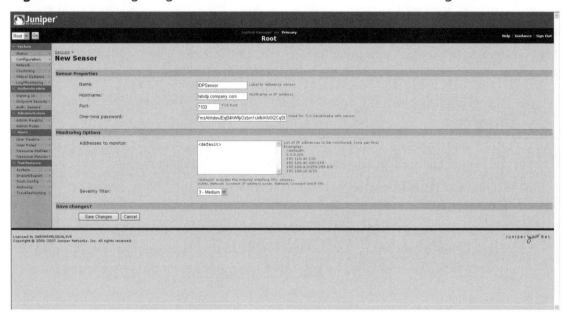

## IVE/IDP Sensor Policies

As we mentioned earlier in this chapter, the IDP is configured to detect attacks and perform whatever action is in the rule base, along with a signal to the IVE if an attack came from it. However, your ability to perform actions on the user session extends beyond the IDP and onto the IVE platform, providing you with some truly powerful integration. Essentially, we can configure the IVE to implement policies on a very granular basis so that we can even provide different actions based on the role the user is in if an attack is detected.

To configure such behavior we configure sensor policies (note that they must be configured for the integration to be able to perform an action on the IVE). We will list the different properties that are available to IVE/IDP integration, and then cover them in an example.

The IVE comes with a default policy which logs all IDP signals. You configure the policies under **System | Configuration | Sensors | Sensor Policies**. Click **New Rules** to create a new policy. See Figure 8.18, which shows a sample sensor policy in the IVE.

- **Events** The IVE categorizes what to do with an attack based on events. We will cover these later in this section.

- **Count** This is the number of events that must occur before the action is triggered.

- **Ignore (just log the event)** This means no action will be taken on the user's session, but the event will be logged in the IVE sensor logs. Note that independent actions may be taken on the IDP sensor (e.g., drop the packet), but the user session on the IVE will not be modified.

- **Terminate user session** This option will promptly end the user's session. Any active connections through the IVE (e.g., SAM or Network Connect) will time out as well.

- **Disable user account** This disables the user from being able to log into the IVE, but it applies only to locally configured accounts.

- **Replace User's Roles with this one** This allows you to replace all of the roles the user is assigned to with a single role. Typically, this is used to perform a quarantine action on the user:

    - **Permanent** You can make the IVE keep this role assignment permanent until the administrator goes into the IVE and removes the user assignment from the quarantine role.

    - **For this session only** This will apply only to this session. If the user logs off and logs back in, he will be in his regular role mappings.

- **Roles** Just like any other policy you apply the IDP sensor policy to appropriate roles. This allows you to respond differently to attacks to different users based on their role membership. Just like any other policy, you can configure these across all roles, selected roles, or all roles other than those selected.

**Figure 8.18** Configuring IDP Sensor Policies in the IVE

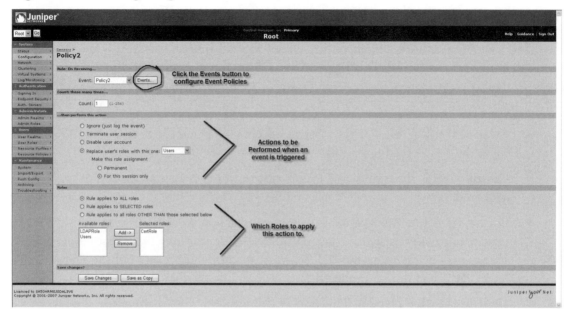

## Events

Each sensor policy must be configured to determine which IDP events should trigger this policy's action. Configuring event policies is just like making custom expressions, and it builds off the same logic. The main difference is that in addition to the standard options that you have in custom expressions, you also have the Juniper IDP variables, which allow you to match attacks based on messages logged to the IVE. You can also extend the logic of the Juniper IDP variables to include the logic of IVE variables in your expressions. Here is a list of the Juniper IDP variables:

- **idp.action** This specifies the action taken on an attack—for instance, none, drop, or close (see IDP Actions in the IDP Security Policy).

- **idp.attackStr** This is the name of the attack in the Juniper IDP attack objects (See IDP Attack Objects in the NSM).

- **idp.category** This is the category into which the attacks are placed in the NSM. Typically, this will be attack for IDP attacks.

- **idp.dstAddr** This is the destination address of the attack.

- **idp.dstPort** This is the destination port of the attack.

- **idp.policyStr** This is the name of the IDP policy that detected the attack. This will be listed in your NSM security policies.

- **idp.policyVersion**  Each IDP policy has a version number, and this number applies here.

- **idp.protocol**  This is the protocol that was used to communicate the traffic.

- **idp.rulebaseStr**  This is the name of the IDP rule base within the IDP policy.

- **idp.rulebaseType**  This is similar to *idp.rulebaseStr*, but this is the actual rule base type as defined in the IDP Admin Guide.

- **idp.severity**  This is the severity of the attack. The IDP Admin Guide covers the various severities for different types of attacks. You can also view the severity of particular attacks in the NSM under the IDP attack objects.

- **idp.srcAddr**  This is the source IP address of the attack (as listed in the IP packet).

- **idp.srcPort**  This is the source port of the attack.

- **idp.timeStamp**  This is the timestamp that the IDP reported regarding when the attack took place.

## Configuring IDP Event Expressions

Just like other custom expressions in the IVE, you use IDP event expressions to match certain conditions in the IVE. In this case, we are defining what attacks to apply to the sensor policy (which will affect the user who sends traffic detected as an attack). Remember that the IDP sensor is responsible for detecting the attack, and must be configured to do so in its policy. If the IDP sensor does not detect an attack (e.g., you only look for major and critical attacks on the IDP sensor, and a medium attack comes through), it doesn't matter what you have configured in the IVE sensor event policy, because it won't receive the signal. On the other hand, you can block attacks on the IDP from IVE users and not necessarily perform an action on their sessions, or apply different policies to different sessions. Think of the event policies configured here as an access list used to match the traffic (events), and the action is configured within the policy.

In this example, we will configure three different event expressions, and apply them to three different sensor policies which will behave differently based on the conditions of the attacks detected. We will assume that our IDP sensor is detecting any attack that it sees, and reporting the appropriate attacks back to the IVE (which is monitoring for any attack using the *<default>* keyword as configured in the sensor properties discussed earlier).

- **Policy1**  Configured to detect any attack of medium, major, or critical severity, for the external contracts group, and will terminate the session

- **Policy2**  Configured to detect any attack of major or critical severity repeated three times in the Users group, and will kick the user out

- **Policy3**  Configured to detect any attack of major or critical severity in the VIP group, and will put them into the quarantine role

1. Go to the **IDP/IVE Policy** screen under **System | Configuration | Sensors | Sensor Policies** and click **New Rules**.

2. Click the **Events** button to bring up a new screen. Make sure the expression selected is **New** under the **View** menu.

3. Specify a **Name** for the policy. In our case, we will call the first policy Policy1. In the **Expression** window we will enter the following information to match the description of the behavior we want to accomplish. Note that you can use the **Expressions Dictionary** to insert statements into the **Expression** textbox. After you create a policy, save it and create the next policy. See Figure 8.19, which shows Policy1 configured in the AdminUI.

   - Policy1: idp.severity >= 3 AND groups = "External Contractors"
   - Policy2: idp.severity >= 4 AND groups = "Users"
   - Policy3: idp.severity >= 4 AND groups = "VIP"

4. After you save the changes you will be back in the **Policy** window. Select the appropriate event policy that you configured. In our example, we are going to configure the following options for each policy (note that you will have to create a policy, then save it and create the next policy):

   - Sensor Policy1: Options:
   - Event: Policy1
   - Count: 1
   - Action: Terminate User Session
   - Roles: If you used separate roles you could apply these to separate users, but if multiple groups use the same role, then you can use the expressions like we did in this example to define the group that the attacks apply to.
   - All Roles
   - Sensor Policy2: Options
   - Event: Policy2
   - Count: 3
   - Terminate User Session
   - Roles: All Roles

- Sensor Policy3: Options

- Event: Policy3

- Count: 1

- Replace user's roles with this one: Quarantine Role

- All Roles

5. After creating a policy, just make sure to save the changes. As with other resource policies, order is important, as the IVE will evaluate the policies from the top down and will apply the actions to the first complete match that it finds.

**Figure 8.19** Configuring IDP Sensor Event Policies

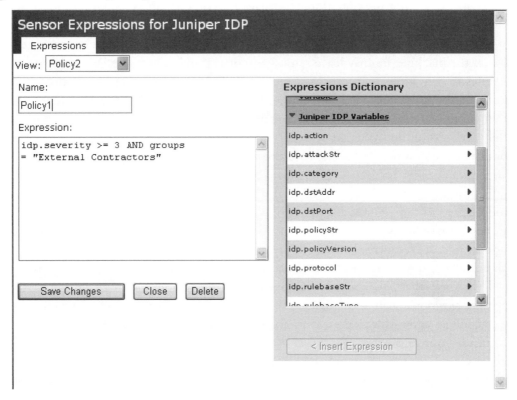

# Summary

As firewalls and NAT have become widely implemented, traditional attacks against internal machines are not directly possible. Therefore, many attackers have been shifting their attack mechanisms to attack clients through indirect methods (e.g., luring clients to malicious Web sites) rather than directly, because they cannot directly access the clients. This shift in attack methodology has forced administrators to alter their defensive practices as well. Administrators are increasingly relying on software on the client machines (antivirus, antispyware, and antimalware software, patch management, firewalls, etc.) to help prevent attacks from external sources. Because many of your users will either have mobile assets that travel to many different networks and/or use machines that you do not manage, you need something to turn to that can provide remote access and help ensure that users are in compliance with your security standards before they can connect to your network. Host Checker helps to ensure compliance on Windows, Macintosh, and Linux machines.

Direct attacks are not the only thing you have to worry about as an administrator. You also have to worry about your intellectual property being stolen or compromised. For instance, if a user logs into a machine, browses for some content on your company intranet site, and then leaves the machine, he may leave sensitive information behind. The IVE implements two features to help protect against this. One is called Cache Cleaner, which removes files remaining on the user's computer, and the other is Secure Virtual Desktop, which creates a virtual environment where everything is contained within the desktop. You have full control over the user's session, and you can prevent the user from saving files to the local machine, network shares, removable media, and so on to help ensure that you can maintain control over your data.

The last topic we discussed was IVE/IDP integration. Although we spent the beginning and middle parts of this chapter discussing how to ensure that a client meets your security policy and doesn't compromise sensitive data, we did not cover what happens if a client tries to attack an internal resource (knowingly or unknowingly). This aspect of IVE security is a capability which ties traditional IPS monitoring with the ability to signal to the upstream IVE to let it know that a user session has violated a security policy, so the IVE can perform the appropriate actions (such as terminating the user session or placing the user in a quarantine). These capabilities allow you to protect internal assets from being compromised by a client that is outside your organization.

Security has always been one of the key aspects of being able to provide remote access to internal resources. As attackers have improved their methods of offense, companies such as Juniper Networks have also improved their products to offer your network even more security. The endpoint security aspect of the IVE has become an extremely popular feature that Juniper has spent a lot of resources to develop and enhance, and you should expect that even more great features will be available in the future.

# Solutions Fast Track

## Host Checker

☑ Host Checker functions on Windows, Macintosh, and Linux machines and provides compliance checking abilities on a remote machine.

☑ The Windows module comes with predefined rules which can check for a wide array of antivirus, antispyware, antimalware, firewall, and operating system-checking packages. It can additionally check for other machine characteristics, such as running processes, files, Registry settings, and ports running on a machine (as well as perform other checks).

☑ You can integrate Host Checker at the realm, role mapping, role, and resource policy levels to provide you with exceptional granularity for controlling how your users interact with the product.

☑ Host Checker offers a wide range of remediation actions, such as enabling a custom message and enabling custom actions (evaluating other policies), as well as other, more powerful actions, such as killing processes and deleting files.

## Cache Cleaner

☑ Cache Cleaner allows administrators to ensure that a client does not leave data in browser caches and other folders on the machine onto which it is connecting.

☑ Cache Cleaner runs on Windows, and has the most features when running through Internet Explorer.

☑ When using Internet Explorer, Cache Cleaner can remove content from individual domains, or can clear out specific files and folders.

☑ When running in browsers other than Internet Explorer (e.g., Firefox) Cache Cleaner can remove files and folders on the client machine to clean up after the client's session.

## Secure Virtual Workspace

☑ Secure Virtual Workspace creates a virtual desktop environment within which all activity can be contained.

☑ You can restrict users' ability to access local drives, shared drives, printers, and removable media when they are connected within an SVW session.

☑ You can control what applications can run within the SVW session, as well as whether users can switch between user desktops.

☑ SVW provides another layer of security to prevent client machines from impacting internal networks by controlling what they can access on their desktop within the connection.

☑ SVW also features the ability to customize the look and feel of the desktop by customizing background colors and images.

# IVE/IDP Integration

☑ The IVE supports integration with the Juniper IDP sensor, which allows the IDP to send signals to the IVE when it detects malicious traffic passing through the IDP from the IVE. This allows you to not only block the attacks, but also proactively enforce a policy on the user's session.

☑ Custom expressions, which are known as events in the sensor policies configuration, are used to define which attacks the IVE will match (functions like an access list).

☑ The IVE can perform several different actions on a granular basis. You can configure the IVE to perform different actions on different users or groups of users and fine-tune the matching with custom expressions. Actions include ignore, terminate user session, disable the account, and assign the user to a different role.

☑ The IVE keeps a record of all the events generated in the sensor event log.

# Frequently Asked Questions

**Q:** Can Host Checker check for individual patches such as Microsoft Updates?

**A:** Host Checker cannot natively check for Microsoft updates, but you can use either third-party checks or IMV checks to evaluate user machines to ensure that they are in compliance with Host Checker.

**Q:** What is the best way to prevent users from getting access to certain roles if they do not comply with security policies?

**A:** Many administrators feel that applying Host Checker policies at the role level allows them to configure checks on individual roles (e.g., a Network Connect role) so that you can allow users access to some roles, but not others based on compliance.

**Q:** Can Host Checker check for antivirus software on a Macintosh or Linux machine?

**A::** The IVE does not currently have predefined checks for Macintosh or Linux, but you can create your own checks by using process checks, and you can determine whether the signatures are up-to-date by doing file checks.

**Q:** Is Cache Cleaner supported on Macintosh and Linux?

**A:** This feature is only supported on Microsoft Windows platforms.

**Q:** Users are complaining that when Cache Cleaner is running, they get browser errors or lose their session states. What is the problem?

**A:** The issue is most likely that Cache Cleaner is removing cookies or other files that the Web browser or another application is using. Your safest bet is to enable the **Clear folders only at the end of session** option in the Cache Cleaner global configuration.

**Q:** Can Secure Virtual Workspace work with Host Checker to ensure that hosts connecting to the IVE and SVW meet security standards?

**A:** Yes, you simply need to apply Host Checker policies at the same (or higher) level as the IVE which can evaluate the client for appropriate policy compliance.

**Q:** What is the difference between *<SVWPolicyName>* and *<SWVPolicyName>.SVWActive*?

**A:** The latter is actively running the SVW environment. Juniper recommends that you select both options when configuring a policy to be evaluated to ensure that SVW is launched.

**Q:** What is the most popular IDP deployment mode for IDP/IVE integration?

**A:** Most organizations use IDP in Inline Transparent mode. This mode is very popular because it is least invasive and the easiest to implement in a network.

**Q:** Can the ISG firewall with IDP modules integrate with the IVE?

**A:** Currently, only the stand-alone IDP devices can function in IDP/IVE integration.

# Chapter 9

# Web/File/Telnet/SSH

## Solutions in this chapter:

- **Clientless Remote Access Overview**
- **Web Access**
- **File Access**
- **Telnet/SSH Access**

- ☑ **Summary**
- ☑ **Solutions Fast Track**
- ☑ **Frequently Asked Questions**

# Introduction

Traditional remote access technologies have often forced administrators to implement all-or-nothing approaches when it comes to remote access. IPSec technologies used to make it very difficult to provide restrictive resources to users in a scalable and easily comprehendible fashion. The IVE really shines through its qualities when it comes to configuring access to resources within your organization—without having to provide users with too much access to your network. Not only does the IVE do a remarkable job of being able to provide least privilege access but also it does so in a manner that can scale across a great number of users. All this can be achieved while still providing an intuitive interface, which will provide more time for administrators to perform daily duties rather than explain to users how to access resources.

In this chapter we focus on a few of the main access methods that the IVE provides. We begin with an overview of these technologies followed by an in-depth discussion of the various access methods. We focus on real-world implementation of these features and the many options that administrators can employ to further customize and control for user experience.

# Clientless Remote Access Overview

One of the main reasons why the Juniper IVE SSL VPN is so popular is because it provides simple methods of deployment for user access. In many cases, you don't even need to deploy a client at all for secure remote user access. Such clientless deployments are the focus of this chapter. The IVE leverages the power of modern Web browsers to provide the interface and communication channel for the SSL VPN session to take place over. Once users have logged on to the IVE, they will then have access to different resources based on the roles configured for them. In particular, we focus on the following four clientless remote access methods in this chapter: Web, file, Telnet, and SSH access.

## Web Access Overview

When you would like to provide access to internal Web sites and Web applications to remote users through a secure channel, Web access is an excellent solution. The Web access component works as follows: The user logs on to the IVE and is presented with a welcome or portal page. If the user connects to other "Web" resources such as an internal Web server through the IVE, the connection will be securely proxied through SSL, and all content will be rewritten so that this behavior is completely transparent to the user. The IVE supports an extensive subset of features to provide a rich user experience, with security and scalability for administrative management. It can handle everything from static HTML to Shockwave Flash and Java Applets. Access to internal Web resources can be preconfigured by administrators, or an administrator can also allow a user to create his or her own bookmarks to such internal resources, as discussed later. If simple access to internal Web resources is what you are looking for, then the IVE's Web access features is your best bet.

# File Access Overview

In the past, administrators usually had to go to great lengths to provide users with remote access to files in a secure manner. The integrated file browsing for Windows and UNIX file shares enables such desired access, with the ability to enforce strict access controls. Better yet, you can configure file access to be available through the Web browser interface of the IVE, without the need to utilize other applications such as SAM or Network Connect. Because you don't need to install any clients on the user machine, you also don't have to worry about needing administrative privileges or specific OS requirements (as long as the OS is one of the supported platforms); everything can be done through the Web browser interface. Users can be given the ability to upload and download files and modify directories within controls set from the IVE, in addition to those imposed by an underlying AAA server such as Active Directory. This means that the IVE can transparently authenticate your users when they try to access file resources. Also, not only can it specify what they can access but also, since this information is passed onto your directory server for authorization, you can still have users comply with access rights that they would normally get with their directory accounts. This provides you with the same level of security that you would normally offer to users, without having to provide any additional user access information.

# Telnet/SSH Access Overview

Telnet access is popular for managing everything from command line terminal servers to network infrastructure equipment such as routers and switches. The IVE has the capability to launch Telnet sessions from the Web interface with the use of a prebuilt Java applet. This allows users from different platforms to access internal (or external) Telnet applications without any need to download any VPN or telnet clients. Note that Telnet is a clear text protocol that can be sniffed and read by anyone who is in the network path of the application. Of course, the Telnet session between the end user's Web browser and the IVE will be secured with SSL, but after it is sent out of the IVE into the network it will be clear text. Where applicable, SSH is a secure alternative to Telnet.

SSH is essentially Telnet that is encrypted with Secure Sockets Layer. This means that the traffic is encrypted from the client to the server. The SSH application is also a Java applet just like Telnet, which can be downloaded on any platform that supports Java. The SSH session is tunneled through the SSL VPN connection from the Web browser to the IVE, but once it leaves the IVE, it is still encrypted by the original SSH session to the destination server. Most applications and network infrastructure gear now support SSH as a secure alternative to Telnet.

# Web Access

Over the years, many applications that were traditionally client based have become "webified." This trend has been largely due to the extensive feature-sets of modern Web browsers, as well as the scalability of Web protocols such as HTTP and SSL. Extensions to Web browser functionality, such as scripting, Java applets, and ActiveX controls, have helped pave the way for a new user Web experience. The other benefit of using a Web browser instead of an application is deployment. Most operating systems ship with Web browsers (often integrated into the OS functionality as well). Since Web browsers are so widely deployed and follow standard protocols and languages, they make excellent candidates for converting applications that must be installed and configured on a user machine to lightweight full-featured clients with which users are often quite familiar.

In this section, our primary focus is the different features available for setting up access to Web resources through the IVE. We begin by discussing Web bookmarks and Web resource policies since they are the building blocks of resource profiles and outline all of the concepts within resource profiles. We follow the Web bookmark and resource policy discussion with an in-depth look at Web resource profiles.

# Web Bookmarks

You will most often find yourself spending time creating Web bookmarks for access to internal Web sites through the IVE. Web bookmarks are a very handy feature since they remove the need for users to know (in advance) where they must browse to. You can also users to create their own bookmarks and use the IVE as a secure Web proxy of sorts.

## Creating Web Bookmarks

Web bookmarks are created within User Roles to provide the user with a link to the bookmarked resource. To create a simple Web bookmark, perform the following steps within the AdminUI.

1. Make sure that Web bookmarks are enabled in the user role. This could be configured in **Users | User Roles | <User Role>**; make sure that **Web** is checked. Next, go to **Users | User Roles | <User Role> | Web**.

2. Click **New Bookmark**.

3. In the following screen, you have several options (Figure 9.1). Begin by filling out a **Name** that a user will be able to reference the bookmark by. Often, this will be

the name of the application for easy reference, rather than the URL itself. The name is what the user will see in his or her Web interface after the portal page is displayed.

4. You have the option of filling out a **Description** that will be displayed in the user interface under the bookmark **Name**. This is useful for providing additional information to the user.

5. Next, you must define the URL for the Web resource. This will follow the same convention that you would normally enter into a Web browser address bar. You can configure this as either a fully qualified domain name or an IP address. For instance, you could configure a Web bookmark to an internal Web server company.local by entering **http://company.local** into the URL field. You can also define resources as HTTPS, use directory and files (such as http://company.local/employees/index.html), and define nonstandard ports such as http://company.local:8080.

6. If you have configured your IVE to show Auto-Allow settings under the **Maintenance | System | Options | Show Auto-Allow**, then you can define Auto-Allow settings for this Web resource. Essentially, this will automatically create a resource policy allowing access to the resource defined in the URL field. This may or may not be necessary based on whether you already allow this in your resource policy fields. You can define whether you want access to be granted only to that specific page or to everything at that level and below in the directory structure tree by selecting **Only This URL** or **Everything Under this URL**, respectively.

7. Lastly, you can define how you want this page displayed. Your options are whether or not to **Open the Bookmark in a New Window** and whether or not to **Display the Web Browser URL in the Toolbar** as well as display settings for the IVE toolbar. These settings allow you to customize the user experience. If you would like the user to still have his or her portal page as an anchor point, then you would probably want to open the bookmark in a new window. Whether or not to display the URL bar depends on if you want the user to see and/or modify the URL he or she is accessing or make it more of a popup-style window. Of course, the IVE toolbar is for IVE-related shortcuts such as accessing the portal page and signing out.

8. Click **Save Changes** to save the bookmark, or if you would like to define additional bookmarks, you can click **Save + New**.

**Figure 9.1** Configuring Web Bookmarks through the AdminUI

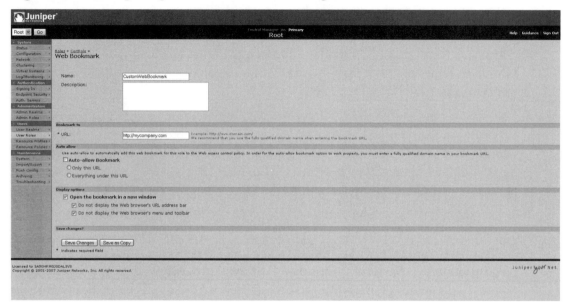

# Web Options

You can configure various options related to end user experience for Web access on a role-by-role basis. This can control the manner in which Web traffic is displayed, user ability to add bookmarks, and content control such as allowing or denying Flash and Java Applets to be passed through the IVE. In this section, we discuss these various settings related to role based Web options.

## User Browsing and Bookmark Options

You can enable users to create their own bookmarks on their IVE portal page, in addition to the capability to give them a Web browser bar in which they can enter their own URLs. If they are given the browser bar, the URLs entered still must pass the Web access list under **Users | Resource Policies | Web | Web ACL**. Any traffic that is browsed through this bar will essentially be proxied by the IVE and go back out to the Internet from there. This can have a performance impact on slow connections and low bandwidth links. The following is an example of configuring the Web options for a role in the IVE; Figure 9.2 accompanies this example:

1. Open the role that you would like to configure the Web options: **Users | User Roles | <User Role> | Web | Options**.

2. To allow users to enter their own URLs to browse through the IVE (access to both internal and external Web resources if allowed by resource policy,) enable the **Users can type URLs in the IVE browse bar** option. Note that this is a new browser bar that appears on the IVE portal page, not the Web browser's address bar.

3. To allow users to create their own persistent bookmarks in their portal page, simply enable the **User can add bookmarks** web option. Of course, any bookmark added, either for internal or for external resource, must comply with the access list for Web resource policies or users will get a message stating that their access is administratively blocked.

4. Lastly, if you would like to prevent users from viewing the actual hostnames of the servers they are contacting, enable the **Mask Hostnames while browsing** Web option.

5. Click **Save Changes**.

**Figure 9.2** Configuring Web Options at the Role Level

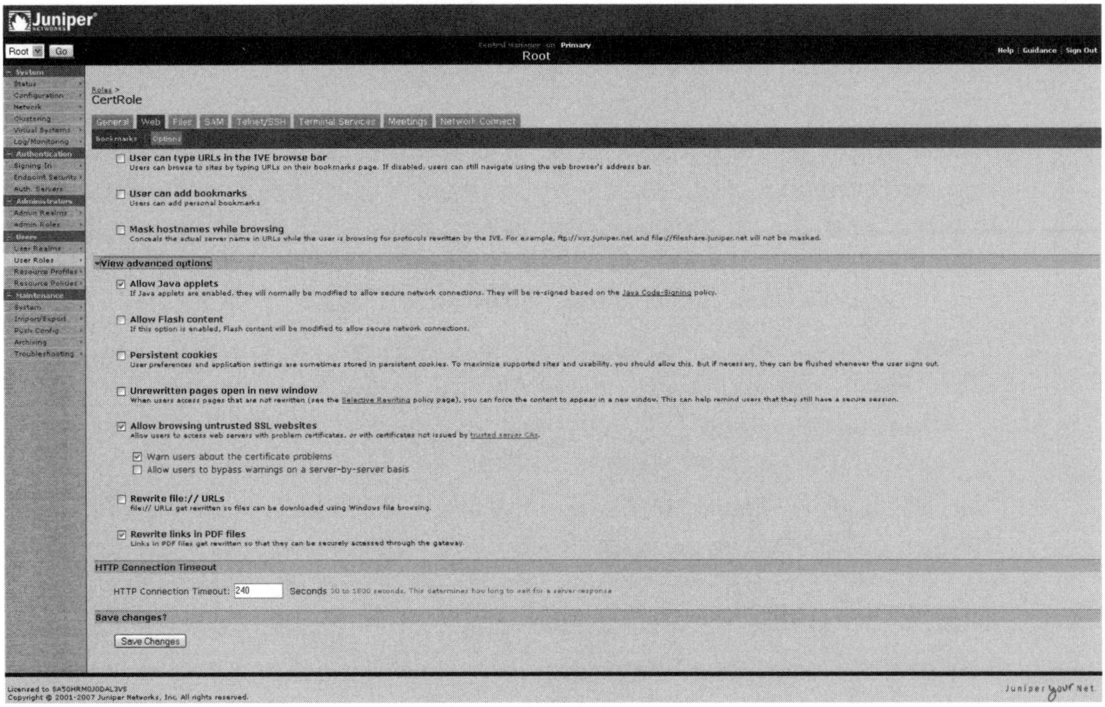

**W**ARNING

The IVE browse bar supports more than just HTTP; it also supports rdp, Telnet, and SSH. This is important to know because if these resources are allowed by resource policy, even though a user might not have a bookmark for them, the user can still launch a session through the browse bar. For instance, a Remote Desktop session could be initiated by entering rdp://172.30.1.50, and it would launch a RDP session to 172.30.1.50 assuming that it is allowed by resource policy. You should be careful about granting users the browser bar without first ensuring that resources are properly restricted via resource policy.

## Advanced Web Options

Each User Role has some advanced options that can be used to tune the user experience when Web browsing through the IVE. The following example shows how to enable the advanced options, such as Flash Content, Java Applets, SSL Access to Untrusted Sites, as well as others (Figure 9.2):

1. To reach the advanced options, you must go to **Users | User Roles | <User Role> | Web | Options** and expand the **View Advanced Options** menu, which is below the **Mask hostnames while browsing** setting. This will display several advanced options that are discussed in this example.

2. You can **Allow Java applets** to be available to end users through the IVE by enabling this option. They will be rewritten by the IVE and resigned based on the Java code signing policy. It is important to note that if the Java applets need to initiate TCP/IP connections, you will need to make a Java ACL that allows them to make those connections under **Users | Resource Policies | Web | Java ACL**.

3. To allow Flash content to be passed through the IVE for this role, you must enable **Allow Flash content** at the very least. A more detailed explanation of allowing Flash content through the IVE is provided later since different kinds of Flash can require more configuration than just enabling this option.

4. Normally, users' cookies are flushed for sites that they browse through the IVE when they sign out for security purposes. This can affect the user experience for sites that require persistent cookies to store user session (such as shopping sites). Thus, you might want to enable **Persistent cookies** to save these cookies across user sessions.

5. You can force unrewritten Web pages to be opened in a new window by selecting the **Unrewritten pages open in a new window** option. We discuss how to force pages to be rewritten or not later.

6. You can allow users to browse to Websites that are not trusted or do not have valid certificates. The IVE has a list of trusted CAs that it will use to validate certificates, as well as using normal certificate checks for valid hostnames and whether or not the certificate has been revoked as well as expired. You can view the Trusted CAs by going to **System | Configuration | Certificates | Trusted Server CAs**. You can enable whether or not to allow users to browse to these sites by setting the **Allow browsing untrusted SSL websites**. There are two additional options: **Warn users about the certificate problems** (highly recommended) and **Allow users to bypass warnings on a server-by-server basis**.

7. If you are browsing through a Windows file share through a Web interface, you will probably want to enable the **Rewrite file:// URLs** if your users are complaining that file browsing or related activities such as opening files through the IVE are not working.

8. If PDFs have links in them to Web resources, you can have the IVE rewrite these links so that they are accessible through the IVE. You can set this by selecting **Rewrite links in PDF files**. Note that this may have an affect on digitally signed PDFs (due to checksums), but the PDF will still be viewable.

9. Lastly, you can configure how long the IVE should wait until it considers an HTTP connection timed out due to no response from the destination server. The default is 240 seconds, and you can modify this by setting a value between 30 and 1800 seconds under the **HTTP Connection Timeout**. It is recommended not to change this setting because it is just the connection between the IVE and the backend server, not the users browser.

10. Click **Save Changes**.

# Web Resource Policies

The Juniper IVE offers a lot of behind-the-scenes functionality that can greatly enhance security and end user experience with regard to Web browsing through the IVE. In this section, we discuss the many resource policy options that are available for the Web access feature set. There are many Web resource policy options; however, we limit our discussion to the most widely implemented and exercised options.

**NOTE**

With Web resource policies, like many other places in the system, you can also use user session attributes to apply dynamically changing policy values or other customizations. For example, you could create a Web access control policy that has the value http://intranet/~<USER>/. This will then be autopopulated at runtime with the real value of <user> (once the user logs on). Thus, if "jsmith" logs in, his acl policies would dynamically be set to: http://intranet/~jsmith/. This functionality can also be done for bookmarks, NC IP pools, and dozens of other areas throughout the AdminUI.

# Web ACL

The Web ACL resource policy is perhaps the most important and widely implemented resource policy that you will use on the IVE. This resource policy controls all aspects of what a user can browse through the IVE Web interface. Whether it is for a bookmark that you create or a URL that the user may enter through the browser bar, it must be allowed in the Web ACL in order for the user to be able to access the resource. By default, the IVE has an "Initial Open Policy" that allows all Web traffic to pass through the IVE for all roles. You can define a different policy for different roles or have them apply to all roles. This gives you great flexibility with regard to granting different levels of access to different users. If you delete the default access rule, you must define access rules to allow access to the desired resources or else the user will see an administratively denied message, and the event will be logged (Figures 9.3 and 9.4).

**Figure 9.3** Message User Will Get If Not Allowed to Access a Web Site by Resource Policy

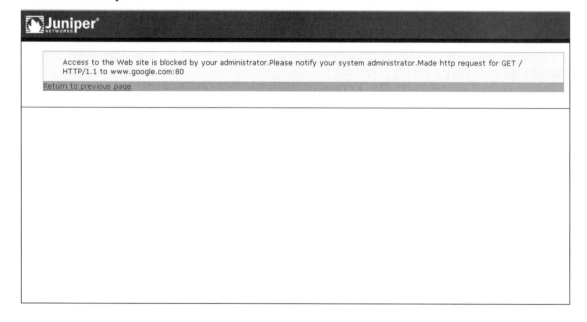

**Figure 9.4** Log Message Generated in the User Access Log When the User Tried to Access the Denied Web Page

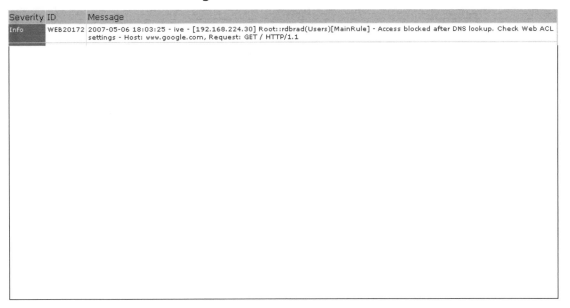

| Severity | ID | Message |
|---|---|---|
| Info | WEB20172 | 2007-05-06 18:03:25 - ive - [192.168.224.30] Root::rdbrad(Users)[MainRule] - Access blocked after DNS lookup. Check Web ACL settings - Host: www.google.com, Request: GET / HTTP/1.1 |

You should pay special attention to your resource policies because even if you create a bookmark to be visible for the user, if a resource policy does not exist, the user will not be able to access that resource. When creating bookmarks, the Auto-Allow feature will automatically generate a resource policy for that resource and within the role for which it is configured so that access will be allowed without manually configuring a resource policy. The following is an outline of the different options when configuring a Web ACL resource policy (Figure 9.5):

1. To create a resource policy, go to **Users | Resource Policies | Web | Web ACL**, which will bring you to the summary window for all resource policies.

2. Click **New Policy**.

3. You must first define a **Name** by which the resource policy will be referenced.

4. Next, you can provide a **Description** for what this resource policy is used for (very helpful especially when multiple administrators control the box).

5. Now comes the interesting part: You must define what **Resources** you would like to either allow or deny access to as part of this resource policy. These are entered into the **Resources** field, one per line, but you can provide multiple resources as well as use wildcards to help define the resources. The format is essentially protocol://<ipaddress>:<port>/<URLpath>/<object>. Therefore, the protocol is the protocol that we are allowing out (HTTP, HTTPS, TCP, and so on). The address can be an IP address or a DNS host name (wildcards accepted). The port can be a single port, a port range (such as 8080 to 8090), multiple ports separated by commas

(80,443,8080), or any (*). Lastly, you can define the directory structure and object if you wish (wildcards are accepted). Let's say you wanted to allow any HTTP traffic to www.google.com; your resource policy could be http://www.google.com. The IVE would fill in undefined options such as the port and directory. This allows you granular control so that you can restrict a user down to only being able to reach a certain level or Web resource and not browse deeper into a directory.

6. Next, you must define how this is allocated to the roles. Just like other policies, you can select that the **Policy applies to ALL roles, Policy applies to SELECTED roles,** or **Policy applies to all roles OTHER THAN those selected below**.

7. After selecting how the resource policy will be applied to roles, you must now select what roles will get this resource policy (unless you selected that it should apply to all roles).

8. The next step is to specify whether you want to **Allow access, Deny access,** or **Use Detailed Rules**. Because the resource policy is evaluated from top to bottom and will stop after a rule is matched, order is important. You may choose to deny access to a resource high up in the rule base as a more specific match so that users cannot reach it when a more general Allow Access rule is matched for other resources below. If the resource doesn't match an allow policy after traversing the entire policy base, it will be denied.

9. Click **Save Changes**.

**Figure 9.5** Configuring Web Resource Policies

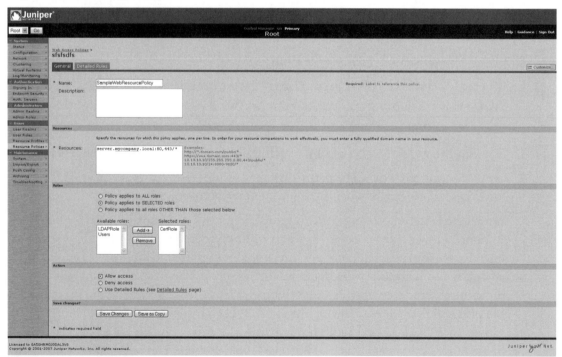

# Java ACL

One of the goals of the IVE platform was to design a flexible system capable of delivering different content formats securely. One of the most popular active content providers used today is Java. Java applets can be used to provide all sorts of different functionality, including running Web-based applications. Often with customized applications, a Java applet will be used as the client piece, which will connect to a server for the main backend application. This is a flexible technique because it can be delivered within a standard Web browser (meaning no client software provisioning), but it also poses some security issues, especially when trying to secure this application through the outside of your network. Fortunately, the IVE can gracefully handle these connections efficiently and securely. Besides encrypting the connection inside an SSL VPN tunnel, the IVE can also control what ports the Java applet can connect with and to what server(s). This is done within the Java Access Resource Policy. In the following example, we configure a Java ACL that is used to allow a Java applet hosted on an internal Web site to be presented to the client, as well as connect back to the backend server:

1. In this example, we create a bookmark for a Web site that hosts our Java applet at java.company.local, as well as a Java ACL to allow the Java applet to connect to the backend server at java-app-server.company.local. We will say that this application uses SSH to connect back to the server on port TCP 22. You don't necessarily have to create the bookmark to use a Java ACL, but we are using one because this is how we are going to direct the user to the Java applet.

2. Begin by creating the bookmark for the Web server that hosts the Java applet. Go to **Users | User Role | <RoleName> | Web | Bookmarks**. You will need to define the **Name, Description**, **URL** (which in this case we will say is http://java.company.local) **Allow Policies,** and **Display Options**. Click **Save Changes**.

3. Next, we create the Java ACL by going to **Users | Resource Policies | Web | Java ACL** and clicking on **New Policy**.

4. Define the **Name** to reference this resource policy, followed by a **Description** (optional, but recommended) for the policy.

5. Next, we want to define the resource for which we are allowing access. In this example, it would be tcp://java-app-server.company.local:22, but you can use IP addresses, port numbers, ranges, wildcards, and so on to define your resources.

6. Just like other resource policies, assign which roles will get access to this policy (**All**, **Selected**, or **Except Selected**) followed by defining whether the access is allowed or denied. If no policy is matched, there will be an implied Deny, so for this example we will select **Accept**.

7. Click **Save Changes**.

## Damage & Defense…

### Preventing Unrestricted Java Applets

Java ACLs are designed to allow an administrator to grant user functionality while restricting users down to only the resources that are needed. Just like a firewall, a Java ACL can be used to limit a user to connecting to certain machines on specific ports. You can leverage this functionality to prevent having to completely open up your network to these applications, thus limiting your attack surface. Note that Java ACLs are designed to work with Java applets, not Java scripts.

## Java Code Signing

If you are rewriting Java applets through your IVE that are signed, you may receive user complaints that they get prompted if the want to trust this certificate (or a similar message) when the execute the applet. This is because the certificate that was used to sign the applet is not a trusted root certificate. (By default, the IVE signs it with its own certificate.) You can import a Java code signing certificate by going to **System | Configuration | Certificates | Code Signing Certificates** and clicking **Import Certificates** and import the code signing certificate for the IVE to use to sign the applets. Next, you will have to create a resource policy to instruct the IVE to resign the applet. Do this by going to **Users | Resource Policies | Web | Code-Signing** and clicking **New Policy.** Then create a new policy to match your Java applet resource, apply it to the appropriate role, and then select **Resign Applets Using Code-Signing Certificate** and click **Save Changes**.

## Caching

Caching Web objects is a common feature implemented in HTTP to help save bandwidth when browsing Web sites for content. Since Web content is usually downloaded to a temporary folder before being viewed, the user will store a copy of this content. If the user then requests the same content at a later time, but nothing has changed, instead of getting the content remotely, it can just pull it up locally, greatly improving performance and saving both network and server resources. The caching directives are usually set by the Web server to instruct the client how to store the objects. Since the IVE intermediates the content, we can modify the directives to clients so that we change the behavior of how the content is stored. Before we discuss an example of configuring caching, let's discuss the following caching options you can control with the IVE:

- **Smart Caching (send headers appropriate for content and browser)** This will attempt to send either the Cache Control: No Store or Cache Control: No Cache based on the Web browser used and the content type of the requested resource. The IVE makes an educated guess as to what will be the best caching option to make the content work. For most multimedia applications, the IVE will use the Cache Control: No Store as the caching directive, which will replace the origin server's cache directives. Other content will result in the IVE replacing the caching directive with either Pragma: No Cache or Cache Control: No Store.

- **Don't Cache (send "Cache Control: No Store")** This option directs the Web browser client to save the file temporarily to disk and then, once the file is open in its respective application (stored in RAM), delete it. This works well for content that is attempting to be opened directly, and not right-clicking a link and saving it to disk. For instance, if you want to be able to click a media file and have it directly open in Windows Media Player, rather than right clicking it, saving it to your computer, and then opening it in the application.

- **Don't Cache (send "Pragma: No Cache")** This action requests that the user does not save the file to disk. The IVE will erase any information in the original caching header that describes the age, date, etag, last-modified, and expires tags.

- **Unchanged (do not add/modify caching headers)** This option forwards the caching headers exactly as they were (if they were) set by the origin server. This may be a good option when caching is causing problems with content, particularly when a user is attempting to open a file directly into an application rather than trying to save it to disk, for example, .wmv, .doc, .pdf, and .ica files.

It is important to understand the different caching actions that can be applied to IVE content with regard to the Web browser interface. Incorrect settings can result in performance issues, and even content not working at all. Most commonly, issues will arise when you are trying to open content directly into an application rather than save it to disk first. Issues can occur because some content is processed differently than other content with regard to opening it. If the caching directives tell the Web browser to not cache and not store, then when the application tries to process the content (such as Windows Media Player trying to open a downloaded WAV file), it may not be able to open the content where it thinks it should have been stored and the user will receive an error message in the application along the lines of not being able to open the file.

Now that we have discussed some options for caching, let's consider an example of creating a caching policy (Figure 9.6):

1. Begin by going to **Users | Resource Policies | Web | Caching**, which will take you to the caching summary page.

2. Click **New Policy** to create a new caching policy.

3. You must define a **Name** for the caching policy to be referenced by.

4. You may define a **Description** of what this caching policy is being used for to help management of the IVE.

5. Next, you will define the **Resources** that will apply to the caching policy. These follow the same convention (protocol://<server>:port/path) as other resources for other policies when it comes to wildcard and resource definition. Often, you will be defining a single type of file that will match for the resource policy. For instance, you might want to apply a specific caching policy to any wmv file, so your resource policy would be \*:\*/\*.wmv. Of course, you could further restrict this down to a specific server as well. For instance, if you wanted to apply this only to an Outlook Web access server OWA.company.local, your resource policy might be https://OWA.company.local/exchange/\*.wmv.

6. Next, you must define how the resource policy will be applied to roles. Just like other resource policies, you can define it to match all roles, selected roles, or any role except the ones selected.

7. The last step before saving this policy is to define what **Action** you would like to take on the resource. As discussed previously, you can perform the following caching actions: Smart Caching, Don't Cache (send Cache Control), Don't Cache (send Pragma: No Cache), or Unchanged (do not modify). Also, you can use Detailed Rules to apply the action.

8. Lastly, click **Save Changes**.

**Figure 9.6** Configuring Web Caching Policies on the IVE

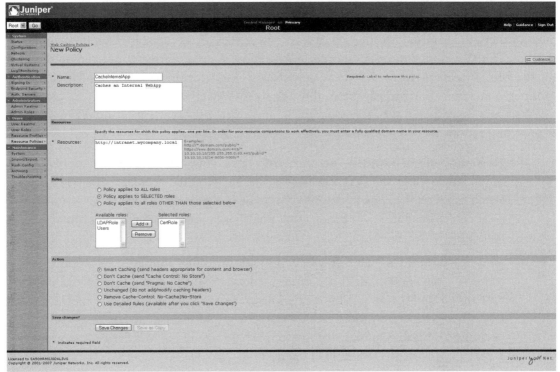

> **NOTE**
>
> There is an additional caching option that you can enable to instruct clients to cache images smaller than a certain size, 10 KB by default. This option is under **Users | Resource Policies | Web | Caching Options**. Setting this policy will override the configuration in the caching policy (for images only.)

## Web Rewriting

Because the IVE is essentially acting as a secure proxy that is intermediating the connection between the end user and the destination Web server, it must perform certain operations to ensure that the content is rewritten properly to reflect this change. All content that passes through the IVE web interface (pass-through proxy excluded, which is discussed later) will pass through the IVE rewriter engine for such processing. Often, changes are made to URL hyperlinks in the content, but other modification to scripting languages, ActiveX controls, and destination content may also be performed. Because the operations can be extremely complex, and the IVE tries to support just about all Web content, you may have to tweak some of the settings relating to the rewriter to ensure that the content is being processed properly. The IVE is intelligent enough to process most content correctly, but certain Web applications, particularly those that don't quite follow standards properly, may need special consideration when trying to pass them through the IVE Web interface.

We begin our discussion of rewriting on the IVE with an overview of the different types of rewriting actions that can be employed in resource policies:

- **Rewrite content (auto–detect content type)** This is the default content rewriting action employed by the IVE. It will automatically select the appropriate rewriting action based on the content that it is rewriting. It is generally a suitable option for most content, and it should be a starting point for rewriting before trying other methods.

- **Rewrite content as** This provides you with several options as to what specifically to rewrite the content as. This is often used when you may be using an extension type that the IVE does not implicitly know. For instance, perhaps you specify *:*/*.cfm, where cfm is a custom Flash format; you could specify the action as **Rewrite content as Flash**. Options that are supported include HTML, XML, JavaScript, VBScript, CSS, XSLT, Flash, DTD, and HTC.

- **Don't rewrite content: Redirect to target web server** This option redirects the user to the target server in the hyperlink when it is matched to the resource defined. For instance, with normal rewriting, if a user clicks on a link through the IVE that is www.yahoo.com, normally the link would be rewritten such that the user session would pass through the IVE, go to www.yahoo.com, back to the IVE, and finally back to the client. Using **Don't rewrite content: Redirect to target web server**, the hyperlink would not be rewritten at all; instead, it would go direct from the computer to www.yahoo.com. This option is mostly implemented when the hyperlinks in question are on the Internet rather than the internal network. This helps send users more directly to resources and can save your organization's bandwidth.

- **Don't rewrite content: Do not redirect to target web server** This is the same as **Don't rewrite content** above, except it displays a note stating this will take users outside the secure domain, and it forces them to click on the link to proceed.

**NOTE**

By default, the IVE rewrites all content that passes through the IVE with the **Rewrite content (auto-detect content type)**. If you remove this policy without applying a substitute, you will likely have users unable to access any Web resources through the IVE. Like all other resource policies, the resource policies are evaluated top to bottom for a match, so listing the most specific matching roles first is usually a good strategy when customizing rewrite policies.

Now that we have discussed the core components for IVE Web rewriting, let's delve into an example in which we specify how to create a rewrite resource policy (Figure 9.7):

1. To create a Web rewrite resource policy, go to **Users | Resource Policies | Web | Selective Rewriting**. This will bring you to the Rewrite policy summary screen, which will show the list of currently configured resource policies to each role.

2. Click **New Policy** to begin configuring the rewrite policy.

3. Begin by defining the **Name** for the policy to be referenced by.

4. Optionally (but highly recommended) you can define a **Description** for this policy.

5. Next, you must define the resources to which you would like to apply the rewriting action. Often with rewriting, you may be defining policies for specific objects and file types, rather than entire sites (although this is always true for policies for which you use **Don't rewrite: Redirect to target web server**). Just like the other resource policies (use the same format protocol://<server>:port/path), you can use wildcards, IP addresses, host names, port numbers, directories, and so on to define the resource that you would like to match.

6. Following the specification of the resource, you must next define which rules it applies to. Just like other resource policies, you can define all roles, selected roles, and all roles except those selected. With the latter two options, you have to select the respective roles from the **Available Roles** and put them into the **Selected Roles**.

7. Next, you define what action that you would like the resource policy to take for resources matching this policy. You can select the following actions: **Rewrite content (auto-detect content type)**, **Rewrite content as** (<select content type>), **Don't rewrite content: Redirect to target web server**, and **Don't Rewrite content: Do not redirect to target web server**. You can also select **Use Detailed Rules**.

8. Click **Save Changes** to complete this policy.

**Figure 9.7** IVE Initial Rewrite Policy Will Attempt to Rewrite All Policies; You Can Customize This Policy or Create New Ones

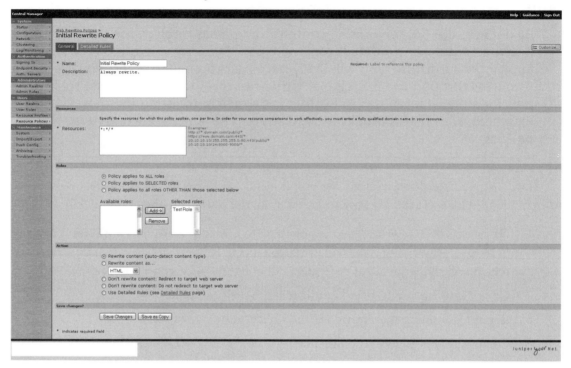

## Web Compression

The IVE has the capability to enhance user experience by compressing Web content that is transmitted to the client. This is particularly useful when the client is connecting to the Internet over low bandwidth links. Additionally, compression can help save bandwidth at the central office where the IVE is deployed by reducing the bandwidth that it needs to send. Compression has many benefits, as well as some disadvantages, so it should be used with caution. Just like caching and rewriting, an improperly configured compression policy can result in problems viewing content through the IVE. Likewise, having the optimal compression and caching policies for your site may help you reduce your end user response times—something everyone will thank you for. In this section, we discuss the various options that are available within a compression policy as well as the default settings and an example of creating a compression policy.

The compression policy only has two options with regard to performing an action on a resource—to either compress or not to compress the content that is matched. Other than that, it is quite similar to other resource policies. Although there are preconfigured compression policies, compression may be turned off on a systemwide level. You can verify whether compression is enabled or disabled by going to **Maintenance | System | Options** and determining whether the **Enable GZIP Compression** option is enabled. If it is not, then no matter what compression options you have configured, they will not take effect. The IVE comes with five preconfigured compression policies. The first four are for Outlook Web Access (OWA), which are predefined because of compatibility issues with OWA and the IVE compression engine, as well as a default policy that will compress everything else. When compression is enabled, content that is matched by the resource policy (and is capable of being compressed by the IVE) will be compressed before the IVE sends the data to the client. The client Web browser will then decompress the data after it has received it on the remote end. To configure a compression policy, perform the following steps (Figure 9.8):

1. Begin by ensuring that compression is enabled on the box. This can be done by going to **Maintenance | System | Options** and ensuring that **Enable GZIP compression** is checked. If it is not, then enable it and click **Save Changes.**

2. Next, go to the compression policy, which is under **Users | Resource Policies | Compression**.

3. Click **New Policy** to create a new compression policy.

4. Begin by defining a **Name** for the compression policy.

5. Optionally, you may provide a **Description** for the policy.

6. Next, you must define the resources to match the compression policy. This follows the same format (protocol://<server>:port/path) as other resource definitions. Note that the IVE can compress the following content types: text/html, text/plain, text/css, text/javascript, text/rtf, application/msword, application/ms-powerpoint, and application/ms-excel.

7. The next step is to define which roles this will apply to. Just like other resource policies, we can apply it to all roles, selected roles, or any role except those selected. When using the last two options, you can select which roles to apply this to by adding/removing them in the **Selected Roles** list.

8. Now we must select what action to take. Assuming that the compression policies are set to default, you will most likely be creating a policy to not compress objects because, by default, there is a catch-all resource policy to compress traffic. If you have removed this policy, then you may be defining a policy to compress certain traffic as well.

9. Lastly, click **Save Changes** to apply the changes.

**Figure 9.8** Configuring Compression Policies in the IVE; This Policy Is Preloaded to Handle OWA js Files

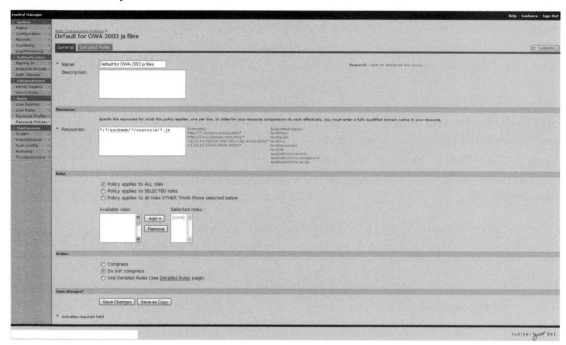

## Single Sign On

Modern-day applications have transformed user activity and productivity within the workplace. One of the common themes for most business applications is to control who can do what, as well as log that information for later use. In order to provide these services, the application must authenticate the user. Authentication alone is pretty simple, but when a user is responsible for working with multiple applications, this can become very burdensome. Organizations from health care to publicly traded companies must balance usability and security (since a user with 20 Post-it notes of passwords on his or her desktop does not do much to enhance security). The same holds true for remote network access. To help improve the overall remote access experience, and balance the needs for authentication, the IVE supports single sign-on (SSO) for most Web applications. This works transparently by passing the requesting server user credentials on the user's behalf. This alleviates a step the user must perform, as well as provides the application with information about the user so it can authorize that user accordingly. Multiple forms of SSO are supported by the IVE; which one is right for your application will depend on how that application authenticates your users. In this section, we discuss the different types of Web SSO authentication mechanisms and present an example of configuring such SSO functionality.

- **Basic authentication** Basic Web authentication is a simply way to prompt users for credentials that should be supported by just about any modern Web browser. Depending on the Web browser, the user will often get a pop-up box requesting credentials before the user is allowed to access the desired page. The IVE can automatically enter the credentials on the user's behalf, so the user never even gets prompted to authenticate and just gets passed into the Web application (assuming the authentication is successful).

- **NTLM authentication** Microsoft has developed a way to transparently pass user credentials through HTTP to authenticate users to Web applications, called NTLM authentication. Since this authentication is normally performed by the Web browser, the IVE must provide this functionality to the backend Web server.

- **Form POST authentication** Some Web applications request authentication within the Web page, and that is where Form POST authentication comes in handy. The IVE can transparently authenticate users to such applications that have a sign-in page. Since these sign-in pages will vary from application to application, you may have to look at the page HTML source to find out what fields are necessary to pass credentials to and map those in the IVE to what credentials should be passed.

- **Header/cookie authentication** Web applications can also use HTTP headers and cookies to authenticate users, and the IVE can support authentication to these applications as well. To set up SSO authentication within headers/cookies, you will need to specify the headers/cookies to add with the appropriate value that the application is expecting.

## Basic SSO Authentication Example

If you have an application that uses basic HTTP authentication, then you can take advantage of the IVE basic authentication SSO capabilities. In this example, we configure an SSO resource policy for basic authentication. We assume that you have already configured a Web bookmark, or the user will be directed to the authentication resource by some other means (Figure 9.9):

1. Begin by going to **Users | Resource Policies | Web | Basic Auth/NTLM SSO** and click **New Policy**.

2. You must define a **Name** for the SSO policy, and best practices recommend that you define a **Description** as well.

3. The **Resources** field is where you will define what resources will have the SSO policy applied to them. Just like other resource policies, this can use IP addresses, wildcards, host names, ports, directory paths, and so on to specify the resource. You can define multiple resources, one per line. For active directory SSO, we recommend using host names rather than IP addresses since the IVE uses DNS for portions of the SSO process.

4. Next, specify how this resource will be applied to what roles. Just like other resource policies, we can apply it to all roles, selected roles, or any role except those selected. When using the latter two options, you can select which roles to apply this to by adding/removing them in the **Selected Roles** list.

5. For this example, we focus on basic authentication. When you **Enable Intermediation**, you have three options. First, **Use System Credentials for SSO** will use credentials with which you logged into your machine. Second, **Use Specified Credentials** allows you to define what credentials to authenticate with. If you only have a single username and password to log into the application, then you can define it in the **Username** field, as well as the **Password** field (not the **Variable Password**). If you want the IVE to use the credentials that the user signs into the IVE with, define **<USERNAME>** in the **Username** field, then define **<PASSWORD>** in the **Variable Password** field. Lastly, you can **Disable SSO**, which will prompt the user for their credentials just as it would normally do so with other applications. If you choose to **Disable Intermediation**, the IVE will not handle these requests, with the exception of Web proxies, which it will automatically authenticate no matter what is selected. Juniper recommends that you do not **Disable Intermediation** due to security risks.

6. Lastly, click **Save Changes** to apply this resource policy.

**Figure 9.9** Configuring Single Sign-on Authentication on the IVE

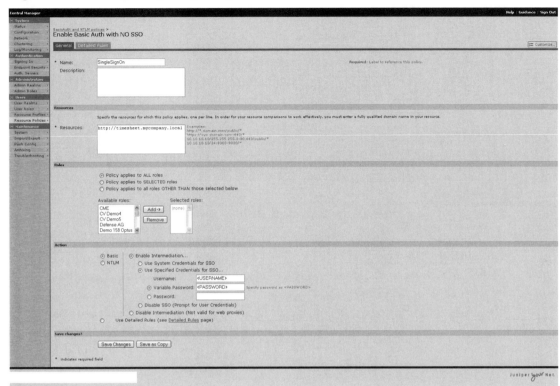

> **WARNING**
>
> You must have properly defined your internal **DNS Domain(s)** under **System | Network | Overview** in order to have AD SSO integration work properly. This is due to the fact that the IVE checks the Web resource domain before passing the credentials.

## NTLM SSO Authentication Example

Web applications that use Microsoft's NTLM authentication can be integrated with the IVE SSO piece. The IVE is capable of handling the authentication in a similar manner in which it handles the basic authentication, as you will see in the following example. We assume you have already configured a Web bookmark or alternate means of directing the user to the resource.

1. Begin by going to **Users | Resource Policies | Web | Basic Auth/NTLM SSO** and click **New Policy**.

2. Just like other resource policies, you must define the **Name**; optionally, you can define a **Description.**

3. Next, specify the **Resources** that will apply to this policy. Juniper recommends that you use DNS names for these resource policies, but you must make sure that the server is a member of a DNS domain that you defined in **System | Network | Overview** page.

4. The next step is to define which roles this will apply to. Just like other resource policies, we can apply it to all roles, selected roles, or any role except those selected. When using the latter two options, you can select which roles to apply this to by adding/removing them in the **Selected Roles** list.

5. For **Action**, select **NTLM**, followed by one of the following actions: **Use System Credentials**, which will use the credentials used to log into the machine, And **Use Specified Credentials**, with options for defining the **Username, Variable Password** (use **<PASSWORD>** ), a static **Password,** and the **Domain.** Most often, you will want to use the authentication that the user used to log into the IVE (if you are using AD or LDAP authentication). Assuming that you want to use the primary authentication for the SSO credentials, you would enter **<USER>** in the **Username** field, **<PASSWORD>** in the **Password** field, and you could either define a specific domain or, if you needed to use the domain that the user logged in with, select **<DOMAIN>** in the **Domain** field.

    Note that <USER> is somewhat different than <USERNAME>. The main difference is that <USER> may be formatted as AD-DomainUsername if you are logging into an active directory realm. For instance, if you have a domain named MYCOMPANY, and a username of BestUser, then the <USER> format could be MYCOMPANYBestUser, whereas <USERNAME> would just be BestUser.

6. Click **Save Changes**.

## *Form POST SSO Example*

In this example, we explore the properties and methods to configure Form POST SSO authentication within the IVE. Form POSTs have some additional fields that are not typical of normal resource policies, which we will explore here.

1. You can reach the Form POST SSO policy by going to **Users | Resource Policies | Web | SSO Form POST** and click **New Policy**.

2. Define a **Name** and **Description** for the resource policy.

3. Next, you will have to define the **Resource** that applies to this policy. Juniper recommends entering a fully qualified domain name for this resource. After the resource is defined, define the **Roles** that are applied to this policy.

4. There are two main actions that can be defined for this policy: **Perform the Post defined below** and **Do not perform the Post defined below**. Normally, you would choose to **Perform the Post defined below** to enable post. The other option is to not post. This is typically performed when you want to have a rule with a specific resource not to post for, followed by a less specific resource policy that you want to perform post authentication.

5. The **Post Details** section is the bulk of the configuration in this example. For Form POSTs to work, you must define which fields in the HTML are used to input the authentication values (most commonly, applications ask for a username and password, but Form POSTs support custom definitions for fields and values). Getting the details right for Form POSTs is usually the most challenging part. Most of the time, your best tool is to look at the HTML source code. Different Web browsers have different options to view the source; for instance, you can view the Web source code in Internet Explorer under **View | Source** and Firefox uses **View | Page Source** to display the source code. Within the source code, you should be able to find the appropriate fields that are used for authentication. Often, you should be able to contact the application developer to get these details if you are having trouble. Additionally, you could use a tool such as HTTPWatch (www.httpwatch.com) to assist with troubleshooting.

6. You must define the Absolute URL that the user's credentials are passed to in the **Post to URL** field. This can often be determined by browsing directly to the resource and either tracking the URL in the address bar or using a browser tool (such as Web Developer, discussed below) to determine the Web resource. There are two options for this field. One is **Deny direct login for this resource**, which will prevent users from accessing this directly. The other option is **Allow multiple POSTs to this resource**, which will send multiple authentication attempts if the application requires authentication for different resources matching this policy. Authentication must be to the same Post to URL server, and the IVE will not authenticate more than one request to the same resource in the same session.

7. Next is the actual Post fields and values. If you want users to be able to modify their SSO information in the **Preferences | Advanced** tab of the UserUI, then the value you place in the **User Label** is what they will see in their interface. The **Name** field is the actual field in the HTML that is used to carry the authentication value. This field name may vary from application to application. Two default values are entered, login and password in the Form POST policy. If your application uses

different fields, then you must define them accordingly. Only one piece of data can be sent per field, so you must often define at least two fields (one for username and one for password). The **Value** field is used to define the actual value that will be presented to the backend server. Here, you can define static values (such as a static username and password) or you can use IVE system variables to specify the values in the fields. The predefined values use the **<USER>** and **<PASSWORD>** variables, which will map these values to the credentials with which the user logged on to the IVE (the primary authentication server). The last value that you must define is whether or not the user can or must modify the data in these fields. If you select **Not Modifiable**, then the user cannot alter these values. If you would like to grant the user the capability of editing these values, select the **User Can Change Value**, or if you want to force the user to change the value, then select **User Must Change Value**. Note that this only applies to the value field. If you predefine a value, it will be shown to the user, but the user will be able to make changes to it.

8.   Click **Save Changes**.

> **NOTE**
>
> If your application is using JSP, be sure it is not using a JSESSIONID pre-auth because the IVE will not have that proper JSESSION ID (cookie) value to send along with the Form POST. In this case, the application may disallow the Form POST and SSO will not work.

## SSO Headers/Cookies Authentication Example

For applications that utilize HTTP headers to pass authentication credentials, you can have the IVE perform SSO tasks to log the user into the application. In this example, we create a resource policy that will authenticate a user to an application that uses header/cookie-based authentication. We assume that you have already created the Web bookmark for the user to reach the resource or will use an alternative method to get the user to the resource.

1.   Begin by going to **Users | Resource Policies | Web | SSO Cookies/Headers** and click **New Policy**.

2.   Define a **Name** and optionally a **Description** for the resource policy.

3.   Next, define the **Resources** that will match this policy. These will follow the standard resource policy input types. Juniper recommends entering a fully qualified domain name for resources in SSO policies.

4. Like other resource policies, you must define what **Roles** apply to this resource policy.

5. There are two **Actions** that you can configure the resource policy to perform: **Append Headers defined below** and **Do No Append Headers defined below**. The former action will append the headers that you define to the HTTP header that is passed as a response to the backend server.

6. The **Header Name** is the field that the IVE will use as the header data type in the HTTP header. You can customize this to the value that suits your application. In order to determine what the header value should be, you can either consult the application documentation/developers or you can connect directly to the application within your network (not through the IVE) and use a tool such as Web Developer, Paros Proxy, or TCP Dump to view the header type that the client should be sending to the backend server. The **Value** field is the field that contains the actual value defined by the header. This is often the authentication credentials. Note that if you need to forward a cookie, you need to set the **Name** field to "Cookie" as well as the value field to "CookieName = CookieValue" according to Juniper.

7. Lastly, click **Save Changes**.

## Tools & Traps…

### Web Page Debug Tools

Web developers have long since developed tools to help debug Web pages and test underlying functionality. As an administrator, you can take advantage of these tools to help glean the appropriate information from the Web application. Firefox offers some excellent (free) extensions that integrate into the browser and can provide a wealth of information. A favorite is called Web Developer by Chris Pederick. You can get this extension from the Firefox extensions page.

# Pass-through Proxy

Certain Web applications may prove too challenging with regard to passing them through the IVE. Luckily, the IVE provides a fallback mechanism that allows you to securely pass traffic through the IVE to internal Web resources, without having to rely on client applications that get installed on the user's machine (such as SAM or Network Connect).

Examples of applications that can prove challenging to pass through the IVE include streaming media applications (such as Flash and streaming Flash), applications that don't follow defined standards, as well as applications with complex ActiveX and/or Java applets. It is not to say that as a whole these types of applications won't work through the IVE, but sometimes there are cases in which this will prove extremely difficult.

Pass-through proxies require slightly more configuration than most other resource policies, and they must integrate with other parts of the system than just roles. In this section, we discuss the components of pass-through proxy, the properties of a pass-through proxy policy, and how to configure one.

## Pass-through Proxy Components

Pass-through proxy works by creating either a virtual host name or virtual IVE (TCP) port for the resource with which you wish to connect. When the user tries to access a resource that is configured by a pass-through proxy policy, the user is redirected to either the virtual host name or the virtual (TCP) port. Thus, here is where the configuration branches off into two options—the virtual host name and the virtual (TCP) port.

Typically, the virtual host name is a more flexible configuration and is better suited to work in most environments, whereas the virtual port requires opening a port on your firewall and requires end user client access to this port (meaning that the remote client must also be able to connect on that port through the firewall or ACL on his or her remote end). The port range for virtual IVE (TCP) ports is 11000 to 11099. So essentially, you simply need to create the pass-through proxy policy for the resource as far as the IVE configuration goes, but you need to ensure that the client can connect to the virtual TCP port on your device. For example, the client would be redirected to https://<yourivednsname>:11099 for the application.

Virtual host names, on the other hand, act as a virtual host from the client's perspective. They are just going to be browsing to a virtual Web site that appears to be hosted on the IVE (which is acting more like a secure reverse proxy). The best configuration is typically to create a virtual IP port under the network settings of your external facing port (under **System | Network | <externalfacingport> | Virtual Ports**). Essentially, you apply an IP address to this new virtual port, and then the IVE can respond to requests that come in on this IP address. You will want to configure DNS to have a host name to point to the IP address of this port, and lastly, you will want to apply the certificate (preferably a wildcard certificate) to this port. Once you have performed these steps, you can then configure the resource policy to handle the pass-through proxy part of the configuration. This may sound complex, but this provides you with more flexibility in the long term and better usability transparent to the user. Here is an overview of the components needed:

1. Virtual IP port created on external facing physical port

2. DNS name(s) associated to the IP address of the virtual port for each pass-through proxy application

3. A certificate to place on the virtual port. Typically, a wildcard certificate works best. Talk to your CA for more details on obtaining one of these.

4. Create a pass-through proxy policy that references the resource and which virtual host name it is applied to.

## *Properties of a Pass-through Proxy Resource Policy*

Pass-through proxy policies have some different fields compared to other resource policies. In this section, we detail the different properties of the pass-through proxy policy, which will help provide the final groundwork before discussing some examples. Figure 9.10 outlines how this is configured in the IVE.

- **Application** This is a field that is used to label the resource policy. It can be thought of as a **Name** field.

- **Description** This field allows you to provide a description for the pass-through proxy policy.

- **URL** This is the URL of the internal server. This accepts only the following format: protocol://<ipaddress/dnsname>:<portnumber>. The following entries would be valid: www.companyintranet.local and https://192.168.212.50:8080. As you can see, you can use either IP addresses or DNS names, with no wildcards. Also, you cannot specify a server path, just the base URL.

- **Use virtual hostname** If you want to use the **Virtual hostname** option as opposed to the **Virtual port**, then you must select the radio button for this option. You must also define the external virtual host name. This **Virtual hostname** is the external DNS name for the internal server for which you create the pass-through proxy policy.

- **Use IVE port** If you want to use the virtual (TCP) port option, then you simply need to define the port number here. The IVE will listen on this port on external connections and, assuming that the session is authenticated, the traffic will be passed to the internal resource. You can enter a port number 11000–11099.

- **Rewrite XML** Instructs the IVE to rewrite URLs within XML data.

- **Rewrite external links** Instructs the IVE to rewrite all external links to pass through the IVE. If this is not enabled, then the IVE will only rewrite the host name for the resource defined in the pass-through proxy policy.

- **Block cookies from being sent to the browser** IVE will not allow cookies to be sent to the remote client but, rather, the IVE will store them, and it will send them back to the server if they are requested.

- **Host-Header forwarding** Instructs the IVE to pass the host name in the HTTP header (**Virtual hostname** mode only).

**Figure 9.10** Configuring Pass-through Proxy Policy (with Virtual Hostname) on the IVE

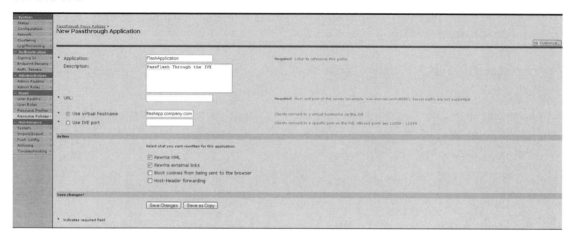

## *Example: Configuring Virtual Hostname Pass-through Proxy*

In this example, we configure a **Virtual Hostname**-based pass-through proxy policy. We are configuring this as a pass-through proxy policy because the destination Web server is on our internal network, serves streaming Flash content, and we need it to be accessible through the IVE Web interface without other applications (such as SAM or NC).

1.  We begin this example by configuring a new virtual port on the IVE to which we will apply the wildcard certificate. In this example, our Internet facing port on the IVE will be the external port. To create the virtual port, go to **System | Network | External Port | Virtual Ports** and click **New Ports**. Note that the virtual port that we are creating should not be confused with creating a virtual TCP port. The latter causes the IVE to listen on another TCP port (11000–11099), whereas virtual ports make the IVE listen on another IP address (TCP port 443,) just like you had another physical port on the IVE.

2.  There are two fields to fill out for a virtual port—the **Name** field and the **IP Address** field. Usually, you will want to make the name the same as the host name of the virtual host name that you want to represent. The IP address will be the IP address for which you will create a DNS record. Click **Save Changes**.

3.  Next, you will need to import a wildcard certificate that you will get from your CA. You can choose to import a wildcard certificate if you have more than one host name you need it to service. This is highly desirable, and with the recent decrease in wildcard certificate costs, you could save a lot of headache by doing this. You can import a certificate under **System | Configuration | Certificates | Device Certificates** and click the **Import Certificate & Key** (assuming that

you did not generate the CSR on the IVE). Installing certificates was discussed in another chapter; you simply need to browse for the certificate and enter the password, or if the certificate and private key are in separate files, you can browse for both and enter the password. Click **Import** next to the upload method you have selected.

4. Now that the new wildcard certificate is loaded, you will want to apply this certificate to the virtual port that you created. You can do so by clicking on the wildcard certificate under **System | Configuration | Certificates | Device Certificates** and ensuring that the virtual port that you created is a **Selected Port** by selecting the virtual port and clicking **Add**. Finally, click **Save Changes**.

5. If you haven't already done so, you must publish a DNS record that points a DNS name to the IP address of the virtual port you created. This DNS name needs to be publicly resolvable and will be used by a pass-through proxy policy to redirect an internal resource to the external proxied address. For this example, the DNS name is flash.company.com.

6. We assume that you have already created a Web bookmark in the IVE or have another mechanism to redirect the user to the IVE virtual host name.

7. As mentioned in previous examples, you will need to define the **Name, Description**, **URL** (which in this case we will say is http://flashpage.company.local) **Allow Policies,** and **Display Options**. Click **Save Changes**.

8. Lastly, we need to create the pass-through proxy resource policy under **Users | Resource Policies | Web | Passthrough Proxy**. Click **New Policy**.

9. Start by defining the **Application** that will be a label for this resource policy. You should also give a **Description** for the policy.

10. The **URL** that you define will be the internal URL. In this example, we said that this was http://flash.company.local.

11. For this example, we are using the **Virtual Hostname** which will map to the DNS name that we created, flash.company.com.

12. We assume that we do not need any of the pass-through proxy options for this example, so just click **Save Changes**.

---

**NOTE**

Juniper typically recommends using the virtual host name method due to its flexibility, even though it does require more steps than the IVE port method.
   Also, you may need to make adjustments on your firewall to allow the HTTPS traffic to reach the new IP address you have assigned to the virtual port.

---

## *Example: Pass-through Proxy with IVE Ports*

In this example, we set up the other method of performing pass-through proxy by having the IVE dedicate a specific (nonstandard) port to listen for requests. These requests will be mapped to the internal resource for which we wish to perform pass-through proxy.

1. In this example, we assume that you have already created a Web bookmark in the IVE or have another mechanism to redirect the user to the IVE virtual port.

2. Now we define the contents of the bookmark. There is nothing special about this bookmark; it should point to the internal resource for which we want to create a pass-through proxy policy. As mentioned in previous examples, you will need to define the **Name, Description, URL** (which in this case we will say is http://flashpage. company.local) **Allow Policies,** and **Display Options**. Click **Save Changes**.

3. Lastly, we will create the pass-through proxy resource policy. Go to **Users | Resource Policies | Web | Passthrough Proxy** and click **New Policy**.

4. Begin by defining the **Application**, which is just a name for this resource policy, as well as providing some **Description** for management best practices. See Figure 9.10, which displays how this appears in the AdminUI.

5. The **URL** will be the internal resource; for this example, http://flash.company.local. In this example, we use the **IVE Port** option. You must select a port (TCP) **11000–11099** for this resource. Lastly, if you need to have the IVE perform any rewriting actions, you can define them. Click **Save Changes**.

> **W**ARNING
>
> If you have an application that needs multiple ports, then you will have to define multiple pass-through proxy policies for each port. Also, the IVE port method may require you to make changes to your corporate firewall to allow traffic to reach the IVE on the new TCP port it will be listening on as defined by your policy. Also, this method requires the client is able to send traffic over this port, which you may not have any control over. Since a client is more likely to be able to connect on the standard HTTPS port rather than a nonstandard port, the virtual host name method is recommended.
>
> Users will not be able to connect to the virtual host name or IVE port directly to log in. They will only be allowed to access pass-through proxy resources if they are configured to be able to do so. The IVE uses security measures such as session cookie authentication to ensure that a user is logged into the IVE and has an active session before he or she will be allowed to access the internal resource. This makes the pass-through proxy functionality more than just a reverse proxy.

# Custom Headers

If you have an application that uses custom HTTP headers, you can force the IVE to allow the custom headers to be sent to the client Web browsers and Web servers. By default, the IVE will not forward these custom headers to the client or to the Web server. This can be accessed by going to **Users | Resource Policies | Web | Custom Headers**. Note that by default this may not be displayed in the Admin Interface. To display this and other hidden options, simply go to any resource policy summary page (for example, **Users | Resource Policy | Web | Web ACL**) and in the upper right-hand corner there should be a **Customize** button that you can click and then select this option to be displayed.

# ActiveX Parameter Rewriting

By default, the IVE will not rewrite ActiveX controls that are contained in Web pages. This may cause issues with the ActiveX controls because it may no longer be pointing to the correct resources. You can use an ActiveX rewriting policy to rewrite various parts of the ActiveX control. These resource policies are contained under **Users | Resource Policies | Web | ActiveX Parameters**. If you have an ActiveX-based application that is not working, this is likely the issue. View the source and search for "clsid." Then search for the parameters, and if any resemble a URL, and were not rewritten properly, make the policy change in the IVE ActiveX parameter rewriting policy to fix it.

# Web Proxy

The IVE can integrate with an existing internal Web proxy server in your environment to help pass content according to your organization's policies. This allows you to perform URL content filtering, caching, and other Web proxy-related functions on IVE Web traffic that passes through the IVE. To do so, you first need to define a Web proxy server under **Users | Resource Policies | Web | Web Proxy Servers**. You will simply need to define the IP address and port number to which the IVE should proxy Web connections. Next, you will need to define a resource policy to specify which Web traffic should be proxied and which should be passed in the clear. This is performed under **Users | Resource Policies | Web | Web Proxy Policies**. Often, you will only want to proxy traffic external to your organization, so you may create a Web proxy policy on top which defines internal addresses as the resources and an action of **Access Web Resources Directly**. The next policy would be placed below the previous policy, match all resources, and have an action of **Access Web Resource Through Web Proxy <ProxyServer>**. This way, you will match any specific internal sites first and pass them directly, and any other sites will be passed through the proxy server instead of directly to the resource. Figure 9.11 shows how this is displayed in the AdminUI.

**Figure 9.11** Configuring Web Proxy Server and Web Proxy Policies in the IVE

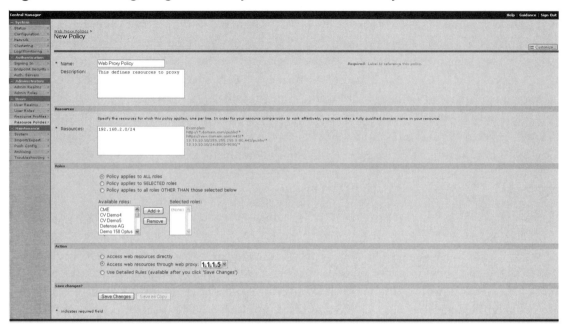

# Launch JSAM

The IVE can automate the launching of JSAM based on predefined resource policies that specify the resources that require JSAM. This allows you to provide flexible content through the IVE without having to have manual user intervention. WSAM and JSAM are discussed at length elsewhere in the book, but just to quickly cover how to configure a Launch JSAM policy, perform the following steps (Figure 9.12)

1. You must begin by enabling JSAM for the user role that you want to create a Launch JSAM policy. Do this by going to **Users | User Roles | <User Role> | SAM | Options** and make sure that **JSAM** is selected. Note that only one SAM policy can be enabled per role. Click **Save Changes**.

2. Next, you can define JSAM applications by going to **Users | User Roles | <User Role> | SAM | Applications**. You can click **New Application**. You will most likely be using a **Custom** rather than **Standard** application. Define the **Name** and optional **Description**. Next, define the **Server Name**, **Server Port**, **ClientLoopback IP,** and **Client Port** for this application. For more information about JSAM applications, see Chapter 5. Click **Save Application**.

3. Lastly, you need to go under **Users | Resource Policies | Web | Launch JSAM** to create the Launch JSAM policy. Note that **Launch JSAM** may not be displayed by default, but you can display it by going under any resource policy, such as Web ACL, and in the upper right-hand corner there will be a **Customize** button that you can click, and a pop-up window will appear with an option to display JSAM. Once you create a **New Policy** for Launching JSAM, you will need to define **Name, Description, Resource** (for which you want to launch JSAM), applicable **Roles**, and, lastly, what action to take. Most likely this will be **Launch JSAM for this URL** to have the IVE launch the JSAM client for resources matching this policy.

4. Click **Save Changes**.

**Figure 9.12** Configuring a Launch JSAM Policy in the AdminUI

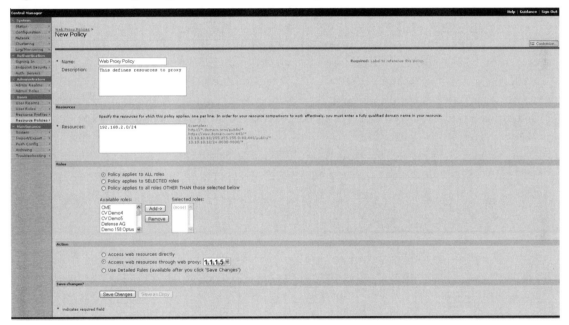

# HTTP 1.1

By default, the IVE disables HTTP 1.1, which is an enhancement of the HTTP 1.0 protocol (see http://www.w3.org/Protocols/rfc2616/rfc2616.html for complete details). HTTP 1.1 adds some additional functionality that may be desirable for the operation of your Web applications. Just like any other resource policy, you can enable HTTP 1.1 across the board or to individual resources through the granular support of resource policies. To configure HTTP 1.1, go to **Users | Resource Policies | Web | Protocol** and create a new protocol with the appropriate resources and an action of HTTP 1.1.

> **NOTE**
>
> The IVE will normally use the same protocol that the client uses (assuming that HTTP 1.1 is enabled). For instance, if the user connects with HTTP 1.0, the IVE will use HTTP 1.0, but if the user connects with HTTP 1.1 and HTTP 1.1 is disabled, the IVE will use HTTP 1.0. If the user connects with HTTP 1.1 and HTTP 1.1 is enabled, then the IVE will communicate with HTTP 1.1 to the Web server.

## Options

There are two options for HTTP resource policies. The first is to allow **IP Based matching for Host Name based policy resources**. This option will allow users to enter IP addresses in addition to host names when browsing for Web content. If you do not enable this and a user enters an IP address (while you've defined host names in resource policies), then the IVE will not match the resource. By enabling this option, the IVE will perform a DNS lookup to determine if the host name in the resource policy matches the IP address provided.

The other option for Web resources is to force **Case sensitive matching for the Path and Query string components in Web resources**. This option will enforce case-sensitive matching, rather than ignoring the case of the URLs that it is evaluating. This may be important for Web servers that enforce case-sensitive files or for Web applications that require case-sensitive requests in URLs.

# Web Resource Profiles

Web resource profiles are probably the most utilized type of resource profiles due to the popular nature of rewriting Web applications through the IVE. The benefits of using resource profiles over traditional role-based bookmarks are discussed elsewhere in this book, so we will spare the details in this chapter. Suffice to say that Web resource profiles can save you a lot of time and make your configuration much less complex; particularly when you are dealing with Web bookmarks.

Some complex Web applications are particularly popular and have led to many support calls to JTAC. Such applications include Microsoft Outlook Web Access Microsoft Sharepoint, Lotus iNotes, and Citrix Web applications. These applications push Web capabilities to a very advanced level and utilize much dynamic content (sometimes not following standards, or implementing proprietary mechanisms for supporting the content). To help accommodate these popular applications, Juniper has made some template Web resource profiles that you can select that will simplify the deployment of these complex applications.

In this section, we discuss the configuration of different Web resource profiles, including the predefined templates and hosting Java applets on your IVE through resource profiles. We also discuss the properties of these different resource profiles and how they can be configured to simplify the configuration and management of your IVE.

# Web Resource Profile Types

As mentioned previously, there are some predefined templates for resource profiles, as well as customizable resource profiles and hosted Java applet resource profiles. It is important to remember that almost every component within resource profiles can be configured elsewhere in the configuration (either as a role bookmark or as a resource policy); therefore, it was important to discuss these components as we did previously, even though resource profiles are usually the preferred way to configure bookmarks within the IVE. Remember that resource profiles allow you to define the same features that you would normally define in role bookmarks and resource policies, but they do so in a wizard-like interface; most important, they allow you to select which roles the profile will be applied to so that you can simply configure a bookmark in one place rather than having to do so in multiple roles or making complex role merging rules. Each predefined template has parameters defined to configure the appropriate resource policy within the profile. For instance, some applications may need special Web caching, compression, and rewriting resource profiles, whereas others may support SSO, pass-through proxy, and so on. Juniper has made much of this process much simpler to configure than the traditional mechanism through role bookmarks.

- **Custom resource profiles** This resource profile type is for creating resource profiles that do not have a predefined template (for example, the rest of the resource profiles discussed in this section). You would use a custom resource profile for creating a resource profile for a standard Web application; you could even use it to define one of the predefined resource profile templates, but you would be responsible for configuring the advanced features that are somewhat automated for you when you use the predefined templates.

- **Hosted Java applet** The IVE can host Java applets in the IVE rather than having to use a separate Web server that you would typically have to maintain. Essentially, you upload the Java applet to the IVE, while the resource profile provides a mechanism for distributing this Java applet across multiple roles rather than having to create separate Web bookmarks within each role.

- **Citrix Web Interface/Java ICA** This is a resource profile template that allows you to easily define resource profiles for Citrix Web Interface. These resource profiles are discussed later along with creating other access for Citrix applications.

- **Microsoft OWA** The IVE has support for OWA 2000, 2003, and 2007 within resource profiles. There are different templates for the different versions because the different versions vary greatly among each other and require different configurations based on the content that they implements.

- **Lotus iNotes** Juniper has also provided support for several different versions of the popular Lotus iNotes platform to simplify the configuration of this application through the IVE. Juniper supports versions 5, 6, 6.5, and 7.

- **Microsoft Sharepoint** Microsoft Sharepoint is a Web portal application that supports a wide range of features for organizations from small business to enterprise. Juniper has provided this template for enabling the IVE to properly handle passing this content through the rewriter while simplifying deployment.

# Configuring Custom Resource Profiles

Whenever you would like to add a Web bookmark to many different roles, you can save time and effort by creating resource profiles. When you are creating a general-purpose profile that is not predefined, you will want to use the custom resource profile. In this example, we outline how to create a custom resource profile.

1. Go to **Users | Resource Profiles | Web** and click **New Profile**.

2. Select **Custom** as the type to define that this is not a type of resource profile that is a predefined template.

3. Define a **Name** that will be used to reference this resource profile elsewhere in the configuration.

4. You can optionally (yet recommended) define a **Description** for the resource profile.

5. Optionally, if you want to define any advanced resource policy settings, you can do so in the resource profile by clicking **Show All Autoallow Policies**. By default, only the **Web Access Control** policy will be displayed.

6. You must define the **Base URL** for the resource for which you are creating a bookmark. If you have this defined and click **Save and Continue** when Auto-Allow policies are enabled, it will usually generate a resource policy for these types if applicable. Note that you may have to make some changes to the policy as appropriate because some components cannot be auto-allowed. For a complete description of what each of these policies does for IVE access, see the discussion of web resource policies presented previously.

7. Click **Save and Continue**. If you have defined any auto-allow policies, the IVE will autocomplete the applicable fields, and you will have to click **Save and Continue** again.

8. Next, you need to select what **Roles** this resource profile will be applied to. Click them from the available roles, and **Add** them to the selected roles.

9. Click **Save Changes**.

10. Lastly, you will be brought to the **Bookmarks** page. Although you don't normally need to do anything on this page, it will show you the bookmark enabled. If you would like, you can define additional **Web Bookmarks** for this resource profile, although the additional bookmarks will be created for the same roles assigned to this resource profile, so if you want the access to be granted differently, you should create the bookmarks in separate rolls.

---

**NOTE**

You can view the auto-created role bookmarks and resource policies that are generated from resource profiles. To view the role bookmarks, go to **Users | User Roles | <UserRole> | Web Bookmarks** and you will be able to see the autogenerated bookmarks. To view the resource policies, go to **Users | Resource Policies | Web | <Resource Policy>**, where the **<Resource Policies>** is the resource policy type such as Web ACL, compression, and SSO. You can perform this for any resource profile type (Web, file, Telnet, SSH, and terminal Services).

---

## Host Java Applet Resource Profile

As discussed previously, the IVE can actually host a Java applet on the IVE without having to rely on a separate Web server or the need to rewrite the applet. There are several different uses of hosting Java applets on the IVE, but you can do so through web resource profiles as follows:

1. Go to **Users | Resource Profiles | Web** and click **New Profile**.

2. Select **Hosted Java Applets**.

3. Define a **Name** for this resource profile and, optionally, define a **Description**.

4. If you don't already have the Java applet uploaded to your IVE, you can click the **Edit List** button, which will bring up a pop-up window to allow you to upload the applet. As of IVE 6.0, only Jar, Cab, Zip, and Class files are supported. You can do so by clicking **Browse** to search for the .jar/cab file locally. If the file is compressed in a ZIP, you should select the **Uncompress** option when uploading the file. Once you have selected it, enter a **Name** for the applet and click **OK** to upload the applet. Finally, click **Close Window** to return to the resource profile.

5. Now select the **Java Applet** you wish to apply to this resource profile from the **Applet to User** drop-down menu.

6. If your applet needs to make network connections, then you would need to make sure that you have a Java access policy. See resource policies for Java access policies for more information on the properties of the auto-allow policy.

7. Click **Save and Continue**.

8. Next, select the roles that will apply to this resource profile by selecting **Role** from the **Available Roles** column and **Add** it to the **Selected Roles**.

9. Click **Save Changes**.

10. A hosted Java applet resource policy does not automatically create a bookmark for the user to click on to launch the page. Normally, you will need to provide the user with a Web page with the Java applet embedded. The IVE can automatically generate an HTML page with the applet embedded so you do not have to introduce another Web server, and you can provide the user with a bookmark on the IVE. To do so, click **New Bookmark** on the **Bookmarks** page of the resource profile.

11. If you are using the bookmark option to generate the HTML for the IVE, you will be brought to another page to generate the bookmark. Begin by defining a **Name** for the bookmark, which users will see within their session as a Web bookmark.

12. Optionally, define a **Description** that users will see to provide them with additional information about the bookmark.

13. Click the **Generate HTML** button to automatically generate a Web page that will host this applet based on the previous information entered in the resource profile. You must either select this option or redirect users to a Web page with the applet in order for this to function properly. You can alter certain parts of the HTML code that is generated for this resource profile if need be. Some Java applets require certain parameters to be passed to them in order to function. These parameters should be provided by the applet developer and must be manually entered within the generated HTML to function.

14. Once the page has been generated, simply **Save** the changes that have been made for your hosted Java applet.

# Outlook Web Access 2007 Example

Microsoft Outlook Web Access has been an extremely popular Webmail platform that integrates with Microsoft Exchange to provide remote clientless access to e-mail. Historically, there have been several vulnerabilities with OWA that can be exploited only requiring access to the Web page without valid credentials. The IVE can help provide security for OWA by proxying access so that OWA is not directly reachable on the Internet. Because OWA is a complex Web application that requires dynamic content and supports a wealth of features, passing it through the IVE with all features working properly has been somewhat difficult in the past. Resource profiles have dramatically simplifies this by integrating all of the necessary components (such as caching and compression changes) into a single profile. OWA requirements through the IVE vary from version to version, but the IVE supports resource profiles for OWA 2000, 2003, and 2007. In this example, we focus on OWA 2007, but you could apply this to the other versions by selecting the appropriate version from the **Type** field in the IVE.

1.  Go to **Users | Resource Profiles | Web** and click **New Profile**.

2.  Select **Outlook Web Access 2007** from the drop-down menu.

3.  Define a **Name** for the resource profile that will be referenced elsewhere in the configuration. Optionally define a **Description** for the resource profile.

4.  Next, you must define the **Base URL** that the IVE will use for the bookmark and auto-allow policies. This should be entered using a fully qualified domain name whenever possible. For example, if our OWA Web server was at email.company. local/exchange, then our base URL would be https://email.company.local/exchange.

5.  Next, you can optionally define the OWA server as a **Managed or Unmanaged Device**. This is in reference to whether the client device is managed or unmanaged to determine how policies such as caching should be applied to clients connecting through this role. Note that other OWA versions have other options in this area for caching.

6.  You have the option of allowing users to **Download** or **Upload** attachments through the IVE. This can help restrict the distribution of confidential content to external parties.

7.  Now click **Save and Continue**. This should propagate the base URL into the appropriate auto-allow polices (Web access, caching, and compression). Historically, changes have been necessary for how the IVE caches, compresses, and rewrites the content for OWA to prevent usability issues (such as hyperlinks in e-mails failing and file download difficulty). You can also define SSO directives when necessary to automate the log-on process. Click **Save and Continue** again to proceed to the Role page.

8.  Specify the **Roles** that this resource profile should apply to, and click **Save Changes**.

9.  You will now be brought to the Bookmarks page, where the bookmark should already be created for the policy. You can add additional bookmarks to this policy if necessary, but it is usually better to define a single bookmark per policy.

## Citrix/nFuse Resource Profiles

These will be discussed at length in Chapter 6 in conjunction with several other options for using Citrix/nFuse through the IVE.

# File Access

Centralized file access is a technology that has been deployed in enterprise networks for quite some time. With the advent of remote access, users have extended the centralized file functionality to external locations. One of the major issues is how to provide file content to remote users securely. In the past, clunky IPSec clients provided secure but not intuitive access for users. SSL VPN technology alone has not improved this problem, but the IVE has implemented a powerful interface for accessing files remotely. In the past, users had to map network drives, which requires additional network configuration. The IVE provides a Web front end that represents the file share, and it allows the user to perform common functions such as downloading, uploading, and managing files (according to permissions).

The IVE provides file access support for CIFS/SMB shares (Windows) as well as NFS (UNIX) shares. This allows you to configure access to most modern network file shares. One of the strengths of creating file access through the IVE is that it does not require any setup on the client side, nor does it require any software—just the Web browser. Like all content distributed by the IVE, it is delivered over a secure connection between the IVE and the client browser. This fulfills the requirement of delivering the remote access to the file shares in an intuitive and secure manner to the users.

In this section, we review the different types of file access that the IVE can provide, followed by configuring file access through the IVE.

## File Bookmarks

As mentioned previously, the IVE supports both CIFS/SMB file shares and NFS file shares. The IVE considers CIFS/SMB shares Windows file shares, whereas the NFS is considered UNIX. The truth is that these are just the protocols, and CIFS/SMB can be implemented on Linux/UNIX/MAC and NFS can be implemented on other operating systems. So when you are configuring file share access, you may have to actually configure access to a SMB share on Linux as a Windows file share. Like Web bookmarks, the file bookmarks that are configured for a user role are displayed in the UserUI. When the user clicks on the bookmark, he or she is taken to a directory tree that follows the file directory structure. Figure 9.13 shows the user interface for browsing files through the IVE, including how to upload files.

**Figure 9.13** File Bookmarks through the IVE User Interface

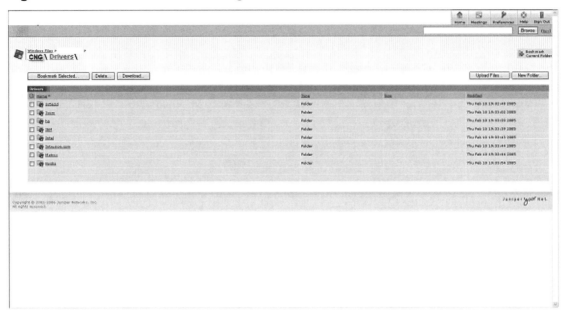

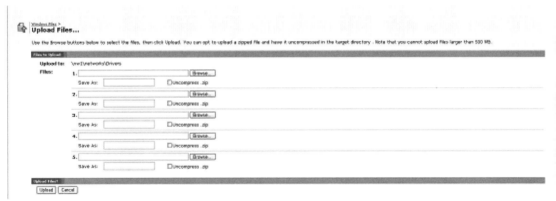

# Configuring Windows File Shares

Windows file shares use the SMB protocol to access the file shares configured on the SMB server. The IVE will act as a SMB client when it gets a request to access the file share on the SMB server. Configuring Windows file bookmarks is quite similar to configuring Web bookmarks on the IVE. The following is an example of how to configure a Windows file share, along with an accompanying screenshot shown in Figure 9.14:

**W**ARNING

Before you begin to configure Windows file bookmarks, you should ensure that you have properly configured DNS, WINS, and Master Browsers for maximum functionality. This can be done by going to **System | Network | Overview** and making sure that **DNS Servers, DNS Domains**, and the **Enable Network Discovery** options are checked. WINS is also recommended if it is present in your network. If necessary, click **Save Changes**.

1. Begin by creating the Windows file bookmarks. To perform this task, go to **Users | User Roles | <User Role>** and make sure that you have enabled **Files, Windows**; if necessary, click **Save Changes**.

2. Now go to **Users | User Roles | <User Role> | Files | Windows Bookmarks** and click **New Bookmark**.

3. You must define a **Name** for the bookmark which will be displayed in the user interface and used within the IVE internally. You can also define a **Description** which is useful for providing the user additional information about the file share.

4. Next, you must define the server that hosts the file share. This is done by defining the **Server/share**. You can define the server and share as \\server\share, or you could define it as smb://server/share. For example, let's say the server is called FileServer, and the share name is FileShare. These resources would look like \\FileServer\FileShare or smb://FileServer/FileShare.

5. You can define a path within the file share if you don't want the user to start off at the root directory of the file share. This is done within the **Path** field. A "/" or blank field will indicate the root directory of the file share. Alternatively, you can specify a directory structure for the bookmark. For instance, if the file directory you wanted to make a bookmark for was \\FileServer\FileShare\folder1\folder2\destfolder, then the path field would contain\folder1\folder2\destfolder.

6. To help enrich the user experience, you can define whether the bookmark should **Appear as bookmark on the homepage and in file browsing**, which will cause the bookmark to appear on the UserUI and when browsing file shares, or you can define the bookmark to **Appear in file browsing only**, which will only display it on the UserUI.

7. You can have the IVE automatically create resource policies within the file ACL. The following options are available: **Enable Auto-Allow Access to this bookmark**, which will automatically create the resource policy for the file

bookmark, and **Read-Write Access**, which allows the user to make changes within the directory to files and folders as well as grant access to subfolders by defining the **Include Sub-Folders**.

8.  Click **Save Changes**.

**Figure 9.14** Configuring Windows (SMB) File Shares

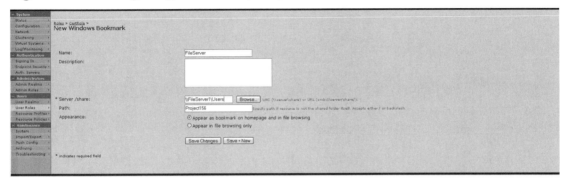

---

**NOTE**

Besides honoring the read–write policy in the file bookmark, users will also comply with other access restrictions made on the file share as well. For instance, if you configure the file share to allow only domain administrators to be able to access the share (this would be done on the file share itself, not in the IVE) and a regular domain user tries to access it through the IVE, the user will not be able to access the files.

---

# Configuring UNIX File Shares

The IVE can also provide access to NFS file shares, which is a format commonly supported by UNIX and Linux operating systems. In this example, we review the different configuration settings that can be implemented in a UNIX file share (Figure 9.15).

1.  To create a UNIX bookmark, begin by ensuring that the user role has access to UNIX file bookmarks. This can be done by going to **Users | User Roles | <User Role>** and make sure **Files, Unix/NFS** is enabled; if necessary, click **Save Changes**.

2. Next, go to **Users | User Roles | <User Role> | Files | Unix Bookmarks** and click **New Bookmark**.

3. You must then define the **Name** that will be displayed in the UserUI as well as referenced internally in the IVE. You can also define a **Description** that will be displayed within the UserUI to help provide additional information to the user.

4. Next, define the host name or IP address of the **Server** hosting the NFS share.

5. The **Path** within the file share should be defined to indicate the directory to which the IVE will direct the user. This can be in the format /folder/folder2. Unlike Windows, UNIX shares use "/" rather than "<0x201D>" to indicate the directory. So if you wanted to make a bookmark for a file server FileServer and place the user in the /Home/FileShare/ directory, FileServer (a resolvable name) would be put in the **Server** field, and /Home/FileShare would be placed in the Path.

6. Just like the Windows bookmarks, you can configure the bookmark to **Appear as bookmark on homepage and in file browsing** or **Appear in file browsing only**.

7. Also, you can define that the bookmark should automatically define resource policies to enable access to the resource with the **Enable auto-allow access to the bookmark**, allow **Read-Write Access**, and/or **Include Sub-Folders** within the bookmark.

8. Click **Save Bookmark**.

**Figure 9.15** Configuring UNIX File Shares

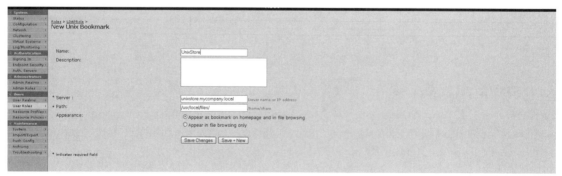

# File Options

There are several options that can be applied to alter the user experience on the IVE with regard to file access. This can be configured on a role-by-role basis. The following are options that can be applied to file bookmarks in the IVE. The options are located under **User | User Roles | <User Role> | Files | Options** (Figure 9.16):

- (Windows) **User can browse network file shares** This allows users to browse through Windows file shares under the Windows file page. This adds the "Windows Files" link in the UI for users and allows them to see all the Windows file shares on the network.

- (Windows) **User can add bookmarks** This allows users to create their own bookmarks within their UI profile.

- (UNIX) **User can browse network file shares** This allows users to browse the network for NFS shares. This adds the "Unix Files" link in the UI for users and allows them to see all the NFS file shares on the network.

- (UNIX) **User can add bookmarks** This allows users to create their own UNIX bookmarks within their UI profile.

- (UNIX) **Allow automount shares** Automount shares defined in NIS (directory server for UNIX) can be accessed by users if this option is enabled.

**Figure 9.16** Configuring File Bookmark Options for Both Windows and UNIX File Shares

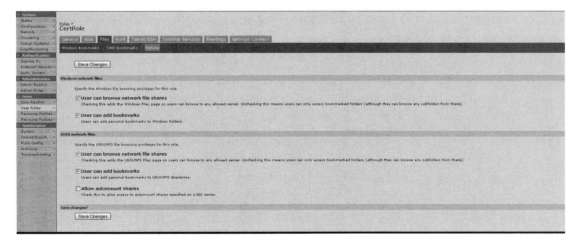

# File Resource Policies

The IVE allows you to configure granular control to file resources through the use of resource policies. Much like the Web resource policies, file resource policies can assist with everything from file access and SSO to compression. File resource policies are required to define who gets access to what, along with additional functionality. File resource policies only apply to file browsing through the IVE interface, and not through other access mechanisms such as SAM or network connect. When adding bookmarks, the auto-allow feature can automatically configure resource policies for access to the resource, and you can do much more with regard to configuring the resource policies. In this section, we explorer the different file resource policies and provide examples for configuring and implementing these features.

## Windows ACL

Windows ACLs are required to allow users to browse CIFS/SMB file shares through the IVE. In addition to the ACLs on the file server, you can control what access the IVE will allow for different resources and roles. There is a default policy that will allow all roles access to any file resource through the IVE. Although this will make it simple to configure file bookmarks without having to create resource policies, it will also open up unrestricted file access to the resources (users must also meet access requirements on the file servers). For purposes of security, it would be best to remove the default rule and create resource policies on an as-needed basis. Creating Windows ACLs is quite simple, especially if you are already familiar with creating Web ACLs. The following is an example of how to create a Windows ACL (Figure 9.17):

1. Windows file ACL resource policies are located under **Users | Resource Policies | Files | Windows ACL** in the AdminUI. You will begin at the resource policy summary screen. Click **New Policy** to define a new resource policy.

2. You must define a **Name** by which to reference the resource policy. This will not be visible to the user but will be used for internal purposes. It is also advised to specify a **Description** of the resource policy for administrative purposes.

3. Next, we must define the **Resource** itself. Windows file ACLs use the following format with regard to defining resources: \\server\share\path, where server is the host name or IP address of the server that the share resides on, the share is the actual share name, and path is the path within the share. The share and path identifiers may be optional depending on the use of wildcards, but you must define the server. So let's say we have a file server fileserver.company.local; we want to

provide access to a share called fileshare, and the base directory the user will see will be called users, so our resource would look like \\fileserver.company.local\fileshare\users. If we wanted to share the C drive on the file server our resource would look like\\fileserver.company.local\c$; this will follow the standard Windows formats for file shares. Note that you may need to use wildcards to define further access within folders. For instance, the previous examples would only give use access to that directory, but if we wanted to give users access to everything below that directory, then we would need to use wildcards. For instance, we would use \\fileserver.company.local\fileshare\users* or \\fileserver.company.local\c$\* to provide access to everything under this directory.

---

**NOTE**

---

You can also use system variables such as <username> in resource policies to dynamically provide users access to their own directories (assuming that they have directories following their usernames) on the file share. For instance, we could write a resource policy \\fileserver.company.local\fileshare\users\ <username>\*, which would give a user access to a directory with the user's username on \\fileserver.company.local\fileshare\users\. This allows you to provide flexible access on a user-by-user basis.

---

4. File resource policies require that you define which roles this resource policy applies to. You can select one of the following options: **Policy applies to ALL roles, Policy applies to SELECTED roles** (select roles from the **Available Roles** list and put them into the **Selected Roles** list to apply), and **Policy applies to all roles OTHER THAN those selected below** (resource policy will apply to all roles except those in the **Selected Roles** list).

5. After defining the resource and what roles it applies to, you must now define what action to take when the resources are matched. You can **Allow access** with optional **Read–only** rights or **Deny access** to the files. (**Detailed Rules** are also allowed.)

6. Click **Save Changes**.

**Figure 9.17** The IVE Comes with an Initial File Browsing Policy That Allows Users to Browse to Any Windows/SMB Share through the IVE File Interface If They Have File Permissions in Their Roles

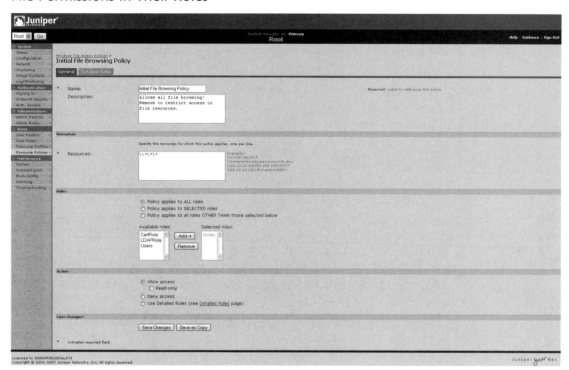

---

**NOTE**

Although you may configure access to resources on file shares, ultimately the access control settings on the file server will have the final say in what users can access, not the IVE. Setting the resource policies on the IVE is useful for restricting users from getting to resources closer to the source, which is often a best practice. This also lets you configure more restrictive access when users are trying to access files through the IVE. Ultimately, if a user does not normally have access to files on a file share, he or she should not get it through the IVE (unless you define SSO to use a different account to access the files). As mentioned previously, file resource POLICIES only apply to file browsing through the IVE, and not through SAM or Network Connect.

---

# UNIX/NFS ACLs

The IVE allows you to control user access to UNIX (NFS) file shares with resource policies just like Windows file shares. The principals are essentially the same with regard to configuring UNIX/NFS ACLs and Windows ACLs, with the exception of the format of the resources. In this section, we discuss the tasks necessary to configure and implement UNIX/NFS resource policies.

1. UNIX/NFS resource policies are configured under **Users | Resource Policies | Files | UNIX/NFS ACL**. When you access this page, you will see a summary of file policies. By default, there is not an initial policy, so you will need to create resource policies (whether through auto-allow in bookmarks or through the UNIX/NFS resource policies). Click **New Policy** to create a new UNIX/NFS resource policy.

2. Begin creating the resource policy by defining a **Name** to reference the policy by, as well as a **Description** (recommended but not required) for administrative purposes.

3. Next, define what **Resources** will be matched to this policy. The UNIX/NFS resource format is different from the Windows (CIFS/SMB) format. UNIX/NFS follows the format server/path. This means that you must define the server with either an IP address or host name, as well as the path to the folder into which you want to place the user. So if we have an NFS server nfsserver.company.local and we want to make a bookmark to the root directory, then we would simply enter nfsserver.company.local in the **Resources** field. If we wanted to make a bookmark that allowed access only to the /home/guest/ folder and no other directories, the resource would read nfsserver.company.local/home/guest/. Lastly, if we wanted to provide access to everything under /home/guest, we could make a resource nfsserver.company.local/home/guest/*. As you can see, the use of wildcards is allowed. You can also use system variables such as <username> in the resource to dynamically allow access to resources that match the username of the logged on IVE user.

4. File resource policies require that you define which roles this resource policy applies to. You can select one of the following options: **Policy applies to ALL roles, Policy applies to SELECTED roles** (select roles from the **Available Roles** list and put them into the **Selected Roles** list to apply), and **Policy applies to all roles OTHER THAN those selected below** (resource policy will apply to all roles except those in the **Selected Roles** list).

5. After defining the resource and what roles it applies to, you must now define what action to take when the resources are matched. You can **Allow Access** with optional **Read-Only** rights or **Deny Access** to the files. (**Detailed Rules** are also allowed.)

6. Click **Save Changes**.

# Windows SSO

The IVE supports SSO for Windows (CIFS/SMB) file shares. This allows the IVE to automatically pass the file server the credentials on the user's behalf, thus saving a prompt for authentication after the user has logged on to the IVE. SSO for Windows file shares is very similar to Web-based SSO. In this section, we discuss how to create and implement an SSO policy for Windows (CIFS/SMB) file shares (Figure 9.18).

1. Windows SSO policies are configured by going to **Users | Resource Policies | Files | Windows SSO** and clicking **New Policy**.

2. You must define a **Name** for the policy and, optionally, a **Description** that is used for administrative purposes and is not visible to users.

3. Under the **Resources** field, you must define what resources apply to this SSO policy. The format can be defined just like the Windows ACL resources. The format for a Windows file share and path looks like \\server\share\path, where you can use wildcards, IP addresses, and host names for the fields of the resource. Whichever method you choose, you need to make sure that it is in fact matching the resources appropriately in order for the Windows SSO policy to be correctly applied to the desired resource.

4. Next, define what **Roles** this SSO policy will be applied to. This follows the standard role allocation that is present for other resource policies.

5. Lastly, you must define how the IVE will authenticate the user to the file server which is requesting authentication. If the file system only needs a single username and password, and you don't need to authenticate different users differently, then you can select the **Use Specified Credentials** option, along with defining a specific **Username** and **Password**. If you need to have users authenticate with their individual credentials, then you should select **Use Specified Credentials** and in the **Username** field enter **<Username>** and in the **Variable Password** field enter **<Password>** (this assumes you want to pass the credentials used from the primary authentication). There is one last option, to simply **Prompt for user credentials**, which the IVE will present the user with an authentication request and intermediate the transfer between the client and backend server.

6. Apply your changes by clicking **Save Changes**.

**Figure 9.18** Configuring Windows SSO File Policies

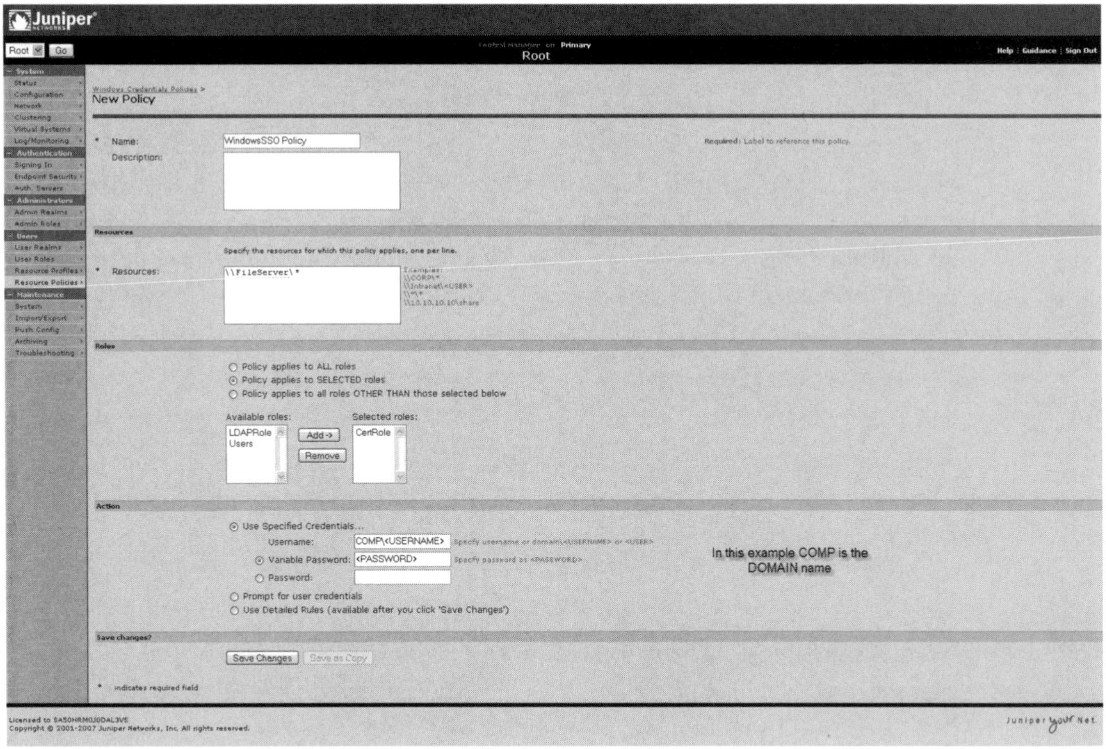

**NOTE**

If your authentication server supports user attributes such as active directory, LDAP, and RADIUS, the IVE can use this to automatically pass your credentials to a backend file server to authenticate the user. You set this up at the Realm level under **Users | User Realms | <User Realm> | General** and have the **Directory/Attribute** set to the appropriate authentication server. Otherwise, you can use other mechanisms such as the Windows SSO to pass authentication credentials to the resource.

# Windows/UNIX Compression

The IVE has the ability to compress files using GZIP between the IVE and the client Web browser. This allows you to save bandwidth and improve performance related to how long it will take for a user to receive the requested file. Note that in more recent versions of the IVE, you can allow the user to ZIP files through the user interface, thus bypassing the need to configure a file compression policy. The IVE comes configured with default compression policies for both Windows and UNIX file resources; however, even though this is enabled, you must still make sure that GZIP compression is enabled systemwide.

1. Go to **Maintenance | System | Options** and make sure that **Enable Gzip Compression** is checked and click **Save Changes** if necessary.

2. After you ensure that this is configured, you can go to **Users | Resource Policies | Files |** and either **Windows Compression** or **UNIX/NFS Compression** and configure a policy to match the appropriate resources to automatically compress. Again, this compression is only between the IVE and the client, not between the IVE and the backend server.

3. Click **Save Changes**.

## Encoding

The IVE supports different international standards for file encoding format. The **Users | Resource Policies | Files | Encoding** menu allows you to select the appropriate file encoding format, which is by default **Western European** (ISO-8859-1).

## Options

The Options menu located under **Users | Resource Policies | Files | Options** allows you to define systemwide options that will apply to resource policies. These include the ability to perform **IP Based Matching for Hostname Based Policy Resources**; **Case Sensitive Matching for All Path Components in File Resources** (which is important for NFS file shares since UNIX/Linux implements case-sensitive files and directories, so an incorrect match could result in problems browsing for resources); and **Allow NTLM V1**, which applies to Windows file shares. NTLMv1, although an improvement from LM authentication, still has inherent vulnerabilities in the protocol. If you do not need this for compatibility reasons, you should disable it to force the IVE to use Kerberos, and not try NTLM if Kerberos fails.

# File Resource Profiles

Just like Web bookmarks, file bookmarks, creating duplicate bookmarks for different roles, or creating confusing role mapping rules to merge roles can be a messy way to manage your device (that is highly prone to errors). File resource profiles can help solve the same dilemma as Web resource profiles for Web bookmarks; that is, being able to define one bookmark that is applied to multiple roles. In this section, we focus on how to create both Windows and UNIX file resource profiles within the IVE.

## Creating Windows File Resource Profiles

In this example, we create a resource profile for a Windows file share, which will be applied across multiple roles. This is helpful when you need to offer bookmarks to the same file share across different roles.

1. Begin by going to **Users | Resource Profiles | Files** and click **New Profile**.

2. For **Type**, select **Windows**.

3. Define a **Name** and optionally define a **Description** for the resource profile.

4. Next, you must define a **Server/Share** that the user will be accessing. You can either enter this in the \\**Server\Share** format as described in the role/resource policy section of this chapter, or you can click the **Browse** button to browse your domain (assuming that you have Master Browsing enabled and appropriate name resolution configured).

5. You can click **Show ALL Autopolicies** to expand the auto-allow policies that are listed. By default, only the **Windows File Access** control policy is listed for this profile. Any autopolicies that you have enabled must have a resource policy in them, or you will generate an error when you attempt to save. In most cases, the auto-allow policy will match the resource that is defined for the server/share. See the resource policies section for Windows file shares for a description of the format for configuring these.

6. Click **Save and Continue**.

7. Next, select the appropriate **Roles** that this resource profile will apply to and click **Save Changes**.

8. The IVE will automatically generate a bookmark, but you can create additional bookmarks for this resource profile. However, they will be assigned to the same roles as the rest of the bookmarks, so if you need to differentiate the bookmarks assigned to the roles, make a separate resource profile.

## Creating UNIX File Resource Profiles

UNIX file resource profiles are essentially the same as Windows resource profiles as far as the configuration is concerned. The main difference is that UNIX file shares utilize NFS, whereas Windows utilizes CIFS/SMB. The format of the file share on UNIX is <server>/<path>, which differs from the Windows format of \\<server>\<share><path>. UNIX file resource profiles are configured by going to **Users | Resource Profiles | Files** and clicking **New Profile**. Select **Unix** as the **Type**. The rest of the configuration mirrors the Windows file resource profiles.

# Telnet/SSH Access

The IVE provides an integrated method to present a simple Telnet client to users through the IVE Web interface. For many years, Telnet has been a popular terminal client application for accessing everything from network infrastructure gear to mainframe servers. One common problem administrators faced was how to provide remote users access to internal applications that use Telnet in a secure and intuitive manner. The IVE provides an exceptional method that automatically provisions access to such internal applications over a secure connection between the IVE and the client. The IVE uses a Java applet that is preconfigured and launched by the user to perform the actual Telnet connection to the desired machine. For more information, see the Java Applet Upload framework, where you can upload even more robust Telnet, SSH, SFTP, RDP, and other Java applets.

The IVE Telnet client follows the same properties as other applications, such as Web and file browsing through the IVE. Telnet is applied to roles, and it has resource policies to restrict access just like bookmarks in the Web interface.

SSH is very similar to Telnet, with the major difference that it is encrypted using Secure Sockets Layer. You could liken the difference between Telnet and SSH to HTTP and HTTPS. Many applications have been moving in the direction of SSH away from Telnet for the added security. Whether it be network infrastructure gear using SSH or other applications, many have implemented this technology to secure terminal connections and other applications between the client and the server.

In this section, we discuss how to configure and implement both Telnet and SSH sessions to provide user access to these applications through the IVE.

# Telnet/SSH Sessions

We start our discussion of configuring Telnet and SSH by setting up user session bookmarks for these applications. Just like other bookmarks, such as Web and file bookmarks, this is done on a role-by-role basis (although you can also use resource profiles to create the bookmarks for different roles).

## Creating a Telnet/SSH Session

In this example, we create a Telnet/SSH session for a user role configured on the IVE. This is very similar to configuring other bookmarks in the IVE, as you will see in this example. Figure 9.19 shows how to configure the AdminUI for an Telnet/SSH session.

1. Before we create the Telnet/SSH bookmark, we need to ensure that Telnet/SSH is enabled for the role we would like to configure the bookmark in. You can perform this action by going to **Users | User Roles | <User Role> | General.** You should see an option to enable **Telnet/SSH**. Make sure that this option is checked, and if necessary click **Save Changes**.

2. Now we will create the bookmark that is referred to as a session for Telnet/SSH. Go to **Users | User Roles | <User Role> | Telnet/SSH | Session** and click **Add Session**.

3. You must define a **Name** for the session that the users will see in their UserUI. You can also specify a **Description** to provide additional information to the users.

4. Next, you must define the **Host**, which is either a host name or IP address of the Telnet/SSH server.

5. After you define the host, you must then define what type of session this is—a **Telnet** session or a **SSH** session. You can only configure one per session, so if you need to have both Telnet and SSH access to the same server, you will have to make two session bookmarks. In addition to specifying the actual session type, you can also specify the TCP port that the IVE will be connecting to on the server. There are well-known ports for both Telnet (TCP 23) and SSH (TCP 22), but if your server uses different ports, then you will have to specify them in the **Port** field of the appropriate session protocol.

6. There is also a **Username** field so you can automatically pass the username to the backend server. You can set a static username or define a system variable such as **<username>** to log into the server.

7. Lastly, you have some options that you can define relating to the visual aspects of the session. You can define a **Fixed** font size (default 12 pixels) or have it automatically **Resize to fit window**. Next, you can define the **Screen Size** of the session (default 80 × 25). Finally, you can define the buffer size of the session (how many lines you will be able to scroll back up and see).

8. Click **Save Changes**.

Figure 9.20 shows what the Telnet/SSH applet looks like when launched.

**Figure 9.19** Configuring a Telnet/SSH Session in the IVE AdminUI to Connect to a Telnet Server

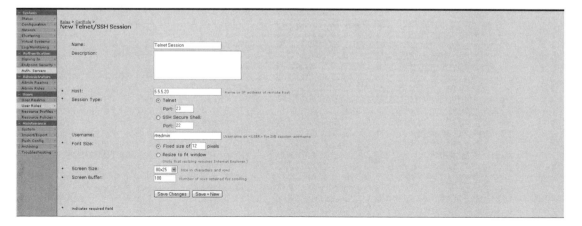

**Figure 9.20** Telnet Applet Published through the IVE Connecting to a Juniper Firewall: The Applet Looks Like a Pop-up Terminal Window Displayed in the Web Browser

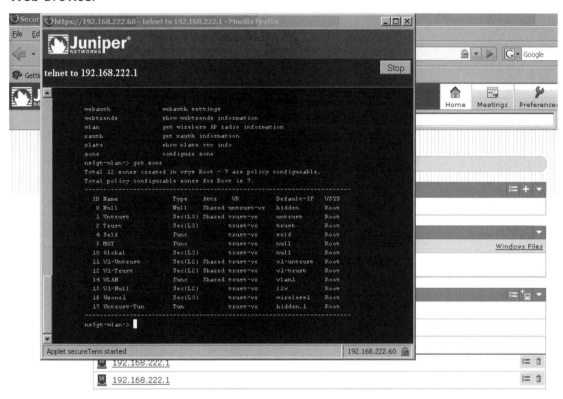

## Telnet/SSH Options

There are two options that you can configure on a role-by-role basis for Telnet/SSH. They are located under **Users | User Roles | <User Role> | Telnet/SSH | Options**:

- You can allow **Users to add sessions**, which works much like allowing users to add bookmarks.

- Also you can **Auto-Allow Role Telnet/SSH Sessions**, which will create resource policies to allow Telnet/SSH sessions that are administratively created. If you allow users to add their own sessions, then you must have a resource policy that allows the connections; otherwise, the user will not be able to access the resource.

# Telnet/SSH Resource Policies

Telnet/SSH sessions work very similar to other access methods through the IVE. Besides being configured within the roles, you must also configure resource policies to allow access through the IVE. This gives you control over who can access what, especially if you allow users to create their own bookmarks. There is only one resource policy that can be configured, along with some additional options that we discuss later.

1. To create a Telnet/SSH resource policy, go to **Users | Resource Policies | Telnet/SSH | Access Control** and click **New Policy**.

2. You must define a **Name** and, optionally, you can define a **Description** for management purposes.

3. Like other resource policies, you are required to specify what **Resources** apply to this policy. The Resource field will follow the familiar format of other resource policies, except you only define the server and port of the Telnet/SSH server. You can use wildcards, IP addresses, host names, and ports/port ranges to define the resource.

4. Telnet/SSH resource policies require that you define which roles this resource policy applies to. You can select one of the following options: **Policy applies to ALL roles, Policy applies to SELECTED roles** (select roles from the **Available Roles** list and put them into the **Selected Roles** list to apply), and **Policy applies to all roles OTHER THAN those selected below** (resource policy will apply to all roles except those in the **Selected Roles** list).

5. Next, you must define whether to **Allow** or **Deny** access to the resource(s) in this policy. Depending on your objectives, you may have to define multiple policies. Note that if you allow users to add their own bookmarks, then you will also need to have a corresponding resource policy to allow that access for it to work.

6. Click **Save Changes**.

## Telnet/SSH Options

The only option for Telnet/SSH resource policies is to enable **IP Based Matching for Hostname Based Policy Resources**.

## Creating Telnet/SSH Resource Profiles

The IVE also allows you to create resource profiles for Telnet and SSH sessions hosted on the IVE. This can help make your life as an administrator much easier when trying to deploy these technologies through the IVE. Telnet and SSH resource profiles are essentially the same configuration, with the exception of what type of profile you decide to create. In this example, we discuss how to create a Telnet/SSH resource profile:

1. Begin by going to **Users | Resource Profiles | Telnet/SSH** and click **New Profile**.

2. First, define the **Type** of profile that you would like to create. Your choices are either **Telnet** or **SSH**. You can only chose one per profile.

3. Define a **Name** and optionally define a **Description** for the profile.

4. You must specify the **Host**, which is the Telnet or SSH server. This can either be a resolvable host name or an IP address.

5. Optionally, you can have the profile automatically create a resource policy to allow the Telnet/SSH traffic to pass through the IVE. The option is titled **Create an access control policy allowing Telnet/SSH access to this server**, and it is enabled by checking the check box.

6. The IVE will automatically enter the standard port numbers for a Telnet or SSH session (TCP port 23 and TCP port 22, respectively). If your Telnet or SSH server uses a nonstandard port, then you must enter the port number in the **Port** field.

7. You can optionally define a **Username** which will be passed to the Telnet/SSH server when logging on to the interactive session.

8. Click **Save and Continue**.

9. Next, select the **Roles** that the resource profile will be applied to by clicking the appropriate roles from the **Available** column and then clicking the **Add** button to add them to the **Selected** column.

10. After you have specified the appropriate roles, click **Save Changes**.

11. You can optionally define additional bookmarks if necessary, but normally it is best left to define the bookmarks in their own resource profile for the most flexibility.

# Summary

Although the IVE may seem complex and detailed at first, Juniper has put forth great effort in balancing functionality, scalability, and security when it comes to the features integrated into the IVE. Once you master the concepts, the rest of your tasks will become much easier. Most of the features in the IVE follow similar conventions with regard to defining bookmarks and resource policies. This allows you to quickly build your skill-set whether you are defining Web rewriting policies or file SSO access. The combination of a role-based access system and granular control of resources allows for policies ranging from very broad and wide reaching to extremely specific. This chapter should help you on your way to developing a well-defined strategy for managing the remote access needs of your organization.

# Solutions Fast Track

## Clientless Access Overview

☑ The IVE supports a Web-based user interface for passing user Web traffic to internal network resources. The access does not require any provisioned clients (other than a Web browser) to be installed on the client machine.

☑ Access to file shares can be securely transported between a client Web browser and internal file shares. Both Windows (CIFS/SMB) and UNIX (NFS) files are supported.

☑ Clientless access to Telnet and SSH applications can be enabled for users who need to have basic access to internal servers over Telnet or SSH without provisioning VPN clients and application software.

## Web Access

☑ User roles allow administrators to enable Web browsing along with other user experience-related settings, such as adding bookmarks, allowing active content, and allowing users to browse URLs through the IVE.

☑ Web resource policies provide the capability to granularly control what a user can access and through which roles. They apply only to Web traffic passed through the IVE Web interface, and not to Network Connect or SAM (which can have their own policies for such access).

☑ Issues regarding Web rewriting, caching, and compression are the most common causes of problems passing Web content through the IVE (besides improper Web ACLs). These policies may have to be tweaked to allow certain content to function properly through the IVE. Alternatively, you may choose other alternatives, such as Network Connect, SAM, or pass-through proxy.

# File Access

☑ File bookmarks enable the administrator to configure access to file shares that can be browsed through the WebUI of the IVE.

☑ File access not only depends on the resource policies of the IVE but also on whether or not the user is typically allowed to access the backend resources in the first place.

☑ Users can be granted access to individual directories and not subdirectories by not using wildcards at the end of resource policies (for instance, avoiding\\server\share\path\*).

☑ Resource policies can enable SSO authentication for Windows (CIFS/SMB) shares. They can be static credentials as well as dynamic system variables that will apply the appropriate attributes of the user trying to access the resource.

# Telnet/SSH Access

☑ Telnet is an application that allows for interactive communication between a client and a server. In the past, Telnet was used for everything from managing network infrastructure gear to providing terminal access to mainframes. Telnet operates in clear text.

☑ SSH is essentially a secure version of Telnet, using encryption to provide a secure communication channel between the client and server.

☑ The IVE supports Telnet and SSH clients through the use of prebuilt Java applets that get opened on the user's machine and then tunnel traffic through the SSL VPN from the client to the IVE. Note that although the communication between the Web client and IVE is secured with SSL, Telnet traffic will not be encrypted when it leaves the IVE destined to the internal telnet server. If possible, SSH is a preferred client.

# Frequently Asked Questions

**Q:** I gave users the ability to create their own bookmarks and browse URLs through the IVE, but they sometimes get messages that the IVE is administratively blocking them; why is this?

**A:** Often this has to do with your Web ACLs under the resource policies. If you have disabled the default, **Allow Any Resource Policy**, then you will need to provide other resource policies to allow this traffic to pass through the IVE. Since users can create bookmarks but not resource policies, you will want to consider what the users should be able to use in advance.

**Q:** I want to integrate my internal proxy/URL content filter to ensure that users are compliant with organizational policies when browsing through the IVE; how can I do this?

**A:** You can create Web proxy resource policies to force appropriate Web traffic to pass through your proxy servers and perform appropriate action.

**Q:** I have a Linux server that uses Samba to host an SMB share; does the IVE support integration with this?

**A:** Yes, the IVE does support SMB integration. You will actually have to configure this as a Windows bookmark instead of UNIX. This is because the "Windows" bookmark is for CIFS/SMB shares, whereas UNIX is for NFS.

**Q:** I noticed that some users are getting access to files that shouldn't be applied to their role; any idea why this could be happening?

**A:** First, check to make sure that the resource definitions in the resource policies are accurate (particularly around wildcards). Also, make sure that you haven't made any mistakes with regard to defining which roles a resource policy should apply to. It is common to select a specific role but leave the **Applies to ALL roles** option checked. If you still can't figure it out, see Policy Tracing under the Troubleshooting menu.

**Q:** Is Telnet access between my client and the backend server encrypted end to end?

**A:** No, the Telnet session is encrypted between your Web browser and the IVE, but once it passes out of the IVE to the internal network, it will be in plain text. This is just the nature of the protocol.

**Q:** The IVE says that there is a compression resource policy enabled, but it doesn't appear that compression is working between the IVE and my Web browser.

**A:** Check to ensure that GZIP compression is enabled on the system by going to **Maintenance | System | Options** and that **Enable Gzip Compression** is enabled.

# Chapter 10

# Maintenance Section

## Solutions in this chapter:

- System
- Import/Export
- Push Configuration
- Archiving
- Troubleshooting

☑ Summary

☑ Solutions Fast Track

☑ Frequently Asked Questions

# Introduction

At the core of the SSL VPN, lies its OS. This, in many ways, is the kernel to the hardware and other I/O, and also keeps all the files and configurations in order. Dual partitions, hardware acceleration, a custom boot loader, and other options are available to fine-tune the OS. These controls are generally global settings for the system to use, and unless otherwise noted, also apply to Virtual Systems since they all share a common hardware subsystem.

# System

The system maintenance menu includes the following components:

- **Platform**  Information, routine maintenance
- **Upgrade/Downgrade**  Manages the boot partitions
- **Options**  Global system parameters, including hardware settings
- **Installers**  Downloadable executables for client agent components

Figure 10.1 shows an example of the System Maintenance Menu.

**Figure 10.1** The System Maintenance Menu

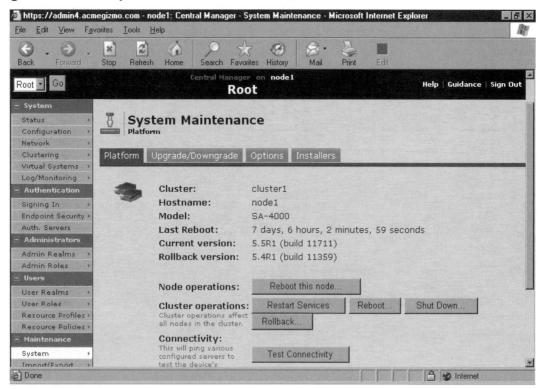

# Platform

The Platform menu provides you with a quick overview of the current state of the system. This gives Administrators a quick overview of what OS the system has booted, and what fallback OSes are available. This includes:

- **Cluster Name**  Used when configured to be part of a cluster
- **Hostname**  Used for Java Applet Upload and Secure Meeting functions
- **Model #**  Based on the hardware profile and license key
- **Last Reboot**  System uptime
- **Current and Rollback Versions**  The IVE uses the concept of a rollback partition. This partition is simply the previous IVE operating system and configuration (before an upgrade took place). If something is wrong with the new version, or there was some need to go back to a previous version, a rollback could be initiated by the Administrator.

## Restarting Services

By navigating to the **Maintenance | System | Platform** menu, you will find **Restart Services.** This function will shut down the IVE OS and then reload it. Please note, however, that the underlying kernel is not restarted and the hardware is not even warm-rebooted. This enables the system to reset and come back online very quickly (generally 10 seconds or less). Some administrative changes will actually do this for you, and will let you know after you have made such a change. This does restart the IVE OS. Therefore, established connections may be temporarily suspended.

## Reboot/Shutdown

Going one step further, the Reboot function actually performs a full reset of the device, including hardware. This often times yields longer bootup cycles since the hardware must reinitialize, and the software must be loaded back into memory. Additionally, all established TCP connections and their state will be lost during reboot. Similarly, when you shut down the system, it is like performing a halt in UNIX. The software turns off, but does not attempt to turn off the power-cycle to the appliance. So after shutting down the system, it must be physically powered off or power-cycled. It is highly recommended that you monitor the serial console during this action, just to better understand the timing of the reboot, and also to ensure connectivity in the event of a failure.

## Rollback

When we speak of rollback, we are not talking about lowering prices. Rollback means using another partition (essentially running an older IVE OS version) on the appliance's hard drive for the next boot. When running, the primary partition contains the *current version* of IVE OS. The *rollback partition* is created during an IVE OS upgrade and preserves all configuration and stored session data. It also includes the old IVE OS, and when a rollback is initiated, the system will reboot and load from the rollback data. It is important to point out here that after you roll back, it is permanent. The good news is, you will be prompted on the Serial Console to confirm this, so don't worry if you accidentally click it.

> ### Warning
>
> *A rollback is permanent.* There is no "rollforward," so be sure to back up the version IVE OS package, and its stored session and configuration data, since it will be lost after the rollback. It is also important to remember that when using the system as part of a cluster, any action will affect the cluster as a whole. So, for instance, if you were to reboot the system, it would initiate a reboot on all members of the cluster.

Lastly, the Test Connectivity button allows Administrators to run a simple "ping" test to the configured AAA servers. This test helps Administrators verify connectivity between the IVE and these back-end servers (see Figure 10.2).

**Figure 10.2** Test Connectivity Results

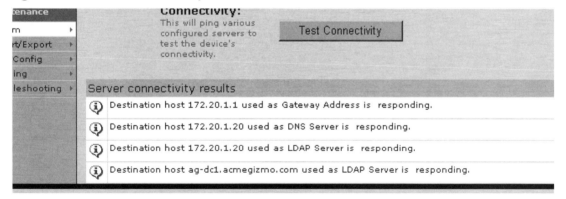

# Upgrade/Downgrade

The Upgrade/Downgrade menu should be used when you want to upgrade or downgrade the system (or cluster). In order to upgrade the system, one must first obtain the software package. This usually requires a service contract, so you may want to check with Juniper Support first. You will first want to download the service package to your PC, and then upload it to the IVE to be installed. The action is a one-step process, so be aware that as soon as you upload the package, it will be installed, and the system will reboot. That is, of course, assuming the package can be extracted properly by the system. You should see a progress meter pop up, so please monitor that for package upload status (see Figure 10.3).

**Figure 10.3** Upload Status

Fortunately, even across reboots, the system maintains its user session states, and when the system comes back online again, users should not be prompted to reauthenticate (although they will need to reinitiate their TCP-based connections). During the upgrade process, you should see some feedback on the screen which basically shows it validating the package, saving all configuration to the rollback partition, and then rebooting the system.

An option to Delete All System User Data will also appear. If checked, this will destroy the entire configuration from the system, forcing the Administrator to reconfigure the system via the Serial Console.

**NOTE**

If the Delete All System User Data option is selected, this will reset all configurations, including the IP address. Therefore, we recommend this option only be employed when you have access to the unit's Serial Console.

If the upgrade was successful, the unit will boot back up in a few minutes, having retained its configuration and user session information. If you were patient and didn't click anything until after you saw the unit come back up on the Serial Console, then when you click, it should take you to where you want, reusing your existing session. You will also now be able to look in the Platform submenu to see the new Rollback and Current versions.

# Options

In the Options list, you will find global system parameters. Some of these may be useful in fine-tuning your deployment (see Figure 10.4).

**Figure 10.4** Options

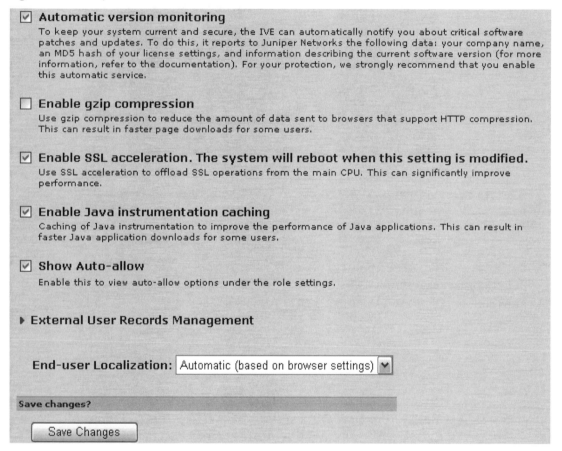

Let's take a minute to walk through these:

- **Automatic Version Monitoring** This feature enables the system to notify Administrators if there is a more recent version available for download. It also lets Juniper better understand what the breakdown is of the install-base, such as what percentage (of those with this enabled) is using 5.3R1. This feature connects to service.neoteris.com periodically to poll the site and see if a new update is available.

- **Enable GZIP Compression** GZIP compression can be used to further enhance a Web application by reducing the amount of bandwidth required and the transfer time, and by increasing the overall end-user experience. When enabled, the IVE Web server can (based on policy) compress certain content using the GZIP standard algorithm. The content is reduced and sent over the wire, and then expanded/ uncompressed by a standard Web browser, such as Microsoft Internet Explorer.

- **Enable SSL Acceleration** When enabled, all encryption routines, including bulk (HTTP data) and handshake (SSL socket), are done in hardware. A specially designed encryption chip is employed, which can perform math logic (crypto routines) far faster than can be done in software. This not only reduces the latency in encrypting/ decrypting content, it also offloads that processing from the system's CPU.

- **Enable Java Instrumentation Caching** Since a large portion of the IVE Access framework is based on Web-based access (often called "core access"), the rewriter becomes a crucial component of the solution. But many applications now employ Java applets, which contain "byte code," that must also be rewritten and then the applet re-signed in order to function properly. Since this can be a very grueling and CPU-taxing process, Juniper provides a feature that enables rewritten Java components to be cached on the system. This way, in deployments where users are frequently accessing these same Java applets, or if everyone accesses the same Java applet, the system won't have to perform the exact same rewrite function every time, and instead it can serve the previously rewritten applet from memory. Also, since the Java byte code doesn't usually contain session-based information (this is contained within the data or applet parameters), there is no worry of caching sensitive information.

- **Show Auto-Allow** This enables or disables the auto-allow option for role configuration. It can be disabled to minimize the information shown on the screen, and also prevent delegated Administrators from accidentally enabling access to a large set of resources.

- **External User Records Management** When the IVE is leveraging a back-end authentication framework (for example, RADIUS), it isn't using stored user accounts or information. But as users log in, a profile is built under their (RADIUS) username. This is stored with the authentication server and serves as a home to persistent passwords, cookies, and other user-related information. This information can grow over time. To fine-tune the system, this can be limited to a smaller number of maintained records, and you can also go in and remove a number of entries, if needed. While using this feature won't impact the functionality of the system, it may change a user's experience (for example, if a cookie is now missing and they log in again, they may need to renew that cookie information when they start browsing). For additional information about this, please contact Juniper support.

- **End-User Localization**  If you don't already know it, the end-user interface is actually localized. That's right, it speaks seven different languages, including English, French, German, Japanese, Chinese (traditional), Chinese (simplified), Korean, and Spanish. This includes all of the IVE pages, and downloaded agents, such as Secure Meeting and Network Connect. Since some companies may have remote workers accessing the system from another country, and using a Web browser in a different language, there needs to be a way to override the Web browser's setting. That's what this option is for. You can choose which language will be used, regardless of the browser setting, or you can leave it set to Automatic, wherein it will serve up content in whatever language the Web browser requests (provided it is a supported language).

# Installers

In the Installers section, you will find what many people are looking for these days: installer files. With the large adoption of SSL VPNs, and the fact that so many customers also issue managed/corporate-issued PCs, the need to build packages and push them out, becomes imminent. Here, you can download the packages and install them manually, or do so by using installer flags, or by pushing them out as part of Microsoft SMS or the like (see Figure 10.5).

**Figure 10.5** The Installer

## Notes from the Underground...

### Administrative Rights Validation

Since the Juniper Installer Service runs as an Administrator, many people believe it could easily be used to install malicious code or other applications. This is not the case. The Installer Service actually verifies the RSA signature and MD5 hash of the signed executable before allowing it to be installed with Administrative rights.

The installer executables include:

- **Juniper Installer Service** This is the Juniper installer service that allows Juniper-signed agents to be installed with Administrative Rights, if required. This package must first be installed by a local Administrator who has Admin Rights to the system. It then runs as a Windows Service, in the background, and installs any package that is properly signed by Juniper and requires Administrative Rights.

- **Host Checker** This is the Endpoint Interrogation tool, employed by many to assess the security posture of the user's PC before and during their session. It provides an extra layer of security and also provides an enforcement point for corporate security policies.

- **WSAM for 9x/ME Platforms** This executable installs the Windows Secure Application Manager for the Win98 and ME Platforms.

- **WSAM for XP/2000 Platforms** This is the same as the previous entry, but is used for Windows XP and 2000.

- **Scriptable WSAM** This is a command-line interface for WSAM and enables a user to launch WSAM, with specific parameters, in an automated fashion. Several flags can be used, including:
  - **–start** Starts the session and exits
  - **–stop** Stops the session and exits
  - **–signout** Signs the user out and stops the session
  - **–version** Prints the version information and exits
  - **–help** Displays the help menu

- **-url <url>** The sign-in URL required for the session

- **-u <user>** The username to authenticate with

- **-p <password>** The password for that username

- **-r <realm>** The realm to authenticate to

- **-reboot** If a reboot is required, reboot automatically (default is to not reboot)

- **-verbose** Diagnostic information

- **-noupgrade** Prevents the installed WSAM client from being upgraded, if desired

- **-loginscript <file>** Script to be run after WSAM is connected to the IVE (for example, to map drives)

- **-postscript <file>** Script to be run post-session, after WSAM exits (for example, to cleanup)

- Service-level status/exit codes are also available for use with other Win32-based applications. For more information, refer to the Admin Guide or contact Juniper Support.

- **WSAM for PPC/WM5** This is the WSAM client for Windows Mobile 5.0. It enables ActiveSync, Terminal Services, and many other IP-based client/server applications to be tunneled securely from the mobile device, over the Wi-Fi or 3G network, to the SSL VPN, and into the corporate resource. Web browsing and file sharing are also available through this interface.

- **NC for 32/64-bit Windows** This is the Network Connect client for Windows.

- **NC for Mac OS X** This is the Network Connect client for Mac OS X. A widget is also included.

- **NC for Linux** This is the Network Connect client for Linux. A command-line version (ncsvc) is also available for these UNIX-based Linux and Mac OS X clients. Specific Linux distributions are supported, so please refer to the Supported Platforms document at http://support.juniper.net/ first.

**NOTE**

Not all versions of Windows, Mac OS, and Linux are supported. For full details, and platform qualification information, please refer to the Supported Platforms Guide.

# Import/Export

In this section, you can do a couple things with the configuration, and with any luck, do so with ease. For beginners, there is the traditional binary import/export. This is broken down into three sections, one for the system, one for users, and one for Instant Virtual Systems (IVS), if enabled. The export is quite straightforward, given that it just tars everything up and you download it somewhere to your PC's hard disk for safekeeping. You can optionally set a password, much like you'd do when exporting a private key from a Web server, which will help protect the configuration (that is, it will prevent someone from stealing the configuration and importing it into their box and then seeing what certain values are). A password is strongly encouraged. So the export is rather simple. The import, however, is where you have some choices to make.

---

### WARNING

Poor configuration management can be dangerous and harmful to your employment. Please be sure to make adequate backups before trying out new data and methods to import. Before proceeding, also be advised that importing and exporting between IVE OS versions is not officially supported, although it may seem to work. Mix and match configurations for different versions at your own risk. It is also important to point out that upon import of a *user's* configuration, current sessions may be invalidated and users may be logged out abruptly. Also, a new *system* or *user* configuration may invalidate a concurrent user's policy evaluations, which could also interrupt their work. For these reasons, it is highly recommended you first test your proposed configuration and then import it only during a scheduled maintenance window.

---

## System (Binary) Import/Export

Binary configuration is, just what it says, binary data. This means you get a blob of data. You cannot choose what you want, nor omit certain logs or state files. You get it all. This also includes a dump of the user sessions and their state. This is great if you want to replicate an entire box elsewhere. Figure 10.6 shows an example of the import/export system configuration options.

**Figure 10.6** Import/Export System Configuration Options

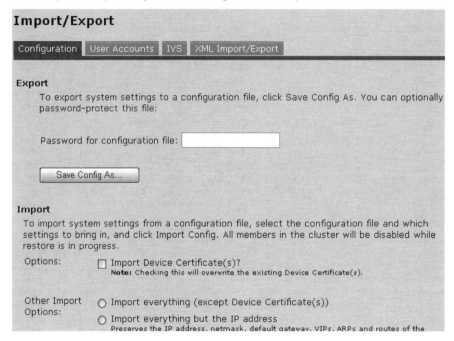

When you are importing, a few of the options available can change the way the binary configuration is imported:

- **Import Device Certificate(s)** This will include the SSL Server Certificate(s) and Private Keys used by the system during export. Upon import, they will be used for all SSL handshaking from that time forward, including renegotiations of the current sessions. This may or may not be desirable, depending on whether you want to enforce this, or whether you don't want to disrupt users (they may get prompted if the imported cert is invalid/untrusted).

- **Import Everything (except Device Certificate[s])** This is a full binary import but excludes the certificate(s) and keys. It does include license keys and network settings.

- **Import Everything except the IP Address** This option is the same, except that it omits the IP addresses of the system. Sometimes when you migrate a configuration from one node to another, you may not want to bring over the network settings (for example, because they differ for the other node).

- **Import Everything except Network Settings and Licenses** Same as the preceding, except that it also omits license keys. This will probably be your most commonly used binary import method, because it imports anything an Admin would normally change.

- **Import Only Device Certificate(s)** This is for those who just want to import certificates (and their respective private keys). For example, let's say you had a wildcard cert on node1, node2, and node3, and now you want to add another node. This is a simple way to get your old wildcard cert/key into the new box (because I know you aren't leaving your wildcard certs/keys sitting around some file server unprotected, right?).

# User Accounts (Binary) Import/Export

User Accounts are actually stored separately within the system. This means, all data for Realms, Roles, Resource Policies, and AAA Services (including cached user entries and stored personal bookmarks) are held within this User config context. Generally speaking, this includes everything that is not system-specific, such as:

- **Sign-In URLs and Policies**

- **AAA Servers and Stored User Data** This includes personal bookmarks, stored cookies/passwords, and customized settings, such as for SSO or Secure Meeting.

- **Endpoint Security Policies and Settings**

- **Realms (Admin and End-User)**

- **Roles (Admin and End-User)**

- **Resource Policies and Profiles**

- **User Session State Table** This is a state table of all active SSL VPN sessions.

---

**W**ARNING

The user configuration, unlike the system, can grow enormously large. With a couple thousand stored user accounts/profiles, the user configuration could easily be 5 MB or larger. Keeping configurations small, such as disabling *personal bookmarks,* helps more easily manage this configuration.

---

This export function works the same way as the system—there's an option to protect it with a password. The import is option-less, and should be straightforward to everyone (see Figure 10.7).

**Figure 10.7** Import/Export User Accounts Options

# IVS Import/Export

If licensed, IVS lets you virtualize the IVE and have multiple portals/VPN configurations running concurrently (see Figure 10.8). The intent is to service subscribers, and provide delegated administration and granular accounting/auditing records. From a configuration management perspective, the same things apply. There must be a way to export the configuration (again, optionally adding in a password) and then import the configuration to another IVE that you want to function in the same manner.

**Figure 10.8** IVS Import/Export Options

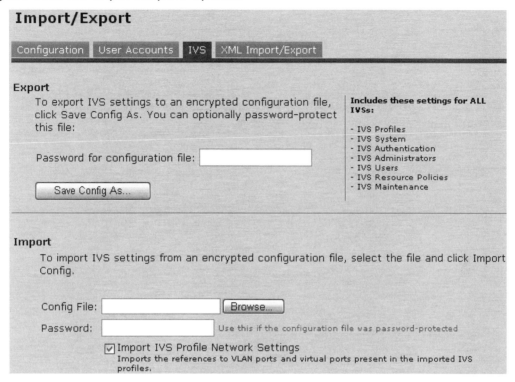

When you are importing, there is an option to import VLAN data. As mentioned previously, there may be instances where you don't want to migrate some bit of configuration, such as the VLAN data, because maybe your VLANs are different at this other node's site. This option provides a little more control over what you normally would get upon import of the IVS configuration.

# XML Import/Export

XML import/export is the topic where those UNIX guys put down their PERL cookbook for a moment and really pay attention. This is a bit more interesting version of Import/Export, and provides you with all of the raw data so you make your own decisions. This framework has also been adopted by several Managed Services Providers who are now offering SSL VPNs as part of their managed services portfolio. The XML framework provides a simple easy-to-understand XML schema, containing all of the system's parameters and their values.

While this may be interesting to read through, it also provides a very standardized way of automating configuration changes. For instance, if I want to import 10,000 user accounts, with the usernames "testuser[1-10000]", I could easily do that and paste it right into the middle of my XML export file, reimport it, and I'm done. I could also build a Web-based front-end that allows personnel to submit some request, and have an updated configuration spit out, ready for approval and system import. This method not only provides a standardized approach, it creates an environment for change control, something many of Juniper's customers deal with on a daily basis.

Since this framework is so extensible, it is very easy to customize what you do and do not like. Juniper has provided a simple Web-based interface so you can choose what components you want included in the XML export. This may be as simple as a single Authentication Server's configuration, or it may be the entire configuration.

---

**NOTE**

The XML export does not actually include every single component of the configuration. Please refer to the Admin Guide or contact Juniper Support for additional details.

---

Let's now take a look at the actual XML schema itself. The following is a sample of a recent schema taken from IVE 5.4R4:

```
- <Network>
  - <Nodes>
  - <Node>
    <NodeIdentifier>us-connect</NodeIdentifier>
  -<DNSResolution>
    <FirstDNSServer>184.14.1.26</FirstDNSServer>
    <SecondDNSServer>184.12.31.19</SecondDNSServer>
    <DNSDomains>acmegizmo.com</DNSDomains>
    </DNSResolution>
    </Node>
    <Nodes>
  </Network>
```

It looks a lot like HTML, right? These Element names actually play a critical role in ensuring that the data belong to the appropriate module. This is so that when you import it, it actually works the way you'd expect. Also, you'll note that the - and +r characters provide a "tree architecture" whereby XML browsers (such as the one embedded into Internet Explorer) can collapse/expand data-sets to make it more easy to browse, and then drill down when you find the right branch. In fact, by completely collapsing all the data objects, you can get a very high-level picture of the system's schema. They also let you use an XML editor, which makes viewing this data very fun, as shown in Figure 10.9.

**Figure 10.9** XML Example

```xml
<?xml version="1.0" encoding="UTF-8" standalone="no" ?>
- <IVE xmlns="http://xml.juniper.net/iveos/6.0R1/ive">
  - <AAA>
    - <ResourcePolicyList>
      - <WebLaunchJSAMAccessPolicyList>
        - <LaunchJSAMAccessPolicy>
          - <RoleSelection>
              <RoleList />
              <SelectionMethod>AllRoles</SelectionMethod>
            </RoleSelection>
            <Action>AllowOrApply</Action>
            <Description />
            <PolicyName>TSWeb</PolicyName>
          - <ResourceList>

                <Resource>http://apps.acmegizmo.com:8080/tsweb/default.htm</Resource>
            </ResourceList>
            <RuleList />
          </LaunchJSAMAccessPolicy>
        - <LaunchJSAMAccessPolicy>
          - <RoleSelection>
              <RoleList />
              <SelectionMethod>AllRoles</SelectionMethod>
            </RoleSelection>
            <Action>AllowOrApply</Action>
            <Description />
            <PolicyName>Ericom WebConnect</PolicyName>
          - <ResourceList>

                <Resource>http://sharepoint.acmegizmo.com:8080/WebConnect5.5/portal/windows/ind
            </ResourceList>
            <RuleList />
          </LaunchJSAMAccessPolicy>
        </WebLaunchJSAMAccessPolicyList>
      - <WebOptions>
          <IPBasedMatching>false</IPBasedMatching>
          <CaseSensitiveMatching>false</CaseSensitiveMatching>
        </WebOptions>
      - <WebCachingPolicyList>
        - <CachingPolicy>
          - <RoleSelection>
              <RoleList />
```

## Tools & Traps…

### XML Automation

With the rise in use of XML and its great portability, it's no wonder many people are building automated frameworks to modify XML on-the-fly. But how do you get it back into the system? Some people were clever enough to find tools like libCurl and Python. These scripts can easily be used to suck down an XML configuration (while logging in the Admin for you), modify it on-the-fly, and then push it back out to the node or multiple nodes. This kind of timesaving technique can improve deployment times and offers great flexibility and automation for SSL VPN Managed Services.

During import, you have three options:

- **Full Import** This is an entire import and replacement of the currently running configuration. If something is not in the XML being imported, it will not be there after the import.

- **Standard Import** This imports any new data and updates any existing data. It is a merge of the configurations, rather than a replacement, and therefore does not remove anything which is not being updated or modified by the imported XML.

- **Quick Import** This imports new data, and will not modify or alter existing data. It is the safest method, but won't replicate a change, only a new object's configuration.

# Push Configuration

Push Configuration builds on the XML import/export framework by providing a mechanism to easily migrate XML configuration pieces from one node to another. Traditionally, *clustering* would do just this; however, with larger deployments, and intercluster management requirements, clustering isn't always the silver bullet. Sometimes a piece of data needs to be replicated from one node to another or from one cluster to another. A manual export/import of the configuration is nice, but for recurring or frequent changes to sets of configuration, it is helpful to have a one-click interface to do the migration for you—especially if it is to 20 other SA appliances on your network. For example, you might want to copy all the new policies to your DR appliance, every night. Push Configuration is designed just for this.

While it does lack a scheduling system, it still provides great value and a slick interface to replicate. You can literally select what data (using the aforementioned XML export interface), and then push it to a node or several nodes. The push attributes are then stored for later reuse, to further simplify this configuration replication process.

> **NOTE**
>
> The *Push Configuration* feature only exists with the Central Manager license. Please note, however, that in newer IVE OS versions, the Advanced license includes Central Manager. Please also note that the receiving node must also contain the Central Manager (or Advanced) license key in order to receive and import pushed configurations.

# Targets

As you begin to use Push Configuration more and more, you will build a target database (see Figure 10.10). These act as bookmarks to use when pushing the selected/entire configuration. Using this is highly recommended if you constantly push configuration to the same node over and over again.

**Figure 10.10** Push Configuration

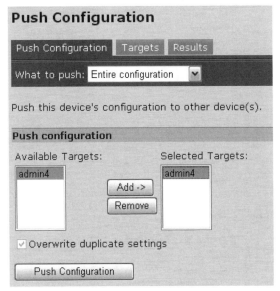

You'll also see there is an option to "Allow this IVE to be a target." What this means is you want this IVE to be able to receive Pushed Configurations (provided the push came with the correct Admin credentials for this box). This should be enabled on any node to which you want to remotely Push Configuration.

# Results

The results page displays recent push jobs and their results. Possible results here include hostname resolution issues, license or version mismatch problems, admin authentication issues, or a note indicating the push was successful. This section may help you identify why a push was not successful, thus allowing you to remedy it so the next push works.

---

**W**ARNING

In most scenarios, Push Config causes the receiving node to restart services. This means all processes will be restarted with the new configuration, which may mean current user sessions may be discarded and users logged out.

---

# Push Config Transport

In order to replicate SSL VPN configurations, or subsets thereof, to other nodes on a network, Push Configuration is used. But how does it work? Push Config actually migrates the configuration using the XML data available via XML Import/Export. In fact, it transports the actual XML as part of this, over an SSL-encapsulated channel. Push Config nearly mimics the process an actual Administrator would take in exporting a config via XML, and logging into another node and importing it and then logging out.

# Archiving

In addition to manual Administrative maintenance, such as exporting a config for backup, or importing a new config, the Administrator may also be interested in taking periodic snapshots of the system configuration, user accounts, and log data.

## Archiving Servers

By configuring an *Archiving Server*, the Administrator is telling the IVE to periodically archive selected data to a remote FTP or SCP server, such as for an off-site backup. The Archive system has separate schedulers for each type of data (see Figure 10.11), including:

- Events Log

- User Access Log

- Admin Access Log

- NC Packet Log

- IDP Sensor Log

- Client Side (Uploaded) Logs

- System Configuration

- User Accounts

- IVS

- XML Configuration

**Figure 10.11** Archiving

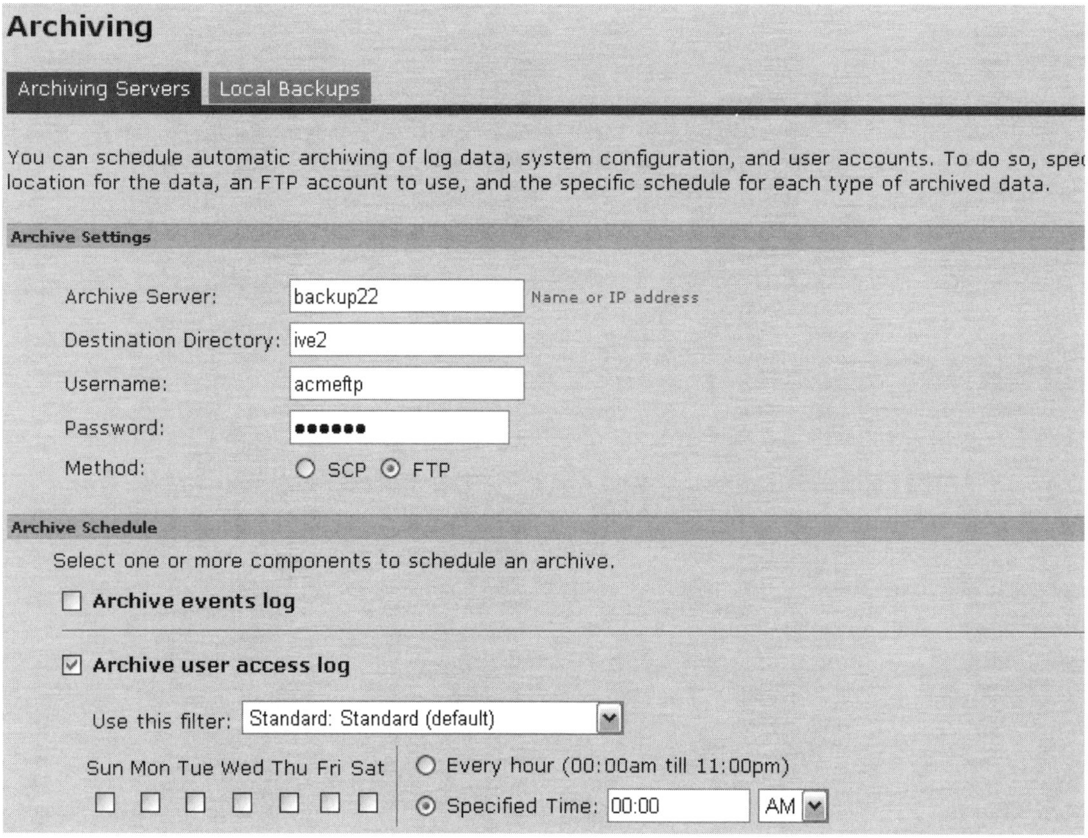

**Archiving**

| Archiving Servers | Local Backups |

You can schedule automatic archiving of log data, system configuration, and user accounts. To do so, spec
location for the data, an FTP account to use, and the specific schedule for each type of archived data.

**Archive Settings**

Archive Server: `backup22`    Name or IP address

Destination Directory: `ive2`

Username: `acmeftp`

Password: `••••••`

Method:    ○ SCP  ⊙ FTP

**Archive Schedule**

Select one or more components to schedule an archive.

☐ **Archive events log**

☑ **Archive user access log**

Use this filter: `Standard: Standard (default)`

Sun Mon Tue Wed Thu Fri Sat    ○ Every hour (00:00am till 11:00pm)

☐  ☐  ☐  ☐  ☐  ☐  ☐      ⊙ Specified Time: `00:00`    `AM`

So, for instance, you could archive the user accounts nightly, and the system configuration weekly. This helps Administrators reduce the amount of data crossing their network, and as a result, having to be stored somewhere.

Archival transport methods consist of either SCP or FTP. (Can you guess which we recommend?) Simply input the path and account credentials for your SCP or FTP server.

## Local Backups

Rather than archiving the configuration to some server that you may not always have access to, you can now back up the configuration right on the device itself. This function works just like the Binary System and User Export/Import functionality works, where a file is stored with the system configuration (a separate one exists for user and IVS data), except that it is on the local IVE disk, rather than on your own PC or FTP server (via Archiving Servers). This means the configuration can quickly and easily be imported since you will always have access to it. These *restore points* can be very handy when you want to try out a configuration for a few days, get feedback, and then decide if you want to keep it or undo it. It could save you a lot of work, in fact.

**TIP**

It is highly recommended that you take periodic (for example, weekly) configuration snapshots, especially if multiple administrators use the system. While all Administrator changes are logged, it is even more important to have a truly working configuration when you need to quickly resolve an outage.

# Troubleshooting

The IVE platform has a wealth of troubleshooting and debugging capabilities available. As a result, just about any problem can be diagnosed by an IVE administrator even without having to know the user's password. Monitoring the state of the IVE individually or as a part of the cluster, long term usage trending, event recording and simulations, packet sniffing, snapshots, and many other troubleshooting tools are all available within the IVE's built-in Web-based administration interface.

One troubleshooting caveat worth mentioning is how licensing can affect what troubleshooting tools are available. The Central Manager (included with an advanced license) adds a few very useful features including a more graphical overview page, as well as per unit graphing if a cluster of IVEs is present. It also adds more intuitive and easy filtering of all logs by making the log events themselves active links to click on and filter dynamically. Additionally, session recording is only available with an advanced license. Since an SA700 cannot be licensed with an advanced license, these options are not available for the SA700; these features are available with an advanced license for SA2000s through SA6000s.

# System Status and Resource Trending

The System Status page and Resource Trending are most commonly used to troubleshoot the following problems:

- If you are exceeding concurrent user license limit, by showing the current and peak number of users logged on
- If the system (or cluster) is overtaxed, by monitoring CPU, memory, hits, and disk space
- If the IVE has rebooted recently, intentionally or unintentionally
- What software version the IVE is running

When you log on to the IVE, a system "dashboard" (the System Status page) is displayed, showing system uptime, software versions, disk space utilization, and the number of signed-in users. If Central Manager is enabled, the dashboard also includes resource trending graphs, showing the number of concurrent users and meetings, hits per second, CPU, and swap space utilization. Central Manager also adds System Status options for all units within a cluster, not just the unit that the administrator is logged on to directly. The system status page without Central Manager is shown in Figure 10.12. Figure 10.13 illustrates the Central Manager.

**Figure 10.12** System Status without Central Manager

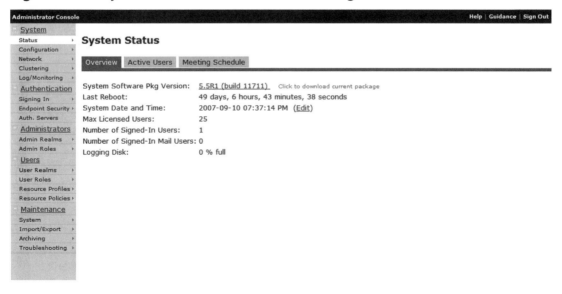

## Figure 10.13 System Status with Central Manager

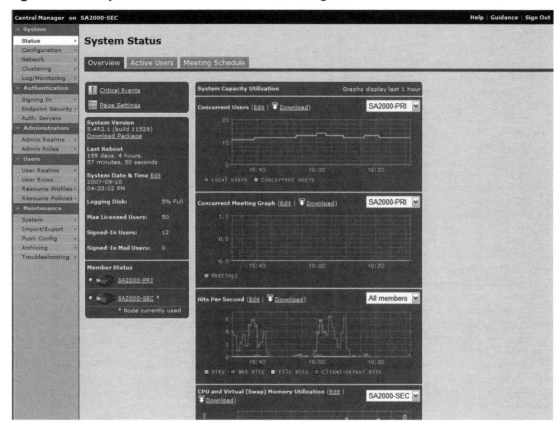

**TIP**

The graphs and the overview page itself displayed in Central Manager are not static; they can be edited. To edit the overview page, click **Page Settings**, and to edit the individual graphs, click **Edit** next to the graph title. This allows you to change colors, naming, thickness of lines, and what variables are displayed. The overview page can also be configured to auto-refresh. The graphs can also be downloaded as an XML file.

Tabs at the top of the status page allow the administrator to see who is logged on to the IVE live by clicking on **Active Users**. User sessions can also be deleted, forcing a user to log out, or their role mappings can be refreshed on the fly. For IVEs with a Secure Meeting License, the *Meeting Schedule* tab is also displayed, showing meetings that users have scheduled on the IVE.

To see more detail on the number of logged-on users and to make sure that the system isn't reaching its peak for its licensed concurrent users, you can view more detailed information by navigating to **System | Log/Monitoring | Statistics** to show the peak number of users broken down by hour over the past week. This is illustrated in Figure 10.14.

**Figure 10.14** Monitoring Statistics

**Monitoring Statistics**

Events | User Access | Admin Access | NC Packets | Sensors | Client Logs | SNMP | Statistics

**Signed-In Users**
Hourly peak load of users

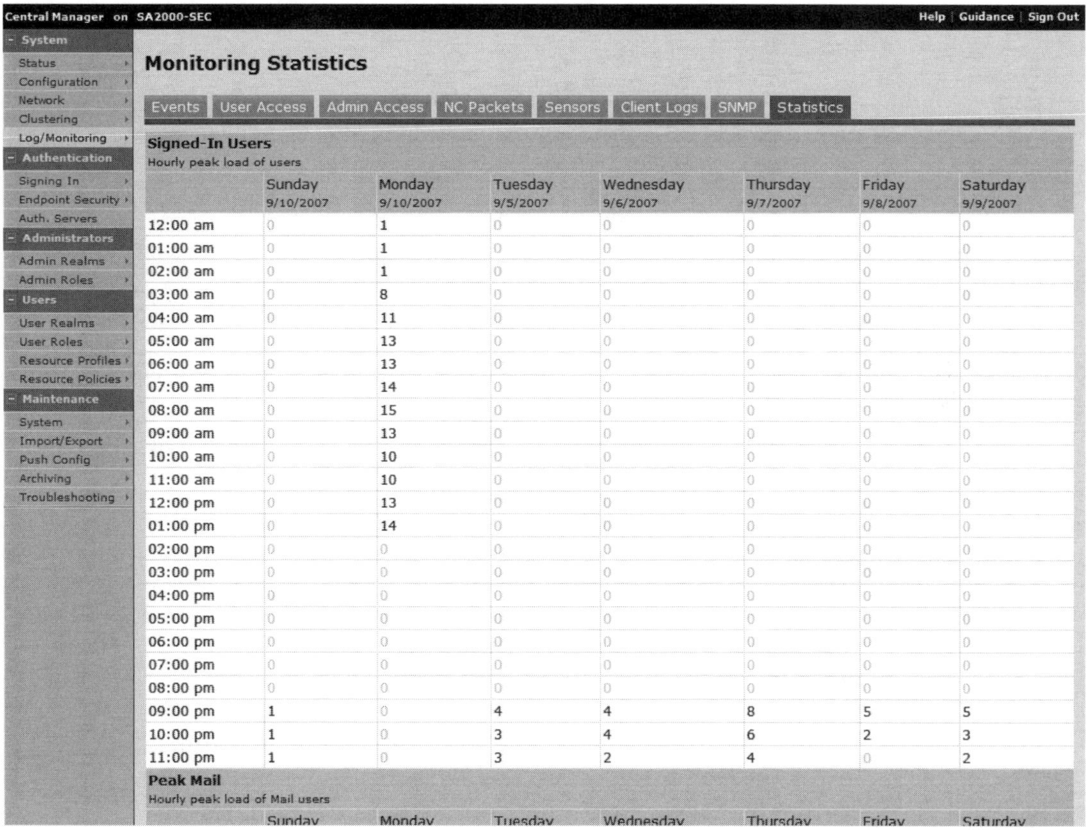

|  | Sunday 9/10/2007 | Monday 9/10/2007 | Tuesday 9/5/2007 | Wednesday 9/6/2007 | Thursday 9/7/2007 | Friday 9/8/2007 | Saturday 9/9/2007 |
|---|---|---|---|---|---|---|---|
| 12:00 am | 0 | 1 | 0 | 0 | 0 | 0 | 0 |
| 01:00 am | 0 | 1 | 0 | 0 | 0 | 0 | 0 |
| 02:00 am | 0 | 1 | 0 | 0 | 0 | 0 | 0 |
| 03:00 am | 0 | 8 | 0 | 0 | 0 | 0 | 0 |
| 04:00 am | 0 | 11 | 0 | 0 | 0 | 0 | 0 |
| 05:00 am | 0 | 13 | 0 | 0 | 0 | 0 | 0 |
| 06:00 am | 0 | 13 | 0 | 0 | 0 | 0 | 0 |
| 07:00 am | 0 | 14 | 0 | 0 | 0 | 0 | 0 |
| 08:00 am | 0 | 15 | 0 | 0 | 0 | 0 | 0 |
| 09:00 am | 0 | 13 | 0 | 0 | 0 | 0 | 0 |
| 10:00 am | 0 | 10 | 0 | 0 | 0 | 0 | 0 |
| 11:00 am | 0 | 10 | 0 | 0 | 0 | 0 | 0 |
| 12:00 pm | 0 | 13 | 0 | 0 | 0 | 0 | 0 |
| 01:00 pm | 0 | 14 | 0 | 0 | 0 | 0 | 0 |
| 02:00 pm | 0 | 0 | 0 | 0 | 0 | 0 | 0 |
| 03:00 pm | 0 | 0 | 0 | 0 | 0 | 0 | 0 |
| 04:00 pm | 0 | 0 | 0 | 0 | 0 | 0 | 0 |
| 05:00 pm | 0 | 0 | 0 | 0 | 0 | 0 | 0 |
| 06:00 pm | 0 | 0 | 0 | 0 | 0 | 0 | 0 |
| 07:00 pm | 0 | 0 | 0 | 0 | 0 | 0 | 0 |
| 08:00 pm | 0 | 0 | 0 | 0 | 0 | 0 | 0 |
| 09:00 pm | 1 | 0 | 4 | 4 | 8 | 5 | 5 |
| 10:00 pm | 1 | 0 | 3 | 4 | 6 | 2 | 3 |
| 11:00 pm | 1 | 0 | 3 | 2 | 4 | 0 | 2 |

**Peak Mail**
Hourly peak load of Mail users

|  | Sunday | Monday | Tuesday | Wednesday | Thursday | Friday | Saturday |
|---|---|---|---|---|---|---|---|

# User Sessions: Policy Tracing and Simulation

To troubleshoot a particular User Session that is having problems, navigate to **Maintenance** and then **Troubleshooting**. The two tools available for troubleshooting user sessions fall under *User Sessions* and are called *Policy Tracing* and *Simulation*. These two tools are most commonly used to investigate why a particular user logging on to the IVE is unable to authenticate or gain authorization or access to a particular resource. Policy Tracing allows the IVE Administrator to specifically track or log what's happening during a *real user session* (meaning the user logs on and the IVE records details for the Administrator to review), and Simulation allows the IVE Administrator to simulate events (and hopefully the problem) by creating a *virtual user session* without needing the actual user's password or requiring them to sign in. The User Session troubleshooting tools are illustrated in Figure 10.15.

**Figure 10.15** User Session Troubleshooting

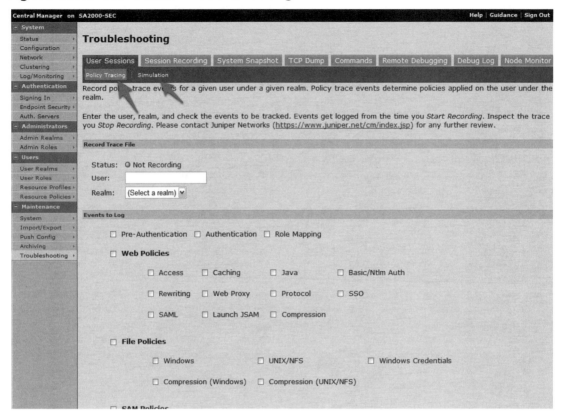

## Policy Tracing

Policy Tracing is most commonly used to troubleshoot the following problems:

- Authentication issues including usernames, passwords, and authentication server issues
- Role mapping issues for a particular user
- Resource policies and conflicts

Start by navigating in the **Admin** console to **Maintenance | Troubleshooting | User Sessions | Policy Tracing**. To begin a policy trace you will need to first define the username and the authentication realm for the user that you want to enable tracing on. The trace will then record in detail the options checked under **Events to Log**. This is illustrated in Figure 10.16. Be careful how many events you choose to log as the IVE can output verbose logs which can make the investigation process very difficult. Only focus on the events that are related specifically to the problem you're trying to troubleshoot. After defining the username, realms, and events to log, click on **Start Recording** at the bottom of the page. The Status will show *Recording…* as in Figure 10.17. At this point the user in question needs to log on to the IVE. After the user has logged on, click on **View Log File** at the bottom of the same page. An example of the Log File view is in Figure 10.18.

---

**NOTE**

Don't forget to click **Stop Recording** after the user is done or you have found what you needed in the log!

---

**Figure 10.16** Policy Tracing Settings

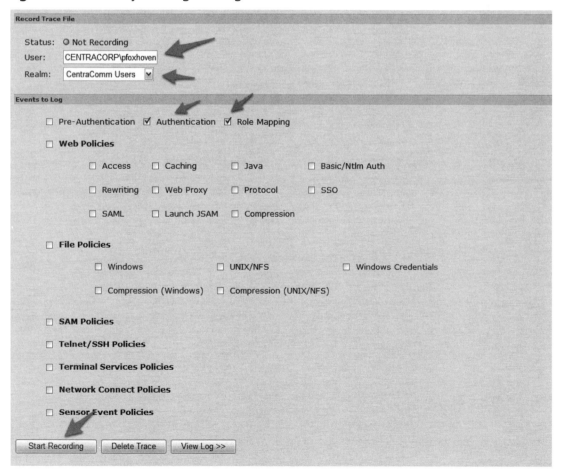

**Figure 10.17** Policy Tracing Recording Started

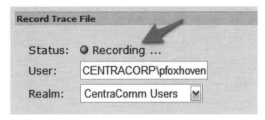

**Figure 10.18** Policy Tracing Log File Viewing

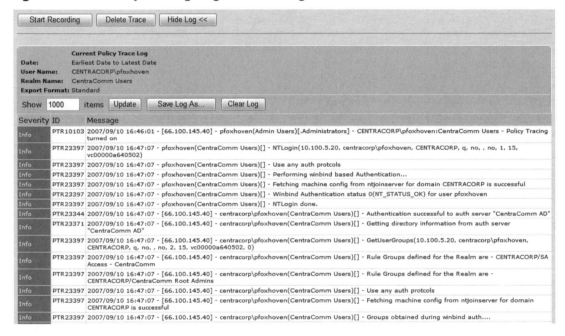

**TIP**

You can use a wildcard character in the username field (such as "$*$") to define what user to enable policy tracing on.

## Simulation

Simulation is used to troubleshoot most of the same problems that Policy Tracing can diagnose, but Simulation allows the administrator to create logs for user sessions without requiring the actual user to sign in, and allows an administrator to create the user session without even needing to know their password. Simulation can take user session troubleshooting one step further, adding more variables to the equation by specifying the sign-in time (to troubleshoot schedules) and many other variables to allow custom expressions to be applied to the session.

Start by navigating in the **Admin** console to **Maintenance | Troubleshooting | User Sessions | Simulation**. Similar to a Policy Trace, you will need to define the username and the authentication realm for the user that you want to enable tracing on, and then the trace will record in detail the options checked under **Events to Log**. Additionally, you can specify a *Query name* to save the simulation settings for future use. As with Policy Tracing, be careful how many events you choose to log, as the IVE can output verbose logs, making the investigation process very difficult. With a simulation you can also define a specific resource to restrict the simulation to, such as a Web, File, or Network Connect resource. This is illustrated in Figure 10.19.

After defining the username, realm, and events to log, click on **Run Simulation** at the bottom of the page as seen in Figure 10.20. If successful, a *Simulation successful* message will appear at the top of the page as in Figure 10.21. After the successful simulation a log file will appear, shown in Figure 10.22.

**Figure 10.19** User Session Simulation

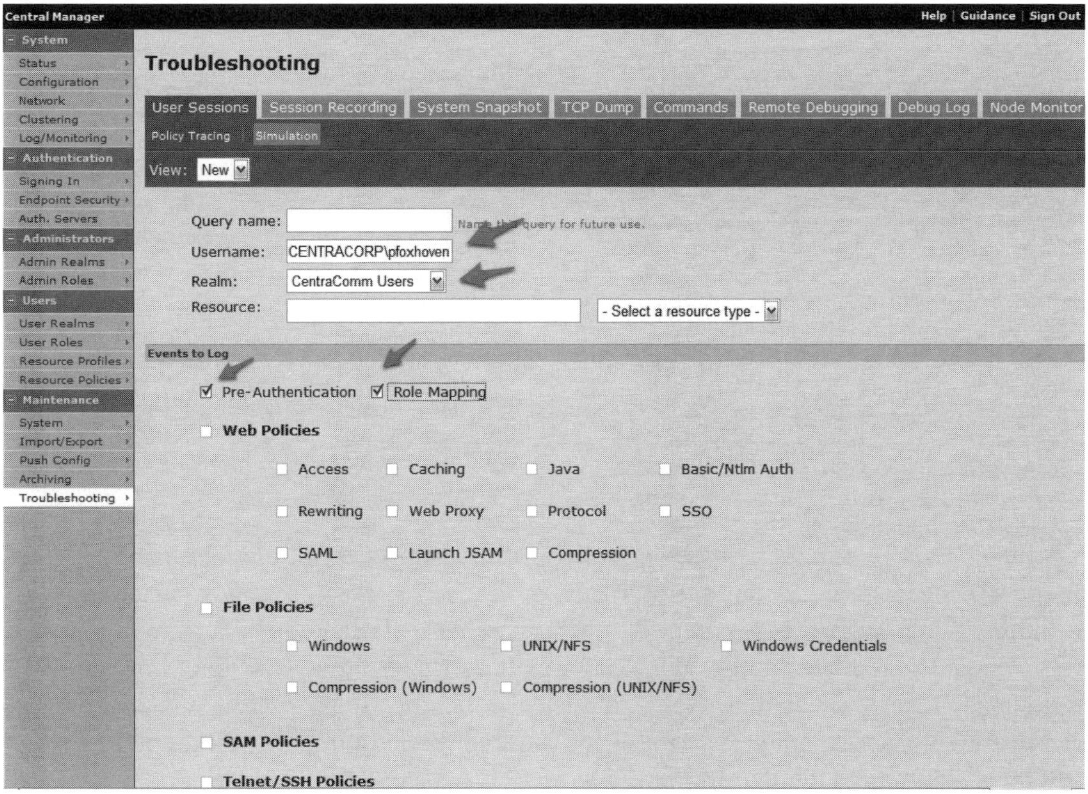

**Figure 10.20** Run Simulation

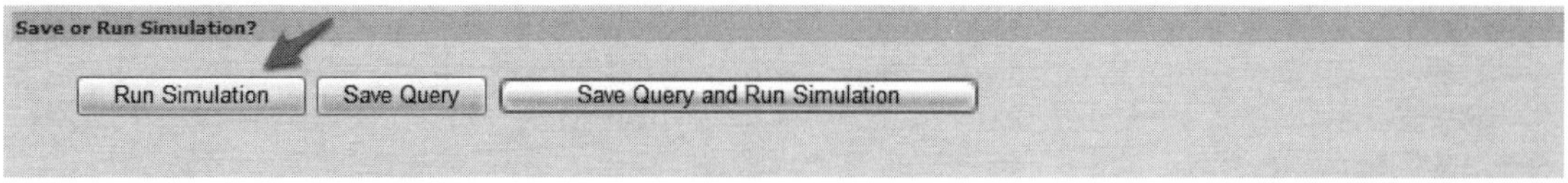

**Figure 10.21** User Session Simulation Successful

**Figure 10.22** User Session Simulation Log File

# Session Recording

Session Recording is most commonly used for the following:

- Troubleshooting issues with web sites being displayed properly through the IVE

- Requests by Juniper Networks Technical Assistance to assist in Troubleshooting the IVE's rewriting engine

- Troubleshooting certain Client/Server Applications

Start by navigating in the **Admin** console to **Maintenance | Troubleshooting | Session Recording**. First define the username of the session that you want to record and the authentication realm for that user. Next, select the **Web (DSRecord)** check box to have the IVE record Web-related traffic. This is most commonly used to troubleshoot how the IVE rewriting engine is rewriting or proxying a particular Web site. If a particular Web site isn't being displayed or working properly, this is the most common option to check. The **Ignore Browser Cache** forces the IVE to not use any caching for the Web content in the log files.

Finally, check the **Client/Server (JCP+NCP)** checkbox to have the IVE record the Java Communication Protocol and the Network Communication Protocol if you need to record particular client/server applications. These settings are illustrated in Figure 10.23.

After defining the username, realm, and events to log, click on **Start Recording** at the bottom of the page. The Status will show *Recording....* At this point the user in question needs to complete the web browsing or client/server application activity in question. After the user has completed this, a trace file will appear in a table to the right of the trace file options as in Figure 10.24. Click on the **Log File** link to download the file for viewing or, more commonly, to send to Juniper Networks Support for further review. An example of the log file is in Figure 10.25.

**NOTE**

Don't forget to click **Stop Recording** after the user is done or you have found what you needed in the log!

**Figure 10.23** Session Recording Options

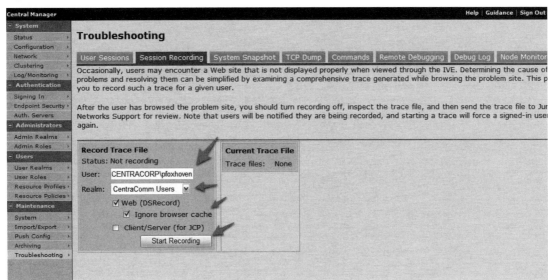

**Figure 10.24** Session Recording Trace File

**Figure 10.25** Session Recording Trace File

```
---- dsrecord.request.before.header:None - 00000.00000 - { 39 } ---- 00000000000000.000000 ----
PackageVersion: 5.4R2.1 (build 11529)

---- dsrecord.request.before.header:None - 20384.00000 - { 619 } ---- 20070910174310.907474 ----
GET /,DanaInfo=www.google.com,SSO=U+ HTTP/1.1
Host: connect.centracomm.net
User-Agent: Mozilla/5.0 (Windows; U; Windows NT 5.1; en-US; rv:1.8.1.6) Gecko/20070725 Firefox/2.0.0.
Accept: text/xml,application/xml,application/xhtml+xml,text/html;q=0.9,text/plain;q=0.8,image/png,*/'
Accept-Language: en-us,en;q=0.5
Accept-Encoding: gzip,deflate
Accept-Charset: ISO-8859-1,utf-8;q=0.7,*;q=0.7
Keep-Alive: 300
Connection: keep-alive
Referer: https://connect.centracomm.net/dana/home/index.cgi
Cookie: DSSignInURL=/; DSID=*********************************; DSFirstAccess=1189457248; DSLastAccess:


---- dsrecord.request.after.header:None - 20384.00001 - { 358 } ---- 20070910174311.15214 ----
GET / HTTP/1.0
Host: www.google.com
Connection: Keep-Alive
User-Agent: Mozilla/5.0 (Windows; U; Windows NT 5.1; en-US; rv:1.8.1.6) Gecko/20070725 Firefox/2.0.0.
Accept: text/xml,application/xml,application/xhtml+xml,text/html;q=0.9,text/plain;q=0.8,image/png,*/'
Accept-Language: en-us,en;q=0.5
Accept-Charset: ISO-8859-1,utf-8;q=0.7,*;q=0.7


---- dsrecord.response.before.header:None - 20384.00002 - { 308 } ---- 20070910174311.69871 ----
HTTP/1.0 200 OK
Cache-Control: private
Content-Type: text/html; charset=UTF-8
Set-Cookie: PREF=ID=cb3df1c1bbdd10fc:TM=1189460591:LM=1189460591:S=t70GjkletGGyOv2Z; expires=Wed, 09-
Server: GWS/2.1
Date: Mon, 10 Sep 2007 21:43:11 GMT
Connection: Close


---- dsrecord.response.before.body:None - 20384.00003 - { 192 } ---- 20070910174311.69923 ----
```

# System Snapshot

System Snapshot allows the IVE Administrator to create a complete image of the current state of the IVE. When running a Snapshot, the IVE runs a series of utilities similar to a *get tech support* or *show tech* option found in many other network devices. Details such as the state of the IVE, the amount of memory in use with paging, details of the processes running, uptime, network and I/O stats, and more are collected into a package that can then be provided to Juniper Network's support. For those concerned about how much information is included in the snapshot, certain details can be omitted, including the system configuration and/or debug log files. Up to ten snapshots can be stored on the system. The snapshots or "dump files" are encrypted for secure transmitting to Juniper. Finally, automatic snapshots can be scheduled to occur automatically after a specified number of hours.

Start by navigating in the Admin console to **Maintenance | Troubleshooting | System Snapshot**. Specify what you would like to include in the snapshot under **System Snapshot Options** and click on the **Take Snapshot** button at the top of the page. It may take a few minutes depending upon the size of your configuration and log files, so be patient. When completed, you will receive a message at the top of the page saying *State snapshot created....* This is all illustrated in Figure 10.26. You can then click on the snapshot created to download the file and provide it to Juniper Networks Support.

**NOTE**

Don't forget to click **Delete the Snapshot** if it isn't needed anymore to preserve disk space.

**TIP**

You can also snapshot an IVE system through the console port if needed.

**Figure 10.26** System Snapshot

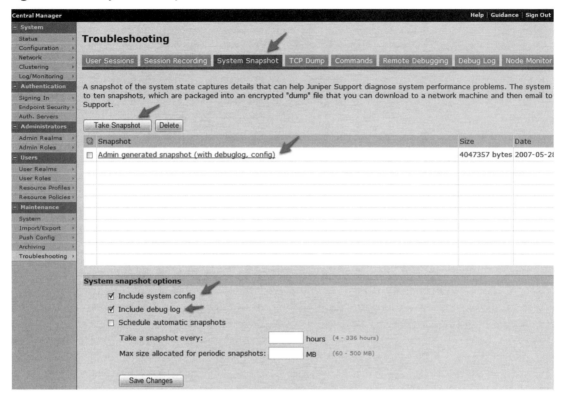

# TCP Dump

TCP Dump is most commonly used for the following:

- Troubleshooting issues with applications transiting the IVE, either Client to Server or Server to Client

- Requests by Juniper Networks Technical Assistance to assist in troubleshooting how the IVE is processing, routing, or rewriting traffic transiting the IVE

- Troubleshooting SAM, Network Connect, and any other application where a "sniff" file might be appropriate

TCP Dump simply allows the IVE to capture packets just as a packet sniffer like *tcpdump* in UNIX/Linux or other common programs like Ethereal would. The administrator can define which interface to capture packets from, whether or not to capture them promiscuously (to increase the level of detail of the capture file), and define filters. It's best to define filters as the capture files can become quite large and hard to parse when troubleshooting a particular issue.

Start by navigating in the **Admin** console to **Maintenance | Troubleshooting | TCP Dump.** Specify the physical port on the IVE that you want to capture packets. If you need to look at packets with a destination of the IVE itself (not passing through), then disable promiscuous mode. If not, make sure it's enabled. If you're not sure, enable promiscuous mode to start with. If you know what traffic specifically you're looking for, it is recommended to define an appropriate filter to specify the port number, protocol, source or destination address, and so on. When completed, click on the **Start Sniffing** button at the bottom of the screen. Figure 10.27 shows an example setup with a filter specified that would restrict the sniffing to only TCP port 80 or, more commonly, HTTP only on the Internal port.

When sniffing has started, the Status will show as *Running*. When you are done, click on the **Stop Sniffing** button. See Figure 10.28 for an example. When completed, you are presented with the dump file and a drop-down list to choose how you'd like to export the sniff from the IVE, shown in Figure 10.29.

**Figure 10.27** TCP Dump Settings

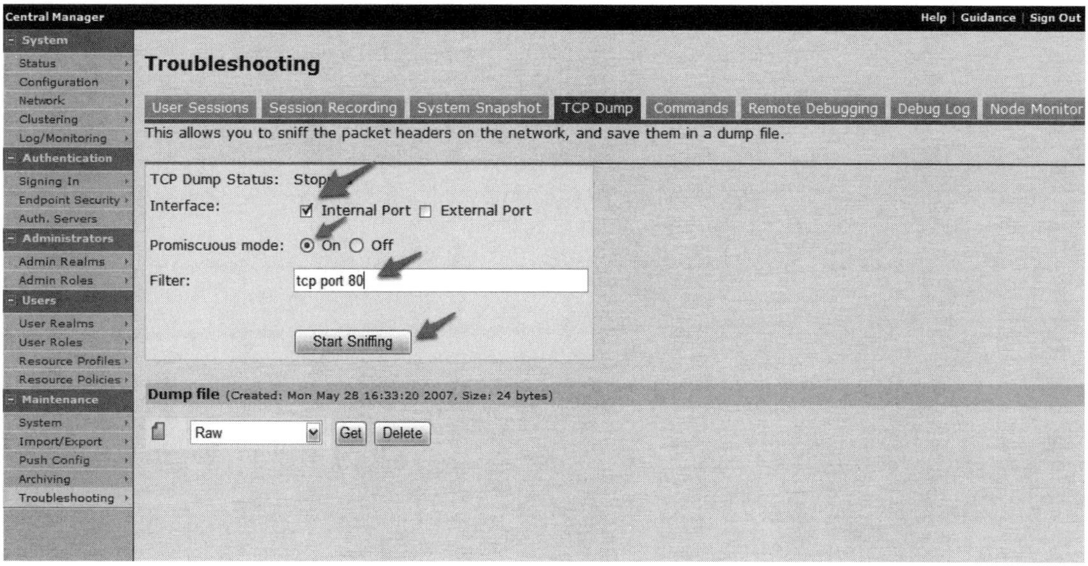


**Figure 10.28** TCP Dump Status

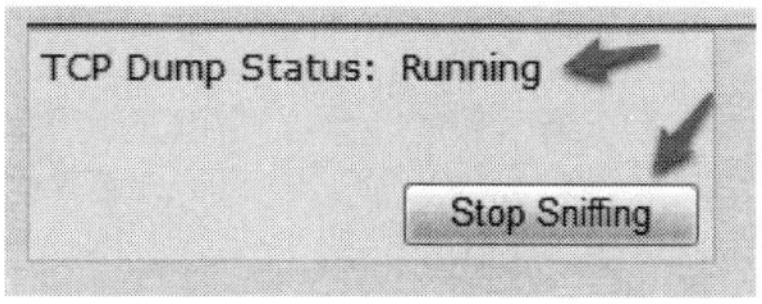

**Figure 10.29** TCP Dump File Exporting

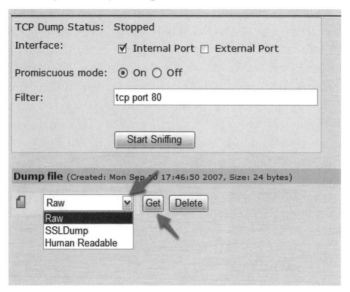

**N**OTE

Don't forget to click **Delete the Dump Files** when they aren't needed anymore to preserve disk space.

**T**IP

For more information and examples of filter expressions to use for TCP Dump, visit www.tcpdump.org/tcpdump_man.html.

# Commands

The Commands tools are most commonly used for diagnosing the following:

- IVE Layer 3 network connectivity to its default and other network gateways and connectivity to servers and other resources shared through the IVE (Ping)

- Tracing the network path the IVE uses to reach the Internet or Internal resources (Traceroute)

- Troubleshooting Layer 2 ARP issues including responses and caching (ARP)

- Troubleshooting DNS Resolution issues (NSLookup)

Start by navigating in the **Admin** console to **Maintenance | Troubleshooting | Commands**. Select the appropriate tool in the **Command** drop down. In the **Target** or **Query** box enter the IP address, domain name, etc., and then click on the **OK** button. The results will be output in the bottom of the same window. See Figure 10.30 for an example.

**Figure 10.30** Troubleshooting Commands

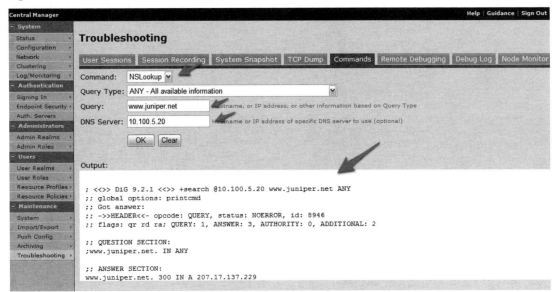

## Remote Debugging

The Remote Debugging tool allows the IVE administrator to provide access for Juniper's Support team to run debugging tools on the IVE remotely. To enable this option, you must first open a Juniper Network's Technical Support case and obtain a debugging code from Juniper that will facilitate the access for Juniper Engineers.

Start by navigating in the **Admin** console to **Maintenance | Troubleshooting | Remote Debugging**. Enter the debugging code obtained from Juniper Networks Support, confirm the host name with Juniper, and click on the **Enable Debugging** button. When finished make sure to click on the **Disable Debugging** button to remove the access. Remote debugging is illustrated in Figure 10.31.

**Figure 10.31** Remote Debugging

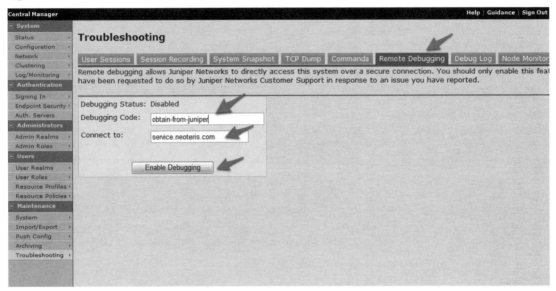

# Debug Logs

Debug logs are a way to enable verbose and very detailed diagnostic logging of events on the IVE. They are most commonly enabled to provide to Juniper Networks Support Engineers by request when troubleshooting internal IVE issues. Debug logs should only be enabled when instructed to do so by a Juniper Networks Support Engineer as it can have a significant performance impact on the IVE. Juniper's Support Engineers will also provide debug log level numbering and event codes to filter the debug files. Debugging logs are not meant to troubleshoot configuration-related issues with the IVE. See Figure 10.32 for an example of the Debug Logs section.

**Figure 10.32** Debug Logs

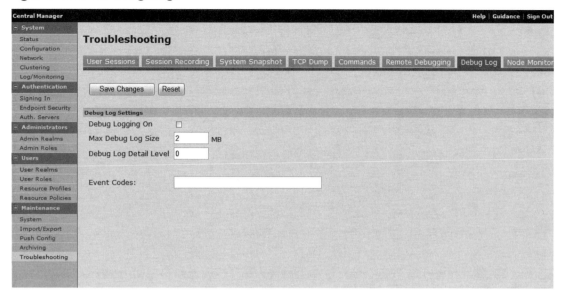

# Node Monitor

Node Monitor is a way to enable verbose diagnostic logging of events on the IVE relating specifically to a cluster configuration. Node Monitoring is typically enabled by request of a Juniper Networks Support Engineer, and Node Monitoring logs are usually requested to be included within a system snapshot. Node Monitoring instructs the IVE to record statistics relating to the cluster to provide to Juniper Support. Figure 10.33 shows an example of the Node Monitor screen.

**Figure 10.33** Node Monitor

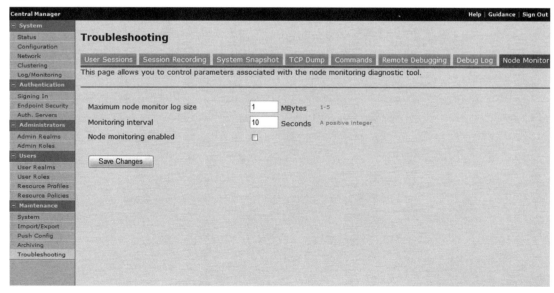

# Cluster: Network Connectivity

The Network Connectivity section under the Cluster tab is another tool that can assist with troubleshooting the operation of an IVE cluster (see Figure 10.34). When you enable the **Cluster Network Troubleshooting** server by clicking on the checkbox and clicking on the **Save Changes** button, the IVE will have nodes connect to the designated cluster server and as they communicate, statistics will output on the same page. These statistics will allow you to determine network connectivity between nodes in a cluster. Please note that you can only enable an IVE to be a server for this tool if that IVE is stand-alone or passive, meaning it is in a cluster but disabled. IVEs already in a cluster cannot be a server. After you enable a server and a node, click the **Go** button on the server and then click on the **Details** link to view the results.

**Figure 10.34** Cluster Troubleshooting (IVE with a Cluster Configured)

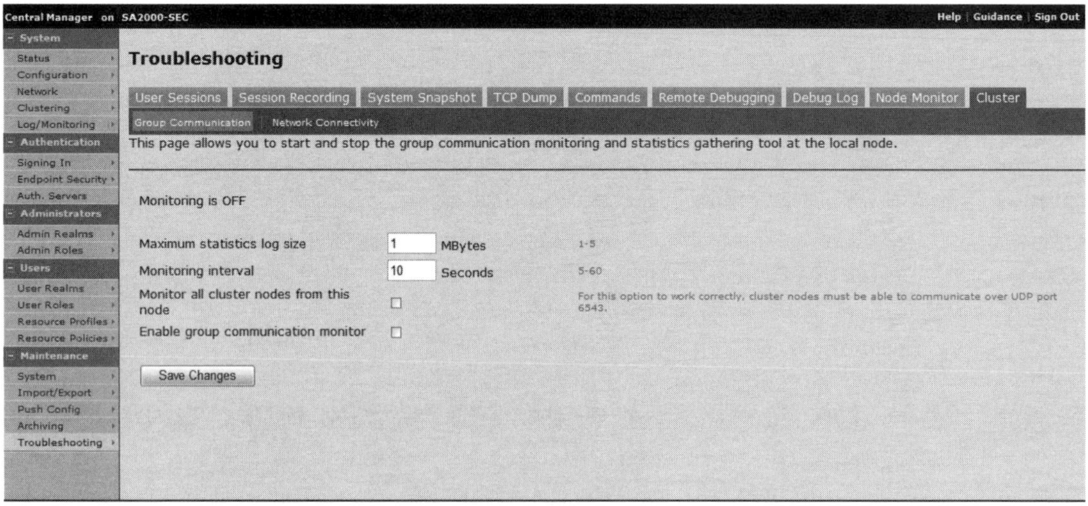

# Summary

It is clear that managing a live system entails quite a bit. This can include basic system administration, such as upgrading or rolling back the unit. However, don't forget about configuration management. This is becoming more and more critical, especially in today's enterprise, and the need for auditable configuration management trails is imminent. Managing multiple boxes is also somewhat challenging, especially if clustering is not being used. Using XML (or Push Config) becomes critical to your ability to quickly and accurately migrate portions or entire configurations from one box to another. Troubleshooting is also highly critical, because if something goes wrong, it could mean a security breach or access control violation. Careful attention must be paid to policy management, and utilities such as Policy Tracing and even Policy Simulation can greatly assist you in ensuring that your policies enforce the right restrictions on your user-base.

# Solutions Fast Track

## System

- ☑ Current and Rollback partitions are used in order to ensure you always have a spare bootable operating system with a previously working configuration.

- ☑ Rollbacks are permanent since there is no "rollforward" function. Be sure to archive your configuration before performing a rollback.

- ☑ While the SSL VPN agents are installed on-the-fly, you can also push them out via SMS or another utility. To do this, simply download the installers from the *Installers* menu. Don't forget the *Installer Service*.

- ☑ Hardware Acceleration (namely SSL) is available as a systemwide option to greatly improve the performance of user transactions.

## Import/Export

- ☑ The system offers a binary import/export function. This function is an all or none import.

- ☑ Also offered is an XML-based import/export function. This allows administrators to select portions of the configuration to export and import, and also exposes the raw data in XML format.

- ☑ Importing the configuration will cause a services restart. Please exercise caution when importing configurations onto live systems.

# Push Configuration

☑ Push Configuration can be used when managing nonclustered nodes or when pushing selected data from a cluster to another cluster or node.

☑ Push Configuration is a licensed feature, and requires receiving nodes to also contain the license.

☑ While this mechanism seems to simply push the configuration to a remote node, keep in mind that the remote node actually performs an import. This means the services will most likely be restarted.

# Archiving

☑ The system's configuration data can all be archived, and it includes a scheduler.

☑ You can also store local backups of the configuration on the node you're working on at the time.

☑ These serve as great change-points that you can later revert back to, should there be a need.

# Troubleshooting

☑ A dashboard containing vital system information is presented when an administrator first logs on to the IVE.

☑ A graphical and more informative version of the dashboard is presented with Central Manager (included with an Advanced IVE License).

☑ The dashboard is commonly used to troubleshoot CPU, memory, hits, disk space, IVE software release, concurrent and peak user-related issues.

☑ Policy Tracing and Simulation tools are used to troubleshoot user sessions on the IVE and are available to assist with understanding why a particular user cannot authenticate or gain access to a particular resource.

☑ Policy Tracing will record information about a session a user creates, whereas a Simulation will allow the administrator to recreate events on the IVE without knowing the user's password or having the user in question involved.

☑ Session recording tools are used to troubleshoot issues with Web content being re-written through the IVE.

☑ Session recording tools troubleshoot certain client/server applications.

☑ A system snapshot is used to create a package to provide to Juniper Networks Support that runs a series of utilities similar to a "get tech support."

☑ Potentially sensitive or confidential information can be omitted from the snapshot.

☑ Snapshots can be scheduled to occur periodically to troubleshoot intermittent problems

☑ The TCP Dump tool is used to capture packets from an IVE session similar to common packet sniffers such as *tcpdump* for troubleshooting applications transiting the IVE.

☑ Commands are Web-based tools that provide an interface to run commands on the IVE including Ping, Traceroute, ARP cache, and NSLookup.

☑ Remote debugging allows the IVE Administrator to provide Juniper's Support Team the ability to run debugging tools on the IVE remotely.

☑ A debugging code must be obtained from Juniper Support before utilizing this feature.

☑ Debug logs are most commonly used to troubleshoot internal IVE issues or problems with the IVE operating system.

☑ Debug logs are recommended to be enabled only at the request of Juniper Support; they can have a significant performance impact on the IVE.

☑ Node Monitor is a tool to enable verbose diagnostic logging of events on the IVE relating specifically to a cluster configuration.

☑ Cluster: Network Connectivity is used to test/troubleshoot network connectivity between nodes in a cluster.

☑ You can only enable an IVE to be a server if that IVE is stand alone or passive (that is, in a cluster but disabled).

# Frequently Asked Questions

**Q:** How do I know what versions my hardware is compatible with?

**A:** Each IVE software revision should have a published Release Notes document. If not, please contact Juniper TAC.

**Q:** How long does it take to upgrade a system to a newer IVE version?

**A:** It depends. At a minimum, expect two to three minutes of downtime. On the high end, it could be 10 minutes. This depends on how much data, such as logs and traces, must be migrated over to the new partition. There isn't actually downtime until the system reboots. During the actual upload of the code and repartitioning, the system continues to service requests. Please remember to monitor the serial console during an upgrade, downgrade, rollback, or factory reset.

**Q:** What does IVE stand for?

**A:** Instant Virtual Extranet. This was the original name of the product when the company was called Neoteris.

**Q:** What is the syntax for TCP Dump?

**A:** Consult www.tcpdump.org for full details.

**Q:** How large is the IVE software package?

**A:** On average, expect it to be around 80 MB.

**Q:** I just want to troubleshoot why a user cannot log on and the *User Access* log under *Log/Monitoring* doesn't show. Why?

**A:** Use **Policy Tracing** and/or **Simulation** under **Troubleshooting | User Sessions**. From here you can enable much more diagnostic logging of Pre-Authentication and Authentication issues.

**Q:** How do I troubleshoot why a user cannot access a particular resource?

**A:** Also use **Policy Tracing** and/or **Simulation** under **Troubleshooting | User Sessions**. Focus on enabling logging of the particular resource they are trying to access—for example, Web Access or Network Connect Policies.

**Q:** I am trying to log on as a user using the Simulation feature. Why do I never see what the user sees?

**A:** While the simulation tool does allow a log-on event to be generated for a particular user without having to know their password, the IVE launches the simulation and outputs the log files. It's not a tool to allow the administrator to completely log on as the user, but allows the administrator to see all of the IVE diagnostic messages as if the user had actually logged on.

**Q:** I'm trying to record a session, but activity that I know should be occurring is not showing in the log file.

**A:** When setting the session recording options, make sure that **Ignore browser cache** is checked as an option. Without this the browser could be retrieving content from its local cache and therefore never requesting the content through the IVE.

**Q:** What file format does the TCP Dump/sniffing tool produce?

**A:** The TCP Dump command on the IVE quite literally runs the widely-used open-source program *tcpdump*. For more information, visit www.tcpdump.org/tcpdump_man.html. The output is determined based on what the user selects when exporting.

# Links to Sites

**www.juniper.net/company/communities/**  Juniper's official discussion forum, which includes IVE communities.

**www.juniperforum.com/**  Discussion forums dedicated to everything Juniper.

**http://kb.juniper.net**  Juniper's Online Knowledgebase with a wealth of IVE notes.

# Chapter 11

## System Section

### Solutions in this chapter:

- **Status**
- **Configuration**
- **Network**
- **Clustering**
- **Virtual Systems**
- **Logging/Monitoring**

☑ **Summary**

☑ **Solutions Fast Track**

☑ **Frequently Asked Questions**

# Introduction

The System menu is where most of the core networking components are configured. This includes the system IP addresses, clustering, logging, Virtual Systems, certificates, and much more. This menu is at the top because typically this is where an administrator must go first, before real Access Management configuration can take place. Also note that some of the menus within the System menu are already populated. This is because they were configured as part of the initial setup on the Serial Console.

# Status

The Status menu offers a quick snapshot of what is going on. On a standard licensed IVE, the Status page displays all of the basic monitoring information, as shown in Table 11.1.

**Table 11.1** The Status Page

| | |
|---|---|
| System Software Pkg Version: | 6.0R1-BETA3 (build 11793) |
| Last Reboot: | 47 days, 22 hours, 24 minutes, 10 seconds |
| System Date and Time: | 2007-07-08 11:05:31 AM |
| Max Licensed Users: | 1000 |
| Number of Signed-In Users: | 1 |
| Number of Signed-In Mail Users: | 0 |
| Logging Disk: | 0 % full |

With Central Manager, however, which is part of the Advanced License now, this information is displayed in a much more elegant form that includes graphical representations of concurrent users, meetings, hits per second, CPU and memory utilization, and also throughput in and out of both interfaces (see Figure 11.1). These graphs are viewable per-node or per-cluster. Also, the data they use may be downloaded by clicking the Download link. This XML data may then be mined for Enterprise reporting or other business needs. We don't recommend reading through it in your free time, though. It can be quite excruciating.

**Figure 11.1** Central Manager—Status

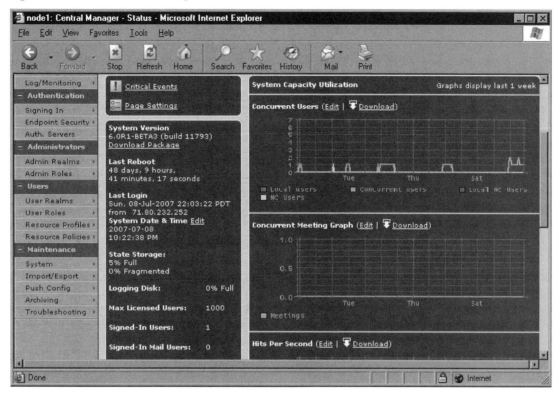

Here you may also edit the page settings, where you can select which options you'd like to display, including:

- Graph options

- The view (think of it as a zoom feature)

- State storage (free disk space for system/state data storage, for future debugging)

- The refresh interval

Critical Events can be used to display the most recent critical events. These are the things you definitely want to look into when first logging in to the system, if possible.

Other functions on this page are for downloading the service package (IVE OS), such as to use it for another node you are managing. You can also see the cluster status here and monitor your nodes to ensure they are communicating properly and are not in trouble.

Lastly, the date and time for the system/cluster are configured here. This is an important step to ensure valid audit data, as well as precise cluster communication and exact policy enforcement information. NTP is definitely something we recommend everyone employ here.

# Active Users

Often times, it's very valuable to learn how your box is working and to see it managing sessions in action. Active Users provides you with just that. In addition, it offers a quick display of which users are using which IP addresses on your network (via Network Connect).

From here, you can view different user-sets, filter the display, and so on, but you can also delete sessions. This is often used when conducting performance or otherwise "load generation" testing on the SSL VPN. We do this to ensure all users get logged out, so the users in the next test can log in as if there were no previously established sessions.

You can also Reset Roles here, which has the system run through all of its current policy information and recheck everything to ensure a user's session is still active and make certain they have access to the IVE features and roles they are supposed to, based on that policy information. It's a way of speeding up recurring checks, and can be helpful if you're trying to visualize policies being enforced upon the right groups of users at the right time.

When looking at the list of users, you may notice some of them display an "!" (exclamation point) next to their name. This is because you have an IDP sensor configured to communicate with your SSL VPN, via something that Juniper calls Coordinated Threat Control. This is discussed later in the chapter, but it is here in the Active Users tab where you can see which users have triggered which IDP sensor events, giving you, the Administrator, the power to alter their session (temporarily or permanently). You may also have chosen to implement automatic action, in which case the system will do it for you.

# Meeting Schedule

Here, you can get a good idea of how the meeting function is used on your SSL VPN deployment. The view can be customized to display:

- Meetings in Progress
- Today's Meetings
- This Week's Meetings
- All Scheduled Meetings

In this chapter, you will find the meetings and their details, along with the conductor and invitees. You can also delete unwanted meetings.

# Configuration

The Configuration menu includes licensing and a place to enable many systemwide options, such as granular controls to further enhance the overall system security.

# Licensing

Under the Configuration menu is the Licensing menu. This is where you can enable IVE features that you've purchased. License options include:

- **Concurrent User Licenses** These are the heart of the system since they provide base user count licensing. These licenses are additive, in that if you have an ADD-1000 and an ADD-500, you'll get a total of 1,500 concurrent users.

- **Cluster User Licenses** The way this licensing works, in a nutshell, is you use the ADD-# licenses to add users to the cluster, then you get another license—the CL-ADD-# license—which entitles other devices to participate in the cluster, dictating that they can support some # of concurrent users for the cluster.

- **Advanced** This license enables several advanced features for a node (or all nodes in that node's cluster). This includes Password Management (interactive user password management via NTLM or LDAP), SAML support, Netegrity SiteMinder support, Advanced Authorization and Delegation Rules, Remote SSO (via Form POST or HTTP headers), Custom Expressions (for policy building and role mapping), and custom sign-in page support (THTML-based). In newer 5.x releases, this also enables Central Manager, which includes Push Config.

- **SAM/NC** This license enables both SAM (J-SAM and W-SAM) and NC (Network Connect) on the node (or all nodes in that node's cluster).

- **Secure Meeting** This license enables the Secure Meeting functionality for the node (or all nodes in that node's cluster). Specific user caps are associated with this. Contact a Juniper Networks sales rep for more details.

- **SSL HW Acceleration for SA-4000** This enables the HW acceleration module, included in every SA4000 appliance, which improves encryption performance significantly.

- **And more…** Contact Juniper Networks for a complete and up-to-date list.

A license key is usually comprised of seven dictionary words—for example, "modem future tree coyote measure sheet currency." This makes it easy for copy/paste, such as from an entitlement e-mail. Once applied to the system, they are validated. Assuming all goes well, they will then be displayed at the bottom of this Licensing UI page. Here you can see the key, a timeframe for when it will expire (or whether it is permanent), and the option to delete the license key. You may need to delete a license key to prove to Juniper you are migrating from one key to another (that is, a larger concurrency level).

It is also important to point out here that the License Keys themselves are actually generated using the HWID (Hardware ID) displayed on the Licensing page. This binding is to prevent the sharing of licenses (which is prohibited by Juniper), but be aware that these keys cannot just be copied and pasted into another device. The actual process typically involves contacting Juniper to get license authorization codes (or in the case of an RMA, new codes that match your old ones) and then using the HWID, they get redeemed from the Juniper licensing page (www.juniper.net/generate_license/). This page binds the HWID and the Authorization code together to form the License key itself (as mentioned earlier: the seven-word strings).

# Security

Under the Configuration menu, you'll find Security. This menu includes many systemwide options that can be used to alter and hopefully improve the overall posture of the system's security. Many of the features here directly impact users, and great caution should be used when making changes to it.

- **SSL/TLS Version** This feature, disabled by default, is here purely for backwards-compatibility reasons (such as if an older Internet browser did not support SSLv3 or TLSv1).

- **Encryption Strength & Options** This may be necessary to support overseas Web browsers, or those which cannot support higher encryption strengths.

- **SSL Handshake Timeout** This may be necessary to ensure that the system's resources are not exhausted if it undergoes an SSL-based DOS attack. This option actually changes the time (wait) for the server before it drops the connection and frees up that allocated memory.

- **Delete All Cookies at Session Termination** The system generally caches cookies to improve usability, and to ensure they are not sent to the user's Web browser (where they serve no purpose). These will be stored on the system, but may optionally be configured to not persist across a user's sessions and instead be deleted upon signout.

- **Include IVE Session in URL** Certain Mozilla Web browsers withhold cookies from a JVM, and therefore the JVM would require the session ID be passed to it via the URL. This reduces security, but increases functionality on these kinds of Web browsers. For more details, please contact a Juniper Networks support representative.

- **Lockout Options** The IVE can prevent brute-force password (guessing) attacks. This is done by rate limiting the number of login attempts from a single IP address.

# Certificates

Certificate Management has always been the crux to any good PKI implementation. It has to be powerful and flexible, and must also be standards-based, for obvious reasons. The IVE employs standard X.509 formatted certificates to support its PKI infrastructure. It also supports standards-based CRL, OCSP, and LDAP mechanism to ensure certificates and certificate information is properly validated. Before we get started, let's define a few terms:

- **PKI (Public Key Infrastructure)**  This is a standardized term that identifies what kind of authentication/encryption framework the system utilizes.

- **CRL (Certificate Revocation List)**  This is a standardized term that refers to a digital list (database actually) of Client Certificates (uniquely identified by Serial Numbers) and whether or not the certificate is still valid (or has been revoked). This is a critical part of any PKI system because it provides an easy mechanism for administrators to enable and disable access even though a user may already have their certificate installed on their remote laptop or PC. This is usually a binary file that is downloaded periodically, and must be refreshed as such.

- **OCSP (Online Certificate Status Protocol)**  This, like CRL, is used to manage a database of revoked/permitted certificates. It differs from CRL, however, in that it is real time, meaning the system looks up a user's certificate in the database in real time to decide whether or not it is revoked.

- **X.509**  This is a standard used in PKI and other frameworks to define IDs, Attributes, and Values of various information. Typical elements include a DN (distinguished name), which is comprised of one or more CNs (common names) and OUs (organizational units).

- **LDAP (Lightweight Directory Access Protocol)**  Another standardized protocol which defines how a system (such as PK) can be accessed remotely, in order to obtain data and authenticate/authorize users. Typically a hierarchy, it looks and feels much like Novell NDS. However, it is more open and standardized.

# Device Certificates

The SSL VPN runs its own purpose-built Web server, and communicates via HTTP/SSL. This Web service requires its own certificate. During initial IVE setup, you were prompted to create a self-signed certificate, which could be used during testing. But ideally, you want to import a signed certificate, preferably by a widely trusted party, known by your audiences. For this reason, many folks go with an organization like VeriSign, Thawte, or Equifax.

Typically, you'd have the original CSR generated at initial setup, and would just get that signed. But when the device generated the CSR, it also generated a Private Key. This key is on the box, but there is no way to retrieve it, for obvious security reasons. Since this security may be too arduous, some users may opt to instead generate a CSR and private key elsewhere (such as on their Corporate CA), get the signed cert, and then import both the signed cert and the private key into the SSL VPN. They may do this for other HTTPS deployments internally, in fact. This process is obviously more susceptible to theft of the private key, but you may find it is a better key management practice, as a backup could then be created and stored in a safe offsite. That way, at least, you have a backup.

It is also important to point out here that the certificates are bound to interfaces (see Figure 11.2). That is, since SSL/TLS begins before HTTP does, there is no concept of a Web server hostname. There is only the IP address that the SSL/TLS service is listening on. For this reason, you need to bind a certificate to an interface. Typically, here you would bind the certificate to both the internal and external interfaces. Nevertheless, it all depends on your configuration—for example, you may be using a VIP, in which case you might want a different certificate bound to that VIP.

**Figure 11.2** Certificates—Binding

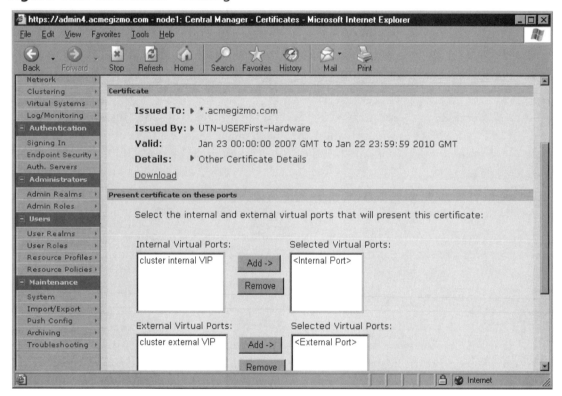

---

**NOTE**

When you import a certificate, you'll need to make sure it's in the PEM storage format. Also, if you generated the certificate yourself, make sure you chose to use the Apache/SSL X.509 format (not mod-ssl).

---

# Trusted Client CAs

Client Authentication is becoming more and more prominent these days. No longer can we trust that just because they know a username and password, they are truly who they say they are. Two-factor authentication is great, but it is rather easy to misuse or give to another. Client Certificates, however, provide greater control over who actually is entitled to use that certificate to authenticate—especially if you enforce strong export or no export protection on the managed devices. This now creates a bind between the actual user and their actual device. This enhances security and also provides very seamless integration into existing PKI infrastructures.

When using Client Certificate Authentication, you have to validate each user's certificate to ensure, at a minimum, the following information:

- It was issued (signed) by a trusted ("known") party ("root/issuing CA").

- It is valid (can also check validity on-the-fly).

- It has correct attributes (based on policies).

- It has an appropriate subject (that is, the username/ID).

Since Certificates are usually issued for some duration of time (years even), and users (employees) may quit long before they expire, it is necessary to manage these Client Certificates properly. Often times, a company may manage a Certificate Revocation List (CRL) or use an Online Certificate Status Protocol (OCSP) service, such as those available as part of Microsoft AD, Sun One Directory, and many more CA infrastructure suites. If you are using one of these, it is necessary to configure it here, because you wouldn't want one of your remote access devices to allow users who had been terminated, now would you?

For imported Trusted CA certificates, you will configure CRL or OCSP, whichever way you like. You have a variety of options in doing so, and can even configure default options to use when auto-importing a Root CA (that is, as the system validates chains, it may download, validate, and import a Root CA for you):

- **None** Do not use CRL or OCSP

- **Use OCSP**

- **Use CRL**

- **Use OCSP with CRL fallback** (recommended)

Now, when a user authenticates using a Certificate Auth Server for a Realm on the IVE, they will be validated against the Trusted CA, which matches the issuer found on the user's certificate. And if CRL and OCSP are used, that provides an even better level of assurance, the user is really able to authenticate here.

Additionally, you may choose here to validate the entire chain of trust, including validating the issuing/root CA cert you've imported, as well as its issuing cert, and so on up the chain, to the top.

Lastly, here you may opt to disallow a Root CA cert you've imported to authenticate users. Say, for example, you wanted to temporarily disallow users from authenticating against this CA, such as for maintenance or an audit.

At this point, if you've configured a trusted Root CA to authenticate user client certificates, you are able to authenticate users, but you may want some additional level of security. For example, you may want to perform realm-level checking to ensure a user's OU (organizational unit) is adequate, or you may want to validate an attribute of the certificate against one found in a user's LDAP repository.

# Trusted Server CAs

Since a majority of the applications used through an SSL VPN may be Web-based, the Core Rewrite functionality of the product is often times used extensively. In addition, since many corporate Web applications work with sensitive information, and also are not directly connected (or even locally connected) to the SSL VPN, there may be a need to provide SSL encapsulation for those Web transactions, perhaps even from end to end.

To support backend HTTPS transactions rewritten and proxied on behalf of the end-users, the SSL VPN gateway needs to act as a client Web browser would—validating that the server is who it says it is, and working to establish a level of encryption for the data channel. Since a standard Web browser, such as IE6, typically has preloaded Root CA certificates and the ability to import new ones, that functionality also needs to be available on the SSL VPN. This is configured in the Trusted Server CAs subtab. If Web browsing to HTTPS sites is enabled and validated (see a Role's Web options), then the certificates here are used to validate signatures of back-end HTTPS sites accessed during a user's session.

# Code-Signing Certificates

Since more and more Web-based applications are using Java, specifically applets, the need to secure these applications further increases. But since the Juniper SSL VPN does not require any forwarding agent for traditional Web-based access, there is nothing to forward Java socket calls. For this reason, the Juniper core rewriter also rewrites Java applets on-the-fly. Since many applets are signed by a trusted party (for assurance it is legitimate code), a rewritten applet would then need to be re-signed.

The IVS provides a couple of options to let you, the Administrator, decide how to sign rewritten applets.

- **Microsoft Authenticode**  VeriSign offers a Microsoft authenticode certificate that is designed to be used to sign Microsoft CABs, including those designed for MS-JVM.

- **JavaSoft**  If using SunJVM applets, you may employ a JavaSoft certificate that can then be used to re-sign Java JAR files.

- **Juniper Web Controls**  There is also an option here to sign Juniper controls. This is for Juniper ActiveX and Java delivery components, which help users install SSL VPN agents on-the-fly, as needed.

# NCP

The Network Communication Protocol (NCP) is used, by many Juniper SSL VPN agents, to communicate between the agent and server. You can think about it like an SSL-based RPC mechanism, used for exchanging application data. This agent list includes Host Checker, W-SAM, and NC, to name a few. NCP has also undergone some improvements over the years, and a newer optimized version (oNCP) became available. NCP can now be configured to run in two modes, auto-select or non-auto-select.

- If in auto-select mode, it will attempt to use oNCP for obvious optimization-related reasons. This method uses compression and some other connection-handling improvements to improve transport efficiency. If a direct connection cannot be made, however, such as if using a Proxy, the fallback non-optimized NCP protocol will be used.

- In non-auto-select mode, it bypasses oNCP altogether. Rarely should this be changed without the guidance of Juniper Networks support personnel.

Since NCP is like an RPC program, it may be waiting long periods for the IVE server to respond. At some point, the wait must be classified as a timeout, and a re-transmit may be issued. For this reason, the Administrator may need to configure how long the interval must be before a connection is deemed timed out.

Additionally, the NCP communications channel may go idle for long periods of time, such as if an application is paused or not running. In this situation, the IVE server will maintain connections, but will want to eventually time them out to free up resources. The idle timer for this scenario can be configured here.

# Sensors (IDP)

As discussed earlier in this chapter, the IVE can be configured to communicate with a Juniper IDP sensor in order to provide additional insight into remote access users who may have launched (accidentally even) a network- or application-based attack. Since the IDP is only capable of seeing what's in the header and payload, and has no concept of a user, much less remote access sessions, it relies heavily upon the SSL VPN to do so for it. When enabled, these two devices can coordinate together to best determine which remote access session caused the application or network attack (or anomaly). This is why the solution is called Coordinated Threat Control.

## Sensors

Under the *Sensors* subtab, you can create the communications relationship between this IVE node (or cluster of nodes) and one or more IDP sensors.

---

**NOTE**

A Juniper Networks IDP sensor can communicate with one, and only one, IVE (or cluster of IVEs); however, an IVE (or cluster of IVEs) can communicate with multiple IDP sensors concurrently.

---

To establish communications between an IVE and IDP, a One-Time Password (OTP) must be initialized on the IDP device. This is done on the IDP ACM (Web-based console). The OTP should be copied and then pasted into the IVE configuration for that IDP sensor. After applying changes to the IDP, the IVE can then have its changes saved, and immediately after, should connect with the IDP sensor. Upon successful connection, an X.509-based certificate exchange will commence, further authenticating the two devices to one another for future session use.

To add a sensor, you'll need the OTP, the IP, and port (usually 7103 tcp). This would also be a good time to ensure your firewall isn't going to block this connection between the SSL VPN and the IDP sensor. When adding a sensor, you will be prompted to choose the *Severity* level. This filters out unimportant or less-critical event notifications in order to reduce the amount of unnecessary traffic on your network. You might set this to 1 initially, just so you can see everything that is being detected. Additionally, you'll want to set the list of *Addresses to Monitor* to ensure the IDP sensor will send events for all IP addresses that may be of interest to the SSL VPN. In other words, this could be any IP address the SSL VPN is servicing (either directly as an Interface of VIP or even via some user's NC session).

From here, you can also see the status of configured IDP sensors (see Figure 11.3). A green indicator means communications are up. A red indicator means communications must be reestablished or that the IDP device is unreachable.

**Figure 11.3** IDP—Sensor Status

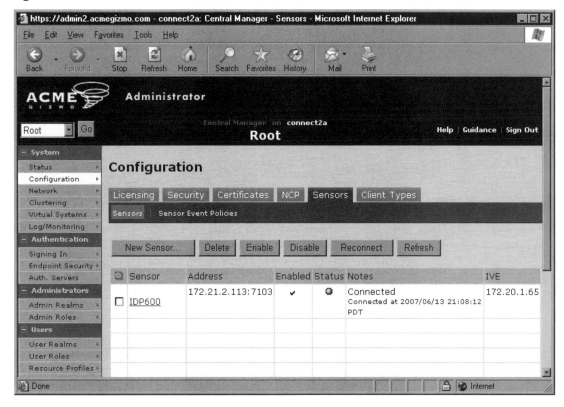

## Sensor Event Policies

Now that communications have been established, the IVE must be configured to act upon IDP sensor events, such as a critical attack notification. To get started, you'll need to create an Event profile. This is typically comprised of a custom Boolean expression, which must equate to true in order to carry out this policy's action. For example, you might say idp.attackStr = 'HTTP:AUDIT:ROBOTS.TXT'. This means that for any notification from the IDP sensor, which includes the Attack String (an attribute in the IDP's event notification) of value 'HTTP:AUDIT:ROBOTS.TXT', take the following action. In such a case, you can choose from several actions:

- Ignore the Event; Log It
- Terminate the User Session
- Disable User Account (requires admin intervention to re-enable)
- Replace Role (Quarantine)
- Replace Role Permanently (requires admin intervention to reinstate)

If "Ignore" is the selected option, no action will be taken and the Active Users tab will show an Exclamation Point, indicating that particular user had caused some kind of IDP trigger. This is a more manual process, but may be used initially to passively monitor and audit notifications being generated by your IDP sensors. Automated actions, however, are configured just like most other IVE functions—they are based on a configured policy. For example, you may want all Critical notifications to disable user accounts, but medium severity notifications may just temporarily quarantine the user and provide them with remediation instructions.

# Client Types

As the definition of remote access begins to more and more blur with that of mobile access, perimeter access devices become more increasingly used by PDAs, Smart Phones, BlackBerries, and other next-generation mobile computing solutions.

Applications aside, the IVE utilizes a variety of Web pages to interact with the user. For example, the authentication page, the portal page, file sharing pages, and even SSO pages. These pages are normally formatted for a full-size PC (or at least a laptop), but become highly unusable and painful to interact with on small form-factor devices.

For this reason, the IVE offers Administrators the ability to provide customized page-sets to users of small form-factor devices. This is all configured based on a Web browser's *User-Agent* HTTP header. For example, the DoCoMo Web browser is typically employed on iMode phones in Japan. Therefore, an iMode (Compact HTML or "cHTML") set of pages would be used to service these Web requests. This can greatly simplify and enhance a user's SSL VPN experience because even though it may lack rich media, images, and cookie support, it does provide a secure, functional environment to run iMode-capable business applications, such as Microsoft Outlook Mobile Access (OMA; not to be confused with OWA).

In order to determine a Web browser's user-agent, you can look in either the User logs (after a user attempts to access) or else in the Policy Trace. For example, a typical Windows XP PC with IE6 would have the following User-Agent HTTP Header:

```
Mozilla/4.0 (compatible; MSIE 6.0; Windows NT 5.1; SV1)
```

Just configure which Web browser user-agent strings you'd like to customize a style for, and select the style from the drop-down list (see Figure 11.4). The different styles are explained in great detail in the IVE Administrators Guide PDF, and also some default string/ style combinations are already listed in the UI for you.

**Figure 11.4** Client Types

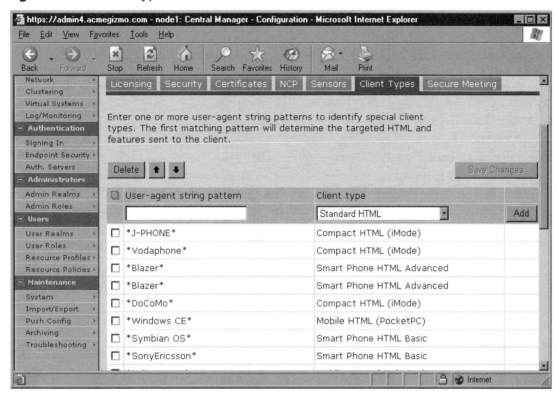

Lastly, there is an option at the bottom here to enable Password Masking. Since cHTML-capable phones usually only have a dialpad keyboard, users may have to press a number multiple times in order to input the correct alphabetic or numeric character. This can be very painful when inputting passwords, because they are generally masked and show up only as a series of ****** characters. Since shoulder-surfing is less of an issue for phone users, and to help alleviate this burden, you as an Administrator may opt to disable (uncheck) this feature so users can actually see the password they're inputting before they click "Log in."

# Secure Meeting

If licensed, Secure Meeting can provide an excellent medium to display remote applications and presentations. In many cases, a conductor is running a meeting, but may have multiple non-IVE users attending the meeting. These users do not log in and authenticate like traditional IVE users (like the conductor), but do require some simple session lifetime options, for idle timeout and maximum session length. These options can be configured on the Secure Meeting tab.

Additionally, for debugging purposes, you may need to retrieve client-side Secure Meeting application logs from attendees. This can be done through the SSL VPN's automated framework; however, it must be enabled. You can enable this on the Secure Meeting tab, but you must also enable Client-Side Log Upload on the Log/Monitoring menu.

With the popularity of Secure Meeting, many folks end up using it daily or even throughout the day. For these scenarios, it can be quite cumbersome to generate a new Meeting ID, and then tell it to everyone over the phone for every meeting you're having. In fact, if you use it to aid in a Tech Support function, it can be even more critical. For this reason, Juniper has come up with the concept of My Secure Meeting. This is an option you can enable so each IVE user can have his or her own Secure Meeting URL that never changes. This way, they can point everyone to the same URL each time. These URLs can also be based on a username or nickname, which is far easier to remember and type in than some random eight-digit string. They will use a built-in prefix and can be configured as follows:

- **Username**  For example, https://meeting.company.com/meeting/kfletcher
- **Sequential Room #**  For example, https://meeting.company.com/meeting/room5
- **Expression**  For example, https://meeting.company.com/meeting/kevin.fletcher

If you want to use the Secure Meeting Email Notification system, you'll also want to configure your SMTP server here. This enables the IVE to relay SMTP messages on behalf of some generic meeting e-mail alias, so that Secure Meeting invitations can be sent to users, even if they are not local to the company. SMTP Auth is even supported for this functionality.

Daylight Savings Time may be honored by some, but not others. That can be configured here along with one other option, which is to allow users to share content in true 32-bit color mode. While this mode does yield higher-quality broadcasts, it does consume considerably more bandwidth, and you may want to limit that here by disabling this Secure Meeting functionality.

To the right of the Secure Meeting page, on newer releases of IVE software, you'll also see the link, Delete Past Meetings. What this does is provide the Admin with the ability to delete old meeting instances from the cache (stored configuration). This frees up disk space and simplifies the meetings database, increasing performance and optimizing the meeting subsystem.

# Network

While L2 and L3 network connectivity is fundamental to the system, it also provides many security-related controls, further enhancing the overall security posture of the solution. Virtual LANs (VLANs), host mapping, static routing, ARP resolution management, and HA are just some of the many features offered by the L2/L3 framework.

Also, please note that in the Network section of the UI, there is a drop-down bar at the top that will display per-page settings for a specific node or the entire cluster. When making changes, be sure to check that the changes you are making apply to the node or to the entire cluster, and select accordingly. If you apply settings to the cluster, it will eliminate the need to add settings to each node, separately. Likewise, per-node configuration will override clusterwide configuration.

## Overview

The Overview page outlines the high-level network settings (see Figure 11.5).

**Figure 11.5** Network Settings Overview

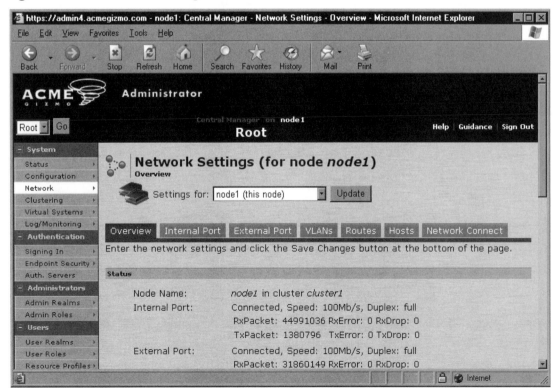

This is composed of:

- **Node Name**  localhost, unless in a cluster.

- **Ethernet Port Status**  Connected or not; Speed; Duplex; Pkt Counters.

- **System Hostname**  This is used by only a few features, including the Java Applet Upload framework, Secure Meeting, and internal system variables.

- **DNS/Domains**  This should be self-explanatory.

- **WINS**  Since the SSL VPN offers a Web-ified File Browsing interface, WINS can be used on the back-end to learn about the Windows network resources. You may also want to configure a Master Browser that can relay the browsing information to the gateway, if it's not physically on that network segment.

- **Network Discovery**  If the IVE detects connected nodes, it will query and build a list of available shares. This helps speed up file browsing, but also creates a bit of chatter on the wire.

# Internal + External Port Management

Managing the Internal and External port (or "Port 1") is fairly simple. The following items must be set up to enable these interfaces:

- IP Address

- Netmask

- Default Gateway

- MAC Address

- Link Speed

- ARP Ping Timeout

- MTU

## Virtual Ports

One of the more confusing topics, an SSL VPN Virtual Port is merely a VIP (floating Virtual IP address) + an Interface Slot, or placeholder to accommodate per-node IP addressing. This concept enables a floating slot instead of just a VIP, and the VIP can be different on different nodes in the cluster—nodes that would assume the VIP in a failover situation. One great benefit of this design is that it supports the concept of WAN clustering, where you may have nodes in disparate IP networks that you want to centrally manage and push policies to.

To set up a new Virtual Port, go to **System | Network | Internal/External Port | Virtual Ports**, then click **New Port**. You'll want to type in a descriptive name, but the important element here is the actual IP address to listen on. Also note that if you're using a cluster, you'll need to set up the Virtual Port as a slot, with IP addresses for the devices in your cluster.

Once you save changes, you may want to revisit the Certificates configuration page, for example, if you want to use a different SSL certificate for this Virtual Port. To modify these settings, choose **System | Configuration | Certificates | Device Certificates**. Once there, you can select your certificate and then choose which Virtual Ports it should be bound to.

## The ARP Cache

Like most IP-based devices, the system must maintain an ARP resolution table, at least temporarily. In extreme circumstances, or for stronger security, you can also hard-code specific IP:MAC entries so ARP is not necessary (and won't be used to resolve those addresses). You can view the dynamic table online or via the Serial Console. You can also modify the table to add and remove static entries.

# VLANs

VLANs may be employed for additional L2 separation, further enhancing the privacy aspects of your network transmissions. Furthermore, VLAN-based routing may be utilized in various Network Edge configurations, such as to route traffic through a multisubscriber network. The IVE supports VLANs with ID 0 to 4096, and can support up to 1024 configured VLANs. For folks using the Virtual Systems framework, VLANs may be easily connected in order to provide further L2 separation of the Virtual Systems.

VLAN configuration is much like the Virtual Port configuration in that there is a common VLAN created for a cluster, and then each node may have its own IP address. To set one up, choose **System | Network | Internal/External port | VLANs**. Like Virtual Ports, you'll need to set these up per-node or per-cluster. Once you create a new VLAN port, you can select a VLAN ID to use when tagging packets, and also the device IP settings used to service those packets inbound/outbound.

> **NOTE**
>
> Please also note that the IP addresses may not conflict (be identical), even if they are configured for use in different VLANs. Overlapping addresses outside of the interface address itself can overlap and will not conflict.

# Routes

The system also maintains a routing table, which is configured on a per-interface basis. Dynamic and inherent routes, such as those for the system IP addresses, will show up in the routing table. Also, any static routes you configure will show up here along with their connectivity (via ICMP) status. Configuring a new static route is the same as you've probably done before. Just be sure to choose which interface it should be routing traffic for.

## Hosts

IP to host mapping is a critical element of any network, and in fact is another avenue of attack for would-be hackers. If you do not trust your DNS, consider adding critical host mapping relationships in manually here for added protection. It may mean the difference between a glitch and an outage.

Adding a new host entry is fairly straightforward. Input the IP and hostname and click Add. If you want to add a comment, you can. If you want to add aliases, simply type the same IP address in with the new alias, and when it is added it will add it to the existing IP entry as another hostname alias for that address. Again, please bear in mind that host entries can be node-specific, so be sure you are viewing the right page (cluster/per-node) before making changes.

## Network Connect

The Network Connect system menu doesn't contain much, except for a configurable IP filter and a server IP. The IP filter provides a way for Administrators to filter out certain subsets/blocks of IP addresses, which this node can service for NC sessions. The primary use case here would be if you had disparate IP networks and wanted to use centralized policies. The policy may have two class Bs within a class A designation, and each node may use only one of the Class Bs on their local segment. Therefore, this filter could filter out just the Class B that is locally connected to this clustered SSL VPN node.

The Server IP is used internally to NC and apparently doesn't conflict with any NC configurations, even those issuing addresses in that space. You can safely leave this as is.

## Clustering

Please note that more details on clustering are included in Appendix A, but we would like to highlight a few things in this chapter as well. When you log in to the Admin UI, you'll see the Clustering menu shown under System, and notice one of the following options: *Create, Join,* or *Status.*

When you see *Create* a cluster, you can do so at anytime, or opt not to. This means that your device is ready to form a cluster, and has appropriate licenses applied. When forming a new cluster, you'll need to choose a cluster name, a name for the node itself, and a cluster password. The password will be used by other nodes to authenticate to the cluster initially. After you create a cluster, you'll need to add additional nodes to the cluster configuration and optionally set up the cluster for Active/Active, or else Active/Passive, which will use configured VIPs. Here, you'll set additional nodes' IP addresses and other pertinent node-specific settings. You may also go back through the other Networking menus to set up node-specific settings for the node to inherit once it joins. You'll also want to add licenses to the cluster so that when the other nodes join, they can retrieve their licenses if they don't already have them. After all of this is done, you can go to the other nodes management consoles and make them join.

When you see *Join* a cluster, this means the device has no existing cluster configuration and no user licenses (which you'd need to form a cluster). This means the device will have to join an existing cluster. You may also see this on the Serial Console during the bootup sequence. With good planning, the node that created the cluster should already have appropriate licenses for each node as well as their respective network and per-node configuration. This way, after the join, your device will configure itself based on what the cluster tells it to.

# Status

On the Status page, you'll find information about the cluster, including all configured nodes, their network settings, and any active cluster VIPs (see Figure 11.6). You can add nodes here, as well as delete them from the cluster. You may also opt to disable a node, such as to take it offline for maintenance. This suspends cluster-related activity for this node, but the idea is that once it rejoins (if so desired), it will synchronize its configuration once again.

**Figure 11.6** Clustering

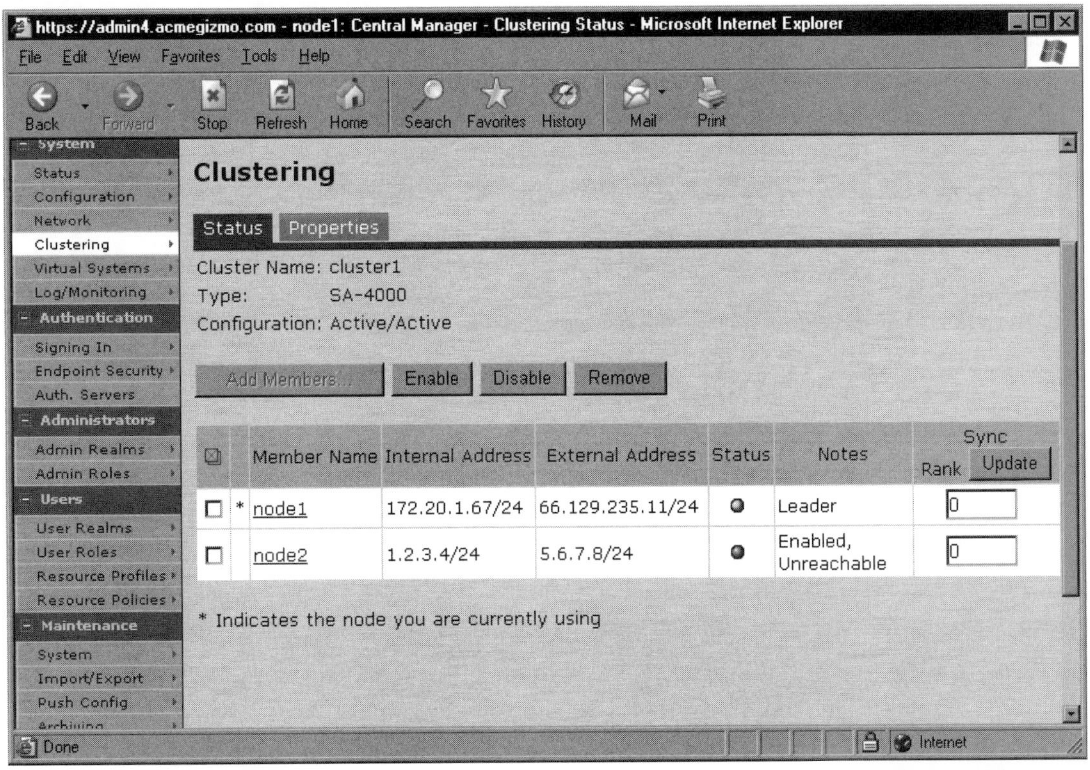

You will also see an option here to set a Synch Rank. When two nodes in a cluster become disconnected from one another, they might each think they are the cluster leader during this "outage." When the outage is resolved, and connectivity restored, there must be an election to determine which node becomes the new leader and holds the true configuration/ state, because (during an outage) the state could change (for example, a user logs out). So the synch rank is to be used to determine which node's configuration and state will be used in this split/re-merge scenario. For this reason, it is recommended that nodes in the most stable environments have the highest synch rank, 255. Synch ranks of equal value will yield a randomly chosen leader.

## Notes from the Underground…

### Cluster Status Icon

The cluster status icon displays a color that lets the Admin know if there is a problem, such as a node is unreachable, disabled, out of synch, or running the wrong version of the OS. If you let your mouse hover over the little icon, a hex code will appear. Each bit is a different flag, and there are about 40 different codes Juniper tracks here. A phone call to JTAC might get you more insight if you're familiar enough with hard-code.

# Cluster Properties

After your cluster is formed, you can configure the format:

- **Active/Passive** This should be used if you have only two nodes in your cluster. This format provides high-availability and mostly seamless failover (remember TCP sessions are not synchronized, just configuration and IVE sessions). It does not provide load balancing, because one node is passive. You may find ways to address/ access the passive node (it is quite simple in fact; just type in the address) but most users will go to the main node, via DNS resolution. A VIP must be configured to use Active/Passive, and we also recommend using an internal VIP, in case the device is accessed internally as well.

- **Active/Active** This turns off the VIP and requires an upstream load balancer to act as the front-end VIP, providing some form of load balancing to the back-end IVE nodes. This could be round robin, but should employ some method of persistence, preferably source IP persistence (also called "sticky"). Also, if using NC, it too will be load balanced, so you'll want to make sure all of a single user's packets go to the same IVE. Products like the Juniper DX can ensure a L7 VIP and an L4 VIP share the same sticky table, which provides a more seamless load-balancing environment for complex SSL VPN connections.

- **Synchronize Log Messages** This can result in a great increase in data being transmitted and synchronized among all nodes in the cluster. Use sparingly.

- **Synchronize User Sessions** This provides seamless failover in that users do not need to reauthenticate even when they are serviced by a different node (in a failover scenario). It also provides synchronization of user session data, such as newly configured bookmarks, personal settings, and so on.

- **Synchronize Last Access Time** This information can be important, but may add to the overhead of cluster communication. You may want to disable this to streamline the communications channel.

- **Disable External Interface When the Internal Interface Fails** In the case where an internal interface has failed, the system cannot service any new, inbound sessions. But most systems cannot relay this information to an upstream load balancer. So, by disabling the External interface, it will signal the load balancer (via inevitable Health Check failure) to stop sending it new requests, because it cannot do anything with them.

- **Advanced Settings** These settings are primarily for WAN or MAN cluster deployments and should be used under extreme caution or under the guidance of Juniper support. They let you increase acceptable latency and connection timers for cluster communications so delays will not disrupt cluster communications. Another way would be to give cluster protocols priority through your firewalls (assuming you control all the hops between clustered nodes).

- **Delete Cluster** This is how you delete the cluster, such as to start over from scratch or to ready a node for it to join another cluster.

# Virtual Systems

Instant Virtual Systems (IVS) provides an alternative approach to managing multiple organizations' solutions. For example, let's say you are a common IT organization supporting multiple individual business units, each with their own needs and services. If you want to centrally manage them, you can, of course, but you could also empower IT representatives from those BUs to manage their own, using a centralized managed deployment. In this case, granular controls must be assigned so the BU owners can only manage those portions of the configuration that pertain to them. Another scenario is as a service provider, where you want to offer managed remote access/VPN services to your existing hosted customer infrastructures.

IVS is the framework that ensures each subscriber's configuration is separate, for both functionality and privacy reasons. Virtual Systems provides cross-sections of the IVE access management system portioned up to offer completely independent systems running within the same physical gateway device.

# Management

At the top is the Root system. This is the system as a whole, and in the Root system, you can define Virtual Systems. A Virtual System is nothing more than the provisioning of a cross-section of the IVE. You may define certain VLANs or virtual ports to use, and you will be required to create one Admin account for that Virtual System. You may also opt to define min and max user count guarantees to enforce service-level agreements (SLAs). A sign-in URL prefix may also be used for all sign-in URLs in that particular Virtual System to distinguish based on the URL. The initial configuration is also something you'll want to check out. It is for creating new Virtual Systems that use another as a template. This allows you to design a Virtual System service offering, and then resell it, dramatically reducing the overhead you incur due to provisioning and setup.

After the Virtual System has been set up, you'll see that the drop-down menu in the Admin UI toolbar now has another Virtual System you can select and manage. This is how you, as a Super Admin of the system, would manage another Virtual System. Alternatively, you could go to that Virtual System's sign-in URL and log in to /admin using the account credentials you set up when you created it. This is how a Virtual System owner/admin would access and manage his Virtual System, since he would/should not have access to log in to the Root system.

# Logging/Monitoring

Chapter 13 contains more in-depth information about logging and monitoring; however, we'd like to go over a few points here as well. One thing to point out up front is that logging and monitoring go hand in hand. Monitoring can tell you when something isn't working, and logging can tell you why. Without this, you wouldn't have a working system, and might as well not have any system at all during that time. It is important to set up your logging system properly, especially if this solution is to handle sensitive data. You never know when you're going to get an unexpected visit from the auditor.

# Logging

The system logs are broken up into several log files: Event, User, and Admin. Each file has its own settings as to which functions should and should not write logs to disk (see Figure 11.7).

**Figure 11.7** Logging

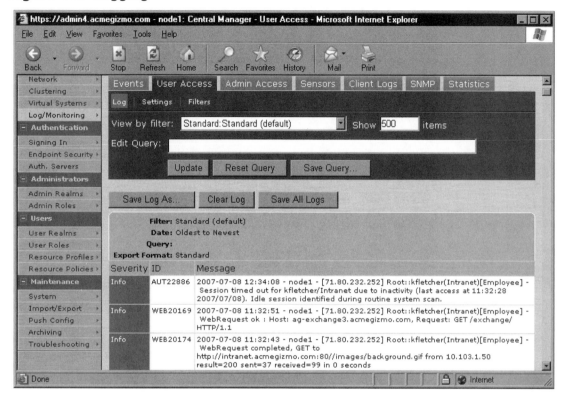

Careful selection here can help reduce the amount of useless log data up-front, before it ever touches a hard disk or tape system. Each log file also has its own SYSLOG options, which are quite flexible. Additionally, you can apply a filter and format to each log file to show only certain data or to format it differently (see Figures 11.8 and 11.9). The filter and format are configured as follows:

- Click the Log\Events submenu.
- Modify or select a new filter.
- Enter a name and then select the date range you'd like to filter out and display.
- Input any query strings to further refine the filter—for example, user = 'bugs'.
- Define an output format, such as the Juniper Standard, W3C, WELF, or a Custom filter with your own delimiters and padding.

**Figure 11.8** Log Filters

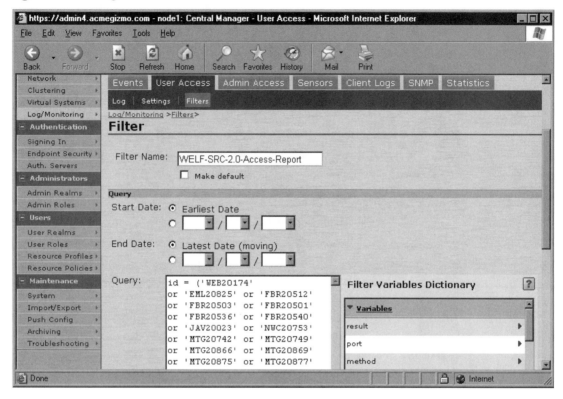

**Figure 11.9** Log Formats

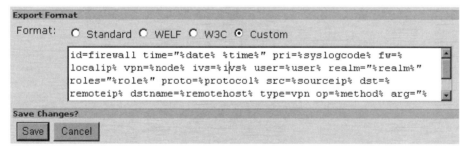

These filters can now be applied to each of the SYSLOG instances. So, for example, you could have W3C formatted data going to server1 while you have all AAA data going to server2 in Standard format.

> **NOTE**
>
> A quick note about disk space and logging. The IVE system has configurable file size limits for the log files. Each log file is then rotated once, as a backup. This means that if you configure the user log to be 200MB, it could take up as much as 400MB after it has been rotated and then filled back up again. Also, the larger the log, the longer it may take to parse through, filter, and display.

## Sensor Logging

If enabled, a Juniper SSL VPN and Juniper IDP sensor may be logically connected to enhance a traditional IDP deployment, by being able to coordinate together to determine which remote access session caused the IDP trigger. Each trigger will yield a notification that shows up in the IVE log. This includes data from the Juniper IDP device, but also includes information about what action may have been taken (based on configured policy). For example, you can see that a user who caused some attack got quarantined immediately. Similar log settings and formats/filters apply here and can be used in conjunction with SYSLOG or to view/save the log data for future use.

## Client Logs

In situations where a client-side agent is not working properly, debugging can be enabled, but the log still resides on that user's PC. With this feature, the Administrator can remotely request that agents upload log data directly to the IVE gateway. This way, they can be consolidated and exported for further analysis, or sent to Juniper support. By enabling the components under the Settings menu, logs will begin showing up in the Client Side Logs framework as soon as logs are generated by end-user agent components. As this happens, there will be a list of available/viewable logs under the Uploaded Logs submenu. From here, they may be downloaded and also deleted afterwards.

## SNMP

Simple Network Management Protocol has been around a while. It plays an important role for the SSL VPN in that it can help alert Administrators to important issues or critical errors the device may endure. For security reasons, no management can take place via SNMP itself; however, simple monitoring may be performed, and some valuable monitoring information may be retrieved and stored by SNMP mining utilities. The two features you can enable/disable are SNMP Queries (to read information) and SNMP Traps (an alerting mechanism to warn Administrators). Basic configuration is also recommended for the SNMP service, to let

SNMP management consoles know what device they are managing, where it is located, and who the contact is.

Additionally, you may configure thresholds for various system resources, such as CPU and Swap Memory. This helps to ensure you are notified when utilization of a resource exceeds that threshold, so you can pay attention to and/or fix something before a catastrophe occurs. You can also configure which severity level log events should be sent as traps, and what SNMP trap servers to communicate with (see Figure 11.10).

**Figure 11.10** SNMP Thresholds

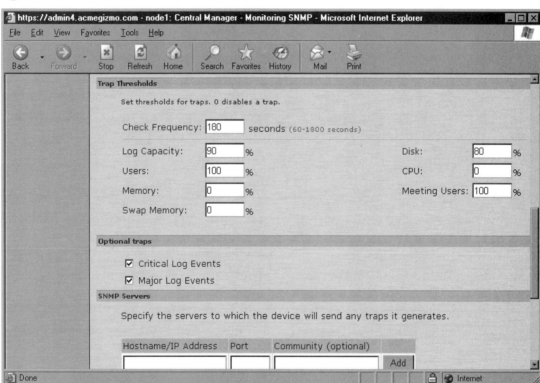

Also note the hyperlink on this page to download the Juniper Networks Private MIB file. This text file can be loaded into any standard SNMP management console, and will map Juniper Private MIB OIDs (Object IDs) into relevant information, such as user counters, cluster information, IVE system information, and OIDs for the SNMP Traps supported.

# Statistics

The Statistics page displays some simple counters of overall system usage (see Figure 11.11). These counters show the last seven days of activity, broken down per hour, per component:

- Concurrent Users

- Peak Email Proxy Sessions

- URL Accesses

- File Accesses

**Figure 11.11** Statistics

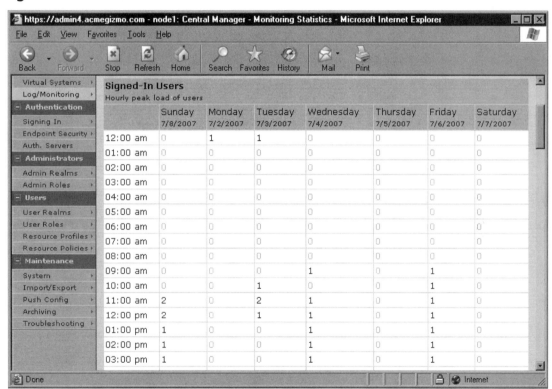

It is rather rudimentary, but could be mined to produce some interested reports, given sufficient data points. In conjunction with the Central Manager Status page, however, you can learn a lot about overall system usage, and more accurately plan future deployments and their capacity needs.

# Summary

As you have seen in this chapter, you can impose many options and controls when deploying an SSL VPN solution. This can include advanced features such as VLANs and Client Certificates, and it can also be deployed to provide managed services using the Instant Virtual Systems framework. Since the SSL VPN is largely a gateway device, it has the liberty of auditing everything that occurs on and through its communications channels. These audit logs are very detailed and can provide the assurance a business demands, especially if an IT audit is about to be conducted. We've also seen how IDP sensors can be spruced up to provide actual usernames instead of just IPs. This functionality is part of Juniper's Coordinated Threat Control solution and makes a great asset to any remote access SSL VPN deployment.

# Solutions Fast Track

## Status

☑ Basic node monitoring, including clustered nodes, uptime, and version information.

☑ Central Manager (part of the Advanced license) provides Graphs and historical XML data.

☑ Active Users can be used to see who's on, what their NC IP is (if applicable), and if they've set off any IDP triggers (if applicable).

## Configuration

☑ System licensing occurs here. Administrators should add licenses to the main cluster node, for user concurrency and to enable features—and also add CL licenses to other nodes which will then join and inherit all the licensed features.

☑ Certificates for Devices and Client Authentication can be configured here. CRL and OCSP are supported, and Root CA certs can be imported for back-end HTTPS trust relationships.

☑ Client types can be configured to provide mobile users with a smaller form-factor IVE display.

## Network

☑ Port Management should be fairly straightforward, with the exception of VLANs, which require some additional configuration both on the device and on the switched environment.

☑ Static Hosts and Static Routes can be managed here, both to increase the availability of the solution, as well as enhance the security by avoiding DNS or ARP poisoning

# Clustering

☑ After creating a cluster, you must add each node's information. Then, nodes can join the cluster.

☑ Active/Passive Clusters utilize a shared, floating VIP, whereas Active/Active Clusters utilize an upstream load balancer to distribute user sessions. Active/Passive can only be enabled in clusters of two nodes.

☑ Many clustering diagnostics and tuning options are available, including Synch Rank and timers. Use them with great caution though. If you have questions, seek expert guidance from the Juniper support team.

# Virtual Systems

☑ Virtual Systems create independent IVE partitions, running concurrently on the same device.

☑ These are usually bound to a VLAN or set of VLANs for logical L2 separation (and security).

☑ Virtual Systems can be managed by the Root Admin (of the entire box) or by individual subscriber admin accounts.

# Logging/Monitoring

☑ Logging is broken up into three separate files: Event, User, Admin.

☑ Each log function has its own settings for what to actually log.

☑ Each log file can use its own filters, formats, and SYSLOG settings.

☑ SNMP is available in an RO mode, using a public string. A private Enterprise MIB is also available for download here.

☑ Statistics track weekly concurrent user usage, based on IVE function.

# Frequently Asked Questions

**Q:** What is WAN clustering?

**A:** WAN clustering implies that at least one of the nodes is in a disparate or separate IP subnet, whether it's in the lab next door, or across the world in some other subsidiary. As long as centralized management is required, you can use clustering, regardless of IP space.

**Q:** How do I download graph data from Central Manager?

**A:** Click the Download link on the page. You'll get XML data, which is a little hard to follow, but can easily be parsed to provide additional reporting.

**Q:** Can I log to multiple SYSLOG servers?

**A:** Yes. In fact, you can even provide data using different filters, and in different formats, to the same or different SYSLOG server/facility.

**Q:** Can I "SET" in SNMP?

**A:** SET is disabled, for security reasons. All management is done via the Admin UI or the Serial Console.

**Q:** Can I connect multiple IDP sensors to an IVE?

**A:** Yes, but each IDP can only communicate with a single IVE or cluster.

# Chapter 12

# Sign-in Policies

## Solutions in this chapter:

- **IVE Sign-in Structure**
- **Sign-in Pages**
- **Sign-in Policies**

☑ **Summary**

☑ **Solutions Fast Track**

☑ **Frequently Asked Questions**

# Introduction

Sign-in policies are essentially the first actions applied when users connect to the IVE. When a user attempts to connect to the IVE, the IVE will use sign-in policies to determine which sign-in page the user should be mapped to and the realms that will be available to choose from (if there are multiple realms configured for that policy). Despite the fact that sign-in policies play such an important role in the function of the IVE, they are overlooked, since they don't usually require much maintenance.

Sign-in pages go hand in hand with sign-in policies and offer extensible options for customizing the user experience when they access the IVE. The IVE allows you to utilize predefined templates for creating sign-in pages, or you can create your own templates, which can be used to manipulate the IVE access capabilities.

In this chapter, we discuss how sign-in policies function, the components of sign-in policies, as well as how to create them. We also discuss how to create standard and custom sign-in pages for both user/administrator access and Secure Meeting pages.

# IVE Sign-in Structure

A logical flow chart can be put together when describing the IVE sign-in structure. As shown in Figure 12.1, a user begins by entering a URL that is hosted by the IVE, such as https://vpn.mycompany.com/sales/. The IVE decodes the encrypted SSL packet and gathers the site information. Based on the site that the user is trying to browse to, the IVE then evaluates the sign-in policies to determine which one matches the user's request. Each policy defines the site the user is trying to access, the sign-in page for that site, the available realms that apply to that policy/page, and, lastly, how the realms are chosen on the page.

When the IVE sign-in page comes up, the user will see the sign-in page itself, along with the appropriate realms that are available to login with. Note that before the user can enter credentials, preauthentication restrictions applied at the realm level may be enforced (such as Host Checker and Cache Cleaner). These steps are going to be our primary focus in this chapter.

**Figure 12.1** Session Access Process

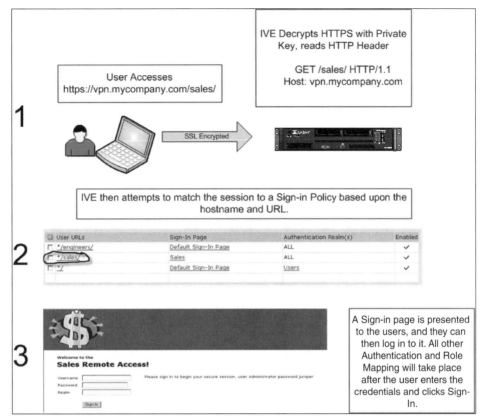

# IVE Licensing

IVE licenses have an impact on some of the features that are available on your IVE relating to sign-in policies. If you only have the baseline license, then you will not be able to create multiple sign-in policies for login (you can only create one Admin, User, and Meeting policy, if applicable. Additionally, you need the Secure Meeting license in order to create Secure Meeting pages. The advanced license will allow you to create multiple sign-in policies in addition to several other desirable features on the IVE.

# Sign-in Pages

A sign-in page is an actual Web page that a user or administrator is greeted with when they access the IVE. Depending on the type of licensing that you have (baseline or advanced), you can create multiple sign-in URLs and therefore you may want to create different sign-in pages for the different URLs to enhance the user experience. As mentioned previously, there are two types of sign-in pages—the standard predefined pages and custom sign-in pages. Standard pages come preloaded with all versions of the IVE, whereas custom pages are created by either creating your own page with an HTML/Text editor or modifying an existing Custom Template. The IVE maps the sign-in page to the appropriate URL based on sign-in policies, which are discussed in-depth later in this chapter.

# Standard Sign-in Pages

Most administrators will find that standard sign-in pages will suit their needs with regard to the sign-in page the user is greeted with. Although standard sign-in pages come preloaded, they do offer you a wealth of customizable options, which allow you to put your own look and feel to the page. This is particularly useful for adding corporate logos, color schemes, and altering the text that is displayed to the users. Making a sign-in page look familiar in terms of logos and color schemes can serve to help orientate the user with your IVE.

The ability to customize the standard sign-in page makes your job much easier, especially if you don't have Web development experience (or time) to create your own custom sign-in pages. The following is a list of the different options for creating standard sign-in pages (Figure 12.2):

- **Name** Every sign-in page must have a defined name that will be referenced elsewhere in the configuration. The name must be unique and should have some useful significance.

- **Page type** A sign-in page can be one of two types: user/administrator or meeting (if you have the Secure Meeting license).

- **Welcome message** The IVE allows you to define a small string of text below the logo but above the portal name in this field. By default, this is "Welcome to the."

- **Portal name** You can define a name for your portal that the users will see, for example "Sales Portal." By default, this is "Secure Access SSL VPN."

- **Submit button** The submit button will cause the IVE to attempt to authenticate the user to the IVE with the credentials entered. You can customize the text of this button by changing the value in this field. By default, it is "Sign in."

- **Instructions** You can provide custom instructions that will be posted on the sign-in page. This is very useful particularly to tell the users how to log on, including which realm to choose. The default message is "Please sign in to begin your secure session."

- **Username** You can provide custom labels for the username.

- **Password** You can provide custom labels for the password.

- **Realm** If you want to refer to the realm label as a different name on the sign-in page, you can define it here.

- **Secondary username**  If you specify a second authentication server, then you can specify alternative labels for the secondary username. This is helpful for informing the user about which credentials should be used to log into the IVE.

- **Secondary password**  Just as you specified the secondary username, you can also define a secondary password. This component allows you to change the label for the secondary password.

- **Prompt for secondary credentials on the second page**  This is an option when you have two authentication servers. It will cause them to authenticate on a separate page after the primary authentication. This is useful for staging the authentication process to make sure that the user passes the primary authentication mechanism before he or she is prompted with the second.

- **Sign-out message**  You can specify the message that will be displayed when the user logs out. By default, this message is "Your session has ended."

- **Sign-in link text**  When the user is logged out for one reason or another, there will be a link that will bring the user back to his or her sign-in page. The text of this link can be modified to state what you would like. The default text is "Click here to sign in again."

- **Logo image**  The logo image is displayed at the header of the IVE sign-in page. By default, this will be a Juniper logo, but you can upload your own logo image as well. You can view the currently applied logo in the Admin page by looking at the **Current Appearance** image when you create or edit a sign-in page. Juniper recommends that the image you provide not be taller than 40 pixels, with a maximum file size of 10 KB. You can use a photo editing application to resize and improve the file compression. You can upload a local image through the IVE admin interface.

- **Background color**  You can change the background color of the sign-in header with this option. You can either define this with the six-digit hex RGB color scheme or you can click the color wheel to visually identify the color you would like to select and the IVE will fill in the six-digit hex RGB color in the field.

- **Missing certificates**  If you use certificate-based authentication, then you can provide an error message if the user does not have a certificate to present to the IVE. The default text of this message is "Missing certificate. Check that your certificate is valid and up-to-date, and try again."

- **Invalid certificate**  If you are using certificate-based authentication and the user presents a certificate that is expired, not signed by a trusted client CA, invalid, or has been revoked, then you can provide a custom error message. By default, this message is "Invalid or expired certificate. Check that your certificate is valid and up-to-date, and try again."

- **Show Help button**  You have an option to provide users with a help interface when they attempt to log in to the IVE. If you want to give them a help button, then you can enable this option.

- **Help button** This is the text that will be displayed as the label for the help button. The default is "Help."

- **HTML file** The IVE help interface is an HTML page that you create and upload to the IVE. This field allows you to browse for the HTML file on your machine and upload it. You cannot include external images in this file because they will not be displayed.

**Figure 12.2** User Standard Sign-in Page Layout

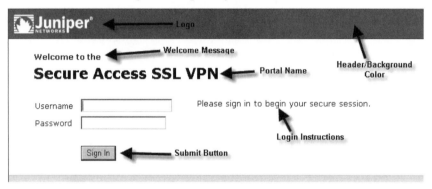

Figure 12.3 shows a screenshot of what an Administrator page looks like. Even though you may use the same page for both User and Administrator Login, the IVE will automatically put in the appropriate text message for the Admin page. The IVE knows when to put this message in based on the type of sign-in policy (using the standard pages versus creating your own custom page).

**Figure 12.3** Administrator Sign-in Page

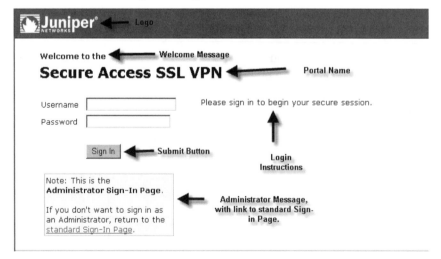

# Secure Meeting Sign-in Pages

If you have a Secure Meeting license for your IVE, then you may wish to either modify the existing Secure Meeting page or create new ones. Just like the standard sign-in pages, there are many parts of the Secure Meeting page that you can customize without having to create a custom Secure Meeting sign-in page outright. In this section, we review the different fields that you can modify as part of a Secure Meeting page:

- **Name** You must define a name for the Secure Meeting sign-in page that will be referenced elsewhere in the IVE configuration.

- **Page type** If you are creating a Secure Meeting sign-in page, then you must select the page type as **Meeting**.

- **Welcome message** Just as you did for standard sign-in pages, you can define a welcome message. The default is "Welcome to the."

- **Portal name** You can define a portal name for your IVE that will be displayed below the welcome message text so that it is contiguous with the welcome message. The default is "Secure Access SSL VPN."

- **Submit button** The submit button will cause the IVE to attempt to authenticate the Meeting user to the IVE with the credentials and Meeting ID entered. You can customize the text of this button by changing the value in this field. By default, it is "Sign in."

- **Instructions** You can provide custom instructions for users right on the IVE Secure Meeting sign-in page. Being able to provide custom instructions spares you the effort of having to create custom instructions with a custom Meeting page.

- **Meeting ID** The Meeting ID is the eight-digit number that uniquely defines a meeting. The user must either enter this manually or click on a hyperlink that will bring the user to the appropriate meeting page. This field allows you to customize the label text that is shown on the Secure Meeting sign-in page.

- **Username** Each Secure Meeting user must have a unique username. This value allows you to change the label text next to this field on the Secure Meeting sign-in page.

- **Meeting password** This is the label text used to specify what you should enter into the Meeting password field.

- **Logo image** The logo image is displayed at the header of the IVE Secure Meeting sign-in page. By default, this will be a Juniper logo, but you can upload your own logo image as well. You can view the currently applied logo in the Admin page by looking at the **Current Appearance** image when you create or edit a sign-in page. Juniper recommends that the image you provide not be taller than 40 pixels, with a maximum file size of 10 KB. You can use a photo editing application to resize and improve the file compression. You can upload a local image through the IVE Admin interface.

- **Background color** You can change the background color of the sign-in header with this option. You can either define this with the six-digit hex RGB color scheme or click the color wheel to visually identify the color you would like to select and the IVE will fill in the six-digit hex RGB color in the field.

The following are two images of standard Secure Meeting pages. The first is from IVE 6.0 (Figure 12.4), whereas the second is from IVE 5.5 (Figure 12.5). The Pre-6.0 pages had a slightly different appearance from the 6.0 versions. Also, there is a message built into the Meeting pages instructing meeting conductors to log in through the "Standard Sign-in Page." This is because only meeting attendees can log in through the Secure Meeting page; all conductors must be users that log in through the IVE to start the meeting.

**Figure 12.4** IVE 6.0 Standard Secure Meeting Sign-in Page

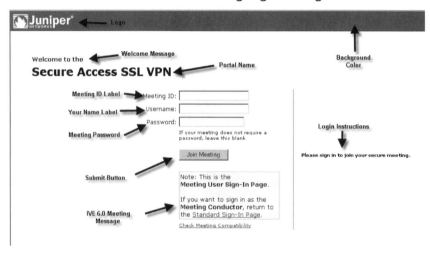

**Figure 12.5** IVE 5.5 Standard Secure Meeting Sign-in Page

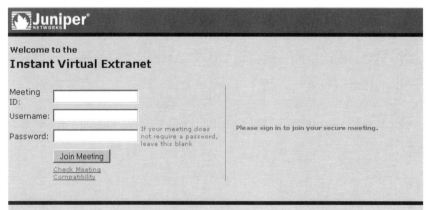

# Configuring a Standard Sign-in Page

In this example, we create a standard sign-in page that will be used by the IVE to present a graphical interface that users will log into on IVE.

1.  To create a standard sign-in page, begin by going to **Authentication | Signing In | Sign-in Pages** and click **New Page**.

2.  You must define a **Name** for your sign-in page that you will reference in sign-in policies.

3.  Next, you must define if this is a **User/Administrator** sign-in page or secure **Meeting** sign-in page (if you have the license).

4.  There are several options for customizing the text in the sign-in page. This includes everything from custom messages to labels and even the text for the buttons (such as the Submit button).

5.  Additionally, you can upload custom logos that help the users identify the site with a familiar organization image. The IVE also supports the uploading of custom HTML files that serve to present the user with help instructions for logging into the IVE.

6.  After you are finished defining the sign-in page, click **Save Changes** to apply the changes to the page.

Secure Meeting pages are almost identical to the standard sign-in pages with regard to creating them. In step 3, you would simply select **Meeting**. Although a few of the optional fields change the name (for example from Password to Meeting Password), this should not be unfamiliar.

**TIP**

If you find that you have made too many changes and want to make a sign-in page revert to the default, go into that sign-in page and click **Restore Factory Defaults**.

# Custom Sign-in Pages

For those organizations with the need to customize the IVE sign-in pages beyond what the standard sign-in page options offer, the IVE provides the ability to create custom sign-in pages. Because the IVE must support properties that can be entered dynamically into a sign-in page based on configuration (such as placing realms into a sign-in page based on the sign-in policy), you actually create custom sign-in pages as templates rather than static HTML pages. For those of you who are familiar with creating HTML Web pages, THTML is very similar and utilizes HTML with some customizable template functions that the IVE will dynamically construct when creating the sign-in page presented to the user. This flexibility provides a framework for you to deliver very robust Web services for your external SSL VPN portal; for example, you could upload the following:

- Splash page or other banner/welcome message

- Maps/locations of offices, very suitable if you're using GSLB

- Labels and content using a different language or using images

- Custom JavaScript or VBScript to provide warnings and alerts or even force users to acknowledge an acceptable usage agreement

In this section, our goal is to provide a high-level overview of what custom sign-in pages are and how they are created. Since custom sign-in pages are a topic worthy of its own book, we do not intend to cover every aspect of custom sign-in pages at length but, rather, give you the tools you will need to create simple pages, and we point you in the right direction for more advanced configurations. We also discuss some of the main caveats with creating custom sign-in pages and IVE functionality.

---

**W**ARNING

We highly recommend that only experienced Web developers or those with experience using template HTML develop custom sign-in pages. The custom sign-in page capability was meant to be more extensive and flexible than simple to implement and maintain. Although most administrators will find that the standard sign-in pages with the customizable options will satisfy their needs, if you require more advanced functionality, we highly suggest that you thoroughly review the custom sign-in page guide, along with testing your custom pages on lab IVEs.

Since custom pages are not developed by Juniper, Juniper may not support them or certain problems associated with custom sign-in pages. You should take this into account before deciding to use custom sign-in pages. If you must use the custom sign-in pages, we highly recommend that you test the pages on a lab system before you upgrade the production system to that version. Sometime Juniper makes changes to the directives that are supported in the THTML, so you will want to test this out before upgrading to a newer version of the IVE.

---

## Sample Custom Sign-in Pages

Juniper offers a few different custom sign-in page template collections that you can download from the IVE. There are four different template examples that you can download from the IVE. These are located under **Authentication | Signing In | Sign-in Pages** and then click **Upload Custom Pages** and they will be listed on the right-hand side. Simply click the link for the template you wish to download to retrieve the collection as a Zip file. The following template collections are available as samples:

- **Sample** This is a basic template of the standard pages that you can customize to fit your needs. It is essentially the template collection that the IVE uses for its standard sign-in pages. It is recommended that in most cases you start with this collection since it contains all of the pages in the standard format for you to work with.

- **SoftID** This template collection is a set of templates based on the RSA ACE token authentication mechanisms. It provides a good place to start for creating your own sign-in pages for RSA ACE authentication.

- **Kiosk** Designed and productized by one of the Technical Marketing Gurus, this sample contains a login page that has a keyboard on the sign-in page. This allows you to not have to enter a password through the hardware keyboard (thus thwarting hardware keyloggers and other software keyloggers that monitor keystrokes). You can even make it jump around the page to further thwart mouse-stroke capture utilities.

- **Meeting Pages** This template contains custom sign-in page templates for Secure Meeting.

Figure 12.6 provides a screenshot of the Kiosk custom sign-in page, which you can download and modify to suite your needs. It includes the onscreen keyboard so that you can bypass having to use a physical keyboard, which is susceptible to both hardware and software keylogging.

**Figure 12.6** Kiosk Custom Sign-in Page Example

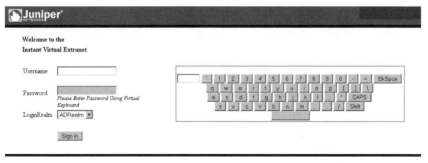

### Defense against Keylogging

Security administrators have been increasingly burdened with having to provide secure access for their remote users to access internal network resources. Often, remote users are not connecting through corporate-controlled machines, so administrators have little control over the state of the machine that is logging into the IVE. Malicious hackers have long since taken advantage of viruses, spyware, and malware to infect and capture confidential information on users machines. One popular technique is to log keystrokes in an effort to capture passwords. There are several technologies that can help mitigate this threat, including RSA SecurID, hardware/software tokens, and even features built into the IVE such as the Kiosk custom sign-in page. Although these technologies don't completely erase such threats, they do provide some power tools to lessen their effectiveness.

Remember, layered security is often the best approach to secure computing. The IVE provides you with features that can help extend your reach when it comes to security, such as Host Checker, Cache Cleaner, Secure Virtual Workspace, and Advanced Endpoint Detection from WholeSecurity. For instance, you can use Host Checker to ensure that antivirus signatures are up to date even on a machine that is not under your corporate control (if the user does not comply with your policy, you can prevent the user from logging into the IVE or from accessing certain roles). You can use these components in conjunction with other technologies, such as antivirus, antispyware, firewalls, and multifactor authentication, to help provide holistic security to your organization and your users.

# Why Does the IVE Use Templates for Custom Sign-in Pages?

A common question that many ask about the IVE custom sign-in pages is: "Why does the IVE use templates for custom sign-in pages rather than straight HTML?" The answer to this question is a bit complex, but we'll shorten it to the following: The IVE uses templates because standard HTML does not give the flexibility to pass information to and from the IVE and dynamically generate pages based on the responses to IVE events (such as IVE sign-in failure). Remember that some of the features that the custom pages must support cannot be hard-coded into the pages but, rather, are created within the pages based on the IVE configuration (for example, which realms are available within custom sign-in pages is based on sign-in policies). Additionally, templates provide for much more flexibility with regard to coding one page, which can vary drastically in appearance based on IVE events (for example, you can write one sign-in page but, based on whether the user passes or fails a client certificate validation check, you can have a drastically different interface).

Essentially, the IVE takes these custom template files and dynamically builds the pages into standard HTML when the user goes to access them based on factors discussed reviously. By utilizing these flexible components, the IVE can provide advanced customization to the user interface while still providing the same functionality that users and administrators expect of the IVE.

# Introduction to Template Toolkit

We've already explained the purpose of using THTML for creating custom sign-in pages, so now we mention a word about using Template Toolkit. Template Toolkit is essentially a processing tool for creating template files across different standards. In our case, we are using Template Toolkit functionality to make template files for the IVE to process and fill in the blanks with content from the IVE as appropriate. After the IVE has processed the THTML files, they essentially end up as HTML for the most part. In fact, the THTML files that you will edit are composed of almost all HTML with the exception of the template code, and other scripting functionality. For more information on Template Toolkit, see www.template-toolkit.org, which not only has the software but also has a wealth of information for creating the templates. Note that the IVE only supports a subset of the template directives, but the Template Toolkit site will still prove very useful for understanding how the templates work. Figure 12.7 provides a screenshot of a THTML snippet from the Sample.zip template toolkit. As you can see, there is logic built into the page based on variables such as LoginPageErrorMessage that can be used to generate the sign-in page based on other factors.

**Figure 12.7** THTML Sample Code

```
</head>

<body onload="FinishLoad(<% setcookies %>)" bgcolor="#FFFFFF" color="#000000" link="#3366CC" vlink="#CC6699"
alink="#3366CC" leftmargin="0" topmargin="0" rightmargin="0" marginwidth="0" marginheight="0">

<table border="0" width="100%" cellspacing="0" cellpadding="3">
    <tr>
        <td bgcolor="<% color %>"><img border="0" src="welcome.cgi?p=logo&signinId=<%signinId%>" alt="Logo"></td>
         <TD bgcolor="<% color %>" align="right"> </TD>

    </tr>
</table>
<table cellpadding="0" cellspacing="0" border="0" width="100%">
    <tr>
            <td bgcolor="#000000" colspan="2"><img border="0" src="<% Home %>/imgs/space.gif" width="1" height="1"></td>
    </tr>
</table>
<blockquote><form name="frmLogin" action=login.cgi method="POST" autocomplete=off onsubmit="return Login(<% setcookies %>)">
        <input type="hidden" name="tz_offset">
        <table border="0" cellpadding="2" cellspacing="0">
            <tr>
                    <td nowrap colspan="3"><b><% welcome FILTER verbatim %></b></td>
            </tr>
            <tr>
                    <td nowrap colspan="3"><span class="cssLarge"><b><% portal FILTER verbatim %></b></span></td></tr>

            <tr>
                    <td colspan="3"> </td>
            </tr>
            <% IF LoginPageErrorMessage %>
                    <tr>
                    <td colspan=3>
                        <table cellpadding=1 bgcolor=#cccc99><tr><td>
                            <table cellpadding=2 bgcolor=#FFFFCC><tr><td>
                            <% LoginPageErrorMessage %>
                            </td></tr></table>
                    </td></tr></table>
                </td>
                </tr>
            <% END %>|
```

# Resources for Custom Sign-in Pages

Since we couldn't possibly hope to fit a complete reference of custom sign-in pages in this chapter, we definitely want to mention some excellent resources for building custom sign-in pages. First, building custom sign-in pages is not meant for those without HTML experience (preferably, you should have lots of HTML or programming experience). Depending on what you want to do, it may be as simple as changing some text in a sample THTML file or as complex as completely rewriting a whole collection of templates. Next, it is definitely helpful to familiarize yourself with the Template Toolkit library mentioned in the previous section. Of course, Juniper also has provided some sample custom pages, mentioned previously, that serve as an excellent starting point for reviewing the raw templates. We highly recommend that you read the *Custom Sign-in Pages Solution Guide*, which is available to registered Juniper support users with active IVE contracts. This guide essentially lays out just about everything that you will need to know about custom sign-in pages, the template directives supported, and all sorts of other related information. Lastly, we highly recommend that when you are developing custom pages, you do so with a lab IVE. This allows you to not interfere with any production environment while you test your new pages. Alternatively, you can also create a separate sign-in URL just for custom sign-in pages that will segment the test URL from your production users.

As mentioned previously, the *Custom Sign-in Pages* document is essentially the official custom sign-in page resource for those wanting to develop custom sign-in pages. This document contains not only the basic instructions for creating custom sign-in pages but also information about the different components of custom sign-in pages. The following is a list of topics discussed in the *Custom Sign-in Pages* document:

- **Template pages** The IVE uses various template pages for everything from the login page to the sign-out page. At the very least, there will be required template pages that are needed for any custom sign-in page template collection to work on the IVE. In many cases, you will need to provide more than the basic subset in order to obtain your desired functionality. The *Custom Sign-in Pages* document describes the functionality of each sign-in page as well as its purpose within the template collection. Some of this information is also contained within the template pages themselves if you look in the Sample.zip template collection. You can download all of the templates in the Sample.zip collection available in the IVE. Open them with Notepad to see what they are all about. It is actually pretty straightforward to code in—think of it like another kind of JavaScript.

- **Template functions** There are several functions that perform different tasks within the IVE custom sign-in pages. These vary from redirecting the user to another page to performing logic within the page. There are many different functions that the IVE uses within different custom pages, so you will want to look through the *Custom Sign-in Pages* guide for a list of these functions, their syntax, as well as examples to help solidify your understanding. Note that these functions are different from the Template Toolkit functions for generating the HTML within the pages.

■ **Template scripts and CGI** There are a handful of scripts that the IVE uses within the templates as well as some Common Gateway Interface (CGI) that is used by the IVE to process user input. The scripts and backend CGI functionality is explained throughout the *Custom Sign-in Pages* guide.

■ **Template variables** The IVE relies heavily on template variables for passing logic between the IVE core system and the custom sign-in pages. These variables range from what type of browser the user is attempting to sign-in with to the result of user authentication to the IVE. There is an extensive list in the *Custom Sign-in Pages* document that should be consulted for capabilities that you can or must use within your pages. A list of required/possible variables should be at the top of each .thtml page.

■ **Error and result codes** Lastly, the *Custom Sign-in Pages* document contains a list of all of the error and result codes that the IVE may return during various tasks, such as authenticating a user or determining if the certificate the user is presenting is valid. Often, these are four-digit error codes and they can be used within Template Toolkit logic to determine what HTML should be displayed within a custom page. Also note that many result variables contain generic error messages. To display custom error message or alternate text strings, simply build a THTML conditional (if) statement to test the login error message's value and if it is what you expect, display some alternative HTML/text instead of displaying the variable.

## Tools & Traps...

### Before You Upgrade

When using custom sign-in pages, you must make some changes to your custom sign-in pages before you upgrade, or else you may create login errors or have users presented with the incorrect login pages. In particular, there are three points that Juniper recommends that you consider before upgrading:

■ The version number in your template must be updated before you upgrade your IVE. Since new variables, functions, and pages may be required in new versions of the IVE, or old variables, functions, and pages may be deprecated, you

Continued

must make sure that your sign-in page has the required currently supported template components. The best way to do this is to update your custom sign-in pages on a lab system first before moving to production to ensure that you do not have any problems. To ensure that you have all of the supported components for the version of code to which you are upgrading, you can also download the Sample.zip template and modify those template files to contain the code that you were using in the old version. This is recommended because you will have less of a chance of leaving out any required variables, functions, pages, and so on that may have changed in the new version. Also, do not skip the validation check, since it helps to ensure that you do not have any issues with your pages when you upgrade.

- You should always review the Juniper release notes before upgrading to a new version of the IVE OS. As Juniper continues to enhance the features of the IVE, new variables and directives may be added or removed from the supported list. You will run into problems particularly when a variable that you are using has been removed after the upgrade. By default, Juniper will check for changes that will impact your sign-in page during upgrade, but this option can be disabled when you upload the custom sign-in page.

- Occasionally, Juniper makes major changes to the user interface between IVE OS versions (such as between IVE 4.2 and 5.0), so you will want to make sure that these changes are acceptable and provide your users with a notification that the interface will be changing.

The best way to ensure that upgrades do not cause issues with your IVE sign-in pages (or virtually any other feature of the IVE) is to set up a test IVE box and perform a lab upgrade. This will allow you to test your IVE without the risk of adversely affecting production systems.

## Uploading a Custom Page

In this example, we show you how to upload a custom sign-in page for either User/Administrator sign-in or Secure Meeting sign-in.

1. To upload a sign-in page that you have stored locally on your machine, begin by browsing to **Authentication | Signing In | Sign-in Pages** and click **Upload Custom Pages**.

2. In the Upload Custom Pages screen, there are a few properties of the page that you must fill out. The first is the **Name** of the sign-in page that will be referenced elsewhere in the IVE configuration.

3. Next, you must define the **Page Type** that you are uploading. This will either be Access (for Users and Administrators) or Meeting.

4. Click the **Browse** button to locate the Zip file containing the custom template files that you created.

5. Normally, the IVE will perform validation checks to ensure that the uploaded pages do not contain any errors that will cause problems for the IVE. If you wish to bypass this validation check, then select the **Skip Validation Checks During Upload**.

6. Lastly, click **Save Changes** to upload the file and incorporate it into the configuration.

---

**W**ARNING

In more recent versions of the IVE (such as IVE 5.4+,) if you upgrade your IVE without upgrading your custom sign-in pages, the IVE will inform you that you should upgrade your custom sign-in pages to the newest version since the version that you are using may be outdated. This is to help ensure that you do not have issues with the custom sign-in pages after you upgrade (for example, new pages may be required in the template because Juniper created new features that require these pages). The IVE may revert back to the standard sign-in page if problems are detected with the custom sign-in page, so make sure that you upgrade your pages when upgrading the IVE. Although there are various ways to upgrade your pages, many believe that the most reliable way is to download the new Sample.zip template collection from the new version of the Juniper IVE and then make the changes in the files to accommodate your needs. Lastly, upload these pages to a lab IVE or a separate sign-in URL so that you can test before applying them to your production IVE/sign-in URLs.

---

# Sign-in Policies

The Juniper IVE utilizes sign-in policies to control how a user is directed to a particular sign-in page when the user attempts to access the IVE. Sign-in policies allow IVE administrators to offer different URLs and portal login pages to the users. This can be particularly helpful when you want to host different login pages on different URLs or even on completely different host names. Sign-in policies essentially offer a layer of abstraction so that you can have the IVE host more than one portal page for the users to log into.

In this section, we focus on how IVE sign-in policies work in conjunction with the IVE sign-in process, as well as how to configure them in some common scenarios. We also discuss how IVE licensing and policy order play an important role in what capabilities you can utilize and how to enhance the behavior of your IVE sign-in process.

# IVE Licensing

Licensing plays an important role with regard to the capabilities that you can utilize with sign-in policies. It should first be mentioned that when you only have the baseline license, you cannot have multiple sign-in policies per access type. This means that you can only have one Admin sign-in policy (defaults to */admin), one user sign-in policy (defaults to */), and one Secure Meeting sign-in policy (if you have Secure Meeting, it defaults to */meeting). Although you can change these URLs, you cannot have multiple per user types. The advanced license is just the opposite and allows you to have multiple URLs for the different sign-in types. In order to configure a Secure Meeting sign-in policy, you must have a Secure Meeting license. Since the SA-700 doesn't support the advance license, you cannot have multiple sign-in policies on that box.

# Sign-in Policy Types and Properties

The IVE has three different sign-in policy types that you can configure: Administrator, User, and Meeting. Of course, you can only configure the latter if you have the Secure Meeting license. The IVE views each sign-in policy type differently; for instance, you cannot configure a sign-in policy that is an administrator policy for users and vice versa. Essentially, sign-in policies of the same type are grouped together in an ordered list evaluated from top to bottom. Before we discuss how each sign-in policy is evaluated, let's take a look at the components that can make up sign-in policies:

- **Sign-in URL** This component defines what URL maps to which sign-in page and the appropriate realms for that page. This field allows you to define the URL in the following format: <hostname>/path. Note that * is an accepted wildcard character when defining sign-in URLs. It essentially acts as a wildcard until a "." is met in the host name. Wildcards cannot be used in the URL path. So, for instance, if your domain name system (DNS) host name for your IVE was somecompany.com, and you wanted users to login on that base URL, you could define the sign-in URL as either somecompany.com/ or */. If you wanted your engineer users to log into a different page, for example, the /engineers page, your sign-in URL could be somecompany.com/engineers or */engineers. So now you might be wondering, why would you want to ever define the host name when you could simply place an asterisk in its place to save the effort of typing out the host name? The answer is because the IVE allows you to host multiple host names on the same IVE interface or virtual port. For instance, let's say your company owns somecompany.com and somecompany.net and both of these map to the IVE in DNS. You could define them with their unique host names if you wanted the IVE to map them to different pages, or if you wanted the IVE to map them to the same page regardless of which one you choose, then you could say */, which would not pay any attention to the host name and just map them to the base URL. We discuss this later in this section.

- **Sign-in page**  Earlier in this chapter, we discussed how to create sign-in pages. The sign-in policy defines which sign-in page a user will be given when he or she attempts to access a specific URL. Let's say you want to offer different sign-in pages for your sales and marketing teams; you could tell your sales team to log into https://somecompany.com/sales and your marketing team to log into https://somecompany.com/marketing. You would create two different sign-in policies—one mapping users who access the sales URL to the sign-in page you created for the sales team and the other mapping the users who access the marketing URL to the sign-in page you created for the marketing team. The sign-in page component of a sign-in policy is the field that distinguishes which sign-in page is mapped to this policy.

- **Meeting URL**  If you have a Secure Meeting license, you can define the Meeting URL for the users who login with this sign-in policy (assuming they have the permission to create and use Secure Meeting). Note that you must define the Meeting URL they will use before you create this sign-in policy.

- **Authentication realm**  For User and Administrator sign-in policies, you must define the authentication realm(s) that will be used in the login page. You can either force the user to type the realm in (more security but more difficult to use) or have the user choose from a list of realms that you provide. In the latter case, if you define multiple realms to be available for the login page, then the user must choose the appropriate realm from a drop-down menu (in a standard sign-in page); if you only have a single realm, then the user will not be prompted for which one to select.

## Components Available to Different Policy Types

Not all of the components listed in the previous section can be applied to each of the different sign-in policy types (user, administrator, and meeting). We list here the components that are available to each policy type:

- **User**  This sign-in policy type supports sign-in URL, sign-in page, Meeting URL, and authentication realm.

- **Administrator**  The Administrator sign-in policy supports the sign-in URL, sign-in page, and authentication realm components.

- **Meeting**  The Meeting sign-in policy only supports sign-in URL and sign-in page (which you are choosing what Meeting page will be displayed for this URL).

# Sign-in Policy Evaluation

To prevent overlaps in sign-in policies, the IVE forces you to define the sign-in policy type when you are creating a sign-in policy. The IVE then groups the different sign-in policies together (Administrator, User, and Meeting). When a user connects to the IVE, it sends the host and path in the HTTP header (which is determined after the IVE decrypts the SSL packets). The IVE then uses this information to match the session to the appropriate sign-in policy. It will always start by determining if the URL matches an Administrator policy first, then a User policy, and lastly a Meeting policy. The user request must make an exact match to the sign-in URL path, although if wildcards are used for the host name field, then the wildcards can match any characters to the "." delimiter. Once a match is made, the IVE stops evaluating the sign-in policies and presents the user with the appropriate page.

---

**NOTE**

You cannot define identical sign-in URLs for the same or different sign-in policy types. For instance, if you have a Administrator policy for which the sign-in URL is */superadmins, you cannot create a User policy called */superadmins.

---

## Sign-in Policy Order

The previous section explained how sign-in policies are grouped together by their type (Administrator, User, and Meeting); now we discuss how order and matching come into play when determining the appropriate sign-in policy to match the user request.

When an HTTPS session is established to the IVE, one of the first tasks that must be completed is to determine which sign-in policy maps to the request. As mentioned previously, the HTTPS request contains both the host and the URL path in the HTTP header. This information is used to map the session to the appropriate sign-in policy. The IVE compares the host and URL path to those of the available sign-in URLs for each policy. The IVE first determines if the session matches any of the Administrator policies, then the User policies, and lastly the Meeting policies. It starts from the top of each policy table and evaluates the policies from top to bottom until it gets a match. Remember that the sign-in URL contains a host/host name portion followed by the URL path in the form \<hostname\>/path. The host name can be a partial or complete host name, whereas the path must be an absolute path. A partial host name can be one that includes wildcards such as *.somecompany.com/, *.egr.somecompany.com/, or a simple */. A complete host name could be vpn.somecompany.com/ or somecompany.com/. The wildcard character can only be placed at the beginning of the host name; thus, whereas *.somecompany.com/and *company.com/ would be valid, some*.com/ would not. Also, the wildcard cannot be used in the URL path.

# Sign-in Policy Examples

We now review two sign-in policy examples to show how the IVE will choose the appropriate sign-in policy based on the request made to the IVE.

## *Example 1: Matching Wildcard Sign-in Policies*

In this example, we examine how the IVE will evaluate three different sessions with the following sign-in policy configuration:

> Admin policies
>
>> */admin/
>
> User policies
>
>> *.somecompany.com/
>>
>> */
>>
>> somecompany.com/sales/
>>
>> */sales/
>>
>> *.somecompany.com/sales/
>>
>> www.mycompany.com/admin/

With the preceding policy configuration, let's look at what will happen when the following access attempts occur:

1. https://vpn.somecompany.com
2. https://www.somecompany.com/sales
3. https://vpn.mycompany.com
4. https://www.mycompany.com/admin

The https://vpn.somecompany.com will match to the first User policy *.somecompany. com/ since the wildcard will match the beginning characters before the .somecompany. com appropriately. This policy would also match to */, but since *.somecompany.com is evaluated before */, it will not match the latter.

https://www.mycompany.com/sales will match to */sales since it is not an absolute match to */, somecompany.com/sales does not match the host name properly, and */ sales is evaluated before *.somecompany.com.

https://vpn.mycompany.com will match to */ since it does not match the host name for *.somecompany.com, and */ is the first policy to match that URL.

Lastly, https://www.mycompany.com/admin will match to the */admin policy. This is because */admin is evaluated before the next policy to match that string, which is www.mycompany.com/admin. The fact that you use "admin" in a User URL does not matter (although that sign-in policy would not bring a session to an Admin page but, rather, a User page if it was matched). What is important to take away from this example is how the policy order and matching a URL with wildcards can take precedence over an exact match.

**NOTE**

The fact that you have completely different host names mapped to the same IVE does not matter (vpn.mycompany.com, www.mycompany.com, and www.somecompany.com). What does matter is that DNS will resolve these host names appropriately to your IVE.

## *Example 2: Matching Admin, User, and Meeting Sign-in URLs*

In this example, we examine another list of hypothetical sign-in URLs and what will happen with various attempts to connect to the IVE in different sessions.

Admin policies

*/Secure/admin/

*/admin/

User policies

*/

*/users/

www.mycompany.com/users/dev/

Meetings

*/meeting/

meeting.mycompany.com/meeting/

We will match the following sessions in the example:

1. https://www.mycompany.com/admin

2. https://www.somecompany.com/Secure/admin/

3.    https://www.somecompany.com/users/

4.    https://www.somecompany.com/users/dev/

5.    https://meeting.mycompany.com/meeting/

6.    https://meeting.mycompany.com/

1.    https://www.mycompany.com/admin will match to */admin since the wildcard will match any host name, and the URL must be an absolute match, so */Secure/admin does not match.

2.    https://www.somecompany.com/Secure/admin/ will match to */Secure/admin/ since we will match any host name for this example and the */Secure/admin is an exact URL match.

3.    https://www.somecompany.com/users/ will match to the */users/ since it does not match any Admin policies, and the URL would not be an absolute match for the */ policy.

4.    https://www.somecompany.com/users/dev/ would not match any of the previously mentioned policies, so the IVE would redirect the session to the base URL matching the */ policy. None of the policies match the correct host name with the exact URL; therefore, no match is made and it will redirect the session to the base URL.

5.    https://meeting.mycompany.com/meeting/ would match to */meeting/ since we will match any host name and the URL makes an exact match to that policy.

6.    https://meeting.mycompany.com/ would actually match to */, which is not a Meeting policy at all. This is because we evaluate the policies from top down. Just because a host name or URL has the name meeting, admin, user, and so on, it does not mean that it will map to that type of policy. Therefore, the first policy to match this session would be the */ policy.

# Creating Sign-in Policies

Now that we have reviewed how sign-in policies function and the role that they play in IVE functionality, we now explore how to create the sign-in policies. We cover three different examples—one for Administrator sign-in policies, one for User sign-in policies, and one for Secure Meeting sign-in policies. Each of the policies has some properties that may not be part of other sign-in policies, which will be pointed out throughout this section.

Before we discuss examples of how to create sign-in policies, we need to mention the components that should already be configured before creating a sign-in policy. Sign-in pages are needed for Administrator, User, and Meeting sign-in policies, whereas realms are needed for Administrator and User sign-in policies. Because these components cannot be created while you are creating the sign-in policy, you must create them *before* you create the sign-in policy. You can always edit the realms and sign-in pages after you create the policy, but a realm and sign-in page must be defined (except for Secure Meeting pages, which do not need the realms) so that you can create the policy without the IVE giving you an error.

# Creating an Administrator Sign-in Policy

In this example, we outline the steps and components that are configured when setting up an Administrator sign-in policy.

1.  We begin this example by going to the Sign-in Policy page under **Authentication | Signing In | Sign-in Policies**.
2.  Click **New URL** to create a new policy.
3.  Select **Administrators** for the **User Type**.
4.  Under **Sign-in URL** you must specify the URL that will match this policy per the properties that we discussed previously in this chapter. Remember, you can only use wildcards in the host name portion of the URL, and the URL path match must be exact.
5.  Select the **Sign-in Page** from the drop-down menu that you want to be applied to administrators who access this URL. Note that you can use the same sign-in page as a User URL, but it will have a different appearance, with an option to go to the standard login if you use the default sign-in page.
6.  Next, you must define how the user is presented with his or her authentication realm. You can either choose **User types the realm name**, in which case the user will have to enter the realm by name into a text box (some consider this more secure since it adds another factor for authentication), or display a list of realms that the user will select from a drop-down menu on the sign-in page. The latter option is called **User picks from a list of authentication realms**. When you select the first option, any realm will theoretically be available on the login page, whereas the second option allows you to restrict which realms will be available. You must add the realms that you want to be present in the login page from the **Available Realms** to the **Selected Realms**. If you do not select a realm, then all will be present.
7.  Lastly, click **Save Changes**.

# Creating a User Sign-in Policy

We now discuss how to create a User sign-in policy. This will probably be the most common type of sign-in policy that you will need to create.

1.  Begin by going to **Authentication | Signing In | Sign-in Policies**, which will bring you to the Sign-in Policy summary page.
2.  Click New URL to create the new policy.

3. Select **User** for the **User Type.**

4. Under **Sign-in URL** you must specify the URL that will be match this policy per the properties that we discussed previously in this chapter. Remember, you can only use wildcards in the host name portion of the URL, and the URL path match must be exact.

5. Select the **Sign-in Page** from the drop-down menu that you want to be applied to users who access this URL. Note that you can use the same sign-in page as a User URL, but it will have a different appearance, with an option to go to the standard login if you use the default sign-in page.

6. If you have a Secure Meeting license, you must define which Secure Meeting policy should be applied to this role. If you want to use a policy other than the default policy (*/meeting/), then you must define it beforehand.

7. Next, you must define how the user is presented with his or her authentication realm. You can either choose **User types the realm name**, in which case the user will have to enter the realm by name into a text box (some consider this more secure since it adds another factor for authentication), or display a list of realms that the user will select from a drop-down menu on the sign-in page. The latter option is called **User picks from a list of authentication realms**. When you select the first option, any realm will theoretically be available on the login page, whereas the second option allows you to restrict which realms will be available. You must add the realms that you want to be present in the login page from the **Available Realms** to the **Selected Realms**. If you do not select a realm, then all will be present.

8. Lastly, click **Save Changes**.

## Creating a Secure Meeting Sign-in Policy

If you have the Secure Meeting license on your IVE, then you can create Secure Meeting sign-in policies. In this example, we show how to create these policies and the components that can be configured.

1. Begin this example by going to **Authentication | Signing In | Sign-in Policies**.

2. Click **New URL** to create a new policy.

3. Select **Meeting** for the **User Type**.

4. Next, select the **Sign-in Page** that will be used for your Secure Meetings. Only sign-in pages that are defined as Secure Meeting sign-in pages (now User/ Administrator sign-in pages) will be available in the drop-down menu.

5. Lastly, click **Save Changes.**

# Sign-in Policy Maintenance

Now that you have created the sign-in policies, we should note a few operations that can be performed when dealing with sign-in policies. All of these operations can be performed under the sign-in policy summary page at **Authentication | Signing In | Sign-in Policies**. Note that many changes require that you click the **Save Changes** button after performing the action for the change to take effect.

- **Deleting sign-in policies** To delete a sign-in policy, simply click the check box next to that policy so it is selected, then click the **Delete** button. You can select multiple policies for deletion. It is not recommended that you delete the defaults because they will be used when all else fails, so if they are missing, there would be no fallback URL to send them to.

- **Enable/disable** A policy is enabled by default when you create it, but you can also disable policies to prevent them from being active, or you can re-enable disabled policies. Simply select the appropriate policy by checking the box next to it and click the desired operation, **Enable** or **Disable**.

- **Moving/reordering policies** Policy order is very important when you have multiple sign-in policies on your IVE. The IVE does not give you an option of where to place a policy when you create it, so you may have to reorder it in the list of policies before it can match the appropriate sessions. By default, new policies are placed at the bottom of the list for their respective type. You can select single or multiple policies and move them around in their respective group. You can use either the **Up Arrow** or the **Down Arrow** buttons to move them accordingly. Remember, you must click **Save Changes** after you reorder your policies for this change to take effect or else it will not be activated and your changes will be lost if you browse to another screen in the AdminUI.

**TIP**

There are two options that you can take advantage of with regard to sign-in policies. Both are under the **Authentication | Signing In | Sign-in Policies** summary page. The first is called **Restrict Access to Administrators Only**, which will effectively disable any user from logging into the IVE. If the user enters the proper credentials, he or she will see a message that states that "Currently only Administrators can Sign On." This might be useful for maintenance or if you are having major issues with the IVE and want to prevent users from logging in while they are being fixed. The other option is to **Display multiple user sessions warning notification.** The default behavior if two users with the same credentials log into the IVE is to terminate the other session. Although this usually isn't a major problem for users who have unique login names, if multiple users use the same credentials (not particularly recommended) then they may not know that they are about to kick the other session offline. To warn the user of this, you can enable this option, which, if there is a successful authentication attempt, will prompt the user to either cancel or continue to login and kick the other session out.

# Summary

Sign-in policies give IVE administrators a flexible mechanism for presenting different content to users attempting to sign into the IVE. By providing a layer of abstraction between the sign-in URL, sign-in page, and available realms, you have many different options for creating separate login pages for users to authenticate to the IVE (license permitting).

There are two types of sign-in pages: standard sign-in pages and custom sign-in pages. The standard sign-in pages should meet the needs of most organizations and have many customizable options. If your organization has advanced needs and would like to put a personal touch on the sign-in page that is not achievable through the standard pages, then custom sign-in pages may be your choice.

By utilizing the powerful features of sign-in policies and sign-in pages, the IVE can provide an extensible interface for administrators to control user login. Juniper has gone to great lengths to enhance customization to provide the best possible experience for users accessing the IVE.

# Solutions Fast Track

## IVE Sign-in Structure

☑ The IVE uses sign-in policies to map sign-in URLs (such as www.mycompany.com/) to IVE sign-in pages, as well as realms that are available in those pages.

☑ Sign-in policies come prepackaged with the IVE, but custom sign-in pages are also supported.

☑ IVE licensing plays an important role because only advanced licenses allow for multiple sign-in pages. You need to know how sign-in policies work because they are used on all platforms (even those with single sign-in policies).

## Sign-in Pages

☑ There are two types of sign-in pages: User/Administrator and Meeting (for Secure Meeting).

☑ Standard sign-in pages allow you to customize many of the features within the page. If you need to make extensive changes to the structure of the sign-in page, you will probably need to use custom sign-in pages.

☑ The IVE comes with some sample custom IVE templates that you can download and modify to fit your needs. Extensive documentation on using custom IVE sign-in pages is available on Juniper's Web site.

# Sign-in Policies

☑ Sign-in policies allow the use of wildcards in the host name part of the URL.

☑ Sign-in policy URL paths must match exactly between what the user enters and what the sign-in URL specifies for a correct match to be made.

☑ Sign-in policies are evaluated from top to bottom in search of a match, so order is important. Sign-in policies can also be enabled or disabled.

☑ Sign-in policies allow you to define how realms are listed on the sign-in page. The user can either be forced to enter the name into a textbox or select the realms that should be available from a list.

# Frequently Asked Questions

**Q:** How can the one IVE host multiple host names on a single box?

**A:** To host multiple host names on a single box, the IVE must be configured to do so with sign-in policies. Additionally, you must make sure that public DNS records are properly configured to resolve the host names to the appropriate IP address on the IVE. Note that you can also use virtual ports to have the IVE listen on multiple IP addresses on a physical interface.

**Q:** I configured a sign-in policy to match a sign-in URL, but traffic never seems to match that policy, and instead maps to another policy. What could I be doing wrong?

**A:** You should first take a look at your sign-in URL and make sure that logically it will match the URL that the users are attempting to login with (especially when using wildcards). Next, check to make sure that your policies are in the appropriate order so that the desired policy is not shadowed by another policy in the list. Lastly, make sure that the user is typing in the correct URL with the correct path when trying to access the IVE. Typically, the IVE will redirect the user to the base IVE URL if an exact match is not made.

**Q:** I created a new realm, but it does not show up in my sign-in URL drop-down menu. What could I be doing wrong?

**A:** You must add the realm to the list of selected realms for the appropriate sign-in policy for it to be listed as a choice in a sign-in page.

**Q:** What is the best method to add company bulletins and other dynamic content to my sign-in page?

**A:** Juniper standard sign-in pages do not support much in the way of adding content, just altering text strings. If you really want to customize the structure of the Web page, you will have to use custom sign-in pages.

**Q:** What are the available template files for creating Juniper custom sign-in pages?

**A:** A complete listing of the various files that the IVE supports is listed in the *Custom Sign-in Pages* PDF available through Juniper. This also includes all of the THTML actions and other advice for creating custom sign-in pages.

# Chapter 13

# Logging

## Solutions in this chapter:

- **Log Types and Facilities**
- **Log Filtering**
- **Log Management**
- **Syslog Exporting**
- **SNMP Management**
- **System Resource Monitoring**
- **Reporting**

☑ **Summary**

☑ **Solutions Fast Track**

☑ **Frequently Asked Questions**

# Introduction

Remote access can extend the boundary of your network, but monitoring and managing your infrastructure cannot simply stop at your ISP router. Whether you are required to sustain records of user activity by regulation or are just trying to troubleshoot an issue, logging is an excellent tool to help provide valuable information to your organization. The IVE provides numerous facilities to perform log related tasks and also provides you with filtering, archiving, and download capabilities for log review and management.

Beyond the on-box mechanisms to process system events and user activity, the IVE also provides a robust SNMP polling facility, syslog log exporting, and system resource monitoring. These features are essential for ensuring that system availability is as high as possible, and they provide you with plenty of information to help keep track of the state of your IVE.

We discuss some third-party reporting tools that can help simplify device management while providing you with historical reporting, event alerting, and long-term log storage.

# Log Types and Facilities

The IVE maintains different log files for different log categories. Each log type is broken down into an intuitive category, which will make your job of investigating IVE events much easier. In this section, we review the different log categories and the information that is contained in the different logs. A thorough understanding of where different logs are stored is essential to help quickly identify system events, user activity, and assist in other trouble-shooting tasks. Juniper also provides additional facilities, such as log filtering, archive, export, and log management features.

## Log Severity Levels

Each IVE log entry is assigned a severity level to help classify the type of event that has occurred. The severity levels follow the syslog severity scheme. The log severity levels are based on the significance of the impact the event will cause on system and user functionality. Logs that are tagged with the level of *Critical* severity indicate that the IVE has experienced an event that resulted in a catastrophic failure of underlying components or an error has occurred that caused the IVE to not be able to process user or administrator actions on the box. When the IVE loses an underlying component of the IVE software, but is still able to handle system tasks, it will log the event as a *Major* event in the system log. This log indicates that the IVE is still functioning, but a significant error has occurred nonetheless. An event that does not result in the failure of a software component or loss of user functionality will be logged as a *Minor* event. An example of such an event would be an interface going active or a default gateway becoming reachable. Lastly, an event that is labeled as *Info*, or an informational event, is any form of user or administrative activity, along with normal system events and processing. The IVE uses watchdog processes to ensure that there is no failure of components of the IVE. In addition, other processes regularly inform the system of the current status, such as the number of users that are logged in. These logs are recorded as informational events.

---

**NOTE**

Licensing plays in important role in the features that you are capable of using on the IVE. With a baseline license, you cannot configure any custom log formats or perform on the box log filtering. In order to filter logs with a basic license, you will need to export them off of the box and use a third-party application. You will also not be able to create dynamic log filters with only the base license. By purchasing the advanced license, you will get the Central Management feature, which allows you to do all of the previously mentioned tasks and has many other features as well, which are discussed throughout this book.

---

# Event Logs

The IVE event log is a general-purpose logging facility that is used to store events related to system operation, including hardware-related events, network events, system statistics and so forth. This log facility is an excellent place to explore when you are trying to determine if any events occurred that affect system availability. If the IVE should need to restart a process, or a system error should occur, it will most likely be recorded in this log.

## Event Log Settings

The event log allows you to configure what type of system events should be recorded in this log. In addition to being able to configure the type of events to record, you can also define a syslog server to export these events to, and you can define the size of the event log file before it is rolled over. By default, the IVE will roll the logs over after they grow to 200 MB, but you can set this to a maximum of 500 MB. The following is a list of the settings that can be configured within the event logs (see Figure 13.1 for the AdminUI configuration of these options; see also Figure 13.2):

## Figure 13.1 Configuring Event Log Settings

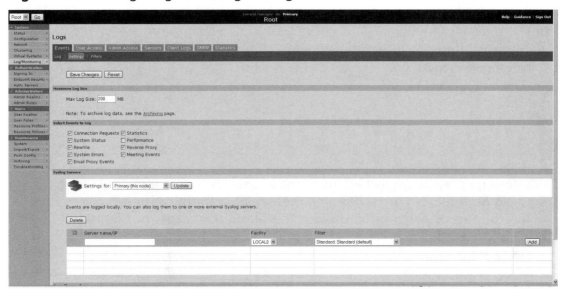

- **Connection Requests** These are logs generated when a user attempts to connect to the IVE. By default, this is turned off due to the large volume of logs that it would generate, but you may want to enable this for troubleshooting and usage purposes.

- **System Status** These logs indicate status information for the IVE, including state changes and other statistics related to the underlying system.

- **Rewrite** This is information related to the IVE rewriter engine and is enabled by default to record events related to the rewriting of content through the IVE.

- **System Errors** As this name implies, this option will record system errors to the event log should they occur. This option is enabled by default and it is recommended that it stay enabled.

- **Email Proxy Events** This log is related to the built-in e-mail client on the IVE, and it will provide information about activities on the e-mail client.

- **Statistics** The IVE continuously monitors the statistics of the box and will record this information, such as the number of users logged in at specific intervals. This information can be logged to the event log by ensuring this option is enabled.

- **Performance** The IVE constantly checks the performance (throughput, memory, CPU utilization, and so on) of the box. Such statistics can be recorded to the event log, in addition to other facilities such as the system dashboard and SNMP. This is not enabled by default.

- **Reverse Proxy** The IVE can function essentially as a reverse proxy, particularly with anonymous authentication enabled. You can record events that take place when the IVE is functioning in this mode by selecting the Reverse Proxy option.

- **Meeting Events** If you have the Secure Meeting module, then you can have the IVE record information such as the number of logged-in meeting users, scheduled meetings, and so on. This option enables you to record these events.

**Figure 13.2** Event Log: Displays Information Related to System Events and States

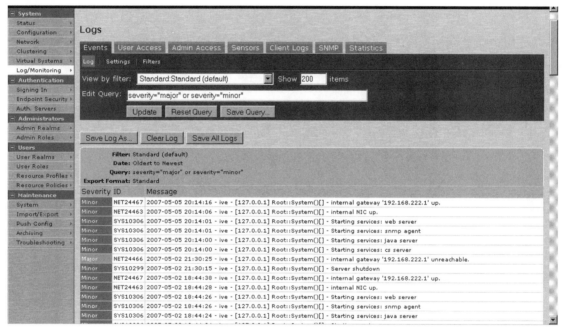

## User Access Logs

Every time a user accesses a resource through the IVE, the user's activities are recorded in the User Access log by default. User access logs are particularly useful for reviewing user authentication, user resource access, and user session timeouts on the IVE. Similar to other IVE event logs, the user access logs are formatted in a manner that is structured to provide as much information as possible in a simple and compact format. User access logs typically contain the following information: event severity, event ID code, timestamp, source IP of user machine (as seen by the IVE), username, realm, role, and access event. Since each log entry contains all of this information, it is much easier to identify a user event and the context (role/realm) in which the event occurred, which is very useful for troubleshooting.

# User Access Log Settings

You can configure what type of information you would like to be recorded to the user access logs. This is useful for removing information that you might think is not necessary to log, and thus save the space in the log file. The user access log is set to increase until 200 MB by default, but it can be set to increase to 500 MB maximum. You can also configure how the IVE handles the user access logs in terms of archiving and syslog export. By default, the user access log will contain the following information (see Figure 13.3 for the AdminUI user log settings; see also Figure 13.4):

**Figure 13.3** Configuring User Access Log Settings

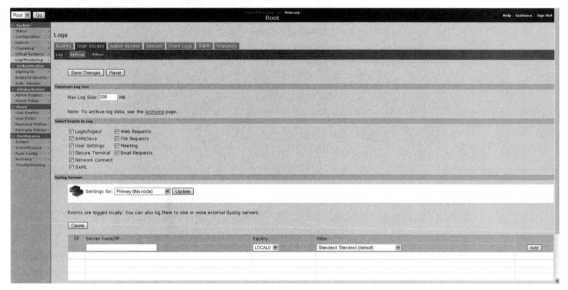

- **Login/logout events**  Generated when a user logs in or out.

- **Web Requests**  Logs generated when a user requests a Web resource through the IVE.

- **SAM/Java**  These events are recorded when a user launches SAM, Java applets, and other tasks related to this functionality.

- **File Requests**  Access to file shares, both Windows and Linux/Unix, is recorded with this setting.

- **User Settings**  Specific changes to user settings in the profile are recorded here.

- **Meeting**  Secure Meeting events from the user are recorded with this setting.

- **Secure Terminal**  Access through the IVE's Telnet/SSH and Windows Terminal Services/Citrix facilities are recorded with this setting enabled.

- **Email Requests**  The IVE e-mail client generates these request logs.

- **Network Connect**  Network Connect events from the user are recorded with this enabled. Events such as IP address assignment and Network Connect establishing and disconnecting a session with the user are examples of such access.

- **SAML**  SAML is short for Security Assertion Markup Language, and it is commonly used to track single sign-on activity on the SSL VPN.

**Figure 13.4** User Access Log Displays Information That Is Logged from User Activity through the IVE

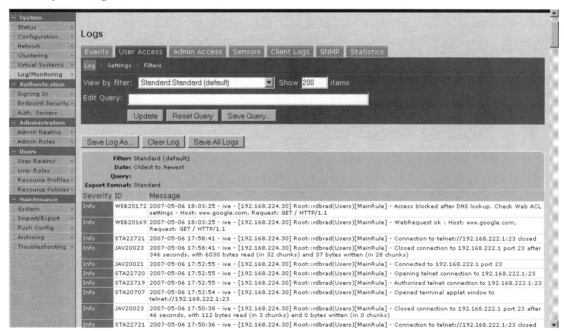

**TIP**

On large systems with lots of user activity, you may notice that it may take a long time to bring up logs, even when the logs are filtered. The reason for this is that the IVE gives higher priority over user-related functionality than system-intensive administrative tasks such as log viewing. This is because the IVE doesn't want to adversely affect user experience accidentally when performing such administrative tasks on the system. If you are having difficulty with the access logs on the IVE, you may want to try exporting the logs with syslog onto a purpose-built system which can help sift through the logs without riding on top of a mission critical application such as the IVE. Of course, you won't get all of the same integrated functionality of the log filtering if you export the logs, but there are other third-party applications that can do this for you, as discussed later.

# Admin Access Logs

The Admin Access logs act as sort of an audit log for administrator activity and changes to the IVE system. This log contains very useful information, such as firmware changes, device reboots, and configuration changes to the IVE. By default, administrators will be recorded when they log in and out of the IVE. Each event will note the log severity, event ID, timestamp, IP address, admin user, realm, role, and a description of the event.

## Admin Access Log Settings

The Admin Access logs have a few settings that can be configured. First, the default log size for the Admin Access log is 200 MB, but it can be set to a maximum of 500 MB. Second, you can configure what events to log, including whether to log administrator changes, license changes, and administrator logins. Third, you can configure Admin log archiving, as well as syslog exporting (see Figure 13.5). The three Admin Access log settings are as follows:

- **Administrator changes** This event will record each change that an Administrator makes to an IVE so that you can audit changes.

- **Administrator logins** Any time an administrator logs into the IVE, it will be logged in the Admin Access log.

- **License changes** When changes are made to the IVE licensing, they will be recorded in this log.

**Figure 13.5** The Admin Access Log Displays Logs Related to IVE Administrator Activity and Can Serve as an Audit Trail of Changes Made to the IVE

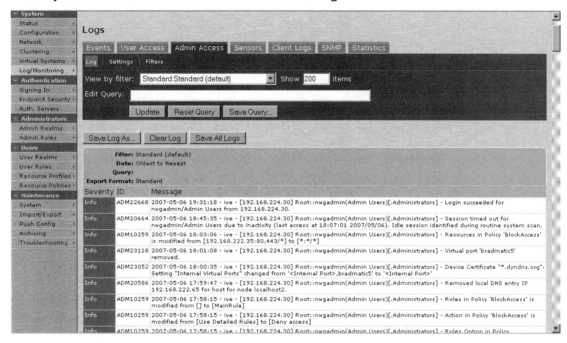

## Damage & Defense...

### Exporting Admin Access Logs

Admin logs may contain some very useful data regarding changes that are made to your system. The problem with storing logs locally is that if something happens to the IVE the audit trail can be lost. The event may be intended, such as an administrator deleting changes to the Admin logs on purpose, or accidental, such as an administrator rolling back an IVE to the previous software by accident. In either case, exporting the logs via syslog to another server can help to reveal activity that took place on the IVE if the logs on the IVE should be inaccessible for one reason or another. The same is true for any networked system but can be particularly useful as a layered security precaution.

# Sensor Logs

The integration between the Juniper IVE and Juniper Intrusion Detection and Prevention (IDP) product has led to a new innovation in security. The ability to stop attacks closer to the source and prevent them from traveling into the network is an excellent feature that Juniper has integrated into its products. The specifics of this integration are discussed elsewhere in this book, but we wanted to include some information about the records that are contained in the sensor logs. These logs contain information related to attack messages that were sent by the IDP to the IVE. When this integration is configured, and the IDP detects an attack, it will signal the IVE that an attack has taken place, and the IVE will determine what user session originated the attack for corrective action as configured in the policy. Notifications of events generated by the Intrusion Detection Server are stored in this log.

# Client Logs

The IVE logging facilities extend far beyond the IVE to assist troubleshooting issues. Since much of the functionality of the IVE also takes place on the client side, Juniper has extended the features to allow the administrator to manage these deployments. Occasionally, users may report strange issues trying to connect or install a client. The IVE has logging features built into the clients, but instead of having to ask the user to search low and high for the log files to upload, there are facilities built into the individual clients to automatically do this with the click of a button. On the IVE side, this log repository will store the uploaded log files for your or Juniper Technical Assistance Center's review.

## Client Log Settings

You can configure which IVE clients can upload logs to your IVE. You have the option to enable client uploads for all of the clients, including Host Checker, Cache Cleaner, Secure Meeting, WSAM, JSAM and applets, Network Connect, and Terminal Services. Of course, you can also set the amount of log space you would like to allocate for client log uploads so that you don't fill up your IVE disk space with client logs. Alerts in the IVE logs can also be generated when a user uploads logs to the IVE so that you will know that this has happened without other user communication.

---

**W**ARNING

Client logs are not migrated during IVE upgrades, so if you need to retain these logs, you must download them from the IVE for long-term storage. Additionally, when an IVE node is removed from the cluster, the IVE logs for that node are deleted and cannot be retrieved. You also have the ability to archive the logs off of the system automatically with the IVE Archiving feature.

---

# Active User Logs

Of course, sifting through the user access logs would be an extremely tedious way to try to determine which users have active sessions on the IVE. Luckily, Juniper also has a logging facility for viewing the active user sessions on the IVE. Simply go to **Status | Active Users** and you will be able to view all active users on the IVE. You can even filter down which users you want to look for if you have a large number of users which are logged in.

Each user entry will show the following information:

- Username
- Realm
- Roles
- Signed In (when the user signed in)
- Network Connect IP (if the user is using Network Connect)

Besides being able to search logs by username, you can also click any of the column headers to automatically sort alphabetically or numerically (depending on the data type for the column). User sessions can also be terminated by selecting the session and clicking the **Delete Session** button. Alternatively, if you need to remove all sessions, you can click the **Delete All Sessions** button to do so (see Figure 13.6).

**Figure 13.6** Active User Logs Display Logged-In Users and Administrators, Realm/Role, Sign-In Time, and Network Connect IP If Applicable; You Can Also End a User or All User Sessions through This Screen

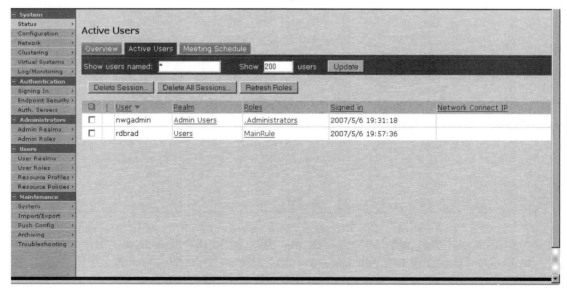

# Meeting Schedule

If your IVE is licensed to use Secure Meeting, then the Scheduled Meeting log is useful to help view what meetings are scheduled. This is useful for resource planning, along with ensuring that your box has enough concurrent meeting licenses to meet your organizations needs. The Meeting Schedule can be viewed under **Status | Meeting Schedule** as shown in Figure 13.7. You can view the meetings that are scheduled on the IVE, along with details such as the **Meeting Details**, **Meeting Role**, and **Attendee Roles**. The IVE has four different filters to help narrow the scope of the meetings that you would like to view. The following filters are provided by Juniper with the IVE:

**Figure 13.7** Viewing Scheduled Meetings in the IVE Meeting Schedule

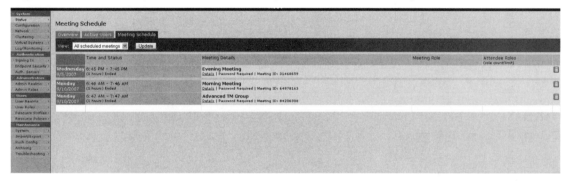

- Meetings In Progress
- Today's Meetings
- This Week's Meetings
- All Scheduled Meetings

Besides being able to view the Secure Meetings, you can also delete any Secure Meeting by clicking on the Trash Can icon to the right of the meeting that you want to delete.

**TIP**

When performing an upgrade to an IVE with very large log files, you might want to consider clearing the log files off of the IVE before you perform the upgrade. Since the IVE will backup all the logs while performing the upgrade, the upgrade can take an extremely long time if the logging is extensive.

Before removing the logs, you will probably want to back them up manually, or if you have been performing log archiving or syslog exporting, then this may already be done for you. By removing the logs beforehand, you can save time when performing the upgrade. Of course, this is not necessary, but just a heads up to help you save time when performing upgrade.

# Log Filtering

In an enterprise environment, you may find yourself overwhelmed trying to sift through log files in search of particular events. The logs are very detailed and offer some great information; that is, if you can locate the entry you are seeking. Luckily, for those of you with advanced (Central Management) licenses, Juniper has responded by integrating log query mechanisms in the IVE. Besides being able to search the raw log entries, you can also configure custom and dynamic filters to display specific log entries in the IVE. Dynamic filtering makes the different criteria of each log entry an active link, which will automatically configure the filter to match that value by creating a filter on the fly. Of course, there is quite a lot that you can do with filtering each type of log facility, so we will delve into examples of how to create filters and common uses for them.

## Log Formats

Before getting into an in-depth discussion, note that the IVE comes with preconfigured formats for log entries, along with the ability to create your own custom log type. Also note that you must have the Central Management capabilities to customize your own log formats.

### Standard Log Format

The "standard" log entry type follows the following format for each log:

%date% %time% – %node% – [%sourceip%] %ivs%::%user%(%realm%)[%role%] %nonRoot% – %msg%

Each variable is contained within two % signs, which serve as delimiting characters, identifying each system variable. In the standard log entry, we are essentially listing the date time, ivenode, source IP, ivs (if applicable) user, realm, role, and the log message. Other characters in the log format are seen as text characters that will be part of the entry. Here is an example of what a log entry looks like with values filled in for those variables:

2007-04-03 13:26:02 – ive – [127.0.0.1] Root::System()[] – internal NIC up.

# WebTrends Enhanced Log File

Juniper has also provided a predefined filter that complies with the WebTrends Enhanced Log File (WELF) format. This is useful if you have a WebTrends reporting server, since you can export these logs to that server and process and report the logs on the WebTrends server, instead of on the IVE. The WELF format is preconfigured as follows:

id=firewall time="%date% %time%" pri=%syslogcode% fw=%localip% vpn=%node% ivs=%ivs% user=%user% realm="%realm%" roles"%roles%" type=mgmt msg="%id%: %msg%"

As you can see, the WELF format is similar to the standard format. Many of the variables are the same; it is just the order that is different.

# W3C Format

This format is a standard by the World Wide Web Consortium for log entries relating to Web site browsing. This filter is unique to the User Access log and is not predefined for other logs. The format on the IVE is as follows:

%date% %time% %sourceip% %method% %uri% %result% %rbytes%

# Custom Log Format

Although the predefined formats might work well for some, Juniper has provided a mechanism for you to log any system event variable for each log entry. This provides you with an extensible method to provide the exact information that you want to see per log entry. A complete list of the different system variables is located in the **Filter Dictionary Variables** above the **Export Format** textbox. Not only can you define different variables but also you can alter the format of the logs. This is especially useful if you want to alter the log entry format for an external log processing application. The system variables can be defined as they are in the other formats, between the % symbol which acts as a delimiter (for example, %date%).

For example, let's say we wanted to see the following information in each log entry: date, time, src IP, user, realm, role, protocol, bytes sent, bytes received, request method, request result, and message. The export format would look like the following:

%date% %time% – [%sourceip%] %user%(%realm%)[%role%] %protocol% – %sbytes% – %rbytes% – %method% – %result% – %msg%

which could result in the following log entry

2007-04-03 13:26:02 – [127.0.0.1] joeuser(userrealm) [userrole] http – 356 – 1412 – GET – 200 – WebRequest ok : Host: www.google.com, Request: GET / HTTP/1.1

Note that the use of characters with the exception of % (the variable delimiter) is viewed as text in the message. Other characters can be used to help the readability of the log entry, or you can use them for parsing the log entries. The msg variable may contain information that is also in other system variables. The output of the msg variable depends on the event, so it may vary from entry to entry, but by using some delimiting variables (such as [ ]) you can identify where this variable starts and ends for your log parsing purposes.

# Log Filtering

Log filters are composed of query attributes, which define what values the IVE should filter for in each entry. These values relate to the system variables for each log entry. You can define multiple query attributes for each log filter, so you can be extremely specific as to what entries you would like to filter on each log entry. Each log filter has the following properties, which control the format and how the log entries are displayed:

- **Filter Name**  This is the name of the filter. It must be unique to other log filter names.

- **Make Default**  This option will make the log filter the default filter. When you open up a log view, such as Event logs or User Access logs, it will automatically apply this filter.

- **Start Date**  This is the beginning date for log entries you would like to view. You can either select the **Earliest Date** option, which will start the logs from the earliest log data that the IVE has on record, or you can select a custom date by specifying the start date.

- **End Date**  The end date defines the limit for the newest log to display. This can either be defined as **Latest Date**, which is the newest logs (which will continue to display new logs each time that the IVE is updated), or you can define an end date in the month, day, year format.

- **Query**  In this field, you specify the variables that you would like to filter. These variables for each log are defined to the right of the query textbox, and most define samples that you can select and click the **Insert Expression** button to add the value to the Query textbox. You can also apply logic to the query string for enhanced capability. See Custom Expressions in Log Filter Queries later in this chapter for details.

- **Export Format**  The last property of a log filter is the actual format of the log. As we discussed in the preceding section, there are predefined and custom formats for these logs.

**TIP**

If you want to alter the fields in the logs but don't want to filter out any entries, simply create a new log filter, with no values in the query field, and define your own custom log format according to the desired log format.

## Applying Log Filters

Once you have created a log filter, you can then apply the filter to a particular log view. Simply open the log that you wish to apply the filter to, and from the **View by Filter** drop-down menu, select the filter that you wish to apply to the log. Additionally, you can define how many log entries you would like to view by specifying the number in the **Show items** text box. Use caution because the number that you view will have an impact on performance viewing logs and how long it will take to generate the page.

## Dynamic Log Filtering

If you have the advanced license, you have the Central Manager feature set, which allows you to dynamically create log filters. This is an excellent feature that is extremely useful for viewing only the information that you want to see, without having to create any log filters ahead of time. Essentially, each value in the log entry will have a hyperlink embedded, so you can simply click on that value and it will automatically construct a filter. The IVE fills in the Query field with the appropriate expression to match the values you have clicked. So let's say that you click the field 'STS20642' and 'Root' in a Event log entry, then it will compose a query string:

(id='STS20642') and ivs='Root'

This string will automatically filter the logs so that you only see log entries with those values. Optionally, you can save this query as a filter by clicking the **Save Query** button, which will bring up a new filter screen with the query attributes already filled in; you can click **Reset Query** to remove the filter; or you can click **Update**, which will refresh the logs to show any new logs that were created and match the log filter since the last refresh. Figure 13.8 shows how a dynamic log can reduce the log received down to specific log entries.

**Figure 13.8** Setting Dynamic Log Filters

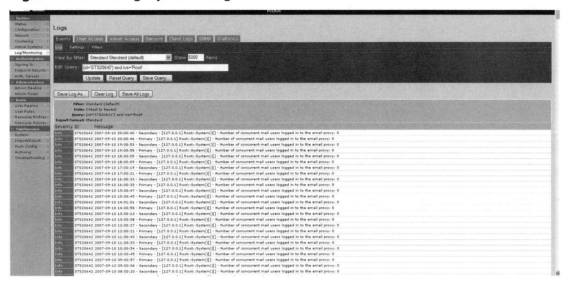

## Custom Expressions within Log Filter Queries

The IVE allows you to apply logic to your query strings so that you can filter on multiple values, with logical conditions. For the most part, you will be interested in the AND, OR, NOT logic when applying logic to filters, so we discuss this here. For a complete list of logical operators and system variables, you can do a search from the Help menu in the Admin interface for Custom Expressions.

- **NOT, !** This will apply NOT logic to a variable to the right of the NOT keyword or the ! symbol, which has the equivalent meaning. Only the log entries where this logic evaluates to true will be displayed. For example, NOT id='STS20641' will display every log entry except those with the ID value STS20641.

- **AND, &&** This will apply AND logic to two variables or expressions, to evaluate that both variables/expressions evaluate to true for a log entry. Only the log entries for which the expression evaluates to true will be displayed. For example, severity="major" AND node = "SecureAccess" will display only major events in the IVE named SecureAccess.

- **OR, ‖** This will apply logical OR to two variables or expressions in a log entry. Only the log entries that evaluate to true for the query will be displayed. For example, result = 404 OR userAgent="Mozilla/5.001 (Macintosh; N; PPC; dk) Gecko/25250101" will only display logs where the Log Entry has a 404 as the result code, or the user agent matches the Mozilla string shown previously.

As mentioned previously, you can apply logic to custom expressions to evaluate multiple conditions. For instance, the same AND, OR, NOT logic can be applied to custom expressions instead of variables. One example would be to create a logical AND between two expressions so that only logs that evaluated both expressions to true would apply (for example, CustomExpression1 AND CustomExpression2). The same could be stated for logical OR and logical NOT. You can have more than one level of nesting for custom expressions as long as the expression has the proper syntax. Remember that depending on the export format you have for the log, not all values may be displayed, but they will still be evaluated in the expression for each log entry.

### Editing the Log Query String

You can edit the Query string of the log filter at any time on a particular log (assuming you have the Central Management capabilities). You can either use a custom filter or use the dynamic filter to specify what values you would like to view, and then simply edit the Query string to reflect the logs you would like to display. This allows for simple changes to be made to the log filter without having to completely re-create the filter. After you have the appropriate string, simply click the **Update** button to apply it.

# Log Management

The IVE has different features to assist managing the logs on the IVE. It is important to first understand how logs are stored on the IVE. By default, the different system logs are limited to a size of 200 MB. When the logs fill up, the log file will be backed up and a new log file will be started. This limit can be raised to 500 MB under **System | Log/Monitoring | <LOGNAME> | Settings**. When you view logs in the log viewer, the IVE will display up to 5000 log entries, and if the current log has less than 5000, then it will display additional entries from earlier logs. The IVE essentially keeps two log files per log type on the system locally.

# Saving Logs

There are a few different ways that you can save logs off of the IVE. This is commonly needed for either storage or troubleshooting purposes, and it is available regardless of the license on the IVE. To manually save any log off of the IVE, simply go to that log under **System | Log/Monitoring | <LOGNAME> | Log** and click the **Save Log As** button as shown in Figure 13.9. This will prompt you where to save the log. Note that you will only save the displayed logs based on the filter (if any) that is applied. So if you need to save all of the logs, clear the query and then save the logs. You can save all of the logs (Event, User Access, Admin, Network Connect, and Sensors logs) by clicking the **Save All Logs** button from any log. This will save all of the logs and download them as a compressed tar.gz

file to your machine. You can configure what events to save for each log type under **System |
Log/Monitoring | <LOGNAME> | Settings** as discussed previously in this chapter. You
can also set up the logs to be sent via syslog (discussed later) or set up an archive schedule so
the logs get sent to another machine, as discussed in Chapter 10.

**Figure 13.9** Saving Log Files on the IVE to Your Local Machine through
the AdminUI

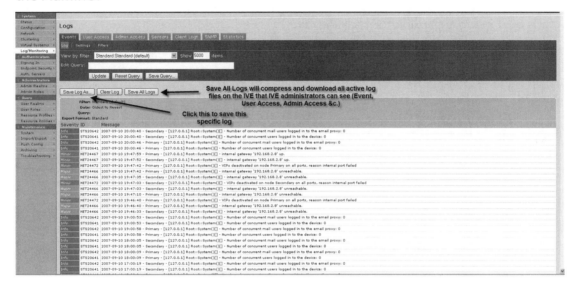

## Deleting Logs

Individual log types can be deleted from the system by going to the appropriate log under
**System | Log/Monitoring | <LOGNAME> | Log** and clicking the **Clear Log**
button. Note that this process is not reversible on the IVE, so if you need to have logs saved
elsewhere, you will probably want to make sure that you are using either syslog exporting
or log archiving to do so.

## Syslog Exporting

The IVE was not meant to be a long-term log storage server, and an IVE under load will
not have the best performance with regard to log filtering. Juniper has provided an excellent
mechanism to solve both issues. You can configure the IVE to export each log type to an
external syslog server that is better suited to store the logs long term. This is also a good way
to be able to monitor any events or changes made on the IVE, especially those that might
result in the IVE crashing or becoming unavailable. For instance, if an administrator decides

to roll back the IVE, you will lose log entries between the time that the IVE was last upgraded and when it was rolled back. By exporting the logs off of the IVE, you do not have to be as concerned about not being able to review logs after the fact.

# Setting Up Syslog Exporting

Configuring syslog exporting on the IVE is a relatively simple task. You can configure syslog exporting for each log type under the configuration settings for the logs (Event, User Access, Admin, NC Packet Log, and Sensors). Simply go to **System** | **Log/Monitoring** | **<LOGNAME>** | **Settings** and you will be able to configure the following settings for syslog exporting for that log type (Figure 13.10 shows how this is configured in the AdminUI):

- **Server name/IP** You must define either a FQDN or IP address for the syslog server.

- **Facility** Specify the facility on the syslog server that is set up to accept the syslog messages from the IVE. This is important because an individual syslog server can accept logs from multiple devices or different logs for each device (such as Event, User Access, and Admin logs), so it is important to specify them accordingly.

- **Filter** You can define a filter to be applied to the syslog messages that are sent from the IVE to the syslog server. By using a filter, you can specify what data should be sent (the query) and in what format (the export format).

**Figure 13.10** Configuring Syslog Exporting in the IVE

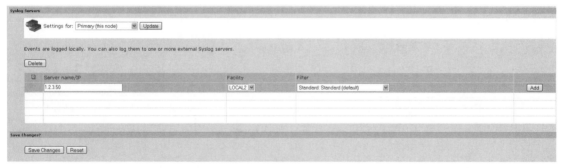

Note that multiple syslog destinations can be defined for a single log type. Additionally, you could send different log types to the same facility on a syslog server, but this probably isn't practical for parsing and reporting purposes. Of course, you must ensure that you are running a syslog server on the device where the syslog entries are sent, and you must also ensure that there is nothing blocking the syslog messages from reaching the syslog server (such as a firewall or our device Access List). The syslog messages are sent to the defined syslog server on port UDP 514.

# SNMP Management

The suite of management capabilities on the IVE extends far beyond simple logging and console dashboards. Juniper has implemented extensive support for SNMP management to make administering the IVE much easier and automated. Most administrators wear many hats and don't have the time to check on the status of the IVE multiple times a day to make sure that it is functioning up to par. Fortunately, SNMP functionality can take a great deal of manual labor out of administering the box and automate such functions even to the point where you are notified whenever an important event happens on the box.

For those of you familiar with SNMP, the IVE has a standard implementation, but where it becomes very valuable is in the support to poll and send traps for a vast number of events and system state values. In this section, we review how to set up SNMP in the IVE, along with the data that can be polled and sent as a trap. We also discuss the systems that can process the SNMP data on the backend to provide you with the data gleaned from the IVE.

# SNMP Configuration on the IVE

There are a few tasks related to the set up of SNMP polling and trapping on the IVE, which is off by default. The configuration for SNMP is under **System | Log/Monitoring | SNMP**. In this screen, you can start by downloading the **Juniper Networks MIB File**, which contains the SNMP MIB for the IVE. For those of you not familiar, an SNMP MIB is a blueprint of the different pieces of information that can be gleaned from the IVE via SNMP. It essentially maps out the various system variables in a type, length, value (TLV) format. This makes it easy to define new values in an extensible fashion. You can load this MIB file into a commercial MIB browser such as HP Openview or freeware such as iReasoning MIB Browser (www.ireasoning.com/mibbrowser.shtml). In the MIB browser, you can view all of the different variables from which you can get data. We discuss a subset of these variables in the following section.

After downloading the MIB, the next task is to enable **SNMP Queries** and/or **SNMP Traps.** SNMP Queries are messages sent from an SNMP polling application (most MIB browsers can send queries as well). When you query (poll) an SNMP enabled device such as the IVE, you define what data you are asking for, and the IVE retrieves it. Examples of data that you can poll for are system uptime, memory and CPU utilization, number of users logged in, and system version. The opposite of SNMP polling is when the SNMP device triggers an SNMP Trap to be sent. This can contain the same type of data as a query response, but it is not explicitly requested by the SNMP polling device. Sending SNMP traps is often useful for alerting, particularly when a system is experiencing an emergency state, is low on system resources, or in response to a particular event. Examples of SNMP traps include sending a trap when memory utilization is high, a critical event has occurred, and the system version has changed.

There are a few necessary and optional fields that are configurable on the **System | Log/Monitoring | SNMP** page. Figure 13.11 shows how this is configured in the AdminUI.

- **System Name** This is a value that you can use to assign the System Name that will be sent in response to an SNMP Query request for it.

- **System Location** This value is useful for specifying the location of the device, particularly if you have several offices with multiple devices.

- **System Contact** This value is useful for defining a point of contact for administering the device. It can be very helpful if you have multiple devices with different administrators. If you have a help desk that monitors the device and notices that graphs for a particular device indicate a problem, the help desk can check who is configured as the System Contact to reach out.

- **Community string** This is the only required field out of the four values. It defines a value that must be specified in a query in order to glean information from SNMP. It works somewhat like a password, but it is important to note that the IVE uses SNMPv2(c), which is not encrypted.

**Figure 13.11** Configuring SNMP Monitoring through the IVE AdminUI

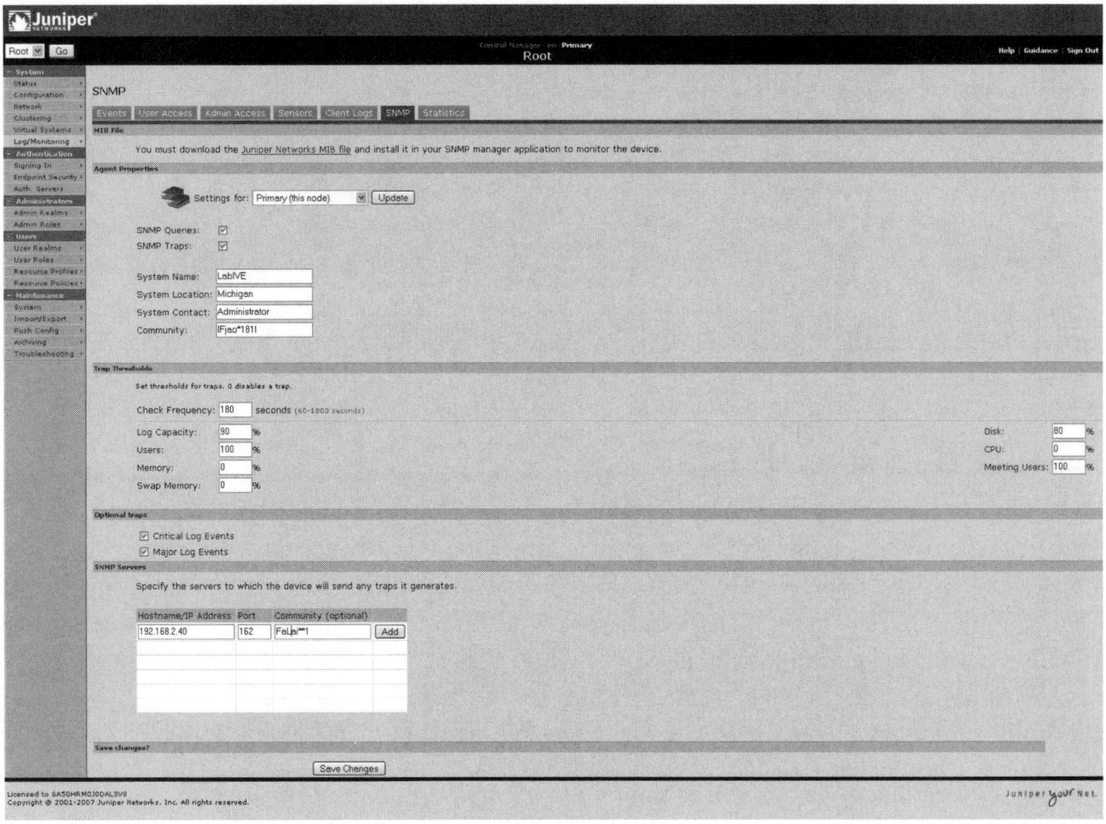

## Damage & Defense…

### Malicious SNMP Queries

SNMP is an excellent tool for providing useful information to administrators, but the same can be said for a malicious person trying to compromise your network. As of IVE 6.0, the IVE has implemented SNMP v2(c) and although it only allows read-only SNMP queries, an attacker could still get useful information from the IVE. Since SNMP v2(c) does not implement encryption to the queries, the SNMP community string can potentially be sniffed from the network. Also, the IVE does not have the capability to only allow queries from certain IP addresses as of version 6.0. To help protect yourself from such malicious activity, make sure that you restrict SNMP queries at a router or firewall level to the IVE to only certain IP addresses. SNMP queries are sent on UDP port 161, and SNMP traps are sent on UDP port 162. You can specify a complex community string so that it cannot be easily guessed by a malicious machine. Additionally, the SNMP data in SNMP query responses is not encrypted in version SNMPv2(c), which must be kept in mind. All in all, SNMP is an excellent tool, and by taking some precautions, you can ensure that you get the most use out of it and mitigate potential threats to your network.

## SNMP Trap Thresholds

SNMP traps allow you to have the IVE send messages in response to system events or system state. In order to trigger the events, we must instruct the system at what levels we would like the IVE to send the traps. If we set the value too low, we will get too many alerts, but if we set it too high, we may not get alerts until the system is already in a critical state. One way to help determine the level at which we should send alerts is to take note of system averages on the Dashboard and then base the thresholds on those but at a higher value. The following thresholds can be set under the **System | Log/Monitoring | SNMP** screen:

- **Check Frequency** This is the frequency with which the system should check the values of the system state to determine if a trap should be sent. This can be set in seconds from 60 to 1800. Zero disables the checks.

- **Log Capacity** This alert defines how much of the space on disk allocated for logs should be utilized before an SNMP trap is sent. The default value is 90%, which is a good value in most cases and should give you enough time to perform maintenance tasks to reduce the log size.

- **Users** You can define a point (i.e., a numerical level based on the percentage of concurrent users active on the IVE) when the IVE will send an SNMP trap. You can use this value to help notify you when you are at a certain percentage of your license capacity. The default value is 100%, meaning that when you have the same number of active users as your license allows, it will send a trap. Perhaps you would like to set a lower value, since at 100% no additional users can log on to the IVE. Suppose you had a 100-user license and you set it at 90%; you could be notified when you had 90 users logged on. At that point you could take action, whether logging out orphaned sessions that have not expired or contacting your Juniper reseller to get additional licenses. One way to help mitigate the number of users logged on would be to set lower timeout values on user sessions so that fewer users who are idle could take away from users who would like to sign on.

- **Memory** This is the percentage of memory that is utilized on the IVE. If the memory utilization becomes too high, you will most likely start running into performance and stability problems. This may result from reaching the limits of the box or from other factors, such as a complex authentication scheme or a bug in the IVE code. Sending an alert will help notify you of this condition. By default, it is 0%, meaning that it is effectively disabled, but a value of 80% would probably suit most organizations well.

- **Swap Memory** This is the amount of memory that is created on the hard disk, also known as virtual memory. When this memory begins to be heavily utilized, you will probably notice performance issues because memory stored on disk is not as fast as memory stored in RAM and must be transferred in and out of RAM to be processed. High utilization of SWAP memory could indicate memory leaks or other critical issues, and it would be a good candidate for sending traps on. It is set to 0% by default, but perhaps a value of 70% would suit most organizations well.

- **Disk** This is the percentage of hard disk space that is full. If you run out of disk space, you will definitely have issues on the IVE. It can affect everything from performance to being able to save user settings such as user-created bookmarks. Although it is usually log files that utilize a majority of disk space, it is useful to know when you are running low so you can take corrective action. It is set to 80% by default, which is probably good for most organizations.

- **CPU** This is the percentage of the CPU processing power that is utilized. This value is tricky because it is not uncommon for a CPU to occasionally spike to 100% for a very brief moment. If you notice that the CPU seems "pegged" at 100% for any amount of time (for example, beyond 30 seconds), this may indicate a problem. You will probably want to check the event logs to determine if there are any critical events. Because this value can lead to false positives, you may want to send a trap only when it reaches 100% and see how that works. If it sends too many alerts because it spikes to 100% without any noticeable performance hit, then you may want to turn it off and rely on other traps.

■ **Meeting Users** This is the percentage of active meeting users on the IVE in relation to the meeting license. If you reach a maximum number of users, new users will not be admitted, so you will probably want to keep tabs on this value to prevent such occurrences. It is set at 100% by default, but this may not allow for corrective action, so perhaps 80% would be a good value for most organizations.

### Optional Traps

You can additionally specify that you would like to receive Critical and Major event log traps. These may be useful to help ensure that the IVE has not encountered a severe error, or a major component has not failed.

## SNMP Server

When you configure SNMP traps, you must define the server to send those traps to. The SNMP server can then take the traps and perform additional processing (such as sending e-mails to administrators). The SNMP server field is pretty straightforward, with the following fields (Figure 13.1 outlines this configuration):

■ **Hostname/IP Address** You must define the FQDN server name or the IP address of the SNMP server to which the IVE will send SNMP traps.

■ **Port** This is the UDP port that the SNMP server will be listening on for SNMP traps. By default, SNMP servers listen for traps on UDP port 162.

■ **Community** Specify the community with which SNMP will use to authenticate SNMP messages.

Lastly, click **Add** to define the server. You can define multiple SNMP servers to receive traps.

## SNMP Objects

The IVE has many IVE objects for both querying and sending trap variables when a threshold has been reached. In this section, we point out a few of the SNMP variables that are particularly useful and worth discussing. For a full list of the SNMP objects, you can go to the Help menu on the Admin console, search for SNMP Agent, and select **Monitoring the IVE as an SNMP Agent**. The following is a list of objects that can be polled or that send traps on the IVE:

■ **logFullPercent** The percentage utilization of the log partition

■ **signedInWebUsers** The number of active users logged on to the Web Interface

- **productVersion** The version of IVE OS code running. This value will change with software upgrades and rollbacks.

- **iveCpuUtil** The percentage of CPU utilization on the IVE

- **iveMemoryUtil** The percentage of memory utilized on the IVE

- **iveConcurrentUsers** Total concurrent users, including those signed in through SAM or NC clients

- **diskFullPercent** Percentage of hard disk that is utilized on the IVE

  IVE Traps

- **iveNearlyFull** When the IVE hits the log percentage full threshold

- **iveLogFull** IVE log is completely full

- **iveMaxConcurrentUsersSignedIn** Maximum number of licensed users logged in

- **iveTooManyFailedLoginAttemps** When a user has reached the lockout threshold on the IVE, this trap will be generated.

- **iveShutdown** The IVE has been shut down.

- **iveReboot** The IVE has been rebooted.

- **iveDiskNearlyFull** The IVE has reached the disk percentage full threshold.

- **iveDiskFull** The IVE disk is completely full.

- **memUtilNotify** This trap is triggered when the memory has reached the percentage threshold to trigger a trap.

- **cpuUtilNotify** Notify when the CPU has met or surpassed the CPU threshold

- **iveNetExternalInterfaceDownTrap** This trap is generated when the external interface goes down. The SNMP logs must be able to go out the Internal or Management interface and be received by the SNMP server for this alert to be received.

- **iveNetInternalInterfaceDownTrap** This trap is generated when the internal interface goes down. Note that you must be able to send the traps through the External or Management interface and these must be received by the SNMP server for this to work.

- **iveClusterChangedVipTrap** This trap is sent when the VIP of a cluster is taken by a different IVE.

## SNMP Management Systems

There are several SNMP management systems available, both commercial and freeware. HP Openview, IBM Tivoli, and What'sUpGold are a few enterprise monitoring systems. Cacti is an open source application that has become a very popular system to query SNMP devices, and it provides historical graphs and statistics on virtually any SNMP object that can be polled. You can find a variety of information, including installation instructions, at www.cacti.net.

# System Resource Monitoring

In addition to the system monitoring that involves exporting data off of the IVE, such as syslog and SNMP, Juniper has also provided some integrated management for the IVE that is worth mentioning. The extent of the capabilities that the Juniper IVE provides depends on whether you have Central Management capabilities available on your IVE. The baseline license allows you to view the number of active users and the maximum number of users that are logged in during each hour of the past 7 days, but not much more in the way of integrated graphing. The Central Management license allows you to extend this capability to providing resource graphs for various system variables, such as the number of concurrent users, memory and CPU utilization, and number of file and URL access hits during a 7-day period. You also have the capability to change some of the properties of the graphs, such as the time period and colors, so that you can have them follow a particular format. Lastly, these graphs may be downloaded in XML format so that you can integrate them into other applications if you wish. In this section, we review all of these capabilities and how to implement them on your IVE.

## System Statistics

The IVE automatically records information about the maximum number of Web and e-mail (IVE Email Client) users that are logged in during 1-hour time intervals for a week. Additionally, the number of URLs and files accessed through the IVE is recorded. If you have the baseline license, you can only view the number of Web users per hour; if you have the advanced/Central Management license, you can view the number of e-mail users, along with URL and file hits. This information is located under the **System | Log/Monitoring | Statistics** menu as shown in Figure 13.12. Each hour of each day will have a value listed in the table, which is related to the maximum number of users/access attempts that were made during that period depending on what table you are looking at. The table order is Signed-In Users, Peak Mail, URL Accesses, and File Accesses, which can be viewed by scrolling down to view each table.

**Figure 13.12** Displaying System Statistics in the IVE

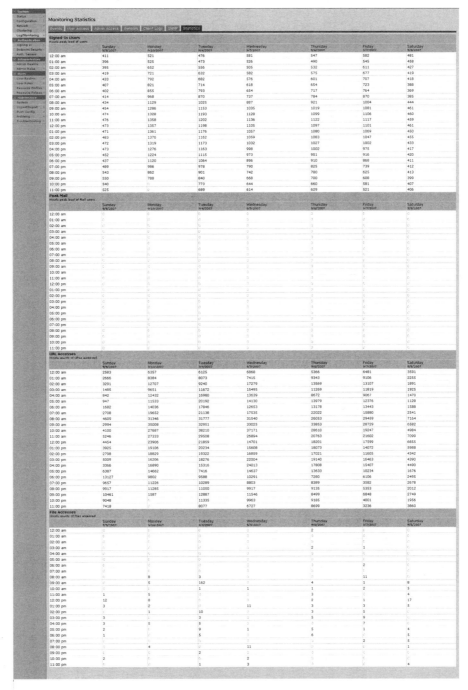

# Central Management Graphs

If your IVE has the Central Management capabilities enabled, then you may have probably noticed some additional graphs located on the Admin Dashboard when you logged in. If you are on another screen of the AdminUI, you can get back to the Admin Dashboard by going to **System | Status | Overview** as shown in Figure 13.13. In this section, we review the different graphs and the available options that can be configured per graph.

**Figure 13.13** The AdminUI with Central Management Enabled

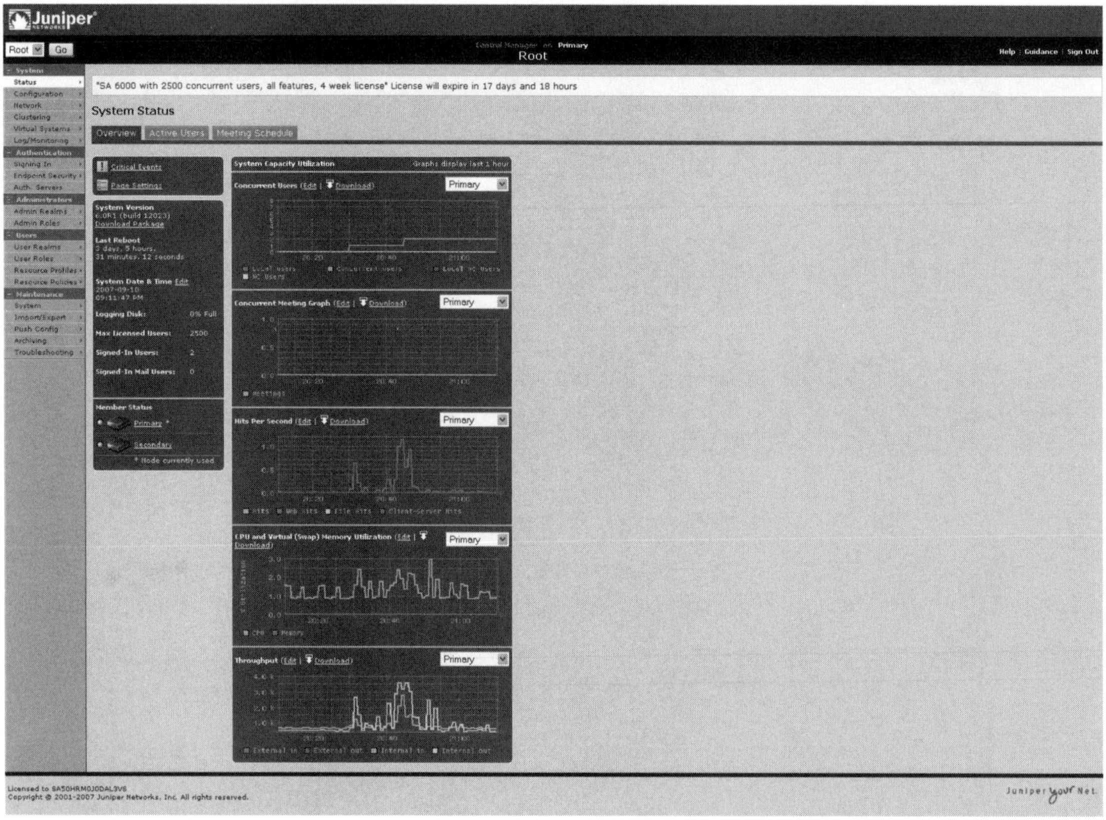

# Common Graph Settings

Before we delve into the different graph types, it is helpful to note a few settings that are common to all of the graphs. First, you can download any graph in XML format by clicking the **Download** hyperlink on that particular graph. Also, you can edit the color schemes for the individual graphs by clicking the **Edit** hyperlink on the graph you would like to modify. The following settings are common to all graphs:

- **Background Color** This is the background color for the graph. There is a color wheel to the right that can allow you to visually pick the background color, or you can manually enter the value for the color of your choice.

- **Major Grid Color** The major grid is both the x- and the y-axis, along with the y vertices at each value along the x-axis and the x vertices along the y-axis. You can specify this color manually or select it from the color wheel to the right.

- **Minor Grid Color** These grid lines are in between the major grid lines on the graph and can be specified, to help provide contrast. You can manually select them or choose from the color wheel.

- **Text Color** When modifying other color values, you may find it particularly useful to be able to modify the text color so that it can be better seen. Just like the other values, either specify the text value of the color or select it from the color wheel.

### Page Settings

You can modify which graphs you would like to see, along with the time period to which these graphs should be scaled, by clicking the **Page Settings** hyperlink on the **System | Status | Overview** page. You can add or remove the following graphs from the dashboard: Concurrent Users, Hits Per Second, CPU and Memory Usage, Throughput, and Meeting. You can also specify what time period you would like all of the graphs to follow. Your choices are 1 hour, 2 hours, 4 hours, Day, 2 days, Week, Month, and Year. Lastly, you can define whether or not to display the state of storage on the IVE, which displays the amount of disk space consumed and the fragmentation of the disk.

## Concurrent Users

The Concurrent Users graph provides information about the number of users who are logged in at any given time. This graph is particularly useful because the IVE uses a concurrent user license model; thus, you may have 500 employees, but if you have a 100 user license, so long as there are not more than 100 logged in at any given time, you will be just fine. This graph can help provide a bit of historical data to help show peak numbers of users at different times depending on the settings. There are two values that you can specify that are unique to this graph, either one of which can be removed by unchecking the check box next to the name of that item:

- **Concurrent Users** This is the number of concurrent sessions on the IVE. You can specify a thickness for the line graph, as well as the color of the line.

- **NC Users** This is the number of users connected through Network Connect. You can specify the thickness of the line, as well as the color.

# Concurrent Meeting

This graph displays the number of concurrent Secure Meeting sessions occurring on the box. This is useful to keep tabs on how you are using the Secure Meeting resources in relation to your licensing scheme. In this graph, there is only one value that cannot be removed, but it can be modified. This is the line for the number of concurrent meetings. You can specify the thickness of the line, as well as the color of the line.

# Hits Per Second

This graph is one way of monitoring the load on the box. Although it doesn't specify the type of transactions taking place, it is still provides some useful metrics into the activity taking place on the IVE.

- **Hits** This is the number of hits to the IVE interface when a user is logged in and during the login process. This value may be removed, or the line thickness and color may be changed.

- **Web Hits** This is the number of Web hits that take place through the IVE. It can be generated by Web bookmarks and other Web-related browsing through the IVE. This value can be removed, and the thickness and color of the line can be modified.

- **File Hits** This statistic is useful for tracking the number of file hits taking place on the box to Windows and UNIX file shares. This value can be removed, or the color and line thickness can be altered.

- **Client/Server Hits** This metric has to do with the client/server application traffic that can be configured to pass through the IVE (non-Web UI interface activity). This value may be removed, or the line thickness and color can be altered.

# CPU and (Virtual) Swap Memory Utilization

This is a very important graph that gives a high-level overview of the CPU utilization and swap memory utilization. This graph can help identify times of resource contention during the day or, on a large timescale, help track trends. This graph has two values that are configurable:

- **CPU** This graph displays the CPU utilization on the IVE during the time period displayed. This value can be removed, and the line thickness and color can be modified.

- **Swap Memory** This is the amount of virtual memory utilization that is currently being utilized by the IVE. The swap memory is memory that is active on the hard disk, usually because there isn't enough space in the physical RAM memory to fit the whole memory image. High swap utilization will often lead to performance issues. This value may be removed from the graph, and the line thickness and color can be modified.

# Throughput

The throughput statistics of the IVE are a very good metric for measuring performance. They can help identify the actual amount of traffic that is processed through the box. The IVE even allows you to graph the different origins of the data, as well as the destinations. You can use the information obtained from this graph in addition to the other graphs to help track IVE performance. The following values are graphed in the Throughput graph:

- **External In** This is a graph of the throughput of data that originates externally and is destined to the internal network. An example of this data would be a user on the Internet browsing an internal Web site through the IVE. This value may be removed from the graph, and the line thickness and color can be modified.

- **External Out** This is traffic that originates outside the IVE, such as a client on the Internet who is browsing to a destination on the Internet. An example would be a user browsing to a public Web site through the IVE Web interface. This value may be removed from the graph, and the line thickness and color can be modified.

- **Internal In** This is traffic that originates on the internal network and is destined for the internal network. An example of this traffic is when a user who, while on the LAN, opens an IVE session and then clicks on a Web bookmark for an internal resource. This value may be removed from the graph, and the line thickness and color can be modified.

- **Internal Out** This is traffic that originates on the internal network and is destined for a resource outside of the IVE. An example would be an internal user browsing to a public Web site through the IVE Web interface. This value may be removed from the graph, and the line thickness and color can be modified.

**NOTE**

You should be careful when trying to calculate the load on your network simply by analyzing the throughput of these graphs. The actual throughput load on your network will depend on how the IVE is set up in your network. For instance, the throughput will be different if you only have one interface configured for the IVE (encrypted traffic enters the device through the internal port and leaves decrypted through the internal port) versus having two network connections—one for the SSL traffic and the other reaching into your internal network. If you use the former example, you may have to count the actual throughput on your network link twice, first when it comes in encrypted and then when it goes back out (to the LAN) unencrypted.

# Reporting

The IVE does not natively incorporate much in the way of reporting beyond some on-box resource utilization graphs. The IVE does not have integrated reporting for performance and storage reasons. Although the integrated reporting for the IVE is somewhat limited, there is a third-party appliance that is purpose built to perform multiple tasks related to reporting, alerting, and log storage for the IVE. The name of the product is the ClearView Reporter by NWG Technologies. In this section, we discuss some of the features of this product, along with other tools to perform reporting on the IVE.

## ClearView Reporter Feature Overview

The ClearView Reporter is a product designed to bridge the gap between the wealth of remote access features on the IVE and the need for enterprise reporting on the SSL VPN. The ClearView Reporter combines the ability for the IVE to export the logs in syslog format with SNMP functionality to gather data from the IVE. It has the capability to perform numerous reports on the data obtained. The IVE can also perform alerting based on various user events. One handy feature is extensive reporting for Host Checker and related log-on events. Since Host Checker can indicate a lot of information about the state of user machines logging into the IVE, as well as compliance with your organizational security posture, the reporting on this functionality is exceptionally useful. To review, the following are features available on the ClearView Reporter (Figures 13.14 and 13.15):

- Enterprise reporting custom developed for the IVE

- Appliance prebuilt with ClearView Reporter software

- Reporting on virtually any logged data on the IVE, including Host Checker

- Enterprise alerting on a large number of system and user events (with configurable thresholds)

- Appliance acts as long-term storage for IVE logs with data retention capabilities

- Supports local, radius, and RSA authentication

**Figure 13.14** ClearView Drill-Down Menu Allows You to Drill Down Logs and Generate Reports at Any Level; Reporting Is Available on Almost All Logs Generated by the IVE

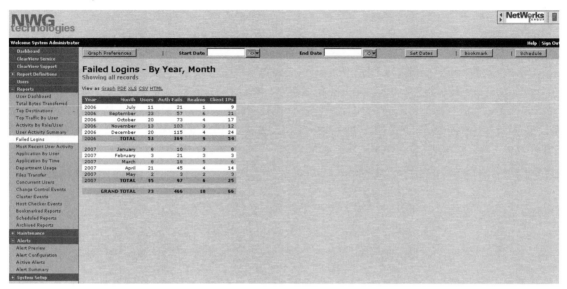

**Figure 13.15** ClearView Alerting Setup Allows for Granular Alert Configuration and Notification Settings

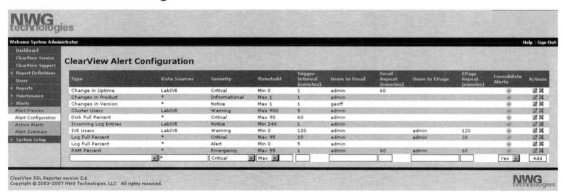

For more information about the ClearView Reporting software, visit the NWG Technologies Web site at www.nwgtechnologies.com.

## Other Reporting Tools

Other tools that are more general purpose and not specifically developed for the IVE are also available and may be useful for reporting purposes. As mentioned previously, there are numerous tools, both commercial (HP Openview and What's Up Gold) and open source such as Cacti, that are capable of performing SNMP polling to gain statistics about the box state, performance, and reporting on virtually any SNMP available object on the IVE. Other syslog-related tools exist for capturing syslog data and can report based on that such as WebTrends and AdventNet Event Log Analyzer. Of course, these tools will require manual configuration to customize the reporting to your needs.

# Summary

Juniper has incorporated several important features in the IVE that can be extremely useful for monitoring everything from user activity to system performance and events. By leveraging the various logging facilities available in, for example, Event, User Access, Admin, and Client logs, you can gain an in-depth understanding of virtually all activity on the IVE device. Additionally, you can rely on other useful features if you have advanced licensing, such as dynamic logging, system utilization graphs, and advanced log formatting options. There are also a wealth of tools available to extend the capabilities of the IVE; these options are both commercial and open source, giving you a wide range of options for maximizing the effectiveness of IVE logging and monitoring functionality.

# Solutions Fast Track

## Log Types and Facilities

☑ IVE contains multiple log files for different types of activity, such as Event, User Access, Admin, NC Packet, Client Upload, and Sensor.

☑ Licensing plays an important role regarding what features are available for logging. Advanced license provides the Central Management capabilities.

☑ You can control which users are logged in with the Active User log. You can remove sessions as well as search for user sessions.

☑ Assuming you have the Meeting functionality enabled on the IVE, you can view the scheduled meetings and remove them as necessary.

## Log Filtering

☑ With the Central Management feature set (advanced license), you can perform extensive log filtering and save such data queries for future user.

☑ Central Manager allows you to perform advanced features, such as altering the log format for log exporting.

☑ You can apply Custom Expressions to log queries to facilitate logic to the query.

## Log Management

☑ In addition to log archiving, you can manually save individual logs, as well as all logs off of the IVE.

☑ You can manually clear logs from the IVE to assist in freeing up disk space.

## Syslog Exporting

☑ You can configure the IVE to export syslogs to an external data repository that is more purpose built for retaining logs.

☑ If you have the Central Management capability, you can configure additional export filtering and log filtering on the syslog entries.

☑ You can configure the syslog to export to multiple destinations for each different log type.

## SNMP Management

☑ The IVE supports both SNMP polling and traps.

☑ You can configure which types of events should trigger traps on the IVE.

☑ Various external tools exist to handle the processing of SNMP traps as well as perform SNMP polling to collect statistics.

## System Resource Monitoring

☑ The IVE contains statistics about the peak number of users who are logged into the IVE at different hours of the day for an entire week. If you have the Central Management capability, additional statistics will be available.

☑ The Central Management feature set allows you to view additional resource graphs on the dashboard, such as information relating to the CPU and memory statistics, throughput, and users logged in.

☑ You can alter the appearance of graphs, including the colors, and time period of the graphs.

## Reporting

☑ The ClearView Reporter by NWG Technologies is an appliance developed for reporting, alerting, and external log storage (from IVE) to fill the gap of reporting functionality available on the IVE.

☑ Other third-party tools exist for a variety of functions related to syslog processing and SNMP polling/trapping.

# Frequently Asked Questions

**Q:** Why is the IVE log screen taking so long to load?

**A:** Juniper has placed more emphasis on maintaining a good end user experience through the IVE than on administrative task performance. This is a benefit so that tasks such as log viewing do not cause user-perceived performance issues. As a work around, you can export the data off of the IVE to process it on a machine that isn't constrained by these limits.

**Q:** Why does it take so long to upgrade the IVE when I have a very large amount of log files on the IVE?

**A:** If you are upgrading the IVE, especially across major versions, you may notice that it takes a long time to perform the upgrade. This is because the IVE performs data backups and other related processing on the logs. To help alleviate this, you should save the logs off of the IVE and clear the log files so they don't have to be processed.

**Q:** Why do some of the SNMP object queries, such as iveWebHits, iveFileHits, and iveNCHits, always increase instead of showing the current statistics for the device?

**A:** These SNMP objects record the number of hits since the device last reset. So essentially, at each reboot, the stats are reset and then count upwards. There are other SNMP objects to show concurrent values.

**Q:** Why doesn't the IVE have integrated reporting?

**A:** The IVE does have some limited reporting facilities, but because reporting (especially in a historical fashion) can be extremely disk, memory, and CPU intensive, it has been left to other third-party solutions to perform these functions off box.

**Q:** Why am I not seeing all of the events in my logs?

**A:** You should check to make sure that some of the events are not disabled for the particular log in which you wish to see these events. You can check each log for event settings by going to **System | Log/Monitoring | <LogName> | Settings**.

**Q:** Why can't I create log queries, perform dynamic log filtering, and save log formats?

**A:** These features require the advanced license, which contains the Central Management feature set.

# Chapter 14

# Enterprise Features

## Solutions in this chapter:

- **Instant Virtual Systems**

- **VLANs and Source Routing**

- **Administration Techniques**

- **Network Connect Considerations**

- **Clustering**

- **Understanding Cluster Communication and Status**

☑ **Summary**

☑ **Solutions Fast Track**

☑ **Frequently Asked Questions**

# Introduction

Virtualization is imminent and is coming in many different shapes and sizes. This appendix does not really discuss the benefits of it (most of which should be obvious), but the bottom line is that you want to get the most out of your capital expenses and if they are sitting around hardly passing any packets, then you are not getting your money's worth. You need to maximize your deployment in order to really reap the rewards of a high-performing business. It is the way of life these days.

Delegated administration is certainly a great solution, but it falls short of offering true control, design flexibility, and, at the same time, enforcing service level agreements (SLAs). This is why Virtual Systems was created. With Instant Virtual Systems (IVS), the administrator gets a truly virtualized architecture that helps to maximize your investment and reduce your operating expenses.

# Instant Virtual Systems

Instant Virtual Systems are a management paradigm that extends the remote access management boundary one level up from where it is today. Think of it as cloning the IVE OS and replicating it (with your desired changes, of course). The system is sliced vertically, and each slice represents a different customer or subscriber or, if you are an enterprise, a division or department because it seems common these days to build centralized IT infrastructures that provide billable services and granular audit trails for compliance.

First, you must get a license for Virtual Systems. This is available for the SA4000 and SA6000, but not the SA2000 or SA700. When enabled, the **System | Virtual Systems** menu will appear. You will also note the term "Root" in the page header now (see Figure 14.1). This means you are in the Root system. As you add virtual systems, you will see them in a drop-down list (on the left) whereby you can jump to different systems to manage them.

**Figure 14.1** The System | Virtual Systems Menu

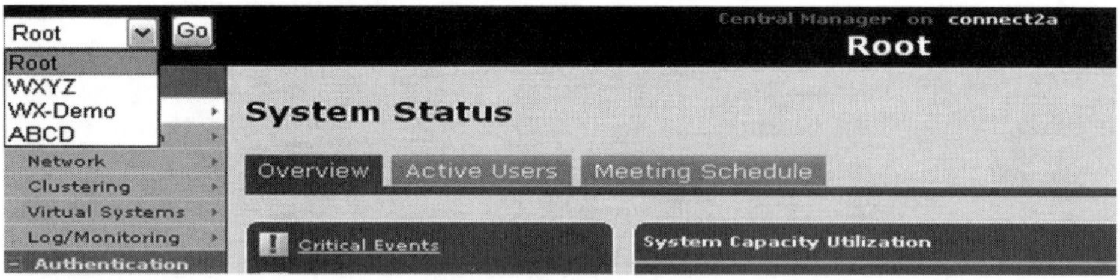

By clicking on **Virtual Systems** you can pull up the list or else create new virtual systems. When creating a new virtual system, you must provide several important elements:

- Name & Description

- Whether it's enabled or not

- Initial Configuration (for example, a template of another virtual system)

- Initial Administrator Account (Recommended)

- User License Allocation

- VLANs

- Sign-In URL Prefix

- Virtual Ports

- NC IP Ranges

Some key points here are Initial Configuration, Administrator Account, and User License Allocation because these ultimately impact how a virtual system can be maximized to get the most out of them. The Initial Configuration is where you begin. This is where you inherit default options and settings, such as certain common group names, common policies, and so on. Some administrators may build generic templates to provide certain levels of functionality—for example, bronze, silver, and gold packages. This may help them develop very structured pricing, and they can still customize it further later on. There may also be different support levels—for example, the customer/subscriber taking the initial ticket, or you doing so. These levels could then be mapped into different templates so that as you get new customers with similar needs, you can quickly and cost-effectively provision them a new virtual system that is already set up the way it needs to be for that level.

Administration is also something you'll want to consider before designing a virtualized offering. There are several ways this could be administered, including the following:

- **Hosted, shared** This model gives you the most bang for your buck. You can continue adding on to your existing deployment until it is at capacity and then add more equipment, scaling very predictably. With some simple routine performance monitoring, you can also determine how responsive the solution is, getting a good idea of what the user experience is like.

- **Hosted, dedicated** When customers require the ultimate in hosting, they need to go dedicated. This provides dedicated hardware and the assurance that no other customers' solutions will interfere. This method should be considered for the most critical systems that cannot be virtualized.

- **Customer premises equipment** CPE is a common model employed by many because of the proximity of the equipment and the location of the management crew. For remote access SSL VPNs, the unit is most definitely at an office, providing remote access to employees and perhaps more. But the management of this device may be offsite entirely. Think of how many IT organizations have worldwide offices with IT organizations at only some of them. Remote management (for example, RDP, ILO, VNC, SSH, and SMS) is critical to running a highly efficient, highly available network. You can't be everywhere at the same time, right?

As the "Root" administrator of the box, you have access to all of your subscribers' virtual systems. You don't, however, want those administrators to have access to all of your subscribers' virtual systems, do you? That is why you want to use Delegated Administration. This built-in administration method provides a separate /admin sign-in portal for your delegated (that is, customer/subscriber) administrators to log in and manage the system. This is provided, of course, that you actually do want to let them manage their own systems versus you doing it for them (for a nominal fee, of course). This is the preferred way of letting subscribers manage their virtual systems, and it ensures there is administrative separation in between.

User License Allocation is really the other half to the SLA equation. The key part of your investment is in user licenses. Managing them effectively, and furthermore having the ability to reprovision user counts on the fly, provides an excellent framework for offering SLA-enforced user concurrency levels.

VLANs must be configured here if they are to be used. If you haven't created the VLANs yet, you can always do that later, come back, and then assign them to your VLAN. By using a VLAN, you get Layer 2 separation and can also plug directly into any VLAN-based routing system.

Because each virtual system will most likely have its own DNS name, or at least some unique name, there must be associated sign-in URLs. This way, a customer of CompanyABC could type in **https://connect.companyabc.com/** and get his or her virtual system, whereas a customer of CompanyXYZ would have his or her own sign-in URL and associated virtual system—both on the same box. These sign-in URLs also may utilize their own associated virtual ports. This is because often the internal port is insufficient because it may have a default or otherwise "Root" SSL server certificate bound to it (remember that SSL server certificates must be bound to a socket because the requested host name will not be known until after the SSL tunnel is established). These virtual ports also will be a part of the clustering failover subsystem, so they will be active only on one node and if **Active/Passive** is employed, they will fail-over to the other node if the first one fails. This is important if you want to offer high availability for your virtual system customers/subscribers.

Lastly, each virtual system can restrict which address NC IP pools can be used by which systems. This may be used if you delegate management of each virtual system and want to let your customer handle his or her NC IP subnet. NC within the virtual system will *not* work if this is not configured properly. The same is true for DNS, which we'll discuss later.

Click **Save Changes**. This takes us to the Virtual Systems list page, where you'll see the newly created virtual system.

Now that the virtual system is defined, you may enter it and proceed with configuration. This is done in two different ways. The first is logging into the [virtual port] sign-in URL with the administrative account you defined in its configuration. This is how normal subscriber administrators would access their configuration. But because you are a Root administrator, you may simply select the virtual system to manage from the drop-down list, which is the second way, and you will assume that virtual system's administrator's role. You can think of this as similar to running "su <vsysname>" in a UNIX environment. You'll see the header change to red and indicate the name of the selected virtual system. Remember, you are the only one who has this functionality because you are a Root administrator. Your customer's administrators will not see the drop-down list or the VS header.

From here, you can configure the virtual system just like your customer would. You might want to do this to set up some basic networking items, such as any special routing, DNS, or host entries for the virtual system. Remember, DNS is not set up initially and must be configured for resolution to work. After that, it's the same as configuring a nonvirtual IVE system.

Now you will quickly find out that some things are missing, such as Cluster and Virtual Systems. These don't exist in the virtual system, only at the root level. The same is true for most of the Maintenance menu. All of the system functions are absent, as well as Import/Export/ Push Configuration. Even the Troubleshooting menu has been stripped down because, for example, you wouldn't want one customer sniffing (via TCPDump) another's traffic, right?

# VLANs and Source Routing

Virtual LANs, or VLANs, are often used to segment L2 networks. This is done by marking the packet with an 802.1q-compliant tag, or VLAN ID. This ID is used by switches and routers and other networking devices to help those devices decide where to forward/route the packet and if any special manipulations are required, such as encapsulating it in an MPLS VPN.

Because the packets for a subscriber can be marked as for a specific VLAN, they can easily be identified throughout the system—not just by the IVE. Traditional LANs utilize a switched infrastructure and are "always connected." In a remote access environment, you don't have that luxury. You must VPN into the network. This means the VPN gateway must do its L2 job on your behalf, such as gratuitous ARPing, or marking the packets for a specific VLAN, just as those LAN switches would do. This enables upstream devices to function without heavy administrative changes. Existing VLAN-based routes and ACLs continue to apply, as if that user was on the LAN.

> **NOTE**
>
> A "gratuitous ARP" is when a network device proactively sends out an ARP broadcast, to the L2 segment, to let all connected devices know that this new device (identified by its MAC address) is now servicing a specific IP address. This means any connected device can now communicate with it. This is often used in clustering/failover because the backup node has to take over servicing a virtual IP.

From a managed services standpoint, this means you can now "virtualize" a customer's data all through your network, from perimeter to customer data center. In addition, it plugs right into your existing infrastructure so you don't need to make heavy changes on other systems, reducing your operating expenses.

# Administration Techniques

As mentioned previously, there are several ways to manage a virtualized solution. Here are some of the different advantages and disadvantages to each. They key, however, is to find a scalable model that suits your needs.

- **Managed service for administration and monitoring** Managing an entity's remote access solution definitely has its challenges. But if that system is one of many that you manage, and you know it inside and out, then it is quite simple and easily scalable. Often, a customer will purchase equipment and let the reseller/integrator manage it remotely. This is different from customer premises equipment (CPE), wherein this managed service is homed on the SP's network, not the customer's. This is usually the preferred method when you, the SP, are also hosting the customer's data center/network infrastructure. Although that is not a requirement here, it does pose challenges if you don't. Those challenges can be overcome using backend MPLS VPNs, however. It is also important to point out here that if you are managing your solutions in this manner, it is wise to explore the shared architecture route to maximize your investment. One other benefit to this administration technique is that you get the luxury of building custom systems to interact with your solution, such as for building, auditing, and monitoring. Because you control it all, you can ensure you get accurate reporting and can easily plan for increased capacity down the road. Additionally, a hidden cost some folks forget is if they are going to sell a hosted service, they may not make up the initial expense until after a year or more. This could thwart a service provider's (SP's) ability to execute and grow. Careful planning and sales options, such as leasing, are important points to consider.

■ **Delegated virtual systems** This traditional virtual systems administration design is commonly used by many organizations, where groups just want to slice the box up and each get their own virtual system and manage it themselves. This way, each gets to leverage an investment that the larger company has made, and each has full control over which users can access what, within their virtual system.

■ **Customer premises equipment** This design is often employed when your customer does not want to share equipment or wants manageability of his or her equipment. Often, this method is coupled with a lease agreement so that the customer may lease-to-own the equipment. The equipment is installed typically at the customer site (network), thus the term "customer premises." The advantage here is that a customer can manage his or her own equipment in addition to having an SP monitor and manage it. The challenge, however, is in having the SP do these tasks remotely (vs. locally if this were a hosted deployment).

■ **HelpDesk considerations** In cases in which an IT organization is managing and monitoring a remote access SSL VPN solution, there may be times when different groups need to log in to the Admin console. The one primary use case we see here is the role of the HelpDesk. Often, this group must provide 24/7 support to the end user and that can mean the need to log in to the Admin console and look at user logs. Because the HelpDesk doesn't "own" the solution—they just monitor it at times—they should not have full control over the solution, nor should they need it. For this reason, delegated administration is strongly encouraged in order to provide separation of duties and also limit what a HelpDesk representative may be able to see/modify. In fact, taking this one step further, some solutions may require varying levels of delegated administration, such as shown in Figure 14.2.

**Figure 14.2** Delegated Administration

# Network Connect Considerations

Because many customers like to use the layer 3 VPN functionality (that is, "Network Connect") of the SSL VPN, this is a crucial piece of the configuration. When you are defining virtual systems, there may be some subscriber VSes that overlap in their IP spaces. Although this isn't a problem for the system to handle, there are some important elements to point out:

- **Node addresses** Although each VS may utilize the same IP address space, the IP addresses that the IVE is listening on (bound to physical or virtual ports) cannot conflict. This means that if CustomerA has 10.0.0.0 and CustomerB has 10.0.0.0, on the SSL VPN the Administrator may need to configure different VIPs, both in that same address space—for example, 10.0.0.1 and 10.0.0.2 for CustomerA and CustomerB, respectively.

- **NC pools** Overlapping IP space is fully supported with NC; however, the NC pools must be set up in order for them to be used by a VS. This is done under **System | Virtual Systems | <VSName>**. Although this may be apparent to most administrators, many forget about it and during their configuration may run into issues when trying to define NC IP profiles from an IP range outside the VS-defined range.

- **IP assignment** Often, customers will want to handle their own IP assignment, which is usually as straightforward as configuring those IP pools in the NC profile. However, in many situations, SPs may want to handle their own IP assignment. For example, if they are providing some additional transport across their network to a customer's circuit, they may need to assign their own IP addresses and then provide source routing or even MPLS encapsulation. To do this, SPs may need to handle IP assignment, and therefore could use their own DHCP service. This may also occur in conjunction with Centralized Authentication, such as if an SP wants to offer managed AAA solutions and use his or her own RADIUS server.

# Clustering

First of all, let's see if you even need clustering. If you want to increase the system uptime, number of users, or throughput beyond what a single system can provide, then a cluster is the way to go and is probably what you are looking for. So if that sounds like you, please read on. If not, then consider just using *XML Import/Export* or *Push Config*, both of which are covered in Chapter 10.

Clustering is simple to understand, really. It is taking one or more units and combining them into a single managed system to provide uptime or high levels of scalability. Terms such as active/active or active/passive are merely used to understand how the cluster has been implemented.

> **NOTE**
>
> Because the IVE Admin Guide, which is publicly available from the Juniper Networks Web site (no support logon required), provides the exact procedure for building a cluster for the specific firmware version you intend to use, we have made no attempts to document those specific and varied procedures here. Instead, we simply encourage you to follow the steps as they are laid out in the appropriate version of the Admin Guide for the version of the IVE software that you are running. In this chapter, our approach is to simply highlight what you need to know, much of which is either not in the Admin Guide or may be hard to find elsewhere.

Perhaps the nicest thing about the IVE's clustering is its flexibility. The standard configuration, known as Active/Passive, provides one active IVE that is servicing all user requests with a second passive IVE that is just standing by in case the active unit should fail. Then there is the more advanced Active/Active configuration, where all systems are processing user traffic at the same time. And finally there is the multi-site cluster that is always Active/Active, but goes the extra mile (actually, many extra miles) by allowing the IVEs to physically reside in data centers around the world. Figures 14.3 and 14.4 provide an overview of these configurations.

**Figure 14.3** Active/Passive Cluster

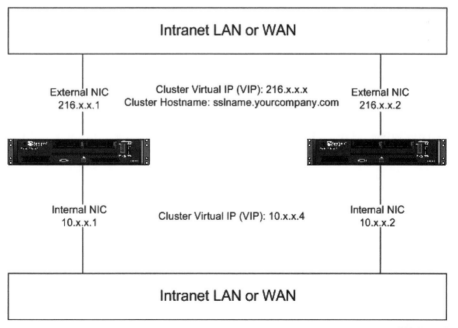

**Figure 14.4** Active/Active Cluster

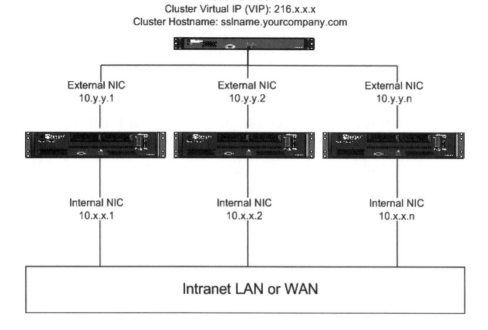

Now, as easy as all of this sounds, things have a tendency to get rather tricky, especially for those that are new to the concept of clustering. We will now cover the key points and guidelines that should help you avoid a great deal of trouble down the road. Also, including our finer points here will prevent us from having to repeat the same as we get in to the more specific configuration guidelines for Active/Passive and Active/Active deployments.

- **Cluster Sizing** SA2000 and SA4000 hardware can only be clustered up to two units, whereas SA6000 hardware can be clustered up to eight units. Note that we said the SA6000 *can be* clustered up to eight units. In reality, several factors determine whether or not going beyond four units in a single cluster would be ideal, and anyone seeking this level of scalability would be well advised to call Juniper and have a skilled Juniper Systems Engineer review this configuration with them, which they will gladly do.

- **Mixed Hardware** If you have the older SA1000, SA3000, or SA5000 hardware, you can't cluster them with the newer SA2000, SA4000, or SA6000 hardware. Yes, we know that the older hardware reports in the admin UI that it is actually the newer series, but that is just the way the newer firmware reports in. And even if you could get it to work today, the next firmware build that you install could possibly break it.

■ **Licensing** Clusters have to be licensed as clusters. You can't take two fully licensed units and then cluster them together. Instead, you have to ensure that one unit is fully licensed—just as though it was going to run on its own—and then add the appropriate clustering licenses (those with "–CL" contained in the part number and/or description) to however many units you want to add to the cluster (up to the supported limit for that configuration). It is vital to understand this before you apply the licenses to any new hardware, because a failure to do so will end up with a call to Juniper's Customer Care group to re-issue the licenses. So when your new hardware and licenses arrive, just remember to assign all of the non-clustering licenses to the first unit, followed by assigning all of the cluster-specific licenses (again, those with –CL in the part number or description) to the remaining units in the cluster. When in doubt, talk to your reseller or Juniper sales representative before entering your serial numbers for each unit in Juniper's online License Management System. And although it is technically a supported configuration to run a cluster without the benefit of the Central Manager feature, which used to be a separate license but became a part of the Advanced license some time ago, we don't recommend you do so.

**T**IP

Build the first IVE in a cluster as you would any non-clustered system: load the base license followed by all feature licenses. Once you have a functional stand-alone IVE, add the remaining units to the cluster, making sure you only apply one unique "–CL" license to each additional unit.

■ **Load Balancing** Anytime you want to configure an Active/Active or Multi-Site cluster, you will have to use a load balancer. DNS Round Robin configurations will not work and are not supported. In the case of multi-site configurations, your load balancer will also need to support Global Server Load Balancing (GSLB), as users will need to be seamlessly directed to any of the available sites. If GSLB is going to be a requirement, check out the Juniper Application Note "GSLB with DX and SA for Large Deployments," which is available from Juniper or any Juniper reseller, for a detailed description of traffic flows and configurations. And if you are planning to use Network Connect with any large number of users, you should definitely look at the DX/SA integration, specifically the "SA Compatibility" option within the IVE, as this will set up the load balancer to allow the high performance ESP mode function. Other load balancers may not be able to support the ESP transport and would, therefore, result in much fewer connections per SA unit.

**TIP**

Depending on your load balancer, you may be able to use the IVE's built-in healthcheck reporting mechanism to inform the load balancer of the IVE's health. This is a Layer 7 health check that can be accessed by configuring the load balancer to query the IVE's *healthcheck.cgi* interface. Check it out in the Admin Guide.

- **Personal Bookmarks**  If you are planning on going beyond a two-unit cluster or will have a two-unit multisite cluster, then you will likely not want to support personal bookmarks, which are those that users enter into the IVE as bookmarks for themselves. The reason for this is that synchronizing thousands of personal settings on a regular basis causes a great deal of cluster overhead, both on the IVEs and the WAN. On top of that, training so many users on how to manage their own bookmarks and ensuring that ACLs exist for each resource that the user wants to access can become a great burden on the administrators and help desk. It's a great feature for smaller companies, but the larger your organization is, the more likely it is that the resource provisioning needs to be managed completely by the administrators, not delegated all the way down to the users. Besides, with the LDAP integration being as detailed as it is and delegated administration being so granular, it is almost always best to allow a limited group of trusted individuals to manage the resources as group settings from within LDAP and the various IVE roles. So, if your organization fits the large deployment profile, I recommend going through the roles and ensuring that the *Allow Users to Create Bookmarks* options are unchecked.

- **Synchronization Settings**  Unless you discover that you absolutely must have them, disable all of the synchronization settings found under **System | Clustering | Properties | Synchronization Settings**. Here's why:

  - **Synchronize log messages**  The IVE can (and does) generate an immense amount of log data: great for auditors, not so great for scalability. Therefore, it is best to just send this data to a *syslog* server on the network, instead of trying to keep all logs synchronized between two or more IVEs.

  - **Synchronize user sessions**  Leaving this setting enabled on a small cluster is probably okay, but for a large cluster the overhead created by trying to maintain potentially thousands of active user sessions across multiple systems just isn't worth the average daily performance hit. Think about it long and hard: do you really *need* all users to have their active sessions remain intact whenever they fail over to another system? Still not convinced? Consider, especially in a multi-site configuration, that the source IP that the application sees for any application that the user was running at the time of the failure will now be seen as coming from a separate IP address, typically resulting in the user having to re-establish their SAM/NC connection and most likely restart their application. It normally is not worth the trouble.

■ **Synchronize last access time for user sessions** This option allows the administrator to see when each user last accessed the cluster, without having to flip through each box separately. This is pretty cool for the smaller configurations, but not as cool as having it go to a robust *syslog* reporting server. Still, if you are going to synchronize anything at all, let this option be the one. But as the IVE Admin Guide will tell you, it is highly recommended to disable this when a load balancer is being used.

# Understanding Cluster Communication and Status

One of the most misunderstood aspects of the cluster is the cluster communication and status. Questions like "What does it mean when the IVE is the Leader?" and "Why can't my IVEs connect to each other over the Internet?" are quite common in new implementations.

Let's first look at cluster communications. The first thing you should know is that all communication occurs over the internal port. And that goes the same for cluster protocol information as it does for the IVE authenticating users or connecting them to resources. So if you set up a WAN cluster, then all cluster communication must communicate over the internal interfaces and across the corporate WAN. Finally, Table 14.1 shows the various ports that the IVE uses to communicate between cluster nodes, just in case you need to open firewall ports to allow the traffic through.

**Table 14.1** Cluster Communication

| Protocol | Port | When | Purpose |
|---|---|---|---|
| TCP/IP | 4808 | Clustering on, Always | P2P encrypted communication |
| | 4809 | Clustering on, Always | P2P clear text communication |
| | 4900-4910 | For a short period during handshake | Key exchange for group communication, state sync where applicable |
| UDP | 4803 | Clustering On, always | Group communication |
| | 4804 | Clustering On, always | Token Heartbeat |

The next thing to understand is what each of the status indicators for the IVE actually mean. These can be seen by looking at the cluster status under **System | Clustering | Status**.

- **Enabled**  As it implies, the node is simply enabled within the cluster. If you want to disable it for any reason, simply select the checkbox next to the **Member Name** and click on the **Disable** button.

- **Leader**  Generally speaking, this is the first unit to come up in the cluster. However, other normal and abnormal operating conditions can still cause a leader election to occur. This election process is of no real importance to end users, and knowing which box is the leader at any given time can generally be placed in the "nice to know" category. But once running, the leader assumes the role of cluster representative, informing the remaining cluster members of configuration and other system updates. There is no difference between the leader in an Active/ Active versus an Active/Passive configuration. Furthermore, administrators can make configuration changes to either unit in the cluster and the configurations will be immediately applied to all cluster members.

- **Active**  In an Active/Passive cluster, this is the active one. If both nodes are showing as active, then the cluster communication between the nodes is likely being blocked or occurring over a high latency connection.

- **Transitioning**  The IVE is moving from the stand-alone to enabled state within the cluster.

# Summary

As you have seen, there are a variety of ways a managed solution may be deployed and configured. This ranges from a traditional single-customer deployment (CPE) to a hosted model and a shared hosted model. Depending on how you manage your IT organization or what services you want to provide as an SP, you may employ one or more of these architectures. However, no matter what method you employ, please note that the SSL VPN will still offer its highly granular access management framework and can be leveraged by many to get the best in SSL VPN remote access.

# Solutions Fast Track

## Instant Virtual Systems

☑ Instant Virtual Systems are a management paradigm that extends the remote access management boundary one level up from where it is today.

☑ Administration is also something you'll want to consider before designing a virtualized offering.

☑ Delegated administration provides a separate/admin sign-in portal for your delegated (that is, customer/subscriber) administrators to log in and manage the system.

## VLANs and Source Routing

☑ Virtual LANs, or VLANs, are often used to segment L2 networks by marking the packet with an 802.1q-compliant tag, or VLAN ID.

☑ Because the packets for a subscriber can be marked as for a specific VLAN, they can easily be identified throughout the system—not just by the IVE.

☑ Traditional LANs utilize a switched infrastructure and are "always connected." In a remote access environment, you don't have that luxury. You must VPN into the network.

## Administration Techniques

☑ Often, a customer will purchase equipment and let the reseller/integrator manage it remotely. This is different from customer premises equipment (CPE), wherein this managed service is homed on the SP's network, not the customer's.

☑ Customer premises equipment design is often employed when your customer does not want to share equipment or wants manageability of his or her equipment. Often, this method is coupled with a lease agreement so that the customer may lease-to-own the equipment.

☑ In cases in which an IT organization is managing and monitoring a remote access SSL VPN solution, there may be times when different groups need to log in to the Admin console. The one primary use case we see here is the role of the HelpDesk.

# Network Connect Considerations

☑ Because many customers like to use the layer 3 VPN functionality (that is, "Network Connect") of the SSL VPN, this is a crucial piece of the configuration.

☑ When you are defining virtual systems, there may be some subscriber VSes that overlap in their IP spaces.

☑ Overlapping IP space is fully supported with NC; however, the NC pools must be set up in order for them to be used by a VS.

# Clustering

☑ Always use the Admin Guide to walk you through creating any cluster, making sure you use the document version for your specific IVE firmware.

☑ Remember that a load balancer will be required for Active/Active clusters and that the Network Connect ESP transport mode (fastest performance and much higher scalability) requires specific configurations that may not be found in all load balancers.

☑ Enabling all of the synchronization options is probably not going to buy you all that much. Resist the temptation to turn on all of these features and only turn on those that you actually need.

☑ Before configuring very large clusters (four or more), contact Juniper Networks and ask for an analysis from one of their SSL VPN specialists. This will help ensure that all design parameters have been taken into account and will provide assurance that the single cluster will meet all expectations.

# Understanding Cluster Communication and Status

☑ All cluster communication occurs over the internal port. If your clusters can't reach each other over their internal ports, then clustering will not work.

☑ High latency and/or high loss connections can cause issues for clusters. These all have to be taken into account, especially with larger clusters.

# Frequently Asked Questions

**Q:** Because the Active/Passive cluster communicates to all back-end using the physical interface IP that it originates from, what is the function of the internal VIP?

**A:** When the IVE is configured in a one-arm format (only the internal port is active) then users are inherently required to connect over the internal port only. Having the internal VIP allows the users to have one IP address and DNS name to connect to. Furthermore, Admins can use the same VIP for management.

**Q:** Can I configure which VLAN the cluster uses when virtual systems (IVS) is in use?

**A:** As the internal port is used, there is no VLAN in use. If you are using a switch between the SA units, then you will need to enable **Native VLAN** on the port, which will place the untagged traffic in a VLAN on the switch.

**Q:** I see that the first cluster member in my two-unit cluster is the Leader, but the second unit owns the VIP. Is this a problem?

**A:** This is a separate role and they are not tied together. It is perfectly legitimate.

**Q:** How do I upgrade a cluster?

**A:** After first ensuring that all cluster nodes are enabled, simply use the Central Manager Admin UI to upgrade the firmware. Once that first node is updated, it informs all remaining nodes that they need to upgrade and will push the new firmware to them. If there are four nodes in the cluster, you will see the first node get upgraded, followed by all remaining nodes at more or less the same time.

**Q:** When I hover over the status indicator (the green dot), it gives me a hex code. What is that for?

**A:** This provides a more detailed view of the cluster status for that node. As these codes are subject to change as the firmware versions change, you will need to look at the admin guide for that particular build to see what they mean. Within the appropriate admin guide you will see a detailed listing of these codes and how to read them. If you think you are experiencing cluster issues, this would be a good place to start investigating. It will also show Support (JTAC) that you are a pro on the system and could easily help you get through the initial call much faster and with less "have you tried this" type of questions.

**Q:** I can ping all nodes in the cluster but one still shows up as being unreachable. What's going on?

**A:** It is likely a simple configuration error. Perhaps a bad cluster password was entered. Or perhaps the group communication mode settings are different. Even a different firmware version can cause issues. Check all of the settings again. When in doubt, go back to the Admin Guide and make sure you are following the exact cluster creation procedure for your specific IVE firmware version.

**Q:** I have a four-unit cluster that is active for all client connections on a daily basis, with four more units just standing by at our disaster recovery site. How can I maintain the configuration across these separate systems?

**A:** Just use the *Import/Export* or *Push Config* options (see Chapter 10) to move the configurations from the production to the backup systems. It would not be desirable to have these become part of the same logical cluster. When using the Import/Export option, just keep in mind that this is done with XML, and the XML options within the IVE have steadily progressed as the IVE has matured. The newer the IVE build, the better the chance that the options you are looking to migrate are present in the XML schema. Also, although the IVE rarely needs to restart its services, certain import options may cause brief service restarts to enable the migrated settings. For disaster recovery sites this is almost never a concern, however, as the target IVEs are not servicing user sessions except during a complete site failover.

# Index

# Syngress: *The Definition of a Serious Security Library*

**Syn·gress** (sin–gres): *noun, sing.* Freedom from risk or danger; safety. See *security*.